The European Commission

3rd edition

edited by David Spence

with Geoffrey Edwards

JOHN HARPER
PUBLISHING

Published by John Harper Publishing
27 Palace Gates Road
London N22 7BW, United Kingdom.

www.johnharperpublishing.co.uk

ISBN 0-9543811-8-1

Typeset in 10/11pt Palatino

Printed and Bound in Great Britain by Cromwell Press Ltd

TABLE OF CONTENTS

CHAPTER 2: THE SECRETARIAT GENERAL OF THE EUROPEAN COMMISSION
by Hussein Kassim

CHAPTER 3: THE COMMISSION AND THE LAW
by John A. Usher

CHAPTER 7: THE COMMISSION AND THE COUNCIL
by Udo Diedrichs and Wolfgang Wessels

CHAPTER 8: THE COMMISSION, POLICY MANAGEMENT AND COMITOLOGY
by Robin Pedler with Kieran Bradley

ANNEXES

TABLES, SURVEYS, GRAPHS AND FIGURES

Tables

Surveys

Graphs

Figures

ABOUT THE AUTHORS

Arjen Boin is Assistant Professor at Leiden University's Department of Public Administration. He writes on institutional design, leadership and crisis management. Recent publications include *Crafting Public Institutions* (2001, Lynne Rienner) and *The Politics of Crisis Management* (2005, Cambridge University Press). Boin heads the Leiden University Crisis Research Center.

Kieran Bradley is Head of Unit for Legislative Affairs at the Legal Service of the European Parliament. He was a legal expert to the European Convention and the Intergovernmental Conference on the Constitution for Europe, has served at the European Court of Justice and has taught at the College of Europe, Natolin and Harvard Law School.

Udo Diedrichs is a Senior Research Fellow and Lecturer at the Department of Political Science, University of Cologne. He has also worked as a senior researcher at the Institute for European Politics in Berlin. His main fields are theoretical and institutional issues of European integration, EU external policy, transatlantic relations, and the Common Foreign and Security Policy.

Geoffrey Edwards is Reader in European Studies and Jean Monnet Chair in Political Science at the Centre of International Studies, University of Cambridge. He is a Fellow and Graduate Tutor at Pembroke College Cambridge. He has written widely on the EU's institutional development and on its foreign and security policies (most recently with Paul Cornish on the EU's Strategic Culture in *International Affairs* vol. 81 no. 4 July 2005). His publications also include *Global Governance in the Twenty-First Century*, co-edited with John Clarke, Palgrave 2004.

Magnus Ekengren is Senior Lecturer at the Swedish National Defence College and was previously Deputy Director of the Policy Planning Unit of the Swedish Ministry for Foreign Affairs. His main research interests are in the fields of European foreign and security policy and the Europeanisation of the nation-state. Recent publications include *The Time of European Governance* (2002, Manchester University Press).

Mark Gray is a member of the *cabinet* of Commission spokesperson Johannes Laitenberger and was formerly a member of the *cabinets* of Commissioners Margot Wallström and Pavel Telicka. He was also a member of the Commission's negotiating teams for the Treaty of Amsterdam and Treaty of

Nice. He has written widely on recent Intergovernmental Conferences and is co-editor of *Rethinking the European Union: IGC 2000 and Beyond*, European Institute of Public Administration, Maastricht.

Martijn Groenleer is a Ph.D. Fellow at the Department of Public Administration, Leiden University. He conducts research on the creation and early development of international and European organisations, in particular European Union agencies. He has been policy adviser with the Dutch Ministry of Foreign Affairs, where he was a member of the task force coordinating the establishment of the International Criminal Court.

Hussein Kassim is Senior Lecturer in Politics in the School of Politics and Sociology, Birkbeck College, University of London. He is a co-editor of 'Preference Formation and EU Treaty Reform', a special issue of *Comparative European Politics* (2004, 2005) and *The National Coordination of EU Policy* (Oxford University Press, 2000, 2001) He has written on the Commission, relations between the EU and the Member States, and European air transport policy.

Richard Lewis is Senior Research Fellow at the Institute for European Studies at the Vrije Universiteit Brussel and Human Rights Fellow at the University of Essex. He was previously Head of the Immigration and Asylum Unit of the Commission. He is the author of several articles on security policy and migration, including 'An Asylum and Immigration Policy for the European Union' (co-author Roscam Abbing, in *Revue des Affaires Européennes* 2001-2002/5).

Sonia Mazey is Senior Tutor and Fellow of Keble College, Oxford. Her recent publications include *Gender Mainstreaming in the EU: Principles and Practice* (London: Kogan Page 2001) and 'Gender mainstreaming strategies in the EU: delivering on an agenda?' *Feminist Legal Studies*, vol.10 (2002)

Simon Nuttall is a Professor in the Department of Political and Administrative Studies at the College of Europe in Bruges. He is a former Director in the Commission's Directorate General for External Relations. His published works include *European Political Co-operation* (Oxford, 1992), and *European Foreign Policy* (Oxford, 2000).

David O'Sullivan was *chef de cabinet* to Romano Prodi and Secretary General of the Commission (2000-2005). He is now Director General of DG Trade.

Robin Pedler is an Associate Fellow of Templeton College, Oxford University and Academic Director of the European Training Institute, Brussels. He was previously Director, External Relations Europe, for Mars. His publications include *European Union Lobbying: changes in the arena* (Palgrave, 2002) and *Shaping European Law and Policy – the role of committees and comitology in the political process*, EIPA, Maastricht, 1996.

John Peterson is Professor of International Politics at the University of Edinburgh. His books include *The Institutions of the European Union* (co-edited with Michael Shackleton, 2nd edition, OUP, 2006) and *Security Strategy and the Transatlantic Alliance* (co-edited with Roland Dannreuther, Routledge, 2006).

Mark Rhinard is a postdoctoral Fellow in the Department of Public Administration, Leiden University, where he participates in a research programme on the transposition of EU directives. His research interests include agenda setting in the EU, policy questions related to security, foreign policy, biotechnology and agricultural issues, and questions of EU implementation and compliance.

Jeremy Richardson is a Fellow of Nuffield College, Oxford. He edits the *Journal of European Public Policy*. His recent publications include the third edition (2005) of his edited volume *European Union: Power and Policy-Making*, London: Routledge.

Michael Smith is Professor of European Politics and Jean Monnet Chair in the Department of Politics, International Relations and European Studies at Loughborough University, UK. He has written widely on the external policies of the EU: his publications include *Europe's Experimental Union* (Routledge, 2000, with Brigid Laffan and Rory O'Donnell), *The State of the European Union*, volume 5 (Oxford University Press, 2000, edited with Maria Green Cowles) and *International Relations and the European Union* (Oxford University Press, 2005, edited with Christopher Hill).

David Spence is Political Counsellor at the European Commission's Delegation to the international organisations in Geneva. He has been lecturer in politics at the Sorbonne, head of European training in the UK's Civil Service College and secretary of the Commission's task force for German unification. He has also worked in the Commission on ESDP and terrorism and was head of training for the Commission's external delegations. He is co-editor (with Brian Hocking) of *Foreign Ministries in the EU: Integrating Diplomats*, Palgrave, 2005.

Anne Stevens is Professor of European Studies at Aston University. After a career in the UK civil service she taught at Sussex and Kent Universities and was visiting professor at the Universities of Paris I, II and the Lille Institut d'Études Politiques. She is author of *The Government and Politics of France* (Palgrave, 3rd edition 2003), author with Handley Stevens of *Brussels Bureaucrats? The Administrative Services of the European Union* (Palgrave, 2001) and co-editor, with Richard Sakwa, of *Contemporary Europe* (Palgrave, 2nd edition, 2005).

Handley Stevens has been Visiting Research Associate at the European Institute of the LSE since 1994, following a career as a diplomat and civil servant dealing extensively with the EU. His books include *Transport Policy in the European Union* (Palgrave, 2004) and, with Anne Stevens, *Brussels Bureaucrats? The Administrative Services of the European Union* (Palgrave, 2001).

Carlo Trojan was Secretary General of the Commission in 1997-2000, having previously (1987-1997) served as Deputy Secretary General. He is now Head of the Commission Delegation to the World Trade Organisation and the United Nations Organisations in Geneva.

John Usher is Professor of European Law and Head of the School of Law at the University of Exeter, having previously held the Salvesen Chair of European Institutions at the University of Edinburgh. Recent publications include *The Law of Money and Financial Services in the EC* (Oxford University Press, 2000) and *EC Agricultural Law* (Oxford University Press, 2002).

Wolfgang Wessels is Professor of Political Science at the University of Cologne, where he holds the Jean Monnet Chair. He has been Director of the Institut für Europäische Politik in Bonn and Director of the Department of Administrative and Political Studies at the College of Europe in Bruges. He was a member of a Commission high level group on CFSP reform and a member of the Commission's group of wise persons on the revision of the Treaty of Maastricht. Since 2004 he has held the Alfred Grosser Chair at the Institut d'Etudes Politiques (Sciences Po) in Paris. He has published extensively on the European Union, particularly on theories and strategies of European integration, the institutional development of the EU and the Common Foreign and Security Policy.

Martin Westlake is head of communications in the European Economic and Social Committee. Having been founding executive coordinator of the Schuman Centre at the European University Institute, he has since served as an official of the Parliamentary Assembly of the Council of Europe, the Council of the European Union and the European Commission. He is an Associate Member of the Centre for Legislative Studies at the University of Hull. He is the author of several books on the EU and on British politics. His recent books include *Kinnock; The Biography*, Little, Brown, 2001, and *European Elections and British Politics* 2004 (with David Butler), Palgrave, 2005. He is co-editor with David Galloway of *The Council of the European Union*, John Harper Publishing, 2004.

David (Lord) Williamson was Secretary General of the Commission from 1987 to 1997. He is now a member of the House of Lords, where he is a convenor of the crossbench peers and chairs the subcommittee on EU social policy and consumer affairs.

PREFACE

David Spence

The European Commission is not good at blowing its own trumpet. Officials mix modesty with diplomacy to avoid trampling on political sensitivities. But there is a job of public diplomacy to be done and my hope is that this book fills a much regretted gap in communication. The book consciously avoids complimenting the Commission in chapters where the human quality of practitioners might otherwise seem prioritised over the administrative structures the book sets out to describe. But, a factual account should not give the impression of faint recognition for Commission officials, particularly those whose lights burn bright – and late – in the Berlaymont. The European Commission would be nothing without the personal abilities and qualities of its staff, many of whom would do academia and the non-governmental world proud, had they not opted for public service.

The third edition of this book took long to appear. I was dogged with repeated bouts of what obituaries call 'a long illness'. Drs. Michael Gebhardt and Jean-Pierre Kains deserve thanks for rescuing the book by rescuing me from fairly certain death when cancer continued to strike with monotonous and frightening regularity over the years since the second edition. My colleagues and friends Lodewijk Briet and Lars-Erik Lundin deserve special thanks for not compulsorily retiring me. Like the oft-quoted Monsieur Jourdain, Briet and Lundin were practising enlightened management before it was thrust upon the Commission between the second and third editions of this book.

The book is a guide to the Commission, but I certainly intend it to be a solid contribution to academic analysis. I have tried to ensure that every chapter was vetted by experts; the chapters by academics submitted to the rigorous control of practitioners, and those by practitioners scrutinised by academic friends. They cannot all be named, but Martin Westlake was generous with time and advice, Carlo Trojan read the whole book and, bringing his wealth of experience to bear, made several pertinent and incisive suggestions. Many colleagues read, commented, adjusted and approved the text for publishing. I must particularly thank Graham Avery, David Tirr, Philippe Willaert, Thierry Bechet, Rainer Lau and Florika Fink-Hooijer for their many technical insights. They have all made this book into an accurate guide to the so-called 'faceless bureaucracy'.

My wife, Arnhild, and sons, Sebastian and William, had to put up with seemingly endless evening and weekend typing and with phone calls from anguished authors, whose texts had been chopped and changed. They have done that with a pleasure and pride that equals my pride in them. But, they deserve to read here my recognition and immense gratitude for their understanding and support.

Very special thanks are due to Suying Lai, who painstakingly read and re-read contributions, ensuring the continuity and coherence of the whole. Her requests to explain what authors meant with their sometimes intricate, when not impenetrable, prose, helped me clarify the thoughts of specialists and make the whole text more readable. In addition, her skilful sub-editing and overall command of the material proved indispensable.

My great regret is that a much admired colleague, Adrian Fortescue, did not live to complete the chapter on justice and home affairs. Adrian imbued the essence of the ideal civil servant. He combined undoubted rigour in his analysis and enormous creativity (without him DG Freedom, Justice and Security would not exist) with the true characteristics of a gentleman-manager. He is sorely missed by friends and colleagues alike.

Finally, my senior colleagues have been indulgent. They have to authorise publication, and they did this without attempting to dissuade me from telling the real story, even if I strayed near to indiscretion. Needless to say, I find this wise. As Beaumarchais wrote many years ago:

> ' les sottises imprimées n'ont d'importance qu'aux lieux où l'on
> en gêne le cours.... sans la liberté de blâmer, il n'est point d'éloge
> flatteur, et il n'y a que les petits hommes qui redoutent les petits
> écrits' (Beaumarchais, *le Mariage de Figaro* act V scene 3).'

If this were not our unspoken motto, this account of the Commission, warts and all, would not have seen the light of day.

David Spence
Geneva, March 2006

FOREWORD

Peter Mandelson

As a 'new boy on the block', I welcome any publication that offers the public honest, objective information about the role that the Commission plays in European integration. The last edition of this book was of immense help to me in reaching the centre of the European maze, and this edition already tops my pile of bedside guides.

Castigated, by turns, for being too bureaucratic and too political, too timorous and too ambitious, criticised for being too overbearing towards the Member States, yet easygoing towards its own occasional hiccups and failings, the European Commission is a scapegoat for Europe's problems and difficulties. Yet, in many respects criticism is simply the price of success. Guardian of the Treaties, executive body of the Community, invested with a monopoly of legislative initiative in many areas, the Commission is Europe's past, present and future – its very heart and soul.

Alongside the key part it plays within Europe's complex institutional triangle, the Commission has also played a prominent role in the emergence of Europe on the international stage. Trade policy was the originating vehicle for the Community's first venture onto the world stage. This is no mere coincidence, for European integration is fundamentally a project for peace and security. And it was underpinned from the very beginning by the idea, deeply rooted in classic liberal thought, that trade is the best way to ensure peace between nations. The European Commission was of major significance – as this book quite rightly recalls – in the emergence of the Community as a single, unified interlocutor with the Americans. So, it has proved critical in the development of an efficient and balanced multilateral trading system.

Gradually, its unquestioned success in trade policy has paved the way for a widening of the Commission's external role and resulted in a fostering of European influence in the world. Sometimes Europe is weakened by the complexity of its architecture and the unavoidable conflicts of competence that it generates both within the EU institutions and between the Commission and the Member States. Yet the overarching goal of creating a Europe with a single voice that can be a 'force for good' in the world is worth all the hassle and pain. As Trade Commissioner, I constantly experience the reality of how much stronger we are when Europe is united and how crucial it therefore is that we find an appropriate answer to the famous question coined by former US Secretary of State Henry Kissinger – 'If I want to talk to Europe, who do I call?' The Constitutional Treaty would go a long way towards achieving this.

As expected by its founders, the Treaty of Rome has not built Europe in a day, but rather provided it with a capacity to face constant new and unpredictable challenges. Today, in an ever changing and globalised world, the enlarged Union has a duty to play a role commensurate with its responsibilities and ambitions. This book shows, in a particularly accurate manner, how the Commission contributes day by day to the permanent renewal of the life of the Union and to making it a genuine model of political integration.

Peter Mandelson
Commissioner for Trade

Introduction. The European Commission in perspective

Geoffrey Edwards

Introduction

At a time of momentous change within the European Union, with enlargement to 25 completed in 2004 and the debates over the Constitutional Treaty during 2003-6, policy making and the institutional balance within the Union have been of critical importance. It is therefore particularly opportune to look again at the position of the Commission. If, in the past, the Commission was claimed as the most original and unprecedented of institutions without which the European Community would not have been constructed (Committee of Three 1979), its position by the mid-2000s was much more ambiguous – regarded as probably vital in the policy process but equally frequently seen as a factor in the inability of the Union to gain legitimacy in the eyes of its citizens. Such divergence of views has followed the Commission from the outset: to Jean Monnet, the first President of the High Authority, the Commission, like the High Authority, was to be an independent arbiter of the European interest (Monnet 1978), while to Walter Hallstein, the first President of the EEC Commission, it was a body committed to economic and political integration (Hallstein 1972). On the other hand, to General de Gaulle, the Commission comprised a group of pretentious technicians (de Gaulle 1971) and to Margaret Thatcher, it was a body intent upon 'the creeping expansion of [its]...authority... twisting the words and intentions of the European Council to its own ends' (Thatcher 1993, 743). Echoes of such divergences continue, their contemporary salience clear in the debates on the Constitutional Treaty during 2005, not least in France and the Netherlands.

If the Commission's stock has inevitably gone up and down over the course of the EC/EU's history, the Delors-led Commission has usually been regarded as the high point – or an aberration (Murray 2004). Neither the Santer nor Prodi Commissions were able to win the respect – nor, though, quite evoke the suspicion – of the Delors Commission, while that of Barroso has yet to make its mark.

Almost inevitably after Delors, member governments preferred a less charismatic Commission President, less intent on fulfilling a vision, than being efficient in the running of the new European Union – 'doing less but doing it better', indeed, became Jacques Santer's slogan while in office. But not only were member governments more alert to the implications of a dynamic Commission, the 1990s saw a much greater assertiveness on the part of national governments with 'Europe' becoming a much more salient domestic issue (Kassim and Menon 2004). The rejection of the Maastricht Treaty by the Danes, and the *'petit oui'* in the French referendum, suggested to many that the permissive consensus that had allowed European integration to proceed had come to an end. While integration deepened – through EMU, developments in JHA, and, arguably, even in CFSP, as well as the gradual extension of co-decision to the European Parliament – much stronger emphasis was placed on the so-called democratic deficit and greater accountability, which inevitably had profound implications for the Commission and its standing. Neither Santer, particularly with his enforced resignation, nor Prodi were able to offset this perceived deficit of both democracy and legitimacy. Their sense of frustration was clear in the Commission's White Paper on Governance, which, almost peevishly, declared:

> 'Where the Union does act effectively, it rarely gets proper credit for its actions... By the same token, Member States do not communicate well about what the Union is doing and what they are doing in the Union. "Brussels" is too easily blamed by Member States for difficult decisions that they themselves have agreed or even requested.' (Commission 2001a, 7).

Few national ministers or even prime ministers and presidents have seemingly been able to resist the temptation of Commission-bashing when unpopular European legislation has been proposed or introduced. Their criticisms may or may not have been justified. They have, though, reflected some of the fundamental changes in the nature of the Union and its Member States and the institutional balance between them.

The Commission and academe

There is a certain irony in the fact that greater academic attention has been given to the Commission only in the period since the Delors Presidency, when it has been so often forced onto the defensive. The dearth of academic literature on the Commission during the period from the late 1960s to the late 1980s was somewhat remarkable when there was no such lack of interest in other EC/EU institutions or policies. Despite being a permanent factor in an otherwise changing constellation of people and coalitions, the Commission, appeared to lose out – with one or two exceptions, notably David Coombes's *Politics & Bureaucracy in the European Community* of 1971, the only full-length study for nearly two decades. The Luxembourg Compromise of 1966 appeared to have set limits both to the integration process and to the independence and initiative of the Commission. It introduced a period of disenchantment with supranationalism in practice. During the period of stagnation in the 1970s, the Commission appeared able, in the face of recession, inflation, and monetary instability, only to propose misguided and unacceptable measures of harmonisation, which simply reinforced that alienation. A federalist Europe may have retained its adherents (even in the UK – see Burrows *et al* 1978), but as a political theory it appeared somewhat passé (Pentland 1973; Harrison 1974). Moreover, neo-functionalism, which to many provided a much needed theoretical explanation of European integration of the 1960s, and which laid such stress upon the central institutions – and especially the Commission – seemed to be wholly inadequate and misguided in a Europe dominated by General de Gaulle and his legacy (Hoffmann 1966). To the extent that explanation and theory received any attention during what has been termed the 'doldrums era' (Caporaso and Keeler 1995), intergovernmentalism and the interactions among Member States seemed to fit broader interpretations of the international system and the role of the nation state within it, especially for many American theorists. For most political scientists and specialists in international relations, the EC was too *sui generis* a phenomenon to encourage closer attention (Rosamond 2000, 98).

But academics are no more or less followers of political change (as well as of intellectual fashion) than others and the changes leading to and engendered by the Single European Act (SEA) led to a refocusing on integration and the role of the central institutions. At issue was the European Parliament, directly elected for the first time in 1979 and intent (largely under Altiero Spinelli's inspiration) on achieving political legitimacy for itself by proposing considerably increased powers in its Draft Treaty on European Union of 1985. The role of the European Court of Justice, with landmark decisions such as the *Cassis de Dijon* case of 1979, was also a crucial point of reference. In addition, a new dynamism came to characterise the Commission, much of it associated with the Presidency of the former French Finance Minister, Jacques Delors. Whatever Delors' personal role in enhancing the Commission's status, the conjunction of political factors provided the support for a heightened Commission profile.

The incoming Commission of January 1985 was able to exploit a number of factors such as the alarm over Europe's increasingly adverse position vis-à-vis US and Japanese competition and the tentative steps towards a research and development programme already being taken (Sandholtz and Zysman 1989) to reinforce the readiness of even the most reluctant of European governments to back a change in the institutional procedures to attain the goal of a single market. It was helped, too, by the new situation created by the resolution of Britain's budgetary problem, in that the Commission found a new ally in deepening the integration process, or at least on proposals making for deregulation and liberalisation. The White Paper on the Completion of the Internal Market was formally presented to the European Council in June 1985 (Commission 1985). The need to expedite decision-making to bring about that completion was perhaps the most critical element leading to the SEA of 1986. The reforms embodied in the SEA drew attention to the interaction of the central institutions, especially the Commission, different interest groups and the Member States.

The *relance* led to a revival of academic interest in integration theories in general and in the Commission in particular, that has continued despite the abatement of the 'Euphoria' that marked the later 1980s and, at least the first year of the 1990s – before, that is, the problems of ratifying and implementing the Treaty on European Union (TEU). Some old approaches were revived, others modified. Neofunctionalism was looked at anew even if it regained few supporters (but see Tranholm-Mikkelsen (1991) or Burley & Mattli (1993)). The realism of political scientists such as Stanley Hoffmann or historians such as Alan Milward (1992; 1993) was modified in the work of those such as Moravcsik (1991; 1993) to become a liberal intergovernmentalism. But there was, too, a movement away from a more IR approach of why and how states integrate towards a more comparative politics approach focusing on policy- and decision-making within the EU as, at least, a proto-political system (Taylor 1989; Sbragia 1992; Hix 1994). Such an approach appeared all the more justified as more and more issues were placed on the European agenda, not necessarily within an EC framework and subject to the 'Community method' of decision-making (see H Wallace in Wallace and Wallace 2000), but through a process of 'Brusselisation' that covered foreign policy, security and many hitherto interior ministry responsibilities that lay at the core of traditional national sovereignty. On the one hand, concepts such as the 'regulatory state' helped to explain processes within the EC framework (Majone 1991; 1993), or more broadly the concept of 'governance' (Marks 1996; Kohler Koch 1999) which took stimulus from both the strengthening of the regional dimension within EC policies and the growing demands from Europe's regions for greater recognition as well as the federal/confederal elements of the Union and its Member States. On the other hand, the reassertiveness of governments and stronger concerns over issues such as democracy within the Union, and its legitimacy, not least in tackling issues so close to core national concerns, led to a host of other approaches taken from both comparative politics and international relations such as institutionalism in its various guises (Peters 1999; Pierson 1996) and, closely linked to it, the concept of Europeanisation (Bulmer 2001; 2005; Featherstone & Radaelli 2003). Disputing all positivist approaches, social constructivism, with its different focus on identity, rules and norms within the Union, was seen as more helpful in understanding it (Jørgensen 1997; Christiansen et al 2001). Such a burgeoning of theoretical interest in the EC/EU since the treaty reforms of the SEA and Maastricht also saw moves towards synthesis (such as Peterson 1995 or Sandholtz and Sweet Stone 1998), as well as dispute.

The challenge of legitimation

Whether disputes over meta-, grand or partial theories have clarified the integration process, especially in the post-Maastricht and post-Delors period, the role of the supranational institutions, particularly the Commission, has been a key variable. Empirically, the role of the Commission has been under the spotlight for much of the period as the Union and its Member States have sought to meet new (and old) challenges in ever continuing rounds of Treaty reform. These challenges provide the background against which the role and functions of the Commission are discussed in the following chapters. They are complex and inter-related. Concern over the collapse of the permissive consensus and increased scepticism towards the EU suggested by the results of the referendums in Denmark and France in 1992 appeared to be echoed in the continuing fall in voting figures in European elections, even in such usually pro-integration Member States as the Netherlands – a process that culminated in the Dutch rejection of the Constitutional Treaty in June 2005. Whether or not the Dutch or French voter in 2005 was simply voting on the Treaty – many seem to have voted also on national political issues – or whether such low turn outs in elections reflects wider disenchantment with politics at any level, the question of the legitimacy of the European construction has inevitably been pushed into central focus.

Of the many dimensions of legitimacy, two are of critical importance to the Commission: the conception of a democratic deficit, and the seeming inability of the Commission to persuade European citizens either of the benefits of integration or its own role in bringing them about. Democratic norms imply at a minimum that the electorate believe they matter within the political system. European elections and the issues raised in them, as well as the voting figures themselves, suggest that the electorate have not yet been convinced. Despite, therefore, the growing role of the European Parliament, and, as Westlake shows in chapter 9, the increased accountability of the Commission to the Parliament with each Treaty reform, direct representation at the European level is not enough. In part, the problem remains the continued invisibility in the public mind of the Parliament itself, but the consequences for the Commission have been serious.

This is all the more so to the extent that there is on the part of the Commission itself what Meyer has termed a 'communications deficit' (Meyer 1999). When compared to many Member States, the Commission is particularly open, making information available at all stages of the policy process. But, as Murray (2004) has suggested, the Commission pays a price for this relative openness: 'Many of the scare stories which pepper the EU's press are exaggerated versions of ideas contained in preliminary, consultative documents...' (p55). Brussels 'bureaucrats' manage still to appear unaccountable and, indeed, still faceless. This last remains the case despite the fact that the appointment of Delors created a habit among the Member States of appointing former national ministers – even prime ministers – to the College of Commissioners, as Spence shows in chapter 1. Commission Presidents now include three former prime ministers (Santer, Prodi and Barroso) – even if two have been from smaller Member States, and the third one of many former prime ministers of Italy. Many Commissioners have, also, sought to remain national figures or at least to appear in their national media – whether to explain current Commission policy or to ensure their political standing on their return. And yet the media seems too often to persist in an image of the Commission as a faceless, distant and alien body.

The inability of the Commission to communicate effectively is, itself, due to a number of factors. Despite Prodi's reforms, the Commission remains ineffectual in its communications strategy. Its reputation was not enhanced by the fact that the Santer Commission was obliged to resign; that for many did not offset the reasons for its resignation – mismanagement and dubious if not corrupt practices. The managerial reforms Santer instigated and which were finally implemented under Prodi by his Vice President, Neil Kinnock, were not of the stuff of national media headlines. Even with a more centralised media service and daily briefings, what headlines there are derive more from the general tendency of national media to report briefings from their national ministers rather than Commission spokesmen. It is in this way that the frequent scapegoating of the Commission takes place, while national ministers can take the credit for any good news. There remains, not least in the British media, the predominant motif of decisions being taken *by* Brussels rather than *in* Brussels, with the role of governments fortuitously overlooked whenever so desired.

The communications deficit masks a much deeper challenge faced by the Commission, which it shares with Member State governments. Whether because of globalisation (Habermas 2001) or the simple complexity of government in the twenty-first century (Scharpf 1999), governments have not only become more reassertive within the EU for fear of an ambitious Commission, but because 'Europe' and the economic model it appears to espouse has become so much more divisive in national politics (*cf* the critique of the 'liberal', Anglo-Saxon model in the French referendum on the Constitutional Treaty). Governments have therefore seen a greater need for assertiveness as a way of masking their own incapacities. On the one hand, the introduction of the euro may have resolved many macro-economic problems; on the other, it has limited governments' freedom of manoeuvre at the national level to respond to economic and social problems – *pace* those who have exceeded the restrictions of the Stability and Growth Pact. And even where common economic and social problems have been recognised, derived, say, from Europe's lack of competitiveness, new approaches have been mooted even if they have so far yielded little. The Lisbon process has meant that issues such as employment policies, pensions, health care, social exclusion/inclusion policies as well as e-Europe are debated at the Union level with best practices, common targets and strategies put forward – but with limited results (Murray 2003). The argument is not that such issues need to be communitarised to achieve results – the role of the Commission within the open method of coordination (OMC) is a highly limited one of monitoring rather than initiating proposals except where Treaty provisions suggest a clear basis. It is simply that it continues to be difficult for governments to act on such electorally sensitive issues at a time when there is already tension between the possible need for 'more Europe' and continued suspicion and scepticism about Europe and the loss of national identity.

Suspicion and uncertainty about the balance to be drawn between Member State responsibilities and what should be done at the European level has been a perpetual concern. A 'journey to an unknown destination' to cite Andrew Shonfield in 1972, may then have been an exciting, inclusive stimulus for many in Western Europe (Shonfield 1972). At the end of the twentieth century, a 'return to Europe' after the Cold War still excited many in Eastern Europe. But whereas Joschka Fischer may have sought to stimulate a new debate on the future of Europe in 2000 (Fischer 2000), the end result of the Laeken Council, the Convention on Europe's Future and the Constitutional Treaty, has been greater suspicion and uncertainty about the end results of the integration process.

That suspicion has been further complicated by the continuous process of enlargement culminating in the accession of ten new Member States in May 2004 and the prospect of further enlargement to include other Balkan states and Turkey. There is, in other words, not only the problem of the lack of a clear idea of the end result, but also the issue of uncertainty about the geographical limits of the EU. The possibility of any state with a 'European vocation' being allowed to accede to the Union once they have met the

'Copenhagen criteria' of being democratic, an open market economy and able to meet the demands of membership, far from being a ringing endorsement of the values of the Union, has become increasingly divisive. The divisions over Turkey's membership seen in France, Germany and elsewhere have been particularly deep.

Such tensions between processes of Europeanisation and continued or reawakened Euroscepticism can be seen in other areas that impinge on the Union's policies in general, and on the Commission and its role in particular. At the rhetorical level, for example, many governments have been clear on the need for a European response to international crime (drug trafficking and people trafficking especially) and terrorism. Not all have been convinced of the desirability of all consequent policy choices or of their justification, even after 9/11 (or the Madrid and London bombings), whether on the extent to which a common arrest warrant should be applicable or over the invasion of Iraq. Public opinion is frequently cited as being in favour of 'more Europe' in terms of security and defence (*Eurobarometer* in Leonard 2005) but few governments have matched even limited rhetoric with increased expenditure. Expectations of greater European activity in different areas sometimes sit uneasily therefore with declared policy aims, with confusion, further suspicion and increased political scepticism often the result.

And amidst all this sits the European Commission. On the one hand, its responsibilities have been increased in nearly every round of Treaty reform, though often shared with Member States. On the other, it has perforce to remain a small bureaucratic body since the Member States have not provided increased resources to match enhanced responsibilities. The result has not necessarily made for greater efficiency either in terms of policy formation or policy implementation. The battle between resources and responsibilities is particularly well-illustrated in chapter 11 where Lewis shows how the communitarisation of JHA issues led gradually to the establishment of a new DG, with a dramatically extended remit in the face of the growing problems of drug and people trafficking and other international crimes, and again in the aftermath of 9/11 in the fight against terrorism. Spence in chapter 14 also shows the impact of an increased EC as well as EU international role.

The role and functions of the Commission

If the above posits some of the challenges faced by the EU and the Commission, one of the questions explored in the chapters that follow is how or whether the basic role and functions of the European Commission have changed over the decades. David Coombes grouped the Commission's roles under five broad headings which have been used as general guidelines ever since. These roles are:

–   an *initiative role*, since with few exceptions within the EC framework, the Commission has the formal responsibility for initiating legislation; it shares that responsibility with the Member States in other areas;

–   an *administrative and management role*, in areas such as agriculture

or competition policy which have been delegated to the
Commission by the Member States;

–   a *mediating role*, i.e., mediating among the Member States and
    between the institutions in order to reach agreement and a
    decision;

–   a *representative role* through its representation of the EC in third
    countries and in many international organisations and participa-
    tion in the representation of the EU through the so-called troika
    (which can often be a team of four);

–   a *normative role* – both as guardian of the Treaties and the *acquis
    communautaire* (i.e., all the Community's legislation and pro-
    cedures) and as the conscience of the Community, which it has
    taken to include proposing ideas and recommendations beyond
    the remit of the Treaties;

Changes and modifications have been inevitable over a 25-year period.
Here we explore some of the more important challenges to and changes in
these various roles which are dealt with in greater depth in other chapters.
    As Coombes pointed out in 1971, such diverse roles have demanded dif-
ferent types of organisation. In a very real sense, the history of the
Commission is one in which it has sought the means of reconciling the different demands laid upon it, with the Member States and their representatives rarely looking on with indifference. Indeed, few if any of the roles
assigned to the Commission under the Treaties have not raised controversy
at some stage or other with one or more of the Member States. As Diedrichs
and Wessels suggest in chapter 7, there have been significantly different
models of relationship between the Commission and the Member States,
with the Commission as putative government of a United States of Europe
at one extreme and as a traditional international secretariat at the other. Too
often the relationship between the Commission and the Member States has
been regarded as a zero-sum game: the acquisition of responsibilities by the
Community equalling the loss of those responsibilities by the Member
States, which is then popularised as the *diktat* of Brussels.
    Such a characterisation inevitably oversimplifies and masks many of the
difficult issues involved in such a multilevel, multifaceted form of governance. On the one hand, for example, as Cini (1996) and Hooghe (2001) have
shown, the Commission and the Council are portrayed as if unitary actors.
Hooghe, for one, has pointed to the very different images of Europe and different attitudes towards supranationalism and intergovernmentalism
among those within the Commission (and see also Egeberg 1999). On the
other hand, there is a wide consensus as Page has suggested on 'the constitutional role' of the Commission, which:

> 'Gives the organisation a legitimacy in political controversies
> rarely given to the permanent administrative organisations of
> nation states – the legitimate authority to be a major independent

actor, and an initiating body, in the policy process.' (Page 1997, 147-48)

Taken too far and such independence is usually challenged by one or other Member State. But there have often been as many radical differences among Member States as within the Commission. Moreover these differences towards the Commission and its roles can vary over time – compare, for example, the Mitterrand-Delors relationship with that of Chirac-Prodi, not least at the Maastricht and Nice IGCs (Endo 1999; Gray and Stubb 2001). But what has been clear is that the Commission's position in the inter-institutional balance has been under discussion in all the IGCs since 1986, particularly those that led to the Treaties of Amsterdam and Nice (see chapter 16).

The Commission as initiator and its competitors

As Diedrichs and Wessels make clear, the interaction between the Commission and the Council is central to Community decision-making – now with the significant empowerment of the European Parliament. The interaction is one that has engendered continuous tension between member governments and the Commission over what has been delegated to the institutions and what powers and influence the Commission therefore has (see, for example, Pollack 2003). It would be a misreading of the Commission's role, as policy initiator, for example, to see it as wholly dependent on the Member States. As Pierson has suggested, 'the current functioning of the institutions cannot be derived from the aspirations of the original designers' (1996, 127), or from a somewhat different angle, as Scharpf declared, powers when not delegated by governments had been 'usurped by the Commission and the Court through interpretations of Treaty provisions which exceeded the original intentions of the contracting governments' (Scharpf 2001). Clearly, however, Commission Presidents, when they have sought to provide leadership, have not always been given the opportunity to do so; and Member States have deliberately sought to down-play the Commission's role not only in the second and third pillars, but also in the framework of monetary union, and in relation to the Lisbon process or Open Method of Coordination.

Nonetheless, the Commission's right of initiative remains central to its independence and to the inter-institutional balance. It was originally set out in Article 155 (EEC) and continued into the Constitutional Treaty in Article I-34, where European laws were to be enacted by the Council and Parliament 'on a proposal from the Commission'. However, although the Commission retains the sole right to initiate legislation within the EC framework (with exceptions given the role of the ECB and ECOFIN – though see below, p 21), it has sometimes been more a formal responsibility than a source of authority. Both the Council (and the European Parliament) have frequently asked the Commission to undertake studies (the Council under Article 208 (ex152) TEC) or propose legislation – there has been a 'trigger mechanism', in other words, embedded in the system from the very outset which enabled the Council in broad terms to set the agenda and undermine or usurp the intended role assigned to the Commission. This became more common in the aftermath of the Luxembourg Compromise of 1966, the establishment of the European

Council, and pillarisation under Maastricht. Michalski (2002) has suggested that by the late 1990s, the Council, Parliament and the social partners were contributing between 20–25 per cent of what became Commission initiatives.

The relationship between the Commission and the Member States has always been unavoidably complex in view of the need for interaction throughout the policy process, from policy formulation through to policy implementation. In terms of policy formulation, even Hallstein during the Commission's 'honeymoon period' of 1958-65 was criticised for *not* continuing the practice of informing, consulting and entering into pre-negotiations with the Member States before a proposal was formally launched (Marjolin 1989, chapter 6). As one of Hallstein's fellow Commissioners put it, the key lay in the two bodies' working together:

> 'The truth of the matter is that, inevitably, the members of the Commission, however dedicated to the European idea, had to take the positions of national governments into account or else risk losing all effectiveness. An essential part of their action ... consisted in reconciling what they considered to be the common interest with what they knew of the concerns of the different governments, including the government of the country to which they belonged.' (Marjolin 1989, 314).

Quite where to pitch any initial proposal, at the highest level of Europe's common interest, or the lowest level of aggregated national preferences, has been a perennial problem confronting the Commission. How to characterise the negotiated outcome has equally been a preoccupation among academics (see, for example, Moravcsik 1993)

Such a constant interaction between the Commission and the Committee of Permanent Representatives (COREPER) was necessary in order that the Commission could be productive; as Hallstein, himself, later put it: 'these constant contacts at different levels help to create an intellectual and psychological climate in which cooperation comes easily and naturally. People become involved and work together to find solutions to the Community's problems in accordance with the Treaty' (Hallstein 1972, 71). '*Engrenage*', this meshing together of a specialised 'European' coterie of national officials, was regarded by neofunctionalists such as Lindberg as an important factor in the integration process (Lindberg 1963, 53-54). The French, indeed, tended to argue that the Community itself would benefit if the Commission was made up of seconded national officials who then returned 'Europeanised' to their capitals (Coombes 1968). Interestingly, they also sought to ensure that foreign policy matters, coordinated through European Political Cooperation when it was established in 1969, would not be contaminated by contact with the Commission – a similar 'red line' was pursued by the British in respect of the Commission and ESDP, with equally limited success (see Spence, chapter 14). But while the Commission bureaucracy may still regard national experts as a mixed blessing (see chapter 6), there are now few national ministries without a European section – whether filled with former detached national experts or not – so pervasive has the European level become. However, this has not necessarily brought with it a significantly increased disposition to agree or convergence of policy; patterns of socialisation are markedly different in different ministries as well as different Member States (see Wessels 2003; Bulmer 2005).

Nonetheless, it has long been an article of faith among many Europeanists that *engrenage* brings with it a greater sense of 'can do' among European and national officials towards resolving the various technical problems presented to them (H. Wallace in Wallace and Wallace 2000). Indeed, it has come about sometimes regardless of the procedural basis on which decisions are actually taken, although, rather naturally from the Commission's perspective, it works most effectively when the 'Community method' is used (i.e. the Commission proposes legislation for the Council and Parliament to adopt by co-decision).

However, the interaction of officials and technicians brings with it certain problems. Altiero Spinelli long ago pointed to the danger of 'bureaucratisation' in terms of a habit of reacting 'suspiciously and fastidiously to intrusions of the political world upon well-ordered administrative activity' (Spinelli 1966, 72). From his perspective, this endangered the role of the Commission as the motor of integration. Once the Commission developed from the small, non-hierarchical, flexible organisation well able to establish easy and close contacts with national officials and technicians, envisaged by Monnet (Mazey 1992), bureaucratisation was inevitable. When faced with the economic and political conditions of the 1970s, it meant the Commission could no longer rely for legislative initiatives on the detailed guidance of the Treaties, thereby reinforcing the tendency towards reliance on precedent within or Member State initiatives from without the Commission (Three Wise Men 1979). The situation was not much improved with the Maastricht pillars, when, if again one takes the Commission line, the transparency, consistency, effectiveness and egalitarianism of the Community method was diluted (Barnier and Vitorino September 2002). Certainly the heavily bureaucratic procedures demanded by national officials and accepted by politicians in the field of justice and home affairs meant that little headway was achieved in the third pillar until after the Amsterdam Treaty (Monar in Monar and Wessels 2001) and, arguably, not until after 9/11 in some areas.

The process of enlargement has compounded the problem. Each round of accessions has inevitably challenged the cohesion and solidarity of the Community itself. For the Commission, there have been two particular problems: in terms of proposing legislation or policy to the Council, there is the question of how to meet the greater heterogeneity of interests, circumstances and aims among the Member States; but the Commission faces a prior question as to what may be politically possible in that the Commission itself is more heterogeneous and subject to more internal differences. This impacts, too, on how the Commission manages and administers policy. There is, in other words, the ever greater complexity of managing a multinational bureaucracy.

Management and efficiency

Spinelli had noted the problem of management even among the original Six when he wrote:

'an elementary human solidarity is always present in greater measure among functionaries of the same nation, with their common habits and language, and subtle currents of xenophobia among functionaries of one country toward those of other countries appear rather easily. This combination of circumstances accounts for the inevitable presence in the bosom of the administration of considerable national loyalty and sometimes even national *omertà* (code of silence).' (Spinelli 1966, 73)

With successive enlargements different mixes of nationalities have brought obvious differences in attitude and behaviour which clearly affect management methods. Colleagues of different nationalities do not always share a collective approach to questions of authority, discipline and basic managerial tradition. Language groups if not nationalities tend to come together at work as they do in leisure activities (Anthropology 1993). As Abélès and Bellier have observed: 'Chaques nationalité a vocation à introduire dans l'instance commune les méthodes de travail que lui paraissent efficaces' (Abélès and Bellier 1996, 434). But language and nationality are not the whole story; politico-cultural differences spill over into the wider policy framework. The culture of openness on the part of the Scandinavians contrasts with, say, the British tradition of passing information on a 'need to know' basis.

Despite his undoubted authority and position vis-à-vis the Council and Member States, Delors did not take the opportunity to introduce some much needed reform in the Commission itself. His personal style, and that of his *cabinet*, inevitably had an impact on the Commission's sense of collegiality as well as its new-found status and sense of purpose. However, in establishing a presidential system and a position beyond that of *primus inter pares*, a degree of tension was inescapable. By the time his second Commission took office in January 1989, Delors had unrivalled control of such policy areas as monetary affairs, and had even divided Lord Cockfield's internal market portfolio among three new Commissioners. He was, in addition, able to rely on a powerful *cabinet*, led by Pascal Lamy, described as 'arguably the single most powerful individual in the Commission after Delors himself' (Ross 1993, 26). The power of the Delors network, run by his *cabinet*, turned the upper reaches of the Commission into an *'administration de mission'* as opposed to an *'administration de gestion'*. As such, it was able to ride above the concerns of the Commission services and, sometimes, of their Commissioners, adding a further layer to the separation between the politics of the College and the bureaucracy of the services (Grant 1994; see also chapter 4). As a result, the need for structural reform within the Commission grew ever more acute and overdue (Ludlow 1993).

It was neither his style nor within his grasp for Santer to follow the Delors pattern. On entering office in January 1995, his Commission was faced not only with the legacy of unpopularity in the aftermath of Maastricht and demands for reform but also with the need to mesh together a Commission of twenty that included Commissioners from the three new Member States (Austria, Finland and Sweden). Some moves to end intra-Commission rivalry and improve coordination within the Commission were agreed early on, at least in terms of the Commission's external portfolios (see chapter 4). But further practical reform tended to take a back seat in view of the demands of the IGC that led ultimately to the Amsterdam Treaty of 1997. The Reflection Group that had been given responsibility for preparing the IGC looked at the wider picture – i.e. both the institutional reform demanded by Maastricht and its implementation, and also at the potential need for change given the prospect of further enlargement to include perhaps an additional ten or even fifteen states. The inability of heads of state and government to agree on the future size of the Commission, which then became one of the so-called 'Amsterdam left-overs' to be dealt with at Nice, somewhat overshadowed the changes that were made relating to the strengthening of the role of the Commission President and the support given to the Commission's efforts at reorganising tasks within the College better to match portfolios and tasks.

With Santer's enforced resignation, it was therefore left to the Prodi Presidency to push through the implementation of the internal reforms he had initiated. Fuller details of the reforms are dealt with in chapters 1 and 17. But what is significant here was the fact that Prodi, through reorganising the College and the top echelons of the bureaucracy through breaking up long-established fiefdoms, as in agriculture, competition etc, sought three outcomes: to ensure a greater independence of the Commission from Member State lobbying; a greater flow of ideas; and greater efficiency. With Neil Kinnock as Vice President, he was determined to reform the bureaucracy with the aim of creating a European civil service based more on merit than seniority and nationality and with better career prospects.

Internal reform of the Commission in the interests of greater efficiency was complemented by concern over the size of the College itself. Continuous and prospective enlargement has meant that there are deemed to be too few portfolios of real substance for the growing number of Commissioners. During the 1990s, therefore, there were growing pressures to reduce the size of the College and delink it from any sense of representation, especially on the part of the bigger Member States. However, even if the French no longer saw an independent but 'representative' Commission as a vital part of the institutional balance to inhibit any resurgent Germany, smaller Member States continued to see it as essential in the prevention of the hegemony of the larger states. Insofar as the Commission has been successful in supporting a European interest against big state dominance, then it has often be seen as the small states' friend. Magnette and Nicolaïdis quote the statement of an Irish foreign minister that if 'the Irish public has a strong sense of the importance of the Commission as a guarantor of fair play and of the common interest' it is not 'that commissioners act as national representatives, but that there is around the table a fair appreciation of the concerns of individual member states' (2004, 13). What they have termed the 'Lilliput syndrome' of the bigger Member States feeling that they are held back by the smaller, may have been most strongly felt in terms of Council voting, but it plays out in relation to the Commission as well. The proposals within the Nice IGC and again in the Convention to establish a smaller, leaner machine were rationalised on the basis of greater efficiency. This was resisted by the smaller states – which were later joined by most of the new Member States but without being able to carry the day. Nice stands therefore, so that once the EU has 27 Member States, the size of the Commission will be limited to 20 (at Amsterdam, the French had suggested a

Commission of 12-14). Given the proposal for strict rotation among the Member States, while smaller states may be concerned about their particular interests, it is a moot point how seriously some of the larger Member States will take the Commission if it has no recognisable national face to show appreciation of their particular concerns.

Mediation and the Commission's rivals

The reluctance of most of the new Member States to envisage a much smaller Commission reflected clearly the argument that smaller countries have traditionally looked to the central institutions and to the Commission, especially 'as defenders of their interests against the tendency of the big countries to dominate' (Grant 2004, 5). Interestingly, Grant went on to suggest that Germany in the past had also regarded itself as a friend of the Commission and of smaller states, noting that under Schröder, Germany's attitude towards the Commission had become more Franco-British and had lost a critical role in relation to smaller states. But what makes the Commission particularly significant for the newer and smaller hard-pressed governments is, as Christiansen has suggested, the continuous growth in the complexity of European governance (Christiansen 2001). However much the Constitutional Treaty had been sought as a means of simplifying EU policy-making, it remains intensely complex with informal processes overlaying already Byzantine procedures. Larger Member States invariably have the resources as well as, usually, the determination to ensure that decisions taken fit the wider picture of national preferences. Smaller states have to rely more on the Commission and like-minded governments to gain the same insurance.

For the Commission, however much it might seek to maintain such an important mediatory role, there have always been difficulties, some built into the system. There has always been, for example, the tension between DGs and Commissioners whether based on nationality, portfolio, or ideological preference. There has not always been any consistent emphasis on ensuring coherence, even with a more presidential system; the Commission itself is as beset by the complexities of technological change and the demands for adaptation, regulation and so on as Member States, large or small. There has also been an inherent tension between initiating proposals that are held to be in Europe's best interests, and then acting as honest broker within the Council framework. Having concluded that a proposal is the best for Europe, and conscious of its right to withdraw and thereby ditch any proposal, the Commission has sometimes been characterised as an nth state (though see Pinder 1975). In the aftermath of the Luxembourg Compromise, the Presidency of the Council also took on a more significant role in mediating among its fellow Member governments, although inconsistently (Wallace and Edwards 1976). Some governments, for example, have regarded it as costly in terms of national preferences (Elgström 2003, chapter 3). Lack of continuity and consistency were major factors in the Constitutional Treaty reforms on a more permanent Presidency. But even without the Treaty, Member States have increasingly looked to each other to collaborate over two or three Presidencies in order to steer a more-or-less coordinated programme through the process. That may still leave the

Commission as a more stable point of reference for other governments, lobbyists etc. But it has been challenged in another direction, too, by the emergence of the Council Secretariat as more than simple note-takers. This may have become particularly clear in the field of foreign and security policy as David Buchan pointed out in 1993, well before the appointment of the High Representative (Buchan 1993). But in general, too, the Secretariat has taken on a much higher profile, however variable the reliance on it of incoming Presidencies.

Yet the Commission has also adapted. While its greater accountability to the European Parliament (EP) since the SEA has alarmed some from the perspective of authoritative regulation, for others it has been more the danger of the Commission's role as mediator between the Parliament and the Council that is of greater significance. If, under the cooperation procedure, it was vital for the EP to win the support of the Commisison, under co-decision it appeared to be more an EP-Council procedure which limited the Commission's role. However, as Westlake in this volume and Corbett et al (2003, 186-194) point out, the Commission's role can be critical in bringing about a result in the conciliation procedures, not least through its more informal contacts between both sides at the outset of the process.

A weakened representative?

The representational role of the Commission has also been challenged both directly by Member States and by policy and institutional innovation. Under the Treaties (Article 133, ex 113 TEC), the Community has exclusive competence within the framework of the common commercial policy for trade in goods. Negotiating in the GATT, and later the WTO, on trade has, as Smith points out in chapter 12, frequently created problems. The French, in particular, have been critical of the Commission if it has appeared to go beyond its mandate in negotiations, especially on agriculture – this despite the close watch officials from member governments have had from the outset over the Commission in the 133 Committee. Prodi's assignment of (the French) Pascal Lamy as Trade Commissioner in place of (the British) Leon Brittan was seen as a deliberately placatory move. However, during the 1980s the GATT had moved beyond trade in goods to consider services (GATS) and intellectual property (TRIPS). The French, again, were to the fore in trying to limit Community competence, and therefore the role of the Commission, and the issue of whether the EC or Member States had competence went to the ECJ. In its decision 1/94, the ECJ appeared to step back from its hitherto more integrative position – including support for responsibilities implied under the Treaties – by limiting EC competence to trade in goods as requested by eight of the Member States (Dashwood and Hillion 2000). Few of the governments could argue that a common position in the WTO was unlikely to be more influential and so accepted the need in such mixed agreements for close coordination. Yet, as Meunier and Nicolaïdis (1999) have argued, it seemed to mark a shift in member governments' attitudes – as well as the ECJ's – towards the balance between the internal distribution of responsibilities and possibly shaping the global economy. The consequence, however, was prolonged renegotiation through the IGCs that led to both Amsterdam and Nice, with still a lack of certainty of outcomes.

What challenged the Commission's role and function even more pro-foundly was when such commercial policies were put more clearly at the disposal of political considerations, through the Common Foreign and Security Policy (CFSP), pillar II of Maastricht. That challenge had, as Nuttall and others have shown, been of long standing and had been a constant pre-occupation of the Commission (and some more supranationally inclined Member States) from the creation of European Political Cooperation, CFSP's precursor, in 1969 (Nuttall 1992 and 2000). The debate over whether politics or economics determined policy might well have been artificial but it had policy-making and institutional repercussions, with turf-fights within the Council structures, between COREPER and the Political Committee, and, of course, between the Community method and intergovernmentalism.

Whereas, however, intergovernmentalism in the third pillar, having been regarded as inefficient and ineffectual, was substantially 'communitarised' at Amsterdam, similar failings within CFSP led to very much weaker calls for any parallel reform. Indeed, as Spence shows in chapter 14, Amsterdam created even greater opportunity for inter-institutional rivalry and competi-tion in the person of the High Representative. It was fortunate that both Javier Solana as the first High Representative and Chris Patten as the Commissioner for foreign policy determined to limit any public spats and to work as closely as possible in tandem. Nonetheless, it became ever more clear that Solana was more than merely the servant of the Council; it became as much a question of him seeking foreign ministers' approval as foreign ministers seeking his advice. The infrastructure Solana created gave him the resources that could provide him with an informational base that was dif-ferent from those of both Member States and the Commission and which allowed him not only to participate with the Presidency and the Commission within the troika but to undertake missions on his own if necessary. Solana's role, for example, in the Orange Revolution of 2004 in Ukraine was particularly telling, especially for the new Member States. The Constitutional Treaty's proposal to create an EU Minister of Foreign Affairs would have developed Solana's position still further, creating additional fears on the part of some within the Commission insofar as the Minister would take on the roles both of the High Representative and Commissioner. Whether an individual could ride two rather different horses at the same time would have been interesting to say the least.

A motor, a conscience and independence

Given such differences and tensions within and about the Commission, it is not surprising that there are very different perceptions of what the Commission's role could and should be. For their part, member govern-ments may accept the Commission's role as motor of integration and the ini-tiator of legislation in the European interest, but they may not always be convinced of its desirability either in general or on specific issues. The inde-pendence of the Commission is guaranteed under the Treaties. That inde-pendence may have been rarely challenged directly since the departure of General de Gaulle, who, for example, refused to allow the reappointment of Hallstein for a third Presidency of the Commission (though Mrs Thatcher, in her time, refused to reappoint one of the British Commissioners, Lord

Cockfield, despite his eagerness to remain to oversee the completion of the single market – a process in which he had been intimately and vitally involved under the first Delors Presidency – seemingly on the grounds that he had 'gone native' (Cockfield 1994)). Moreover, the disputes over new Commission Presidents, with Santer and Prodi being very much compromise candidates (see chapter 1), suggest that member governments remain alert both to the Commission's independence and the significance of the President. Indeed, whether as a result of or despite such concerns, successive treaty reform has led to what has been termed a growing 'presidentialisation' within the Commission, with the President being given increasing responsibilities for the accountability of the Commission as a whole.

Independence can be interpreted in different ways, not least when a government believes that its voice is not being heard on an issue of vital national importance, or if its interests are more generally being dismissed through ignorance or lack of familiarity. But there are also very different national traditions in terms of the nature of the relationship between government and non-governmental bodies, social partners or other interests, with some firmly institutionalised through economic and social councils, and others, ostensibly at least, equally firmly kept at arm's length. Given the Commission's need for expertise, whether from government departments or interest groups, it is often open to challenge for being too close to particular interests or influences; it is inevitably a fine line between providing information and lobbying. Yet acceptance, in general, of the Commission's independence remains a vital factor if it is to retain the authority to remain the motor of integration and set the Community agenda within the parameters of the Treaties and beyond.

Pushing beyond Treaty limits has frequently been successful; it has also been a major factor in arousing and maintaining suspicion of the Commission. Over the years, not least during the Delors period, a number of steps have been used to extend the Community's competence and therefore the role of the Commission. An initial use of Article 308 (ex 235 TEC), which allows the Commission to propose Community action not foreseen in the Treaties, has then led the Commission to seek to bring about a change in the legal base and a consequent shift from unanimity to majority voting. This was the case, for example, in environmental legislation, a specific legal base for environmental legislation being introduced under the SEA, initially requiring unanimity, which was then switched to qualified majority voting (QMV) under Maastricht. Similar progressions have occurred in other fields, such as social policy – with the new Labour government of 1997 finally signing up to the Social Chapter of Maastricht in 1997 – and in health, consumer protection, education and other areas not originally delegated to the Community. In other cases, the Commission initiated research into particular areas of social policy, vocational training and education to bring about closer cooperation, or sought to take advantage of imprecise drafting. Pressure from outside the EC/EU, as in the case of the G24 and the coordination of aid to Central and Eastern Europe, has led to an acceptance, at least in principle, that new areas ought to be brought within the European framework, with the Commission then managing to put this into practice by delineating the content in so-called 'whereas' clauses or 'recitals' in

Community legislation, which set out the legal and political basis for the proposal.

Not all such measures have been met with success – the Lisbon process, for example, owes much to member governments seeking an alternative route. But whether a government seeks to reject a proposed policy on procedural grounds (does the Community have competence?) or substantive grounds (is the policy desirable in itself?), it can become politically divisive, both in domestic political terms and among the Community institutions, and, frequently, the Commission becomes suspect or scapegoat. British ministers, for example, have often led the way with criticisms of the way in which the Commission has sought to move into 'every nook and cranny of society'. Such labelling of the Commission as a self-aggrandising, mismanaged, corrupt and sometimes simply 'foreign' or 'alien' bureaucracy inevitably undermines its standing and authority.

The counterpoint to such aggrandisement throughout has, of course, been Member States' use of the veto. The Luxembourg Compromise of 1966 had no legal validity but has 'hovered' in the background, to use a former British Foreign Secretary's term, ever since. From the outset it had a massive political consequence insofar as it removed the obligation to accept QMV where a Member State declared that 'a vital national interest' was at stake. It meant that the predisposition to accept compromise inherent in QMV was lost, thus diminishing the Commission's ability to pursue what it saw as the European interest. The Commission was forced to take account in formulating its proposals of the minimalist position of each Member State. It was no longer a question of unanimity in the Council to amend a Commission proposal (under Article 149 of the Treaty of Rome) but unanimity to achieve acceptance. It meant a more complicated and more dependent relationship with the Council of Ministers.

And yet, since the 1980s and the SEA, QMV has increasingly become the norm within the EC framework, a framework that has also seen considerably wider responsibilities. That, however, according to commentators such as Majone, has not necessarily extended the Commission's authority or reduced the complexities it faces. Many of the competences moved to the European level are shared with the Member States or have been moved on a much more flexible, less harmonised, less 'communitarian' basis (Majone 2002). Other agencies have been established to implement policies, with the Commission left struggling to coordinate them in the interests of coherence. At the same time, Majone and others (for example, Héritier 2001) have pointed to the challenge posed to the Commission by the move towards co-decision with the EP on so many issues decided by QMV, in the sense that it risks compromising the Commission's credibility as regulator – Majone going as far as to term it 'the perils of parliamentarisation'. For its part, the Commission has been attempting to (re-) enhance its executive role, charging the Council and the Parliament to focus more on defining the essential elements of policy and controlling the way in which those policies are executed. The Parliament, that is to say, should enhance its role in feeding the views of its electors into the political debate in a 'better use of powers' (Commission 2001a).

If the Luxembourg Compromise has slowly been transformed into more consensual and even majoritarian decision-making, the role of the European

Council has grown ever more significant. It began as a deliberate challenge by Giscard d'Estaing to take up the political leadership of the Community. The primary aim was for heads of state and government to articulate Europe's strategic and long-term goals. To deal with the growing problems caused by structural economic change compounded by global monetary instability, oil crises and the soon-to-be-realised threat of recession, Europe, as Bulmer and Wessels (1987) put it, fell back on what had been called its 'ultimate resource', the leaders of Europe themselves. However, in addition to these 'cosy fireside chats', i.e., informal exchanges on strategic aims, heads of state and government also began to frame if not take decisions and to settle issues outstanding from other Councils. While, by the end of the 1970s, the Commission President had become a fixture in all parts of the discussions, it was not until the Delors Presidency that the Commission was able to make any serious impact. But, as Ludlow has suggested, it was not simply Delors strengthening the Commission's long-term capacity for leadership, it was providing leadership through the European Council (Ludlow 1991, 117).

Nonetheless, the Delors factor can be seen as vital in reviving the Commission's authority. It has been equally important in maintaining the idea of an independent Commission regardless of subsequent Commission Presidencies. As Delors himself suggested during the celebrations in Rome to mark the thirtieth anniversary of the Community, the Commission was a 'strategic authority' established by the founding fathers to 'guarantee the continuity of the [integration] project despite the political or geopolitical hazards'. Acting as the 'custodian of European interests ... [and] as a repository of past achievements', the Commission had a unique obligation to point 'the way to the goal ahead' (EC Bulletin 1987). However, that obligation could not be carried out in isolation; as Delors also put it, this time when speaking to the European Parliament in January 1988, 'the Commission itself cannot achieve much but it can generate ideas. Its main weapon is its conviction' (Commission of the European Communities, 1988).

Delors' role was therefore critical not only in terms of a more independent authority but one authorised to be the motor of integration. His Presidency has been much discussed (see for example, Grant 1994; Ross 1995; Endo 1999; Drake 2000, though also see Moravcsik 1999). He held office longer than any of his predecessors. He was in the enviable position, at least until 1991, of having a vision of a Community which was shared with those of critical political importance and which appeared to fit with what was politically possible, whether in terms of the completion of the internal market and a more cohesive social space, brokering the budgetary agreements or preparing the report on EMU. He was also able to assert a much stronger Commission identity both within the EC and on the broader international stage, and, with the end of the Cold War, articulated a strong sense of Europe's destiny. He had the political authority and determination to pursue his own vision, and was well able to exploit his relationship with President Mitterrand and with Chancellor Kohl, especially in view of his early, positive role over German unification when he was able to take advantage of the reticence of other European leaders (Spence, 1991). It was the Commission, too, that was given responsibility for coordinating the G24 assistance to Central and Eastern Europe, and so on.

What enhanced his stature even further and distinguished him from other Commission Presidents was the perception of Delors as a potential President of France, and not merely as President of the European Commission. Malfatti may have resigned from the Commission in order to contest Italian parliamentary elections, and Romano Prodi, too, returned to domestic politics, though he did not quite resign before doing so in 2004, while Roy Jenkins returned to Britain to help establish the Social Democrat Party. But few other Presidents were regarded as having much of a political future. In being spoken of as a successor to President Mitterrand – at least until the changes in the Left's fortunes in France and the set-back of Maastricht, to which the French electorate agreed by only the narrowest of margins – Delors had, for a time, unprecedented political leverage. Even Stanley Hoffmann, very much from the intergovernmental camp of commentators, was led to suggest that 'while the Community's progress has depended on a series of bargains among its main members, Delors has skilfully prodded them and enlarged the opportunities for further integration' (Hoffmann 1991).

Spence tracks the subsequent impact of Commission Presidents in chapter 1. Santer, despite his effort to do less better – and the flood of legislation to bring about the completion of the single market did wane – inevitably suffered from being compared with Delors. It was not enough not being Delors, nor even being a former prime minister among prime ministers and presidents. The catchwords were consolidation and subsidiarity rather than reform and new initiatives – except perhaps within the Commission itself – which failed to win back to the Commission any wide public acceptance.

Prodi was appointed with strong support among the Member States and the EP, even if with a difficult brief to steer the Commission out of the slough into which it had sunk. Given that support, he sought also to ensure a heightened capacity to generate ideas and proposals and to recapture some at least of the intellectual high ground. He did so, *inter alia*, by launching a new initiative on 'shaping the new Europe' in February 2000, an initiative that was to evolve into the Commission's White Paper 'European Governance' in July 2001. Led by Jérôme Vignon (the former head of the Forward Studies Unit) a small team supported by 12 inter-service working groups formulated ideas that were to improve the effectiveness of the EU and reconnect the EU institutions with European civil society (Wincott 2001a). The White Paper adopted five principles of good governance: openness, participation, accountability, effectiveness and coherence. Yet, as Metcalfe has pointed out, it was not a particularly *white* paper in that it gave little idea of any blueprint for the application of the principles it had adopted, but instead invited participation in their development as if almost a (British) green paper (Metcalfe 2001). Insofar as some of its suggestions were aimed as much at the Council and the Member States as to the European Parliament and itself, such modesty of purpose was probably wise.

The White Paper's central thrust was the revival and reinforcement of the Community method. Given the pressures that created alternative trends, as in the enthusiasm for OMC, this suggested a conservativism on the part of the Commission or, as one critic, put it, both 'institutional self-interest' and 'a remarkable lack of concern about the real challenges confronting the

Union and its Member States' (Scharpf 2001). But Prodi's efforts to initiate a new debate were also overtaken by events that commanded far greater media attention. Joschka Fischer's speech on a 'lean' federal future of Europe given in May 2000 evoked responses from many other European leaders. One of Fischer's conclusions, though, was that the 'Monnet method', i.e. communitarisation, 'has proved to be of only limited use for the political integration and democratisation of Europe' (Fischer 2000, 17). Nonetheless, the Commission, through consulting widely on its proposals, clearly hoped to have an influence both on those taking part in the Future of Europe debate and the wider public – although it did not help in either by launching the White Paper at the beginning of the summer holidays. However, in its general tendency to look back towards tried methods, the Commission appeared only to have marginalised itself in a debate that became dominated by Member State governments, from the Laeken Council in December 2001 and eventually within the Convention to the IGC that finally agreed the Constitutional Treaty in June 2004.

The Commission's normative role, whether in terms of more grandiose ideas or pushing into nooks and crannies, has important implications for its other role as the collective conscience of the Union. While irritating to those who find themselves on the 'wrong' side, the Commission's role in seeking to ensure conformity of implementation across the EU, to prevent, especially, distortions of the market, and Member States backtracking on what they had agreed in Council, has long been accepted. But just as there is a built in tension between the Commission's role in initiating legislation and then seeking to mediate within the Council or between the Council and the EP on the same proposal, so the normative and conscience roles sometimes sit uneasily together – though it has often been the Court of Justice in accepting the extended logic of the Commission's position that has received the more public opprobrium.

The Commission's relationship with the Court is discussed further by Usher in chapter 3. Here we want to point only to the sometimes delicate political balancing act involved in taking a Member State or the Council to the European Court of Justice. After all, the Commission doesn't always win. In decisions such as 1/94, the ECJ took, from the Commission's perspective, a particularly disappointing attitude, rejecting the bulk of the Commission's case both in terms of the Treaty base and the Treaty's implied powers. If, in that case, the Court was seen as being somewhat inconsistent and incoherent (Meunier and Nicolaïdis 1999), in Case C-27/04, when the Commission took the Council to Court on the way it dealt with French and German breaches of the Stability and Growth Pact, the Court was positively Solomonaic. On the one hand, it declared 'the action inadmissible insofar as it concerns the Commission's claim that it should annul the Council's failure to adopt decisions to give notice to France and Germany.' On the other hand, the Court annulled 'the conclusions adopted by the Council in which the Council held the excessive deficit procedures in abeyance and modified the recommendations previously made by it to each of those Member States for correction of their excessive deficit'. (ECJ 2005) But the point here was that the Commission had appeared increasingly squeezed out of a significant role in monetary policy, between the ECB and ECOFIN. Even though the decision was welcomed by the Council as well as by the Commission –

if only for what it offered in terms of clarification – the Court did acknowledge that the Commission had an enforcement role that could not be easily dismissed by the bigger Member States.

Conclusion: back to legitimacy

Such battles with Member States and/or the Council have marked the EC/EU's history. As suggested above, the Commission has not always emerged stronger. There remains a profound communications deficit. There remains, too, the still more intractable issue of legitimation. Given the tendency for general scapegoating, it is surprising in some respects that the Commission is still trusted to the extent that it is – and interestingly sometimes rated more highly than the Council (Wessels 2003, 5). The 'legitimacy deficit' emerged after the difficulties of ratifying Maastricht, and much of the 1990s was spent by governments and the EU institutions attempting to 'reconnect' the governed to governance. They had little success – if one takes European election voting figures as the point of reference or the fate of the Constitutional Treaty in France and the Netherlands. And the Commission is having to bear its share of responsibility, a fact brought rudely home to it in the Committee of Experts' second report on the Commission after its resignation in 1999. While the Committee may have been writing about management procedures in relation to the Financial Regulation, the Commission's shortcomings were termed 'extreme' and appeared only too easily applicable to its management as a whole (Committee of Experts 1999 point 2.0.11). Meyer has argued convincingly that while much attaches to the downfall of the Santer Commission because it confirmed suspicions of mismanagement, nepotism etc at the core of Europe (and see, too, Connolly 1995), it revealed even more importantly 'the long term inadequacy of institutional structures and practices to cope with increasing media attention and parliamentary scrutiny.' (Meyer 1999, 618). Legitimacy was thereby pushed back to the forefront of public discourse.

One of the problems in dealing with the issue of legitimacy and 'the legitimacy deficit' in the Union, however, is that the terms are used in so many different ways. Barker (2003), for example, has distinguished six different uses of the concept of legitimacy, while Jachtenfuchs et al (1998) Beetham and Lord (1998) or Føllesdal (2004) have tended to settle on three or four – generally through indirect legitimation by member governments via the Treaties; through representation via various parliamentary bodies, both European and national; through effective technocratic problem solving; through a decision-making process procedurally inclusive of or at least open to those to whom policy is directed; and through some form of a collective political identity. The temptation of sticking to a simple definition of popular acceptance, i.e. of democratic legitimacy, still runs up against the argument raised by Barker and Shore (2000): 'Conflating the normative with the empirical – how things ought to be with how they are – is typical both of the way the EU represents itself and of the way it is represented in many textbooks in the burgeoning field of European integration studies'. (Shore 2000, 126). Whatever hopes there might be for the widest possible readership of textbooks, what one frequently ends up with are competing discourses within the media, from which elites just as much as the public take most of their information: a Commission claiming its legitimate role but not often heard; member governments either claiming national success as providing legitimacy for their decisions within the Council or lambasting the Commission for its failings; sectoral interests claiming either victory or defeat – the latter in terms, say, of demonstrating farmers usually being more likely to grab the headlines; and the media itself adding its own spin depending on its assessment of what its audience, its owners or its ideological or party inclination demand.

It may be that the electorate rightfully expects more of a new system of governance than from the old governments – why else was integration necessary? But its reference point seemingly remains that of national political systems, strong on democratic control and accountability, with policies somehow connected to social justice (Lehning and Weale 1997, 10). It follows that the European system should have the same characteristics. However, as Barker puts it: 'Whilst the EU may govern, it does not follow that it has subjects in the way that a state does. And yet talk of a "legitimacy deficit" describes just such a governing relationship or, rather, decries its absence' (Barker 2003, 160). If the European system of governance was not – except perhaps on the part of federalists – intended to replicate a state-like political system at a different level, processes of legitimation were inevitably to be different. Yet since Maastricht, the EU and the Commission have been criticised for the erosion of what they had never had.

What, however, has opened both the Commission and Council (including the European Council) to criticism has not only been what they claimed for themselves in terms of their legitimacy and legitimation but how they have claimed it. The Commission, for example, at least in respect of those contributing to the White Paper on Governance, has regarded legitimacy as closely tied to democratic norms. Jérôme Vignon, chief advisor on the White Paper, wrote of the crisis of democracy that it was:

> 'not first and foremost a question of *deficit*, that is the absence of a parliamentary institution analogous to that found at the centre of national public life...the crisis of European political legitimacy originates principally from the procedures of the European Community, which have become formal rather than genuine... the current management of complexity by the national and community powers in charge of Europe, though admirable in many respects, does not really do justice either to the richness of knowledge or to the diversity of contexts in Europe.'
> (European Commission 2001a, 4) (emphasis in original)

Given such a perspective, the emphasis of the White Paper on the Community method as the best means of legitimating the EU (and the Commission) comes as less of a surprise.

Moreover, within the *Cahiers*, Renaud Dehousse argued strongly that what was required was less emphasis on legitimation by *output* ('People no longer accept that the quality of decisions is all that matters...') nor even simply on *input* legitimation, i.e. a say in policy choices ('often inspired by an idealised, Rousseauian, vision of parliamentary democracy in which representatives of the people serve the collective interest of a polity and translate it into legislative decisions'). Dehousse called for an input-oriented approach supplemented by a *process*-oriented one, which would open up the post-legislative bureaucratic phase and emphasise transparency and participation throughout (Dehousse 2001, 185-86).

Introducing greater – any – transparency to implementation could end some of the secrecy surrounding the policy process. It might also allow greater insight into the limitations of the Commission's role in implementing legislation and focus more attention on the responsibilities of the Member governments which, to such a large extent, share in implementing EU policies. On the other hand, while others, too – not least the European Parliament – have seen mileage in opening up comitology (see, for example, Allio 2003), the emphasis once more is on the technical and procedural dimensions, that while vital to the process, may not be key in terms of winning wider trust and acceptance. After all, despite the existing opportunities for openness in decision-making (i.e., rather than policy implementation) brought about by the moves towards codecision between Council and Parliament, the emphasis within the EU remains heavily on technical expertise. MEPs have frequently sought to be effective scrutinisers of proposed legislation – rather at the expense of establishing the Parliament as the 'grand forum' of the Union. Given the continuing national preoccupation of the EU's media, European-level political communication has often suffered as a result. The consequence has been that there has been little sense of connection between technocratic governance and the governed. There is therefore a sense, as Barker put it, that:

> 'The attention paid to legitimacy has obscured the equally important question of legitimation as an activity carried out to a significant degree not for the communication to subjects or the world outside the ruling organization, but for the self-identification and legitimation of those within it...' (Barker 2003, 167).

The Convention and the Constitutional Treaty sought to open up to a wider Europe a number of avenues in terms of the simplification of laws, a clearer division of powers – as well as, in the interests of efficiency rather than democracy, a smaller Commission. The demise of the Treaty as it was presented to the Member States in 2004-05 leaves the Union with structures and procedures under the Nice Treaty – a Treaty accepted by all Member States, even if the Irish agreed only at the second attempt. But the Nice Treaty was regarded as sufficiently unsatisfactory to lead to the innovation of the Convention and the Constitutional Treaty, so continued work within its framework is hardly the best way of seeking a greater sense of legitimacy. Yet, this is the unavoidable backdrop against which the Commission will be constrained to operate until further notice.

1. The President, the College and the *cabinets*

David Spence

Introduction: the historical and political context

Whether the European Commission is a proto-government in a would-be federal system or a civil service in an intergovernmental confederation of states, it is a politically contested EU institution. Its role, responsibilities, legitimacy and size have long been controversial issues, and there have been many attempts to resolve the dilemmas arising from the unwillingness of governments to grapple with a series of resulting operational conundrums described in many of the chapters in this book. 'Administration de mission', as was Delors' Commission, or 'administration de gestion' as those since Delors have been; that, for Commission watchers, has been the prime question since the Treaty on European Union (Maastricht) established two inter-governmental pillars rivalling the Community pillar. This undermined the Community method in which the Commission retained the sole right of legal initiative, a symbiotic relationship with the Council and the European Parliament and the claim to embody the originality of Europe's suprana-tional ambitions. Maastricht created roles for the Presidency of the Council where adopting the Community method would have secured roles for the Commission, and it created confusion in the public mind about which European institution was really in charge of what. Most importantly, there were now new major obstacles to efficient management of EU business (Piris 1994) – a high price to pay for the principle of enhanced intergovern-mentalism and a pressing reason for renewed reflection on the institutional framework.

The Treaty of Amsterdam was the result. One positive feature for the Commission was the enhancement of the role of the Community by the laying of foundations for a shift of justice and home affairs from the inter-governmental third pillar into the supranational Community pillar. Yet, Amsterdam's simultaneous reinforcement of the second, intergovernmental pillar gave the Secretary General of the Council and High Representative for the CFSP tasks which would have been the Commission's had the CFSP been made subject to the Community method. On the other hand, the Commission's right of initiative seemed no longer in doubt and its institu-tional position actually appeared strengthened. The Santer Commission thus set about achieving a major streamlining of the institution's executive and managerial functions based on a declaration at the Amsterdam Council on improving the organisation and functioning of the Commission. This sounded promising, but progress in reform was marred by the subsequent fall of the Santer Commission, which both left a good deal of unfinished business and also revived critical interest in a further review of institutional arrangements. Thus, in August 1999, President-elect Prodi appointed yet another group of three wise men to make proposals to yet another Intergovernmental Conference (IGC) in preparation for what became the Treaty of Nice. The group was composed of senior politicians charged with considering whether the limited agenda so far identified for the IGC was adequate.[1] As far as the Commission's structure was concerned, the Three Wise Men's report again went over paths well-trodden since the Spierenburg Report of 1979, and it reiterated the arguments made in the previous context of the Treaty of Amsterdam. Unfortunately, the Treaty of Nice also failed to resolve the relevant issues. Indeed, it added further issues to the agenda.

The failure of three Intergovernmental Conferences and Treaties within seven years adequately to resolve the questions European governments had created for themselves paved the way for the subsequent 'European Convention' and the Draft Constitution for Europe. The Convention again took the same issues forward that Spierenburg had identified some twenty-five years earlier. Commissioners Barnier and Vitorino (2002) put it to the Convention that the Community method 'is the most original element and the key to success of the European project (and is) still essential for the effective operation of the EU'. Member States' positions on the Commission and the Community method have always varied according to traditional interests and views. The smaller states have broadly been keen to prevent a reduction in the Commission's powers and prerogatives (Nicolaïdis and Magnette 2005). Indeed, in many ways they have wished to enhance them. The larger states, led alternately by France, the UK and Germany, have raised fundamental issues surrounding the Commission's constitutional status and have frequently been keen to clip the Commission's wings.

The Constitutional Treaty whose ratification faltered so spectacularly in 2005 thus followed a long series of reports and impassioned debates. This chapter investigates the issues involved and outlines the legal and political framework governing the appointment, tasks and accountability of the Commission. It compares the current reality of the Nice Treaty with the 'might have been' clauses of the Constitution. The relevant questions revolve particularly around:

- the powers and profile of the Commission President
- the powers of Commissioners
- the principle of collegiality
- the role of the European Council and the European Parliament in the appointment of the Commission President
- the appointment of Commissioners and the distribution of portfolios
- the status of vice presidents
- security of tenure of Commissioners
- accountability of Commissioners
- interaction between Member States and Commissioners

- the number of Commissioners
- the role of *cabinets* as intermediaries between Commissioners and the services, the Parliament and the Member States.

The powers and profile of the Commission President: opportunities and constraints

The President's role is fundamental to the operation of the Commission and the coherence of the EU *per se*. But his is no easy task. History since the Luxembourg Compromise of 1966 has shown the continued risk of the Commission being reduced to the 'secretariat' that some Member States have always wanted it to be. It is, in other words, an issue of leadership. As Commissioner Mandelson has argued succinctly, 'the unique position of the College as envisaged in the Treaties, as a political body to give political leadership to Europe from the standpoint of the European interest, has been eroded by a pincer movement: loss of control over its agenda to its own Services pursuing special interests, however legitimate, on the one hand, and a loss of leadership to the Council on the other' (Mandelson 2005). The question is how the Commission President responds to the leadership challenge.

The President convenes meetings of the Commission, establishes the agenda (or excludes items from it), chairs the College, chairs groups of Commissioners, approves the minutes and the Commission's decisions, determines how important issues are and whether streamlined processing of issues is appropriate, receives the accreditation of heads of non-EU states to the European Communities and is a member of the European Council. He is also the representative of the Community at meetings of the G8, troikas and political dialogue. Thus, much depends on the personality and personal clout of the incumbent. A strong President can have his own way. A weak President is perforce obliged to preside over dissent, occasional incoherence among his team and, in the case of Santer, over outright censurable practice or at the very least inappropriate behaviour. As Nugent perhaps understates it, 'a forceful and activist President can do much to enhance the Commission's general standing and leadership capacities' (Nugent 1995). A President lacking these personal attributes may well produce a correspondingly opposite effect. President Prodi suffered greatly at the hands of the press, and this reflected on the Commission itself. As the *Financial Times* put it, 'the EU executive... has dwindled while he (Prodi) has been at the helm... at European summits he is a peripheral figure' (*Financial Times* 2003a). The Prodi Commission may have been full of strong individuals, but it was collectively weak. On the contrary, Delors' Commissions each contained several weak figures but they were collectively strong – thanks in both cases to presidential ability and style.

As the charge of being peripheral suggests, the Commission President's effectiveness is judged very largely by his ability to interact successfully with Heads of State and Government in the European Council. He does not possess their democratic credentials, but he is as able, in principle, to command the respect of European civil society and the media by his powers of communication and his authority as leader of the Commission and master of the technical dossiers before the College and the European Council. The

President of the Commission must be able to persuade his interlocutors – prime ministers, presidents, national parliaments and the European Parliament and, not least, the media and the public – that a supranational approach can not only make a difference, but be a substantially better option than a merely national focus. Choosing 'sexy' issues – not least those that are likely to capture the enthusiasm of political circles wishing to make the Commission's success their success – and providing the imagination and managerial skill to see the task through are essential. Choosing, at the right time, to focus on the internal market, energy supplies, the environment or foreign affairs can leave a lasting image in political and public minds. The President can thereby seal the Commission's fate by either making it the leading permanent political actor on the European stage or relegating it to a secretariat role, obsessed with the details of procedures, deadlines and finances.

Within the Commission itself, the President has to preserve a balance between three potentially conflicting pressures: effective chairmanship of the Commission, maintenance of collegiate consensus and leadership of the policy orientation of the Commission. Tension between such objectives exists, of course, for every head of government and for the Presidency of the Council. For them, as for the Commission President, the requirement of collegiality means spending effort in seeking consensus. But, the option open to a head of government of imposing a policy position on his peers, is not open to the President of the Commission, just as this option is not open to the EU Presidency in relation to its peers in Member States. Commission Presidents frequently find it difficult to persuade Commissioners to adopt their preferred policy position. And even though the President may call for a vote at an appropriate moment in the discussion or seek to adjourn a final decision, he has no monopoly on these procedural weapons. His strength and standing are crucial to his success in imposing a view.

It was long believed that enlargement would increase the size of the Commission beyond what would allow for effectiveness and that this would pose even more challenges to the Commission's leadership. But enlargement seems to have 'ended up giving the Commission fresh doses of sorely needed vigour and vitality' (Peterson 2005). Barroso's managerial skills and the quality of the new Member States' Commissioners provide the explanation. But it came at a price. The objective of College efficiency has seen an increase in the number of written procedures, an increase in Commissioners vying for visibility and arguably less substantial debate in meetings of the College itself.

The 2004 accession states mostly appointed leading members of their political classes to the College: four of the ten original 'shadow' Commissioners (appointed without portfolios in May 2004) were former foreign or finance ministers, and another two were former European affairs ministers. Of the three new Commissioners then appointed to the Barroso Commission, one (Kovacs) previously served as foreign minister, another (Vladimir Spidla of the Czech Republic) was a former prime minister and a third (Piebalgs) had been Latvia's ambassador to the EU. Thus, most 'accession Commissioners' had in-depth knowledge of EU affairs, having helped negotiate their country's accession to the Union (Peterson 2005). The current Commission actually includes three former prime ministers, five former foreign ministers and three former finance ministers. Running a ship with several former captains in the crew clearly requires the real captain to be more than *primus inter pares*. Much therefore depends on the personality and leadership qualities of the Commission President, but this has often proved a prime weakness. It has made the College's effectiveness dependent on the personal authority of the President, who, since he is formally *primus inter pares*, lacks formal political independence and managerial control. So the President actually starts off with inbuilt constraints. As Kinnock put it, 'It's a bloody awful job – and I've had enough bloody awful jobs for a lifetime!' (Westlake 2001, 670). True, under the Presidency of Jacques Delors, the President of the European Commission emerged as a powerful figure on the European and international stage. Yet, even as 'the most successful Commission leader in the history of the Community' (Ross 1995, 14), and despite the history-making achievement of a 'Delors effect' (Ludlow 1991), Delors held a position significantly subordinated to the Commission's collegial structure. As he put it himself, even in the selection of his team's mandate his power was hampered:

> 'Il y a toujours un exercice difficile de répartition des portefeuilles, puisque…le président de la Commission n'est que le primus inter pares' (Delors 1994, 221).

In sum, however, the powers of the President, despite the constraints of his formally equal position with that of the other Commissioners, are considerable, but their successful use clearly depends on the quality of political leadership and on propitious political circumstances – and these change. The current situation is perhaps best summed up by a Commissioner:

> 'My political judgement may be wrong. But my sense is that the Commission today has a golden opportunity to assert … fresh political leadership. The Commission has of course limited powers of its own to act. And those that it has, it must use sparingly to maximum effect. I am not advocating a bout of regulatory hyperactivity on the Commission's part. What we need is focus and impact' (Mandelson 2005).

Much of the focus and impact is determined by the Commission President. And it is overall political circumstances and the balance of national forces which, in turn, determine both the appointment and the options open to the President in managing the College and the extensive powers and responsibilities of Commissioners themselves.

The Three Wise Men's Report of 1999 stressed that the authority of the President of the Commission had been increased at Amsterdam, but that 'in order to enable the President to cope effectively with an increased membership, it would be advisable to go further'. Should the President's right to hire, fire and reshuffle be untrammelled? Where would be the borderline between a request from him to resign on substantive grounds or on the basis of a simple difference of views? When should the President of the Commission represent the EC or the EU abroad and when should some other authority carry out this task? In a national government, apart from the constraints of coalition politics, the Prime Minister is free to select his team and the buck really does stop with him. Delors reportedly remained aloof from some of his colleagues and had open disagreements with several of his Council-appointed team. Had he possessed the right to sack individuals, it is highly likely that he would have used it. What is the likelihood that censure of a Commissioner in office will soon be possible? Where should the EU buck really stop? The following sections answer these questions.

The appointment of the President – the international politics of national choice

The Treaty always provided that the President be appointed by 'common accord' of the Member State governments for a fixed term. From the signature of the Treaty of Rome until agreement at the Maastricht Intergovernmental Conference this term was four years for each Commission member. The President and Vice-Presidents were appointed for two years, but this was more or less automatically renewable. In general, the provisions for the appointment of the Commission provide for a strong role for Member States and for the European Parliament (EP), yet without establishing a fully fledged parliamentary system of executive accountability.

Former Commission President Delors once proposed that the candidate for President should emanate from the European Parliament itself, with each political grouping proposing a candidate and the group with the majority thus providing the Commission President, but this is unlikely to be on the cards for the foreseeable future. In a contribution to the Convention, the Commission did, however, propose the election of the President by a two thirds majority, to be subsequently approved by the European Council (Commission 2002g). At present the Parliament approves (ratifies) the choice already made by Member States after a process of hearings. On the Commission's proposal the logic would have been reversed.

The Commission actually relies on a mix between three sources of legitimacy – the European Council, the Council and the European Parliament. After the enlargement to the UK, Denmark and Ireland, the Tindemans Report to Council in December 1975 recommended that the Commission President be appointed by the European Council, that his appointment be confirmed by vote in the European Parliament and that he only then appoint his team, again in consultation with the Council (Tindemans 1976). This recommendation went into limbo. There followed in 1979 the Spierenburg Report (Spierenburg 1979), the product of an independent review body appointed by the Jenkins Commission. Spierenburg recommended reducing the size of the College and the Commission's departments, strengthening its Presidency and modernising its personnel policy. Contemporaneously, the Report of the Three Wise Men appointed by Heads of Government (Wise Men 1979) into the functioning of all the institutions went over the same ground as Spierenburg. It drew similar conclusions, which were subsequently repeated in the European Parliament's Draft Treaty establishing the European Union (Spinelli 1984), and the Council's Dooge Report (Dooge 1985). The latter, produced at the same time as the negotiations on enlargement to the Iberian peninsula, culminated in the Single European Act of 1986. Again, the recommendations were to no avail. The procedure for appointment of the Commission President, and his subsequent role in the designation of the other

Commission members, were thus frequently debated. It took the Treaty on European Union to begin the process of change.

Before Maastricht the re-appointment of the President was a straightforward matter, if not quite a formality. Member States were obliged to go through the formal renomination procedure half-way through the four-year term of a Commission in order for the President to continue in office. The Treaty on European Union (TEU) extended the period of appointment of the President and the Commission to five years to coincide with the term of the European Parliament, carefully ensuring further political sniping by omitting to provide that the Parliament be elected before the Commission was appointed. But, it did begin a trend for the European Parliament to approve the nomination of the President and his Commission, a new power, which was continually to strengthen the President's independent standing vis-à-vis Member States, yet made the post more vulnerable to pressure from the Parliament (Westlake 1998a).

In 1994, the Santer Commission was the first to submit to these new procedures. The Parliament accepted Santer's nomination as President by only a slim majority in July 1994, largely because it sought to mark its disapproval less of the nominee himself, than of the procedures employed by the Member States in his nomination. The rejection of the Belgian Prime Minister Jean-Luc Dehaene by the British after he had been very publicly supported by the French and Germans, and his replacement by Santer, whose views were, ironically, very similar to those of Dehaene, led the EP to stress the need for greater transparency and accountability. Santer's response was to encourage a series of hearings of individual Commissioners similar to American Congressional practice. This took place in January 1995. The Parliament, though, was beginning to be tough. Its hard questioning of Ritt Bjerregard was widely approved, and Santer was pressured into relieving Padraig Flynn of his chairmanship of an equal opportunities commission and chairing the meetings himself. He was also constrained to renegotiate a code of conduct with Parliament. The EP then endorsed the Commission as a whole by a large majority.

Subsequently, the Amsterdam Treaty introduced amendments to lend greater legitimacy to the President through an adjustment to the appointment process. It introduced three new features. The governments of the Member States were to nominate by common accord the person they intend to appoint as President of the Commission; *the nomination shall be approved by the European Parliament*. The governments of the Member States would, *by common accord with the nominee for President*, nominate the other persons whom they intend to appoint as members of the Commission and significantly, *the Commission shall work under the political guidance of its President*. In part as a result, the process of hearings reached considerable sophistication with the Prodi Commission in September 1999 – though with the press also anxious to contribute to the debate by hunting in the nooks and crannies of the candidates' former careers.[2] Thereafter, the Treaty of Nice introduced substantial changes to the appointment procedure, including a change to majority voting in the European Council for the nomination and appointment of the President of the Commission and subsequent approval by the European Parliament.

Apart from enhanced efficiency, this endows the presidential nominee with a dual legitimacy – based on formal executive and legislative agreement. The Council agrees by qualified majority a list of the other members of the Commission based upon proposals from the Member States, and in agreement with the President-elect. In a final step, the President and the nominated members of the Commission must be approved by the European Parliament before they are officially appointed by the Council, acting again by qualified majority. But, while this makes the appointment of the Commission easier to achieve, as no single country can exercise a veto, it does risk the disgruntlement of governments with a Commission President or member whom they had initially rejected. This may be considered a hindrance that democratic principles make unavoidable but, significantly, there is a further dual bind attached to the issue of greater parliamentary influence over the appointment procedure. Given the already shaky support for the office of the Commission President in public opinion, and given the low turnout that characterises European elections, the implications of a President elected by a slim majority of parliamentarians, themselves elected with a low turnout, is unlikely to lend the office of President of the Commission and the Commission itself much credibility. Indeed, the notion of legitimacy itself might then come under more scrutiny. As one academic has already underlined, the EU institutions have never really been legitimate in any normal sense of the word (Barker 2003). Thus, making the Commission dependent on the majoritarian politics of the European Parliament might merely prove a sham rather than a contribution to the revitalisation of the Commission itself. In addition, as the current Head of Delegation of the Commission Delegation in Washington, former Irish politician John Bruton, commented to the Convention, there would be a risk of unhealthy tension between the Commission and the parliamentary minority that had opposed the election of the President (Bruton 2003).

Whether the selection procedure for Commission President produces the best candidate for the job is also a moot point. It has been rare in the history of the Commission for the strongest candidate to be chosen. In 1994 a special summit was called to appoint Jacques Santer, Luxembourg's little known Prime Minister, as President. There had been many hesitations in capitals. After the first attempt at the EC summit in Corfu had collapsed when John Major had vetoed the candidacy of Jean-Luc Dehaene and other high profile runners had also fallen by the wayside either for lack of support or because of informal vetoes by France and Germany, Santer had become the clear choice of Helmut Kohl, the German Chancellor, but only as a President no one was prepared to veto. As Patten later put it, 'We blocked the nomination of the Belgian Prime Minister, Jean-Luc Dehaene… and got instead a Luxembourger, who was less able and arguably more federalist than the wily Belgian' (Patten 2005, 82).

Since Nice, however, the possibility for heads of government to nominate the Commission President by qualified majority voting has begun to change the context of the nomination. Yet, President Barroso was also far from the first choice. French President Chirac had openly backed Luxembourg Prime Minister Juncker as Commission President as early as February 2004. In May 2004, a month before the selection of the new President of the Commission to succeed Romano Prodi in November, the situation was still very open. After a series of trial balloons four names remained in the public frame – Guy Verhofstadt, Chris Patten, Antonio Vitorino and Pat Cox. Each had drawbacks, raising the possibility of a last-minute compromise candidate emerging at the summit on June 17-18, perhaps even Irish Prime Minister Bertie Ahern himself, then President of the Council, though he denied his interest. According to the EU's informal rotation principle, the Commission presidency was to go to a centre-right politician from a small, north European state, after being held for five years by a centre-left former Italian prime minister. Juncker and Verhofstadt had the right background, but the former rejected nomination in March. Verhofstadt, a centre-right Flemish liberal, free-marketeer and consistent balancer of Belgium's budget, had alienated pro-American EU partners the previous year by opposing the Iraq war and launching a four-nation European defence initiative seen as divisive. Perhaps not surprisingly Verhofstadt remained President Chirac's preferred choice, but Britain, Poland and Denmark saw him as too close to France and too federalist. He soon declared that he wanted to keep his job of Prime Minister. The way was then opened for another mooted Belgian candidate, Jean-Luc Dehaene, but he had already been barred by the United Kingdom in 1994. Despite the fact that he had meanwhile become deputy to Giscard d'Estaing in the praesidium of the Convention, he stood no chance.

Patten, a pro-European Conservative, then emerged from the shadows after UK Prime Minister Tony Blair decided to hold a highly risky referendum on a planned EU constitution. Patten had just spent over four years as External Relations Commissioner. He thus knew the house well. He was a witty orator and respected administrator, who might have used the Brussels platform to help convince sceptical British voters to back the constitution and perhaps even join the euro. The deputy Secretary-General of the Council, de Gaulle's nephew, Pierre de Boissieu, broke the news gently to Patten: 'They think you are very good, but "they" can't accept you as President' – an English-speaking Commission President highly critical of EU farm subsidies would have been a hard sell in Paris and the UK was neither in the euro-zone nor in Schengen, as the French sarcastically pointed out. 'Let's be clear', said Patten, 'you can't accept a British President'... 'in response I got a wintry smile' (Patten 2005, 25-26). It would anyway have been difficult for Tony Blair to explain his support for a Conservative to the Labour party.

Vitorino, a former Portuguese defence minister, had won praise for his work on integrating EU crime-fighting, counter-terrorism, asylum and immigration policies, as well as his role in the Convention. But although backed by a centre-right Lisbon government, he was a socialist and the majority of EU governments were of the centre-right, as was the majority likely to emerge from the approaching European Parliament elections. Barroso, then Portuguese Prime Minister, declared at one point that he was not a candidate and that Vitorino was Portugal's choice. Political arithmetic ruled out former Finnish Prime Minister Paavo Lipponen, who announced his interest, but was not well known and not well supported. Cox, a 51-year-old former TV presenter, had just finished a 30-month stint as president of the EP. As a French-speaking liberal he would have had no trouble winning parliamentary assent, but he had never served in government and was seen by some as too lightweight to run the Commission. Finally, the Austrian Wolfgang Schüssel emerged briefly as a candidate, though he was unlikely to win Franco-German approval after his recent alliance with Haider's

extreme right party. Barroso was again a candidate no one was prepared to
veto.

In the long run, it may be that parliamentary influence on the appointment
of the President will increase, but as things stand in 2006, the EU is in for a long
stalemate in terms of its continued institutional development. The Parliament's
ability to vote on the President is a way of influencing the Commission's
agenda, as parliamentarians are thus perfectly able to make their ratification of
a President conditional on his or her amenability to their programme. This
might be seen as a potential drawback for the Commission's independence
and integrity, but it is offset by the perspective of an enhanced relationship
between Commission and Parliament and thus increased legitimacy. If a
Commission President could claim democratic legitimacy on the basis of parliamentary support, the Commission would be in a stronger bargaining position with the Council in times of disagreement. But, whether parliamentary
majorities will ever determine the colour of the Commission President remains
to be seen. The 1999 parliamentary elections brought a large majority for the
right (though eleven of fifteen national governments were of the opposite persuasion) and there were rumours before the election (indeed, before the
Commission's resignation) that the German government, as President of the
Council, had agreed to consult the heads of Parliament's political groups on
the nominee for President. Member States were then faced with the threat by
the Christian Democrat European People's Party (EPP) that if EU heads of state
and government nominated someone from a political party which lost the election, they would not win the backing of Parliament (*European Voice* 1999b). The
issue became whether to move the planned Cologne Summit on 3–4 June (due
to nominate the President) till after the European elections on 10–13 June, so as
– formally at least – to reflect the views and possibly political colour of the
newly elected Parliament. Having failed to achieve a change in the date, the
President of the European People's Party, Wilfred Mertens, subsequently
wrote to Prodi attempting to make the Parliament's later assent to the College
in September conditional on sufficient representation of the new parliamentary
majority in the new Commission. The idea was not new. The Parliament had
argued during the 1996 IGC that the President of the Commission should be
directly elected by the Parliament on the basis of a list submitted by the
Council and German MEP Elmar Brok had actively developed an idea of
Delors' for a 'European president', arguing that the political parties should
float candidates for the Commission presidency and that voters should have
the right to decide (*Guardian* 1999). Governments may at some point envisage
such far-reaching reform, and since the role of Parliament has already been
considerably enhanced, despite low public support for the Parliament and the
Commission, calls for deepening links between the democratic process and the
nomination of the Commission President and the College are likely to continue. In the distant future, a parliamentary role in the nomination of
Commissioners is thus not to be excluded.

The appointment of members of the Commission – Commissioners' interests and national interests

The selection of individual Commissioners lies with Member States, and
a firm convention has evolved that Member States do not interfere in each

others' choices. A decision is then made by the Council of Ministers, normally the General Affairs and External Relations Council (GAERC), on the nomination of all the new Commission members just before the expiry of the term of office of the outgoing Commission. The December meeting of the GAERC is the normal vehicle for formal nomination. In the run-up to the formal nominations there are two principal sources of external lobbying on the President-elect. One is from existing members of the Commission desirous of renomination, for there is no time limit on the period which an individual may spend as a member of the Commission. The other is from governments, though, importantly, during its term of office the Commission can expect to see national elections in most of the Member States and a change of government may lose a Commissioner his national government's support.

Presidents of the Commission have always sought to influence Member States' choice of Commissioners, since they naturally want some say in the appointment of colleagues with whom they will work. But, if Amsterdam changed the rules, allowing the President more influence and leeway, their subsequent efforts to influence the appointment procedure have actually met with mixed success. This is hardly surprising. For Member States, nomination of Commissioners is a useful piece of political patronage. It can be used to reward loyal service or to remove from the domestic scene individuals whose services are no longer required for a variety of reasons, but who cannot be safely dismissed altogether – Spidla, Kovacs, Brittan and Michel spring to mind.

While they cannot control the composition of the Commission, Commission Presidents do have a significant, if not predominant, influence on the initial distribution of portfolios, however. Commissioners' portfolios are agreed by consensus amongst the Commissioners and once the initial allocation has been made, it is very difficult to change it. Even Delors, who had considerable powers over the allocation of portfolios, had neither the power to shift responsibilities nor to reshuffle his team. He was therefore not able to benefit from the powers of political patronage familiar to every national leader. Such powers are arguably growing, however, since the Amsterdam Treaty adjusted the rules. Presidents Prodi and Barroso have enjoyed a greater margin of independence since then, as discussed below and in chapter 19.

The smaller Member States have always viewed a post in the Commission as an important political job in its own right. However, until recently, many governments from the larger states tended to view a post in the Commission as carrying relatively little kudos. Yet, with the growing powers of the Union and its increasing relevance to domestic politics, it has become the norm for Commission nominees to have held ministerial posts of Cabinet rank in their national administration, and while Commissioners are formally chosen by heads of government, appointments are subject to a high level of national political bargaining. And it is not only in those Member States in which coalition government is the norm, but also in systems where the executive is based on one or two parties, that the head of government may not be able to exercise a free hand. President Mitterrand, for example, was reportedly obliged to appoint Christiane Schrivener in 1992 when his own first choice decided to opt for a national position, and, according to press reports, UK Conservative back bench pressure on Prime Minister John Major was one of the reasons why Neil Kinnock, the former Labour Party leader, was not nominated for the post of (second) British Commissioner in 1993, though he was successful in joining the Santer Commission in 1995 and staying on for the Prodi Commission.

In a submission to the IGC in May 1997, the Commission argued strongly that the President's role in determining the membership of the Commission had to be increased, and that the other Commissioners should be designated by agreement between the President and the governments of the Member States rather than simply nominated without recourse. The Three Wise Men's report of 1999 also argued that the President 'should have more effective influence in the nomination and selection of Commissioners. He should be given clear authority to organize, co-ordinate and guide the working of the institution'. Twenty years previously, the Spierenburg Report had also advocated that the President-elect be able to veto nominees for the College, with Member States obliged to nominate a second candidate if the first proved unacceptable to the President. As to the European Parliament, though not formally required to, Delors always waited for votes of confidence from the Parliament before allowing Commissioners to take their oaths of office before the Court of Justice. With Amsterdam this became the rule. Amsterdam introduced a new right of the President to select (and potentially dismiss) members of his own team. Declaration 32 to the Treaty 'considers that the President of the Commission must enjoy broad discretion in the allocation of tasks within the College, as well as in any reshuffling of those tasks during a Commission's term of office'. Whereas the Commission President was formerly 'consulted' on nominations for Commissioners, he now has the right, in principle, to disagree and to settle alone the distribution of his team's portfolios. Prodi underlined at Cologne his decision that 'pick and mix' portfolios would be avoided and that the portfolios would be created and candidates for them sought thereafter, rather than attributed a portfolio after their initial selection.

Significantly, however, a series of untoward circumstances during the appointment procedures for the Barroso Commission began to set different precedents. Barroso reputedly instructed his nominees to avoid, in their parliamentary hearings, taking a view on Turkey or on the fate of the Constitution if it were not ratified. The aim was to remove at least two 'hot potatoes' from the hearings. But there remained enough other heated issues for Parliament to demonstrate its new muscular image and where Barroso was not so fortunate. The Parliament insisted that Neelie Kroes relinquish all her previous corporate responsibilities so as to ensure there was no genuine, potential or perceived conflict of interest. It was decided that special arrangements would be made in sensitive antitrust cases, involving companies Kroes had worked for in the past, such as the US firm Lockheed. To ensure potential decisions by the Commission would be fair and impartial, Kroes was asked to abstain and pass responsibility for such cases to another Commissioner, perhaps to President Barroso himself. But, this was not the end: unfortunately for the President, the Parliament had got wind of a 'harmless' holiday he had spent with a Greek shipping magnate, an old friend of his, and began to go down the track of censuring the Commission (*European Voice* 2005d). MEP Daniel Cohn Bendit wrote an open letter to

Barroso, asking him to reassign shipping dossiers initially removed from Kroes and put under his own direct authority, to the (French) transport Commissioner, Jacques Barrot. He was also required 'to provide an overview of the dossiers in question as well as of the associated decisions taken so far by your Commission' (*European Voice* 2005d).

Barrot thus entered the portfolio-shuffle scene for a second time. He had joined the Commission towards the end of the Prodi term, replacing Commissioner Barnier as regional policy Commissioner when he resigned early to become French Foreign Minister. Barrot was then offered the justice and home affairs portfolio by Barroso. After refusing it, he accepted the transport portfolio. This caused some consternation in France about France's reduced influence in the lead portfolios – despite the fact that transport is one of the largest EC budget posts. It took an intervention by Barnier, by then Foreign Minister, to counter the criticisms in France about France's loss of prestige (*Le Figaro* 25 August 2004). The European Parliament had criticised Barrot strongly since he had not revealed a previous conviction in France. Other notable pressures on the President to adjust portfolios surrounded the appointment of Latvian Commissioner Pielbags instead of Kalniete and the shift in portfolio of Kovacs from energy to taxation and customs.

However, the most important case of the President being obliged to re-arrange his portfolio priorities was the Buttiglione affair. During the nomination proceedings, a hearings committee voted by 27 to 26 against Buttiglione as Commission Vice-President and Commissioner for justice, liberty and security, after he made several declarations demonstrating somewhat antediluvian views on women and homosexuality. This was set to build a firm precedent for parliamentary power to enforce a re-shuffle of portfolios and even censure a nomination. Barroso resisted, proposing a mere reshuffle of responsibilities. But, in a second vote, the committee members were asked if they would favour Buttiglione as a Commissioner, were he given a different portfolio. The vote on this was still 28 against and 25 for. Despite the fact that there was no legal recourse for the European Parliament, Barroso withdrew Buttiglione after several contortions, including the suggestion that, like Kroes with certain commercial dossiers, Buttiglione be relieved of responsibility for sensitive issues regarding discrimination. But what worked for her, i.e. the removal of certain companies from her ambit, did not work for Buttiglione. In his case, issues of fundamental principle were at stake. Barroso abandoned him. He was replaced in the end by Italian Foreign Minister Frattini and a new College was presented for parliamentary approval.

In the old days, Catholic leaders such as EU founders Konrad Adenauer of Germany and Robert Schuman of France or former EU Commission President Jacques Delors tended to translate their religious beliefs into a secular concern for social welfare and justice. Recently, conservative Catholics have stressed the more controversial sphere of personal morality. This is where Buttiglione came a cropper, whereas Barrot, also a staunch Catholic, was not tested on the linkage between his religious views and the transport portfolio he took on. In the old days also, stability could be guaranteed, since the distribution of portfolios was usually expected to remain in the same hands for the duration of a Commission, and tenure covered both membership of the Commission and individual executive responsibilities within it – except, of course, when the enlargement of EC membership required new members to be added to the Commission and there was a need to redistribute portfolios to make room for them. Now, seemingly, such stability and personal security cannot be guaranteed.

Independence, security of tenure, resignation and censure

One of the central objectives of the founding fathers of the Community was to underline and accentuate the freedom of individual Commissioners to take policy positions without influence from their home governments. In line with Monnet's vision of the Commission as a supranational policy-making body, the Treaty lays down that members of the Commission 'shall be completely independent in the performance of their duties'. To underline the point, it also states that 'each Member State undertakes to respect this principle and not to seek to influence the members of the Commission in the performance of their tasks'. Commission members must accept not to engage in any other occupation during their term of office and to refrain from any action incompatible with their duties. They give a solemn under-taking to this effect before the European Court of Justice at the start of their term of office.

Thus, in principle, Commissioners are independent of outside influence, and enjoy a remarkable security of tenure in office. The Treaty does make provision for a Commissioner to be compulsorily retired or deprived of his right to a pension only on a decision of the Court of Justice if he or she 'no longer fulfils the condition required for the performance of his duties or if he has been guilty of any serious misconduct'. But, this procedure had never been activated in the history of the European Economic Community, nor of its predecessor, the European Coal and Steel Community, until a case against former French Prime Minister and Commissioner Edith Cresson was brought in November 2005, though Commissioner Bangemann came close to it when he left Delors' Commission to join the board of the Spanish Telefonica. It is certainly not a regular sanction for use against inefficient or difficult Commissioners.

Outside this legal clause of dubious practical value, neither the President, other members of the Commission, the Council of Ministers, nor the European Parliament can legally remove an individual member of the Commission, though many advocated such a power with regard to Commissioner Cresson in the Santer Commission. After all, had it existed, the College would not have been obliged to resign. While the joint resigna-tion might justify reams of reflection on the principle of collegiality, the facts were rather simple. The French government was not going to allow the French Commissioner to carry the can. As her fellow Commissioner Van Miert argued, 'Paris's strategy was clear: avoid at all costs that Cresson be the sole Commissioner to resign, even if that meant tarring the whole College with the same brush' (Van Miert 2000, 252). The political implication is that, unlike a minister in a national government, a Commissioner may not need to retain the political support of the President, his colleagues, his gov-ernment or any parliament, whether national or European, in order to remain in office. Nor, on the other hand, can he hope to take over the port-folio of a colleague through the strength of his performance or lobbying abilities. Yet, the strength of the goal of maintaining the national image can come in handy. A high degree of political independence and security of tenure is seemingly contingent at least on the national pride of the Commissioner's 'home team'. Influence of Member States' governments on the Commission may be weakened by concern to be seen as neutral. In any case, while a newly-appointed Commissioner owes his post to his national government, there is no certainty that the same government will still be in office five years later when decisions on reappointment are made. National pride may be sacrosanct – though that also may depend on which nation is concerned. There may be no political advantage to be gained by the maintenance of excessively close links, but there is no doubt that they exist – and may prove useful. Yet, overt attempts by governments to influence 'their' Commissioner are inevitably greeted with scorn and derision in the European Parliament and the press.

In national politics, governments depend on parliaments for their appointment and their continued existence, and since Maastricht and the 1999 Santer Commission resignation, the European Parliament has begun to move EU politics in the same direction. Member States may still appoint Commissioners and the Parliament currently has no authority to decide which Commissioner receives which portfolio, and thus no formal power to veto an appointment. But the experience of parliamentary influence on the Commissions appointed since the Maastricht Treaty shows that the Parliament has gradually achieved such a de facto role. The power of the Parliament has become evident at times of appointment, resignation and crisis, and there are day to day operational implications in the changing relationship between the Commission and the Parliament, which the resignation brought about. In contrast to the retrospectively pedestrian hearings of the Santer Commission, there was an air of conditionality present in the questions posed by the new Parliaments in July 1999 and 2004. The 1999 Parliament targeted former Delors *chef de cabinet* Pascal Lamy, mooted trade Commissioner, blaming him not so much for wrong-doing as for being responsible for Delors' mode of management (Hearings 1999). Vice-President designate Loyola de Palacio also stood accused of tolerating abuses of flax subsidies when Spanish Agriculture Minister and was obliged to comment on the issue before Parliament. Philippe Busquin was accused of involvement in the Agusta affair. Commissioners had to state their readiness to resign should the President require it and their senior staff and *cabinets* were even put under pressure (*European Voice* 1999a).

Parliament's role in the appointment of the Barroso Commission is described in the previous section. But it is the supervisory role of the Parliament, in particular in scrutiny of Commission proposals and in budgetary control, which has increased significance. This has changed radically since the Maastricht Treaty. As Westlake argues in chapter 9, the Parliament now exhibits a penchant for a more politicised approach to business. The relationship between the Commission and the EP is no longer only adversarial on occasion. Parliament's scrutiny may be part of the consensus-building which has operated between the Commission and the EP since the Single European Act, but Commissioners and their policies were not traditionally subject to the detailed critical scrutiny that is now the norm. They were not held to account in the same way as national politicians and there was anyway nothing, bar courtesy and political fall-out, to prevent the Council of Ministers from reappointing the same individuals to the Commission, if ever they were obliged by Parliament to stand down. Now, if the political majority assenting to the appointment of a new Commission found that the work of its budgetary committee later revealed Commission weaknesses and errors, there is no longer a guarantee that the Commission would be able to rely on the same majority if support in a confidence motion were needed. The relationship between the Commission and the Parliament is thus clearly more political than hitherto.

The European Parliament has the important right to censure the Commission as a whole, but this still cannot be used to enforce the removal of individual Commissioners, a restriction which considerably weakens the effectiveness of its power of censure. Amongst other things, concern that the power to censure might be misused on political grounds to attack members of a particular party has prevented its extension. Commissioners can however be asked to account for their policies before committees and the full European Parliament and more and more frequently Parliament places operational funds into 'the reserve', freeing them only when policy concessions are made to Parliament. The budget for the external delegations is an example (see page 408). So far, the Santer case remains the sole example of parliamentary censure leading to the resignation of the whole College. But there have been frequent threats. In 2003 revelations regarding dubious practices at Eurostat led Prodi to remove the Director General and several senior officials from office, but the risk was clearly his own removal (with the College) if he did not act (Merritt 2003).

In the Santer Commission, the list of alleged improprieties, if not all to do with corruption and fraud, had been long and it fed public anxiety in a way that fostered the view that Parliament's role should be increased. The Commission seemed unable to run a recruitment system without some candidates receiving the exam questions in advance. A Commissioner (Bangemann[3]) was accepting fees for speeches; another (Cresson) had employed friends with official money for private political purposes. It took the Commission until November 2005 to press the European Court for sanctions, including loss of her pension rights. There had also been cover-ups in the 'mad cow' affair. A Commissioner (Flynn) had expressed the view that it was hard to live on his salary – despite the relative generosity designed to help maintain a stable membership of the college by discouraging its members from being lured into the private sector by the prospect of higher pay. Another (Bjerregaard) had published a diary of life in the Commission without consulting Santer. Evidence linking Commission officials with the Mafia and even one related suicide had been published (Aubert 1995) and former Commission officials had written books denouncing malpractice, dishonesty and alleged harassment by senior colleagues (Connelly 1995; Alexandrikis 1996.) One (Buitenen) had 'blown the whistle' on corruption and been rewarded by suspension from office.[4] In addition, journalists had turned from reporters to investigators and had become keen to expose malpractice (Nicolas 1999). But, the immediate cause of the Commission's resignation was the attempt to avert the threat of a vote of censure by the European Parliament and thus the sacking of the whole Commission.

To a certain extent, the Commission had brought the potential of a censure motion upon itself by its brinkmanship in December 1998. In a report on the 1996 budget discharge the Parliament had refused discharge, posing several conditions for agreement. A vote on the issue was due on Thursday 16 December. A Commission declaration on 15 December summed up the situation and it is worth recalling for the record, for it was a warning blast from a sinking ship, both as far as the Santer Commission was concerned and for the Commission's ability to ride roughshod over the Parliament. 'Après moi le déluge' was perhaps the intended message.

> 'The draft report proposing the discharge of the budget con-
> tains a certain number of additional demands concerning the
> internal management of the Commission. In substance, most of
> these demands coincide with the objectives that the present
> Commission has been pursuing, with great determination and
> for some time already in the context of the 'Tomorrow's
> Commission' initiative. The chances of these reforms succeeding
> in 1999 depend very largely on the credibility and authority of
> the Commission. The Commission would be seriously under-
> mined if the Parliament does not vote the budget discharge
> tomorrow and redirects back the issue to its Budgetary Control
> Committee. ... The Commission therefore considers that it is very
> important both for its proper functioning and for it to perform its
> interinstitutional role that it obtains the budget discharge tomor-
> row... *If the budget discharge is not given, the European parliament*
> *must clarify the situation by proceeding to a vote on a censure motion,*
> *as specified in Article 144 of the Treaty'*. (Emphasis added.)

If censorship of the College as a whole has only been used once, there-after the idea of parliamentary censorship of individual Commissioners, often aired in the past and equally often dismissed during successive IGCs, came to be regarded as essential. The political cost of the whole College resigning, instead of individual Commissioners who were to blame, had been a high price to pay for the ineptness of one or two Commissioners. The right to censure a Commissioner would have proved helpful by requiring individual members of the Santer Commission accused of corruption to resign, without causing the 1999 constitutional crisis, which obliged the whole College to depart. Santer's Commission would then have remained intact until the end of its mandate on 4 January 2000 and been remembered for its reforms and other successes, such as the introduction of the euro and the beginning of the enlargement pre-negotiations, rather than for its his-tory-making resignation.

When he addressed the Cologne Summit in June 1999, Prodi stressed that it was likely that the Parliament might in the future require guarantees from individual Commissioners that they would resign if an individual motion of censure by the Parliament required it.[5] His view was that he, Prodi, and not the Parliament should decide. He would require Commissioners' commit-ment in advance to resign if he required it. The European Parliament would then be free to censure the Commission as a whole, if it disagreed with the Commission President's decision. During the 1999 parliamentary hearings each Commissioner did affirm his or her readiness to resign at Prodi's request – a considerable *de facto* reform and one which subsequent IGCs discussed, with a view to *de jure* treaty amendment. The report of the Three Wise Men in October 1999 also argued that 'this informal arrangement should be formalised in the Treaty, so as to confirm the authority of the President, with due respect for the collegial character of the Commission. This would also clarify the respective powers of Parliament and President regarding the performance and tenure of Commissioners' (Three Wise Men 1999).

It would, of course, be unusual for any national government to allow ministers to be sacked by Parliament, though the converse is painfully true; governments can usually dissolve parliaments. Not so in the EU context. It would be unlikely for the Commission to gain the right to require the dissolution of the Parliament and call an election. The Commission does not play a purely governmental role and it is also unlikely that it ever will. It is unlikely that the Parliament will acquire the right of individual censure in the foreseeable future, though many in the Parliament have advocated the right, both while Commissioners are in office as well as on nomination, and one can see the point. The Commission proposed in the Convention that both the European Council and the European Parliament should have the right of censure over the Commission. On this basis, there would be 'equivalent rights both for the appointment and for monitoring the action of the Commission... (allowing the Commission)... to continue to exercise its functions independently and also to assert its political accountability' (European Commission 2002g, 18), but the Constitutional Treaty left the question of an individual Commissioner's resignation in the hands of the President without specifically referring to the Parliament, as was already the case in the Nice Treaty.

Commissioners' relations with Member States

Monnet's original intention was for the Commission to stand collectively above the pressures of national governments. Though individual Commissioners should explain their countries' views and problems with policy proposals, the Treaty insisted that there could be no instruction involved. But, Commissioners are appointed by their governments. They often serve two five-year terms. The UK has maintained a mixture of single and double terms, with only Leon Brittan staying for a third term. Commissioners may, of course, resign but they cannot be sacked by their appointing government, the Commission President, the European Parliament or anyone else. Yet, in order to be effective the Commission must function in a political as well as a legal and administrative context. Commissioners are not ambassadors for their Member States but they do articulate policy concerns that reflect their domestic political backgrounds or specific points of national concern. In this way the Commission takes account of differing national sensitivities in formulating a European policy. This is important to its overall effectiveness, and it is no one-way street. As one Commissioner concludes, 'We alone can persuade the Member States to live up to their responsibilities' (Mandelson 2005). This is no easy job, and the boot is often on the other foot, with the Commission being blamed for Member States' own shortcomings. As one academic comment puts it, the plaintive 'The Commission Made Me Do It' is a frequent national apology for politically unwelcome national action (M.P. Smith 1997).

Member States also try to influence Commissioners in very public ways.

The acrimonious debate in 2005 between President Chirac and the Barroso Commission is but one example. Chirac blamed the Commission for not acting when Hewlett Packard sacked a large number of French employees, though the Commission's power to act was non-existent and the French themselves had rejected a Barroso plan to set up a European unemployment fund for precisely this purpose. Chirac had previously blamed Commissioner Bolkestein for lessening the chances of popular support in the French referendum on the Constitution. Likewise, the French criticised Commissioner Mandelson for overstepping his trade mandate in the same period (as they had criticised Leon Brittan when he held the same portfolio). Pressure on Commissioners over individual political issues is thus some-times intense. On 12 October 2005 Chirac wrote a formal letter to Barroso complaining about Mandelson's handling of negotiations within the World Trade Organisation. French citizens had 'le sentiment que la commission ne défend pas avec suffisamment de détermination et d'énergie leurs intérêts' argued Chirac. Mandelson retorted that France was shooting itself in the foot. (*Le Monde* 14 October 2005). The French press was not alone in high-lighting the link between the French refusal to agree the Constitution in May 2005 and Chirac's subsequent attempt to make the Commission France's whipping boy, and Barroso found considerable sympathy when he answered that it was sheer populism to lay the blame for national short-comings at the feet of the Commission. As to the principle of national influ-ence on individual Commissions, in any case, as Patten has wryly put it, on the whole Commissioners are 'surprisingly restrained (or discreet) in defending national positions, with one or two exceptions whose flag-waving diligence usually backfired' (Patten 2005, 123).

So, it is important, therefore, that the Commission or an individual Commissioner is not seen as the captive of a purely national interest. A Commissioner suspected of too close a relationship with one Member State is likely to face a more critical audience in the Commission for his policy proposals and also likely to be ridiculed by the press. Member States have not only the right to criticise the College, but, presumably also the duty not to use it as a whipping boy and also to give credit where it is due. But this does not always go without saying. As Commissioner Wallström put it at the end of the first year of the Barroso Commission 'the Commission is only as strong as the support it gets from the Member States. Sadly, this has been lacking in the first year. Frankly, this helps nobody. The new Commission is based on the principle of partnership – this needs to extend to all Member States' (Wallström 2005).

There is also the obverse accusation of the Commission interfering in a Member State's affairs. Indeed, when Competition Commissioner Neelie Kroes publicly backed Angela Merkel in the 2005 German elections, it was not well received in German opposition circles. Yet, Commissioners' links with their national political parties and national governments play an important role by offering a channel of communication and influence in both directions. Member States explain their particular concerns to their nominated Commissioners, thereby hoping to influence Commission policy in their preferred direction. Likewise, a Commissioner may persuade his national government of the need to support Commission policy, or at least to search for an acceptable compromise, particularly in his own area of responsibility. Good domestic political contacts allow a Commissioner to influence the policy debate in his home Member State. As Leon Brittan once explained, 'I am frequently consulted by Jacques Delors about what is going on in Britain. It would be bizarre if I could not answer... I think that it is important that whoever holds my job should play a part in British public life since the EC itself is part of British public life...' (*Financial Times* 1990).

A relevant question is whether powerful Presidents have to come from France or Germany. The markedly successful Presidents Hallstein and Delors did. And it is at least worth reflecting whether Santer's, Prodi's and perhaps Barroso's lack of a direct link into the Franco-German motor may retrospectively prove to have been part of the cause of their comparative weakness, as, indeed, was the fact that they were by no means the first choice of the Member States. Gaston Thorn, Delors' predecessor, led a some-what lacklustre Commission and was not considered for reappointment. Chancellor Kohl was unsuccessful in persuading others of the advisability of a German, though there was a strong case for one, since there had been no German President since Hallstein. Belgium promoted Vicomte Davignon, a Vice-President under Jenkins, but Belgium's previous President, Jean Rey, had been a Walloon, so it was time for a Flemish President, despite Davignon's high personal profile. In any case, France did not favour Davignon and Germany had bad memories of Davignon's previous passage through the Commission, where he had tried to restructure the European steel industry in the 1980s. Ortoli had been a recent French President, so, arguably, it was too soon for another. Yet, Mitterrand proposed former External Relations Commissioner Claude Cheysson, which brought about Margaret Thatcher's wrath and opened the way for Mitterrand's former finance minister Delors, whose federalist and socialist credentials seemed to have escaped her, such was her enthusiasm for a man who had brought managerial sense through fiscal prudence to Mitterrand's early flights of left-wing fantasy.

In allocating posts among the team, the President balances national and personal preferences and tries to give some political shape and direction to the Commission.[6] There is competition for the portfolios with the 'big' dossiers of Foreign Affairs, Economic Affairs, Trade, Agriculture, Competition and the Internal Market. Governments are obviously keen for their nominees to have politically advantageous portfolios in the belief that this will open up a channel of influence for them on key issues. There is considerable evidence of governments lobbying the President on behalf of their Commissioners during the intense period of activity preceding the allocation of portfolios in a new Commission. The national Permanent Representations to the Community play a major role in this process. During the appointment of the Barroso Commission, the media discussed almost daily the idea that the previous German Commissioner Günter Verheugen should be a 'Super Commissioner'. There was an amusing background. The Spanish minister of finance, Rodrigo Rato, was, despite the defeat of his party in the recent elections, his country's candidate as head of the International Monetary Fund. President Chirac seemed to have vetoed the nomination of Rato, favouring the French candidate Jean Lemierre, then President of the European Bank for Reconstruction and Development. The German press recounted that the French finance minister, Francis Mer, and the German, Hans Eichel, had made a deal for Berlin to support Lemierre for the IMF in exchange for French support for the nomination of a German as Vice-President of the Commission responsible for economic questions in the future Commission. Günter Verheugen had let it be known that he wished to remain in the Commission as economic 'super Commissioner'.

In practice, the influence of national governments and of the European Parliament on Presidents Prodi's and Barroso's selection of Commissioners underlined both continuity and change. National pressure remained similar. German Christian Democrats, for example, pressed Prodi via the European People's Party (EPP) in the European Parliament for a right-wing Commissioner, despite German Federal Chancellor Schröder's wish to appoint a socialist and a green and thus reflect the governmental coalition. Having allegedly accepted the EPP view, Prodi is said to have been in open conflict with Schröder, though Schröder had the last word. There was also disagreement between the French, German and British governments over the four external relations portfolios – trade, enlargement, development and foreign affairs. In addition, Prodi is said to have wished for candidates with economic and business experience, only to be faced with several candidates with purely political backgrounds.[7] He later said he was pleased that almost all the members of his team had been members of their parliaments, that three quarters of them had been ministers and that his College exhibited considerable legal, diplomatic, business and political party experience (Prodi, 21 July 1999.) Pleased he might have been, yet he had asked the Irish government to replace its first candidate, former justice minister Maire Geoghegan-Quinn with serving attorney-general David Byrne, a commercial lawyer, and the French nominee, Michel Barnier, is said to have been appointed despite Prodi's support for the continuation of Yves Thibault de Silguy (*European Voice* 1999c). Deals are thus done on the basis of extraneous influences, such as how to reflect in the College a balance with appointments to other European posts. The debate and dissension surrounding candidates for the post of NATO Secretary-General, European Central Bank President, UN and EU special envoys to parts of the former Yugoslavia and the Secretary-Generalship of the Council of Ministers (and the post of deputy) have all, at times, been part of the international equation.

As to the effect of European office on the national careers of individual members of the Commission, views differ. Whether becoming a Commissioner or even President of the Commission is an honour or a handicap depends on a Commissioner's country of origin and the political context. While the Barroso Commission may include three former prime ministers, five former foreign ministers and three former finance ministers, in many cases the move to Brussels is a form of consolation prize. No matter how successful they are in their career in the Commission, UK Commissioners often have been, or become, national has-beens in terms of political office. In other cases, a post in the Commission is a privilege and by no means an indication of political fatigue, as Santer, Rey, Prodi or even Barroso have shown. Page and Wouters demonstrate that only 23% of Commissioners reinsert successfully into national politics (Page and Wouters 1994, 445-461), but it is rare, though not unprecedented, for a Commissioner to resign before the end of his mandate in order to return to a post in national government or the private sector. In the Delors

Commission, Bangemann and Ripa di Meana did. Under Prodi, Anna Diamentopoulou did. She left the Commission to campaign in the Greek legislative elections, formally resigning on her election. She was replaced by Stavros Dimas on 16 March 2004 for the remainder of the mandate of the Prodi Commission, until 31 October 2004. Shortly afterwards, Commissioner Pedro Solbes announced that he had accepted an offer to return to Spain as minister of the economy and deputy prime minister in the new socialist government, though he had said he had been planning to stay until the current Commission's term ended in October. France is remarkable in that several Commissioners subsequently became ministers (Deniau, Cheysson, Barnier) or even prime minister (Barre). Delors broke this mould. Whereas the likelihood of a brilliant political career subsequent to the job of Commissioner was hardly an option for his predecessors, except Raymond Barre, it clearly was for Delors. He was perhaps the best President of France the French never had. He had Mrs Thatcher to thank for that, for his lode star for national power was his passage through the European Commission. As for Italy, with the exception of Franco Malfatti, who resigned from the Commission to contest Italian parliamentary elections, previous Commissioners rarely had particularly promising subsequent political careers. Romano Prodi, who while Commission President had planned his political future by assuming leadership of a group of Italian centre-left parties, came under fire in March 2004 for saying he would bring Italian troops back from Iraq if he were in power. The then Italian Foreign Minister, and later Commissioner, Franco Frattini accused Prodi of an 'illegitimate' use of his position as EU Commission President. He nevertheless leads Italy's socialist opposition, though whether he will lead Italy's next government is not a foregone conclusion.

Coordination and policy-making within the College

Overall, the way the Commission is organised has increasingly come to resemble that of a national government, with only defence not explicitly covered by a Commissioner. As a result, a striking feature of the European Commission today is the much greater variety in the workload compared with the Commissions of yesteryear and consequent increased policy responsibilities among the College. Some Commissioners, such as the Agriculture Commissioner, have important executive responsibilities and are involved in constant negotiation with the Member States. The Agriculture Commissioner is probably the closest to a national minister. DG Agriculture functions like a national ministry, with a large number of executive as well as policy staff. At the other end of the spectrum, Commissioners with responsibility for areas whose direct policy competence is limited or disputed, such as energy, audio-visual or social affairs, are likely to have a less direct role, with no executive responsibility and a relatively small policy staff. In general, areas such as foreign affairs or competition policy provide greater scope for a high public profile and this means that the Commissioner carries more weight among his colleagues. Some policy areas, such as the budget and financial control, provide the Commissioner with detailed insight into a range of the Commission's activities, thus enabling him to intervene competently in areas outside his own responsibility. But, importantly, as with a national government, the notion of a team breaks down without commitment to collegiality. As Commissioner Wallström has put it, 'with a larger number of Commissioners, the principle of collegiality is more important than ever. With the multi-national, multi-lingual, cross-party nature of the Commission it naturally takes time to gel. It is also normal that different Commissioners have different views. But, on the main issues, full debate must take place in the College and then the agreed position must be defended by all Commissioners' (Wallström 2005).

When, in the 1996 IGC, the issue of individual censure motions arose, the Commission maintained that this would destroy collegiality. Most Member States agreed with the Commission, but this was certainly out of reluctance to give the Parliament more powers rather than to enhance collegiality or as a resolution of the issue of censure *per se*. The principle of collegiality, advocated by the founding fathers of the Community and by its first President Walter Hallstein, remains important for the operation of the Commission. Behind it lies a complex notion of collective responsibility and a multiplicity of operational consequences. As far as possible the Commission tries to reach a consensus on issues. For this, it needs to act as a team in the way a national government does. This is not an easy task given that the College is characterised by a variety of cleavages – national, political, ideological and sectoral. As Smith has emphasised, this means 'it is almost entirely unhelpful to examine the College using the lens of political party affiliation' (Smith 2003, 142). One might add that any other single lens would be equally unhelpful.

Mandelson put this point into perspective soon after taking up his post, pointing out that 'the multi-national, multi-lingual, cross party nature of the Commission is bound to mean that the body takes time to gel' – a situation not helped in the Barroso Commission case by the Buttiglione affair which 'revealed a remarkable political fissure over values within the broad church of pro-Europeans'. But as Mandelson pointed out, despite having 'a reputation for being a British politician who was well networked on the Continent' he himself knew only fellow Commissioners Almunia and Hübner, had come across others such as Verheugen and Wallström at conferences, but none of the rest. And, as he put it, 'none of us had served for the full period of the previous Commission. We were pretty much all new boys and girls... compare the difference with another set of new boys and girls coming to office in Britain when New Labour won the election in 1997. We'd all known each other for a pretty long time' (Mandelson 2005).

Collegiality, therefore, is hard to achieve, but necessary and attainable. It was intended to produce discipline in support of decisions taken, despite the possible distaste of individual governments. But linked to the absence of a right of Parliament or the Council to censure individuals, it may be little more than a shelter from individual accountability.

To facilitate discretion, Commission meetings are closed to outsiders and simple majority voting is the rule. In principle all voices carry the same weight in discussions, though, inevitably, Commissioners from the larger countries are able to comment more authoritatively on likely national political reactions to certain sensitive proposals and their views on the general political situation within which the Commission works also tend to command more attention. Nevertheless, the requirement that an absolute majority of Commissioners must provide positive support and, if necessary, vote in favour of a proposal, means that influence is inevitably limited by members' individual ability to persuade others to vote for their proposals. Even the President has only one vote in Commission meetings. It is therefore possible for the President to be outvoted on specific issues. Apart from threatening to resign, as Delors apparently frequently did, he has no means of preventing this, and once a decision is taken the President is then as bound by collegiality as any of his colleagues. Voting may be less satisfactory than achieving consensus in the Commission, but it is regularly used to resolve contentious issues. Any member of the Commission may request a vote on a subject under discussion in the College. Voting is then confidential, though total votes in favour or against and abstentions are recorded formally in the Commission minutes and do, on occasion, become more widely known.

The requirement to find a majority of votes in support of a measure is rendered difficult by the likelihood that two or three Commissioners are likely to be absent on business from any one weekly Commission meeting. Voting is by a show of hands and votes cannot be taken by proxy. So the presence of the Commission member at the time that the vote is taken is necessary for it be registered. Thus, in practice, it is usually safer for Commissioners to have more than a simple majority in favour of their motion. Commissioners who are not present may be represented by a member of their *cabinet* so that they have a record of the debate, but *cabinet* members may not formally speak in debate or vote, and the Commission may choose to meet in restricted session to discuss personnel questions or particularly sensitive issues. Only Commissioners themselves may then be present. Despite all this, the emphasis in the life of the College is on consensus. Voting is rare. As in any process of political decision-making by qualified majority vote, it is clearly not the vote in itself which is important, but the *possibility* of a vote that is crucial. Knowing that a vote can be called obliges Commissioners to seek compromise beforehand. Thus the Commission has admitted that in 2000 there were only 3 occasions when a vote was called, out of 572 decisions, in 2001 3 out of 426, in 2002 4 out of 221 and in 2003 1 out of 125 (European Commission, 2003 annex 1).

Supporting collegiality is also a matter of Commissioners' self interest. Each Commissioner is aware that at some point he or she may need the support of a majority of colleagues. So there is continuous lobbying and coalition-building among Commissioners. Ideological outlook or national experience may predispose agreement between certain Commissioners, but discussion is ultimately on an issue-by-issue basis so no Commissioner can afford to take another's support for granted, nor allow unnecessary ill-feeling to develop, even when there is disagreement. The requirements of continuing collegiality mean that no single issue can be made into a make or break question of confidence. Commissioners know that they must go on working with one another. Despite the elaborate structure of *cabinet* meetings to prepare the Commission agenda, debate within the College itself is frequently critical to the policy outcome. And the effectiveness of each member's contribution is determined by several factors: their own portfolio responsibilities, their reputation amongst other Commissioners, wider political factors and their personal interest in the subject. A Commissioner's portfolio is of considerable importance in determining his or her weight in general policy-making. All the more reason for effective coordination within the collegial framework, a task made more complex with enlargement, since written procedures have increased and direct confrontation has consequently been made less frequent, despite the omnipresent risk.

Vice-Presidents: coordinators or policy supremos?

Before 1993, the Commission appointed six Vice-Presidents, but there was no clear deputy. Amusingly, failure to agree on the nomination of Vice-Presidents at the start of the Delors III Commission in January 1993 meant that there were no deputies at all for a while. It took until 30 June to decide the six Vice-Presidents of the new Commission, a decision then valid only until 1 November 1993 when the Treaty on European Union entered into force, entitling the Commission to appoint only one or two Vice-Presidents. Apart from the title, and a slightly larger salary, the post of Vice-President actually brings no substantive advantages within the College, except the right to replace the President in the chair of Commission meetings during his absence. It was partly for this reason that the TEU reduced their number from six to two, by tacit agreement the two longest serving Commissioners.

Member states have traditionally viewed Vice-Presidents essentially as potential coordinators or representatives rather than policy leaders. But the Commission stressed in the 1996 IGC (preparing what became the Treaty of Amsterdam) the importance of bestowing actual policy roles on Vice-Presidents, arguing that it could further improve its overall policy management by better use of Vice-Presidents. The Commission's starting point was the need for three Vice-Presidents, responsible for external affairs, economic affairs and overall integration and citizenship. These were three areas where Delors and Santer had both retained overall responsibility for coordination. The fact that there were five Commissioners responsible for aspects of external relations, for example, underlined the need for authoritative coordination and highlighted the inefficiency of current arrangements. A Vice-President for external relations also matched neatly the Commission's advocacy of a higher profile for itself in the Common Foreign and Security Policy (CFSP) as part of a proposed new troika consisting of the Commission, the Presidency and the High Representative for the CFSP. The other two Vice-Presidents would cover the obvious gap in the provision of high level responsibility for the image of the Commission in public opinion and a potential vacuum in responsibility after the introduction of the euro. But, the Amsterdam Treaty actually produced no change in the status quo. Only the foreign affairs Vice-President appeared in the Amsterdam conclusions, Declaration no. 32 mentioning 'in particular the desirability of bringing external relations under the responsibility of a Vice-President'. The other two apparently desirable Vice-Presidencies disappeared for a time without trace – as, in fact, the external relations Vice-President did in practice.

The External Affairs Commissioner has always been seen as a major figure in the College, attending the General Affairs Council with the foreign ministers of the Member States. However, as in national governments, the nature of the job obliges the External Affairs Commissioner to spend a good deal of time abroad, so he or she is unable to attend all Commission meetings. This possibly diminishes his or her influence, a fact compounded several times since spring 1993, when the external affairs portfolios were split; first between external trade and foreign relations and then further on both geographical and functional lines, as chapter 14 describes in detail. The prospect of a clear deputy President emerging was thereby diminished, despite the effort to make the External Relations Commissioner the coordinator of other Commissioners in the Relex family. Santer appointed two Vice-Presidents, Sir Leon Brittan and Manuel Marín, both of whom held external relations portfolios. But he kept the formal coordinator role for himself. Prodi appointed two Vice-Presidents, neither of which was an external relations Commissioner, though he returned to the system of the Relex Commissioner coordinating the other foreign affairs Commissioners. Barroso in turn reversed the latter policy by keeping the high political coordination for external affairs to himself, while formally nominating the Relex Commissioner, Benita Ferrero-Waldner, as routine coordinator, a move not exactly destined to engender prestige and authority for the supposed coordinator – anyway no longer a Vice-President.

Over time, the Commission's view on Vice-Presidents has not quite echoed Spierenburg's analysis in 1979. Spierenburg underlined the lack of cohesion between Commissioners and the imbalance between portfolios, arguing that poor coordination among Commissioners and their lack of encouragement of senior officials had led to a dearth of coordination among Directors General and a resulting growth in the power and role of the *cabinets* (see below). Spierenburg argued that the lack of coordination at College level could be remedied by systematic and permanent working parties of Commissioners with a Vice-Presidency actively responsible for directing coordination – a principle only partly implemented under Santer[8], toyed with by Prodi and rejected by Barroso. Spierenburg's idea for the Vice-Presidency was a kind of chief executive, responsible for management of work programmes, coordination and supervision, leaving representation and chairmanship to the President himself. Commissioners without a formal portfolio, for example second Commissioners from the large Member States, could assist those under particular pressure. Spierenburg's analysis found general approval at the time, but his recommendations were ignored. On the contrary, Delors went so far as to create a parallel command structure via his *cabinet* rather than address the issue of reform (Ross 1995) and all Commission Presidents since him certainly avoided the idea of a coordinating Vice-President.

By the time Prodi was confirmed as Commission President, ideas had moved on however. The British government, for example, was insisting that one of the Commission's Vice-Presidents should have responsibility for reform of management, personnel and budgets (UK Government Paper 1999). Defying the Amsterdam conclusion in Declaration 32, Prodi, in a speech to the European Council in Cologne, announced his intention to create only two new Vice-Presidencies and then based on policy responsibility, rather than managerial criteria. The first would cover the management of the reform of the Commission, linked to a related portfolio such as internal audit, financial control, fighting fraud or the budget. The other would take responsibility for relations with the European Parliament, linked either to overall oversight of institutional reforms and/or a new service for Citizens' Europe. This sounded coherent. That the widely supported Amsterdam idea of a strong Vice-President for external affairs was abandoned was perhaps linked with the appointment of former NATO Secretary General Javier Solana as 'Mr CFSP' and Secretary General of the Council. A strong Commission Vice-President for external relations might have been viewed as a clear Commission attempt to create an institutional and personal rival. The fact that lack of coordination in external affairs had led to obvious managerial inefficiencies in the Commission was seemingly not reason enough to alter the position. Whether this was insightful decision-making on Prodi's part, the realisation of the power politics involved, or whether, contrary to the protocol in the new Treaty, he was obliged by Member States to take this stance, remains a moot point.

In fact Prodi's proposals were anyway diluted. The two Vice-Presidents, Kinnock and Loyola de Palacio, had portfolios mixed in curious ways. If the Commission were aiming at implementation of the principle of joined-up government, this was hardly apparent in the appointments it made. Kinnock was given the reform portfolio after convoluted discussion on his taking on the role of Commissioner responsible for relations with the Parliament alongside a meatier policy-oriented responsibility (Westlake 2001, 695), but the linked portfolio of the Intergovernmental Conference went to Barnier, who also handled regional policy. Responsibility for relations with the European Parliament, arguably also a dossier linked to reform, was given to Loyola de Palacio along with the energy and transport portfolios, both of which had warranted a sole Commissioner's responsibility hitherto and neither of which sported a specifically umbilical link with democratic control. The overall effect of the change, because of its seeming lack of coherence, in fact lent credence to the idea that Vice-Presidents should be policy coordinators, apart from begging the question of whether the tasks chosen for these two Vice-Presidents were really worthy of Vice-Presidencies rather than other tasks. Of course, the new Vice-Presidency for relations with the Parliament did raise the profile of the Commission in the Parliament. It provided a means of keeping close to parliamentary affairs, trouble-shooting and thus heading off potential embarrassment, though how energy and transport related to this inter-institutional task remained a mystery. Increasingly, however, closeness to parliamentary committees enables compromises to be worked out at an earlier stage and obviates Parliament blocking legislation. An obvious spin-off is the increase in the Commission's role as mediator between Parliament and Council, allowing it to regain some ground lost as a result of the direct relationship between Council and Parliament introduced by the co-decision procedure in the Maastricht Treaty and enhanced since then.

A different implementation of the Vice-President principle would be to make groups of Commissioners subject to overall coordination and management by a Vice-President. Such policy-making groups existed in the 1960s and the principle was again tried under Prodi, though it failed to make an impact on Commission business, since the groups had little or no influence over the political agenda of the Commission, precisely because of missing authoritative coordination and leadership. It was perhaps for this reason that Barroso avoided the mooted idea of clusters of Commissioners. There had been an idea (Grevi 2004) for a shift to fortnightly meetings of the

College and weekly meetings of Commissioner groups chaired by Vice-Presidents. A weekly meeting between the President and the Vice-Presidents would square the coordination circle. It would allow a strategic approach to the issues on the Commission agenda with an enhanced scrutiny of political options at the highest level before policy is decided. This would turn the current less than optimal coordination process into a more streamlined and effective machine. The number of Vice-Presidents (and corresponding groups) could be decided according to the main strategic priorities of the Commission and the overall work programme, with the key criterion being avoidance of clashes of competence. Not only would efficient coordination thus be engendered, but there would be a strong likelihood of a more rational decision-making process allowing for national singularities and closer links with the services as part of the enhanced process of policy preparation. Barroso did not choose to move in this direction. The Vice-President issue is thus more complex than it appears at first sight. Certainly, Barroso has had to grapple with the complexity of the Vice-Presidency versus Commissioner clusters issue, actually appointing five Vice-Presidents (Wallström, Verheugen, Frattini, Barrot and Kallas). The decision not to make Ferrero-Waldner, the Relex Commissioner, a Vice-President was made in light of the mooted later-to-be-introduced post of Vice-President for External Relations and Foreign Policy thought imminent because of the Draft Constitution. Hope and fate clearly played a hand, where charity might have produced a more sensible managerial result.

The size of the Commission: principles, reasoning and justifications

Given the extent of debates about the numbers of Commissioners, it must be concluded that 'size' is a key issue. The College of Commissioners consisted until the last enlargement in 2004 of 20 members. It is now 25 strong, awaiting the arrival of a Romanian and Bulgarian Commissioner, when it will reach the symbolic number (see the Nice Treaty below) of twenty-seven. Originally, the larger states, France, Germany, Italy, Spain and the United Kingdom, had two Commissioners and each of the other Member States one. The usual custom in the larger states was for both government and opposition to be represented. Two votes in a College deciding policy by absolute majority not only allowed the larger states greater weight in the policy-making process but also enabled parties out of government in their home country to retain representation in the Commission. The greater weight of the big five was the stumbling block not only to overall fairness, but to managerial efficiency. Indeed, the problem, as one Commissioner commented over thirty years ago, was that 'inefficiency could hardly be organised in a more costly way' (Dahrendorf 1972, 85). Since the IGC leading to the Nice Treaty the large Member States have played off the size of the Commission against the weighting of votes in the Council. Institutional progress between Amsterdam and the Draft Constitution came largely to depend on abstruse mathematical equations of dubious relevance and perplexing convolution.

The Treaties always laid down that the number of Commissioners may be increased or reduced by unanimous agreement in the Council. This allowed the number of Commissioners to increase with each enlargement of the

Community. The 1991 IGC on Political Union saw the first open discussion on reducing the number of Commissioners from the larger Member States from two to one. It was part of an ongoing debate about the efficiency of the Commission as a policy-making body, in which critics argued that it was difficult for the then College of seventeen Commissioners to be effective in decision-making. In the event the efficiency arguments in favour of a smaller College were outweighed by the desire of four of the five larger Member States (the United Kingdom reputedly being the exception) to retain two Commissioners in the College. It was agreed at Maastricht that the question of allowing every Member State only one nominee in the Commission would be discussed again in the event of further enlargement of the Community's membership. So the discussion at the time of the 'EFTAn' enlargement did not lead to change. The question was then on the agenda of the Reflection Group preparing for the 1996 IGC, when it began to be linked to the qualified majority rules used in the Council and then remained part of the logrolling process in the negotiations for the Amsterdam and Nice Treaties and the Draft Constitution.

The accepted wisdom had long been that the number of Commissioners was already too great before even the EFTAn enlargement, so the enlargements of 2004 and 2007, set to more than double the number of Commissioners, were looked on as a considerable challenge. In a declaration to the Amsterdam conclusions, France, Italy and Belgium made resolution of the outstanding issues for overall institutional reform the *sine qua non* of the next enlargement. If the pundits had been right over the years and the Commission was in need of reform, further enlargement created a situation where further delay would undermine the nature of the EU system itself. There were four issues of principle at stake: national representation, the equal status of Commissioners, guaranteeing the Commission's autonomy and the need for efficient coordination. Optimal size depends on a balance between legitimacy through national representation and operational efficiency (Petite 1996). Over the years all Member States have wished to retain the right to appoint a Commissioner regardless of size, budget contributions and political clout in the Union. They have argued that legitimacy and national public acceptance require it. Indeed, the smaller Member States have made it abundantly clear that their vision of the EU was not domination by the larger countries. Those who accepted the counter-argument that operational efficiency risks being seriously hampered if, in an enlarged Union of 27 by 2007 and within a further ten years perhaps 35 Member States, all Member States retain a Commissioner, hoped quietly that their own country would not lose out.

The justification for the original arrangements was threefold: democratic accountability, individual workload and national balance. Commissioners have quasi-ministerial tasks. They need to travel within and outside the EU to represent the Commission. They are obliged to retain and cultivate links with their countries of origin and national Parliaments. The existence of three institutional locations, Brussels, Strasbourg and Luxembourg means wasted travel time, and Member State clout should, anyway, be reflected in the number of Commissioners. These are, indeed, sound arguments for retaining a somewhat larger College, perhaps divided into teams of junior Commissioners led by senior Vice-Presidents.

The Commission's increasing dependence on Parliament requires resources for it to be effective. The College always meets during the parliamentary session in Strasbourg and some Commissioners are on hand as a *'permanence'* for the other days. In addition, Commissioners are frequently present in Brussels at parliamentary committee meetings to defend and advocate Commission policies. Traditionally, Parliaments claim the right to hear representatives of governments holding political rather than administrative office, so it is appropriate for Parliament to be addressed by Commissioners. In a reformed system, junior Commissioners could conceivably appear in minor debates and defend legislative proposals at committee stage as they work through the co-decision procedure. Appearance in plenary session on major issues of policy could then be left to full Commissioners, with the appropriate *cabinet* member responsible for parliamentary affairs effectively working to both levels of Commissioner and providing an enhanced liaison function between the DGs and the Commissioners. In addition, while overall policy coherence might not be a foregone conclusion under this system, the advantages of an 'inner cabinet' system, as practised by Member States, would be undeniable. Junior Ministers are a widespread ministerial category in national political life and there are good reasons for the Commission to envisage a similar system, not least the fact that the competence and workload of the Commission have increased exponentially to cover all ministerial responsibilities in Member States. A 'presidential team' system, with permanent Vice-Presidents co-ordinating teams of sector-based Commissioners might resolve the numerous issues arising. It would have the advantage of making the core of the College (the Vice-Presidents) resemble a national governmental cabinet, while also ensuring proper co-ordination within and between groups of Commissioners.

The size of the Commission: competing views

But, the treaties never made provision for political or geographical weighting in the Commission, as they did for the Council and the Parliament. It would clearly contradict the independence of Commissioners anchored in the Treaty of Rome if national interests were reflected in College discussions. The risk has always been that College meetings would come to resemble a Council meeting, a kind of bureaucratic Committee of Permanent Representatives, almost a COREPER III (Piris 1994, 480), with *cabinet* members lower down forming a parallel to Council working groups. Peterson cites a senior official to the effect that *cabinets* are already 'like mini-Councils within the Commission' (Peterson 1999), and Ross (1995) points to several examples of Commissioners lobbying harder than objectivity would require for their own national position in Commission decisions. But there are surprising exceptions to the flag-waving principle. When national push risked becoming Community shove during the BSE crisis, both UK Commissioners refrained from blocking Commission decisions. They did not emulate the UK's non-cooperation within the Council (Westlake 1996). The report of the Three Wise Men in October 1999 concluded that the 2000 IGC should avoid the danger of the College becoming 'an assembly of national delegates' (Three Wise Men 1999) and a report by a senior official (Petit-Laurent) had analysed earlier how the Commission might function with thirty members, which it did in fact during the final few months of the Prodi Commission as 'stagiaire-Commissioners' from the acceding countries arrived.

One starting point for analysis has to be the fact that there is no intrinsic need for each Member State to have a Commissioner. After all, the Commission supposedly represents the European interest, not that of the Member States, and Commissioners are formally appointed 'on the grounds of their general competence'. One could conceive, for example, of a small College of highly qualified, democratically appointed Commissioners with national proportions maintained, perhaps, at the next level down, that of Directors General. This view, argued forcefully, though anonymously, by Commissioner Dahrendorf in 1972 (Dahrendorf 1972) would require rethinking the question of national balance and the concomitant removal of states' automatic right to a Commissioner. Spierenburg recommended that in 1979, but to no avail. Later, Commission President Roy Jenkins, who authorised the report, bitterly remarked, 'the position of too many Commissioners chasing too few jobs, with which I was confronted in 1977, was exacerbated by the Greek entry of 1981 and the Spanish and Portuguese entry of 1986' (Jenkins 1991, 376). It was thus not surprising that the Dooge Report of 1985 also recommended only one Commissioner per Member State, but equally unsurprising that the resulting Single European Act made no adjustment, despite Margaret Thatcher's argument that 'a Commission of 17 is liable to be too large for efficiency or to provide all members with serious portfolios' (Thatcher 1985) and the British House of Lords Select Committee on the European Communities' admonition that 'it must be doubted whether the members of such a large body can work efficiently and harmoniously together as a "College"' (House of Lords 1985). The subsequent Maastricht Treaty negotiations still did not heed the calls, though it did of course extend Commission competences. The debates in the 1996 IGC and thereafter seemed to demonstrate that it was highly unlikely that there would ever be such agreement, despite the compelling case for a smaller, tighter operation making for better coordination, easier agreement and clearer conclusions, not to mention kindling team spirit and projecting a better image. Yet a protocol to the Nice Treaty suddenly took a step in this direction by announcing that when the number of Member States reached twenty-seven, a review would break the strict ruling of one Commissioner per Member State. The Nice proposal is reviewed below.

Commission size issues in the 1996 IGC

Historically, the 1996 IGC produced the most focused arguments. A team of German academics argued that Commissioners should not be appointed on a national quota basis at all (Weidenfeld 1994, 38), and the French MEP Jean-Louis Bourlanges actually advocated total severance of the ties between Member States and Commissioners (Bourlanges 1996). Karl Lamers, foreign policy spokesman of the Christian Democratic Union (CDU)/Christian Social Union (CSU) in the German Bundestag, identified ten to twelve EC policy areas, recommending that the total number of Commissioners be reduced to fit the portfolios. Since the national right to a

Commissioner would thereby vanish, there would have to be 'an unwritten rule whereby a Member State which does not have a Commissioner during one legislative period should be considered for one during the next' (Lamers 1995, 43), a prescient idea which re-appeared in the Convention. British Commissioners had long advocated such a change (Brittan 1994, 238–43; Tugendhat 1985, 201). Brittan proposed twelve senior Commissioner portfolios, with rotating assistant (or junior) Commissioners without portfolio. To lend weight where it was believed due, the larger countries, on this hypothesis, might always have a senior Commissioner, with the remaining senior and junior Commissioners drawn, on a rotating basis, from the other states. Brittan proposed that each full Commissioner have two votes. Each junior Commissioner, disallowed from voting against his or her senior Commissioner, would have one. At least half the number of Commissioners and half the votes would be required for approval of a Commission decision. This, he argued, would result in a streamlining of administration, an acceleration of the reallocation of staff and funds between competing priorities, operational improvement, and more coherence in the Commission's image to the outside world. Stricter appliance of the principle of subsidiarity might also result, since controls would have to be introduced ensuring that one current function of Commissioners, to guarantee consideration of their national administrative cultures, would be maintained. If this relatively full description of Brittan's proposals seems somewhat indulgent, given the actual Treaty outcomes, the point of its inclusion here is to demonstrate that many wheel-re-inventing discussions might have been more profitably based on a reading of more daring texts written in the twenty-five years since Spierenburg by Commissioners with first-hand experience of the shortcomings of the current system.

The larger Member States were, of course, always reluctant to relinquish their second Commissioner. Former Commissioner Etienne Davignon somewhat cynically argued in the run-up to Amsterdam that, despite the apparent German, French and British agreement to reduce to one Commissioner, 'they may have managed to come to an agreement because they were certain that in the long run one country or another would oppose the idea' (Davignon 1995, 16). Nonetheless, the circulation of ideas outside the Commission for reform of its size began to have an effect on the inner circles. The German government felt some embarrassment at the idea that the largest country in the EU might occasionally end up with no Commissioner if the College were to consist of only twelve members. At the Noordwijk special European Council on 23 May 1997, the Germans persuaded the others that the status quo was preferable to an endless quarrel, but the smaller countries would not agree to a new system without guarantees of national representation. The Commission's proposal was similar to those of Brittan and Lamers. It also argued that the President should allocate portfolios to members and be able to make changes during the Commission's term of office. In the Commission's proposal, unlike in Brittan's proposal, all Commissioners would be fully involved in debates and voting. Junior Commissioners would have the same voting rights as those with portfolios, and would participate fully in College discussions.

Such potential changes pose a series of questions. Whether Member States would need to be compensated for losses/gains made in the number or status of 'their' Commissioner (an issue discussed in Westlake 2004; chapter 14), was key. In addition, a further point of contention has been how a 'revolving' system of senior nominations might work, and how the danger of the large states filling the more important posts might be averted. Yet it is clear that a system of junior and senior Commissioners would certainly ensure that all states remain represented, small members incapable of permanently filling big posts would be appeased, the current workload of the large-portfolio Commissioners would be reduced and external representation would be more frequent at political level.

The Amsterdam and Nice Treaties, the Prodi Commission and the Convention

The Amsterdam Treaty skimmed the surface of the issues. It settled the question of the larger Member States having two Commissioners with a 'protocol on the institutions with the prospect of enlargement of the European Union', which read:

> 'Article 1
> At the entry into force of the first enlargement of the Union . . . the Commission shall comprise one national of each of the Member States, provided that, by that date, the weighting of the votes in the Council has been modified, whether by re-weighting of the votes or by dual majority, in a manner acceptable to all Member States, taking into account all relevant elements, notably compensating those Member States which give up the possibility of nominating a second member of the Commission.

> Article 2
> At least one year before the membership of the European Union exceeds twenty, a conference of representatives of the governments of Member States shall be convened in order to carry out a comprehensive review of the provisions of the Treaties on the composition and functioning of the institutions.'

Soon after the Amsterdam Treaty's implementation, a European Parliament report in 1999 advocated that:

> 'a more systematic attempt should be made to identify "real" portfolios, and then to adjust the structures of the Commission and of its Directorates-General (DGs) to those real needs... [and that] Teams of Commissioners should be established for each subject area, with senior and junior Commissioners on the model of full Ministers and Ministers of State in national governments.' (Herman 1999)

But as Prodi took office, these issues were far from resolution. Commenting at the Cologne European Council, Prodi argued that the idea that it was not possible to carve out substantial jobs for nineteen Commissioners needed to be dispelled. Each portfolio, argued the new President, would carry with it a significant area of work; the main challenge was 'squeezing all the work of the Commission into nineteen portfolios' (Prodi 1999c). While some portfolios would be unchanged, others would be re-grouped to remove overlap and duplication, and there would be a grouping of DGs under the responsibility of single Commissioners. This remained to be seen.

The Nice Treaty ended the rule by which Germany, France, the UK, Italy and Spain had two Commissioners. Nice ruled that the Commission would be made up of one national from each Member State until the EU includes 27 countries. In practice this means until 2007 when Bulgaria and Romania are expected to achieve formal membership. Thereafter, a rotation system was to be applied, based upon equal treatment of all EU states and reflecting the geographical and demographic profile of the EU. Thus, when the EU had 27 members, EU governments were to agree unanimously the number of Commissioners, but this had to be fewer than the number of Member States. At the same time, the President of the Commission was to be appointed by qualified majority as opposed to the rule hitherto of consensus in the European Council, and his nomination was to continue to be subject to approval by the European Parliament. The subsequent Convention proposed a College of a maximum fifteen members on the basis of a list compiled from nominations from Member States, with each entitled to nominate three nominees, thus taking geographical and political aspects into consideration. Nice's idea of an egalitarian rotation thus disappeared as the political debate continued. Likewise, the Nice provision that the College should act under the President's guidance also disappeared. This led to considerable criticism (*EU Observer* 2003). The Commission's view on the issue of size had also meanwhile evolved. In 1999 it had argued that the 'current way in which the Commission operates, with new powers vested in its president to give political orientation... and decision-making in the College on the basis of a simple majority of the members creates an important balance which is likely to be disturbed if the number of Commissioners is increased' (Commission 1999c). Yet, by the time of the Convention the Commission had come to favour a system in which all Member States would be represented with a member of equal status (Commission 2003, 6). The Convention itself was in favour of a functional distinction between a limited number of European Commissioners with voting rights in the College and Commissioners without voting rights. On this basis, not all EU Member States could benefit from 'their own' European Commissioner. In the end, however, the IGC 2003/2004 changed the Convention's draft. It proposed a rotation system in which two thirds of the Member States would have their nationals represented in the Commission.

The Commission risked losing more than it could possibly gain with the proposed Constitution. As one contribution to the Convention had put it, there could be 'a countdown to extinction' (Convention 2003a). The Convention proposal was a system of equal rotation with fifteen rotating Commissioners (including the President and the new Minister of Foreign Affairs) and non-voting Commissioners from other Member States. Art. 1-25 (3a) of the Convention's draft foresaw that 'Member States should be treated on a strictly equal footing as regards the determination of the sequence of, and the time spent by, their nationals as Members of the College' and 'consequently, the difference between the number of terms of office held by nationals of any given pair of Member States may never be more than one'. This arrangement was to be valid from 1 November 2009, thus leaving the following (Barroso) Commission composed as foreseen at Nice, i.e. with one Commissioner per Member State. The Commission is currently reflecting on the fact that the 2007 enlargement requires new legislation on numbers of Commissioners in order to implement the Nice Treaty provisions.

Prodi shared with colleagues his fear that the IGC needed to review certain articles of the Convention's draft: 'the Draft Constitution proposes a Commission' made up in a way that will – in my opinion and that of the whole College – make the institution representing the Union's general interest less able to do its work effectively and credibly... it creates a distinction between Commissioners which might split the College and damage trust' (Prodi 2003). The Commission itself argued that 'the outcome of the convention was not a finished product' and that 'The approach advocated for the composition of the Commission... does not appear viable in the light of the way the Commission really operates... With equality for all the Member States... being a settled point in the Convention, it must be possible to find a form of composition which is better suited to the dictates of legitimacy and effectiveness of Commission action... [the composition proposed by the Convention is]... complicated, muddled and inoperable, [and] threatens the basis of Collegiality'.[9] If the Commissioners without voting rights were to manage a portfolio, the Commission could not see how they could effectively exercise their responsibilities without being able to participate in the collective decision. And if they did not have a portfolio, the Commission 'wondered what their role within the College could be'. It posed a string of practical questions to the IGC:

> 'Are the non-voting Commissioners Members of the Commission? What are their rights? May they attend meetings of the College, and take part in discussions? May they suspend a written procedure? Are they empowered to take decisions on behalf of the Commission? Can they be given specific responsibility for an area of activity involving the right to give instructions to a Commission department? What is the nature of their relations with the President (who is, according to the text, personally responsible for their activities, in direct contradiction to the principle of collegiality, in spite of the fact that the Convention rejected proposals for introducing the individual political responsibility of Members of the Commission)?'

The issue had become too complex for the EU public or even for the average EU official to comprehend. The heightened complexity was in part due to the fact that the size of the Commission was now inextricably linked with the issue of weighted votes in the Council. In an effort to reach an acceptable compromise the Commission admitted that, 'The fact is that it is not necessary, in terms of maintaining collegiality, for all the Members of the Commission to be involved in all the decisions adopted on behalf of the Commission' and it therefore proposed:

> 'to generalise and formalise the decentralisation of decision-

making within the Commission, by structuring the College into a number of Groups of Commissioners, while taking whatever steps are necessary to guarantee collegiality and consistency of policy. The College, embracing all the Members of the Commission, would address only the most important issues and would therefore have only a limited number of decisions to take. Other Commission decisions would be taken by groups of Commissioners, each of them acting in fields which are proper to their competences within the general guidelines laid down by the College'.

The Commission's view was that this arrangement would relieve the burden on the full College meetings, enhance policy coherence, and still ensure that the most sensitive issues had the benefit of a collegial decision. In a letter from President Prodi to the Irish Presidency (24 April 2004) an amendment was suggested to Art. 1-25 suggesting that from 1 November 2014 the Commission should comprise its President, the Vice-President for Foreign Affairs and sixteen members. This formula was acceptable at least until the new Central European members had been fully integrated into the EU.

In the end, the Constitutional Treaty maintained the Nice Treaty's composition of the Commission – one Commissioner per Member State – until 2014. From then on, the Commission was to comprise a number of Commissioners corresponding to two thirds of the number of Member States. The members of the Commission would be chosen according to a system based on equal rotation among the Member States, which had already been decided in the Nice Treaty. Article 4(1) of the protocol on enlargement annexed to the Nice Treaty made provision for one Commissioner per Member State until the EU reached 27 members. Thereafter:

'the number of members of the Commission shall be less than the number of member States. The members of the Commission shall be chosen according to a rotation system based on the principle of equality, the implementing arrangements for which shall be adopted by the Council, acting unanimously'.

The rejection of the Constitutional Treaty in successive referendums has given EU officials and the public alike time to learn the mathematical equations necessary to understand how their institutions will work if the Treaty is agreed at some point in the future. Meanwhile, the Nice Treaty applies and it can be expected that the Commission will propose appropriate changes to cope with further enlargements as they occur.

The *cabinet* system

The role and success of Commissioners is intimately bound up with that of their *cabinet*s or personal teams of advisers. A good *cabinet* can boost the standing of an otherwise poor Commissioner, and a poor *cabinet* can compromise an otherwise good Commissioner. So, it is no coincidence that the most effective Commissioners have traditionally been those with the best-staffed and best-organised *cabinet*s. Of course, the effectiveness of any one *cabinet* also depends on the skill and political nous of their Commissioner, so this is a two-way process. But a Commissioner's reputation does depend largely on *cabinet* efficacy in providing sound advice and guidance.

Delors' former *chef de cabinet*, later Commissioner, Pascal Lamy, referred to the *cabinet* system as the 'jardinier de la collégialité', though Machiavelli identified somewhat more personal stakes arguably applicable to Commissioners long ago.

> 'The choice of servants is of no little importance to a prince, and they are good or not according to the discrimination of the prince. And the first opinion which one forms of a prince, and of his understanding, is by observing the men he has around him; and when they are capable and faithful he may always be considered wise, because he has known how to recognize the capable and to keep them faithful. But when they are otherwise one cannot form a good opinion of him, for the prime error which he made was in choosing them.' (*The Prince*, chap. XXII)

Aside from their use to Commissioners in terms of personal impact, the strength, importance and thus relevance of the *cabinet* system to the Commission's own system of internal governance results from two observable trends; the growing complexity of policy demands on the Commission and the seemingly inevitable general tendency of small, easily manageable and personally loyal groups of advisors to be placed outside mainstream bureaucracies, a common characteristic of governance in Member States. In the Commission *cabinets* have increasingly been drawn into the detail of policymaking, monitoring and implementation, adding thereby to their traditional centrality in the political processes of the Commission and the complex interaction of Community institutions. They were always a high level focus for lobbying from sectoral and national interests. They always helped coordinate policy and mediate among competing interests both within the Commission and outside. And they have thus always provided a useful lens through which to view the intricate and informal processes of Commission policy-making (Ross 1993). How far they have been drawn into the nitty-gritty of management has been a function of individual Commissioners' approaches and the overall management style of the President.

Historical origins

A system of personal advisers or ministerial *cabinets* giving political support and advice to Ministers was a familiar part of the politico-administrative systems in most of the founding Member States. While the system was not so well developed in Germany, it was well established in Italy, Belgium and France. Monnet encouraged a dynamic and fluid system of policy advice during the early years of the ECSC, yet the elitist *Cabinet* system he perhaps unwittingly encouraged was a product of the strong French administrative influence on the Community in the early years. *Cabinets* were perceived as a natural support mechanism for members of the High Authority, and key *cabinet* members were highly influential in both policy advice and political negotiations. Thus, the EEC Commission appointed in 1958 inherited private offices largely based on the pattern of French ministerial *cabinets*.

Europe's high fliers were to take to this French system like ducks to water. But in the early days, Hallstein, the new President, was still keen to keep the *cabinets* small, realising that large interventionist *cabinets* would be likely to jeopardise good working relations between Commissioners and civil servants for all the reasons described below that did, in fact, later become apparent. Hallstein also anticipated that since the *cabinets* were chosen by Commissioners largely from their own nationals, they risked becoming poles of attraction for national interests within the Commission and thus inhibiting the development of the European identity which he was trying to foster (Mazey 1992). He was clearly right about that risk. He also viewed the Commission as a collective body in which all members ought to be well briefed on general Community policy in addition to their own portfolio concerns. Commissioners were expected to have a high public profile and to make regular visits around the Community, accompanied by members of their *cabinets*. On occasion, Commissioners sent their *cabinet* members to represent them. All this was easy in a world where Community competence was limited and, for example, a good lawyer could remember all the cases that had come before the Court of Justice. Its impossibility today is a good reason for a system of junior Commissioners to provide the representative function, instead of allowing it to slip to *cabinets* or senior administrators.

The early *cabinets* evolved rapidly as new policies became established, Community competence expanded and the powers of the institutions began to be more clearly delineated. The functions of *cabinet* members thereby became more and more wide-ranging and varied. They dealt with lobbyists, liaised with national governments, developed policy initiatives, wrote speeches and generally organised the work of the Commission. *Cabinets* acted as the political antennae for Commissioners by keeping them alerted to politically sensitive or difficult issues and acted as a filter for parties and pressure groups at both national and European level. In the early days, Commissioners had ancillary responsibilities for two other policy areas than their main portfolio, so each policy area was discussed by a triumvirate of Commissioners. As they came increasingly to rely heavily on *cabinet* members for advice, Commissioners' dependence was heightened in areas outside their main sphere of responsibility. If the practice of policy responsibility beyond the immediate portfolio of an individual Commissioner in the end proved unworkable and became defunct, the expectation that Commissioners should nevertheless be well briefed over a range of policy areas persisted. It underlies the notion of collegiality and it has made the *cabinet* system indispensable. Thus, *cabinet* jobs became top jobs in the Commission. Members of *cabinets* do not get their hands dirty with resource management and budgets. They get the chance to work closely with the College, to concentrate on the intellectual challenge of defining the European interest and defending their own politician. They thus get to test their personal political skills, and they achieve the clear prospect of 'parachutage' into a managerial post in the services when their period in the *cabinet* comes to an end, if not higher office elsewhere, including, for some such as Pascal Lamy, as EU Commissioner.

Tasks and task masters

The internal workings of a *cabinet* reflect the personality and working style of both the Commissioner and of the *chef de cabinet*. Some *cabinets* meet their Commissioner on most working days and enjoy regular and direct access to discussions on all policy issues. Others tend to filter papers through the *chef* who handles issues with full delegated authority from the Commissioner. Thus, *cabinets* are involved to different degrees in assisting Commissioners with their policy responsibilities and enhancing the presentation of the Commissioners' public image and political philosophy. They are responsible for coordination and liaison with Member States and with the services. They thus provide a combination of private office secretariat, political advice and additional policy input. Just as they are an undoubtedly important mechanism for coordinating policy within the Commission, they also ensure that the Commission's policy is effectively presented. Patten gave his *cabinet* a good deal of credit for his own effectiveness in communicating precisely and with consummate style. His notes and 'communications' to the College or the foreign ministers were redolent of the 'elegant and witty clarity of my *chef de cabinet*'s prose style' (Patten 2005, 157), but then he did have, on his own admission, 'the best that Britain's Foreign Office and Treasury could have provided'. *Cabinet* members write speeches and articles and ensure that the Commissioner has effective communication with his or her own government and with national public opinion. The latter is one of the most delicate and controversial of the *cabinets*' functions.

Cabinets are frequently suspected, not always unjustly, of leaking internal Commission documents to their national administrations. In return, they receive detailed briefing on their own government's concerns about a particular proposal before a Commission debate takes place. They are certainly in constant contact with the national Permanent Representation in Brussels and, on occasion, with ministries in the Commissioner's home state. But it would be misleading to see this process as instruction given to the Commission by a government. More often it is a process of negotiation between *cabinets* and national governments within the parameters of their respective positions. In this the *cabinets* are constantly lobbied by pressure groups of their own and other nationalities to raise points of particular concern at inter- and intra-*cabinet* meetings. Although key interest groups obviously have close contact with the *cabinet* of the Commissioner with policy responsibility for their area of concern, they naturally also exploit contacts in other *cabinets* and DGs. Europe-wide lobbyists focus on *cabinets* before the Commission makes a decision, duplicating, albeit at a higher level, the pressure which will already have been exercised on the Commission officials who have prepared the issues for discussion. The Permanent Representations of the Member States and of non-EU countries represented in Brussels tend to make lobbying at *cabinet* level a priority (see also chapter 10).

Performing the significant role of monitoring the work of Commission officials and liaising between the Commissioner and his or her staff makes the *cabinets*' work particularly contentious. Policy submissions and opinions are channelled from the services through the relevant *cabinet* member to the Commissioner and views from the Commissioner are channelled back down to the services. *Cabinets* are past masters at building synergy, finding majorities and constructing package deals with other Community institutions and with Member States. The result, in principle, is that policy choices have joint political and administrative ownership. There are sometimes differences of view. Senior civil servants object to receiving instructions from (sometimes young and inexperienced, albeit intellectually high flying) *cabinet* members. They also object to the frequent practice of *cabinet*s circumventing senior staff and dealing directly with middle-ranking or even junior staff at the hub of a given policy area. Commission officials have often expressed the view that *cabinet* members interfere too much in the detail of their work and take over too much of the substantive policy-making. Yet, *cabinet* members rightly feel that it is essential for them to become familiar with dossiers in order to advise their Commissioner. Tension between policy advisers and administrative officials is common to most systems of policy-making. Over time, advisers find that their pattern of relationships with permanent staff institutionalises the tension. Though the direct link between the Commissioner and his permanent civil service in the Directorates General is clearly vital, there are thus risks to be avoided.

Formally, there is an institutional buffer, which may prevent tension arising. The administrative effectiveness of a *cabinet* working with its own Directorate General depends to a considerable extent on efficient liaison with an official who is not a member of a *cabinet*; the Director General's Assistant. This is a post akin to that of a private secretary in a British ministry, responsible for supervision of the Directorate General's internal structures and procedures, coordination with other Directorates General and shielding the Director General from time-wasters. Briefing requests from the *cabinet* and their day-to-day contact with the Directorate General thus customarily transit through the Assistant, who is chosen by the Director General himself. When it does not, it means either the *cabinet* or the services are actually running the show. Under Delors, the President's *cabinet* was extremely powerful. After Delors there was a good deal of work to be done in re-establishing proper hierarchical relations between services, *cabinet*s and Commissioners. Rectification resulted from the need to end the existence of the parallel administration on which Delors' *cabinet* had relied. This is discussed in chapter 4. New rules for *cabinet*s was one answer. But, after the Santer and Prodi Commissions, it was the services which seemingly needed to be brought back to order. As one Commissioner put it:

> 'I hope I don't put too many noses out of joint by saying that since the glory days of Delors, the Commission has not been led from the top down... my guess is that power within the Commission has inexorably shifted to the Services. Indeed I believe that through the shocks of the Santer resignation and the subsequent upheavals, it was the Directors General who kept the Commission show on the road and I readily acknowledge this. The consequence has been a loss of cutting edge in policy and a reluctance to make hard choices instead of endless compromises. Priorities have not been set by Commissioners who take an overall political view. They have been set by individual Services with their own entirely legitimate, but focused set of interests and concerns' (Mandelson 2005).

Whether Mandelson's view is a valid comment on the whole Commission or merely a reflection of the situation in some policy areas is a moot point. It was certainly a rapid conclusion, for when he expressed it he had not yet been Commissioner for a year, though his *chef de cabinet* had been a member of Leon Brittan's *cabinet* in the Delors days, when rivalry between the intellectual and managerial styles of Delors and Brittan was becoming an integral part of Commission folklore. Certainly, Santer's managerial style, unlike Delors', involved insisting on senior officials and *cabinets* finding compromises before the College met, as opposed to Delors' penchant for the intellectual fray at the most senior level. In almost Socratic enthusiasm Delors thrived on divergence, argument and winning cerebral battles. His *cabinet* members were willing disciples. If the services' power and influence has bounced back since this dialectical heyday, it is still the *cabinets* that are expected to ensure effective coordination within the Commission's administrative structure. But, these days, if the proper hierarchy between *cabinets* and services is upset, it may well be due to a managerial bilious attack rather than a new chronic ailment. Managerial style at the very top of the Commission clearly affects the services, but the way this happens is still a matter for conjecture. There is little hard evidence to explain trends, and commentators inevitably concentrate on the writings of Ross, one academic with an insider view, though his experience was limited to the Delors era. Bygone days may help ask the relevant questions, but they are a poor guide to the *cabinet* system some fifteen years later. But, the growing reluctance of *cabinets* to be really involved and thus share the burden of accountability introduced by recent reforms might well be evidence of a trend from political valour to managerial discretion.

Selection and composition

Cabinet members are appointed by and directly responsible to their Commissioner and retain their posts at his personal discretion. They have no security of tenure. Governments and political parties are much exercised by the composition of Commissioners' *cabinets*, since they have become a vital point of contact for the Member States within the Community system. It was originally agreed that Commissioners' *cabinets* should consist of two members, plus a secretary and typist, and the President's *cabinet* should consist of four advisers plus two secretaries. But, Commissioners soon began detaching high-flying civil servants from the DGs to serve in their *cabinet*, and the *cabinets* thus gradually acquired a major influence over the day-to-day running of the Commission. In turn, there was a growth in the number of members and in their seniority and calibre. *Cabinets* are now usually a mixture of internal Commission staff, seconded to the *cabinet* for the Commission's five-year term, and outsiders on secondment from national administrations or the private sector. The latter tend to spend an average of two to three years in a *cabinet*. As to the former, a passage through a Commissioner's *cabinet* is an undoubted key to a successful career in the Commission. A high proportion of senior staff in the Commission has seen service in one *cabinet* or another. In the 1990s the Commission financed a *cabinet* of six members for each Commissioner, at least one of whom had to be a national of another Community Member State. In practice, some had as many as eight members, with the additional posts funded by the Commissioner's home administration through secondment or occasionally through a system of temporary attachments. Santer's *cabinet* was actually ten-strong with nine different nationalities; the exception that proved the rule. It was Prodi who reduced the formally allowed number of *cabinet* members to six. He also required the deputy head of *cabinet*, or 'sous-chef' as a culinary metaphor would have it, to be of a different nationality to the *chef*.

It is not only the incumbents who seek fame and excitement by distributing their CVs at the beginning of new Commissions. The Permanent Representations of the Member States spend considerable time supporting their own nationals. And Commissioners are not left to their own devices. In the United Kingdom, the Cabinet Office draws up a list of civil service candidates for *cabinet* posts with British Commissioners and offers the list to other prospective Commissioners. In France, new Commissioners who have previously been national ministers often take members of their former ministerial *cabinet*s with them to Brussels and the SGCI (the Secretariat Général pour la Coordination Interministerielle des Affaires Européennes) plays a similarly influential role in proposing *cabinet* members. The Permanent Representations of the Member States in Brussels are also a valuable source of candidates both for *cabinet*s and for senior posts in the Commission's administration. There is a lot riding on the access to policy-making afforded the smart *cabinet* member, so the large Member States have recently supplied new Commissioners with a list of even forty or more candidates. One prospective *cabinet* member is reputed to have received a refusal for a *cabinet* post for which he had not provided an application. It was always the case that the British Foreign Office placed one its own high fliers in the post of *chef de cabinet*. Millan and Kinnock diverged, however. They appointed a high flying Commission insider, Philip Lowe, who has subsequently been Director General of several DGs.

The routines of cabinet business: menus and cuisine interne – from special chefs through sous-chefs to full chefs

Each *cabinet*'s coordinating role is governed by the timetable of the Commission's weekly meetings, normally held on Wednesdays. Issues requiring a Commission decision must be signalled at least nine days in advance of the relevant Commission meeting, usually at the *chefs de cabinet* meeting held at the beginning of the previous week. An updated outline agenda is circulated each week by the Secretariat General. Indicative longer-term timetables of the Commission are also circulated. These are designed to help prevent excessive bunching of major issues at particular meetings, to enable all and sundry to manage their own diaries and to set indicative timelines for ending routine coordination by authoritative decision-making. Under the rules of procedure any Commission member has the right to insist that an item of business be placed on the agenda of a particular meeting, so the management of business is therefore not exactly easy to plan. In practice, July and December tend to be particularly busy months and September and January relatively quiet.

Substantive sectoral policy proposals are discussed at meeting of representatives of all Commissioners' *cabinet*s, known as 'special chefs' meetings.

These are chaired by a member of the President's *cabinet*. They can last for between one and 12 hours, or occasionally even longer, depending on the complexity and political sensitivity of the issue under discussion. During a normal week there are likely to be six or seven such *cabinet* meetings, made up of *cabinet* members responsible for the issue under discussion. Papers for these meetings have to be circulated 48 hours in advance and provide an initial summary of the positions of those Directorates General which have been consulted. Other *cabinet*s are thereby made aware of how much opposition remains to a proposal, where it comes from and why. They can thus alert their Commissioner (or their capital) accordingly. It is not unknown for a *cabinet* to disavow the objections of its own Commissioner's DG in a meeting of its *chefs de cabinet*. The irresolvable issues of rival services often transmogrify at a flick of the magic wands of non-specialist but politically canny *cabinet* members. The conclusions of these meetings are drawn up by the President's *cabinet*. They provide a first indication of the likely outcome in the Commission. It is then open to individual *cabinet*s to place formal reserves on all or some of the conclusions, but not to have the conclusions rewritten. The special *chefs* meeting therefore provides considerable scope for the President's *cabinet* to construct a consensus around its own desired outcome, a task which, at this stage, does not yet require the support of the Secretary General. Writing the minutes is an important facet of policy-making.

Coordination between the Commissioners' *cabinet*s takes place within a tight time-scale and with firmly fixed procedures. The conclusions of special chefs meetings form the input into the Monday *chefs de cabinet* meeting. This meeting differs from the special *chefs* in that it is chaired by the Commission's Secretary General and takes place under the watchful and authoritative eye of the legal service. At this level, the permanent civil service input from the Directorates General remains important. But the parameters for debate have been set previously by the special *chefs* meeting, although the President's *chef de cabinet* undoubtedly plays a major role in setting the agenda, as does the Secretary General. A delicate balance is thus struck in proxy between collegiality and Presidential authority. The meetings of *chefs de cabinet* follow the same agenda as the subsequent full Commission and seek to achieve consensus on as many points as possible in advance of the Commission meeting on the following Wednesday. Those points on which unanimous agreement is reached at the chefs meeting nonetheless remain on the Commission agenda as so-called 'A' points – for agreement without discussion. This reflects the principle that the College of Commissioners itself takes all formal decisions, except where a specific delegation of powers, known as an *habilitation* or 'delegated procedure' (see chapter 4), is given to one or more members. It is indeed open to any Commissioner to seek to reopen an item marked down as an 'A' point at the beginning of the weekly Commission meeting. However, as 'A' points reflect a consensus among Commission members, it is rare for this to happen, except as a political gesture, perhaps accompanied by a dissenting statement for the minutes. In such politically sensitive cases it is not unusual for the College to follow the Council example of 'false B points', where 'A' points are disguised as 'B' points for public (the very specialised sectors of the public, that is) consumption. In internal Commission parlance, these are 'C' points.

Non-contentious issues can also be agreed through the written pro-cedures described in chapter 4. Here, all *cabinets* receive copies of a draft proposal and a deadline is provided for objections. If there is none, the decision is agreed formally without further discussion. If one or more *cabinets* object, the procedure is suspended while bilateral discussions take place to see whether the difficulty can be resolved. If it cannot, then the writ-ten procedure is abandoned and discussion of the proposal is shifted back to the normal *cabinet* procedure involving oral discussion either to settle the issue or, if not, to prepare for Commissioners to do so. Written procedures are normally used for minor issues, such as amendments to customs pro-cedures, agricultural or internal market regulations. In cases of urgency and with the agreement of the President's *cabinet*, the 'accelerated written pro-cedure' may be used, allowing for the Commission to take a decision within 48 hours. This is useful for urgent but non-contentious issues such as the authorisation of humanitarian aid. Finally, as an anti-climax to these bureaucratic meanderings, Commissioners get to discuss the high political dossiers, as really contentious issues arrive on the agenda of the College meeting.

Advantages of the cabinet system

This chapter posited at the outset that the work of the *cabinets* is shaped by the functions, standing, prestige, experience and calibre of the Commissioners themselves, and that the converse was also true. While the *cabinets* can to some extent counterbalance a Commissioner's shortcomings and are used by Commissioners to strengthen their own performance in areas where they might otherwise be weak, in practice it is very difficult for advisers to manage the successes and failures of policy-makers in the serv-ices. The *cabinet* system lends important credibility to the notion of colle-giality and if it did not exist, it would have to be invented. It has many advantages. Problems of working in a multinational bureaucracy and with officials from various administrative backgrounds have always been diffi-cult for Commissioners, but they are attenuated by *cabinets* acting as inter-locutors and buffers between the Commissioner and the services.

In the early years of the Community, it became apparent that for a policy to be successful tough negotiation with politicians, civil servants and interested parties in the Member States was vital. Without political support for them, policies are untenable. And it is the *cabinets* which identify key interests within the Member States and construct deals with Commission officials from DGs with divergent views. There was an undoubted advan-tage in letting this kind of job fall to the Commissioners' *cabinets*, since until the Permanent Representations of the Member States became established in the mid-1960s as a clearing house for national interests, the Commission was in frequent direct contact with national elites, the work being coordinated and supervised by the *cabinets*. There is thus a long tradition. National politicians and pressure groups put considerable pressure on the *cabinets* to advance their claims and the *cabinets* have thereby become both a pressure point for national and sectoral interests and a focus for the accommodation of national and Community interests (Ritchie 1992), including that of the Commissioner's own political party, which may also have a liaison member in the *cabinet*, a job frequently combined with work on European Parliament issues. To sum up, *cabinets* are the prime mechanism for intra- and inter-Commissioner coordination. It is easier for policy disputes to be sorted out at the level of *cabinets*, if previous coordination between the services has failed. These are all clear advantages.

Disadvantages of the cabinet system – cabinet-service tensions

But there are problems. As the policy competences of the EC grew in the 1960s, the patterns of decision-making became increasingly institutionalised and bureaucratised, and problems of coordination and lack of strategic direction grew acute in a system where the lines of political responsibility and accountability were never clearly drawn. While there were obvious advantages to the *cabinet* system, and while they clearly increased the political weight of Commissioners by providing a pool of reliable and politically loyal advisers, there were thus also drawbacks. Advice is only good if leaders are prepared to use it, but empowering advisors by strengthening *cabinets* often implies reluctant services must accept that *cabinet* members are acting on the authority of the Commissioner, whether they like it or not. They must refrain from questioning the *cabinet*'s style and methods. Like it or lump it. But, increasingly, Commission officials came not always to accept willingly the authority of the *cabinet* to supervise, monitor or override their views. And the problem increased as the number of *cabinet* members increased and the profile of the Commission changed. This happened when Delors left and Member States became clearly content to keep the Commission in an ill-defined 'rightful place'.

Even in the 1970s, the Spierenburg Report had found that *cabinets* shielded Commissioners from their services, usurped the responsibilities of Directors General and questioned proposals without consulting the responsible officials in the services. Henceforth, argued Spierenburg, no policy document should be edited without consultation of the appropriate Director General and there should anyway be no radical departure from the theme of the basic proposal. Spierenburg also criticised the *cabinets*' widespread interference on appointment issues and the 'undue' attention to nationality factors, itself compounded by *parachutage* (see page 201) of *cabinet* members into plum jobs in the services. While not offering a solution to the problem of *parachutage*, Spierenburg recommended reinstatement of officials only into their former posts on leaving the *cabinet*. While not dismissing the fact that *cabinet* members would have acquired considerable skills while working in *cabinets*, there should, it was argued, be fair competition for posts. The Spierenburg Report thus drew attention to the dangers inherent in the proliferation of *cabinet* members. Lowering the morale of the services and creating a barrier between the Commissioner and the DGs was perhaps an inevitable result of *cabinets*' institutionalised relationship as hierarchically superior to the services. The danger was that this risked inhibiting the ability of *cabinets* and services to be innovative. On the one hand, the *cabinet* system could distance the Commissioner from his administration, as it is often easier for him to take decisions with hand-picked advisers than with permanent civil servants. On the other, if initiative and profile lay with the *cabinets*, why would the services attempt a proactive approach? Prodi's attempt to place Commissioners geographically with their staff was an attempt to remedy this. But, if distance from their Commissioner may lower the commitment and morale of the services, proximity is not necessarily an indispensable remedy either. It facilitates potential interference and thus engenders an inevitable concomitant rise in *cabinet* micro-management of the services' day-to-day business.

Another potential disadvantage resides in the fact that some (not the seconded officials from the services) *cabinet* members have no security of tenure and they are not always endowed with the insider knowledge of the Commission official. They are reliant on Commissioners for their job and this might conceivably limit their willingness to give critical advice. The Commissioner might end up cocooned from the complex realities of policy formation and implementation. Thus, it is clearly difficult for the *cabinet*s to strike a successful balance between developing a long-term strategy and responding to current and pressing issues, even if they often possess a high level of technical expertise and political nous and can thus offer the Commissioner a well-informed choice of policy options and help prevent the risk identified by Mandelson of policy being determined by officials with their own priorities, departmental interests and sectoral commitments. Of course, the services are rightly preoccupied with defending the interests of their own departments. But, this means they are frequently reluctant to accept adjustment to policy resulting from a more general view of the Commissioner's or the Commission's interest, a phenomenon well-known in ministerial circles in Member States. This is why Commissioners and their *cabinet*s became increasingly interventionist under Delors in supervising and controlling the work of the services, and why, to their discredit, *cabinet*s increasingly took over dossiers and intervened closely in the work of officials. This had the effect of damaging morale in the Commission bureaucracy. There has since been an indubitable trend for civil servants not to accept or at best to openly doubt the authority of *cabinet*s to supervise or monitor them. And there is a further source of sensitivity. The extent to which a *cabinet* may be perceived as using its policy role to inject national preferences into a draft proposal prepared by the officials before it is discussed more widely, can raise hackles. It can be interpreted positively as a demonstration of the *cabinet*'s wider political approach, but it can also be seen as revealing undue sympathy for a particular Member State's position. The growth of lobbying at the Community level intensifies the problem.

Yet another problem is the tendency of *cabinet*s themselves to become bureaucratised. This is a matter of pressing concern given the growing numbers of *cabinet* personnel. With twenty-five Commissioners, total *cabinet* staff currently number no less than one hundred and fifty and more likely two hundred. This means increasing functional specialisation within *cabinet*s and growingly institutionalised patterns of relationships between the permanent bureaucracy and the *cabinet*s and amongst *cabinet*s themselves. Clearly, many of the advantages of a flexible and dynamic think-tank begin to be lost once an advisory body becomes institutionalised. Nevertheless, given the nature of the Commission as a collegiate body and the need to provide personal support to Commission members often unused to the Brussels working environment, it seems likely that *cabinet* influence will continue to grow unchecked in importance and be supported by increasingly powerful and proactive Commissioners.

Reform proposals, current cabinet developments and the Barroso Commission

Questioning the *raison d'être* of the *cabinet* system raises the issue of the power of Directors General, both in relation to *cabinets*, the Secretary General and to Commissioners themselves. On the one hand, the *cabinet* system has arguably led to a usurpation of power, frequently rendering the Directors General powerless and even sidelining the Secretariat General. One academic observer with inside experience of the *cabinet* system commented of the Delors years that *cabinets* 'meddle too much in the services' business. Sometimes skilful *cabinets* become "shadow *cabinets*" for their Commissioners' administrations, undercutting the autonomy of the appointed leaders of the Directorates General. *Cabinet* members, including the most junior of them, often reworked and rewrote the work of the services – sometimes "just for the fun of it" in the words of the Assistant Secretary General, Carlo Trojan' (Ross 1995, 161). On the other hand, this is the converse of Mandelson's view cited above. So, times may therefore have changed. It is important to stress the ten-year (and two Colleges) interval between the two observations in addition to the nature of the providers of the insight. But, the issues identified by Ross clearly needed to be resolved. Santer's *chef de cabinet*, Jim Cloos, and Carlo Trojan, meanwhile promoted to Secretary General, set up a steering committee of *chefs de cabinet* and Directors General. The aim was to analyse how to avoid the excesses of the present system by keeping the *cabinets* in the political process and out of the day to day running of the services. Trojan's 'Commission de Demain' paper gave formal recognition to the problems and suggested limiting the *cabinets'* interventions, possibly by means of a code of conduct. It also raised the possibility of reducing the number of cabinet members, and thus improving relations between services and *cabinets* and acting as a built-in brake on *parachutage*. The paper further suggested the inclusion of the relevant Directors General at the weekly meeting of heads of *cabinet*.

Pressure for change in the *cabinet* system also came from the Parliament. The Herman Report argued that reform of the *cabinet* system should go beyond that promised in the Trojan reports under President Santer. '*Cabinets* [should] have no more than six members, and with only one or at most two members of the same nationality as their Commissioner... [and that] *cabinet* members from outside the Commission should be put on the same footing as normal applicants to the Commission before moving on elsewhere within the Commission and that those who are Commission officials should have a normal career progression when leaving the *cabinet*, and should not be able to jump more than one grade'. Prodi later arrived at the same conclusion. The first report of his Committee of Wise Men also made extensive criticism of the *cabinet* system, while the second focussed on working practices in general, including tendering procedures and staffing policy to cover increases in workload. On appointment, Prodi promptly initiated another review of the *cabinet* system and himself appointed an Irishman, David O'Sullivan, *chef de cabinet*.[10] O'Sullivan described the purpose of the review as achieving 'a clear distinction between political responsibility and the managerial function' (*European Voice* 1999). It seemed likely that the outcome would be *cabinet*s of reduced size and a more multinational composition. Commissioners and their *cabinet*s were located with their services and there was an attempt to ensure a mix of nationalities. Under Prodi, to give immediate effect to the announced new reform era, 1000 staff moved offices in the summer of 1999 and Commissioners left the Commission headquarters in the Breydel building and were decentralised to be close to their Directorates General – a sign, argued many, of a divide and rule strategy, that presidential power was to remain at the centre, with the College fragmented and thus more manageable. A more charitable view was that the new proximity would, as Prodi argued, enhance the relationship between Commissioners and *cabinet*s at the political level and Directors General and the services at the managerial, administrative level. It was, on either account, more than a symbolic gesture at reform, and overall it led to the *cabinet* system becoming even more central to the process of Community policy formation; a centrality already evident in the Delors Commissions in which several Commissioners augmented their official quota of *cabinet* posts with additional members financed from national governments or political sources.

The Barroso Commission presented Commission watchers with a new series of parameters. Prodi's aim had been to avoid the nepotism of the Santer years, and the *cabinet*s got caught up in the process. Either the *chef* or the deputy *chef* had to be of a different nationality from that of the Commissioner. Under Barroso there must now be three nationalities in any *cabinet*, gender balance and three posts reserved for Commission officials rather than outsiders brought in by the Commissioner or their foreign ministry. The resulting changes produced *cabinet* constellations, which would be unrecognisable to old Commission hands. There were four German *chefs de cabinet*, serving Verheugen, Michel, Reding and Potocnik, and two German deputy *chefs*, serving Barrot and Ferrero-Waldner. They were almost all young Commission officials. France had one *chef de cabinet*, in the Barrot *cabinet* and two deputy *chefs* in the Mandelson and Kroes *cabinet*s. The UK had three *chefs de cabinet* (Mandelson, Grybauskaite and Ferrero-Waldner) and one deputy *chef*. Spain had two *chefs de cabinet* (Almunia and Spidla). The *Financial Times* summed it up nicely: 'Brussels has become the scene of a medieval hiring fair with a sharp-suited, international twist – a chaotic scramble for some of the European Union's most influential jobs' (Parker 2004).

Some concluding remarks on the evolution of the College, its President and the *cabinet* system

The *cabinet* system clearly has many benefits for Commissioners and the high calibre of *cabinet* members means they are well qualified to assist the Commissioner in policy evaluation and provide an invaluable source of advice across the whole range of Commission issues. But the advantages of *cabinet*s need to be set against the inherent drawbacks of the system. With the growing number of *cabinet* members and their increasing role in policymaking there is still the danger of a parallel bureaucracy, similar to the system under Delors described in chapter 4. Relations between *cabinets* and permanent Commission officials are inevitably delicate, though their aim ought to be the same – enhancing simultaneously the effectiveness of the Directorate General and the Commissioner's profile, by ensuring that policy decisions are made rapidly and effectively, by providing informal guidance on the Commissioner's wishes and by supporting all concerned in the debate on policy priorities with other services. However, the distinction between policy guidance and interference is not always clear-cut. Commission staff tend to hold firm views on what policy line is best, and the risk of conflict between the *cabinet* and permanent officials is likely to remain real for some time to come. Essentially, however, the *cabinet* system is there not only to protect and enhance the Commissioner, but because the system is intended to enhance the Commission itself and the leadership of EU business by the Commission President. Efficient coordination should enhance Commission leadership. The problem for Barroso's leadership, as Peterson describes in chapter 19, was that Barroso was a *pis aller*, accepted reluctantly by some Member States and resignedly by others. He was the candidate, as the *Economist* put it, 'whom nobody was ready to veto' (*Economist* 2005).

The Barroso Commission took office on 18 November 2004, three weeks after Member States signed the Constitutional Treaty and six months after the enlargement of the EU to ten new countries. The Commission seemed at first sight on the crest of a new wave destined to sweep European integration back into the public consciousness and thus boost its flagging status after the ignominious demise of the Santer Commission and the lacklustre Prodi Commission. But popular rejection of the Constitution by the Dutch and the French and a new debate about the disadvantages of further enlargement, particularly to Muslim Turkey, changed the parameters. The Commission, as usual, bore the brunt of Member States' unwillingness to prepare the terrain for what was, after all, their decision to widen and deepen the EU by doubling the membership and revising the Treaties four times in one decade. Barroso was first boxed into one corner by the European Parliament and then boxed himself into others. He had to remove two nominated Commissioners before they took office and he chose to focus on the Lisbon Strategy, which was mainly Member State competence, susceptible only to catcalls from the Commission's ringside seat. He also chose to focus on areas where the Commission had limited rights of initiative; a decision he further aggravated in his first year by withdrawing some one hundred proposals where the Commission did have the right to set the agenda, and doing it in the name of 'Better Legislation'. Somehow, went the unspoken message, 'Europe' was indeed the Europe of the States and not the Europe of the Union. Meanwhile, Barroso's Commissioner for Communication, Margot Wallström, was attempting to demonstrate the contrary with a plan 'D', standing for Democracy, Dialogue and Debate.

As for leadership within the Commission, turf battles continued and a major re-shuffle in November 2005 saw heads roll and scores settled under the cover of the new principle of senior staff rotation. Yet, in his favour, President Barroso was seemingly trying to make the Commission more modest after the Delors years had stamped 'aggrandisement' on the Commission's t-shirt, ironically undermining through his outstanding leadership the efforts of his successors in maintaining the image of European leadership in a far more turbulent environment. By 2006 it was difficult to avoid the conclusion that Barroso was leading a European civil service, an *administration de gestion*, rather than an *administration de mission*, the 'proto-government' many had long feared. This was perhaps no bad thing, but in leadership terms it was a large step away from the heady days when the world looked to Delors for leadership and guidance. By 2006 the EU had become preoccupied with improving its public image and making understanding of EU issues more accessible to the public. Whether the Commission and the Member States could hear themselves speak when they maintained that the Constitution did need ratifying in the long run, and whether they understood what they were saying, are moot points. The rejection of the Constitution in two countries seemed to indicate that the public was listening, but that they were not hearing the 'right' message.

Endnotes

[1] The senior politicians were former Belgian Prime Minister Jean-Luc Dehaene (once vetoed by the UK for Commission President), David (Lord) Simon and former German President Richard von Weizsäcker. The secretary of the group was the respected former Belgian Permanent Representative, Philippe de Schouteete. See Three Wise Men (1999).

[2] Philippe Busquin of Belgium, for example, was obliged to deny a *Sunday Times* (12 September 1999) allegation that he had misled Parliament in denying being questioned by judicial authorities in the Dassault–Agusta case.

[3] Bangemann left the caretaker Commission hurriedly in June 1999 to join the Spanish telephone company Telefonica. The following month, COREPER discussed whether he should forfeit his pension rights.

[4] The Marta Andreasen case discussed in chapter 17 is an example of this lesson not being learned.

[5] In March 1999 the leaders of the European socialist parties (thirteen of fifteen governments) had called for the Parliament to be given the right of individual censure. A parliamentary resolution confirmed that this was the Parliament's position later in March.

[6] Smith, A. *Les Commissaires européens: technocrats, diplomats ou politiques*, Sciences Po, Paris, 2002 provides a general sociology of Commissioners and their *cabinets*.

[7] Philippe Busquin (B), Anna Diamantopoulou (Gr), Loyola de Palacio (Sp) and Margot Wallström (S).

[8] Six groups of Commissioners with overlapping responsibilities were created in the Santer Commission: 1) Growth, competitiveness and employment; 2) trans-European networks; 3) cohesion; 4) information society; 5) environment; 6) external affairs.

[9] The quotations are from Opinion of the Commission, pursuant to Article 48 TEU on the IGC (Com (2003) 548).

[10] O'Sullivan's appointment, apparently on a recommendation of former Commissioner Peter Sutherland, was a break with tradition. Presidents had always had compatriots and Commissioners have usually chosen (or had chosen for them) compatriots as *chefs de cabinet*.

2. The Secretariat General of the European Commission

Hussein Kassim[1]

The Secretariat General (SG) occupies a pivotal position within the European Commission and the wider system of EU governance. It provides administrative support to the College, offers a channel for two-way communication between Commissioners and the services, and oversees interdepartmental coordination. As well as conducting tasks of routine administration, the SG prepares the Commission's input into treaty reform negotiations (Dimitrakopoulos and Kassim 2005), assumes responsibility for competencies new to the Commission, and takes charge of complex, sensitive or controversial policy dossiers. Though formally responsible to the College, the Secretary General, the Head of the SG, enjoys a special relationship with the Commission President, providing a source of advice and information, and a conduit between the Commission President's *cabinet* and senior management in the services. The SG is also responsible for the coordination of the Commission's relations with other EU institutions, monitoring the progress of legislative proposals and reporting developments to the rest of the Commission. In managing relations with, in particular, the Council of Ministers and the European Parliament, as well as national governments and other bodies and actors, it contributes to the overall coherence of EU governance (Christiansen 2001). In short, the SG plays a crucial coordinating role in a fragmented institutional environment.

Though its importance is widely acknowledged, not least due to the renown of its first Secretary General, Emile Noël, the SG has rarely been the subject of detailed analysis. This chapter takes a step towards remedying this neglect. It looks at the origins and early development of the SG, investigates the evolution of its responsibilities, and considers changes in its organisation and *modus operandi*. It examines the functions performed by the SG, and offers an evaluation of its effectiveness. The chapter makes three contentions: first, that the SG played a crucial role in the institutionalisation of the Commission, the formation of its institutional identity and the regularisation of its operation; second, that the SG's responsibilities have evolved in response to external demands, while its *modus operandi* has varied with the leadership style of the Commission President and the Secretary General's conception of the Secretariat's role; and third, that for reasons often beyond its control the SG is more successful in the performance of some responsibilities – notably, its support of the College and its management of relations with other institutions – than others, with interdepartmental coordination perhaps the most problematic.

Historical background

Any account of the SG must begin with the legendary figure of Emile Noël, who, as Executive Secretary of the Commission of the European Economic Community (EEC) from 1958 until 1967, and Secretary General of the merged executive until 1987, was for three decades the Commission's most senior official. Noël had a profound impact on the Secretariat and the Commission administration more generally. His personal qualities, experience and individual standing were key factors in establishing the authority of the Secretariat, bestowing an influence on the body that reached beyond its formal functions (Siotis 1964, 233-4), but his style could not be emulated. The task he left to his successors was to 'de-singularise' the SG, transforming it into a more orthodox administrative unit.

Origins

An Executive Secretariat (ES) was created in the ten-week period following the first meeting of the Commission of the EEC, held on 15 January 1958, when the administrative structures of the new executive were put in place. The ES occupied a position alongside eight functional departments (responsible for external relations, economic and financial affairs, internal market, competition, social affairs, agriculture, transport, and overseas development) and two horizontal services (the Legal Service, and administration and personnel). Not modelled on an existing body, national or international, it was constructed to meet three requirements. The first was the ambition of Walter Hallstein, the first Commission President, that the Commission should be 'une grande administration' that would be the equal of any national civil service. Only a body that was expert and organised would be able to act as 'a new factor in European and international politics' (Noël 1998, 132). Collegiality was the second. It had been agreed at the outset that, even though specific portfolio responsibilities would be allocated to individual members, Commission decisions would be taken collectively at a weekly meeting of the College devoted expressly to that purpose (Noël, cited in Poullet and Deprez 1977, 160; CEC 1958, 21-2; Noël 1992; Berlin 1987, 35). A secretariat would be needed to prepare and service these meetings (Doc. 40/58, cited in Commission 1958). The third requirement arose from the Commission's institutional setting. The EEC was one of three Communities, each with a set of institutions. The design of the EEC created an interdependent relationship between the Council of Ministers and the Commission, which called for close and constant interaction, while the Commission also needed to maintain regular contact with its counterparts in the European Coal and Steel Community and the European Atomic Energy Community. The Secretariat would be responsible for managing these relations at the official level. Its tasks were formalised by and detailed under Article 16 of the Commission's internal Rules of Procedure, which were drafted in late February 1958 (CEC 1963). The Executive Secretary or deputy Executive Secretary would attend all meetings of the College, unless the members of the Commission decided otherwise (Article 9), countersign the minutes (Article 10) and authenticate decisions adopted by the Commission (Article 12). Overseeing the publication of the Official Journal was a further responsibility (Coombes 1970, 249-50),

By the end of July 1958, the ES had taken shape. Three functional divisions were established: the Registry (known within the Commission by its French name, *le Greffe*) to prepare the work of the College; a second unit to ensure the services were informed of Commission decisions and that they implemented them, to liaise with departments and to keep Commissioners informed of Community business; and an external relations division to maintain contact with other EEC institutions, the High Authority and the Euratom Commission. A fourth unit provided general administrative support. A deputy Executive Secretary was appointed to assist the Executive Secretary and to assure continuity of Commission business when the Executive Secretary was away from Brussels.

The SG under Noël

For thirty years, Emile Noël headed the SG, imposing his imprint on its structure and operation. Noël's authority derived from two main sources: his post-war career in European public service and his personal qualities. Before his appointment to the Commission in February 1958 when still in his thirties[2], Noël was already a high-flier. After a stint at the Council of Europe as Secretary of the General Affairs Committee (later the Political Committee), he became director of the Secretariat of the Constitutional Committee of the ad hoc Assembly, the body that produced the draft treaty for the European Political Community, linked to the ill-fated European Defence Community. Between 1955 and 1956, Noël headed the *cabinet* of the French Socialist, Guy Mollet, then President of the Consultative Assembly of the Council of Europe, during which time he moved increasingly within federalist circles.[3] When Mollet was made French Prime Minister, Noël followed him to Paris, serving first as his *chef de cabinet* and then his deputy Director. In this latter capacity, Noël was part of the French delegation to the Conference on Euratom and the European Economic Community, participating in the drafting of the Treaties of Rome. Not only was Noël a witness at the creation of the Communities, which contributed to his standing, but those who worked with him paid testimony to his personal qualities (see, e.g. Sutherland 1996; Delors 1996; Meyer 1994): a formidable capacity for work, an outstanding memory for detail, and his ability to craft compromises – 'l'homme de la solution'. As a former colleague, Max Kohnstamm, observed: 'He was like a monk from the Middle Ages, with a total devotion to a cause. He had one object in mind: European integration, or, as Jean Monnet described it, "Yesterday force, today law." '

Noël believed in an activist role for the Commission and that the Secretariat should play a leadership role vis-à-vis the services. This implied extensive and energetic involvement on his part as head of the ES, which took place mostly behind the scenes and by working with officials that he trusted and not necessarily through the hierarchy. Noël's view was that the ES would operate most effectively if it were small and flexible. He favoured a light structure, without directorates, that enabled him to work directly with desk officers. As one interviewed official commented, 'the ES was in many ways a support structure for the Executive Secretary, [and there was] a strong sense among the staff of working directly to the Executive Secretary'. A further feature of the ES associated with Noël was its support for campaign activities that promoted European integration. The ES had a small budget, which it used to support university exchanges, town twinning and academic research. In addition, Noël acted as ambassador for the Community. He received notables visiting Brussels, and sought to explain the purpose, functioning and achievements of the Communities to the outside world through seminars and articles in academic journals. The publication of his short guide to the Community, *Comment fonctionnent les institutions des Communautés européennes*, illustrates how he considered this to be a personal responsibility.

Noël personally carried out many of the ES's key responsibilities. He advised the Commission President, took the minutes at the College's weekly meetings, reported decisions of the College to the Directors-General and the assistants of the Directors-General, chaired the Monday meeting of the *chefs de cabinet*, and represented the Commission in COREPER, as well as in plenary sessions of the European Parliament. He also chaired the promotions committees for Commission officials. Later, with the institutionalisation of summitry, Noël accompanied the Commission President to meetings of the European Council, the only Commission official permitted to attend. He represented the Commission throughout the long process that led to the merger of the executives in 1967 and, after Hallstein's departure, it became a tradition for incoming Commission Presidents to visit Brussels for a personal briefing from the Executive Secretary (Jenkins 1989; Delors 1996, 2004: 170).

The ES made a central contribution to the institutionalisation of the Commission in the decade after 1958. The registry emerged as the keeper of the organisation's institutional memory, the SG drafted (Meyer 1994, 263-4), regularised and safeguarded Commission procedures, including its internal rules of procedure and the Staff Regulations. As Commission responsibilities increased, and with them the size and complexity of the organisation[4], the demands on the Secretariat multiplied. In response, the Secretariat General, as the ES became known after the merger, was forced to expand, growing from four unit in the early 1960s to nine in 1975, 11 in 1978, 12 in 1982 and 13 in 1983. For the first time (in 1968), the post of Director was created in the SG and, in 1973, as part of the exercise to accommodate officials from the new Member States, a second deputy Secretary General was appointed.[5] A unit dedicated to internal coordination was created in 1978 with the aim of programming Commission action. Furthermore, the SG assumed new responsibilities, as the Community's competencies expanded. Following the Hague Summit, in the first instance of what was to become standard practice, the Secretariat took temporary charge of a new policy field – European Political Cooperation – before a permanent home was found.[6]

The growing institutional complexity of the Community also forced structural change in the SG. Increasing internal differentiation within the Council, such as the division of COREPER into two bodies in 1962 and the steady proliferation of Council formations throughout the decade, combined with an increase in the number of days spent in working groups (from 1,233 in 1967 to 1,403 in 1970, stabilising at around 2,000 in 1974), multiplied the number of Council meetings requiring a Commission presence. As the Secretary

General could not attend both, it was left to the deputy Secretary General to represent the Commission in COREPER II. Meanwhile, in the early 1970s the SG began to devote more substantial resources to monitoring developments in, and working with, the EP. A dedicated coordination unit was set up in the Secretariat, which worked closely with the *Groupe des Affaires Parlementaires* (GAP), a body that brought together the members from each *cabinet* responsible for relations with the EP (Westlake 1994, 12).

Under the first Commission President, Noël had played a key role in the formative years of administration, but after Hallstein's departure in 1967 Noël became as indispensable for his leadership qualities, experience and memory as for his organisational abilities. Whereas members of the Hallstein Commission had been veterans of the post-war drive for integration, this was not true of their successors. In this context 'Noël supplied the institutions with some of the political vision which the commissioners often lacked' (Grant 1994, 102). His 'voice was often decisive in meetings of the College, and always important where internal promotions were concerned' (Middlemas 1995, 221-2). The SG's influence and that of Noël reached its apogee in the early 1980s. As one observer commented:

> 'It is not a service, like the Legal Service, that has official power over the DGs. However, because of its central position, the authority of its leader, and the fact that nothing happens within the Commission without him intervening in one way or another, the SG has become the memory of the institution, its principal adviser, its mediator and its overall guardian. Over the years, in this way it has acquired a dominant position within the services, and this to such an extent that virtually nothing can be done against the wishes of the Secretariat General' (Berlin 1987, 69. *Translated from the original*).

The arrival of Jacques Delors in 1985 led, however, to a dramatic change in the SG's status. As well as an activism not witnessed in Brussels since the days of Hallstein, the Delors' era brought a personalised style of leadership, centred on the President's *cabinet* (see, e.g. Dinan 1997, 253), and characterised by the mobilisation of personal networks (Ross 1995, 37, 64; Endo 1999, 114). Despite their respect for Noël, the relationship between the Delors *cabinet* and the Secretary General was often tense (Endo 1999, 117). In contrast to his predecessors, Delors had no need for Noël's services as adviser or 'fixer'. The latter role was ably assumed by Pascal Lamy, the President's *chef de cabinet*. In addition, the Delors team grew increasingly irritated 'by the same old ways in which Noël conducted the in-house business, in particular his conciliatory run of the *chefs de cabinet* meetings' (Endo 1999, 117). There were constant clashes between the Commission President's *cabinet*, which sought to establish itself as the nerve centre of the Commission, and the Secretary General (Endo 1999, 43), who was unhappy with Delors' apparent disdain for collegiality. Noël retired from the Commission in 1987. One of his last tasks was to represent the Commission at the Intergovernmental Conference that negotiated the Single European Act (SEA).

The SG after Noël

Noël's departure led to a transformation of the SG's structure, operation and style. His successors – David (now Lord) Williamson (1987-1997), Carlo Trojan (1997-2000), David O'Sullivan (2000-2005) and Catherine Day (2005-) – each brought different conceptions of its role to the Secretariat and had to confront particular challenges. All, however, sought to make the SG more efficient and more like an ordinary bureaucratic body.

The Williamson era

Prior to his appointment to the post, David Williamson had held senior positions in the UK civil service and the Commission. A former Head of the European Secretariat in the Cabinet Office, where he had served under Margaret Thatcher, Williamson had experience of senior office in the Commission as deputy Director General of DG VI (Agriculture). One of his priorities was to improve interdepartmental coordination, which was widely regarded as problematic. Noël had preferred to use personal networks – he was 'not a methodical manager' (Grant 1994, 102) - but this was by definition an unsystematic approach. Williamson encouraged the formation of *ad hoc* inter-service working groups, as a way of overcoming departmentalism. Given the formidable structural and cultural obstacles to cooperation, it is unsurprising that he was only partly successful (Endo 1999, 118-9).[7] If improving routine coordination proved problematic, Williamson did succeed in easing the flow of information within the organisation and in making the annual work programme more meaningful (Ludlow 1991). No longer was the latter the occasion for 'an annual opening up of filing cabinets' (Ross 1995, 267-8). Rather than accepting the overly ambitious wish lists submitted by DGs, the SG began to return for revision those that were unrealistic.

Williamson scored other notable successes. At the Brussels European Council in February 1988, he was instrumental in resolving the budgetary dispute over the UK's contribution. He worked closely with the Commission President in negotiating the major financial packages, Delors I and Delors II, with the Member States. He played a role in the negotiations leading to the accession of Sweden, Finland and Austria. He was also appointed personal representative of the Commission President to the group of personal representatives at the Maastricht and Amsterdam IGCs. In addition, Williamson adapted the SG to the institutional changes resulting from the SEA and the TEU. The SEA had strengthened the EP's role in the legislative process by introducing the cooperation procedure. Williamson responded by instituting a system, located in the SG, for monitoring and recording developments within the EP – the first time that the Commission had kept records on parliamentary business. Other new tasks included responsibility for monitoring the implementation of single market related measures, as well as the application of Community law, especially in relation to state aid, and the coordination of protection against fraud. The SG was also handed responsibility for administering the cohesion funds. In the wake of the TEU, a unit was established in the SG to handle relations with the new Committee of the Regions. The Secretariat provided a home for the Task Force for Justice and Home Affairs, took charge of biotechnology, as well as the 1993 Delors White Paper, and was given the task of handling Commission action in relation to the BSE crisis. Community action with regard to German unification was coordinated by the deputy Secretary General, Carlo Trojan (Spence 1992). In short, by the time that he left office, Williamson had succeeded in depersonalising the SG and adjusting it to the demands of two major treaty reforms.

The SG under Trojan

Carlo Trojan was appointed Secretary General after ten years' service as deputy Secretary General, two years as deputy Director General in DG VI (Agriculture) and terms in the *cabinets* of three Commissioners (Lardinois, Vredeling, and Andriessen). He had a clear vision of the type of body he wanted the SG to become: smaller, less compartmentalised with better internal communication and greater staff mobility, and concentrated on its core function of serving the College with a more forceful and pro-active role in coordination. Trojan's conception coincided with the recommendations of two key reports, the first drafted by the Commission's Inspectorate General and the second produced as part of the 1998 'Commission of Tomorrow' ('DECODE') exercise: non-core activities should be transferred to other departments and the SG should concentrate on coordination, providing a venue for resolving inter-department conflicts and encouraging DGs to consult each other seriously rather than simply exchanging notes.

As a result, the Fraud Office (UCLAF) was moved out of the SG to become a free-standing entity (OLAF), and the *bureau de stages* transferred to DG IX (Personnel and Administration). Similarly, the drugs coordination unit and the unit responsible for coordinating structural funds were moved out of the SG. Securing a more interventionist role for the SG in coordination proved more problematic. Such an elevation would have run counter to the norm of departmental equality by elevating the SG above other DGs, and challenged the supremacy of the College. Unsurprisingly, it found little support. Trojan was only partially successful, therefore, in re-shaping the SG. However, he did preside over Agenda 2000, the multi-disciplinary package designed to prepare the Union for enlargement to Eastern Europe. He also oversaw preparations for the adaptation of the Secretariat to the new circumstances of the Treaty of Amsterdam. By granting the Commission President for the first time the power to determine policy choices, the Treaty implied that the SG should intervene earlier in interdepartmental coordination.[8] Trojan left the SG in May 2000, two months after the resignation of the Santer Commission, and became head of the Commission's delegation in Geneva four months later.

The SG under David O'Sullivan

On his appointment in May 2000 David O'Sullivan became only the Commission's fourth Secretary General. O'Sullivan had begun his career in Ireland's diplomatic service before moving to the Commission, where, as well as holding positions in DG I (External Relations), DG V (Social Affairs) and DG XXII (Education, Training and Youth), he served in the *cabinets* of Commissioners Sutherland and Flynn. When Romano Prodi became

Commission President, O'Sullivan was appointed *chef de cabinet*, a position he held for twelve months before moving to the SG.

Table 1: *Secretaries General and Deputy Secretaries General, 1958 – to date*

Executive Secretary		Deputy Executive Secretary	
Emile Noël	1958-1967	Winrich Behr	1958-1959
		Axel Herbst	1960-1963
		Helmut Sigrist	1964-1967
Secretary General		**Deputy Secretary General**	
Emile Noël	1967-1987	Helmut Sigrist	1967-1968
		Klaus Meyer	1969-1976
		Christopher Audland	1973-1981
		Michael Jenkins	1981-1983
		Horst-Günther Krenzler	1983-1987
David Williamson	1987-1997	Carlo Trojan	1987-1997
Carlo Trojan	1997-2000	Bernhard Zepter	1997-2002
David O'Sullivan	2000-2005	Maria Pia Filippone	2000-2002
		Philip Lowe	2002-2002
		Enzo Moavero-Milanesi	2002-2005
		Eckhart Guth	2002-present
Catherine Day	2005-present	Alexander Italianer	2006-present

Source: Secretariat General of the European Commission, private correspondence (26 January 2005); Organigrammes of the Commission of the European Communities (various dates)

O'Sullivan took up his position in the SG at a time when the Commission faced a number of serious challenges and morale within the organisation was low. The Santer team had resigned and the Member States had instructed the incoming Commission President, Romano Prodi, to implement a thoroughgoing reform programme.[9] This was a process in which the Secretary General would be a leading figure and which implied changes in the SG itself. By the end of the Prodi Commission, O'Sullivan had overhauled its organisation and operation, redesigning its structures and making personnel changes. Even before the reform White Paper was launched, the SG began working on the simplification of Commission procedures. (Prodi had announced his intention to eliminate unnecessary bureaucracy at the Cologne European summit, some months before assuming office.) The task was entrusted to a second Deputy Secretary General, Maria Pia Filipone, and lines of responsibility within the SG re-configured accordingly. Initial action was directed towards twelve areas, including the delegation of decision-making authority to Directors General, financial control, openness, access to documents, relations with lobbies, and revising the Manual of Operating Procedures. At the same time, O'Sullivan began to modernise and streamline the Secretariat itself, moving out responsibilities that fell outside its core business. The SG was also the service most directly involved in the follow-up to Prodi's early attempt to address problems in the functioning of the Union, drawn together in the White Paper on European Governance.[10]

Work on administrative reform began immediately (on Commission reform, see Stevens and Stevens, chapter 17 of this volume; see also Kassim 2004a, 2004b; Levy 2002). The Secretariat was involved at every stage of the process – for example, it was a key actor in the peer review exercise that Prodi carried out to evaluate the distribution of resources across Commission departments[11] – with O'Sullivan seeking to promote a sense of common ownership of the reform among Commission services by ensuring their participation in discussions.[12] It was itself the object of some of the main reform measures (Commission 1999b, 41), some of which, including improving internal coordination, responded to specific recommendations of the Committee of Independent Experts (1999, para 7.11). It contributed to the reform White Paper and was identified as the service responsible for formulating and implementing a number of decisions, notably under the chapters concerning creation of a culture of service and improving strategic planning specified therein. Once the Task Force for Administrative Reform reached the end of its two-year 'sunset' term, moreover, the SG took over the central role for coordinating the reform. This function is performed by the Secretary General, who chairs the Activity Based Management (ABM) steering group, which (unusually) brings together officials and *cabinet* members, namely, the Directors General and Heads of Cabinet of the central services (SG, DG ADMIN, DG BUDG).[13]

The creation within the SG of Strategic Planning and Programming (SPP) was the centrepiece of the planning chapter of the reform White Paper. SPP is a system designed to integrate activities and resources within the administration and to enable the Secretariat to programme action across the Commission and monitor and verify policy implementation. It is organised around an annual policy cycle, with an early identification of priorities, the aim of which is to strengthen the SG's coordinating role, enabling it to intervene at an earlier stage, encouraging DGs to cooperate even before proposals have been drafted, convening meetings of officials and *cabinet* members, and arbitrating in inter-departmental disputes.[14] Against the background of greater delegation and decentralisation, also key themes of the reform (see Commission 2000), the introduction of these new techniques and their location in the SG reinvent the SG's internal coordination function.[15] The responsibilities of the other Deputy Secretary General, Bernhard Zepter, who represented the Commission in COREPER, were expanded to strengthen the role of the SG in this regard.[16] For its involvement to be acceptable to the DGs, however, the Secretariat had to establish its ability to 'add value'. Propagation of the idea that the SG was 'a service at the service of other services' signalled the cultural change that O'Sullivan sought to bring about.

The new conception of the SG's role and the responsibilities it assumed as part of the reform process were reflected in a revised mission statement:

> 'The principal mission of the Secretariat General is to ensure the delivery of the Commission's political priorities as defined by the President. It works pro-actively to deliver strategic planning and programming, guarantee effective internal policy coordination,

manage the collegial decision-making process and coordinate the position of the Commission with other institutions. It has specific responsibility for driving forward administrative simplification and for managing the future of the Union debate, including the followup to the White Paper on European Governance. It is also responsible for monitoring issues of horizontal interest (e.g. institutional questions, openness policy, relations with civil society, data protection), providing official information on the decision-making process and reporting on the EU's activities. The Secretariat General is at the service of other services and the College, acting as a force for cohesiveness in the Commission.'[17]

As a result, from 2000, the SG has had a more pronounced presence in the work of the services. The emphasis in the reform programme on improved planning and programming, better use of resources and more effective delivery has reinforced its central coordinating and monitoring role.

The Secretariat General today: functions, responsibilities and organisation

Although it continues to perform its traditional functions, the SG has acquired new tasks and undergone a degree of restructuring as a result of the reforms undertaken by the Prodi Commission. It has both internal and external responsibilities.

Internal responsibilities

Servicing and supporting the College: The SG is the gatekeeper of the College's agenda – its 'heartland' in the words of one interviewed official – which the Registry prepares for the coming month in a weekly meeting between a senior member of the Commission President's *cabinet* and the Secretary General. The nature and outcome of these meetings depends to a considerable extent on the personalities of those involved, the style of the Commission President and the latter's opinion of the readiness of issues for discussion. Delors, for example, worked according to strict criteria in deciding which topics were ripe for discussion, though his judgement in individual cases was not always shared by other Commissioners (Grant 1994, 103). A rather different dynamic was evident under Prodi, who was less concerned to control the College's agenda. SG officials reported that there was little direct contact or strategic discussion between SG management and the President's *chef de cabinet*, and that items were put on the College agenda after clearance with the appropriate member of the President's *cabinet* by an SG desk officer. The SG is also responsible for record-keeping and for producing the documentation that circulates through the College. As well as preparing meetings of the College and of the *chefs de cabinet*, the Registry distributes relevant documents and drafts the minutes of the College's meetings.[18] The SG has a long and jealously guarded tradition of neutrality, though the requirement that minutes be approved by the Commission President before they are circulated has occasionally provoked questions on that score. The Registry also manages all decisions taken by the Commission by whatever procedure, oral, written or *habilitation*, as discussed in chapter 4. It finalises formal texts and is responsible for formal transmission of documents to other EU institutions and relevant bodies.

Maintaining and enforcing administrative procedures: The SG draws up new procedures and regularly revises and updates the *Manual of Operating Procedures*, detailing every aspect of the Commission's operation. It also ensures compliance with the rules of the house, while reducing and eliminating unnecessary bureaucracy. It is also charged with safeguarding the rights and competence of the Commission, remaining constantly alert to potential intrusions on Commission prerogatives by other institutions. With respect to comitology, for example (see chapter 8), it monitors legislative proposals and issues guidance to the services on which procedures are acceptable.

Strategic planning and programming (SPP): The SG was historically responsible for planning and programming the work of the Commission, but it only recently acquired the means to take a more directive approach with the new techniques and mechanisms introduced by the Kinnock reforms (see chapter 17). SPP enables the SG to programme action beginning at the end of year n-2 with the submission by departments of their priorities for year n. Proposed action is discussed by the College, led by the Commission President, who then confirms the Commission's objectives in the form of an Annual Policy Strategy (APS). The APS is the basis for the allocation of resources (human and financial) according to the policy priorities it sets out. It structures the preliminary draft budget and forms the basis of the dialogue between the Commission, the EP and the Council, which takes place in the first half of year n-1. In light of these discussions towards the end of year n-1, the Commission adopts its work programme for year n. The work programme is broken down into operational plans for each service (Annual Management Plans), which detail and schedule objectives, so that progress can be monitored and evaluated by the SG, and in relation to which the Directors General report in their Annual Activity Reports their progress and success.

The SG provides administrative support to the President throughout the process, collecting proposals from the departments, circulating the draft programme for comments, and monitoring the implementation by DGs of their action plans. It also runs the three networks that underpin SPP:

> – the resource directors group, introduced under MAP 2000 and SEM 2000, meets fortnightly, with the deputy Secretary General for coordination in the chair, to discuss reform-related issues, especially concerning personnel, and to support regular meetings of a group of Directors General;
> – the interservice coordination group, which meets monthly at director level, presided by the same chair, oversees and polices the implementation of the work programme and discusses sensitive issues arising from the work programme;
> – the Activity-Based Management (ABM) network, chaired by the head of unit in the SG responsible for SPP.

Horizontal coordination: Though its desk officers monitor the progress of proposals and make sure that the services meet deadlines for the transmission of documents and otherwise behave correctly, formal responsibility for taking the lead in interdepartmental consultation lies with the case officer (*chef de file*) in the operational department. The SG usually takes action only where problems arise. It intervenes to ensure that officials in other interested departments are consulted, by suggesting that an exchange of view or a meeting takes place. Although a more pro-active role in coordination for the Secretariat was an aim of the reform, it is not clear whether this has yet been achieved. A more interventionist style depends upon a close working relationship with the Commission President's *cabinet* and political backing from the Commission President. Under the Prodi Commission, uncertainty about whether the Commission President would hold to the agreed line in the face of pressure and erratic communication limited the SG's effectiveness.

The SG's involvement continues when a dossier moves to the political level. The Secretary General himself chairs the weekly meeting of the *chefs de cabinet* (on a Monday), which runs through the dossiers on the College's agenda in advance of its Wednesday meeting. The *chefs* meeting offers a last chance to resolve outstanding difficulties before the full Commission. An official from the Secretariat is also present at meetings of the 'special *chefs*' (see chapter 1), chaired by a member of the President's *cabinet*.

Vertical coordination: The SG relays decisions of the College to the Commission administration through a number of channels. Electronic transmission has replaced the recorded summary that was previously used to inform officials of the outcome of the weekly meeting. There are also regular (five or six a month) meetings of the Group of Directors General, a body significantly upgraded under O'Sullivan. Whereas in the past these meetings were, in the words of one official, 'a rather sterile conduit for relaying the outcome of the College meeting', they are now 'a dynamic forum for discussion of management and policy issues' and 'the exchange of ideas between horizontal and operational DGs'. Proceedings have been formalised, and written 'operational conclusions' are circulated within twenty-four hours. Each meeting has a single theme – they tended to be reform-related under the Prodi Commission – and the meetings under O'Sullivan are more interactive than under previous Secretaries General. Third, the Secretary General chairs a meeting of the assistants of the Directors General. This enables him to stay abreast of departmental needs and problems arising in day-to-day administration.

Direct responsibilities: Permanent direct responsibilities include monitoring the transposition of directives by Member States and handling suspected infringements of the Treaty. The SG is also charged with freedom of information, publication of official documents, as well as administrative support for Commission participation in treaty reform (Dimitrakopoulos and Kassim 2005). Responsibilities temporarily residing in the SG relate to the Lisbon strategy, negotiation of the Financial Perspective and services of general interest.

External functions

Post box: The SG provides a formal contact point for communications with representatives of national governments, the Council Secretariat and the Secretariat General of the EP, and other bodies.

Representing the Commission in the Council, the European Council and at IGCs:

The Secretary General plays a key personal role in representing the Commission. He is present at meetings of the European Council, where he contributes to drafting the Presidency conclusions, and the Economic and Finance Council. He also attends plenary sessions of the European Parliament and accompanies the Commission President at IGCs. A Deputy Secretary General attends the General Affairs and External Relations Council, while an official from the SG is present at every meeting of the Council at ministerial level. The Secretary General no longer represents the Commission in COREPER I, a function now performed by the SG director responsible for relations with the Council. The Commission continues to be represented by a Deputy Secretary General in COREPER II, while a senior SG official represents the Commission in the Antici and the Mertens Groups.[19] Though in the distant past the SG represented the Commission at all levels of the Council, today officials of individual DGs are the main Commission representatives.

The SG Directorate F monitors the progress of proposals through the machinery of the Council and, when they reach COREPER, ensures that the Commission's stance is coordinated with the views of other DGs. It ensures that Commission officials with the necessary expertise attend meetings. Difficult issues are discussed in the Groupe de suivi pour les Affaires du Conseil (GrAC), created in 2001, which brings together the member of each of the *cabinets* responsible for institutional questions. The GrAC, essentially a trouble-shooting body, meets twice monthly and is chaired by a member of the Commission President's *cabinet*.

Representing the Commission in the European Parliament and other EU bodies: SG officials monitor EP developments in committees, in plenaries and in the planning bodies of the Parliament (Conference of the Presidents, meetings of EP committee chairs, the Neunreither group and trialogues[20]). They circulate information on the progress of proposals within the Commission and ensure the right Commission officials attend EP committees and plenary sessions. The SG services the Parliamentary Affairs Group, which prepares the Commission's positions vis-à-vis the EP, for agreement by the College. It organises the follow-up to EP decisions and assists the Commission President and the Commissioner responsible for relations with the EP at inter-institutional meetings. It also handles parliamentary questions, which it forwards to the appropriate Commission department and ensures that an answer is forthcoming. The Commission's position in all co-decision cases is prepared by the SG in liaison with the relevant DG. The SG performs a similar function in relation to the Economic and Social Committee and the Committee of the Regions – attending its meetings, reporting on developments, and ensuring that the Commission is represented.[21] When an issue comes to decision by the College, the SG informs all institutions involved in the legislative process.

Inter-institutional relations: As well as these routine contacts, the SG is involved in continuous dialogue with its counterparts in other EU institutions (seven in all) on issues of common interest. Regular meetings of the Secretaries General were initiated by O'Sullivan as part of a strategy to promote and strengthen inter-institutional cooperation. Administrative reform, particularly changes to the staff regulations, has been a frequent discussion topic. The creation of the European Selection Panel Office to manage recruitment to the European administration, including the organisation of the *con-*

cours, and of the European Administration School to provide in-house training for new recruits and managers, was a direct result of these consultations. Discussion of potential cooperation on issues such as library provision or the commissioning of research are other regular topics.

Organisation and operation

The SG was re-organised in early 2005 following the appointment of the Barroso Commission. Directorate C, responsible for programming and policy coordination, was split into two, the names of some divisions were changed, and the Task Force on the Convention on the Future of Europe was disbanded, with one of its three units becoming Directorate H, responsible for institutional affairs. The SG currently has eight directorates (see table 2).

Table 2: *The changing structure of the Secretariat General, 2000-2005*

2000	2001	2003	2005
Deputy Secretary General with special responsibilities for Directorates C, D & E	Deputy Secretary General with special responsibilities for Directorates C, D & E Deputy Secretary General with special responsibilities for Directorates A, B, & G		Deputy Secretary General with special responsibilities for Directorates A-E Deputy Secretary General with special responsibilities for Directorates F-H
Reporting to Sec Gen or Deputy Sec Gen	*Reporting to Sec Gen or Deputy Sec Gen*	*Reporting to Sec Gen or Deputy Sec Gen*	*Reporting to Sec Gen or Deputy Sec Gen*
Administrative Unit – Financial & human resources, mail & archives – IT – IGC – Coordination of co-decision	– Information on IGC, dialogue on Europe – IGC on reform of institutions	Protocol service, mediation service, personal data protection, Task Force: the future of the Union and institutional matters	
Directorate A	*Directorate A*	*Directorate A*	*Directorate A*
Registry – Meetings of the College & follow up – Written procedures – Secretariat of ECSC Consultative Committee	*Registry* – Meetings of the College & follow up – Written procedures – Secretariat of ECSC Consultative Committee	*Registry* – Meetings of the College & follow up – Written procedures – Electronic transmission of documents	*Registry* – Oral procedure & circulation of documents – Written procedure, habilitations & delegations – Electronic transmission of documents

Directorate B	Directorate B	Directorate B	Directorate B
Horizontal matters; institutional aspects; Community law; information	Simplification of working procedures & methods – simplification – transparency – relations with civil society – modernisation of archives	Relations with civil society – relations with agencies – application of Community law – openness & professional ethics, – archiving systems & the historical archives	Relations with civil society – Application of Community law – Transparency & relations with civil society – Archiving system & historical archives – [deontology]
Directorate C	Directorate C	Directorate C	Directorate C
Coordination – coordination & planning of Commission work – transparency & access to documents – organisation & management, secretariat of reform group of Commissioners	Policy planning & coordination – strategic planning – coordination of policies – annual report & publications	Programming & Commission policy coordination – SPP & coordination, – policy coordination, – publications – IRMS	Programming & administrative coordination – SPP – Coordination of administrative & budgetary policies – Annual report & publications – Secretariat of Audit Committee
Directorate D	Directorate D	Directorate D	Directorate D
Relations with the Council – Relations with Council I – Relations with Council II	Relations with the Council – Relations with Council I – Relations with Council II – Coordination of codecision	Relations with Council – Relations with Council I – Relations with Council II – Coordination of codecision	Policy coordination – Lisbon Strategy Task Force – Policy coordination I – Policy coordination II
Directorate E	Directorate E	Directorate E	Directorate E
Relations with the Parliament, the Economic & Social Committee, the Committee of the Regions, & trade & industry	Relations with the Parliament, the Economic & Social Committee, the Committee of the Regions, & trade & industry	Relations with the European Parliament, European Ombudsman, ESC & COR	Resources & general matters – Programming & resources – Mail & documents – IT – Information & databases

Directorate F	Directorate F	Directorate F	Directorate F
Forward Studies Unit (reports directly to the Commission President)	Forward Studies Unit (reports directly to the Commission President)	[No Directorate F; Forward Studies Unit no longer located in the SG]	Relations with the Council – COREPER I – COREPER II, G7/G8 – Codecision
Directorate G	Directorate G	Directorate G	Directorate G
	General affairs & resources – Mail – Information – IT	Resources & General Matters – Programming and resources – Mail, documents & internal information – IT & databases	Relations with the European Parliament, Ombudsman, Economic & Social Committee, Committee of the Regions, & national parliaments
		Task Force on the future of the Union & institutional matters	Directorate H
			Institutional affairs – European constitution – Institutional affairs & better regulation – Governance

As a central service, the SG falls under the direct responsibility of the Commission President. The relationship between the latter and the Secretary General is on a different footing from that of other Commissioners and their Directors General. The Secretary General has defined institutional responsibilities that give the officeholder greater autonomy than most Directors General, while performance of tasks, such as preparing College meetings, require closer and more direct contact with the Commission President than is typically the case for a Director General and Commissioner. The division of work between the two Deputy Secretaries General has varied considerably, reflecting the concerns that confront the Secretariat. Currently, one is responsible for Commission relations with other EU institutions (Directorates F, G, H), the other for internal coordination (Directorates A, B, C, D, E).

Evaluating the Secretariat General

Any examination of the SG inevitably raises two questions: how powerful is it, and how effective? The SG is clearly an important body within the Commission and within the Union more broadly, but it is not powerful in a political sense. It lacks the resources (staff, technical expertise) to develop firm views on policy choices, while the relative weakness of the Commission Presidency, as well as the Commission norms concerning collegiality and departmental equality, mean that it does not have the authority to impose its own views on Commission departments. Moreover, any influence that it can exercise is conditional on the confidence of the Commission President, the College and the Directors General, and the relationship between the Secretary General, on the one hand, and the Commission President and his *cabinet*, on the other. The SG's influence within the wider EU system is also contingent. Although, historically, it was a central repository of institutional memory and technical expertise, this is no longer the case. Successive treaty reforms, introducing new competencies that the Member States have been concerned to insulate from the 'Community method', have turned the Council Secretariat from a mere manager of procedure into a repository of substantive policy expertise. This has been most visible in the area of external EU relations, where rivalry between the SG and the Council Secretariat has become increasingly intense, as chapter 14 underlines.

In terms of its effectiveness, the SG performs relatively efficiently given its small size and the difficult conditions under which it operates. These difficulties are most evident in relation to internal coordination. It is too soon to judge the effectiveness of the SG's role in strategic planning and programming, since this is a relatively new and complex operation, which needs to be embedded.[22] However, in terms of routine inter-service consultation, the SG is only partly successful. Partly, this is due to the fact that it cannot pull rank. Authority is an important resource for any central coordinator. Unlike comparable bodies at the national level (the Cabinet Office in London or the Secrétariat Général du Gouvernement (SGG) in Paris), the SG cannot draw on the unquestioned authority of a powerful chief executive (Spence 2005). Even if the Commission Presidency has been strengthened, as chapter 1 argues, the principle of collegiality implies that the Commission President cannot impose decisions on his colleagues. Partly, the Secretariat's capacity is limited by stretched resources. But, an additional difficulty derives from the segmented nature of the Commission. DGs operate like fiefdoms; they are concerned principally with advancing their own proposals and are reluctant to share information. Their 'silo mentality' presents a persistent challenge.

The SG is, by contrast, relatively effective in carrying out its external responsibilities. Authority is less of a problem and the SG can rely on institutional pride and the willingness of officials and members of the Commission to cooperate in presenting a united front once a decision has been adopted by the College. Yet, even here, there are difficulties. For example, the SG's ability to ensure that Commission officials toe the agreed line in the Council is limited by the fact that monitoring only begins when a dossier reaches COREPER. Officials in Council working group are effectively 'off radar'. If they are unhappy with what the College has decided, there is little to stop them re-opening issues or trying to return to an earlier version of the text, of which they were probably the author. Similar possibilities exist when a proposal moves to the Parliament. An official may use informal contacts with members of the concerned EP committee to promote his or her favoured version of the text rather than the proposal formally adopted by the College. Furthermore, the loss of its representational monopoly in the Council in the wake of Maastricht's creation of the three-pillar structure has made performance of this task considerably more difficult.

Conclusion

Though its responsibilities have evolved and developed since its creation in 1958, the SG has always been at the heart of the Commission. It performs a series of roles that are fundamental to the operation of the organisation and is the only body with a general overview of developments across the Commission and in other EU institutions. Indispensable to the work of the College and close to the president, it was always 'the only body (other than the Commission itself) ... responsible for taking a view of the organisation as a whole' (Coombes 1970, 250). Every decision must in some way pass through the Secretariat, and nothing in the Commission can happen unless the SG takes the necessary action. Never merely an organiser of business, its work has been central, first to establishing the Commission as an administration, and second to enabling the Commission to carry out its responsibilities under the treaties.

The SG may not be as powerful or effective as central coordinating bodies in national administrations. Yet, whatever its shortcomings, these need to be set against the sheer range of its responsibilities. In contrast to the Cabinet Office in London or the SGCI in Paris, the remit of which is restricted to the internal functioning of the governmental apparatus, the SG must not only manage internal coordination in a collegial organisation, where Commissioners, unlike ministers, lack the authority to take decisions individually, but must also handle interactions with outside bodies in a constantly changing institutional environment that is more complex, and where the policy agenda is longer and more varied than in a Member State. In addition, the SG simply does not have at its disposal the resources – administrative tradition, party discipline, the authority that flows from centrally concentrated power – available to its counterparts in national capitals. Despite its undoubted central role, therefore, the SG remains a modest, back-stage actor in contrast to the growingly high profile of the Council's own Secretariat General (Westlake 2005, 349).

Endnotes

[1] Three members of the Commission, thirty officials and four *cabinet* members, serving and retired, generously shared their insight and experience in interviews between June 1997 and April 2004, granted on the basis that they would not be identified. I should like to express my gratitude to them all. I am also indebted to Lord Williamson, to participants in the panel, 'Building the European Commission: the creation and early development of a supranational actor', ECPR standing group, Bordeaux, 26-28 September 2002, especially Andy Smith, and to Dionyssis Dimitrakopoulos, Anand Menon, David Spence and Martin Westlake for their comments on an earlier version of this chapter. Special thanks are due also to officials of the Secretariat General and the Historical Archives of the European Communities as well as to Hagen Streb for supplying some of the data for table 1. The fieldwork for this project could not have been completed had I not been awarded a small research grant by the Nuffield Foundation and a major research grant from the British Academy. I gratefully acknowledge both.

[2] It was agreed that as the Commission President was a German, its top official should be a Frenchman (interview, 29 May 2001).

[3] For example, Noël was involved in the Action Committee for Europe and remained in touch with Jean Monnet throughout his life.

[4] The number of Commission departments and administrative units increased from 100 divisions and specialised services in 1958 to 124 in 1967 (Poullet and Deprez 1977, 149 and 144). The number of officials rose from a post-merger figure of 5,149 officials, compared to 2,924 before the merger, to just over 5,000 in 1969, to nearly 7,000 after the first enlargement (Poullet and Deprez 1977, 144) and to more than 15,000 by 1987 (Page 1997, 23). With the first two enlargements, the College grew from nine members (1967-1970, 1970-1973) to thirteen (1973-1977, 1977-1981) and then fourteen (1981-85). One veteran official recalled that, when he was recruited in 1961, he was welcomed to the Commission by the Secretary General himself rather than the Director General of his department (interview, 16 April 2001a). This would have been unthinkable a decade later.

[5] One of the tasks entrusted to the latter, a UK civil servant, was the codification of the rules of 'the house', the product of which was the *Manual of Operating Procedures*, the authoritative guide to the rules and internal processes of the Commission. The Manual has been revised and up-dated several times since.

[6] It retained this responsibility until the creation of DG IA twenty years later

[7] He was fully aware of the difficulties that his efforts were likely to encounter. As Spence noted in the first edition of this book, quoting Leonard 1990, Williamson 'presided over the most important of the inter-departmental committees established in the late 1980s in the aim, as he once confided, "not to mould a technically perfect administration, but one that will work"'.

[8] 'Reinforcing internal coordination', unpublished internal paper of August 1999.

[9] The terms of the mandate issued to Prodi are worth recalling: 'The Commission should speedily put into effect the necessary reforms, in particular for the improvement of its organisation, management and financial control. In order to do this, the next Commission ought to give urgent priority to launching a programme of far-reaching modernisation and reform. In particular, all means should be used in order to ensure that whenever Community funds, programmes or projects are managed by the Commission, its services are suitably structured to ensure highest standards of management integrity and efficiency', *Bulletin of the European Union* 3,1.39 I

[10] The White Paper on European Governance (COM (2001) 428) was published on 21 July 2001. Follow-up initiatives addressed: better regulation; comitology; information; better implementation; alternative regulation; access to documents; corporate governance; and corruption. For critical analyses, see Wincott (2001), Joerges (2000), and Joerges et al (2002).

[11] One of Prodi's stated objectives was that, in order to ensure effectiveness, the Commission should act only where it had appropriate resources.

[12] Private correspondence, 16 June 2004.

[13] It is also 'a clearing house for texts of a horizontal nature, linked to resource management, before they go into inter-service coordination to ensure that the horizontal services share a common line on the main questions' (private correspondence, 9 June 2004).

[14] The purpose of these meetings, which bring together the members of each cabinet responsible for the subject area in question, is to make as much progress as possible on an issue before it goes to the *chefs de cabinet*.

[15] By involving the SG early, it was hoped that the number of meetings of the 'special chefs' could be reduced. It was widely believed that such meetings were held too often and that the number could be reduced, if opportunities were created to resolve issues downstream, so limiting the involvement of *cabinets* in routine decision making. A further innovation was to routinise mixed meetings of officials and *cabinet* members.

[16] The number of desk officers was increased to eleven.

[17] See http://europa.eu.int/comm/dgs/secretariat_general/mission/index_en.htm.

[18] The Prodi Commission decided that the latter should be made available on the Europa website.

[19] For details of these preparatory meetings of Councils see Westlake, 2004.

[20] On all these institutional arrangements see Corbett, Jacobs, and Shackleton *The European Parliament*, 6th edition, John Harper Publishing, 2005.

[21] The SG is also in regular touch with the Court of Auditors, though the financial DGs are the Court's principal interlocutors within the Commission, and the Ombudsman.

[22] Though see Levy (2002).

Postscript

The Secretary General of the Commission: a personal comment by David Williamson
(Secretary General 1987 - 1997)

Whether Britain is at the heart of Europe is sometimes questioned, but that the Secretary General and the Secretariat General are at the heart of the European Commission can surely not be questioned. I consider myself very privileged to have served in this important post for ten years.

The organisation of the Secretariat General and the changes over the years are examined elsewhere in this volume. As a contribution to the history of this period, I wish only in this memoir to give a flavour of the other responsibilities which the Secretary General carried during my years in that post.

The role of the Secretary General as *primus inter pares* among the Directors General and as commanding the confidence of the College of Commissioners meant that he had a special place in the whole range of important European Union activities at the highest level. This was reinforced by tradition, notably because for a very long time – from the founding of the Commission until 1997 – the post of Secretary General was held by only two people, the great Emile Noël and myself (and there are still only five Secretaries General up to today: Emile Noël, myself, Carlo Trojan, David O'Sullivan and Catherine Day).

Over a period of ten years as Secretary General I participated in every major European Union event. I was present at every meeting of the Heads of State and Government in the European Council and participated in the drafting of the conclusions. I was present at every meeting of the Foreign Affairs Council and at meetings of the Economic and Finance Council; I was at every plenary session of the European Parliament and at the many hundred meetings of the European Commission itself.

In addition, the President of the Commission and the College as a whole decided, on a number of important subjects, to allocate specific tasks to the Secretary General as representative of the Commission. For example, Emile Noël represented the Commission at the highest official level in preparation of the Single European Act, which brought in the single market. I was one of the Commission representatives at a similar level for the preparation of the Treaties of Maastricht and Amsterdam. This involved many months with the personal representatives of the Heads of State and Government in the group which was the principal forum for negotiating the draft Treaties. It was for me the part of my job which carried some of the greatest responsibility and the greatest workload. I also, on many important occasions, worked directly with the Commission's President and his *chef de cabinet*, for example in preparation of summit meetings both in the European Council and with the Presidency of the Council, in the negotiation with the Member States of major agreements such as the 'Delors packages' involving the financing of the regional and other structural funds, and in more recent years the negotiation of the series of enlargements of the Union.

The workload of the Secretary General also increased when the Secretariat General provided a cradle for some baby policies, which later grew into strapping youngsters before moving off elsewhere in the organisation. For example, the common foreign and security policy was at first handled within the Secretariat General; the important work on justice and home affairs began as a task force in the Secretariat General; and the Cohesion Fund (now in DG 'Regional Policy') began in the Secretariat General.

The Secretary General is at the crux of the system and, in order to have influence, he had to command the confidence of the President of the Commission, for whom he acted in a sense as a Director General, and of his *chef de cabinet*. I consider myself very fortunate to have worked closely, during the golden years of progress of the European Union, with Jacques Delors, one of the greatest Europeans of his generation and with Pascal Lamy, his brilliant and very active *chef de cabinet*. The Secretary General had also to command the confidence of the College as a whole; the Secretaries General have always considered themselves to be the servants of the College, honour bound to reflect as accurately as possible its wishes. The Secretary General had to command the confidence of the services and in particular the Directors General; he is an important source of their information and, in last resort, the channel by which they can make their views known to the President. Finally, the Secretary General had to have a strong base and very able people in his own Secretariat General so that, both within and outside, he had a demonstrable grip on the important responsibility he held.

Although the Secretary General had an important role in the internal organisation of the work of the Commission, it is also important to understand the Secretariat General's responsibilities in relation to the other European institutions and the Member States. The external face of the Secretariat General is probably less well known except by those who deal directly with it. It was, however, a considerable source of responsibility for the Secretary General. It co-ordinated all the Commission's relations with the Member States in the Council of Ministers and always directly represented the Commission at the operationally vital level of COREPER II and I (the Permanent Representatives and Deputy Representatives of the Member States) and in other bodies in the structure of the Council, e.g. the Antici Group. Apart from the President of the Commission, the responsible Commissioner and their *cabinets*, the Secretariat General was the most important point of contact for Member States in their negotiations of legislative or similar proposals presented by the Commission, although the Secretary General clearly worked closely with the Directorates General concerned. I would say that in my period as Secretary General and over a wide range of issues, Carlo Trojan, the Deputy Secretary General at the time, was the principal voice at official level of the Commission in its dealings with Member States and in the defence of its proposals before them.

The other major institutional partner of the European Commission was the European Parliament. All relations with the Parliament were handled by the Directorate in the Secretariat General, which also handled the transmission of documents (including parliamentary questions) and recorded and informed the services of the key points both from plenary sessions and from the vital committee work. Because of the very wide and frequent contacts between the European Commission and the European Parliament, a large number of officials from the operational Directorates General were often present in parliamentary committees (sometimes as many as 100 officials in a 'committee' week), and the Commissioners themselves attended when required. But the overall handling of the arrangements and contacts was centralised in the Secretariat General.

This short overview is sufficient to show that the role of the Secretary General has in the past gone far beyond the role of an organiser of business and that it always had the potential to extend into areas of real importance to the Commission as the motor of the common interests of the Member States in the progress of the European Union.

The Secretary General of the Commission: a personal comment by Carlo Trojan
(Deputy Secretary General 1987-1997 and Secretary General 1997-2000)

Before my appointment as Secretary General in 1997, I served for ten years as Deputy to the then Secretary General, David Williamson. I have always considered the period I spent as Deputy Secretary General a privileged one, since it gave me the opportunity to be closely involved in a wide range of policy areas, both within the Commission and in relation to Member States.

The principal roles of the Deputy Secretary General were twofold: representing the Commission in COREPER II – the ambassadorial level committee of EU Permanent Representatives of Member States – and ensuring policy coordination within the Commission itself. Both roles demanded the confidence and trust of the Commission President and the Secretary General. And they involved close working relations with Commissioners, Directors General, Permanent Representatives, and the Secretary General of both the Council and Parliament.

I was thus closely involved in the policy coordination and negotiation of major 'packages' such as Delors II, German unification and Agenda 2000. Participation in both COREPER and the weekly *chefs de cabinet* meetings enables the Deputy Secretary General to keep the College informed of the state of play in the Council and to feed the latest Commission considerations into the COREPER process. Together with David Williamson, I also attended practically all General Affairs Council and Ecofin meetings and became increasingly involved in the preparation of European Councils where, at the time, the Secretary General and *chef de cabinet* of the President played a key role in drafting conclusions.

Taken together, these diverse roles of the Deputy Secretary General gave me a bird's eye view of all major issues confronting the European Union. However, I was much less involved in the overall management of the Commission or the Secretariat General itself. David Williamson had the extraordinary talent of combining the roles of manager and policy adviser. Nonetheless, I was tasked with chairing a major screening operation of the Commission services (DECODE) and towards the end of the third Delors Commission, together with David Williamson and a number of colleagues, assisted Commissioner Karel Van Miert in preparing a report for the incoming Commission President on the functioning of the Commission. Many of the findings of both exercises re-emerged when I was appointed as Secretary General in 1997.

Far too little attention has been given to the achievements of the Santer Commission due to the circumstances which led to its collective resignation on 16 March 1999. Yet, it was the Santer Commission which paved the way for the recent major enlargement to twenty-five Member States, the passage to the third phase of EMU, and the successful introduction of the euro on 1 January 1999.

The Santer Commission also played a major role in the somewhat underrated Treaty of Amsterdam, which put employment and justice and home affairs definitively on the European Union's agenda and introduced some important institutional changes. The Santer Commission also initiated a far-reaching programme of administrative reform: SEM 2000 (Sound and Efficient Management) and MAP 2000 (Modernisation of Administration and Personnel Policy). It may arguably have been too little, too late, but it was nevertheless Erkki Liikanen who laid the foundation for the comprehensive administrative reform subsequently implemented by Neil Kinnock under the Prodi Commission.

Agenda 2000 was far more complex than the two previous major financing packages. It had to deal with both existing policies and the perspective of an unprecedented enlargement with ten new Member States. The Santer Commission had to square the circle between the objectives of achieving stabilisation of expenditure, reforming outdated policies, and adjusting the balance between national contributors. The package was negotiated in the context of the introduction of the euro and the necessity of keeping budgetary deficits down at national level. The fact that the Santer Commission achieved a deal at the Berlin European Council a few weeks after its collective resignation was a considerable achievement.

It is fair to say that administrative reform was not one of the priorities of the successive Delors Commissions. Until the nineties, the Commission was essentially an 'administration de mission'. As communism fell, it was called upon to manage a very high level of direct funding without the appropriate management experience and without sufficient human resources. Moreover, over the years additional tasks were given to the Commission by Member States, and it acquired new competences through successive Treaty changes.

In fact, the tasks of the Commission evolved over the years, making it an administration much more comparable to national civil services. But neither the administrative organisation nor its management followed this evolution. The Santer Commission was the first to address the mismatch between management capacity and administrative reality. Erkki Liikanen was the first Commissioner to invest seriously in the financial reform process.

At the time – as Secretary General – I personally experienced how difficult it is to implement administrative reform in a multinational institution with 15 different nationalities and backgrounds, and with a total lack of uniform administrative culture. In national organisations or even multinational companies, there is at least one culture, one corporate identity, and one working language. Moreover, organisational and management reforms usually occur periodically over the years. In the Commission, implementing change depends on a severe budgetary squeeze or on the house being on fire. In fact, we had both towards the end of the Santer Commission. The fall of the Commission not only marked a switch in the balance of power between Commission and Parliament, but it also constituted a major incentive for comprehensive administrative reform – a task successfully implemented under the Prodi Commission.

The Secretary General of the Commission: a personal comment by David O'Sullivan
(Secretary General 2000-2005)

Over the past few years the Commission has undergone a profound transformation. In a relatively short period of time, major Treaty revisions have been adopted and have entered into force. The European Union has grown significantly in membership and responsibilities. Internally, after a long period of slow adaptation, the political crisis that led to the resignation of the College in 1999 required the Commission to take a harder look at itself, at its working methods, its lines of responsibility and its overall accountability.

Today's Commission is built on the solid foundations laid down by successive generations of committed Europeans. The achievements of Emile Noël as Secretary General cast a long shadow over his successors. The man who held the post for over thirty years so dominated the life of the institution that it was always going to be an almost impossible act to follow. And yet my two predecessors rose admirably to that challenge. David Williamson assumed the mantle with ease, combining the best tradition of British public service with the unique character of the emerging European administration. Carlo Trojan took over after a brilliant ten-year stint as Deputy Secretary General, and it fell to him to steer the institution through some of its more testing moments.

But the achievements of David and Carlo cannot disguise the reality – the Commission of Emile Noël has gone forever. When I look at the photo of the first Commission, ten people gathered around what could be a family dining table, I am struck by the very different picture that the institution represents today. During the transition between the Prodi and Barroso Commission, I found myself dealing with two Presidents, 40 serving or nominated Commissioners, 650 members of Cabinet and two buildings!

The Commission which began as a cottage industry in the 1950s, grew under Noël's stewardship into the mature administration which enabled Delors to launch the single market of 1992 and the Euro a decade later. Yet, as Carlo Trojan points out, the 'administration de mission' created by Noël came under increasing strain as the nature and scope of the European project evolved in the 1990s. To gauge the extent of the change, let's consider two simple indicators: in less than 25 years the Commission doubled its personnel and has seen its responsibility for the budget of the Union multiply, in the same period of time, by a factor of ten!

Against this background, it is not surprising that the role of Secretary General of the Commission has also changed significantly, keeping pace with the evolving role of the institution and with the new powers of the Commission's President in giving leadership to the College.

This book deals extensively with the role and tasks of the Commission, its internal organisation and its recent reforms. I will therefore limit this contribution to some observations on how the role of the Secretary General has developed in recent years based on my personal experience.

Today's Secretariat General (SG) has a clear focus on the core tasks of planning, inter-institutional relations and co-ordination. It is less a manager of individual actions or an 'incubator' for new policy areas than was often the case in the past. These changes have a direct impact on the Secretary General in his roles as 'Chief Executive Officer' of the SG, as Secretary of the College, as *primus inter pares* amongst his fellow Directors General and as a privileged interface with other institutions. This is not to deny that some of the essential features of the job have remained constant – I am thinking in particular of the need for a close and trusting relationship with the President and the College or of the need for versatile and able personnel in the Secretariat General.

In my view, the changes in the role of the Secretary General are linked to three main developments: the growing role and new tasks of the European Union as a whole, the process of political maturity within the Commission as an institution, and increasing scrutiny and visibility of the work of the Commission.

Over the past decade, the European Union has seen a significant evolution in terms of responsibilities, procedures and membership. Better to serve the interests of the Union, the Commission has also refocused its role and its input in the inter-institutional process, within the limits laid down in the successive Treaty changes.

The Union, created in Maastricht just over a decade ago, has taken on the new responsibilities agreed upon in Amsterdam and Nice and is now in the exciting phase of ratification of its first Constitution. In the areas of monetary policy, justice and home affairs and foreign and security policy, to name just the most striking examples, the Union has made unexpected progress and is setting itself even more ambitious objectives. Moreover, discussions in a Union of 25 require qualitatively different preparatory work from that which took place just over ten years ago for the Community of the 12.

This increase in number of Member States and in areas of responsibility has required stronger inter-institutional co-operation and a certain degree of specialisation. All institutions have refined their capacity to deal with these new areas: for the Commission, this has led to a new equilibrium between the SG and sectoral services.

The Secretariat General remains the guarantor of collegiality, at the service of the President. I consider that the biggest challenge for the SG today is that of policy integration, bringing together different policy strands at the earliest possible stage of preparation to ensure that when proposals arrive at the College for decision they are coherent with the overall political goals.

As an institution, the Commission has experienced over the past ten years an unprecedented expansion in the range and quantity of its tasks. In parallel, the Commission has reached a new level of political maturity. This development has also transformed the role of the Secretary General.

Internally over the past five years the Commission has undergone the most thorough reform it has ever known, touching all aspects of financial management, personnel policy, programming and planning. Under the leadership of President Prodi and Vice President Kinnock, the administrative reform launched in 1999 set out a vision for the modernisation of the institution, matching tasks with resources and ensuring accountability and transparency. Five years on, the reform has been a success: the process of transformation towards a modern and adaptable administration has been set on the right tracks. As President Barroso has pledged to the Parliament, the Commission remains committed to the highest standard of accountability and transparency.

Administrative reform has also had important repercussions on the role of the Secretariat General: the process of decentralisation included financial procedures and key aspects of personnel management. Directors General have become individually more accountable. In a more decentralised and transparent system, the Secretariat General has a stronger role in planning and quality control.

The Secretary General maintains his role as 'Director General' of the SG. In this function I focused the activities of the SG on our core tasks of co-ordination and service to the President and the College, reducing as far as possible the number of other responsibilities that had been accumulated in the SG 'by default'. And with my fellow Directors General, I shared the responsibility for the implementation and delivery of the reform requested by the College.

Lastly, more scrutiny has led to more political visibility for the Commission and a better division of political and administrative responsibility within the institution. A clearer division of tasks between the political level of the College of Commissioners and the administrative level has developed. Under the close scrutiny of public opinion and the European Parliament, the Commission has made enormous progress.

To some extent this has been a process of 'normalisation' for an institution that in less than five decades developed from a small body to a large administration with multiple tasks, numerous centres of expertise and growing responsibilities. The reform has clearly put political overview of the actions of the Commission in the hands of the individual Commissioners and of the President of the Commission.

Power must not only lie with the politician but must also be seen to do so. Suggestions that the real power lies with 'faceless bureaucrats' are no longer acceptable.

The Secretary General ensures that the goals set at the political level are translated into clear administrative actions, guarantees the best possible level of internal control and monitoring, and ensures that clear reporting lines are fostered between the political level and the administration. In many ways, the SG today is taking up this central role of co-ordinator of a modern complex administration and in doing this it acts as an extension of the President's powers over the internal organisation and the political guidance of the College.

The experience of 2005 also confirmed that at a time of transition from one Commission to the next, the Secretary General is called to play a role of continuity and institutional stability. The choices of President Barroso for the organisation of his College have clearly confirmed the pivotal role of the Secretariat General for the functioning of the College, now and into the future.

There will never be another Noël, but maybe in the modern era that is to be welcomed rather than regretted.

3.   The Commission and the Law

John A. Usher

Introduction

Politicians critical of 'creeping federalism' in the Community, have some-times pointed to the European Court of Justice (ECJ) as the most 'federal' of the Community's institutions and the most effective locomotive of European inte-gration (Heseltine 1989). But it is argued here that as regards the legislative and administrative functions in the Community, it is still true to say (as Commission President Malfatti informed the European Parliament in 1970) that 'the Commission is, at one and the same time, the guardian of the Treaties and the motive force of integration', even though at first sight it is now subor-dinated to other institutions: following the Amsterdam and Nice amend-ments, its members are appointed by the Council subject to the approval of the European Parliament, and the Parliament has shown that it is prepared to exer-cise both its power of censure (in relation to the Santer Commission) and its power to block new appointments (in relation to the Barroso Commission).

Under Article 211 of the EC Treaty, the first duty of the Commission with regard to the proper functioning and development of the single market is to 'ensure that the provisions of this Treaty and the measures taken by the insti-tutions pursuant thereto are applied'. In its unique position as proposer and enforcer of Community legislation, the Commission has the opportunity to fulfil this duty both in the legislative process and subsequently in ensuring the observance of the legislation itself. Moreover, this chapter argues that Article 211 has conferred on the Commission both legislative powers and enforcement duties that are not apparent from the substantive Treaty provisions. In exer-cising these powers and duties, the Commission is assisted by its Legal Service, an overarching service separate from the specific Directorates General. Under art. 21 of the Commission's Rules of Procedure, the Legal Service must be con-sulted on all drafts or proposals for legal instruments and on all documents which may have legal implications, and its agents represent the Commission in legal proceedings before the European courts.

The Commission and the legislative process

a) Council legislation

The fundamentals of the Commission's position in the legislative process under the EC Treaty are set out in Article 250(1) and (2). Here, the Commission's sole right of legislative initiative is set out. Under these provisions, the Council, on the one hand, must act unanimously if it wishes to amend a Commission proposal, and the Commission, on the other hand, may alter its proposal at any time during the procedures leading to the adoption of a Community act. As with amendments made by the other institutions, the question arises of when an amendment is so fundamental as to constitute a new proposal. In the context of a dispute between Parliament and the Council, it has now been held that where a Council amendment altered the substance of a proposal compared with the version seen by Parliament, it must be resubmitted to the Parliament unless the change was requested by Parliament itself (Case C-65/90, 1992).

Of course, in the day-to-day process of negotiation in the Council of Ministers and its subsidiary bodies, the Council working groups and COREPER, there is a constant process of negotiation involving a collaborative process of adjustment of the Commission's proposals. The Commission is an equal partner in the process, albeit deprived of a vote on the outcome, but it nevertheless retains a veto power in its ability to withdraw the proposal itself unless satisfactory compromise is reached (despite the surprising silence of the Treaties on the matter). Indeed, if the precedents under the original system of legislation are followed, the Commission could, if it believed that amendments pursued by the Council effectively changed the nature of its proposal, simply withdraw its proposal. It did precisely this in November 1986 with regard to the Erasmus scheme for student exchanges. According to Commissioner Marin, who was responsible for the matter, this was done to prevent the Council from depriving the scheme of all significant content (EC Commission 1986).

Discussion of the changes in the legislative process brought about by the cooperation procedure introduced by the Single European Act and the co-decision procedure introduced by the Maastricht Treaty and amended by the Amsterdam Treaty has concentrated on the relationship between Parliament and Council. While the cooperation procedure is now virtually defunct except in the area of Economic and Monetary Union, its terminology is ambiguous about the powers of the Commission after the adoption of a common position by the Council: under art. 252 (d) the Commission must 're-examine the proposal on the basis of which Council adopted its common position' in the light of the Parliament's proposed amendments, and it then forwards to the Council its re-examined proposal. This appears to imply that there is still a Commission proposal which can be amended or withdrawn. However, under the co-decision procedure, which is nowadays effectively the normal legislative procedure (and was expressly recognised as such under the Treaty establishing a Constitution for Europe) it is clear from the terms of art. 251(2) and (3) that it is the Council's common position which is at issue in the second reading, and not the Commission's proposal (De Grucht 2003). The role of the Commission is rather to deliver an opinion on any amendments proposed by the Parliament, although if it delivers a negative opinion on a particular proposed amendment, the Council may only adopt such an amendment if it acts unanimously. However, if Council and Parliament are unable to reach agreement on the second reading, and the matter moves to conciliation, then under art. 251(4) it is the Commission which is entrusted with taking 'all necessary initiatives with a view to reconciling the positions of the European Parliament and the Council.' Its role therefore remains of vital importance. Even under the co-decision procedure, it is still the Commission that drafts the original proposal, and in the second reading stage, whether or not the Commission delivers a negative opinion on a proposed Parliamentary amendment will determine the majority required in the Council to accept or reject that amendment. Furthermore, the Commission retains its original power to amend or, in practice, withdraw its proposals at least up to the adoption of the common position, which is a powerful negative weapon.

b) Treaty base

Differences of opinion on the appropriate Treaty base under which proposals for Community legislation are made are a regular source of conflict between the Commission and Member States. Indeed, officials from some national administrations are given explicit instructions to check whether proposals (and even impending proposals or 'gleams in the Commission's eye') do not establish precedents leading to an increase in the Commission's power or the spill-over of responsibility from an exclusively national arena to the sphere of Community competence. Arguments about competence are matters of day to day negotiation in Community business. They are the practical evidence of the continuance of the dispute between supporters of supranationalism and intergovernmentalism.

According to Article 7 of the EC Treaty, each Community institution 'shall act within the limits of the power conferred upon it by this Treaty'. Further, Article 253 provides that acts of Community legislation 'shall state the reasons on which they are based'. The European Court's role is to ensure these articles are respected and, in this context, it is interesting to note that the express grounds for annulment of acts of the Community institutions under Article 230 are 'lack of competence, infringement of an essential procedural requirement, infringement of this Treaty or of any rule of law relating to its application, or misuse of powers'. 'Competence' is thus a crucial issue – and it is a matter which was dealt with expressly in arts. I-11 to I-18 of the 2004 Treaty establishing a Constitution for Europe. In the meantime it has been and remains an area where the tension between the Commission's two main roles is clearly articulated. As a civil service, the Commission would naturally give way to its political masters. As an independent political animal, the Commission is keen to extend its power and play a politically strategic role in setting the goals of the Community itself. For that purpose, it clearly suits the Commission to choose a Treaty base enabling it to expand Community competence and to enhance its own power. This means a constant quest to identify potential for new areas of competence, and a vigilance to prevent perceived erosion of Community competence in the context of the present three-pillar structure of the EU. Thus in Case C-170/96, the Commission sought the annulment of a Council Decision relating to airport visas adopted under the Third Pillar on Justice and Home Affairs (as it then was). The Commission's argument was that there was an express provision of the EC Treaty on visas under which the decision should have been adopted, and although that argument was unsuccessful, the European Court held that although it had no jurisdiction under the Third Pillar at that time, it could nevertheless use its jurisdiction under the EC Treaty to check whether the other pillars were being used to circumvent Community powers. This approach has been extended to acts adopted under the Second Pillar (CFSP) in Case C-91/05, where the Commission is seeking the annulment under Article 230 EC of a Council Decision implementing a Council Joint Action on the European Union's contribution to combating the destabilising accumulation and spread of small arms and light weapons. The Commission's argument was that the contested decision affected Community powers in the field of development aid, since the Cotonou Agreement between the Community and the ACP States already covered actions taken against the spread of small arms and light weapons, and the Commission had concluded, pursuant to the same agreement, a Regional Indicative Programme for West Africa, giving support to a regional policy of conflict prevention and good governance, and providing for a moratorium on the import, export and production of light weapons in West Africa. In the Commission's view, this meant that the Council had no competence to adopt the contested act under the Second Pillar. Moreover, the Commission sought a declaration of illegality under Article 241 EC of the Joint Action itself as an act of a general legislative nature on which the contested CFSP decision was based.

In the context of the third pillar, the Amsterdam Treaty introduced Article 35 EU, giving the Court an express jurisdiction to review the legality of framework decisions and decisions adopted under Article 34 EU. The grounds for annulment are the same as those under art. 230 EC, and rights of action are given to the Member States and to the Commission. The Commission has also used this provision to prevent the erosion of Community competence. In Case C-176/03 it sought the annulment of Framework Decision 2003/80 on the protection of the environment through criminal law, claiming that the Community legislature was competent under the environmental provisions of the EC Treaty, notably Article 175, to require the Member States to prescribe criminal penalties for infringements of Community environmental protection legislation if it took the view that that was a necessary means of ensuring that the legislation is effective. Indeed many of the relevant provisions of the EU Framework Decision had been taken from the Commission's proposal for an EC Directive on the matter. In responding to this claim, the Court noted (following its airport visas judgment) that it was its task to ensure that acts adopted under the third pillar did not encroach upon the powers conferred by the EC Treaty on the Community, and that it was common ground that protection of the environment constitutes one of the essential objectives of the Community. It concluded that the relevant provisions of the framework decision had as their main purpose the protection of the environment and they could have been properly adopted on the basis of Article 175 EC. In those circumstances, the entire framework decision encroached on the powers which Article 175 EC confers on the Community, and it therefore had to be annulled. The Commission has subsequently indicated that in its view the Court's reasoning can be applied to all Community policies and freedoms which involve binding legislation with which criminal penalties should be associated in order to ensure their effectiveness (COM (2005) 583 final).

In the context of the EC Treaty, the Commission has in tactical terms sought legal justification for the selection of Treaty bases requiring qualified majority (QM) voting rather than unanimity. This not only removes the potential for one or two Member States to block the Commission's proposals. Choosing a QM Treaty base implies that compromises resulting from negotiations are likely to be based somewhere above the lowest common denominator of agreement between Member States and thus somewhat closer to the Commission's initial proposal. The Commission's power to propose legislation gives it the further power to indicate the Treaty base under which it is to be enacted. Determining the Treaty base has important consequences in two respects: the legislative procedure (and majority) to be used; and the question of substantive competence. As to existing jurisprudence, a clear example in the area of legislative procedure is that of health measures relating to agricultural products. This was traditionally dealt with by legislation made jointly under Article 94 on the approximation of laws and Article 37 on agricultural legislation. While Article 94 requires unanimity, Article 37 allows a qualified majority decision to be taken. The United Kingdom challenged two pieces of Council legislation adopted under Article 37 alone, which it thought should have been adopted under Article 94 by unanimity as well (Case 68/86 & Case 131/86). These pieces of legislation related to the hormone content of meat and to the treatment of battery poultry (Council Directives 85/649 and 86/113). Although the United Kingdom 'won' because of procedural irregularities, on the substantive issue the European Court made it clear that a mere practice of the Council could not create a binding precedent with regard to the correct legal base, and that agricultural legislation could, and should, take account of requirements such as the protection of the health and life of humans and animals.

There is some authority for saying that there is an additional factor to take into account in determining whether to enact legislation under Article 95 (or another provision involving QM in Council and the cooperation or co-decision procedure with the European Parliament) where the alternative legal base does not involve an enhanced role for the European Parliament. This arose from a dispute between the Commission and the Council on the appropriate legal base to be used in a case concerning environmental legislation. The issue (Case C-300/89) arose from the enactment of a Directive on titanium dioxide waste by unanimity under the original version of Article 130s (now art. 175), when the Commission had proposed that it should be adopted by QM under what is now Article 95. The Court's view was that it was not possible to use procedures involving both unanimity and the cooperation procedure for the same legislation. To do so would defeat the very object of the cooperation procedure, which was to increase the Parliament's participation in the legislative process as a matter of fundamental democratic principle. Requiring the Council to act throughout by unanimity would certainly diminish Parliament's influence, since under the cooperation procedure unanimity is normally only necessary where the Council wishes to override Parliament or the Commission. It normally only requires a qualified majority in Council to carry the Parliament's view. The Court in fact found that Article 174(2) envisaged that legislation under other provisions could (indeed should) have the aim of protecting the environment, and that Article 95 envisaged the need for a high level of environmental protection single market legislation. The Court therefore held that the Directive should have been enacted under Article 95, but the message may be taken to mean that where alternative Treaty bases are available, preference should be given to that which enhances the democratic role of the Parliament.

However, this would appear not to be an absolute rule, and it is not illegitimate to use Article 175 where the internal market effects of environmental legislation are subordinate in nature. This appears from Case C-155/91, where the Commission and Parliament claimed, on the basis of the judgement in the titanium dioxide case, that Council Directive 91/156 on waste should have been enacted under Article 95 rather than Article 175. It might have been thought that since the Court had held in Case C-2/90 that each region, commune or other local authority could take measures to ensure the treatment and elimination of its own waste as near to its place of production as possible so as to limit its transport, that questions of the movement of goods did arise. However, the Court took the view that the Directive was intended to achieve the precise opposite of the free movement of waste within the Community, that is, that each Member State should eliminate its own waste at the nearest point of disposal. While admitting that certain aspects might affect the internal market, the Court held that these effects were subordinate to the overall aim of protecting the environment through effective waste management. Attractive as the democratic appeal of the titanium dioxide case may be, it is the policy objective which remains the main determinant of Treaty base, though there is often scope for more than one view of the predominant policy objective.

This question was analysed in depth in the judgment of the Court in Case C-376/98 annulling European Parliament and Council Directive 98/43 (OJ 1998 L213/9) on tobacco advertising and sponsorship, which resulted from the Commission's longstanding proposal to ban all forms of tobacco advertising. The Directive was enacted under three provisions of the EC Treaty: art. 57(2) on freedom of establishment of the self-employed, art. 66 applying the same provision to services, and art. 95 on the internal market. These are now arts. 47(2), 55 and 95, and while the current texts contain amendments, they do not relate to the points at issue. It was well-known that the Federal Republic of Germany had opposed this Directive in the Council (Hervey 2001) and it continued its opposition in the judicial arena, bringing the present action. In support of its application, Germany put forward several lines of argument, alleging, in particular, that art. 95 of the Treaty was not an appropriate legal basis for the Directive, and infringement of art. 47(2) and art. 55 of the Treaty. However, since the applicant and the defendants stated that their arguments regarding art. 95 also applied to the interpretation of arts. 47(2) and 55 of the Treaty, the Court took the view that it was therefore appropriate to consider the pleas alleging that arts. 95, 47(2) and 55 of the Treaty did not constitute the proper legal basis for the Directive together. As summarised by AG Fennelly, the first argument was that the Directive was, in reality, a measure for the protection of public health, whose effect on the internal market, if any, was merely incidental to its principal aim – reflected in its content – of reducing smoking. The second argument was that, in any event, the Directive was not a valid internal-market measure, for a number of reasons. First, there was no significant inter-state trade (or none at all) in either the advertising services or advertising media at issue, relative to trade within each Member State, with the result that varying national legislations posed only a negligible potential obstacle to such trade and did not cause an appreciable distortion of competition. Secondly, Germany claimed that the Directive effectively resulted in a total prohibition of tobacco advertising – about 98% of such advertising by value, including that with exclusively domestic effects – resulting in an impediment to freedom to trade in advertising-related goods and services.

In relation to the argument that the Directive was really a health measure, the Court observed that the first indent of art. 129(4) (now art. 152(4)(c)) of the Treaty excluded any harmonisation of laws and regulations of the Member States designed to protect and improve human health. It accepted, however, that that provision did not mean that harmonising measures adopted on the basis of other provisions of the Treaty could not have any impact on the protection of human health. Indeed, the third paragraph of art. 129(1) (now reflected in the first indent of art. 152(1)) provided that health requirements were to form a constituent part of the Community's other policies. However, it emphasised that other articles of the Treaty could not be used as a legal basis in order to circumvent the express exclusion of harmonisation laid down in what was then art. 129(4) of the Treaty.

More generally, the Court held that it was clear that the measures referred to in art. 95(1) were intended to improve the conditions for the establishment and functioning of the internal market. In its view, to construe that article as meaning that it vested in the Community legislature a general power to regulate the internal market would not only be contrary to the express wording of the provisions it had discussed, but would also be incompatible with the principle embodied in art. 5 of the EC Treaty that the powers of the Community are limited to those specifically conferred on it. It further declared that a measure adopted on the basis of art. 95 of the Treaty must genuinely have as its object the improvement of the conditions for the establishment and functioning of the internal market. If a mere finding of disparities between national rules and of the abstract risk of obstacles to the exercise of fundamental freedoms or of distortions of competition liable to result therefrom were sufficient to justify the choice of art. 95 as a legal basis, judicial review of compliance with the proper legal basis might be rendered nugatory. The Court would then be prevented from discharging the function entrusted to it by art. 220 of the EC Treaty, namely ensuring that the law is observed in the interpretation and application of the Treaty.

On the other hand, the Court accepted that if the conditions for recourse to arts. 95, 47(2) and 55 as a legal basis were fulfilled, the Community legislature could not be prevented from relying on that legal basis on the ground that public health protection was a decisive factor in the choices to be made. On the contrary, it pointed out that the third paragraph of art. 129(1) (now art. 152(1)) provided that health requirements were to form a constituent part of the Community's other policies and that art. 95(3) expressly required that, in the process of harmonisation, a high level of human health protection was to be ensured.

The Court concluded that it was therefore necessary to verify whether the Directive actually contributed to eliminating obstacles to the free movement of goods and to the freedom to provide services, and to removing distortions of competition. As AG Fennelly put it, the real issue in these proceed-

ings was not whether health protection figured prominently in the motivation of those promoting its adoption, but whether the internal market constituted, on its own, a sustainable legal basis for the Directive.

In the context of this internal market argument, it was accepted that as a
result of disparities between national laws on the advertising of tobacco
products, obstacles to the free movement of goods or the freedom to provide
services existed or might well arise. In principle, therefore, a Directive prohibiting the advertising of tobacco products in periodicals, magazines and
newspapers could be adopted on the basis of art. 95 with a view to ensuring
the free movement of press products, on the lines of Directive 89/552 on
television services, art. 13 of which prohibits television advertising of
tobacco products in order to promote the free broadcasting of television programmes. The Court added, however, that for numerous types of advertising of tobacco products, the prohibition under art. 3(1) of the Directive could
not be justified by the need to eliminate obstacles to the free movement of
advertising media or the freedom to provide services in the field of advertising. That applied, in particular, to the prohibition of advertising on
posters, parasols, ashtrays and other articles used in hotels, restaurants and
cafés, and the prohibition of advertising spots in cinemas, prohibitions
which in its view in no way helped to facilitate trade in the products concerned.

The Court further held that the Directive did not in any event ensure free
movement of products which were in conformity with its provisions, since
under art. 5 of the Directive, Member States retained the right to lay down,
in accordance with the Treaty, such stricter requirements concerning the
advertising or sponsorship of tobacco products as they deemed necessary to
guarantee the health protection of individuals.

On the broader issue of competence, and in particular whether the
Directive was justified as a method of eliminating distortions of competition, the Court stated that it was required to verify whether the distortion of
competition which the measure purported to eliminate was appreciable,
citing its decision in the titanium dioxide case discussed above. The Court
emphasised its view that in the absence of such a requirement, the powers
of the Community legislature would be practically unlimited. It observed
that national laws often differ regarding the conditions under which the
activities they regulate may be carried on, and this impacts directly or indirectly on the conditions of competition for the undertakings concerned. In
the Court's view it followed that to interpret arts. 95, 47(2) and 55 of the
Treaty as meaning that the Community legislature could rely on those
articles with a view to eliminating the smallest distortions of competition
would be incompatible with the principle that the powers of the
Community are those specifically conferred on it.

The Court then examined whether the Directive did actually contribute to
eliminating appreciable distortions of competition. It did accept that the fact
that sponsorship is prohibited in some Member States and authorised in
others could give rise, in particular, to certain sports events being relocated,
with considerable repercussions on the conditions of competition for undertakings associated with such events. However, it held that such distortions,
which could be a basis for recourse to art. 95 of the Treaty in order to prohibit certain forms of sponsorship, were not such as to justify the use of that

legal basis for an outright prohibition of advertising of the kind imposed by the Directive. The point was made rather more bluntly by AG Fennelly. He suggested that art. 95 was not an appropriate legal basis for a measure whose effect on the harmonisation of the conditions of competition was merely incidental, and concluded that Community rules whose sole effect in a given sector was to prohibit the relevant business activity could not be said to equalise conditions of competition in that sector, whatever may be their effects on competition in some related field.

The Directive there at issue has subsequently been replaced by EP and Council Directive 2003/33 which is limited to prohibiting tobacco advertising in the press, in radio broadcasting, in information society services and through tobacco-related sponsorship. It may also be observed in this sector that in Case C-491/01 the Court upheld the validity of Directive 2001/37 (OJ 2001 L194/26) in so far as it laid down maximum tar, nicotine and carbon monoxide yields for cigarettes and in so far as it requires packets of cigarettes and other tobacco products to display a prominent warning, on the basis in particular that unlike the tobacco advertising directive, it contained a provision guaranteeing the free movement of products complying with its requirements. Furthermore, in Cases C-210/03 and C-434/02 it upheld the total ban in that Directive on the marketing of tobacco products for oral use.

Leaving on one side the scope of internal market legislation under art. 95, while the Commission may perhaps claim some responsibility for extending the bounds of Community competence by proposing the use of general Treaty provisions such as Articles 94 and 308, it must be emphasized that those provisions do require unanimity in the Council. So it can hardly be claimed that the Commission is solely responsible for expanding Community competence and thereby expanding its own power.

c) Delegated powers

There is a further important provision relating to the Commission's legislative powers in art. 202 of the EC Treaty, which was introduced by Article 10 of the Single European Act. This sets a framework within which the Council may delegate powers to the Commission. The Council has, of course, been delegating powers to the Commission from the outset. The best known example is the system of management committees used in the common organisation of agricultural markets. Management committees enable the Council to delegate discretionary powers to the Commission with a requirement to consult a committee representing the interests of the Member States (see, for example, art. 25 of Council Regulation 1784/2003 on the market in cereals). This pattern has been followed in other areas, but with variations, so that there are nowadays many different committee procedures, described fully in chapter 8. The committees must either be consulted by the Commission, have their approval sought by the Commission or must be informed by the Commission in particular circumstances. The basic aim of Article 10 of the SEA was to provide an overall framework for such delegation of powers and for the committees to which the Commission should refer its proposals. This would prevent the creation of ad hoc systems, each marginally different from the other. Article 10 required the structure of such 'comitology' to be laid down in advance by the Council, so that the system used in any particular legislation follows one of the patterns laid down beforehand (Nicoll 1987).

The initial Council Decision (87/373), adopted in 1987, has been replaced by Council Decision 1999/468. This provides for just three basic types of committee procedure: an advisory committee, a management committee and a regulatory committee. The advisory committee is just that: the Commission may seek the opinion of the committee and its members, but is not bound by it. The management committee system is mainly used in the agriculture sector. The Commission presents to the committee a draft of the measures it wishes to take, but it is able to implement its measures immediately even if the committee votes against them, subject to the possibility of the Council taking a different decision within a fixed time limit. Under the third procedure, the regulatory committee, the Commission may only introduce its measures if the committee has approved them. If the committee does not approve, the Commission is required to refer the matter to the Council, which again has a time limit within which to act. Only if the Council does not act within that time limit may the Commission adopt its own measures.

When the proposal for the 1987 Council Decision came before the European Parliament in October 1986, the Parliament decided by a majority of 235 to 36 to reject that part of the proposal allowing for regulatory committees. The Parliament took the view that the existence of such committees diminished its own power of control over the Commission. Following the enactment of the Decision, Parliament sought its annulment, but was held not to have *locus standi* (Case 302/87). Parliament's rules of procedure require amendments to proposed legislation on the internal market to foresee advisory committees, with management committees acceptable at second reading. This view was shared by the Commission. In its opinion of 21 October 1990 on amendments to the Treaty, the Commission argued that 'as far as delegation of powers to the Commission is concerned, efficiency demands that both the letter and the spirit of the Single European Act be fully applied in practice... only two formulas should be allowed under the Treaty; the advisory committee and the management committee' (COM(90)600 final).

The important point of principle in this seemingly recondite issue is that the European Parliament is not involved in any of the committees, which are composed of Member State representatives. These are usually the same people who sit in the Council working groups which prepare the Council decision. Since the Parliament's ultimate power of control lies in censuring the Commission, the committee procedure offering maximum power to the Commission simultaneously offers the largest degree of Parliamentary control and censure. Needless to say, the Council takes the opposite view, opting frequently for the regulatory committee. However, under the 1999 Decision, the European Parliament must be informed by the Commission of committee proceedings on a regular basis. To that end, it must receive agendas for committee meetings, and copies of draft measures submitted to the committees for the implementation of instruments adopted by the co-decision procedure. Furthermore, in the specific context of the regulatory procedure, if the European Parliament considers that a proposal submitted by the Commission pursuant to a basic instrument adopted in accordance with the co-decision procedure exceeds the implementing powers provided for in that basic instrument, it shall inform the Council of its position, and the Council should only continue if it thinks it appropriate. In any event, if the European Parliament indicates, in a Resolution setting out the grounds on which it is based, that draft implementing measures, the adoption of which is contemplated and which have been submitted to a committee pursuant to a basic instrument adopted under the co-decision procedure, would exceed the implementing powers provided for in the basic instrument, the Commission must re-examine the draft measures. Taking the Resolution into account and within the time-limits of the procedure under way, the Commission may submit new draft measures to the committee, continue with the procedure or submit a proposal to the European Parliament and the Council on the basis of the Treaty.

The Commission must also inform the European Parliament and the committee of the action which it intends to take on the Resolution of the European Parliament and of its reasons for doing so.

In practice, the Council was not willing, notwithstanding the scrutiny and supervision afforded by the comitology, to limit itself to the adoption of the framework legislation for the achievement of the internal market by the end of 1992, and leave it to the Commission to enact the detailed implementation. It was, however, prepared to do so in the areas of agriculture, the customs tariff, and the updating of technical standards. In the Commission's submission to the Council in 1991 on the operation of the comitology system decision, the Commission commented bitterly on the fact that despite the commitment to speed and efficiency in implementing the internal market, the Council had been extremely reluctant to accept the Commission's adherence to the principle of advisory committees for all internal market matters.

d) Original legislative powers

Whatever express legislative powers the Commission may have enjoyed under the now-defunct ECSC Treaty, it is commonly held that under the EC Treaty 'the Commission proposes but the Council disposes.' Like most generalisations, it was subject to exceptions, only one of which remains in force. This is art. 86(3) of the EC Treaty, which relates essentially to the application of the competition rules to public undertakings. It was nevertheless perhaps belief in the generalisation that led the United Kingdom to challenge Commission Directive 80/723 on the transparency of financial relations between Member States and public undertakings, issued under Article 86(3)EC, on the basis that under the scheme of the Treaty only the Council could issue directives containing general legislative provisions imposing new obligations on Member States. The aim of Commission directives, it was argued, was merely to deal with a specific situation in one or more Member State. This argument did not find favour with the European Court. In its judgment in Cases 188–190/80 [1982], the European Court held that the limits of the powers conferred on the Commission by a specific provision of the Treaty are to be inferred not from a general principle but from the wording of the provision in question, analysed in the light of its purpose. The purpose, in this case, was found to be to enable the Commission to perform effectively the duty of surveillance imposed upon it (i.e. with regard to the payment of unlawful State aids, which it treated as a matter of competition policy in the structure of the EC Treaty).

A similar broad view of the Commission's powers under Article 86(3), which were stated to be 'normative', i.e. law-creating, was taken in Case C-202/88 *France v. Commission* with regard to a Commission Directive on competition in the market in telecommunication terminals. It was stated that the possibility that there might be Council legislation under other provisions did not restrict the powers of the Commission under Article 86(3). On the other hand, in interpreting that provision, the Court held that while the Commission could require *exclusive* rights of importation etc. to be abolished, it could not require *special* rights to be abolished in the absence of further precision, and could not use Article 86(3) to deal with the unilateral conduct of undertakings.

Even where the only express power of the Commission is to make proposals there have also been interesting developments. Specific examples may be cited from the agricultural sector in situations where the Council failed to do what it should have done. One illustration relates to the common fisheries policy. Under Article 102 of the 1972 Act of Accession, the Council should have adopted legislation 'with a view to ensuring protection of the fishing grounds and conservation of the biological resources of the sea' by the end of 1978. Such legislation was not in fact adopted until 1983. In the meantime, the Commission had put forward proposals for a common fisheries policy suggesting total allowable catches (TACs), and amended these proposals from time to time. It would appear that the Commission was prepared to authorise national catch quotas which followed the proposals, as is evidenced by Case 287/81. Eventually, the Council issued a series of Decisions on fisheries activities in waters under the sovereignty or jurisdiction of Member States. These required Member States to observe the TACs laid down in the Commission's proposals, as e.g. in Council Decision 82/739. More contentious, however, was the fact that the Commission itself published a declaration (OJ 1981 C 224/1) to the effect that it considered its proposals to be legally binding on the Member States. Whatever the view of the Council in the matter, no published retraction of this declaration was ever made.

The ramifications of accepting that Commission proposals may eventually become legally binding in themselves are immense, but the tactic did not meet with the approval of the Court. The European Court had to consider the matter in Case 346/85 *United Kingdom v. Commission*. This arose from the Commission's refusal to allow the Agricultural Guidance and Guarantee Fund to meet United Kingdom expenditure in relation to fisheries activities not in accordance with the Commission's TAC proposals. In its judgment, the Court stated categorically that unilateral proposals by the Commission were not rules of Community law. It emphasised, in particular, that legislation with financial consequences should be certain and of foreseeable application. A similar view was taken in Case C-303/90 *France v. Commission* where the Commission appeared to impose obligations on Member States by a 'Code of Conduct' on the implementation of a Council Regulation. It was found that the Code went beyond what was required by the Regulation, and that in any event the Regulation did not confer implementing powers on the Commission. More recently, it was found in Case C-

233/02 *France v. Commission* that Guidelines on regulatory cooperation agreed between the Commission and the US authorities were not legally binding.

Matters did, however, go somewhat further in the cereals market. Under the system used until 1992, prices had to be set for each marketing year by the Council, and 1985 saw the basic prices being set by legislation adopted unilaterally by the Commission. Under Article 37(2)EC, legislation on the common organisation of agricultural markets is adopted by the Council acting by a qualified majority on a proposal from the Commission. It was further provided at the time in Article 3 of Council Regulation 2727/75 on the common organisation of the market in cereals, that the target and intervention prices for each marketing year should be fixed by the Council under the same procedure. In 1985 the Commission proposed for the first time that some of these prices expressed in ECUs should actually be reduced. The Council was unable to reach agreement on the matter by the appropriate date. This was not unusual. Indeed, it was often necessary to 'stop the clock' when prices were likely to rise or stay the same, which meant paying the previous year's prices on a temporary basis. But much greater difficulty arose if the aim was to reduce the guaranteed prices. If the previous year's prices were to be paid in such a case, producers would be paid an excess which would have to be recovered (with considerable administrative rigmarole) once the new lower prices were agreed. The matter came to a head in June 1985. Under the version of Article 3 of Regulation 2727/75 then in force, the intervention prices valid on 1 June in Greece, Italy and certain regions of France had to be adjusted in the light of the intervention prices fixed for August. This was the first month of the new marketing year. In the light of the Council's failure to act on its proposals, on 20 June 1985 the Commission adopted Decision 85/309 on 'precautionary measures' with regard to the buying-in of cereals in Greece, Italy and those regions of France, requiring the Member States to reduce certain of the previous year's prices by 1.8 per cent. This was replaced by Commission Regulation 2124/85 adopted on 26 July 1985 (i.e. just before the start of the marketing year) applying general 'precautionary measures'. These fixed lower prices in the cereals sector other than for durum wheat. In October 1985, the Commission exercised its express power under Article 13 of Regulation 2727/75 to fix import levies on cereals, adopting in Regulation 2956/85 levies calculated from the basic prices it itself had enacted. Interestingly, no Council legislation was adopted in the matter until Council Regulation 1584/86 of 23 May 1986 fixing the cereal prices for the 1986-87 marketing year. This expressly continued some of the prices fixed by the Commission.

In adopting its 'precautionary measures' the Commission declared in the recitals to the Decision and to the subsequent Regulation that it was acting under Articles 10 and 211 of the EC Treaty. Article 10 requires the Member States to take all appropriate measures to ensure fulfilment of the obligations resulting from the action taken by the institutions of the Community, to facilitate the achievement of the Community's tasks, and to abstain from any measure which could jeopardise the attainment of the objectives of the Treaty. Article 211 empowers the Commission, inter alia, to ensure that the provisions of the Treaty and the measures taken by the institutions pursuant thereto are applied. This is the 'guardian of the Treaty' function. Presumably, therefore, the rationale of the Commission's action was that the failure of Member States in Council to fix the cereal prices in due time constituted a breach of their duties under Article 10 and that the Commission's duty under Article 211 was to ensure the application of the common organisation of the market in cereals. That no direct challenge to the Commission's legislation was mounted either by the Council as such or by any of the Member States is particularly remarkable.

Certainly, the cereals price issue is not the only case of the use of this technique. Subsequent examples of the same technique may be found for example, in the sheepmeat market in 1990. Likewise, in 1991 in the market in oils and fats a Council Regulation gave the Commission express power to act if the Council had not taken a Decision by a specific date. However, the problem has not in practice arisen subsequently: during the 1990s regulations were adopted which largely fixed prices for a series of years, and the question does not arise under the single payments system introduced by Council Regulation 1782/2003.

Inaction on the part of the Member States in agricultural price-fixing cases forms an interesting contrast to the alacrity with which Germany, France, the Netherlands, Denmark and the United Kingdom sought the annulment of Commission Decision 85/381. This established a prior communication and consultation procedure with regard to migration policies concerning nationals of non-Member States which the Commission claimed to be able to issue under the original Article 118 of the EC Treaty (see, for example, Case 281/85). It could well be that in the price-fixing case the Commission's legislation provided a mutually convenient solution to a difficult political problem. Nevertheless, if the legal basis for the Commission's action does indeed authorise the enactment of legislation by the Commission in circumstances where the Council should have acted but has not done so, the potential scope for such Commission legislation is enormous. It might, on the other hand, be argued that such legislative power should be restricted to matters such as the common organisation of agricultural markets which are entirely subject to rules of Community law.

In any event it is clear from Case 63/83 *R v. Kirk* that where the Council's failure to act does not leave a legal vacuum but leads to the cessation of a derogation from the basic rules contained in other Council legislation (in this case the principle of equal access to the waters of other Member States), the Commission has no power to breach that Council legislation.

Enforcement of Community Law

a) Against other institutions

While the Commission has express powers to take enforcement proceedings against Member States and, in specific circumstances, against individuals, it may be suggested that on occasion the Commission has taken legal action against another Community institution not so much to protect or increase its own powers as to deal with what it has perceived to be an infringement of Community law by that other institution. A couple of recent examples may be given. In Case C-11/00 *Commission v. ECB*, the Commission sought the annulment of the ECB's Decision on fraud prevention, which had been adopted on the basis of the view held by the ECB that its independence under the EC Treaty meant that it was not subject to EP and Council Regulation 1073/1999 concerning investigations conducted by the European Anti-Fraud Office (OLAF). The Court in fact held that while the ECB had independence in relation to the exercise of its specific powers, that did not have the consequence of separating it entirely from the EC and exempting it from every rule of Community law; in the result it was found that the adoption by the ECB of its own Decision infringed the general Regulation on OLAF investigations.

Similarly, in the context of the Stability and Growth Pact which applies in the eurozone, the Commission brought Case C-27/04 *Commission v. Council* to seek, inter alia, the annulment of Council 'conclusions' which held the excessive deficits procedures against France and Germany in abeyance. While the Court accepted that the procedure might de facto be held in abeyance if there was not a majority in the Council to take the matter forward, it held that there was no power under the Treaty provisions on the excessive deficits procedure or under the secondary legislation on the Stability and Growth Pact formally to decide to hold the matter in abeyance. The Court therefore annulled the Council's conclusions.

b) *Against Member States*

Under Article 226 of the EC Treaty, if the Commission considers that a Member State has failed to fulfil an obligation under the Treaty, it shall deliver a reasoned opinion on the matter after giving the State concerned the opportunity to submit its observations, and if the State concerned does not comply with the opinion within the period laid down by the Commission, it may bring the matter before the Court of Justice. As the EC Treaty was originally drafted, there were two significant differences from Article 88 of the ECSC Treaty. Under the ECSC Treaty the Commission itself could find a Member State in breach, subject to review by the Court. Under the EC Treaty it is the Court which determines whether there is a breach. Further, while the ECSC Treaty provided from the outset for financial penalties to be imposed (though this never seems to have occurred), the original version of the EC Treaty did not.

The Commission's powers in this respect have been changed by virtue of the amendment introduced by the Maastricht Treaty in the shape of what is now art. 228 of the EC Treaty. This provides a supplementary procedure if a Member State has breached the Treaty and has not taken the necessary measures to comply with a judgment of the Court of Justice. In such a case, the Commission shall, after giving that State the opportunity to submit its observations, issue a second reasoned opinion specifying the points on which the Member State concerned has not complied with the judgment of the Court of Justice. If the Member State concerned fails to take the necessary measures to comply with the Court's judgment within the time-limit laid down by the Commission, the latter may bring the case for a second time before the Court of Justice. In so doing it must specify the amount of lump sum or penalty payment which it considers appropriate for the Member State concerned to pay. If the Court of Justice finds that the Member State concerned has not complied with its judgment it may impose a lump sum or penalty payment. There could hardly be a starker illustration of the primacy of Community law. This power was first exercised in Case C-387/97 *Commission v. Greece*. Initially, the sanctions only involved penalty payments running from the date of the second judgment, which, it may be suggested, is hardly a great deterrent. However, in his Opinions in Case C-304/02 *Commission v. France* delivered on 29 April 2004 and 18 November 2004, AG Geelhoed suggested that even where the Commission only asks for such a penalty, the Court should have power to go beyond what the Commission has requested, and impose a lump-sum payment.

This approach was followed by the Court in its judgment given on 12 July 2005. The case involved the failure by France to comply with a judgment given against it in 1991 in Case C-64/88 *Commission v. France* finding that it had failed to carry out controls ensuring compliance with technical Community measures for the conservation of fishery resources. The Court imposed a periodic penalty payment at the rate suggested by the Commission, albeit on a half-yearly rather than a daily basis, but added a lump sum penalty of 20 million euros 'in the light of the fact that the breach of obligations has persisted for a long period since the judgment which established it and of the public and private interests at issue'. The Commission welcomed this judgment 'as it will undoubtedly strengthen the Commission's efforts at ensuring the effective application of Community law in all policy areas' (Press release IP/05/917), but the judgment also illustrates that the Court is in no way bound by the penalties suggested by the Commission.

In any event, it has long been the case that the Commission itself may impose indirect financial sanctions where Community money is involved. Cases 15 and 16/76 *France v. Commission* involved a Community aid for the distillation of table wine. The French government had taken the view that the aids payable under Council Regulation 766/72 were inadequate, and supplemented them with national aids. The Commission then initiated the procedure under Article 226 EC against France in relation to the breach of a Treaty obligation involved in the payment of national aids, but did not pursue the matter when the aids ceased to be paid. However, when it came to the discharge of the EAGGF accounts, the Commission refused to accept liability for the amounts of aid payable under Community law, on the grounds that the national measures had had the effect of distorting the distillation operation by extending it. Before the Court, the French government claimed that the EAGGF should meet the proportion of the aid granted which corresponded to the rates fixed by Community rules. But it was held that it was impossible to ascertain the extent of the effect of the combined national and Community aid due to one or other component part and that it was impossible to establish with certainty what quantities of wine would have been distilled in France if the national measure had not been adopted. With regard to the discontinuance of the proceedings under Article 226, the Court pointed out that this did not constitute recognition that the contested conduct was lawful. So, by adding a national element to a Community aid, France found itself having to finance the whole amount. On the other hand, if a Member State does not add its own national aid, but pays a Community aid to recipients falling outside its scope, the Member State will not necessarily lose the whole aid. In Case 49/83 *Luxembourg v Commission* it was held that where the Member State had acted in good faith it might still obtain reimbursement to the extent that it could prove that the aid was properly paid – but the burden is on the Member State.

In the context of state aids, recourse by the Commission to Article 226 is not necessary. The Commission has power under Article 88(2) itself to decide that a Member State should abolish or alter an aid. Moreover, the Commission may go to the Court directly if the Member State does not comply. The use of art. 226 is also excluded in the context of the excessive deficits procedure under art. 104 of the EC Treaty. Art. 104 does however empower the Council, acting on the basis of a Commission recommendation, to impose specific sanctions on Member States which fail to comply with measures for deficit reduction judged necessary by the Council.

Article 226 proceedings have not always been automatic. The Commission enjoys a certain discretion under Article 226 if a Member State appears to be in breach of its Treaty obligations. However, it would appear from the statistics in the annual Reports to the European Parliament on Commission monitoring of the application of Community law that a change in attitude occurred in 1979. Before then, a positive decision was required to take action. Since 1979, it seems that a positive decision is required not to take action. Be that as it may, a very small proportion of Article 226 letters give rise to cases before the Court.

Any legal challenge to the Commission's exercise of its discretion in this matter is very difficult to mount directly, although indirect remedies may be available. Article 226 does not require the Commission to issue a binding decision. Rather it requires it to issue a reasoned opinion to a defaulting Member State, an act which has no binding effect under Article 249 of the EC Treaty and which is not susceptible to judicial review under Article 230. The conclusion drawn from this in Case 48/65 *Lutticke v. Commission*, was that since the opinion itself could not be challenged, a letter sent to a complainant refusing to issue such an opinion could not be subject to an action for annulment either, although it did constitute a 'definition of position' so as to block an action for failure to act under Article 232 of the EC Treaty. If the Member State does not comply with the opinion, the Commission is then empowered, but not required, to bring the matter before the Court. Hence the Commission has a discretion which does not appear to be susceptible to direct challenge, although a complainant Member State could bring an action against the defaulting State in its own name once the Commission had issued an opinion, or has failed to do so within three months, under the terms of Article 227, as in Case 141/78 *France v. UK*. A Member State can act under this provision even where the Commission agrees with the approach of the State against which a complaint has been made, as in Case C-388/95 *Belgium v Spain*.

On the other hand, indirect challenge to the exercise of the Commission's discretion may be mounted by invoking the direct effect (if such there be) of the relevant Community rule before a national court against the defaulting Member State or one of its agencies. The practical result may well be that the validity of national legislation is put indirectly at issue before the European Court. The Court recognised this possibility of private policing in the leading case of *Van Gend en Loos* itself, stating that 'the vigilance of individuals to protect their rights amounts to an effective supervision in addition to the

supervision entrusted by [Articles 226 and 227 of the EC Treaty] to the diligence of the Commission and the Member States'. One effect of this has been
to prevent a settlement of enforcement proceedings brought by the
Commission against a Member State from being final, if private interests are
involved. In Joined Cases 80 and 81/77 *Ramel v. Receveur des Douanes*, French
wine importers were able to invoke the direct effect of the relevant provisions of EC law to challenge levies imposed by the French authorities on
imports of Italian wine in 1975-76. They did so before the French courts and
thence on a reference for a preliminary ruling before the European Court
(Article 234), even though the Commission had withdrawn an action it had
brought against France under Article 226 alleging that the imposition of
such levies was in breach of France's Treaty obligations. Further, in Joined
Cases 142 and 143/80 *Italian Finance Administration v. Essevi* it was recognised that an individual may invoke the direct effects of a Treaty obligation
even against conduct of a Member State which the Commission had
regarded as permissible in its opinion given under Article 226.

   Indirect challenge may also be mounted through an action for damages.
In Case 14/78 *Denkavit v. Commission*, it was alleged that the Commission
had failed to act sufficiently urgently to require the abolition of certain
Italian measures, thereby incurring liability to the applicants. The Court in
its judgement was apparently willing to accept that if there was no justification for the Commission's conduct, and this improperly contributed to the
maintenance of an obstacle to trade between Member States, then the
Commission could incur liability. It was, however, held that in the circumstances, since the Italian measures related to additives in animal feeding-
stuffs, it was reasonable for the Commission to wait to receive the respective
reports of a standing committee and of a scientific committee on animal
feeding-stuffs.

c) *Against individuals*

   The power of the Commission to enforce Community law against individuals relates essentially to competition law. Again there are differences
between the Treaties, since the Commission's powers in this area were
trimmed after the initial years' experience of the ECSC. Unlike Articles 65
and 66 of the ECSC Treaty, which clearly gave the Commission sole jurisdiction to apply their rules, the EC Treaty does not confer on the
Commission exclusive powers with regard to the competition rules it contains. Rather, Article 83 of the Treaty provides for the Council to take
measures to give effect to the substantive rules contained in Articles 81 and
82. The point, *inter alia*, was to define the functions of the Commission. Until
such measures were adopted, EC competition rules were to be enforced
either by the national authorities, under Article 84, or by the Commission 'in
cooperation with the competent authorities of the Member States' under
Article 85. The Commission's powers to enforce the competition rules alone
were originally conferred on it by Council Regulation 17/62. Although this
Regulation conferred exclusive power on the Commission to grant exemptions under Article 81(3), it otherwise maintained the competence of the
national authorities to apply the prohibitions in Article 81(1) and Article 82
unless proceedings have been initiated before the Commission itself (under

Article 9 (3)). Furthermore, the regulation was not universal in its application. Council Regulation 141/62 excluded transport from its scope, and although specific rules for road, rail and inland waterway transport were enacted in 1968, air and sea transport remained excluded until power to enforce the competition rules in the context of sea transport was eventually conferred on the Commission by Regulation 4056/86. This was done with regard to air transport by Regulations 3975 and 3976/87.

Thus, in its 1980 *Report on Competition Policy*, the Commission noted that when it was faced with a complaint from a Danish airline, Sterling Airways, alleging abuse of a dominant position by Scandinavian Airlines System (SAS), it had to fall back on the system envisaged in Article 85 of the EC Treaty and seek the cooperation of the competent national authorities in order to be able to investigate the complaint (Commission 1980, 94-96).

Of greater practical importance is the fact that it became clearly established by the European Court that the prohibitions contained in Articles 81(1) and 82 of the EC Treaty produce direct effects, and hence may be invoked by parties to litigation before national courts irrespective of the terms of the implementing Regulations (see Cases 12/73 and the second *Brasserie de Haecht* case). Indeed, much of the case-law on competition rules has evolved in the context of questions referred for preliminary rulings by national courts rather than in direct actions seeking the annulment of Commission competition decisions.

Nevertheless, the role of the Commission remains of fundamental importance for those subject to general EC competition rules. The Commission is the only body which directly enforces those rules at the Community level in the interests of Community policy, rather than national policy or private interest. Until Regulation 17 was replaced by Regulation 1/2003, it was the only body which could grant exemptions under Article 81(3), and it may, under Article 23 of Regulation 1/2003, impose fines of up to 10 per cent of turnover. The example might be taken of the fine of 75 million ECU imposed on the packaging firm Tetra Pak for an abuse of a dominant position (Commission Decision of 24 July 1991).

Be that as it may, in 1992 the Commission indicated both in 'soft' legislation and in its formal decisions, a desire for a greater role to be played by national courts and authorities in the application of Community competition rules. In December 1992, the Commission adopted a Notice on the Cooperation between national courts and the Commission in applying Articles 81 and 82 of the EC Treaty (OJ 1993 C39/6). For the most part the Notice appeared simply to codify the case-law of the European Court on the matter, while indicating the remedies available at the national level (for example, damages) which the Commission itself could not give. On the other hand, the Commission did offer, in the context of Articles 81 and 82, to advise any national court which wished to consult it, as to its 'customary practice' in relation to the Community law at issue (Commission 1992 para 38). This might appear to create an unofficial system of references for preliminary rulings parallel to that created by Article 234 of the EC Treaty in relation to the European Court, though the Commission did emphasise that the answers it gives are not binding on the courts which requested them (ibid para 39). The clear underlying aim, justifiable within the framework of subsidiarity now anchored in Article 5 of the EC Treaty, is that the Commission should be able to concentrate on cases of Community interest.

In the context of decisions given in individual competition cases, in November 1992, in the *SACEM* case, which involved complaints about fees charged by a French copyright agency, the Commission made public (in *Agence Europe* No 5868, 30 November 1992) the fact that it had referred the matter to the French competition authorities to deal with. The basis for the referral was that the effects of any abuse of a dominant position in that case would mainly be felt on French territory.

The logical conclusion of this process was the replacement of Regulation 17 by Regulation 1/2003, which fully enables national authorities to apply the EC competition rules set out in arts. 81 and 82 of the EC Treaty, and allows them as well as the Commission to grant exemptions under art. 81(3). The Commission therefore no longer has an exclusive competence with regard to the administration of the general competition rules under art. 81 and 82.

The area of mergers is somewhat different. Here, it seems an exclusive competence has been created and maintained by secondary legislation, in the guise of the Commission's exclusive jurisdiction to administer the system. The EC Treaty was silent on mergers, although certain types of takeover were eventually held to constitute an abuse of a dominant position (see Case 6/72). More generally, in 1990, a system of merger control under the EC Treaty came into operation by virtue of Council Regulation 4064/89, which has now been replaced by Council Regulation 139/2004. Under this legislation, notably Articles 1 and 21, the EC Commission has exclusive competence with regard to mergers with a 'Community dimension' and Member States are in principle prohibited from applying their national legislation. 'Concentrations with a Community dimension' are defined as those where the aggregate worldwide turnover of all the undertakings concerned is more than €5 billion and the aggregate Community-wide turnover of at least two of the undertakings involved is more than €250 million, unless each of the undertakings concerned achieves more than two-thirds of its aggregate Community-wide turnover in one Member State. In the present context, Article 21(2) of the Regulation grants the Commission sole jurisdiction, and art. 21(3) prohibits Member States from applying their national legislation to such 'concentrations'. Member States are, however, entitled under Article 21(4) to protect legitimate interests, defined as including 'plurality of the media', by measures compatible with the general principles and other provisions of Community law.

Furthermore, by virtue of Article 9 of the Regulation, the Commission may refer a notified concentration to the national authorities with a view to the application of national competition law. It may do so where it considers that a concentration threatens to affect significantly competition within that Member State's market, where that market presents all the characteristics of a distinct market, whether or not it constitutes a substantial part of the common market. The reason for this is that in the context of the EC's internal market, the area of a particular State is not necessarily a relevant criterion in determining whether competition is adversely affected. Conversely, however, under Article 22 of the Regulation, a Member State may request the Commission to take a decision with regard to a concentration which has no

Community dimension. It may do so where such concentration threatens to affect significantly competition in the Member State concerned and where such concentration affects trade between Member States. It would appear that Belgium referred the 1992 takeover of Dan-Air by British Airways to the Commission under this provision (*Agence Europe* No. 5880 16 December 1992).

Duties on the Commission

That the Commission's status as guardian of the Treaties may lead to the imposition of duties as well as the conferment of powers in its relationships with the Member States has been clearly shown in Case C-2/88 Imm. *Zwartveld*. This involved a request by a Dutch court for the European Court to give it assistance in a case before it. The judge was investigating an alleged fraud involving breaches of the Community fish quota system and the fish marketing system and claimed that in order to proceed with his investigation he needed access to certain reports prepared by Commission officials and required those officials to give evidence before him.

The Commission refused to transmit the reports to him. He then sent a request to the European Court asking it to order the Commission to produce the documents and to order the inspectors to give evidence. The Dutch judge was obviously aware of the difficulty of finding a legal base on which the European Court could act and invoked Articles 1 and 12 of the Protocol on the Privileges and Immunities of the European Communities. Article 1 provides that the property and assets of the Communities shall not be subject to legal measures of constraint without the authorisation of the Court of Justice, while Article 12 provides, among other things, that the immunity of Community officials with regard to acts performed by them in their official capacity is subject to the jurisdiction of the Court in disputes between the Communities and their officials and other servants. The judge also invoked the Council of Europe conventions on assistance in criminal matters, arguing that, although the Community itself was not a party to these conventions, they should, nonetheless, be considered as an integral part of the Community legal order. This, in itself, indicates an interesting development of the Court's well-known case law holding that the principles underlying the European Convention on Human Rights are general principles which must be recognised within the Community context, even though the Community itself is not a party to the Human Rights Convention (see, for example, Case 36/75 at p. 1232).

The Commission's view was that the Dutch judge's application was inadmissible. It argued that the Treaty must be regarded as exhaustive with regard to the remedies available before the European Court. It emphasised that the only way a national court could bring a matter before the European Court was by a reference for preliminary ruling under Article 234 of the EC Treaty, but in this case Article 234 was not relevant because the Dutch judge was not seeking the interpretation of a provision of Community law. The Commission also suggested that Articles 1 and 12 of the Protocol on the Privileges and Immunities of the European Communities were not relevant in this context.

Asked by the Court as to its substantive reasons for refusing to produce the reports or to allow its inspectors to give evidence, the Commission took the line that its inspectors' reports were internal documents which did not necessarily reflect the Commission's position. In addition, their communication could harm relations between the Commission and Member States in the delicate area of supervision of the fisheries market. In addition, the Commission invoked Article 2 of the Protocol on Privileges and Immunities, which provides that the archives of the Communities shall be inviolable, claiming that it contained no exemptions so that the Court had no power to lift that immunity.

With regard to the appearance of its inspectors as witnesses, the Commission indicated that it was neither willing to indicate the identity of its inspectors nor authorise them to give evidence, for it might affect their work and the degree to which they were able to exercise effective supervision on behalf of the Community. On the other hand, the Commission did declare its willingness to prepare a report for the Dutch judge to the extent that this would not compromise the Commission's supervisory functions. The Commission also indicated that it might designate specific officials to give evidence before the Dutch judge, but he in turn refused to accept this offer.

Following a procedure analogous to a reference for a preliminary ruling under Article 234 of the EC Treaty, the Court invited the Community institutions and the Member States to submit observations. The case aroused a great deal of interest with observations received from the Council, the Parliament, France, Germany, Greece, Ireland, Italy, The Netherlands, Portugal and the United Kingdom.

The Court's own reasoning began with a reference to the famous case of *Costa v. ENEL*, emphasising the passage in that judgment which held that the EC Treaty had created its own legal system which became an integral part of the legal systems of the Member States. The Court then referred to its judgment in *Les Verts v. European Parliament*. Here, despite the silence of the original version of Article 173 of the EEC Treaty which referred only to acts of the Council and the Commission and not to acts of the European Parliament, it had held that the general scheme of the Treaty was to make direct action available against all measures adopted by the institutions which are intended to have legal effect. Therefore, an action for annulment must lie against measures adopted by the Parliament intended to have legal effects with regard to third parties, a view subsequently incorporated into the text of the current art. 230 (into which the old art. 173 has evolved). It pointed out that the EC is a Community based on law. Neither the Member States nor the institutions might escape from judicial control over the conformity of their actions to the Treaty, which the Court described as a constitutional charter.

It argued that the relationship between the Member States and the Community institutions is governed, by virtue of Article 10 of the Treaty, by the principle of loyal cooperation. This not only requires that Member States take all necessary measures to guarantee the effective implementation of Community law, including the use of criminal penalties; the principle also requires the Community institutions to observe reciprocal duties of loyal cooperation with the Member States. The Court argued that this duty to cooperate was of particular importance in the relationship with national judicial authorities responsible for ensuring respect for Community law within the national legal order.

In the light of these arguments, the Court held that the privileges and immunities of the Communities were not absolute and that the specific privileges and immunities accorded to Community officials were for their own personal protection. The Protocol could not therefore be used to avoid the duty of loyal cooperation owed to national judicial authorities. The Court suggested that where a request for information or evidence came from a national judge investigating alleged breaches of Community law, it was the duty of any Community institution to give active support to the national judge by handing over the documents and authorising the officials to give evidence. This was particularly so in the case of the Commission, since it is entrusted with ensuring that the provisions of the Treaty are applied.

In seeking to establish its own authority to order the Commission to comply with this basic duty of loyal cooperation, the Court invoked Article 220 of the Treaty, under which the Court is required to ensure that in the interpretation and application of the Treaty the law is observed. The Court held that by virtue of this provision it must ensure that an appropriate remedy be available to enable it to exercise judicial control over the Commission's performance of its duty of loyal cooperation towards a national judicial authority. The Court therefore held that it had jurisdiction to examine whether the refusal to cooperate was justified in the light of a need to avoid interference with the operation and independence of the Communities. The Commission was ordered to deliver the documents requested by the Dutch judge and to authorise its officials to give evidence before him, unless it could show that there were imperative reasons relating to the operation or independence of the Communities which would justify the refusal to deliver the documents or to authorise the giving of the evidence. The duty of the Commission in this respect was thus clearly established.

Conclusion

The intention of this chapter has been to illustrate the pivotal role of the Commission in the Community legal framework, albeit one subject to the jurisdiction of the European Court (and, in competition matters, to that of the Court of First Instance). In some areas the Commission has made bold innovations, such as its 'precautionary' legislation on agricultural prices, though that path does not seem to have been followed further. It may also be suggested that it has adopted a policing role with regard to the activities of other EU institutions. On the other hand, the successful culmination of the Commission's policy to divest itself of some work in the competition area is evidence of caution, and perhaps even an example of the principle of subsidiarity being applied in practice. A more prosaic explanation, however, is that it reflects the fact that the Commission has not been given the level of staffing necessary to carry out its myriad supervisory duties. In the light of this, the fact that the European Court, through the doctrine of direct effect, has allowed the private policing by interested individuals of certain breaches of Community law which fall within the supervisory jurisdiction of the Commission, may be seen as offering a degree of relief to the Commission rather than as a challenge to its pivotal role as guardian of the Treaties.

Citations for Chapter 3

Commission Regulation 2124/85 (26 July 1985) on general 'precautionary measures'.

Commission Regulation 2956/85 (OJ 1985 L285/8) on import levies

Commission Regulation 3890/90 (OJ 1990 L367/154) on the sheepmeat market

Commission Directive 80/723 (OJ 1980 L195/35) on the transparency of financial relations between Member States and public undertakings

Commission Directive 85/309 (OJ 1986 L163/52) on 'precautionary measures' with regard to the buying in of cereals in Greece and elsewhere

Commission Decision 85/381 (OJ 1985 L217/25) on migration policies

Commission Decision of 24 July 1991 (OJ 1992 L72/1)

Commission Rules of Procedure (OJ 2000 L308/26)

Commission Press Release IP/05/917 of 12 July 2005 on the judgment in Case C-304/02 *Commission v. France*

Council Regulation 17/62 (OJ Sp.Ed. 1959-62 p 87) on the enforcement of competition rules

Council Regulation 141/62 (OJ Sp.Ed. 1959-62 p 291)

Council Regulation 2727/75 Articles 25-27 (OJ 1975 L281-2/1) on the organisation of the market in cereals

Council Regulation 1584/86 (OJ 1986 L139/41)

Council Regulation 4064/89 (OJ 1989 L395/1) on merger control

Council Regulation 1720/91, Art.4 (OJ 1991 L162/27) on the market in oils and fats

Council Regulation 1073/1999 (OJ 1999 L136/1) concerning investigations conducted by the European Anti-Fraud Office (OLAF)

Council Regulation 1/2003 (OJ 2003 L1/1) on the implementation of the rules on competition

Council Regulation 1782/2003 (OJ 2003 L2709/1) on the single payments system

Council Regulation 139/2004 (OJ 2004 L24/1) on mergers

Council Directive 85/374 (OJ 1985 L210/29) on liability for defective products

Council Directive 85/649 (OJ 1985 L382/228) on the hormone content of meat

Council Directive 86/113 (OJ 1986 L95/45) on the treatment of battery poultry

Council Directive 87/102 (OJ 1987 L42/48) on consumer credit

Council Directive 88/314 (OJ 1988 L142/19) on consumer protection in the indication of the prices on non-food products

Council Directive 88/315 (OJ 1988 L142/23) on consumer protection in the indication of the prices on foodstuffs

Council Directive 91/156 (OJ 1991 L78/32) on waste

European Parliament and Council Directive 98/43 (OJ 1998 L213/9) on tobacco advertising and sponsorship

EP and Council Directive 2001/37 (OJ 2001 L194/26) on tobacco products

EP and Council Directive 2003/33 (OJ 2003 L152/16) prohibiting tobacco advertising in the press, in radio broadcasting, in information society services and through tobacco-related sponsorship

Council Decision 82/739 (OJ 1982 L312/17)

Council Decision 87/373 (OJ 1987 L197/33)

Council Decision 1999/468 (OJ 1999 L184/33)

Case 26/62 *Van Gend en Loos* [1963] ECR 1, 13

Case 6/64 *Costa v. ENEL* [1964] ECR 585

Case 48/65 *Lutticke v. Commission* [1966] ECR 19

Case 48/72 *Brasserie de Haecht* [1973] ECR 77

Case 6/72 *Continental Can v. Commission* [1973] ECR 215

Case 127/73 *BRT v. SABAM* [1974] ECR 51

Case 36/75 *Rutili* [1975] ECR 1219

Cases 15 and 16/76 *France v. Commission* [1979] ECR 321
Cases 80 and 81/77 *Ramel v. Reçevoir des Douanes* [1978] ECR 297
Case 14/78 *Denkavit v. Commission* [1978] ECR 2497, 2505
Case 141/78 *France v. UK* [1979] ECR 2923
Cases 142 and 143/80 *Italian Finance Administration v. Essevi* [1981] ECR 1413
Cases 188 to 190/80 *France, Italy and U.K. v. Commission* [1982] ECR 2545
Case 287/81 *Kerr* [1982] ECR 4053
Case 49/83 *Luxembourg v Commission* [1984] ECR 2931
Case 63/83 *R v. Kirk* [1984] ECR 2689
Case 294/83 *Les Verts v. European Parliament* [1986] ECR 1339
Case 281/85 *Germany v. Commission* [1987] ECR 3203
Case 346/85 *United Kingdom v. Commission* [1987] ECR 5197
Case 68/86 *UK v. Council* [1988] ECR 855
Case 131/86 *UK v. Council* [1988] ECR 905
Case 302/87 *European Parliament v. Council* [1988] ECR 5615
Case C-2/88 *Imm. Zwartveld* [1990] ECR I-3365
Case C-64/88 *Commission v. France* [1991] ECR I-2727
Case C-202/88 *France v. Commission* [1991] ECR I-1223
Case C-300/89 *Commission v. Council* [1991] ECR I-2867
Case C-2/90 *Commission v. Belgium* [1992] ECR I-4431
Case C-303/90 *France v. Commission* [1991] ECR I-5315
Case C-155/91 *Commission v. Council* [1993] ECR I-939
Case C-388/95 *Belgium v Spain* [2000] ECR I-3121
Case C-170/96 *Commission v. Council* [1998] ECR I-2763
Case C-387/97 *Commission v. Greece* [2000] ECR I-5047
Case C-376/98 *Germany v. EP and Council* [2000] ECR I-8419
Case C-11/00 *Commission v. ECB* (10 July 2003)
Case C-491/01 *R v. Secretary of State for Health ex p. BAT and Imperial Tobacco* (10 December 2002)
Case C-233/02 *France v. Commission* (23 March 2004)
Case C-304/02 *Commission v. France* (12 July 2005, Opinions of AG Geelhoed delivered on 29 April 2004 and 18 November 2004)
Cases C-210/03 and C-434/02 *R v. Secretary of State for Health ex p. Swedish Match* (14 December 2004)
Case C-27/04 *Commission v. Council* (13 July 2004)
Case C-91/05 *Commission v. Council* (commencement of proceedings 21 February 2005)

4. The Directorates General and the services: structures, functions and procedures

David Spence

Introduction

This book focuses on the various roles, responsibilities and functions of the Commission and its interinstitutional relationships. It is not a book about policy, but about procedures, despite the attention given to the specific Commission roles in second and third pillar matters, where the Commission has roles different from those in the first, Community pillar. The aim of this chapter is to provide an understanding of the structures and procedures typical to all Commission Directorates General (DGs), whatever the policy area. It provides an overview of the organisation of the Commission services and their working environment and reviews the process of decision-making within the Commission overall.

The Directorates General and other services

To begin with, the use of certain terms needs to be defined and explained. Depending on the context, the term 'European Commission' may refer to the College of Commissioners or more broadly to the whole organisation comprising the College and the administrative organisation that supports its work. The administrative organisation is often referred to as the Commission's 'services'. The services are divided into DGs with relatively stable operational responsibilities, temporary task forces, ad hoc groupings and specialist administrative services not large or important enough to form a Directorate General. As chapter 1 underlines, Commissioners have the support of *cabinets* to assist them and to link the work of the services to that of the College of Commissioners.

The whole edifice is supervised and coordinated by the Secretariat General, much in the way the Cabinet Office functions within the UK's domestic system or Prime Ministers' offices act in other countries. There is a fundamental difference, however. The Secretariat General of the Commission (SecGen) *does* supervise the work of the services and it does ensure a degree of coordination, but the degree to which it does this is not comparable to the coordinating function of the Cabinet Office, which both chairs inter-ministerial meetings and provides an arbitration function – stretching the term 'coordination' from mere information sharing, as in the Commission, to authoritative setting of policy. In the Commission this role is part of the inter-*cabinet* coordination described in chapter 1. The SecGen also manages formal relations between the Commission and the other EU institutions, ensuring for example that the relations between individual Directorates General and their institutional environment, whether the European Parliament or the Council and the Member States, is properly and efficiently coordinated at the most senior level. The role of the SecGen is considered exhaustively in chapter 2, but this chapter makes some further reference to its function as the nerve centre of the Commission as a whole and the summit of the system of Directorates General and services.

A former Secretary General once described the Commission's organisation as 'basically a structure of mini-Ministries called Directorates General' (Williamson 1991). The analogy with the organisation of national governments is useful, but only as a first approximation. Directorates General have responsibilities (competences in Commission terminology) for particular areas of European policy, but they are usually at the service of the real policy-entrepreneurs, the Commissioners and their *cabinets*. The latter interact with their opposite numbers in other *cabinets*, and with the political world outside the Commission, while administrators are supposedly problem-solvers, technicians in command of the facts to be used by their administrative and political hierarchy. Outwardly, DGs do resemble national ministries and their desire for independence gives rise to similar problems of coordination with rival/partner DGs to those faced within national civil services. However, the roles and responsibilities of DGs are not defined in the same way as national ministries. In the main, they are not executive organisations with direct links to the public. Although frequently the target of criticism as the epitome of bureaucracy, they are also not conventional machine bureaucracies with large staffs engaged in continuing routine administrative work. Instead, they are strategic nodes in politico-administrative networks working with and through national administrations as well as with other institutions and organisations at the European level.

Organisationally, DGs have identities of their own, some more clearly and permanently defined than others. They are not merely parts of a monolithic bureaucracy. Over time, an administrative structure has emerged where the 'vertical' DGs with responsibility for a given policy in terms both of legislative initiative and subsequent management have become semi-autonomous organisations with hierarchical management structures. The size and internal organisation of the DGs varies. DGs typically have between 400 and 900 staff, but there are many exceptions (e.g. DG Informatics which has over 2000). Large DGs are large because their area of responsibility falls for the most part into 'Community competence'. The smaller the DG or service, the more it is likely that the policy area is 'mixed competence', i.e. shared with Member States, or where executive functions and budgets are small. Development is an area of mixed competence, but the size of the budget for overseas development justifies the importance of the DG in functional terms, even if in terms of human resources, now that project management has been hived off to a separate DG in Brussels and to the Commission Delegations abroad, it remains remarkably small.[1]

Essentially, however, DGs do not implement policies. That is the role of national administrations. But they do devise policy, whether incremental (the consequence of previous policy) or innovative. Commission policy is a mix of policy entrepreneurship and routine graft from the bottom of the internal hierarchy of the DG.

The development of DGs since the beginning of the Prodi Commission in 1999 has been amusing. Before that, DGs were known by their chronological number rather than their functional title. A sentence such as 'if DG I is to do that, it must be sure to get DG IA and DG IB on board, and clearly needs to consult DG III before deciding a line to take' would have been fairly common. This was comfortable for insiders, for EU lobbyists and EU-nerds in general, but it completely foxed the public and probably contributed to its alienation from the 'faceless' (if not numberless) bureaucracy of Brussels. In order to fill the obvious gap between those in the know and those wishing to know, Prodi decided to move from the numbers system (which was in fact helpful in one sense, since it was not based on a linguistic definition) to a system where the titles of DGs resembled the titles of ministerial equivalents in Member States. But, this meant the titles varied according to the language used, a delineation further confused by the decision to shorten these often unwieldy names into code-like abbreviations. Some, like DG Fish, are fun, but others, such as DG Sanco, are mystifying. DG Sanco is the internal term for DG Health and Consumer Affairs, from the French 'Santé et Consommateurs' – a new alienation for English speakers and other language speakers for whom 'SANCO' means, of course, nothing! Table 3 on the following page juxtaposes the DGs with numbers and names used in the Santer, Prodi and Barroso Commissions, including the abbreviations used internally. The table is more than a guide to the DGs. It demonstrates the shifting administrative sands in the Commission's management apparatus.

The number of DGs and services has grown since the original 9 in 1958. There are currently 28 DGs and 12 services. In addition, there are 22 separate Community agencies, described in chapter 5. The considerable expansion of Community competence and the concomitant increase in the number of services explain why. On the other hand, some DGs have disappeared after a seemingly short run-in time. This has to do with attempts to streamline the organisation and thus enhance efficiency. To use the dreaded, but comfortable, abbreviations and numbers (readers are directed to table 3), DG EAC was created out of DGs X and XXII, and DG Enterprise (now renamed DG Enterprise and Industry) was created from the merger of DGs III and XXIII. Further, as chapter 14 describes in detail, the external relations DGs were rationalised. After DGs IA and IB were created, DG IB was almost immediately eliminated, and DG IA became DG External Relations (Relex). In addition, DG Enlargement was created by taking certain country desks from the previous DG IA and adding them to the previous Enlargement Task Force, then transforming that Task Force into a full-blown DG. Meanwhile, a truncated DG Trade was created as foreign political relations became a specific concern of DG Relex, the inheritor of the former DG IA, thus leaving trade almost back where it was when it was called DG I.

Table 3: *Directorates-General under the Santer, Prodi and Barroso Commissions*

Directorates-General Santer Commission	Number	Directorates-General Prodi Commission	Directorates-General Barroso Commission	Abbreviation
External Relations: Common Commercial Policy and Relations with North America, the Far East, Australia and New Zealand	DGI	Trade	Trade	DG TRADE
External Relations: Europe and the New Independent States, Common Foreign and Security Policy and External Missions	DG IA	External Relations	External Relations	DG RELEX
External Relations: Southern Mediterranean, Middle and Near East, Latin America, South and South-East Asia and North-South Co-operation	DG IB			
Economic and Financial Affairs	DG II	Economic and Financial Affairs	Economic and Financial Affairs	DG ECFIN
Industry	DG III	Enterprise[1]	Enterprise and Industry	DG ENTR
Competition	DG IV	Competition	Competition	DG COMP
Employment, Industrial Relations and Social Affairs	DG V	Employment and Social Affairs	(renamed) Employment, Social Affairs and Equal Opportunities	DG EMPL
Agriculture	DG VI	Agriculture	(renamed) Agriculture and Rural Development	DG AGRI
Transport	DG VII	Energy and Transport[2]	Energy and Transport[3]	DG TREN
Development	DG VIII	Development	Development	DG DEV
Personnel and Administration	DG IX	Personnel and Administration	Personnel and Administration	DG ADMIN

Table 3: *Directorates-General under the Santer, Prodi and Barroso Commissions (continuation 1)*

Directorates-General Santer Commission	Number	Directorates-General Prodi Commission	Directorates-General Barroso Commission	Abbreviation
Information, Communication, Culture, Audiovisual	DG X	Press and Communication[4]	Communication	DG COMM
Environment, Nuclear Safety and Civil Protection	DG XI	Environment[5]	Environment	DG ENV
Science, Research and Development	DG XII	Research	Research	DG RTD
Telecommunication, Information Market and Exploitation of Research	DG XIII	Information Society	Information Society and Media[6]	DG INFSO
Fisheries	DG XIV	Fisheries	Fisheries and Maritime Affairs[7]	DG FISH
Internal Market and Financial Services	DGXV	Internal Market	Internal Market and Services[8]	DG MARKT
Regional Policies and Cohesion	DG XVI	Regional Policy	Regional Policy	DG REGIO
Energy	DG XVII	See footnote 2		
Budgets	DG XIX	Budget	Budget	DG BUDG
Financial Control	DG XX	Financial Control[9]	Internal Audit Service[10]	IAS
Taxation and Customs Union	DG XXI	Taxation and Customs Union	Taxation and Customs Union	DG TAXUD
Education, Training and Youth	DG XXII	Education and Culture[11]	Education and Culture	DG EAC
Enterprise Policy, Distributive Trades, Tourism and Cooperatives	DG XXIII	See footnote 1		
Consumer Policy and Consumer Health Protection	DG XXIV	Health and Consumer Protection	Health and Consumer Protection	DG SANCO

Table 3: *Directorates-General under the Santer, Prodi and Barroso Commissions (continuation 2)*

Directorates-General Santer Commission	Number	Directorates-General Prodi Commission	Directorates-General Barroso Commission	Abbreviation
		Justice and Home Affairs	(renamed) Justice, Freedom and Security	DG JLS
		Enlargement	Enlargement[12]	DG ELARG
			Humanitarian Aid[13]	DG ECHO
			Informatics[14]	DG DIGIT
			Interpretation[15]	DG SCIC
			Translation[16]	DG T

[1] DG Enterprise was created from the merger of DGs III and XXIII.

[2] DG Energy and Transport was created from the merger of DGs VII and XVII and adding nuclear safety from DG XI.

[3] Adding space from DG RTD, security-related research from DGs INFSO and RTD and application of treaty rules on free movement of goods from DG MARKT.

[4] DG Press and Communication was created from the merger of the communication units of DG X with the spokesman's service. The audiovisual policy and media programme units of DG X went to DG EAC. It was renamed DG Communication in February 2006.

[5] While civil protection remained in DG XI (renamed DG Environment), nuclear safety moved to DG TREN.

[6] Adding from DG EAC audiovisual policy and media programme units upon the inception of the Barroso Commission.

[7] Adding responsibility for law of the sea from DG RELEX.

[8] Adding free movement of capital from DG ECFIN and responsibility for business related services and management of notifications by Member States of draft rules on services from DG ENTR.

[9] Transformed into the Internal Audit Service (but still a DG) in July 2001 as a result of the Kinnock reforms.

[10] See footnote 9.

[11] Adding from DG X audiovisual policy and media programme units upon the inception of the Prodi Commission.

[12] Adding the Western Balkans Directorate from DG RELEX.

[13] Formerly the Humanitarian Aid Office.

[14] Created on 1 May 2004 from the former Informatics Directorate.

[15] Formerly the Joint Interpreting and Conference Service.

[16] Formerly the Translation Service.

Table 4: *Special Services and Units under the Santer, Prodi and Barroso Commissions*

Santer Commission	Prodi Commission	Barroso Commission	Abbrev.
Secretariat-General	Secretariat-General	Secretariat-General	SG
Inspectorate-General	Inspectorate-General[1]		
Legal Service	Legal Service	Legal Service	SJ
Forward Studies Unit	Group of Policy Advisors	(renamed) Bureau of European Policy Advisors	BEPA
Joint Research Centre	Joint Research Centre	Joint Research Centre	JRC
Spokesman's Service	See footnote 4, table 3		
Translation Service	Translation Service	Became DG Translation	
Joint Interpreting and Conference Service	Joint Interpreting and Conference Service	Became DG Interpretation	
Statistical Office (Eurostat)	Statistical Office (Eurostat)	Statistical Office (Eurostat)	ESTAT
Informatics Directorate	Informatics Directorate	Became DG DIGIT	
European Community Humanitarian Office	European Community Humanitarian Office	Became DG for Humanitarian Aid	
Euratom Supply Agency	Falls under DG Energy and Transport		
Office for Official Publications of the European Communities	Office for Official Publications of the European Communities	Office for Official Publications of the European Communities	OPOCE
Task Force for the Accession Negotiations	Became DG Enlargement		
Joint Service for the management of Community Aid to Non-Member Countries	Common Service for External Relations	EuropeAid Co-operation Office	AIDCO
	European Anti-Fraud Office	European Anti-Fraud Office	OLAF
		Office for Infrastructure and Logistics in Brussels	OIB
		Office for the Administration and Payment of Individual Entitlements	PMO
		Office for Infrastructure and Logistics in Luxembourg	OIL
		European Communities Personnel Selection Office	EPSO

[1] The Inspectorate General was abolished by the Kinnock reforms. Its function of 'internal management consultancy' of the Commission was in theory transferred to the new Internal Audit Service, but it has failed so far to manifest itself.

Even more complicated is the case of some services which seem to disappear. The Internal Audit Service (IAS), for example, is not the same as the now eliminated DG Financial Control. It is a separate DG whose Director General has the title of 'Internal Auditor of the Commission'. This service carries out independent audits of the Commission's management and control systems, governance and risk management. It reports directly to the Commission via a committee of Commissioners and external experts, the Audit Progress Committee (APC)[2]. The IAS has no role in the verification and control of individual transactions, as did DG Financial Control before. As chapter 17 describes, the Commission's reform programme of 2000 abolished the central financial control of all transactions, carried out *ex-ante* by DG Financial Control, and integrated this function in a decentralised form into all the DGs and services of the Commission. As such, most of its staff thereby moved to posts in other DGs now fully responsible for the *ex-ante* control of all transactions in their policy field. At the same time, however, the Commission set up a new central service, located within DG Budget, to design and oversee all relevant financial, legal and control issues in the Commission and to support the DGs in applying the new rules. This Central Financial Service (CFS) issues the minimum internal control standards and the relevant baseline requirements for procurement and subsidies etc. Twice a year, the CFS draws up a report giving an overview on the state of internal control in the Commission DGs and services.[3]

It is hoped that the reader gets the picture. Surprisingly, perhaps, for the general reader, to old Commission hands this all makes sense and is not gobbledegook!

Relations between Commissioners and their services

A distinctive feature of the organisation of the Commission was long the disparity between the overall responsibilities of Commissioners and the functions of individual DGs. Portfolios of Commissioners have historically often included several DGs and services, and they have also varied from one Commission to the next (see Annex E for an overview of portfolios in the Barroso Commission). This made for a lack of continuity and, given so many changes in the short history of the Commission, for a certain sense of impermanence. This impermanence has affected hierarchical patterns, as individual services change Commissioner and portfolios are created to match the ambitions of new Commission Presidents and national government pressures. Impermanence was also aggravated by the fact that while Commissioners had long been housed together in the Commission's Berlaymont and then Breydel buildings, under Prodi they were housed with 'their' DGs. This was a sign for some that presidential power was to remain at the centre, with the College fragmented and thus more manageable. The formal line was that relations between Commissioners, their *cabinets* and their DGs would be enhanced by proximity, but when the disadvantages of consequent lack of easy informal consultation and coordination between Commissioners and *cabinets* was realised, Barroso reversed the trend – the famous Berlaymont housing the College and regaining prominence after more than ten years of enforced asbestos clearing and reconstruction not unlike the process of reform in progress since the end of the 1990s.

Impermanence has also been one of the prime problems of management accountability and efficiency in the Commission. DGs did not always report to the Commission through an individual Commissioner, but often through several. They consequently often suffered managerially from split staff loyalties and internal divergences.[4] The principle of collective responsibility by the College was not reflected at all in management structures in individual DGs, nor was there therefore ever a corresponding collective *esprit de corps*. Commitment to the collective responsibility of the services as a bureaucratic support to the collective responsibility of the College of Commissioners was obviated by an alternative commitment to the principle of the management accountability of individual DGs and services to individual Commissioners. True, national ministries function in the same way. But, unlike ministers in national governments, Commissioners have often not been the final authority for 'their' DGs because there has not always been direct correspondence between the responsibilities of DGs and the overall portfolios assigned to Commissioners. Chapter 14 describes some of these challenges as they pertain to the field of external affairs.

The lack of continuity in Commission portfolios has sometimes produced excessively rigid and over-centralised management systems within DGs in order to cope with the constant changes. For Directors General, maintaining control as Commissioners with different objectives pulled parts of DGs in varying directions was no easy task. It would not be so dramatic if authoritative coordination were in place, but as we shall see below, where there is coordination it is often formalistic, rather than reflecting the true need for coordination to arbitrate within a strategic long-term approach to policy-making, rather than information-sharing in a knee-jerk environment resulting from the pressure of 'tomorrow's meeting'.

Parallel procedures and political power

This is one cause of the emergence of 'parallel' procedures that have characterised some Commissions, and notably Delors'. 'Parallel procedures', or what Berlin called an 'informal parallel administration' (Berlin 1987, 301), describes a situation where personal networks and the privileged place of the *cabinets* in an extremely hierarchical command structure form the basis of a set of informal rules of procedure, which command the respect, despite the resentment, of Commission staff. Delors' *chef de cabinet*, Pascal Lamy (himself later a Commissioner for Trade and since 1 September 2005 Director-General of the World Trade Organisation), ran the Commission through such 'parallel' procedures. As one inside observer commented, 'to achieve its end, the presidential *cabinet* had to be willing to break through official chains of command and responsibility. "Reaching around" Commissioners and/or their *cabinets* was common practice. The same was true of "reaching into" the administrative services, whose leadership was refractory or left something to be desired'. The *cabinet* clearly believed it needed to. Thus, the President's *cabinet* has been much more than *primus inter pares*. Lamy is said to have run the '"the house" through his control over the Commission agenda (with Williamson) and his ability to command attention from General Directors of the administration' (Ross 1993). Moreover, the President's *cabinet* 'had to be willing to break through official chains of command and responsibility' by 'reaching around'

Commissioners and 'reaching into' the work of both the services and the other *cabinets*. The problem, as one of Delors' *cabinet* members put it, was that 'we are supposed to win, and we usually do. Part of this is because we are better than most other *cabinets*... But we are supposed to be tougher than the other *cabinets* too. This means we have to fight all the time. I find it hard to fight all the time'. (Lodewijk Briet in Ross 1994, 508-10). Clearly, policy entrepreneurship is facilitated if innovative or normative decision-making can rely on the automatic agreement, whether through conviction or loyalty, of the bureaucracy.

Parallel procedures imply that when speed and efficiency are required, Task Forces are set up independently of DGs. When issues are tactically inconvenient, a view from the Legal Service can stymie a proposal's progress. Inter-service groups function effectively on one reading, but they are unable to sway a powerful DG's view on another. In any case, the best coordination by the services has often run foul of *cabinet* objections at a later date. If a draft proposal is inconvenient or unacceptable to one or other Commissioner, *cabinets* may re-draft it, often running roughshod over their own services. The Spierenburg Report showed awareness of this phenomenon twenty-five years ago when it stated:

> 'although the usefulness of these private offices is not disputed, some aspects of their operation are starting to cause difficulties and are even threatening to disrupt, quite substantially, the smooth running of the Commission services: Cabinets 'shielding' Members from their services, Chefs de Cabinet usurping the responsibilities of Directors General, meetings of Chefs de Cabinet (and indeed of junior Cabinet staff) questioning proposals without consulting the officials responsible for them, interference in appointment procedures with undue weight being given to nationality factors, and so on.' (Spierenburg 1979)

As the traditional tools of the bureaucratic system are gradually being reformed (see chapter 17), there is an emerging dichotomy between the principles of justice and fairness in the allocation of tasks and the bureaucratic rewards of leadership status on the one hand and the continuing need for enhanced efficiency on the other. The question for the operators of the 'parallel administration' was always how to ensure maximum effectiveness of the bureaucratic structure in the delivery of their own policy entrepreneurship. A key challenge for the implementation of the Kinnock reforms will surely be the ability of the reformed bureaucracy to deliver effectively to the policy entrepreneurs. Without effective bureaucratic structure, policy entrepreneurs will otherwise continue to rely on 'parallel' methods to get their way. Some have argued (Berlin 1987; Spierenburg 1979) that the clash between the verticality of command structures in the DGs and the horizontality of the collegial system of Commission decision-making militates in favour of a reinforced Secretariat General, a service with a horizontal mission, but with a degree of respect in DGs that produces a de facto verticality in its operational style. The alternative was seemingly enhanced *cabinet* leadership, though enhanced synergy between *cabinets* and the SecGen would obviously be a formidable machine.

For leadership to succeed the mechanisms for assigning responsibilities among DGs and making DGs accountable for exercising them need to be as well developed as those in the most efficient national governments. This is not to suggest that bureaucratic politics in the form of competition for responsibilities and jurisdictional conflicts among DGs can ever be eliminated. But there was clear scope over the years for improvement in management and organisation which the Spierenburg Report identified as early as 1979. Spierenburg argued that the workload of the services had increased inexorably, but that the distribution of staff did not reflect the differential growth of the workload. He deplored the proliferation of services and DGs and suggested merging several DGs into a small number of large administrative units in order to facilitate coordination between related sectors. The fact was, he argued, that 'the Commission is being managed in a manner and with techniques which are inappropriate in present circumstances and can only be more so after enlargement' (Spierenburg, 1979). Yet, management reform could only be taken seriously as an operational concept rather than as lip service twenty-five years later. The 1996 IGC was actually committed to addressing these unresolved issues and this very fact demonstrated that the Commission does not have a totally free hand to put its own house in order. National governments take a close political interest in the internal reorganisations of the Commission. From a Member State's point of view, reshuffles of Commissioners and of Directors General need to be closely supervised so that national interests are defended. When the staff problems described in chapter 6 are added to these issues it will be readily understood that the development of a European civil service and an efficient management system have been fraught with difficulties that the Kinnock reforms outlined in chapter 17 are hard to put to remedy.

In mitigation it has to be stressed, however, that much of what we know about the operation of the Commission has been based on the years of the Delors Commission (e.g. Abeles 2004 and Ross 1994). New research is needed on the evolution of management style since Delors and since the Kinnock reforms. Delors' style was dramatic-political. There are, after all, not many Commission Presidents who could address his Directors General as Delors reputedly did in 1991. He met all Directors General every six months and is said to have threatened once:

> 'If I could hire and fire here, I'd go after at least five or six of you… I know which ones among you don't take me seriously and those who do… I know who you are… I see everything and I think about what I see. In a government I'd be able to remove people. But here you are all barons, it is hard to shake you up… But, I'll get you nonetheless… there are some of you who seem to have barely progressed since elementary school. DG III and DG IV are worse here than the others… I have no intention of letting you get away with it.' (quoted in Ross 1994, 121)

Management structure and hierarchy in the Directorates General

The formal picture of the internal organisation of a DG or other service is a conventional pyramid-type hierarchy. While this standard representation ignores significant differences in organisation and management between the

DGs, it does provide a starting point for analysis. Each DG is headed by a Director General (staff grade traditionally A1 but since the Kinnock reforms AD15/16) and is divided into directorates, headed by Directors (former A2s, now AD 14/15), who report to the Director General. Each directorate is composed of several divisions, or 'units', normally headed by an AD9 to 13 (formerly A5/A4/A3). Heads of unit sometimes have deputies or heads of sector. There are simply not enough units for the qualified staff available, so posts as deputies and heads of sector are consolation prizes for staff deserving some form of title, but unluckily not amongst the chosen few heads of unit. In a differently staffed world, such heads of sector could be heads of unit in their own right and command a team of support staff. Their areas of responsibility are often large and important, but resources simply do not permit the creation of more units. To be in charge of the whole of disarmament policy, including policy-making in such key sectors as non-proliferation, weapons of mass destruction (which commands considerable budgetary resources), representation of the Commission in a series of Council working groups and as spokesman of the Commission in the G8 non-proliferation working group, would normally justify a separate unit. But these tasks fall to one official as head of one individual sector within an overall 'security unit' in DG Relex – with no support staff.

In the larger DGs there is a Deputy Director General (often of equivalent grade to the Director General) whose role is to coordinate, mediate and filter demands on the Director General, as well as take responsibility for a regional or functional area. In the Delors III Commission, DG I (External Economic Relations) had a German Director General, four Deputy Directors General of differing nationalities and also a Chief Advisor of Director General grade. In the current Barroso Commission, in DG Competition, the British Director General Philip Lowe has three Deputies, for Mergers, Antitrust and State Aid.

Despite promises to eliminate the posts, Chief Advisers (*conseiller principal*) have responsibility for a precisely determined area of policy with quasi-independent status within the DG, where they may report directly to the Director General or even the Commissioner, thus skipping the formal hierarchy and bypassing Directors or Directors General. Chief Advisers often owe their status to the fact that they are too senior to be ditched without personal or national acrimony, but the formal structure of the DG has no place for them. Demotion is rarely if ever an option. In any case, Chief Advisers are usually prominent and deserving staff with excellent service records. They have the enviable status of responsibility for a precise subject area without the managerial and administrative responsibility which comes with a post in the formal structure. In the case of DG I during the Delors III Commission, for example, the Briton, Alan Mayhew, supervised relations with the newly independent states of the former Soviet Union, relations with the countries of Central and Eastern Europe and the trade and aid programmes in these areas. On the other hand, some Chief Advisers are not noted for their creativity or high responsibility. Too experienced to demote, often too old or not good enough for managerial posts, they serve time until another suitable job – or retirement – beckons.

Structures and roles of other services

DGs are formally based on a particular policy field such as competition, development, the environment and trade, etc. These 'vertical' services/DGs are complemented by horizontal services, such as the Legal Service, the Secretariat General or, prior to its integration into DG Press, the Spokesman's Service. Though equivalent to DGs, these central services are not known as Directorates General. Nor are the other services, outside the DG structure, which may be forerunners of new DGs – various 'Task Forces', some of which prove to be transitory project teams and disappear when their mandate or negotiating role is over, for example the Enlargement Task Forces and the Intergovernmental Conference Task Forces. The Enlargement Task Forces have usually fallen under the direct authority of a Commissioner and figured in the official Commission organigramme. Because of the expertise they develop, they have provided the organisational resource for new directorates charged with subsequent waves of enlargement. The Enlargement Task Force dealing with British, Irish and Danish membership in 1973 was subsequently converted into Directorate (H) within DG I and made responsible, under Commissioner Natali, for the enlargement negotiations with Greece and then Spain and Portugal. The Enlargement Task Force for the Eftan countries in the Delors III Commission was under the direct authority of the Commissioner for External Political Relations, Hans van den Broek. The Head of the Task Force, the Dane Steffen Smidt, enjoyed Director General status during the negotiations, which lasted one year from March 1993 to March 1994, though he did not have the formal title. Such was the exponential expansion of the EU that these ad hoc arrangements later resulted in the creation of a permanent DG (DG Enlargement), but Smidt himself moved on, becoming Director General for development, then personnel, then fisheries before taking Article 50 (see below).[5]

The important feature to retain is the relative independence of such 'horizontal' teams in the 'vertical' structure of the DGs and the fact that they sometimes report directly to a Commissioner as opposed to a Director General. A typical exception to this model was the Task Force for German Unification, constituted under the chairmanship of the then Deputy Secretary General, the Dutchman Carlo Trojan. This Task Force never entered the organigramme, lasted a mere seven months and resembled an ad hoc inter-service group rather than a fully constituted Task Force with offices, secretaries and seconded staff. But, other Task Forces or small units in the Secretariat General prefigured later establishment as a full DG, for example the Task Force in the early 1980s dealing with information and telecommunications technology, which reported directly to Commissioner Narjes. Other examples were the Task Force for Small and Medium Enterprises, which later became DG XXIII, the Task Force for Education, Youth and Training, which became DG XXII under Edith Cresson in 1994, and the Justice and Home Affairs and European Political Cooperation units in the Secretariat General, both of which became full Directorates General as Commission competence expanded (see chapters 12 and 14). Whether such transformations are planned or simply emerge, given the factors discussed below, is a moot point. One task force, 'Coordination of Structural Funds', became a DG, but was short-lived, disappearing in the Delors III Commission. Significantly, it was, by definition, a 'horizontal' DG, rather than the longer-lived vertical DGs which were subject to its coordinating ambition. Its demise is symptomatic of the general difficulties of securing effective coordination within the Commission mentioned above.

Internal and external influences on the functions of DGs

Mention of coordination raises the question of the organisational division of labour within the Commission. Problems of coordination depend on how competences are allocated between the DGs and the patterns of interdependence that a particular allocation gives rise to. There are three key considerations at work in the allocation of competences among DGs: administrative logic, the politics of the College of Commissioners and the interests of the Member States. Conventional administrative logic of the kind that has influenced public management reforms at the national level prescribes the grouping together of closely related tasks within organisational units to maximise interdependence and facilitate coordination across organisational boundaries. European integration is specifically concerned with policy areas of high interdependence and many responsibilities are hard to assign unambiguously to one DG or another. Therefore, strong interactions among DGs take place in all phases of policy development and management. Moreover, the widening range of Community competences continually reopens the issue of whether the new policy areas will be assigned to new DGs or incorporated in existing ones. The expansion of Community competence has led both to the growth of existing DGs and to expansion of the number of DGs.

A second major influence on the creation of new DGs and structural reorganisations is the need for Commissioners to have a worthwhile job to do and an administrative structure at their command. Most restructuring operations take place when new Commissions take office, rather than as a result of perceived management need or administrative logic (Berlin 1987, 54). They are the product of 'windows of opportunity' (Nugent and Saurugger 2002). The creation of a DG for consumer affairs was reputedly motivated by the expansion of the Commission to 20 members after the 'Eftan' enlargement to include Austria, Finland and Sweden. How much similar factors played a role in the separation of fisheries (which became DG XIV) and the harmonisation of food production standards (until 1993 DG III and thereafter DG XV) from DG VI (Agriculture) in 1977 would be interesting to research. Likewise, the disaggregation in 1967 of the former DG IX for 'administration' into three separate DGs (DG XIX for Budgets, DG XX for Financial Control and DG IX for Personnel and Administration) made operational sense from the 2005 perspective of vastly expanded budgetary and human resources, yet it seems likely that creating portfolios for the increase in numbers of Commissioners after the merger of the institutions in 1967 may have played the key role at the time of their creation.

The external political environment is a third factor influencing the internal organisation of the Commission and the division of competences among DGs. Although, in principle, the Commission is a supranational organisation, the intergovernmental dimension cannot be ignored. Member States seek to maintain or strengthen DGs of political importance to them and try to ensure that their own nationals are in positions of power. Sensitivity to the views and expectations of external stakeholders is extremely important for an organisation at the centre of national webs of political and organisational pressures. It is the unstated justification of the principle of one Commissioner per Member State. Equally, the danger of compromising organisational goals and being captured by powerful external interests must be borne in mind. In the case of the Commission these are live issues. The major organisations in its environment are the national administrations of the Member States. Well-developed intergovernmental networks are essential to the success of European policies, and the Commission must be continually involved with its national partners throughout the process of policy development and subsequently in the process of jointly managing agreed European policies. But the interests of the Member States in securing a power base or resisting changes vital to their interests in the internal organisation of the Commission can create organisational rigidities and inflexibilities. These can work against the effective use and occasional reallocation of the Commission's limited human resources. They may even block reform efforts, not to mention demoralise staff seeking fair shares and promotion by merit.

This is not to suggest that real change never occurs. On the contrary, there has been a history of structural changes since the Commission's inception (Berlin 1987), and profound changes have resulted from the Prodi Commission's widely discussed management reform, though whether the profundity of the reforms matched their proliferation remains a moot point. The real problem was long the fact that the Commission seemed unable to respond quickly enough to the urgent demands for reform and restructuring arising from the pressures for further deepening and widening of European integration. In mitigation, the constraints on the Commission just described are not conducive to effective management or effective use of scarce human resources. As chapter 17 underlines, criticism of rigidities was rife for years, whether from the Court of Auditors, the Member States (particularly the net contributors to the Community budget), disabused Commission officials or the press. Critics underlined the apparently large numbers of underemployed staff in the Commission, the clear lack of staff in key areas of emerging policy responsibility, the inability of the Commission to decide a rational redeployment policy and the large numbers of external staff employed on a range of temporary contracts in order to cope with the resulting staff shortfall in key areas. Thus, whether the 'screening' of 1991 and subsequent reforms were responses to internally perceived needs to restructure and enhance efficiency, or whether pressure from outside the Commission was the real catalyst, is relevant. *The Economist* epitomised public criticism throughout the 1990s, claiming in 1990 that:

> 'Sloppy management means that the Commission cannot ensure that the best people are used where they are most needed. Some departments (Directorates-Generals or 'DGs' in Euro-speak) are overworked, while others take it easy. Officials in charge of external relations, agriculture and some bits of competition policy have too much to do. Those at fisheries, information and administration have time to twiddle their thumbs.' (*Economist* 1990)

and in 1998 that

> 'The general impression given of the Commission is of an organ-
> isation with which anybody likes to do business. It likes spending
> money, it tends to botch the paperwork, and it frequently loses
> interest in the final result. It tries to manage too many programmes
> with too few resources' (*Economist* 1998).

However, as reform attempts at the end of the 1990s demonstrated, it is
easier to identify the problems than solve them. European integration
imposes political requirements on the organisation of the Commission that
complicate the process of management. A mix of nationalities in a DG and
within individual units is the norm. Commissioners are usually of a different nationality from the Directors General who head the services for which
they are responsible. Deputy Directors General and Directors are usually of
yet other nationalities. The purpose, clearly, is to ensure a wide spread of
nationalities in senior positions and the avoidance of nationality clusters,
with concomitant charges of complicity in the defence of one national
interest (Willis 1983, 8). A more generous view would be that such clusters
would prevent the expression of other national administrative styles and
viewpoints in the articulation of Commission policy. There are, however,
some exceptions to the rule. Thus, in the Delors III Commission, the Belgian
Commissioner Karel Van Miert, whose responsibilities included personnel
and administration, had a Belgian Director General, Frans de Koster. While
the criticism may be unfounded that this Belgian duo avoided discussions
and official reviews of national balance in staffing because of the relative
advantage to Belgian nationals of the current system, particularly in the B
grades, the existence of the criticism itself underlines the public relations
importance of maintaining balance in the upper echelons.

Yet, there is a management price to be paid for these political benefits.
Cultural diversity has costs – difficulties in communication; different, possibly incompatible, assumptions about how to deal with superiors and subordinates; incongruent expectations about how to manage conflicts; and
culturally-defined differences in the approach to coordination among DGs.
Inadequate skills and capacities to cope with these problems are potent
sources of frustration, unproductive conflict and inadequate coordination. In
a multicultural organisation like the Commission, which works under pressure and public scrutiny, differences cannot always be smoothed over. It is not
unknown for a Director General to be required to leave the service after the
appointment of a new Commissioner, usually for reasons of incompatibility.
The staff regulations allow for this in Article 50, which states that 'a senior
official may be retired in the interests of the service'. Thus, it may be made
clear to a senior official that there is no suitable employment available for him
and that the 'interests of the service' require his retirement, a technique frequently used when posts are required for other nationals after enlargements.
Since the financial consequences of the measure are quite advantageous, it has
also been known for senior staff to seek, or at least hope for, Article 50 to apply
to them. Disagreement over policy and an inability to communicate satisfactorily in a common language are often reasons for infrequent but nonetheless
occasional partings of the ways. The departure of German Director General
Dieter Frisch from DG VIII (Development) after the appointment in 1993 of

the Spanish Commissioner Manuel Marin was a case in point. The resignation of the Director General for Agriculture and his replacement on the appointment of Commissioner Andriessen in 1985 was a similar case. There have been many others. Peter Wilmott, Director General of DG XXI was constrained to part from his Commissioner Mario Monti in 1995; Commissioner Emma Bonino had to part with José Almeida Serra, Director General for Fisheries (DG XIV); and Social Affairs Commissioner Anna Diamontopoulou had to release Allan Larsson, Director General of Employment and Social Affairs, in 2000. Thus, analysis of the issue of Commissioners' relations with their services is incomplete without mention of Commissioners being obliged to sever relations with Directors General. The *Financial Times* irreverently envisaged one such event in the Barroso Commission. 'Mandelson has a dire relationship with Peter Carl, his Danish Director General... Mandy has often clashed with his officials over tactics in trade talks' (*Financial Times* 2005c). Carl was indeed replaced in a general reshuffle of Director General posts in November 2005. But, lest we stray into personnel issues covered in chapter 6, the point has been to stress the important implications for internal management that result in discontinuities linked to personal and political interest in periodic restructuring operations.

Over time, however, persisting structures have emerged. 'Vertical' DGs with responsibility for a given policy in terms both of legislative initiative and of subsequent management created fiefdoms and management structures of a typically bureaucratic nature. Studies have shown that there is no single administrative culture, but many competing management 'cultures' based on language and nationality, though often centred over time in specific policy locations, which thus become imprinted with the characteristics concerned.[6] There have often quite simply been 'national flags' on certain jobs over long periods of time. It is not surprising that inertia has often characterised such policy areas, with DGs resisting coordination of policy and collaboration with other DGs in specific areas. Objectively, the associated conservatism has formed a bulwark against root and branch reform, which the Kinnock measures are still at pains to remove.

Decision-making – from initiation to first draft

A useful way to gain a picture of the functioning of the Commission is to trace the development of proposals within the services through to the point of endorsement by the College of Commissioners. Given the collegial nature of the Commission and the resulting collective responsibility for decisions, sensitive matters must come before the full Commission at its weekly meetings. Yet, the Commission can also delegate powers for decision-making to a Commissioner in the way that powers are delegated to individual ministers of a national government. Clearly, if all decisions in Community life had to be discussed in a full meeting of the Commission, there would be administrative overload, paralysis of the decision-making process and the submergence of important subjects in the myriad of managerial and administrative tasks for which formal Commission decisions are required; hence the need for thorough preparation by the services in advance of consideration by the College and the development of alternative procedures to relieve it of routine and non controversial work. Before analysing the decision-making process within the Commission, it is helpful to stress that decisions are not only about new legislation or new policy proposals. They can also be about high political issues, such as bringing a court case against a Member State or a firm. The next section reviews the procedures involved in the framework of the Commission's Treaty guardianship role.

Procedures in the framework of the Commission's role as Guardian of the Treaties

As Usher outlines in Chapter 3, the Commission may institute legal proceedings against a Member State before the Court of Justice for alleged non-fulfilment of Treaty obligations. Member States generally respect the Treaty and most violations are due to misunderstandings, misinterpretations or to delays in transposing Community legislation into national law. Deliberate non-compliance nonetheless exists, either because the Member State concerned has intentionally misread the terms of a directive, believing it has a case for an exemption from the legislation or because it may wish to gain time before full implementation. The areas of competition, environment policy and the internal market are prime examples. Member States and the Commission are generally reluctant to pursue cases before the Court of Justice and most disputes are thus resolved at an early stage – albeit 'early' can sometimes mean years, since the procedures leading to a full court action take several months.

The Commission may become aware of an infringement for a number of reasons: an individual, a company or a Member State may complain, or an investigation by Commission officials may uncover possible violations. The Commission then needs to decide whether to take action. Such a decision would be subject to the procedures described below – either a decision in the Wednesday meeting of the College or a written procedure. Thereafter, the Commission sends a 'letter of formal notice' – there are more than one thousand letters of notice annually – requesting the Member State concerned to explain the alleged breach. The Member State then has approximately two months to reply. If it fails to reply or provides an unsatisfactory explanation, the Commission issues a 'reasoned opinion' outlining why it considers the Member State to be in violation of the Treaty. Again, the Commission usually gives the Member State two months to comply. Most cases end with such a letter of notice or a reasoned opinion.

The prime purpose of the infringement procedure is not to secure a court ruling that the infringement has taken place, but to persuade the Member State to conform. In almost 85 per cent of cases the infringement proceedings are terminated after the first two stages – formal notice and reasoned opinion – and thus before a reference to the Court of Justice takes place. Litigation is the final resort. Member States are reluctant to let legal proceedings begin, and the Commission is similarly reticent for fear of alienating public opinion in Member States, where its role is often contested by large parts of the public. On the other hand, sustained non-compliance by a Member State does require formal action and a refusal by the Commission to prosecute may alienate precisely those interest groups whose sympathy the Commission needs in its more general task of creating legitimacy for the

European institutions and European integration itself. Nevertheless, political deals between the Commission and Member States are common. To save the British government possible embarrassment and to help establish good relations with London during the UK Presidency in the second half of 1992, for instance, the Commission reputedly requested the Court to postpone a number of highly publicised environmental law cases against the UK. On the other hand, under pressure from environmentalists, the Commission made threatening noises just prior to a British general election over the ecological implications of plans for a road building scheme at Twyford Down.

Taking decisions – the preparatory process

Whatever the purpose of a proposal, the preparatory process follows broadly the same lines. However, it is worth noting that proposals may serve one or other of three purposes. Some are simply attempts to articulate the European interest by statements or white papers on policy issues. Others are legislative initiatives which either propose the creation of completely new legislation or propose technical legislation which specifies existing rules in more detail. Thirdly, the Commission is called upon to decide policy with regard to its own legislation in the framework of delegated powers. This is discussed by Pedler and Bradley in chapter 8. Procedures decided within the framework of the Commission's role as 'guardian of the Treaties', mentioned above, are fully discussed by Usher in chapter 3.

Legislative initiatives and decisions to take Member States to court are highly political. The College debates proposals, and one Commissioner will be required to defend agreed proposals in discussions in the Council of Ministers. In both institutions, there is voting, negotiation, coalition-building and package deals. As for more technical legislation, officials from the Commission services debate the issues with national officials, and the Commission and Council are often called upon only to rubber stamp their officials' decisions. On the Commission side this is done by written procedure, rather than oral discussion in the College, and on the Council side there are 'A' points in Council meetings (Westlake 2004, 37-8).

The Commission's decision-making procedures provide for six overlapping phases in the process of policy formulation: the initiation phase, the drafting phase, inter-service coordination, agreement between specialised members of *cabinets*, by *chefs de cabinet* and finally the College itself. The adoption of proposals for action follows the same administrative procedure, whether the decision concerns new policy orientations, minor amendments to existing legislation, the management of agricultural markets or a decision to bring (or threaten to bring) a legal action in the European Court of Justice. The adoption of the proposal by the College under Article 2 of the internal rules of procedure is the outcome, but it is the journey, rather than the arrival of the proposal that requires explanation.

The real institutional initiator of a policy proposal in any given area can be the Commission, the European Council or the Council of Ministers. Once the seed for a policy has been sown, however, the Commission has legal responsibility for the formal draft and one DG takes the lead in initiating discussions with actors inside and outside the Community institutional framework. Mazey and Richardson (see chapter 10) describe the environing 'policy networks' with which a lead DG interacts. The usual internal route for a new proposal is for a Directorate General of the Commission to set up a consultative committee of 'technical experts'. Some experts are independent consultants from academia or interest groups. Others are desk officers from the national governments, who may well turn up later in a Council working group to discuss the resultant proposal. Often, to the irritation of Commission officials, they may argue a somewhat different case in the later stage than they did in the initiation phase, since inter-ministerial coordination in the national capital may lead to modifications in the initially more technically informed and often more flexible national position.

Since several initiatives are usually in progress at the same time, there is often a sense of overload in national government circles. A belief can develop that time is too short to attend all of these committees and, in any case, the key debate will take place at a later stage when a firm proposal is on the table. But being reactive can be a risky strategy for a national government. An important element of pre-negotiation takes place in the Commission's committees. It is here that the main lines of the ultimate intergovernmental bargain begin to emerge, setting the agenda and establishing parameters for subsequent discussion in the formal negotiations. Hence, it is unwise for national governments to let others make the running. It is better to try to influence the Commission early and obviate the need for rearguard action later in the negotiations. The strategic issue is to ensure that a national viewpoint gets due consideration in the Commission proposal.[7] For the private sector, squaring the lobbying circle means influencing all governments early in the initiation process as well as the Commission itself. There are thus many varied and competing pressures on a DG in the initiation phase, as national officials take on a role of representation of the interests of groups in their countries (insofar as these are compatible with government policy), which, if they have prepared the ground thoroughly, will have lobbied the Commission services already.

Drafting and inter-service coordination

The drafting phase takes place when consultation is well under way. Middle-ranking officials in the leading Directorate General begin the drafting process. There is a strong tendency for firm positions, emerging in technical experts' groups, to be incorporated in the draft text. Clearly, under qualified majority voting, if only a minority of Member States persists in a given view, pressure will not be high on the Commission to dilute its position. The draft finds its way up the 'hierarchy' to Director General level for endorsement. Drafting overlaps the process of coordination among DGs. It is rare that a DG is solely responsible for a legislative proposal, so coordination with other DGs is a constant feature.

The importance of coordination in the Commission is stated in the Commission's rules of operational procedures, which stipulate that:

> 'Any department preparing a Commission decision or proposal must take account of the fact that the Commission as a whole will bear responsibility for the measure in question and must act accordingly, i.e. in conjunction with other departments as appropriate. Underlying this requirement is the principle that the

administration is 'one and indivisible': although each sector is the
responsibility of a different Member, the administration as a whole
serves the Commission as a whole.'

The lead department is thus well-advised to make informal contact with
other departments as soon as drafting begins. Formal inter-service meetings
and consultation later ensure coordination. Formally constituted 'inter-service groups' build a permanent coordination structure. In addition to ad hoc
inter-service consultations, there were 48 formalised inter-service groups in
1990. By 1993 there were 63 groups. In 2006 there were 224. The Secretariat
General maintains a full list of inter-service groups and is responsible for
supervision of coordination meetings and ensuring appropriate departments
are correctly consulted and in a timely manner. Formally subject to a
Commission decision, inter-service groups are now set up only with the
authorisation of the Secretariat General. The numbers of such formally constituted groups naturally understate the extent of coordination through more
informal means, such as email and ad hoc meetings between colleagues.

In addition, several Commission services are involved as a matter of routine in decision-making and therefore have to be part of the coordination
process for any proposal. The Directorates General for Budgets and Financial
Control must be consulted on all proposals with financial implications.
Likewise, the Directorate General for Personnel and Administration must be
formally involved if a proposal has implications for personnel. The
Commission's Legal Service must be consulted before a proposal reaches the
agenda of the College or enters a written procedure. The role of the Legal
Service is formally to ensure conformity with the Treaties, coherence with
existing legislation and with agreed procedures in other areas of Community
business. While these requirements may be considered a routine task, the
third relates to political desiderata such as the maintenance of an agreed
Commission line on competence, on legal base or on comitology (see chapters
3, 8 and 14). Ensuring that the Legal Service is in agreement with the principle
at issue is clearly, therefore, one way of ensuring respect and acceptance for
the proposal. The Legal Service reports directly to the Commission President,
and collaboration between the President's *cabinet* and senior officials from the
Legal Service provide a vital agenda-setting function. A favourable opinion
from the Legal Service on a text is a clear political advantage. An
unfavourable opinion means either that the text must be amended or an
accompanying explanatory statement be provided and that proposals may
not follow the written or delegation procedures described below. For new
legislation, the lawyer-revisers (*juristes-linguistes*) must also be involved to
ensure coherence of the proposal in the official languages of the Union.
Preparation of the text by DG Translation may not have covered all the legal
nuances.

The problem of managing coordination is common to every modern
administration, but within the Commission it is particularly difficult. An
increasingly diverse and interdependent set of interests has to be taken into
account and, while much is done within the framework described above,
there are inadequate capacities for effective coordination. The shortfall in
capacities for managing coordination in the Commission is part cause and
part consequence of a wider systemic weakness in the management of
European policies, the EU's 'management deficit', in principle dealt with by

the management reforms introduced by Kinnock (see chapter 17). As other chapters underline, European integration has a record of moving to new commitments without building the capacities to deal with them effectively. Upgrading the Commission's coordination capacities would not eliminate the capacity deficit, but it would be an important step towards remedying this increasingly serious problem, described in the case of the Common Foreign and Security Policy as the 'capability-expectations gap' (Hill 1993 and Hill and Wallace 1996, 5).

The structural disparity between the responsibilities of Commissioners and those of DGs mentioned above has been a complicating factor. Inter- and intra-organisational coordination has been confounded by mismatches between the portfolios of Commissioners and the responsibilities of DGs. This adds to the tasks of coordination and makes for difficulties in developing effective institutional procedures for joint decision-making to deal with differences and resolve conflicts. In the case of DG I, under Delors there were two Commissioners, the Briton, Sir Leon Brittan, responsible for external economic affairs and trade policy and the Spaniard, Manuel Marin, mainly responsible for cooperation and development policy but also responsible for North-South Relations, Mediterranean policy and relations with Latin America and Asia. Marin was also lead Commissioner for DG VIII (Development). As for external political relations, these were the responsibility of yet another Commissioner, the Dutchman, Hans van den Broek, operating through a separate DG, DG IA. Rivalry between these three Commissioners and the three Directors General involved slowed considerably the creation of a unified foreign service in the Delors III Commission and led to some cynicism and embitterment of staff. Subsequent coordination issues within the 'Relex family' in the 1990s and after 2000 demonstrated how difficult it was to ensure effective coordination reaching beyond mere information exchange to authoritative arbitration. Chapter 14 describes the issue in full.

The problem of inadequate coordination capacities was recognised not only in the reports of outsiders such as Spierenburg (Spierenburg 1979). In 1988, the Commission held a seminar in Erenstein to debate the need for increased coordination and for simplification of procedures. The resulting committee discussions continued to stress the ongoing need to improve interdepartmental coordination, and various formal procedures were created to monitor the progress of coordination in relation to particular proposals. At the weekly meeting of Directors General and at the weekly meeting of assistants of Directors General, the schedule of implementation of the Commission's work programme is reviewed and issues about to be brought to the College are noted. By the time proposals reach this stage, coordination should have taken place to ensure that differences have been settled and that major policy issues can reasonably be put before the Commission for speedy and uncomplicated decision. Yet, despite this commitment to interdepartmental coordination, it has often been argued that the system was flawed because some DGs acted independently and there was not enough central control to restrain them. On this analysis, some DGs are powerful enough to override objections from others. Their status is based on the preponderance of their issue areas in the Commission since its inception, their large staffs, their financial responsibilities and finally the excellence, professionalism and commitment of staff in these areas. Thus, the argument goes, these DGs are able to pursue their own line and resist coordination because the Secretariat General lacks arbitration authority. Coordination is contested territory. It is not clear where responsibility for coordination lies – formally it lies with the SecGen, in practice it has often lain with the lead department or in the President's *cabinet*. This is not to suggest that coordination should necessarily be equated with central control and handed over to a single hierarchical authority. Rather the problem is how to ensure that DGs work together effectively.

High level decision-making – cabinets, chefs de cabinet and the College

Coordination is where DGs and Commissioners' *cabinets* with their different outlooks, interests and agendas must come together. If a sharp distinction could be drawn between administrative and political coordination, perhaps the process could work more smoothly. But, given the unique responsibility of the Commission for policy initiative and the interdependence of different strands of policy, such a separation is not feasible. The crucial coordination phase of the policy preparation process suffers from confusion about the roles of top officials in DGs and their counterparts (or adversaries) in Commissioners' *cabinets*. While the relationship may sometimes work well, the inadequacies and rigidities of the organisation on one side and the capricious nature of the political process on the other often make for frustration and unsatisfactory performance.

Delors' (and his *chef de cabinet*'s) response to these shortcomings was to try to circumvent the bureaucracy by adopting a very direct style of leadership rather than attempting to reform and strengthen the organisation and management of the Commission. Whatever short-term gains this produced in terms of political commitments to further integration, it left a legacy of unresolved management problems and an organisation where the quality of coordination was far from optimal. It was not surprising that President Santer espoused the theme of consolidation; doing things better rather than doing more. The 1996 IGC was supposed to address the question of effectiveness, but it took the resignation of the Santer Commission and the Kinnock reforms for the nettle to be finally grasped.

Before submission of a proposal to the College of Commissioners, internal rules of procedure provide for a series of formalities to be completed and for the text to be circulated no later than noon on the Thursday before the Commission meeting. The Secretariat General's registry division, known by its French term 'greffe', is responsible. The preparation of the text itself is the responsibility of the lead DG and it is presented by the lead Commissioner – on occasion in consultation with other named Commissioners, where portfolios overlap. It is expected that strong efforts will have been made to achieve as much agreement as possible through coordination processes. Whatever differences of opinion that remain after inter-departmental consideration are outlined in an explanatory note which accompanies each document. The presence or absence of such differences of opinion between Directorates General influences the way proposals are subsequently handled. Prior agreement permits the use of written or delegation procedures.

At this final stage of preparation, and before submission of the draft to the

College of Commissioners, their *cabinets* will have become involved. The lead Commissioner's *cabinet* may well have been involved already in the drafting process, and will certainly have closely vetted the text. But the other cabinets are now an important formal port of call for the draft, so the text transits via the Secretariat General to all other *cabinets* for vetting and control. At this stage, the process of inter-*cabinet* negotiation takes place and a last effort is made to reach an agreed draft in 'special chefs' meetings – that is meetings with the individual *cabinet* members who have responsibility within their *cabinet* for the subject matter concerned. It should be remembered that the *cabinets* will seek to defend both their own Commissioner's interest and the Commissioner's national interest. They will be fully briefed by 'their' permanent representation and national officials about what is at stake. Thereafter, the key preparatory meeting for the College is the *chefs de cabinet* meeting on Mondays, chaired by the Secretary General. Just as in COREPER before a Council meeting, agreement on most issues may already be possible. This enables non-controversial issues to proceed to the Commission as 'A points', which are not formally discussed, as opposed to 'B points' which require discussion. Textual amendments arising from prior *'specials-chefs'* meetings or the meeting of Heads of Cabinet can be dealt with in the remaining time before the College meets to formalise the resulting decision. This, of course, is a cosy view. Depending on personalities, whether in the College, the *cabinets* or in the services, 'blood needs to be kept off the Commission floor' (Ross 1994, 119). As one senior official noted in a specific case:

> 'all of us were getting incessant instructions on what to do from *cabinet* members, not even from the *chefs de cabinet* either. And they kept introducing fundamental changes into the document. This kind of thing has the effect, over time, of "deresponsibilising" the services, we lost our willingness to take risks and think things through… Furthermore, the cabinets are always pursuing their own national interests...' (quoted in Ross 1994, 119)

Whatever the politicking, submission of a proposal to the full College then follows. Where full agreement has not been reached in advance, Commissioners debate the outstanding issues, settle what they can agree and put other issues on the agenda of a future meeting or refer them back to the services and *cabinets* for re-drafting. In addition to meetings of the full Commission which adopt texts, there are two kinds of formal meetings of Commissioners to settle policy lines where the whole Commission need not be involved. The first, 'restricted', group (*groupe restreint*) would be composed of a small number of Commissioners, mandated by the College on grounds of the specificity of the subject at issue. In the period immediately following the announcement that the unification of the two Germanys was likely, a group restricted to President Delors, the External Affairs Commissioner Frans Andriessen, the Commissioner for Economic Affairs Henning Christophersen and the Internal Market Commissioner Martin Bangemann met frequently to decide on a coordinated Commission strategy in the ongoing debate about the nature of the unification and the overall implications for the Community. Subsequently, an 'open group' (*groupe ouvert*) was constituted under the chairmanship of Commissioner Bangemann to analyse the implications of German unification for all aspects of the *acquis communautaire*. An open group is 'open' to all Members of the Commission who wish to participate. The system resembles the original system of the ECSC and the early days of the EEC when groups of Commissioners fell into eight or so categories approaching each of the issue areas as a mini-College, rather than the more individualised approach of today. It was only after 1970 that the current system of individual portfolios began to emerge. The group approach was a system to which Prodi attempted to return (see below).

Habilitations

For reasons of efficiency and convenience, not all matters are decided by all Commissioners, though their endorsement is required. There are two other procedures by which decisions may be taken which avoid the necessity of meetings of the College: 'habilitations' and written procedures. The purpose of the delegation procedure, known internally in the Commission by the French word 'habilitation', is to relieve the College of discussion of decisions on routine matters, usually with a narrow margin of discretion and which present no political problems. Article 27 of the internal rules of procedure allows the Commission to delegate a power of attorney to one Commissioner, formally to commit the Commission. The *habilitation* procedure is usually used in areas of a managerial or administrative nature. A condition of the exercise of the mandate remains the ultimate collective responsibility of the College. Questions of principle or general policy, as mentioned above, are customarily dealt with in the Wednesday meeting and cannot be the subject of *habilitation* procedures. Typically, *habilitations* occur either for purely technical issues, often in the agricultural sphere, or where political and substantive differences on a text have been removed by previous discussion and compromise, so that all that is required is a final adjustment of the policy. Personnel and financial decisions are excluded from the procedure.

Written procedures

Written procedures are a much used decision-making process for items not requiring discussion at the weekly meeting of Commissioners and where a delegation procedure is not necessary. It is used where the relevant Directorates General have agreed the proposal and the Legal Service has given its approval. Written procedures are initiated by the Secretariat General at the request of one or more Members of the Commission. The request is submitted by the head Directorate General to the registry service in the Secretariat, the *greffe*. The *greffe* ensures that formal requirements have been completed as follows:

(1) approval of associated DGs;
(2) favourable opinion of Legal Service;
(3) examination of legal form and terminology;
(4) preparation of a summary list indicating agreement at appropriate levels;
(5) setting a time line;
(6) sending different language versions to lawyer-revisers;
(7) circulation of the proposal to Commissioners and concerned DGs.

Thereafter, if no reservations are made by Commissioners through their *cab-*

inets before the expiry of the time limit, the Secretary General records approval of the measure, draws up the final text incorporating drafting changes by lawyer-revisers and includes mention of the decision in a daily memorandum to Commissioners listing all items agreed by written procedure.

There are two sub-types of written procedure: ordinary and expedited. 'Ordinary' written procedures allow five working days for agreement after distribution of the text. Allowing for the administrative work of the *greffe* to take place, this means that a decision by ordinary written procedure occurs 10 days after receipt of the request. The 'expedited' written procedure (*procedure écrite accéleree*) is authorised by the President on a request from the Secretariat General. Here, three days are allowed for texts where legislation is urgently required. The 10-day ordinary procedure is thus reduced to five. Expedited written procedures 'for finalisation' enable urgent measures agreed by the *chefs de cabinet* meeting or by the College to be adopted rapidly. The time limit can be as little as one day. 'Expedited written procedure by special circulation' enables the Commission to take decisions at short notice in response, for example, to natural disasters or requests for emergency aid etc. A 'special' version of this procedure is reserved for Commission responses to Council common positions under the cooperation procedure.

Simplification

One issue which has dogged discussion on procedures is the overriding need for simplification of legislation and the avoidance of unnecessary bureaucracy. While the procedures described in this chapter are likely to remain the same, the output and quality of legislation are set to change. Commission Vice President Günter Verheugen has stressed the Commission's commitment to deliver better regulation (Verheugen 2005) and made a commitment to ensuring internal procedures take on the principles involved. The Commission has strengthened its internal quality standards for new proposals, including tighter rules for impact assessments. In 2005, close examination of 215 proposals still in the legislative pipeline was carried out and a list of proposals to be withdrawn or modified was set to be presented. In addition, the screening of more than 30 policy sectors containing legislation was undertaken. Of 60 legal acts already identified as having a potential for simplification, more than half were presented for final decision on simplification by the European Parliament and the Council. Since most of the measures impacting negatively on competitiveness are national, the Commission also set up a high-level group of national regulatory experts to ensure better cooperation between EU institutions and Member States' governments on regulatory reform. The group began work in September 2005, while the Commission began a separate consultation process to identify the views of concerned sectors. Revised internal rules to strengthen impact assessments accompanying Commission proposals were also introduced. Officials now need to factor into their proposals administrative costs, evaluate alternative options, such as 'no EU action' (except where the Treaties define an obligation to act), and envisage simplification of existing EU legislation and alternatives to 'traditional' instruments (e.g. co-regulation or self-regulation). The aim was increased coherence and quality of proposals. In addition, the Commission began research on an initial list of 144 simplification proposals identified by a Council Working Group, so that a list of priorities for 2006 and 2007 could be established.

Conclusion: post-Nice changes

The College is neither a mere rubber-stamp of deals struck by officials in its name nor an omnicompetent group deciding for itself on all matters of principle and detail. The College depends on the efficiency of its services. For the Commission to do its job of dealing with major policy issues, it has to do its preparatory work well. The College, argue the cynics, only has cognisance in the final stage of a dossier's journey through the system. Despite the fact that Commissioners may vote on proposals and that a mere simple majority suffices to carry a measure, the principle is consensus, so the justified case of the specialist official may be drowned by bureaucratic power structures on its way up the hierarchy and in the political compromises emerging from *cabinet* and College discussion. It would be senseless to deny the criticisms of present arrangements. These include the setting of time limits for coordination proceedings which render real preparation and discussion impossible, and the organisation of meetings without due notice or at such a high level of officialdom that the detail may remain undiscussed as the lead department attempts to achieve a political settlement. In addition, where a strong DG is in the lead, it may not attempt to seek consensus, but simply try to impose its view. In doing so, it may restrict access to information, so that DGs with a marginal interest are, in fact, marginalised.

Prodi promised that after the Nice Treaty was implemented (it came into force on 1 February 2003), Commissioners' areas of responsibility would be reorganised around core tasks essential to the functioning of the Union. The idea was not new. The Santer Commission contained several such groups, such as external relations and equal opportunities. Work would, Prodi argued, be prepared by groups of Commissioners responsible for a general policy area, mirroring the changes that were likely to be made to the structure of the Council. A number of Vice-Presidents were to be appointed to supervise each group of areas. Each Vice-President would work closely with two or three Commissioners depending on the scope of the fields covered. The aim was to introduce the changes from the beginning of 2004 and ensure that the Commission's decision-making process was rationalised along the same lines. This meant that while fully complying with the principle of collegiality, decision-making could be modernised with Vice-Presidents preparing the decisions to be taken by the Commission, meeting at least once a week to prepare the meetings of the College and to take decisions that the College has authorised them to take. The full Commission would continue to meet once or twice a month to set the political priorities and plan the work, and all decisions in principle would be taken by the College, as well as those it is required to take under the Treaties. The Vice-Presidents supervising groups of Commissioners would take on an increasingly important role in implementing political priorities and decisions. Finally, Prodi promised, there would be no question of a 'directoire' of larger Member States within the Commission. The President should and would choose the best and brightest irrespective of their country of origin (Prodi 2002). It remains to be seen whether Commission President Barroso will deliver on the Prodi proposals.

At the beginning of 2006 it looked unlikely.

This chapter has reviewed the common, everyday structures and procedures in the Commission and also widened the discussion in chapter 1 on the role of *cabinets*. Importantly, despite the seeming simplicity of the structures and procedures, what made the Commission effective in the Delors years was the existence of a parallel, informal system which ensured that real power remained outside the services, focused in the *cabinet* system and providing a tight command structure. It was as if Commissioners' *cabinets* let the services play the game of policy-making, consultation of interest groups and inter-institutional relations, while reserving both judgement and the exercise of real power to themselves. The first edition of this book eleven years ago hypothesised that the move towards a system without the need for a parallel administration might come when a Commission was appointed with two significantly different features from those of the Delors Commissions: first, the absence of a dramatic-political President and second, the absence of an ever-expanding administrative agenda. Internal administrative reform and the consolidation of the resulting civil service ethic might then be possible. Although Santer, Prodi and Barroso cannot be described as quite so 'dramatic-political' as Delors, the agenda has not shrunk over the last ten years. On the contrary, enlargement, the euro, the Stability Pact, the creation of the European Security and Defence Policy, the shift of parts of Justice and Home Affairs into the Community arena and the overall reform of the Commission have kept the agenda brim-full. The jury thus remains out.

Endnotes

[1] There are only 242 staff working in DG Development in Brussels. See the comparative figures for the staffing of Commission Directorates General at table 6.

[2] Information is available on its website http://europa.eu.int/comm/dgs/internal_audit/ index_en.htm

[3] More information on the CFS is available on the DG Budget website: http://www.cc.cec/ budg/index-en.htm

[4] An MA thesis at the College of Europe illustrates well the difficulties and turf battles arising. See Gordon, T. 'Empire Building within the Commission', unpublished manuscript, 1995.

[5] A full chronological account of the steps which led to Smidt's resignation can be found in a speech to the European Parliament by Commissioner Franz Fischler on 23 May 2002 entitled 'The Reform of the Common Fisheries Policy'. In addition to the case of Smidt, the speech includes a useful summary of the last stages of decision-making in the Commission. To counterbalance this view see eufactsfigures.com/july2002.

[6] These mainly anthropological studies began by an invitation by Delors to three anthropologists to spend time in the Commission in 1993 to research 'the existence or not of a specific Commission culture, plus the weight of the different languages and national cultural traditions, and their impact on working relationships, and how a European identity might emerge in such a context' (Abélès et al 1993 and Abélès 1994).) Subsequent studies by Cini (1996, 2000 and 2004) have taken the research further. Less anthropological and more political-science oriented was the study by Ross (1994 and 1994a).

[7] The issue of how Member States coordinate at the various levels in the process are analysed in Kassim 2000a and Spence 2004.

5. The European Commission and Agencies

Martijn Groenleer

Introduction[1]

The establishment of over twenty agencies at the European level is one of the most prominent institutional innovations of recent years within the European Union. Agencies are independent administrative bodies, geographically dispersed throughout the Member States, which play a key role in implementing European legislation and regulating European policies. They thus fulfil a variety of functions and a broad range of tasks.[2]

The delegation of tasks to European agencies raises a series of intricate questions. Why were they created? What tasks do they perform? What is their relationship to the Commission? The key issue underlying these questions is how to strike a balance between the autonomy of agencies and the accountability they must render. To contribute to the effective delivery of European policies, agencies must take account of the needs and interests of their principals (the Commission, the Council, and the Parliament), but in doing this, their independence may be compromised, and their credibility and legitimacy undercut. How agencies deal with this tension is important for the role they play in European governance.

This chapter aims to shed light on this issue. It provides an overview of European agencies, tracing their historic origins and the reasons for their creation, and setting out a framework for their analysis and a description of their main characteristics.[3] It also discusses the tension between autonomy and accountability; analysing the implications for the organisation and functioning of agencies. The concluding section examines future issues concerning European agencies.

Agencies at the European level

There is no agreed definition of a European agency.[4] On its website, the EU offers the following definition of a European Community (EC) or first pillar agency: 'A Community agency is a body governed by European public law; it is distinct from the Community institutions (Council, Parliament, Commission, etc.) and has its own legal personality. It is set up by an act of secondary legislation in order to accomplish a very specific technical, scientific or managerial task which is specified in the relevant Community act.'[5] Their legal status enables EU agencies to function as independent units, outside the Community institutions. This position contrasts with bodies that work within the Commission infrastructure, such as the Joint Research Centre (JRC), the Statistical Office of the EU (Eurostat), the EU Anti-Fraud Office (OLAF) or the European Community Humanitarian Aid Office (ECHO) (cf. Kreher 1997, 228). These bodies are also relatively independent, but are not endowed with their own legal personality.[6]

Table 5: *Overview of European agencies*

Community (first pillar) agencies	Mandate/function
European Centre for the Development of Vocational Training (CEDEFOP); Thessalonica, Greece; Council Regulation (EEC) No 337/75, 13 February 1975.	Provide information on and analyses of European vocational education and training systems, policies, research and practice.
European Foundation for the Improvement of Living and Working Conditions (EURO-FOUND); Dublin, Ireland; Council Regulation (EEC) No 1365/75, 26 May 1975.	Provide social policy makers with information on the developments and trends in living and working conditions in Europe.
European Environment Agency (EEA); Copenhagen, Denmark; Council Regulation (EEC) No 1210/90, 7 May 1990.	Collect, prepare and disseminate information on the state and trends of the European environment.
European Training Foundation (ETF); Turin, Italy; Council Regulation (EEC) No 1360/90, 7 May 1990.	Support the reform of vocational training in partner countries and translate EU policy into training and labour market instruments for third countries.
European Monitoring Centre for Drugs and Drug Addiction (EMCDDA); Lisbon, Portugal; Council Regulation (EEC) No 302/93, 8 February 1993.	Collect and disseminate information on drugs and drug addiction in Europe.
European Medicines Agency (EMEA); London, United Kingdom; Council Regulation (EEC) No 2309/93, 22 July 1993.	Protect public and animal health by evaluating and supervising medicinal products in Europe.
Office for Harmonisation in the Internal Market (OHIM); Alicante, Spain; Council Regulation (EC) No 40/94, 20 December 1993.	Provide legal protection across all countries of the European Union by registering Community trade marks and designs.
European Agency for Safety and Health at Work (EU-OSHA); Bilbao, Spain; Council Regulation (EC) No 2062/94, 18 July 1994.	Promote the development, analysis and dissemination of information that improves occupational safety and health in Europe.

Overview of European agencies – cont.

Community (first pillar) agencies	Mandate/function
Community Plant Variety Office (CPVO); Angers, France; Council Regulation (EC) No 2100/94, 27 July 1994.	Grant rights ensuring industrial property protection for eligible new plant varieties.
Translation Centre for the Bodies of the European Union (CdT); Luxembourg, Luxembourg; Council Regulation (EC) No 2965/94, 28 November 1994.	Provide translation services for other EU agencies and bodies.
European Monitoring Centre on Racism and Xenophobia (EUMC); Vienna, Austria; Council Regulation (EC) No 1035/97, 2 June 1997. (To be converted into European Union Agency for Fundamental Rights.)	Provide the EU and its Member States with information and data on racism, xenophobia and anti-Semitism at the European level.
European Agency for Reconstruction (EAR); Thessalonica, Greece; Council Regulation (EC) No 2454/99, 15 November 1999.	Manage the main EU assistance programmes in Serbia and Montenegro and the former Yugoslav Republic of Macedonia.
European Food Safety Authority (EFSA); Parma, Italy; EP and Council Regulation (EC) No 178/2002, 28 January 2002.	Provide independent scientific advice on all matters with a direct or indirect impact on food safety.
European Maritime Safety Agency (EMSA); Lisbon, Portugal; EP and Council Regulation (EC) No 1406/2002, 27 June 2002.	Provide technical and scientific advice to the Commission in the field of maritime safety and prevention of pollution by ships.
European Aviation Safety Agency (EASA); Cologne, Germany; EP and Council Regulation (EC) No 1592/2002, 15 July 2002.	Assist the EU and its Member States in establishing and maintaining a high, uniform level of civil aviation safety in Europe.
European Network and Information Security Agency (ENISA); Crete, Greece; EP and Council Regulation (EC) No 460/2004, 10 March 2004.	Assist the Community in ensuring high levels of network and information security.
European Centre for Disease Prevention and Control (ECDC); Stockholm, Sweden; EP and Council Regulation (EC) No 8517/2004, 28 April 2004.	Identify, assess and communicate current and emerging threats to the health of European citizens from communicable diseases.
European Railway Agency (ERA); Lille-Valenciennes, France; EP and Council Regulation (EC) No 881/2004, 29 April 2004.	Reinforce safety and interoperability of railways in Europe.
European Agency for the Management of Operational Cooperation at the External Borders (FRONTEX); Warsaw, Poland; Council Regulation (EC) No 2007/2004, 26 October 2004.	Assist Member States in the implementation of Community legislation on the control and surveillance of the EU's external borders and coordinate operational cooperation between Member States.

Overview of European agencies – cont.

First pillar agencies continued	Mandate/function
Community Fisheries Control Agency (CFCA); Vigo, Spain; Council Regulation (EC) No 768/2005, 26 April 2005.	Ensure effective use of EU and national means of fisheries inspection and surveillance.
European Chemicals Agency (ECA); Helsinki, Finland; Proposal for an EP and Council Regulation (EC) COM(2003) 644/15, 29 October 2003.	Manage the technical and scientific aspects of the EU's chemical policy (REACH) to ensure the consistency of decision-making at the European level.
European Institute for Gender Equality (EIGE); site to be decided; Proposal for an EP and Council Regulation (EC) COM(2005) 81 final, 8 March 2005.	Support the EU and its Member States in the fight against discrimination based on sex and the promotion of equality between men and women, as well as raise awareness of gender equality among EU citizens.

Second pillar agencies	Mandate/function
European Institute for Security Studies (ISS); Paris, France; Council Joint Action, 20 July 2001.	Assist in the creation of a common European security culture and to enrich the strategic debate in the Union.
European Union Satellite Centre (EUSC); Torrejón de Ardoz, Spain; Council Joint Action, 20 July 2001.	Support European Union decision-making, particularly in the context of the European Security and Defence Policy (ESDP) through the collection of space related information.
European Defence Agency (EDA); Brussels, Belgium; Council Joint Action, 12 July 2004.	Support the Member States in their effort to improve European defence capabilities.

Third pillar agencies	Mandate/function
European Police Office (Europol); The Hague, The Netherlands; Europol Convention, 26 July 1995.	Enhance police cooperation between Member States.
European body for the enhancement of judicial co-operation (Eurojust); The Hague, The Netherlands; Council Decision, 28 February 2002.	Enhance judicial cooperation between Member States.
European Police College (CEPOL); Bramshill, United Kingdom; Council Decision, 22 December 2000.	Enhance cooperation in law-enforcement training between Member States.

Executive agencies	Mandate/function
Intelligent Energy Executive Agency; Brussels, Belgium; Commission Decision (2004/20/EC), 23 December 2003.	Implement the tasks concerning Community aid under the Intelligent Energy programme.

Overview of European agencies – cont.

Executive agencies (continued)	Mandate/function
European GNSS Supervisory Authority; Brussels, Belgium; Council Regulation (EC) 1321/2004, 12 July 2004.	Manage the European satellite navigation programmes (such as Galileo and EGNOS).
Executive Agency for the Public Health Programme; Luxembourg, Luxembourg; Commission Decision (2004/858/EC), 15 December 2004.	Implement the tasks concerning Community aid in the field of public health.
Education, Audiovisual and Culture Executive Agency; Brussels, Belgium; Commission Decision (2005/56/EC), 14 January 2005.	Manage Community action in the fields of education, audiovisual and culture.
Executive Agency for the Trans-European Transport Network (TEN-T) (*proposed*); Brussels, Belgium	Implement tasks involved in the management of co-financing granted to the TEN-T.
Other agencies	**Mandate/function**
Euratom Supply Agency; Luxembourg, Luxembourg; Statutes of the Euratom Supply Agency, 6 November 1958.	Ensure a regular and equitable supply of nuclear fuels for Community users.

EC agencies are different from European organisations created on an intergovernmental basis such as the European Space Agency (ESA) and the European Patent Office (EPO), which confusingly use the word 'European' in their title. The Commission is involved differently with each of these non-EU agencies. ESA is an independent organisation, yet it maintains close ties with the EU through an ESA/EC Framework Agreement. ESA and the EU also pursue a joint European strategy for space and are together developing a European space policy.[7] As for EPO, although it is an independent organisation, the Commission participates in its Administrative Council as an observer. In contrast to these intergovernmental organisations, EC agencies are part of the broader EU legal framework. However, they are different from the European institutions that are explicitly mentioned in Article 4 of the Treaty Establishing the European Community (TEC) – the Commission, the Council, the Parliament, and the Court. The present Treaty does not specify a legal basis providing for the creation of agencies.

Community agencies are created by a decision based on secondary law, in other words, by legislative decision-making in the form of a Council regulation (Geradin and Petit 2004; Kreher 1997, 227; Vos 2000, 1121).[8] Each Community agency has its own regulation, in which the specific mandate, objectives and tasks of the agency are specified. Most early agencies are based on Article 308 of the TEC.[9] This general provision requires that the consultation procedure be applied to create an agency (Kreher 1997, 232). The consultation procedure implies limited potential influence for the European Parliament during the legislative decision-making process and unanimous decision-making by the Council.[10] By contrast, more recently established agencies are usually based on specific Treaty provisions, which provide for the co-decision procedure and imply majority voting. By relying on specific Treaty provisions, the Commission can limit the mandate, function and task of the agency to the scope of the specific Treaty provisions. Under Article 308 of the TEC, however, the Council possesses extensive powers to determine the action to be undertaken by the Community (Geradin and Petit 2004, 43; Lenaerts 1993).

In addition to Community agencies, several Council (or second and third pillar) agencies have been established. The Council agencies that fall under the Common Foreign and Security Policy (CFSP) of the EU are created by a Council Joint Action. The legal basis for agencies in the area of justice and home affairs varies from a Council Decision, to a Convention or a Council Regulation. They all operate under the authority of the Council. The establishment of Council agencies led to much debate on the pros and cons of EU as opposed to EC agencies: the creation of an EU satellite agency, for example, clearly risks duplication and rivalry with the JRC's satellite research section. Former Commission President Prodi warned that the creation of agencies on which the Council can confer power may create conflicting centres of power. If agencies are created, 'this must be done by maintaining the logic of the Community system. Those agencies must operate under the authority of the Commission which is answerable to [the European Parliament] for their actions.'[11]

The emergence of European agencies

Community agencies

The first Community agencies, the European Centre for the Development of Vocational Training (CEDEFOP) and the European Foundation for the Improvement of Living and Working Conditions (EUROFOUND), both aiming to promote social dialogue at the European level, were created in 1975. With a limited mandate and few discretionary powers these agencies are relatively weak (Kelemen 1997, 1).[12]

Until the end of the 1980s, the creation of more European agencies was hindered by the restrictive interpretation of the Meroni judgement, rendered under the European Coal and Steel Community (ECSC) Treaty in 1958 (Dehousse et al. 1992; Lenaerts 1993). In the Meroni judgement, the European Court of Justice set out criteria that had to be met before the European institutions (in this case the High Authority of the ECSC) could delegate powers to other bodies or agencies.[13] In order not to disturb 'the institutional balance which is characteristic of the institutional structure of the Community', the Court ruled that the institutions may only delegate power to bodies or agencies 'if it involves clearly defined executive powers the exercise of which can, therefore, be subject to strict review in the light of objective criteria determined by the delegating authority.' By invoking the Meroni judgment, the

Commission, in particular its Legal Service, thwarted any attempt by other EU institutions to confer autonomous decision-making power to agencies (Dehousse 2002; Majone 2002a).[14]

The end of the 1980s witnessed renewed interest in the idea of establishing European agencies. The adoption of the Single European Act in 1986 provided the Commission with a significant increase in workload. The shortcomings of 'a purely legislative approach to market integration' became increasingly clear (Majone 2002a, 329). However, restrictions on the Commission's personnel budget, imposed by the European Parliament and the Council of Ministers, made it difficult for the Commission to expand its support staff (Kelemen 2002, 101-102). In January 1989, Commission President Delors therefore launched a wave of agency creation. The first new Community agency created was the European Environment Agency (EEA). The Council approved the EEA regulation within ten months, and the relative ease of its approval spurred proposals from other Commission DGs (Kelemen 2002, 101-102). By 1999, ten new agencies had been established.

Since the Prodi Commission took office, the EU has engaged in a new wave of agency creation. The BSE crisis in 1996 and the resignation of the Santer Commission in 1999 revealed serious shortcomings in the capacity of the European Commission to deliver effective and legitimate policies (Majone 2000; Vos 2000). In an attempt to restore the perceived loss of credibility and legitimacy of the Commission, the new Prodi Commission launched a process of reforms of which the creation of new agencies was part (Vos 2000). By the end of 2004, six new Community agencies had been established.

Council agencies

In addition to Community agencies, Council agencies assist EU Member States to advance their work in pillars II and III. To promote the development of the CFSP, the Member States agreed at the European Council in Cologne (1999) to place the European Institute for Security Studies (ISS) and the European Union Satellite Centre (EUSC), formerly part of the Western European Union (WEU), under the newly created office of the High Representative for the CFSP. In 2004, a European Defence Agency (EDA) was established, again under the responsibility of the High Representative.[15] In the area of justice and home affairs, EU Member States created a European Police Office (Europol) in 1995, a European Police College (CEPOL) in 2000, and the European body for the enhancement of judicial cooperation in criminal matters (Eurojust) in 2002. These EU agencies were all set up under the authority of the Council to support cooperation between the national authorities of Member States. While the Commission enjoys structured relations with them (membership of the board, etc.), it undertakes no executive functions and plays second fiddle to the Council and the Member States. The creation of Council agencies enhances a trend that may serve to undermine the Commission's role within the Community sphere.

Why agencies?

Agencies are not unique to the EU system. States regularly create agencies. In the United States, the first agencies were established more than a century ago, and agencies have proliferated in most Western European countries as well (Pollitt and Talbot 2004; Pollitt et al. 2004; Van Thiel 2001). A variety of reasons explain why the EU has used the agency option.

Functional needs

Agencies are designed to meet functional needs: they organise independent expertise at the EU level, increase transparency of EU policy-making, and facilitate both Europe-wide cooperation between stakeholders and efficient and flexible implementation of EU legislation (Kreher 1997; Majone 1997a; cf. Pollack 2003). Indeed, the creation of European agencies should be seen as part of the debate on reform of the EU institutional framework and the future of European governance (Flinders 2004; Vos 2000).

They are created to answer the call for independent expertise of a highly technical/scientific nature not readily available within the Commission: 'the independence of their technical and/or scientific assessments is [...] their real *raison d'être*. The main advantage is that their decisions are based on purely technical evaluations of very high quality and are not influenced by political or contingent considerations.'[16] As non-majoritarian institutions, not directly accountable to voters or to their elected representatives, agencies are said to be insulated from the political process (cf. Dehousse et al. 1992; Majone 1997b; cf. Moe 1990). They are delegated the technical and managerial functions of the Commission, leaving an 'unbundled' Commission to focus on the political dimension (cf. Spence 2000). This insulation aims to ensure policy continuity, which is imperative to policy credibility (Majone 2000).

Another major justification for agency creation is to remedy the perceived shortcomings of the committee framework described in chapter 8. After all, '[t]he Council-Commission-Comitology process is among the least transparent policy-making processes in the democratic world' (Shapiro 1997, 291). The BSE crisis clearly demonstrated the downside of this process, when anonymous experts were propelled into a decision-making position (Grönvall 2001). In contrast to the comitology system, 'the agency option appears substantially more transparent' (Kreher 1997, 242; cf. Thatcher 2002b). By giving increased visibility to EU decision-making, agencies may meet the demand for public accountability, thereby increasing the legitimacy of EU policy-making.

The lack of policy coordination and cooperation between stakeholders throughout Europe constitutes yet another reason to establish European agencies. Before, stakeholders were essentially excluded from the EU policy-making process. Agencies can more easily establish or maintain (formal or informal) networks that ensure contact with stakeholders (Dehousse 1997; Majone 1997a; 1997b), thus encouraging the European-wide exchange of information and best practices and spurring further administrative integration in Europe (Chiti 2000; Kreher 1997; Yataganas 2001). Moreover, several agencies' management boards include stakeholders other than the Commission and the Member States (e.g. the social partners, business and consumer groups). By offering ways of involving stakeholders, agencies can increase the perceived quality and acceptability of their work.

The creation of agencies is supposed to contribute to the efficient and flexible implementation of Community policies, particularly in areas requiring frequent decisions based on technical or scientific considerations and where uncertainty is great (Majone 1997a). Agencies can be more efficient than the Commission because they are usually smaller organisational entities. They also have more flexible staffing structures, allowing them to replace staff more easily and thereby maintain a high level of expertise.

Inter-institutional politics

Functional considerations alone cannot account for the establishment of European agencies. The political interests of the agencies' principals (the Commission, the Council, and the Parliament) also play a role in their creation and design (Kelemen 2002; cf. Pollack 2003).[17]

In the early 1990s, the agency option was a welcome solution to a pressing problem. Both Commission Presidents Delors and Santer expected that 'Eurosceptic' Member States would not support an expansion of the Commission's staff necessary to cope with the increased workload. By delegating tasks to agencies instead, the regulatory capacity of the EU could increase without the otherwise concomitant expansion of the size of the Commission, and the agency option was acceptable to the Council (Kelemen 2002, 101-102). EU Member States expected that through the creation of European agencies they could wield more influence and exert more control on EU law-making and implementation. The management boards of the agencies would largely be composed of Member States' representatives and the agencies would be distributed among locations in the Member States (Kelemen 2002, 99-101).[18] Whether this has actually resulted in more influence and control for the Member States continues to be debated.[19]

Until the mid-1990s, the European Parliament did not play a major role in the establishment of new agencies (Kreher 1997). Emerging as a legislative actor alongside the Council after the Maastricht and Amsterdam Treaties, the Parliament began to assert its influence over the creation and design of new agencies, particularly by using its budgetary powers. It became aware that 'the delegation of extensive implementation powers to agencies controlled by member state appointees threatened to undermine the Parliament's influence at the implementation stage' (Kelemen 2002, 104). The increased role of the Parliament vis-à-vis the Council led to a change in the Commission's position on the creation of new agencies by the end of the 1990s. With the support of the Parliament, the Commission no longer saw the need to expand its activities by delegating significant regulatory powers to agencies if it could also enlarge the EU's regulatory capacity without setting up new agencies with extensive powers (Kelemen 2002; cf. Majone 2002a). The Commission's changed position is, for example, reflected in the limited scope of powers granted to the European Food Safety Authority, the first agency created through the co-decision procedure.[20]

Organisation and functioning

There is no single model for a European agency. Existing agencies vary, for instance, in the size of their budget and in the number of staff they employ. The Reconstruction Agency for the Balkans (EAR) has by far the largest budget, almost €277 million in 2005. By contrast, the agency with one of the smallest budgets, the Monitoring Centre for Racism and Xenophobia

(EUMC), had less than €10 million in 2005. Whereas the Plant Variety Office (CPVO) and the EUMC had around 40 employees in 2004, the Medicines Agency (EMEA) and the Office for Harmonisation in the Internal Market (OHIM) employed about 360 and 670 staff members respectively. Despite their differences, the existing agencies share a number of common characteristics with regard to their mandate and function, structure and composition, and budgetary provisions (Geradin and Petit 2004, 41-43; Kreher 1997; Vos 2003).

Mandate and function

The Commission has identified two types of Community agencies: executive and regulatory. Executive agencies assist the Commission in the management of Community programmes; they are subject to strict supervision by the Commission.[21] Regulatory agencies are 'required to be actively involved in exercising the executive function by enacting instruments which contribute to regulating a specific sector.'[22] Within the category of regulatory agencies, the Commission makes yet another distinction between agencies with the power to enact legal instruments binding on third parties and those that have no independent power of decision.

None of the current European agencies would qualify as a full-blown regulatory agency. Most have a limited mandate laid down in the constituent act together with its objectives and tasks. Only three agencies have decision-making powers: the Office for Harmonisation in the Internal Market registers Community trademarks and designs, the Plant Variety Office grants Community plant variety rights, and the Aviation Safety Agency issues certificates for aeronautical products. Two other agencies, the Medicines Agency and the Food Safety Authority, do not have decision-making powers of their own, but the Commission has to base its decisions on the scientific opinions issued by these agencies (Majone 2002b; Vos 2003, 121). By rendering services to industrial sectors, these five agencies facilitate the operation of the internal market.

All other existing agencies have predominantly advisory functions, which fall into four broad categories (Kreher 1997, 236-237; Vos 2003, 119-121; Yataganas 2001, 26). One group of agencies collects, analyses and disseminates information in their respective policy fields.[23] A number of these agencies, such as the Environment Agency, the Drug Monitoring Centre (EMCDDA) and the Monitoring Centre for Racism and Xenophobia, also create and coordinate European information networks, connecting national focal points in the Member States.[24] A second group consists of agencies that execute programmes and tasks for the European Union within their respective fields of expertise.[25] A third group of agencies brings together representatives of employers, employees, Member States and the Commission to inform and support the formulation of EU social policy.[26] A fourth and new group of agencies performs safety and/or interoperability tasks (Geradin and Petit 2004, 43-49).[27]

Sometimes the constituent act of an agency determines its priority areas, but usually the agency has to translate the statutory objective into more detailed priorities, for instance, in the form of (multi-)annual work programmes. The constituent acts of agencies do spell out procedures for the adoption of the work programme. In some cases, the administrative or management board has to consult or seek the opinion of the Commission;[28] in other cases, the management board has to take into account the Commission's priorities.[29] The Maritime Safety Agency (EMSA) is an exception. In this case, the Commission has to agree with the agency's work programme. When the Commission disagrees, EMSA's administrative board has to re-examine the programme and adopt it either with a two-thirds majority, including the Commission representatives, or by unanimity of the representatives of the Member States.[30]

Structure and composition

European agencies have rather similar organisational structures. Power is divided between an administrative or management board, an executive director, and one or more scientific/technical committees.

Administrative or management board

All agencies have an administrative or management board. The board formulates the strategic objectives of the agency. It also formally adopts the agency's annual work programme, report and budget, and it usually appoints the executive director of the agency (see below). The composition of the board is specified in the constituent act; in most cases, the board is primarily composed of representatives of EU Member States. In addition to these national representatives, the board includes representatives of the Commission and in some agencies also representatives of the European Parliament and other stakeholders, such as the social partners.[31] But the number of member state representatives always exceeds the number of representatives of the European institutions. Most boards are headed by a member state representative; in only two cases (the ETF and the CdT) does a Commission representative head the board. Most agencies also grant observer status to representatives of other EU institutions, other EU agencies, or third countries.[32]

Practical problems have arisen in relation to the large size of some management boards (notably those including the social partners), the lack of discussion on issues of strategic importance, and the difficulties of ensuring a permanent high-level representation of stakeholders.[33] The size problem, increasingly urgent after the enlargement of the EU in May 2004, is addressed in new agencies. The boards of newly created executive agencies are supposed to comprise only five members appointed by the Commission; newly created regulatory agencies would have a 15-member board.[34]

The executive director [35]

All agencies are headed by an executive director who bears responsibility for day-to-day management, staff and personnel matters, the preparation of a draft budget, annual work programme and report, and the implementation of the budget. The executive director is also the legal representative of the agency. There are several appointing procedures for an agency's executive director, indicating the degree of formal autonomy an agency has in relation to the Commission or the Member States (Kreher 1997, 234-5). In the most commonly used procedure, the power of appointment is shared between the Commission and the management board: the Commission proposes and the board appoints the executive director.[36]

Technical or scientific committees

The actual work of agencies is usually done by committees of scientific or technical experts in a particular field or area. The committees assist the board and the executive director in scientific or technical matters by rendering opinions or issuing recommendations. The members of the committees are usually appointed by the board of the agency on the basis of their specific expertise.

Budgetary provisions

Agencies enjoy a varying degree of budgetary autonomy (Kreher 1997, 235-6). In their early years, agencies receive funding from the Community budget to cover their expenses, but afterwards agencies develop different sources of funding. Most agencies are financed from the general EU budget through a Community subsidy. Some agencies also receive (voluntary) contributions from national and international organisations or Member States.

Four agencies are entirely or partially self-financed: the Medicines Agency and the Offices for Harmonisation in the Internal Market and Plant Variety charge their clients fees for the services they provide;[37] the Translation Body receives financial contributions from its clients, mostly other agencies, for its translations. While these agencies have a relatively high degree of budgetary autonomy, they are not completely free in setting the fees they charge; the power to fix the fees is divided between the Commission and the Council, in accordance with a procedure laid down in the constituent acts.

Autonomy and accountability

Significantly, the delegation of tasks to independent European agencies has met with little criticism. This is remarkable because 'agencification' at the national level has evoked considerable critique (Flinders and Smith 2003; Pollitt and Talbot 2004; Pollitt et al. 2004; Thatcher 2002a; 2002b; Van Thiel 2001). The potential added value of the agency option has to be weighed against possible disadvantages of European agencies, demonstrated by the ongoing tension between autonomy and accountability.

Autonomy

The independence of European agencies is considered to be one of the main justifications for their creation. Yet several agencies have experienced difficulty in gaining a reputation as autonomous organisations performing their tasks independently of the Commission or the Member States (cf. Selznick 1949). The Environment Agency, for instance, has 'continuously tried to demonstrate its independence, in particular from the Commission and specifically from DG Environment.' In institutional terms, however, the Environment Agency for most stakeholders 'is the Commission' (Arthur Andersen 2000). The independence of the Food Safety Authority (EFSA) is impinged upon by a so-called administrative review clause, inserted by the Council in two draft regulations and already legislation in two acts. The clause empowers the Commission to require EFSA to withdraw its decisions or undo its acts.[38]

The Commission, in turn, sometimes considers agencies to have too much autonomy, developing and pursuing priorities different from the Commission's priority needs. In the academic literature, this is known as 'bureaucratic drift' (Calvert, McCubbins and Weingast 1989; Epstein and O'Halloran 1994). Bureaucratic drift can occur because agencies' constituent acts do not always clearly define their objectives, often do not specify their tasks in detail, and rarely spell out their policy priorities (cf. Wilson 1989). The Commission, for instance, believed that the Monitoring Centre for Racism and Xenophobia in its early years had given too much weight to establishing a profile as a campaigning organisation, instead of concentrating on 'its role as the data collection body foreseen by the Regulation.'[39] The disparity between agency activities and Commission policy has made the Commission sometimes turn to other information sources or, as in the case of the Monitoring Centre for Racism and Xenophobia, to propose more clear objectives and tasks.[40]

The autonomy of agencies is also affected by stakeholders other than the Commission. Their participation in the work of an agency is, of course, essential for the agency's legitimacy: stakeholder representation in the management board can ensure that the agency's decisions and activities are accepted and supported by the key actors in a given field or area. But, it is difficult for an agency to meet the various expectations and demands of stakeholders without compromising its independence. Indeed, there is a risk that the agency is (too) easily influenced or even 'captured' by those whom it is supposed to regulate (Baldwin and McCrudden 1987, 45-50; cf. Thatcher 2002b). A disproportionate degree of agency autonomy and strong representation of other stakeholders in the management boards of agencies thus risks reducing Commission control over the agencies.

Accountability and control

The autonomy of European agencies raises questions regarding their accountability and control. Their principals may delegate them tasks for certain functional and political reasons, but what prevents agencies from developing in ways not intended by their principals, pursuing their own interests and avoiding accountability and control? Some scholars point to the danger of placing too much power in the hands of appointed bureaucrats who cannot easily be held accountable for their actions (cf. Everson 1995). Their fear of uncontrolled bureaucracy is strengthened by the image of agencies serving to create 'jobs for the boys'. After the loss of influence and prestige by the Commission, agencies provide a safe haven for senior Commission bureaucrats with a career still ahead (cf. Majone 2002b).

Even if agencies only have an advisory function or information role, it is clear that their activities have important implications for policy-making. Agencies influence policy choices and political interests: their data, findings and information are often political rather than objective and neutral. They are sometimes said to be politically motivated and vulnerable to political manipulation. This, in turn, has raised concerns about their credibility and legitimacy, paradoxically one of the reasons to establish independent agencies in the first place (Everson 2001; Shapiro 1997, 283-4).

Moreover, a new feature with the Barroso Commission is that agencies now figure prominently in the portfolios of individual Commissioners. This arguably makes it difficult to determine who should be held accountable in case of trouble. Kreher (1997), for instance, mentions the potential case of a new medicine with European-wide approval causing problems. It is not unlikely that a blame game would ensue from the fragmentation of power between the Commission, which takes the decision to approve a medicinal product, and the Medicines Agency (EMEA), which is responsible for providing the Commission with scientific advice on the evaluation of medicinal products. This is especially so since EMEA's recommendations on the authorisation of medicinal products are usually rubberstamped by the Commission, following a written procedure (Dehousse 2002). Interference by the Commission, even on an occasional basis, could undermine the legitimacy of EMEA and the credibility of the authorisation system (Everson et al. 1999, 198).

Principals do, of course, have various mechanisms at their disposal to control agencies (Curtin 2005; Everson et al. 1999; Kelemen 2002; Vos 2003; Yataganas 2001). Besides representation in the management board and the power to propose or appoint the executive director, the Commission can make sure that its needs are addressed through its involvement in the preparation of the agency's work programme.[41] In the case of the Environment Agency, for example, the Commission expressed reservations regarding 18 of the 93 projects proposed in the agency's first multi-annual work programme. These projects were subsequently excluded.[42]

The European Parliament can use its budgetary powers to exercise financial oversight. It has regularly withheld funding, for instance pending the decisions on the locations of agencies (cf. Brinkhorst 1996). It has also frequently demanded information on the financial situation of agencies, as happened in case of the Reconstruction Agency after allegations of corruption surrounding its work. Some of the new agencies, such as the Aviation Safety Agency and the Border Agency, have to send the Parliament their annual report. The Parliament can also invite their executive director to report on the work of the agency. All agencies are subject to internal and external budget control: the Commission's financial controller carries out an internal audit of the agencies and external control of the agencies is performed by the Court of Auditors of the European Communities. The Court of Justice exercises judicial oversight by its review of actions taken by agencies.

Member States control agencies through their representatives in the administrative or management boards, and they can further exercise influence over agencies through the networks of national authorities (Kelemen 2002). As agencies often rely heavily on the cooperation of national authorities in their respective policy areas, this may make them responsive to the demands of such national authorities and their governments (Everson et al. 1999; Majone 2002b; Yataganas 2001).

The European institutions thus have various mechanisms at their disposal to hold agencies accountable. It is questionable, however, whether the principals other than the Commission can effectively control agencies through the mechanisms they have. The European Parliament, while it is gaining influence, still has rather limited formal powers to control agencies; member state governments may be bypassed by agencies that liaise directly with national authorities brought together in European networks.

Conclusion: the future of European agencies

While the creation of European agencies may have a significant impact on the EU's capacity to govern, further delegation of tasks to independent EC/EU agencies is clearly not a panacea for the problems the EU still faces with regard to efficiency, credibility and legitimacy. The agency option is merely complementary to other means of EU governance, in particular the committee system. Agencies are thus likely to be used on a case-by-case basis and have a carefully designed institutional structure ensuring their accountability (cf. Curtin 2005). But, the establishment of independent agencies at the European level does have important implications for the EU institutional framework. It would be too simple to assume that the creation of agencies implies a weakening of the Commission's executive role. Indeed, by bolstering the credibility and legitimacy of EU policy-making, the growth of agencies may very well strengthen the Commission vis-à-vis the other European institutions.

Endnotes

[1] The author is grateful for critical comments on earlier drafts of this chapter by Arjen Boin, Mark Rhinard and David Spence.
[2] See table 5 for a list of European agencies as of 2005. Whereas this chapter primarily focuses on Community agencies, this list also includes other agencies at the European level.
[3] The agencies examined in this chapter are designated by different terms (such as centre, foundation, institute, office, authority, and agency). This may lead to some confusion, particularly as the same terms may be used to designate other bodies which do not conform to the definition of an agency.
[4] Even though agencies are mentioned in the draft Constitutional Treaty, the Treaty does not define agencies, nor specify a framework for agency creation and design. Agencies are, for example, mentioned in Article I-50 ('Transparency of the proceedings of Union institutions, bodies, offices and agencies'). Europol and Eurojust are explicitly mentioned under Article III-272, III-274, and III-276.
[5] See European Union, 'The Agencies of the European Community', available at http://europa.eu.int/agencies/index_en.htm.
[6] Newly created *executive* agencies, such as the Intelligent Energy Executive Agency, the Executive Agency for the Public Health Programme or the Education, Audiovisual and Culture Executive Agency, are not legally independent either. They are subject to supervision by the Commission.
[7] See Commission of the European Communities, White Paper – *Space: A New European Frontier for an Expanding Union. An Action Plan for Implementing the European Space Policy*, COM(2003) 673, Brussels, 11 November 2003.
[8] Newly created executive agencies, however, are based on a Commission Decision.
[9] Except the European Environment Agency that was created on the basis of Article 175 TEC.

[10] In two cases, EMEA and CPVO, the Commission proposed to base the creation of agencies on a different article of the TEC, which would have implied the use of the cooperation procedure and qualified majority voting in the Council. The legal basis was however changed by the Council during the drafting stage.

[11] See European Commission, Romano Prodi, President of the European Commission, Plenary Session of the European Parliament, Strasbourg, 3 October 2000, Speech/00/352.

[12] These Community agencies were not the first European agencies to be established. One early agency, the Euratom Supply Agency, acting under the supervision of the European Commission and operative since 1960, was created under the Euratom Treaty.

[13] See European Court, *Meroni & Co., Industrie Metallurgiche, SpA v High Authority of the European Coal and Steel Community*, Case 9-56, Judgment of the Court of 13 June 1958, at 150-152.

[14] As the Meroni judgment was rendered under the ECSC Treaty, both its validity and applicability under the present Treaty are debatable.

[15] The question of responsibility is particularly relevant with regard to the creation of the post of EU Foreign Affairs Minister, combining the functions of the High Representative for the CFSP and the External Relations Commissioner: it is not yet clear under whose responsibility – the Commission or the Council – the existing CFSP agencies would fall and where, institutionally, new agencies in the area of foreign policy should be established (see chapter 14).

[16] See Commission of the European Communities (2002), Communication from the Commission, *The Operating Framework for the European Regulatory Agencies*, COM(2002) 718 final, Brussels, 11 December, p. 5.

[17] The European Court of Justice plays a limited role in the establishment of agencies.

[18] Not all proposed agencies were acceptable to the Member States. In the mid-1990s, a European Telecom Agency was proposed to regulate the liberalised EU telecom market. This proposal, supported particularly by some members of the European Parliament, was blocked by Germany, France and the UK, unwilling to transfer authority from existing national agencies to agencies at the European level (Kelemen 2002, 110).

[19] Dehousse (1997, 2002), for instance, claims that in the EC context powers are usually not taken away from a Community institution but transferred vertically, from the national to the EU level. He therefore argues that the concept of delegation is ill-suited to situations in which powers are conferred upon independent agencies; Europeanization would be a better description of this process (but see Eberlein and Grande 2005, 94-96).

[20] The creation of a European Cartel Office proposed by Germany and Italy was opposed by the Commission, for fear of losing its extensive powers in the field of competition regulation (Geradin and Petit 2004, 14; Kelemen 2002, 111). Several other agencies are still under discussion and might be set up in the future. Examples include a European Procurement Agency and a European Securities Agency.

[21] See Council Regulation (EC) No 58/2003 of 19 December 2002, *Statute for executive agencies to be entrusted with certain tasks in the management of Community programmes.*

[22] See *Operating framework for regulatory agencies*, p. 4. See also Commission of the European Communities (2005), *Draft Interinstitutional Agreement on the Operating Framework for the European Regulatory Agencies*, COM(2005) 59 final, 25 February 2005.

[23] This group includes ETF, EU-OSHA, and ECDC. It also comprises EU agencies such as Europol, EUSC and ISS.

[24] Such as EEA (EIONET), EMCDDA (REITOX) and EUMC (RAXEN).

[25] This group comprises CdT and EAR.

[26] This group includes CEDEFOP, EUROFOUND and EU-OSHA.

[27] This group includes agencies created during the second wave, such as EMSA, ENISA, EBA and ERA.

[28] In the case of, for instance, ETF, EAR, EEA, EMCDDA and EASA.

[29] In the case of, for instance, CEDEFOP and EFSA.

[30] See Article 10, para 2(d) of the regulation establishing EMSA. See table 5.

[31] In cases in which the social partners are involved, the total number of board members is highest; the number of board members is lowest in agencies with decision-making powers.

[32] Third countries may also be granted full membership of the agency, such as in the case of EEA.

[33] The creation of an executive board was seen by some agencies as a solution to these problems.

[34] Comprising six members appointed by the Commission, six members appointed by the Council, and three members (without voting rights) representing stakeholders. See *Statute for executive agencies* and *Operating framework for regulatory agencies*.

[35] In two cases, OHIM and CPVO, the executive director is referred to as president.

[36] The director of new executive agencies is appointed by the Commission.

[37] Considering the public character of the services it renders, EMEA, in contrast to OHIM and CPVO, is not supposed to become entirely financed by fees. This would make the agency too dependent on the pharmaceutical industry (Vos 2003).

[38] See letter to the Council, the Commission and the European Parliament on 19 May 2004, www.efsa.eu.int/mboard/initiatives, published 2 June 2004, last updated 7 September 2004, accessed on 9 November 2004; Response to the Management Board from the Commissioner for Health and Consumer Protection, David Byrne, 24 June 2004.

[39] See Commission of the European Communities (2003), *Communication from the Commission on the activities of the European Monitoring Centre on Racism and Xenophobia, together with proposals to recast Council Regulation* (EC) 1035/97, COM(2003) 483 final, Brussels, 5 August, p. 17.

[40] Plans to transform the European Monitoring Centre on Racism and Xenophobia into a European Agency on Fundamental Rights have caused concerns over duplication in the area of human rights. Terry Davis, Secretary-General of the Council Europe, commented: 'With all the best will in the world I can't understand what it is going to do.' See *Financial Times* (2005), 'Too Many of Us in the Human Rights Business, European Leaders Are Told', 7 February.

[41] The Communication on the proposed *Operating framework for regulatory agencies* stresses that work programmes of such agencies must be subject to the Commission's prior agreement.

[42] See Institute for European Environmental Policy and European Institute for Public Administration, *Evaluation of the EEA. An IEEP/EIPA Study*, Final Report to DG Environment, Part 1: Main Report, August 2003, pp. 24-25.

6. Staff and personnel policy in the Commission

David Spence and Anne Stevens

Introduction

The personnel policy and practices of the European Commission are a reflection of an unresolved tension between the original aim of supranationalism and the reality of encroaching intergovernmentalism. The Commission's bicephalous nature as a civil service in the classic sense and yet a policy initiator, the motor of integration and guardian of the European interest, has, perhaps inevitably, meant that its status is contested. Its recruitment and management procedures underline the originality of Commission officialdom, serving as it does a supranational polity.

The creation of a supranational 'Europe' is linked by some (perhaps especially those who work for it) with the need for a permanent, and above all 'independent' European civil service. However, while Member States may pay lip service to this ideal, none of them shows much sign of abandoning either the importance attached to ensuring that national mentalities, reflexes and interests are represented, or the practice of seconding or even 'parachuting' national officials into the Commission's administration with a resulting exacerbation of divergent administrative cultures. That has inevitably intensified the varying perceptions of Commission officials about the role of their institution. Indeed, their seeming inability to promote a clear image to the general public about what their role could or should be, may be a causal element in the European Union's failure to gain public support. The 'No' votes in the French and Dutch referendums of May and June 2005 had many complex causes, but a perception of the Commission and its officials as bureaucratic and remote certainly contributed. This chapter reviews the original ethos of the Commission as a supranational civil service and confronts the intentions and management assumptions of its creators with the reality of administrative life and practice after fifty years of operation.

The origins and ethos of the Commission administration

The Commission's administrative infrastructure was based on that of the High Authority of the European Coal and Steel Community, set up in 1952. It was no accident that the French system served as a model, given the role in the creation of the High Authority's organisation of its first two presidents, Jean Monnet and René Mayer, both senior civil servants from France. When the European Economic Community and the European Atomic Energy (Euratom) Community were established in 1958, each had its own separate High Authority or Commission, and these were only merged into one, the European Commission or, more precisely, the Commission of the European Communities, in 1967. Within five years of this merger came the first enlargement to include Denmark, Ireland and the United Kingdom (1973), followed by Greece (1981), Spain and Portugal (1986), and Austria, Finland and Sweden (1995). The impact of the 2004 enlargement to ten further countries is still making itself felt. However it is certain that, like each of its predecessors, it will mean a readjustment of the Commission's staffing and organisation. Each has introduced new management styles, adding to the diversity of views on the Commission's role and creating still further management tensions based on diverse cultures and management methods. Enlargements have thus contributed to successive re-definitions of the self-image of the official and the role of the institution itself. The ideal of a neutral European civil service standing above the interests of the Member States has persisted, but with the 2004 enlargement, it is arguably facing its greatest challenge yet, if only because the the 25-member EU is – painfully – implementing parallel, often enlargement-related, processes of administrative and management reform (see chapter 17).

To meet this ideal of neutrality and to ensure from the outset that European officials were independent of national governments, a special category of European civil servant had to be created. Monnet wrote in the 1950s of 'un nouveau type d'hommes [qui] était en train de naître dans les institutions de Luxembourg comme dans un laboratoire ... c'était l'esprit européen qui était le fruit du travail en commun' (Monnet 1976, 551). Daniel Strasser captured well the essence of this in terms of staffing and administration when he wrote:

> 'It was normal to give the status of civil servant to those who are a prefiguration of what will one day be a civil service of a European Confederation. Of course, doing that is more costly and more of a constraint than a system of contracts would be, but it is a modest price paid for the construction of one of the pillars of Europe.' (Strasser 1980, 429)

There is with hindsight a certain inevitability about the adoption, to ensure quality and independence, of a statutory framework which states that officials operate 'solely with the interests of the Communities in mind; [they] shall neither seek nor take instructions from any government, authority, organisation or person outside [their] institution. [They] shall carry out the duties assigned to [them] objectively, impartially and in keeping with [their] duty of loyalty to the Communities' (Staff Regulations 2004, I-8 article 11(96)). The emerging policy-making bureaucracy drew, to an important extent, upon former members of the civil services of the Member States. 'The essence of a continental European bureaucracy was in its creation of a distinctive social class...' and such bureaucracies 'are associated with formalism and hierarchy – the insistence that rules and procedures be observed' (Page 1997, 7-8). Both these features demand a clear statutory definition in order to entrench them. As Jacques Rueff, then a judge at the ECSC Court of Justice with special responsibility for managing its budgetary and administrative questions, said in 1953 'We have, rather blindly, chosen the option of a statutory framework (a *statut*) by analogy, because we want to create a situation closer to that of national administrations than that of international organisations. We felt that supranational civil servants (*un corps de fonctionnaires supranationaux*) were, in fact, almost national civil servants, whose nationality was supranationality' (quoted in Conrad 1992, 64; author's translation).

This conscious attempt to endow the Commission with a supranational ideology or mission was confirmed by Walter Hallstein, the first President of the Commission of the European Economic Community, in 1958. Hallstein was unashamed to include 'theory, doctrine, utopia, forecasts, planning, futurology (and) vision' in his writing, nor to admit that for him the final stage was 'full and complete federation' (Hallstein 1972, 11 and 295). The collective memory of these early halcyon years has remained important in the self-perception of Commission staff. It contributed strongly to the sense of identity and singleness of purpose of a generation of officials from the original Six 'for whom "building Europe" was a direct, personal response to the horrors of the second world war' (*The Economist* 23 November 2002). It can, however, also create barriers to younger generations for whom the very language used and the symbols of the past, redolent though they may be of early definitions of purpose, and evocative of an identification with building something new, frequently fall flat in the face of the need to deal with continuous technical and administrative details of legislation.

Paradoxically, however, the Hallstein period also saw the entrenchment of the *cabinet* system which has long served to reinforce national interest and representation within the Commission structures. Indeed, the *cabinets* were virtually the first administrative services to exist for the new EEC Commission, during the period between January and March 1958 when the division of responsibility between Commissioners was being decided. Hallstein fought against the development of large *cabinets* on the grounds that, since it was accepted that *cabinet* members would be of the same nationality as the Commissioner, they would work against his aim of strengthening 'l'esprit communautaire' (Lemaignen 1964, 49-50 cited in Mangenot 2001, 37).

For many years the European Commission remained a mix of the French and German systems, though not without some influences from other Member States (Stevens 2001, 32), but French administrative style and practices predominated, notably in the *cabinet* system, the Secretariat General, the personnel structure, interservice groups etc. (Dubouis 1975). French was the main working language of the Secretariat General. Thus, instructions in French from the core of the European administration imbued the institution with a mentality which looked to French culture and administrative norms as the unstated model of public administration. These entrenched reflexes have in recent years been challenged by the growing influence of British and Scandinavian Commissioners and officials in the area of administration, by movements for reform which take some of their inspiration from the new public management approaches which have flourished in the English speaking world and by the increasing use of English within the Commission.

Commission personnel policy

The Commission remains a very small organisation given its responsibility for the development, management and control of Community policies. It is, however, surprisingly difficult to state with any certainty how many people really work for the European Commission.

Table 6: *Distribution of officials and temporary agents by DG and category*

	A	B	C	D	Total
College	179	32	206	3	420
Secretariat General	155	85	178	39	457
Legal Service	183	24	96	6	309
DG Press and Communication	168	129	134	12	443
Bureau of European Policy Advisors	12	3	10		25
DG Economic and Financial Affairs	209	101	107	5	422
DG Enterprise and Industry	346	129	192	11	678
DG Competition	316	81	153	4	554
DG Employment, Social Affairs and Equal Opportunities	270	102	141	4	517
DG Agriculture and Rural Development	379	191	275	10	855
DG Energy and Transport	362	242	226	7	837
DG Environment	244	84	138	5	471
DG Research	645	211	265	13	1134
Joint Research Centre	770	494	378	27	1669
DG Information Society and Media	399	111	248	11	769
DG Fisheries and Maritime Affairs	112	83	66	4	265
DG Internal Market and Services	211	49	99	3	362
DG Regional Policy	236	106	142	7	491
DG Taxation and Customs Union	151	85	93	5	334
DG Education and Culture	203	122	205	19	549
DG Health and Consumer Protection	337	79	175	6	597
DG Justice, Freedom and Security	153	51	88	2	294
DG External Relations	335	111	209	15	670
DG Trade	193	99	86	6	384
DG Development	131	26	79	6	242
DG Enlargement	100	37	58	2	197
DG EuropeAid Co-operation Office	277	165	193	10	645
DG Humanitarian Aid	54	49	39	2	144
Statistical Office	227	177	150	6	560
DG Personnel and Administration	156	149	303	43	651
DG Informatics	81	136	127	4	348

	A	B	C	D	Total
DG Budget	147	124	126	6	403
Internal Audit Service	43	14	13	1	71
European Anti-Fraud Office	106	102	61	3	272
DG Interpretation	508	33	74	16	631
DG Translation	1570	51	439	20	2080
Office for Official Publications of the European Communities	67	247	177	30	521
Office for Infrastructure and Logistics in Brussels	31	62	246	112	451
Office for the Administration and Payment of Individual Entitlements	20	70	156	7	253
Office for Infrastructure and Logistics in Luxembourg	12	25	100	46	183
European Communities Personnel Selection Office	15	27	52	2	96
Total without Unified External Service	**10113**	**4298**	**6303**	**540**	**21254**
%	47.6%	20.2%	29.7%	2.5%	100.0%
Unified External Service*					
Legal Service	1	1			2
DG Economic and Financial Affairs	2				2
DG Agriculture and Rural Development	1				1
DG Research	10	1			11
DG Information Society and Media	1				1
DG Health and Consumer Protection	1				1
DG External Relations	584	218	74		876
DG Trade	3	1			4
DG Development	21	1			22
DG Humanitarian Aid	1				1
European Anti-Fraud Office		2			2
Total Unified External Service	**625**	**224**	**74**		**923**
%	67.7%	24.3%	8.0%		100.0%
Grand Total	**10738**	**4522**	**6377**	**540**	**22177**
%	48.4%	20.4%	28.8%	2.4%	100.0%

* Unified External Service includes staff from all DGs serving outside the EU in Commission delegations. See chapter 15 and Annex J.

Source: Commission Statistical Bulletin, July 2005. Figures are for 2004.

Table 6 gives the authorised staff numbers for the Commission in 2004 and suggests that it employed the equivalent of 22,177 people. But this would be an underestimate. An internal review (*Designing Tomorrow's Commission* – DECODE) of the Commission's organisation and operation (European Commission, 1999b), based on a census of staff in April 1998, reckoned that there were in fact 31,013 people working for the Commission at that time (see table 7), including temporary and locally employed staff. The figure is not likely to have been notably less several years later. Moreover, numbers will rise further over the period to 2010, to accommodate the enlargement with ten new Member States that took place on 1 May 2004. The Commission's target over the period is to recruit 3,441 additional officials or temporary agents and 350 external staff. (COM C(2003) 436/5 and European Commission press release IP/05/488 27 April 2005).

Table 7: *DECODE figures for European Commission Staffing 1998*

Type of staff	Numbers
permanent and temporary staff	20,880
auxiliary staff	1,033
detached national experts	760
casual staff	606
local agents	2,133
in-house service providers	1,836
extra-mural service providers	3,765
TOTAL	**31,013**

Source: European Commission, 1999b, p. iii

The majority of Commission staff are concentrated in Brussels and Luxembourg, but there are information offices in Member State capitals and in regional centres including Munich, Edinburgh, Cardiff, Belfast, Milan, Barcelona and Marseilles. The DECODE figure for permanent and temporary staff includes 1,834 staff at Joint Research Centre establishments spread over five centres throughout the Community with smaller numbers of staff attached to some national centres. It also includes 606 officials at the Commission's 123 delegations to non-member countries and to the international organisations to which the Commission is accredited. By 2005 that figure had risen to 990. The figure for local agents includes 1,919 staff at Commission delegations abroad. By 2005 there were 3,765 (see annex J).

The Commission likes to compare its relatively modest size favourably with that of other administrations. Martin (Martin 1995) notes that in the mid-1990s there was less than one European civil servant (0.8) for 10,000 European citizens, while there were 322 national civil servants for the same number of citizens. But such comparisons are of doubtful relevance. The Commission is directly responsible for the implementation of very few policies – in most cases that is the responsibility of the Member States – and that is what generally requires large numbers of staff.

Small size may be an advantage. Administration is close to the effective players in the Community game and discussion, explanation and lobbying take place within a closely-knit web of contacts. But there is a reverse side of the coin. Combining knowledge of the situation of the individual region, firm or citizen, and managing the enormous number of contacts with Member States in the administering of policies, inevitably stretches staff resources. In a situation where the geographical and sectoral scope of policy-making and implementation is still steadily expanding, management on a shoe string is faced with the inevitable contradiction of reduced efficiency and disheartened staff. There is now a general recognition that the Commission's understaffing was one of the prime causes not only of the emergence of what almost amounted to a parallel administrative regime with its own salary scales, promotion prospects and procedures, but also of severe abuses of the system. The post-1999 reform programme (see chapter 17) is attempting to tackle this in a number of ways.

The statutory framework

The conditions of service of officials and temporary agents of the Commission are set out in the 'Regulations and Rules applicable to Officials and other Servants of the European Communities', determining their rights and obligations, career structure, pay scales and social security and pension arrangements. The rules, originally agreed in December 1961, were based on the experience of the ECSC, and took definitive form in Regulation 259/68 of 1968 following the merger of the three Communities. This constitutes a single *statut*, which now applies to officials of all the EU institutions except the European Investment Bank and the European Central Bank. A very substantial revision of the *statut* was one of the products of the post 1999 reforms. Council Regulation (EC, Euratom) No 723/2004 of 22 March 2004 was implemented on 1 May 2004, the date on which 10 new Member States joined the EU.

The *statut* is an EC Regulation, running in its consolidated English version to 167 pages and consisting of nine Titles (containing well over a hundred articles) and thirteen Annexes. Like many of the analogous texts in the Member States, most of which possess a statutory framework for their civil servants, it is essentially a framework law. The *statut* is thus shorter than, for example, the non-statutory codes of terms and conditions for British civil servants (Stevens 2001, 46) but it is less flexible. There is a parallel regulation setting out the conditions for other employees – temporary staff, auxiliary staff, local staff and special advisers – and a raft of other, more detailed implementation rules in each institution.

Since the texts are a Regulation adopted by the Council of Ministers, amendment entails laborious procedures involving consultation first with staff representatives and then with the inter-institutional staff regulations committee, before a Commission proposal can be put to the Council of Ministers. The *statut* is subject to parliamentary consultation and views in the Council may be very divided, especially given the different administrative traditions in the Member States (Page 2003). As the Commission itself pertinently remarks of the process of amendment '[i]n the ensuing melée, unexpected delays can occur. Past reform efforts have sometimes foundered in the thickets of these procedures' (European Commission 2002, 62).

Reform could not however be indefinitely postponed, because, firstly, the *statut* to some extent embodied the assumptions of the period when it was agreed. Moreover there were then only six Member States whose administrative cultures, if varied, shared many of the same roots. By the turn of the century the *statut* was increasingly anachronistic. Secondly, following the 1999 events, demand for reform had acquired substantial political, as well as administrative, impetus. While many of the measures deemed necessary would have been possible within the framework of the old *statut*, a complete revision was an important symbol of the importance of organisational and cultural change (Coull and Lewis 2003, 8). Progress was not rapid (see chapter 17) but the process was completed some two years after the Commission put its first detailed proposal to the Council in April 2002.

Statutory staff

Statutory staff comprise the officials and temporary agents covered by the 'Staff Regulations of officials and the Conditions of Employment of other servants of the European Communities'. The *statut* provides a basis in law for all the formal events of an official career, from appointment to resignation or retirement, and for the relationship between the EU institutions and their employees both individually and collectively.

Permanent officials

Permanent officials are normally expected to serve with the Commission until they reach the normal retirement age, which is now set at 65 although an official may opt to retire after 63, and may exceptionally be retained until 67. When the staff structures were established in the 1950s they were based on those then prevailing in France, which had themselves been strongly influenced by the contemporary British civil service. Staff were consequently divided between four categories – A/LA, B, C, D, each divided into grades. Staff in the A category carried out the Commission's policy work and filled all senior positions. LA staff filled posts in the Commission's translation services or, as interpreters, in the Interpretation and Conferences Service common to all institutions of the Union except the Parliament. A and LA staff required a university degree or equivalent qualification. Staff in category B, responsible for executive tasks such as the Commission's own financial and personnel services, required education to university entrance level. Category C covered secretarial and clerical staff. Messengers, drivers, and other manual staff belonged to category D. In principle staff were recruited at the lowest grade in their category and were able to expect a reasonably guaranteed career progression taking them to A4, B1, C1 or D1 respectively, a point they were likely to reach around the age of 50 (European Commission 2002, 23). Promotion across the boundaries between categories was not the norm.

These category structures came to seem increasingly outdated – the D category was abolished in the French system in the early 1990s. Purely secretarial functions, which occupied many category C officials, are increasingly redundant while the requirement for other forms of support has grown; the persons occupying posts in categories C and B are increasingly well-qualified, while the messenger and housekeeping functions undertaken by category D have either dwindled as communication becomes electronic, or can readily be externalised. One of the main innovations of the new *statut* is thus their abolition and replacement by two 'function groups', situated on a linear 'single spine' on to which all existing officials will be transferred via transitional arrangements with their salaries protected (see chapter 17). The system is not, however, fully linear since there is still a division between a lower (Assistant – AST) group and a higher (Administrator – AD) group with an examination barrier between them and a quota (20 per cent of newly appointed officials each year) limiting movement between the AST and AD groups (Coull and Lewis 2003, 4). Nevertheless, the new structure is intended to remove a number of bottlenecks and allow officials recruited at relatively low levels to progress much further than would previously have been possible (see chapter 17)

In the AD grades there is (again as in the French system) no strong link between grade and function, although a revised Annex 1 to the *statut* sets out typical posts for each grade (see annex F). However, for example, 'Head of Unit' appears as a possible post for grades AD 9 to 14. There is considerable flexibility in the level at which policy work can be done and where AD 9 – 14 are not Heads of Unit there is no expectation that they will have more junior staff working for them. Staff in the most senior posts, from Directors General down to and including all Heads of Unit, are, however, expected to manage the staff reporting to them, though some very senior staff, e.g. a Principal Adviser at AD 13 or 14, may have no staff beyond immediate secretarial support.

Recruitment and training

The Staff Regulations (Articles 27 and 29) require the Commission 'to secur[e] for the institution the services of officials of the highest standard of ability, efficiency and integrity...' and to do so, if they cannot fill vacant posts by promotion or transfer, 'follow[ing] the procedure for competitions on the basis either of qualifications, or of tests, or of qualifications and tests'. Special arrangements are in place for recruitment to the most senior management posts (see below). The practice of recruitment via 'objectively' marked competitive tests is based on the *concours* system which evolved in France for entry to the higher civil service. However, alongside this the EU imported features from other systems. Success in a *concours* does not lead directly to appointment to a post. Instead it opens a place on a 'reserve list'. The Staff Regulations provide in Article 30 that 'the Selection Board shall draw up a list of suitable candidates. The appointing authority shall decide which of these candidates to appoint to the vacant posts.' The reserve list normally contains about twice as many candidates as the number of posts to be filled, a feature deriving from Belgian precedents. The appointing authority's discretion not to take candidates from the list in the order of their competition results follows the Italian model (Ziller 1988).

The organisation of the Commission's services was for a long time predicated on the notion that, as a permanent and independent civil service, it offers a steadily ascending lifetime career. This notion is particularly important to the staff unions, which have always been hostile to the recruitment of staff at mid-career level, where newcomers compete with existing staff seeking promotion.

Their pressure is one of the main reasons why the Commission continues to limit the general open *concours* to the lower grades (1-4 for the AST group, 5-8 for the AD group). The institutions may organise competitions for entry to grades 8-12, but only for 20 per cent of entrants each year. This notion also explains the long persistence of upper age limits – for Commission administrator entry grade *concours* the limit was 45 – which some Member States have felt themselves compelled by equal opportunities legislation to abolish, and which the EU Ombudsman roundly criticised (*European Voice* 13 July 2000). The 2000 White Paper *Reforming the Commission* (section IV.4, p. 17) reiterated the Commission's commitment to abolishing such limits, although the trade unions and some of the other institutions remained doubtful. It took another letter from the Ombudsman (*European Voice* 21 December 2000) to induce the Commission to take a unilateral decision to abolish all age limits from April 2002 (European Commission 2002, 7). It was, however, a retired Director General who voiced a widely-held opinion in a letter to *European Voice* (25 April 2002) in the spring of 2002:

> 'What I find… astonishing is that the EU institutions, some of them with strong reluctance, have given in [to the demand for the abolition of the age limit] or seem about to do so.
>
> …If ever [candidates over the former age limit] are hired [in the entry grades] they will work on the same job with the same salary as a young beginner aged 22 – 23. Anybody who has some experience of staff management would know that such a situation will create frictions, jealousy and envy almost from the first day.'

Whilst some competitions may be open to a very wide range of candidates, others may be more restricted. For example, at the time of enlargement, there are always competitions limited to nationals of the new Member States. The Commission aimed to recruit 814 new officials from the new members in 2004 and 715 in 2005. The first competitions produced 1,081 new employees for the beginning of April 2005. A second round of competitions followed in 2005 for recruitment in 2006 (European Commission press release IP/05/488 27 April 2005). Targets were set for the distribution of the new recruits amongst Directorates General. A competition may be structured so as to reserve some appointments for candidates with degrees in particular subjects such as law, economics, or statistics, or for people with particular types of experience such as external relations or aid management (e.g. in March 1998, for the Commission) as well as specialist staff ranging from interpreters, doctors, veterinarians, mineralogists and accountants to nuclear inspectors. This was the pattern adopted for recruitment from the new Member States, with some ten separate competitions organised, including, for example, for those with expertise in economics, business management or statistics, and for those with expertise relevant to the management of the structural funds.

For purely administrative tasks, the Commission traditionally favoured competitions for specialists, but lawyers or economists in countries such as the United Kingdom are not particularly attracted to the civil service and are unlikely to be willing, after passing the *concours*, to wait for an extended period on a 'reserve list' to be selected for a post. In 1991 the Commission was persuaded to open competitions for young generalists. The British had been lobbying for the change for years as one way of remedying their chronic under-representation (Denman 1990). However, the impact of successive enlargements, the very considerable time (often well over a year) and expense involved in completing the procedures, and the rather low turn-over in a relatively small administrator level staff contingent, have all militated against the Commission's stated policy of holding such competitions at regular pre-announced intervals. One consequence has been an enormous volume of applications when such competitions are announced. The 1993 A7/A8 *concours* had 58,000 candidates of whom 1,800 reached the second stage and 600 reached the final oral examination for a total of 200/250 places on the reserve list. In 1998 there were 30,000 candidates. The high numbers have to be reduced to manageable proportions – no more than two or three thousand – by the pre-selection stage. This has consisted of two or more multiple-choice papers; one designed to test knowledge of any specialist expertise which may have been required, whilst the others test more general administrative skills, knowledge of the EU institutions and policies, and finally the candidate's chosen second language. The marking scheme allows the various elements to be differentially weighted, but all candidates must reach the pass mark in all papers, usually 50 per cent.

All the tests, except the language test, are the same for all candidates. In 1993 the cultural problems which this posed were tackled by multiple choice questions on general culture somewhat akin to those of the board game *Trivial Pursuit*. The resultant criticism produced the more focussed tests of 1998/9 but even highly knowledgeable generalist UK candidates on that occasion were floored by questions requiring detailed knowledge of the staff regulations for which their broad and non-legalistic approach had not prepared them. The competition took place on the same day in eleven languages and at as many as 38 different centres across the EU. So when cheating was reported at the tests in September 1998 in Rome and in Brussels – some candidates left the room and used mobile phones to check their answers – the whole competition had to be annulled and re-run six months later at vast expense. The linguistic, logistical and legal difficulties of organising recruitment within a very tightly regulated framework are formidable, so that even quite simple and technical competitions, such as one for English language interpreters held in 2000-01, can take nine months or more. The Commission's 2000 White Paper acknowledged several of the main problems of the *concours* when it spoke of the need for better logistical organisation and recognised the need to have tests that take 'full account ... of the multicultural dimension of the EU as well as gender'.

The technical complexity of organising recruitment across fifteen, and now 25, Member States in ways that do not unfairly discriminate against certain nationalities or one sex is very considerable. Moreover, until 2003 each individual institution organised its own recruitment, duplicating procedures but without coordination. Spurred on both by the pressures for a reformed and more professional human resources policy, and by the prospect of massive and complex recruitment following enlargement, the various institutions agreed in mid-2002 to set up a joint European Personnel Selection Office, operative from 1 January 2003 (Decisions 2002/620 and 621). The EPSO (see www.Europa.eu.int/EPSO.html) now runs all except the most specialised of the open competitions and has the task of developing more streamlined, automated on-line procedures. Its creation has resulted in savings, with recruitment costs budgeted at some 11 per cent less than had previously been spent across all the institutions involved (COM (2004) 93F, 31).

Given the explicit linkage in the early period between the creation of an independent civil service and the furtherance of the integration process it is perhaps surprising that training did not figure more prominently in the provisions for officials, especially since the French, on whom so much of the early Commission organisation was modelled, had in the 1940s created a National Administrative College (Ecole Nationale d'Administration – ENA) expressly to underpin a new ethos amongst officials. Only rather limited training has been provided, which until the 1990s was heavily concentrated on language skills development (Stevens 2001, 105-8). The late 1990s saw training and development take off in the Commission both in terms of the funds available and the possibilities on offer. The Kinnock reform programme strengthened the link between appraisal, training and career development as part of an integrated process and envisaged the creation of a 'European Civil Service training centre'. The other institutions also expanded their activities in this area considerably and opened discussions that led to the creation of the European Administrative School (EAS).

The School, which is organisationally attached to the European Personnel Selection Office (EPSO) but is operationally independent, formally came into existence on 10 February 2005 when the founding texts were published in the Official Journal (edition n° L37 of 2005). Its initial mandate is to provide training programmes for officials of all EU institutions at three career moments: on arrival; when they have been identified as having the potential to progress from the grade of assistant to that of administrator; and on appointment to a management position.

The School handles both the organisational and logistical aspects of its training and development programmes and is also responsible for their design, development, delivery and evaluation. Although many of the training events will be outsourced, it has an internal training capacity and also has an advisory role. The EAS has offices in both Brussels and Luxembourg.

Mobility, hierarchy, and career structure

Once embarked upon a lifetime career as a Commission official some mobility between jobs is normal, though the scope for very specialised staff to change their area of work is limited. Although staff have been encouraged to move between areas of work, at least within Directorates General and often between them, the achievement of staff mobility has been a particular weakness within the Commission's personnel management. Between 1990 and 1997 an average of only 800 staff (about four per cent) moved from one Directorate General to another each year (Williamson Report 1998, 48). This creates real difficulties of two kinds. First, the institution finds it difficult to adjust staffing levels to changing requirements. A 'screening' exercise in 1991, intended to identify over- and under-staffed areas, had rather little effect. *Designing Tomorrow's Commission*, launched by the Santer Commission in 1997 and completed in 1999, was an even more thorough-going study with the same intention. Its impact combined with the attention directed to the Commission's use of resources by the diagnoses of the causes of the 1999 resignation, and its results were consequently more far-reaching. In the first year after its publication there were over 650 redeployments between DGs to priority areas. Second, lengthy tenure in 'sensitive' posts with personnel or financial responsibilities increased the danger that cosy, unhealthy or even corrupt relationships could develop. As part of the reform of internal controls Directorates General have been required to identify such posts, and compulsorily move anyone who has occupied one for more than seven years. This has not always been easy, since the technical expertise that has to be replaced may be in short supply (COM (2004) 93F, 8).

The long standing difficulties in securing mobility arose from two main causes. First, while mobility was expected and, indeed, can be a key way of ensuring career progression, the initiative has normally lain with staff themselves. Leaving career management in the hands of the individual member of staff may suit the most confident and ambitious, but it may also open the door to patronage and favours. Conversely, those who are more cautious or less well connected tend to regard mobility as more of a threat, detrimental to their career prospects and tantamount to a disciplinary measure. If they chose to remain in the same post for a very long time, it has been extremely difficult for management to move them against their will, particularly if they had satisfactory reports, as nearly all staff have done. Secondly, sideways movement between Directorates General for administrative category officials could be seen as potentially setting back promotion since Directors General submitted lists for consideration by the promotions committee and were less likely to include newcomers whom they did not know. Increased expectation and greater ease of mobility has thus been one of the key objectives of the reforms of the early 2000s (see chapter 17). Moreover, the activity based management approach introduced in 2002-3 (ibid) is intended to ensure that regular assessment of areas of strain, oversupply and redeployment will become a routine management task. In 2003, 5.8 per cent of officials were moved to priority areas.

Promotion up to a certain level is also considered a normal expectation. Formally, promotion has required the existence of a vacancy to be filled at the higher level (although this may be derived from the allocation of budgetary resources rather than the definition of a post) and has been supposedly based on a combination of seniority and merit, with evidence for merit coming from the reports drawn up on all staff at least once every two years. In practice over many years reporting was not necessarily undertaken when it should have been, and was too bland to produce meaningful distinctions between candidates. This had the consequence that seniority has been the main factor at the lower levels, with officials effectively guaranteed movement up to a senior (but not managerial) grade over a period, on average, of 17 to 20 years. Considerations other than seniority became more important when promotion, for example to a head of unit post, meant a change in function and the acquisition of management responsibilities. The annual promotions round (except for the highest levels) are overseen by promotions committees with representation from both management and the staff side.

The relative slowness, but also automaticity of promotion, tended to provide little incentive to seek to achieve outstanding performance. A survey in the late 1980s found a widespread perception that the way to achieve promotion was to have the right connections, followed by seniority, luck, the right nationality, service in a *cabinet*, the will to succeed, ability, qualifications, knowing when to keep quiet and – last of all – producing results and hard work. Despite widespread acknowledgement of these features over at least a decade it proved extremely difficult to tackle them, not least because the problems included those of mentality as well as structures. A former Secretary General of the Commission – who as such was chairman of the joint boards for all B grade promotions and all A grade promotions up to A3, and of the Central Committee on Nominations for appointments as head of unit and director – insists that 'merit (and to a lesser extent seniority) was the basis for ... promotions and nationality played no significant part whatever' and that he 'refuse[d] to attend any meetings of *cabinets* intended to discuss the distribution by nationality of head of unit' (personal information). A new integrated appraisal and promotion system intended to recognise and reward merit and avoid the disincentive to mobility hence forms a key aspect of the reforms of the early 2000s. It has been implemented since 2003 (see chapter 17), but well informed internal observers conclude that 'whether it is a success in reality will not be clear for at least a decade' (Coull and Lewis 2003, 4) since it challenges both the Commission's internal culture and the Member States' concern about the position of their nationals within the Commission's services (see below).

Promotion's counterpart, demotion, is as unusual amongst the staff of the Commission as it is in national civil services. So is the removal of underperforming officers – indeed, only one official has ever actually been dismissed for failure to perform. As in Germany and France, for example, permanent officials of the Commission are well protected both by the legal framework, and by a legitimising belief in the rigour of the initial recruitment process – if they were no good they would never have got through in the first place (European Commission 2002, 54). The position has been further complicated by the persistent system of national protection via the *cabinet* system running through personnel policy in practice. As one official observed 'it is theoretically possible (to fire someone) but when I fire someone, I am not firing him, but a nationality, I am not firing a civil servant, but an Italian ... The only way to get rid of him is to promote him and "sell" him to someone else' (quoted in Michelmann 1978, 489). That one consequence has been undue protection for poor performance is quite widely recognised, not least in the Kinnock reform programme, which acknowledges that absenteeism, poor timekeeping and similar problems were condoned rather than being tackled through the only mechanism available – the disciplinary procedures – which were 'tantamount to using a sledgehammer to crack a nut' (European Commission 2002, 54). It remains to be seen whether the new procedures to deal with what is described as 'wrongdoing', involving the annual appraisal system, a corrective plan and recourse to a disciplinary board in the case of two successive negative appraisals, will be effective in countering the impact of national protection in individual cases.

The hierarchy

The nature of the promotions system highlights some of the features of the hierarchical structure within the Commission's services. Drawn out on paper the Commission's structure has many of the characteristics of a classic Weberian pyramid. Each Directorate General or Service is headed by a Director General, with a number of Directors heading its functional divisions, and units within those consisting of a head of unit and several desk officers. Support is provided by AST group (formerly B and C category) officials, though not in large numbers, so the base of the pyramid is rather narrow. However, the reality is more complex, in a number of ways.

First, there may be units, such as that for the management of the Directorate General's own resources, outside the pyramidal structure. Until the late 1990s it was usual for Directors General to have an Assistant, usually at a rather senior (A4) level (Sasse, et al. 1977, 153) but with a more frequent than normal turnover, attached to their own offices. The Assistant had key functions in the management of the Directorate General and the deployment of personnel, and in the smaller Directorates General was also often responsible for the financial management of the Directorate. From the late 1990s the increased emphasis on good management resulted in the setting up of resources units under Resource Directors, within the normal hierarchy of the Directorate General.

Second, one or more policy advisers, operating outside the pyramidal framework, may be attached to the Director General or one or more of the Directors. Usually at AD14 (A3) level, they are justified by the Commission on the grounds that their special policy expertise is required. They are surprisingly numerous. In 1998 the DECODE team found 15 principal advisers and 167 advisers, 'a great many of them [with] only minor or poorly defined tasks to perform'. In 2002 there were some 150 posts for advisers established within the organisational framework and a further 100 advisers in 'personal' posts (European Commission 2002, 19 section 2.4.2). In effect, such posts have often been used as a way of providing an honourable move sideways. It may be that the previous post is now required for a person of a different nationality. It may be that no operational or managerial position commensurate with someone's seniority can be found. It may be a solution pending the resolution of problems – the former Director General of Eurostat, Yves Franchet, was moved into an adviser post (prior to retirement) when the organisation became engulfed in scandal. It may be a way of easing someone's passage towards retirement, particularly since early retirement in the interests of the service is really only possible by mutual consent (*European Voice* 27 February 2004). A reshuffle in 2004 resulted in several former Directors General and deputy Directors General moving into adviser posts, in at least one case specifically as a prelude to retirement (Commission Press Release IP 04/229). The reform documents promise a review to ensure that such posts will in future only exist where there is a genuine operational need. But with increased mobility they are likely to continue to be too useful in allowing for flexibility and contributing to the complex political game of placating all interests, for their numbers to diminish substantially.

Finally the notion of hierarchy implicit in the pyramidal model of bureaucracy is not necessarily shared across all the national cultures from which Commission officials are recruited. Terms such as 'hierarchy', 'accountability', 'subordination', 'co-operation', 'common interest', even if they are in the everyday language of the Commission, are susceptible to different interpretations according to whether they are perceived in the 'Northern' countries, more familiar with the concept of management, or in the 'Southern' countries (Bellier 1999, 254; Bellier 2000a, 57). The hierarchical superior and the manager are two different entities – the first occupies a position, the second a function – sometimes united in the same person on whom staff pass a different judgment according to their knowledge of the various national styles (Bellier 1999, 255). It is not difficult to find anecdotes of the confusion which arises when very differing sets of (often unexpressed and unarticulated) assumptions and preconceptions encounter each other (Pollitt and Bouckaert 2000, 190), especially when even the vocabulary carries a different baggage in different languages. For example, if the Weberian norms of structured management are deeply embedded, a veneer of informality may easily be applied, to soften the harsher underlying realities. The lack of the trappings of deference does not, however, mean that the constraints of obedience are absent. Maryon McDonald tells of a female French official in the European Commission who, finding her British superior rigid and unsympathetic, was all the more bewildered when he asked her to 'stop calling him "Monsieur" and call him "Jim"' (McDonald 1997, 63). In a multicultural organisation, moreover, there has been space for alternative hierarchies and cultures with 'their own precedence, reciprocities and proprieties' (McDonald 1997, 67-68). As one of McDonald's interviewees reported, 'It seems to be something to do with personal rank and honour, but precious little to do with management' (ibid, 64) 'Shame, naivety and stupidity' are ascribed to those who do not know how to work such a system (ibid, 68). To officials who understand, or learn to understand, such structures the Commission can seem open, exciting and 'democratic'. It may leave even relatively junior officials with a great deal of scope to make proposals, to 'do creative and exciting things' (ibid, 65). To those to whom the norms of such a system are unfamiliar it can seem more like 'anarchy' (ibid, 63), a system without rules, without guidance, without a clear assignment of tasks. The unwritten understanding of what one can do oneself and what should be passed on, and to whom, acquired in different systems comes to seem invalid. Since such understandings are by their very nature uncodified, unwritten, and deeply rooted in the culture within which they develop, there is no coherent or readily comprehensible alternative.

The consequence can be that whether they come from structured or hierarchical backgrounds, Commission officials can experience their working environment as riven with internal politics, highly personalised, anarchic and insecure (Stevens 2001, 175-6). In consequence there is no single agreed management style, such as one would expect in a national civil service. For example, the different administrative cultures present among the Commission staff are marked in the way notes are written, or information conveyed. Submissions may be written in a classic French cartesian style or follow a more British sequential approach on the basis of check lists, of arguments for and against, or of questions and answers with supporting evidence. Some DGs resemble feudal systems and their most senior staff are often described as the 'barons' of the system. Guarding information is a means of retaining power and, as in national systems like those of France and Germany, the right to sign letters and other documents is a cherished privilege of senior staff and the 'best practice' recommendations of the 'who signs what' quality circle which reported in 2003 (COM (2004) 93F, 30) are unlikely to have a speedy impact. On the other hand, there are senior managers working on the basis of delegation of responsibility to their staff, using an open flow of information.

Posts at the top

Posts at the most senior levels (now AD 14 – 16) have always been subject to somewhat different rules from those at lower levels. In normal circumstances posts at Director level have very largely been filled by promotion from below, but promotion does occur much more directly into a specific post than at lower levels. In April 2004, 18 such posts were advertised by name (Director General of the Joint Research Centre, Directors in Energy and Transport, Agriculture, Environment...) but confined to nationals of the new Member States (European Commission press release IP/04/519). By April 2005 five Directors General or Deputy Directors General, out of a target of 10, had been nominated, as had seven Directors or Principal Advisors (European Commission Press release IP/05/488 of 27 April 2005). Instead of the joint union/management promotions committee a Consultative Committee for Nominations, composed of a group of Directors General under the chairmanship of the Secretary General, decides. The unions have been refused staff representation in this committee on the grounds that the filling of such posts is a prerogative of the leadership at 'political' (College of Commissioners) level. The new single spine structure (see above) collapses the former A3 – A1 levels, assimilating existing A3 posts to point 14, and allowing for Directors and Directors General to be located between points 14 and 16. These are the levels at which national and political influences have customarily played a major role (see below).

Pay and pensions

When the European Coal and Steel Community was established, the salaries of its officials were set at relatively high levels, both so as to attract good staff to a new and untried institution, and to ensure some parity with the private companies of the sector. This pattern of relatively high salaries has continued in the Commission (Georgakakis 2002, 8). Commission salaries are at or – in some cases – well above, the levels for roughly equivalent officials in national capitals. However, they are in general in line with what such officials would receive if posted to a diplomatic mission in Brussels. The structure is much complicated by special allowances added on to basic pay. In this the pay structure mirrors that of many diplomatic services and national systems in many of the Member States. The reform proposals simplify these, removing rent and transport allowances, for example, and reducing the cost of allowing for annual journeys to the place of origin of the official (provided it is over 200 kilometres from the location of the official's post). Commission officials are not subject to national income taxes, but pay a progressive income tax, which rises to 45 per cent of salary in the top bands, as an EU tax. In 1981, at a time when the Community budget was causing dissent between Member States, and there was, in a period of recession, a tendency to cut back on public expenditure, the negotiations on the 'method' by which salary levels are fixed (see below) resulted in industrial disputes including a ten-day strike by officials of the Commission. As part of the settlement a so-called 'crisis levy' was introduced to mitigate the impact on the budget of salary rises. It was retained, again after demonstrations by the unions, at 5.83 per cent and renamed the 'temporary contribution', when the 'method' was renegotiated in 1992 (Georgakakis 2002, 8). The revised *statut* (Article 66a) provides that from 2004 it will be replaced for eight years by a 'social' contribution which will start at 2.5 per cent and rise over the period to 5.5 per cent. Across-the-board annual salary increases have since 1981 been determined by a system called the 'method' which takes and applies an average of the percentage purchasing power increases awarded to officials in national public services. This is now formalised within the regulatory framework (Staff Regulations 2004 Annex XI), in the hope of avoiding conflict with the unions over salary levels. Pre-tax basic salaries in 2004 ranged from €2,325 a month (approximately £19,000 a year) for the lowest level of the lowest grade (the new linear spine grade 1) to €16,094 a month (approximately £131,300 a year) at the highest possible level. An Administrator at the lowest level of the entry grade (AD5) received (before levies) €3,810 a month (about £31,000 a year) (Staff Regulation 2004 article 66; for 2005 figures, see Annex G).

The Commission operates an unfunded final salary pension scheme involving a contribution (9.25 per cent of salary) and accrual at the rate of 1.9% of the final basic salary per year of service, so that approximately 37 years' service produces the maximum pension of 70 per cent of the final basic salary. Retirement before 63 reduces the pension payable. Officials appointed before the implementation of the new *statut* enjoy slightly more favourable conditions, but changes were insisted upon by the Council, on the grounds that officials of the EU should not be exempt from the 'modernisation' of pension schemes that was being implemented throughout most of the Member States. The main concern will in fact have been to cut the cost of the Staff Regulations package. The changes were opposed by the unions, who called a one-day strike in May 2003 (*European Voice* 22 May 2003) but there was not much stomach for a prolonged fight since most of the impact falls on new staff who have no voice.

There are substantial disincentives to retirement below 60 (moving to 63 with the reforms) and considerable incentives not to retire until 65, and relatively few do leave before that age. Article 50 of the Staff Regulations does allow for early retirement, with compensation, for A1 and A2 officials where the interests of the institutions require this, although this provision is not easy to enforce against resistance (*European Voice* 27 February 2004). In the interests of flexibility and mobility the new Regulation allows the Commission each year to award their full accrued rights to a small number of early retirees at other grades, and in 2002-3, when the Council refused to allow the

Commission the number of new posts they felt they needed to cope with enlargement, early retirements were actively sought in the interest of freeing up posts for nationals of the new Member States. As the Court of Auditors observed, this was hardly consonant with the EU's declared strategy of encouraging the retention of older workers (Dinan 2003, 39).

Staff representation

As the European civil service was originally inspired by the French and German civil services, staff representatives are involved in all aspects of personnel policy and management. Unions thus play an important role in the administrative life of the Commission. A Central Staff Committee, elected by the staff, is the contact point between the administration and the staff representatives. It appoints staff representatives to a variety of committees, ranging from the management committee of the nursery for staff children, the disciplinary and promotion committees, to selection boards involved in the recruitment competitions. In practice it is the trade unions who put up lists of candidates for the Central Staff Committee.

The union structure is highly fragmented and membership is not high (in 1999 no more than 35 per cent of the staff and possibly as few as 18 per cent), although all officials may express their preferences through their votes for one or another of the union lists for the Central Staff Committee. Nevertheless, industrial conflict and strike action are not uncommon, as in 1998 and 2003 (see chapter 17).

The unions have thus been militant, particularly in defence of established procedures and conditions, but they play a much less crucial role in relation to individual grievances. Informal networks, especially national networks, may be a more efficacious resource. Moreover, much personnel administration is a matter of legal interpretation and officials may contest decisions they consider harmful by formal procedures, first within the Commission and, in the final resort, before the European Court of Justice. Such cases – of which there were, over the period 2000-03, between 110 and 124 a year – were, from its creation until 2004, delegated to the Court of First Instance, making up between 25 and 35 per cent of its total case load. As the burden of business on the Court has increased, and given the specialised nature of this jurisdiction, the Council of Ministers decided in November 2004 to create a European Civil Service Tribunal as an integral but separate part of the Court of Justice. This Tribunal comprises a panel of seven judges appointed by the Council (Council Press Release C/04/254 of 2 November 2004). Legal proceedings are, of course, inevitably protracted and cumbersome. There is also a mediator who intercedes between the administration and its officials on working conditions and relations with management. The mediator is supposedly completely independent, and officials seeking advice or pursuing complaints have access in confidence. The Kinnock reforms have attempted to reinforce the mediator's independence and increase the office's staffing, partly in a bid to decrease the number of cases that go to the Court.

Temporary agents and non-statutory staff

Permanent employment as an official is not the only form of employment relationship between the Commission and those who work for it. There have been essentially four other categories of employment, and a group of 'work experience' trainees known as *stagiaires*. There are
–   temporary agents;
–   auxiliary, local and casual staff;
–   freelance and consulting staff;
–   detached national experts.
The proposed new Staff Regulation will add a further category – contract staff – which it is hoped will rationalise and supersede some of the previous categories. The Reform White paper (COM(2000) 200) rightly observed that the 'situation is confusing, untransparent, and expensive' (p.14).

Temporary agents serve under contract with the Commission for a limited period of time and are divided into the same categories and grades as permanent officials. Indeed, the staff statutes apply equally to them. Their conditions of employment are the same, except for the limited period of employment and the fact that, in the A category, they cannot normally be appointed to management functions. The reform process is attempting to ensure that almost all posts (except those in the anti-fraud office) are converted into permanent posts, even if some of them may be filled by employees on time-limited contracts. Thus, in 2001 100 permanent posts were created by the conversion of operational credits into provision for posts and a further 90 existing temporary posts were converted into permanent ones (COM(2003) 40 final/2).

The Commission nevertheless intends to retain the four longstanding types of temporary employee. Temporary agents filling temporary posts are recruited for specific jobs of a transitory nature. Selection procedures consist of a public call for applications, an evaluation of the candidate's professional experience and an interview with a selection board. Temporary agents may also fill permanent posts where a permanent post is vacant, there is no internal candidate to fill it and competition reserve lists have been exhausted. This is a rare occurrence in category A, but is more frequent in the B and C categories. Contracts for these temporary agents are limited to two years, with extension possible for a maximum of one year. *Cabinet* temporary agents are recruited from outside the Commission directly by the Commissioner, and serve on his or her private staff for the duration of the mandate. Finally, temporary agents recruited under the research budget of the Commission have usually been scientific experts recruited on indefinitely renewable five-year contracts, a system dating from the 1970s when the need for greater flexibility in such appointments became apparent because a permanent cadre of nuclear scientists recruited by Euratom could not readily be re-assigned to the new research priorities. Many research staff, provided they have been working for at least six years and can pass a competition, are being established as permanent officials. Those DGs that recruit staff on the research budget of the Commission (Research, Information Society, the Joint Research Centre, Energy and Transport, Enterprise, and Fisheries) will have between 10 and 35 per cent of their permanent posts reserved for temporary staff on contracts of not more than three years. In future all research staff recruitment will be handled by the European Personnel Selection Office.

Auxiliary staff are taken on to replace officials temporarily absent (on secondment, sickness or maternity leave, for example) or to deal with a sudden and temporary peak in workload. Their contracts have in the past been limited to one year but three years will now be the norm, and their use will be confined to the Commission's central services, since the employment of auxiliary staff will not be possible where contract staff are employed.

Employees at the Commission's Representations in the Member States and its Delegations in third countries have constituted a separate group of auxiliary staff, which is now to be subsumed into the new category of contract staff. Casual staff from employment agencies will not be ruled out, though resort to them will be discouraged and they will be limited to no more than six weeks in any one department. At the other end of the scale there will continue to be provisions for the occasional employment of freelance special advisers, for example as special representatives of the Commission in the crisis areas of the world.

During the 1980s and early 1990s the SEA, the single market and the evolution of the situation in Eastern Europe increased the tasks of the Commission considerably, yet few if any provisions were made to increase the human resources necessary to deal with them. As a result, the Commission services were faced with the choice between simply not doing the work, or finding other means to secure the necessary manpower. In 1992 a report for the Parliamentary Committee on the Budget stated that almost one third of the staff working for the Commission came from outside and were paid in part from the operating section of the budget (Elles 1992, 611) – the so-called 'mini-budget' device (see chapter 17). In some instances, this was the result of a genuine shortage of human resources. In others, it became a convenient way of hiring and firing and introducing a carrot and stick management ethic. The possibility of not having a contract renewed is doubtless an incentive to achievement. The problem in terms of public service ethic is that the system of recruitment of such external personnel was almost totally discretionary, and there was no central control of their qualifications.

The 1999 crisis in the Commission, and the revelations in the reports of the European Parliament Committee of Independent Experts set up to consider the allegations against Commissioners and their services, threw a highly critical light upon these practices, and inspired a number of the reform proposals. These took three forms: first, a statement by Commission President Prodi that the Commission would refuse to take on new tasks unless the administrative means to undertake them were provided; second, the introduction of the activity based management system which is intended to show up instances of mismatch between tasks and resources; and third, a clear statement that the Commission's central services would concentrate on its core roles – the right to initiate policy proposals and guardianship of the Treaties. Other tasks would be 'externalised' – hived off to executive agencies (see chapter 5) which, although managed by permanent officials, would be staffed in the main by a new category of 'contract' staff.

Under a new Title IV within Part II of the Staff Regulations – Conditions of Employment of other servants – contract staff may be employed at all levels ranging from the equivalent of the previous Category D up to a ceiling at the middle of Category A. Such staff may cover a wide range of functions – from nursery nurses in the crèches and messengers to the implementation of policy in executive agencies and the Commission's overseas offices. They are recruited by a relatively simple procedure – monitored by a joint union-management committee – involving press and internet advertisement and interview by the local agency concerned, and employed on the basis of contracts running for a maximum of five years, renewable for a further five years, and then, provided they can prove an ability to work in three languages, convertible into open-ended contracts, but without access to the status of a permanent official. The career structure will have 18 grades in four function groups, which are roughly equivalent to the old A-D categories, but the ceiling will be set at a point equivalent to the middle point of Grade 8, below the level at which management responsibility might be exercised (European Commission 2002, 44-46; Staff Regulations 2004, Part II article 93). The intention clearly is to produce more flexible employment arrangements for staff engaged in service delivery functions at all levels, and to confine employment within the 'European Civil Service' to those required for its core functions.

So-called 'Detached (seconded) National Experts' – staff on secondment from various administrations or private companies in the Member States – form a distinct category of temporary staff with their own terms and conditions. They remain paid by their employer, though the Commission covers their living expenses in Brussels. They may work at the Commission for a period of not more than three years and not less than three months. The seconded national experts system is justified and defended by the Commission as a two-way information system, designed to foster closer relations between the Commission and national administrations by allowing civil servants from each side to learn about the other's procedures and administrative culture (Hay 1989, 50). The arrangements are one way of ensuring that the Commission is not regarded merely as a collection of 'foreigners' with power to determine the national policy-making agenda. Together with more general attempts at achieving a geographical balance of staff (see below), the Commission has taken seriously the need to ensure that its methods are understood in Member States and that secondees may return to imbue their own administration with an understanding of the purpose and priorities of the Commission. With subsidiarity and the increasing trend to decentralised management of EU policy, the Commission seems set to develop further its links with the national and regional administrations.

The disproportion between outward and inward secondment, and the scale of the latter, suggest that in fact the recruitment of DNEs has also been a crucial means of dealing with budgetary stringency and filling gaps within the A grades. Numbers of outward secondments have remained small, in the region of 20-30 a year since the early 1980s, although the ambition is to increase this to about 50, but inward secondments grew rapidly from about 1985 onwards. The figure was generally thought to have stabilised at around 600-650 since 1991, but the DECODE report found 760 such staff in May 1998 (European Commission 1999b, 9). In 2001 the number of incoming DNEs was equivalent to 777 person years and in 2002 to 892. In 2005 the number of DNEs had risen to 955 persons. The significance of these numbers lies in their concentration, since they account for about 15 per cent of non-language and non-research A grade staff, and much higher proportions than that in some Directorates (see Petit-Laurent 1994, 13). The DECODE report showed that by 1998 the heaviest concentrations of DNEs were to be found in the more technical Directorates such as statistics, nuclear safety, customs and taxation. This remained the case in 2005, but there were also more than 40 DNEs each in the Directorates responsible for enterprise and industry, employment, social affairs and equal opportunities, agriculture and rural policy, energy and transport, environment, research (topping the list with 99 DNEs), the Joint Research Centre, internal market and services, health and consumer protection (Commission Statistical Bulletin 2005).

The necessarily close collaboration between the Commission and national administrations requires a good level of mutual understanding and collaboration. However, the presence of so many national experts is not without disadvantages: some Member States are over-represented, and some people fear that such a strong representation of national civil servants and their exercise of authority on behalf of the Union could weaken the independence of the European civil service (Cassanmagnago-Cerretti 1993, 6-9; Penaud 1993, 67; Petit-Laurent 1994, 14). Moreover it makes little sense if the system is used as a short cut by national civil servants to join the Commission staff, as a number of them have done.

The desirability of spreading knowledge of the Commission's aspirations and networks widely throughout European administrative – and industrial and commercial – elites also motivates the Commission's *stagiaire* scheme which takes young graduates, mostly from the EU countries, but also from more than 50 countries outside the Union, on five-month work placements. The scheme started in 1960. The intention is that they should acquire an understanding of EU ideals and decision-making processes, which may be useful to them in later careers. The networks and contacts which the *stagiaires* undoubtedly acquire, give them an advantage should they later find themselves on a reserve list following a competition. For the private sector, maintaining close contacts with *stagiaires* or employing them at a later date provides privileged access to information and inside knowledge. *Stages* and *stagiaires* are thus much sought after.

In the early decades, traineeships were sometimes a fast route to a job in the Commission, via extensions to the traineeship period or part-time contracts at the end of the stage. This allowed access to the informal systems of recruitment discussed in the next section. In 1993 extensions were discontinued and a lapse of one year was introduced before temporary contracts could be offered to former *stagiaires* (an exception being made for interpreter *stagiaires* who are trained in-house).

Side doors to the Commission: *sousmarins* and others

Numerous indicators attest to the attractiveness of permanent employment in the Commission. These include the high numbers of candidates for general open competitions, the low rate of early retirement, and efforts made, for example, by some *cabinet* staff, DNEs, and consultants to remain within the Commission's employ at the expiry of their contractual or secondment periods. Pay and employment conditions (for example social and medical coverage) are good, and, as Stacia Zabuski found in the European Space Agency, working in a multinational organisation can seem 'exciting' and staff may fear that a return to a mono-national environment would be narrow or boring (Zabuski 2000, 181). But entry into permanent officialdom is far from easy. The front door methods of recruitment (see above) involve highly infrequent and very uncertain general competitions for entry only to the lowest grades in each category, which were until 2002 subject to strict age limits. Their only alternative for a career in the Commission was to obtain a temporary agent contract, which opened up the possibility of permanent establishment via special entry competitions organised only for staff already in employment under statutory contracts. But given the limited number of such competitions, and the fierce competition within them, only the very best, or those with the greatest contacts in high places – *piston*, as it is known – were likely to succeed.

During the 1980s and 1990s one informal route to full official status, despite its implications for a European civil service, was transit via one or other non-statutory 'atypical contract'. If, for example, an individual, say, a seconded national official, was sought by a Directorate General yet could not take the normal competition route to official status, e.g. on grounds of age, he or she might be employed on a contract as a consultant, thereafter obtain the status of auxiliary agent, graduate to a full temporary agent contract and thus be eligible for an internal competition for establishment, for which the age requirements are waived. The various stages gave the person concerned the epithet *sousmarin* (submarine) in the Commission jargon. The point is that such individuals were from the outset always destined to join the statutory staff of the Commission, though avoiding some of the more difficult formal hurdles involved.

The trade unions inveighed against such practices, as undermining the ethos and morale of a 'European Civil Service' and opening the door for favouritism and abuses. The use that was made of 'side-door' procedures for former members of the Commissioners' *cabinets* was widely and particularly resented (see below and Joana and Smith 2002, 78). These protests, but perhaps even more the changed climate in the Commission since the departure of Delors in the mid 1990s, have largely put a stop to such procedures. Special internal competitions are now rare. The Commission is likely to draw a lesson from the experience of the Committee of the Regions. In 2002, anxious to recruit quickly to posts filled by temporary officials whose contracts were about to expire (61 out of 231 permanent posts were held on temporary contracts), the Secretary General proposed an internal procedure, not an open competition. One of the unions called a strike and the Chair of the Committee of the Regions, Sir Albert Bore, overruled the proposal. Thus the side door to entry has been all but closed. Yet the role of national influence in recruitment and career prospects remains pronounced. Old reflexes fade slowly – in March 2002 a former Commissioner from the Delors era wrote to Commission President Prodi: 'I enclose the CV of a young lady...She is highly intelligent and very presentable. I wonder if you could put her name into the system to see if anything can be done' (*European Voice* 9-15 January 2003).

National balance

The two basic criteria for selection of Commission staff were originally allegiance to the European ideal and a high level of competence. The ideal remains and is an integral part of the Commission official's self-perception. Liesbet Hooghe's detailed study of 137 Commission officials at Grades A1 and A2 led her to conclude that 'strong, often personal, factors, lead them to perceive European integration as a momentous and positive development' (Hooghe 2001, 51-52). However, while their work may be infused with the spirit of independence and neutrality essential both to the self-esteem of the institution and to the maintenance of respect for its policy-making methods and political priorities, there are tensions over the proper balance between resource allocation and power-sharing between the state, region and 'Europe', which can pose problems for officials and the services. Hooghe found that 25 per cent of the 105 top officials for whom she had data 'lean strongly towards intergovernmentalism' (ibid, 78).

Moreover, nationality has always been a key element in the recruitment and deployment of officials. The role of 'national balance' within the Commission remains a sensitive issue. Formally the notion is eschewed in favour of what amounts to a euphemism – geographical balance. 'Nationality' with its link to 'nationalism' which 'in this milieu is something you should "go beyond", something you can "overcome" is accepted as an important factor and widely discussed informally, but is unacceptable in formal discourse, so 'Europe's administration is officially a world not of different nations and nationalities but of "geographical balance" (McDonald 1995, 52). The 'right to appropriate representation (geographical balance)' (European Commission 2002, 38) is recognised most strongly in relation to new Member States, so that competitions restricted to particular nationalities or languages can be legitimated, and can be found, for example, in the general terms of reference of the European Personnel Selection Office.

In strictly pragmatic terms geographical balance is justified by the argument that it is essential, if the Commission is to avoid distance and alienation from the EU's citizens, that there should be persons on the staff who can act as 'interpreters' between the EU and the polity and society where their roots and early experiences lie. As one of her interviewees explained to Liesbet Hooghe, officials 'who do not know their own country … are less valuable to this institution. … they are there to reflect their national cultures and values' (Hooghe 2001, 91). Similar reasoning, as we have seen, underlies the secondment schemes which result in the presence of so many detached national experts within the Commission's services. Similarly the right of Commissioners to make temporary appointments to their *cabinet* is used to ensure that the national interests of his or her country of origin are represented and protected, even if this is only one function of the *cabinet* and not necessarily the prime one (Joana and Smith 2002, 52).

The question of national balance takes on a rather different aspect when it is seen to affect the recruitment and career opportunities of individuals. There are no formal arrangements to ensure balance but 'nationality is a central criterion for promotion in the Commission and this is likely to make it a critical resource – or handicap – for top officials' (Hooghe 2001, 29). In the lower grades, factors influencing the choice of candidates relate more obviously to competence, personal networks and the interest of the service, although Page concluded that the imbalance amongst applicants and amongst those who were successfully declared eligible for recruitment and placed on the reserve list was markedly higher than the imbalance amongst officials in post, and suggested that this indicated that attention was paid to national balance at the point of actual selection of eligible candidates for a specific post (Page 1997). Despite the absence of a statutory system of nationality quotas in the Commission, informal quotas for the top three grades existed as early as the High Authority (Conrad 1992, 68), the aim from the outset (*pace* Monnet) being that Member States had a modicum of certainty that their interests were respected, or at least that their national administrative concerns and methods were recognised. Coombes describes how a gentlemen's agreement existed to divide posts between the original six Member States on the basis of proportions contributed to the Community budget (Coombes 1970, 141). This meant that for the original Six, the French, Germans and Italians provided 25 per cent each and Benelux provided the rest. On enlargement, the UK was to have joined the other three large States and Benelux with 18.4 per cent each, leaving Ireland and Denmark with 4 per cent each. A similar approach was adopted for 2004, where a communication approved by the College of Commissioners explicitly recognised that 'Representation of the new Member States in the Commission's staff must be fair and balanced, i.e. reflecting their relative weight in the enlarged Union' (SEC/C(2003)436/5 14 February 2003 p. 2). Ensuring this in fact required a time-limited waiver, approved by the Council of Ministers, of Article 27 paragraph 3 of the Staff Regulation, which forbids the reservation of any posts for nationals of a specific country.

The application of any general division of the spoils is complicated, first, by the acknowledged desirability of staff immediately below or above a given senior post being of a different nationality (Page 1997, 59). Even at lower levels there is a concern to avoid obvious national clusters. In 1997 Page concluded that his detailed study of category A officials provided no evidence for the 'colonisation' of any parts of the institutions by officials of any particular nationality. The Commission planned to distribute posts for nationals of the new Member States to be recruited between 2004 and 2010 across the Directorates General by setting targets both for total posts and for middle management posts, based in the latter case on the number of new posts allocated to the DG by the resource allocation method, and on their capacity to absorb new recruits.

Secondly, individual Member States may regard some areas as more crucial than others and may exert stronger pressure to retain staff in certain key policy areas. Moreover the European Court of Justice has indicated that while Article 27 of the Staff Regulations provides for a wide geographical distribution of posts, there could be no justification for an appointment on nationality grounds alone. Thus, if there is general acceptance that an element of national balance must exist, reserving a post under national quotas and thus eliminating otherwise excellent candidates actually breaks the rules (ECJ Case T-58/91, 1993), hence the waiver regulation required for the 2004 enlargement,

The distribution of posts in different categories in 2004 is shown in table 6. Table 8 shows the fluctuations over time of the distribution of posts in the

A category among the Member States. The A category is that in which the mismatch between the proportion of officials of each nationality and the proportion within the EU of the population of that country is smallest.

Table 8: *Percentage of 'A' Grade staff by nationality*

	1974	1980	1989	1994	2002	Proportion of EU 15 population
France	18.5	20.2	16.5	16.5	15.1	15.63
Italy	18.2	17.4	13.4	13.1	12.6	15.28
Germany	18.7	19.0	14.9	13.8	12.1	21.72
Belgium	13.1	13.5	12.1	12.0	10.9	2.72
UK	14.9	14.5	11.7	11.4	10.7	15.84
Spain			10.1	10.5	9.8	10.65
Greece			4.7	5.4	5.6	2.79
Netherlands	6.3	6.0	5.4	5.5	4.6	4.24
Portugal			3.9	4.1	3.6	2.72
Sweden					3.1	2.35
Ireland	3.9	2.9	3.3	3.4	2.9	1.02
Denmark	3.8	3.0	2.4	2.9	2.7	1.41
Austria					2.6	2.14
Finland					2.5	1.37
Luxembourg	3.1	2.9	1.6	1.0	0.7	0.12

Sources: Calculated from Spence 1997a, 83 for 1974 to 1994; 'Employer of the Month: European Commission' 2002, 37 for 2002; 'Population and Living Conditions, Theme 3 First Results of Demographic Data Collection for 2001', 2002 for population.

It is scarcely surprising that the B, C, and D categories which undertake support tasks include disproportionate numbers of the nationals of the countries in which the main bulk of the employment occurs. Only Italy is as substantially over-represented in these categories as Belgium and Luxembourg, a phenomenon explained by the existence of a sizeable Italian community in Belgium before the creation of the European institutions, by general Italian willingness to migrate and by the support mechanisms provided by the existence of a substantial group of compatriot colleagues.

The mechanisms for the maintenance of national balance and the placing of candidates in key posts are complex. For some nationalities strong social networks play an important role. Hooghe notes that nationalities with a strong sense of identity – she cites the Danish, Spanish and Irish – are particularly likely to foster social events and occasions which 'are invaluable for nurturing professional contacts' (Hooghe 2001, 106). The *chefs de cabinet* are much involved in the career prospects of officials of their Commissioner's nationality. They know many of the staff concerned and are particularly closely involved in the complex manoeuvres and deals which may be associated with appointments at the top two levels. Their machinations have been described by a *cabinet* member as 'like a game of chess, played by *chefs de cabinet*, who know the people and the vacant posts and keep it all pretty much in their heads'. The system has been more bluntly described as 'horse-trading' and denounced for leaving posts above A4 level unfilled for months (*Financial Times* 30 September 1996). Jean Joana and Andy Smith (2002, 70) speak of the Commissioners as 'managing' the officials from their countries and note how much time it consumes. One former *chef de cabinet* complained to them it was as much as ten per cent of each (long) working week which 'is ridiculous ... I spent a lot of time rebuilding the morale of marginalised, bitter and discontented officials and trying to persuade the Secretariat General that it was necessary to find a place for them' (Joana and Smith 2002, 119 footnote 1, author's translation).

Equally, the Permanent Representations of the Member States often do what they can to advance the cause of their nationals. The French have long been, and continue to be, very adept at this, and in 2004 French nationals occupied some 16 per cent of the top posts. In Germany, realisation of the importance of strategic placements came somewhat later, and in 2004, despite constituting 21 per cent of the EU-15 population, Germany held only 13 per cent of the top posts (*European Voice* 2-8 December 2004). The UK's worries over imbalance took some 15 years to become acute. Between 1986 and 1991 the UK was the most seriously under-represented Member State in candidates and in those proceeding successfully to the reserve list (although its candidates were somewhat more successful at this stage). Since the end of the 1980s, the European Staffing Unit of the Cabinet Office and the Permanent Representation in Brussels have instituted a successful pro-gramme of advice and support. Sweden, learning from the example of others, planned its objectives for securing key posts well in advance of accession. In 2004, reflecting the greater openness and transparency towards which the reform process had pushed the Member States, specific posts at the most senior levels (two Directors General, for the Joint Research Centre and for the Information Technologies and Telecommunications DG, six Deputy Directors General and ten Directors) for nationals of the new Member States were identified and advertised (Commission Press Releases IP 04/229 and IP 04/519), and it was intended to fill a further 19 Director posts (*European Voice* 2-8 December 2004). Progress in actually doing so was slow, however. Seven months after enlargement only four out of over a thousand management posts at the level of head of unit and above had been filled by nationals of the new Member States.

Amongst the consequences of the Member States' efforts to achieve pro-portionate representation in senior posts, and to occupy key positions, was the tendency for certain posts to become informally appropriated to specific nationalities – marked out, so the metaphor went, by 'national flags': German in Competition Policy, French in Agriculture, Italian in Financial and Economic Affairs (Page 1997, 54). As the Commission itself somewhat disingenuously admitted in 2002, the procedure for appointments to senior posts '[f]or several decades... mirrored the established, rather complex European decision-making process. It ultimately led Member States to share out management posts at the Commission among themselves under a sort of quota system, even reaching the stage where Member States were almost claiming certain posts as being theirs by right' (European Commission 2002, 26). This practice was strongly linked to what is known as *parachutage* –

dropping an outsider into a particular post. *Parachutage* has taken three forms. First, an outsider is brought in to fill a very senior post, in the interests of national balance. This is analogous to the procedures which exist in both France and Germany for appointing to very senior official posts on the basis of political allegiance. Page's detailed study, using biographical data on 2,300 officials in all the institutions mostly at grade A4 and above (Page 1997, 20), showed that in the A1 and A2 grades of the European Commission 70 per cent of the posts were filled by officials who did not start in the basic career grades (A7-A8). Even below the top two levels (where *parachutage* is provided for in the Staff Regulations), he estimates that 45 per cent of A3s and even one in three of all A4s did not begin their careers at A7 or A8 level. Page's definition of a parachutist encompasses all those who did not start at the normal career grades, so many of his sample had in fact had a substantial period of service in the Commission before arriving at the top.

Parachutage can, secondly, be used to describe the placing of those who have served in *cabinets* in senior posts. It has been generally recognised that statutory officials who have served in a *cabinet* with a heavy workload, unsocial hours and no weekends, but acquiring valuable experience, deserve promotion on returning to the services. Indeed, such service is often an extremely valuable step on the career ladder and Joana and Smith found that, at least until the 1999 crisis, most such officials did, indeed, obtain promotion (Joana and Smith 2002, 77). However, the parachuting into a service (usually at a fairly senior level) of someone from outside the regular staff after a spell in a *cabinet* has been liable to be greeted with a degree of cynicism and resentment. Moreover, to accommodate the *cabinet* members senior posts were kept vacant for a long period and new posts created, to be filled by those with *piston* (powerful support) but without the qualifications normally required. The extent to which this occurred at the end of the Delors Commission gave rise to much criticism. In the light of the furore the Santer Commission adopted a new Code of Conduct for *cabinet* staff which inhibited direct movement by temporary employees into permanent status, and whereas fewer than 20 per cent of former *cabinet* members left the Commission when their *cabinet* was disbanded after the final Delors Commission in 1995, over 35 per cent of those who had served in the Santer Commission's *cabinets* between 1995 and 1999 did so (Joana and Smith 2002, 78).

The Prodi Commission's reforms paid considerable attention to attempts to rectify some of the more objectionable features of these practices. In addition to the Code of Conduct, a new procedure for appointment to posts at A2 and A1 (now AD 15/16) was introduced (Commission Decision of 21/12/2000, SEC(2000) 2305). This procedure can involve external advertisement. In 2001 70 per cent of A2 (now AD 15) vacancies were advertised and in 2004 specific vacancies were advertised, but confined to nationals of the 10 new Member States. A rapporteur at the grade of the post to be filled draws up a short-list, and candidates are interviewed by an Advisory Committee on Appointments, chaired by the Secretary General. The process up to this stage may explicitly take 'broad geographical balance' and 'measures to encourage the promotion of women' into account. Following interviews, the Commissioner responsible for the DG concerned is presented with a short-list from which to choose, in agreement with the

President of the Commission and the Commissioner responsible for Personnel and Administration.

Under Prodi, it was decided that the incumbency in any post of any Director or Director General should be limited to five years with seven as a maximum. This resulted in a flurry of movement, involving the transfer or departure of a number of long-serving Directors General, and the hauling down of several 'national flags'. For example, Guy Legras, its long serving French Director General, left the Agriculture Directorate General. The policy has continued, so that, for example, a major reshuffle of senior posts in the spring of 2002 included a UK national replacing a German at the head of the Competition Policy Directorate General in 2002, despite reported attempts by the German Chancellor Schröder to have the previous incumbent stay as long as possible. One of the conditions of the success of this reform is the abandonment by Member States of their ingrained attachment to ensuring the presence of their own nationals, or at least persons thought to be sympathetic to their approach, in key positions. In the 2002 reshuffle, controversy arose over the removal of Danish Steffen Smidt from the head of the Fisheries Directorate General. It was widely alleged, though robustly denied by the Commissioners, that his removal resulted from Spanish pressure. Spain strongly objected to a proposed fisheries policy reform (*European Voice* 2-8 May and 23-29 May 2002; *The Economist* 12 May 2002). In the upshot the application of the new appointment procedure led to the subsequent appointment of another Scandinavian to the post.

As in a number of Member States, the possibility of reshuffles depends upon a mechanism for handling the position of those removed. Some transfer between services. By the end of 2003, when no Director General had been in their post for more than five years, there had been 116 transfers in the top two grades since 1999 (COM(2004) 93F, 9). Others are moved to posts as advisers or (more rarely) persuaded to take Article 50 retirement (see above).

It is possible that, whilst retaining the principle of broad geographical balance, the reforms of both promotions and senior appointment procedures will achieve their overt objectives, which are to remove all national flags and to greatly diminish the impact of the informal networks, whether national, party political or others. Nevertheless, it does remain the case that in a system heavily influenced by informal networks, staff who have the necessary pull (or *piston*), especially with the *cabinet* of their own national Commissioner, have been able to progress rapidly. The converse is also true; informal networks can form harsh judgments against which there is no appeal, and in a highly competitive environment senior staff who are thought to have made errors of judgment, or who fail to keep their support networks in good repair, are liable to find themselves rather suddenly faced with a requirement to 'take Article 50'. The circumstances of such events are frequently shrouded in a degree of mystery, barely concealing suggestions of cabal and back-stabbing, but the risks and the rewards at this level are recognised as considerable, and the departure terms are generous.

Moreover, as a consequence of successive enlargements staff have been recruited in a series of national waves, following the growth of the European Union, leading to an uneven age profile, with undesirable consequences for promotion prospects and career development. These upheavals have had the effect of temporarily blocking almost all normal recruitment from sources other than the new Member States (Hay 1989, 25 and 39).

National balance has always been a key feature of both the formal arrangements, and to a much greater extent the informal operation of the Commission's staff and personnel policy. Having recognised the nefarious impact of many long-standing practices the Commission is seeking to render the processes more transparent, and thereby achieve a more accept-able equilibrium between necessary attention to the specificities of each Member State and a genuinely merit-based and 'European' system. Against the power and influence of Member States, who have their interests to pro-tect, and who may not wish to accept at European level assumptions which challenge traditional domestic practices, it can take a long time to change the rules and even longer to inculcate a new culture (Cini 2001; Cini 2004a).

Gender and ethnic balance

EU legislation in relation to equal opportunities between men and women has, since the 1970s, been progressive and often well in advance of what the Member States might otherwise have done. Legislation in relation to racial discrimination has followed more slowly, but an EU-wide directive was introduced in 2000. Given the forward-looking role of the policy-makers, it is surprising that the Commission's own personnel practices sug-gest limited impact. In 2002 women comprised 29 per cent of heads of unit and Directors and approximately 22 per cent of all A grade officials (see General Report of the European Union 2001 and 2002) and in July 2005, 38 of the 283 officials in grades AD15/16 were women (13 per cent). The 2005 figure of nearly 14 per cent for women in post at grades AD 14 and above did, however, represent an advance on the 2002 figure of 11 per cent (Commission Statistical Bulletin 2005 and European Commission 2004b) and two of the first four appointments from new Member States at that level in 2004 were women (*European Voice* 2-8 December 2004). This represents slow, but steady progress from 3 per cent in the four higher grades in 1993 and, in the A grades overall, 11.3 per cent in 1992 and 6.1 per cent in 1982 (*Courrier du Personnel*: 11.2.1993). The first of three positive action pro-grammes to monitor progress and raise awareness began in 1988, and in line with general EU policy the Commission is now attempting to ensure that issues of gender equality are 'mainstreamed' throughout its personnel policy. The advancement of equal opportunities for both sexes in the Commission may be rendered particularly difficult by the fact that it is largely staffed by expatriates. Distance from homeland may deprive a work-ing woman of access to informal support mechanisms for family responsi-bilities, although the Commission does maintain childcare facilities. Similarly, some parts of the Commission persist with a long working hours culture. Finally, the extent to which career moves and advancement may depend upon informal contact, networks, acquaintanceships and rec-ommendations can place women in a disadvantageous position. Some net-works – those based on nationality for example – are gender neutral. Others, such as those based on political allegiance or career profile, are more strongly male-biased and while there are few women in senior posts there may be a dearth of mentors and sponsors for younger women (Stevens 2001,

114). The European Commission presented on 3 March 2006 a 'Roadmap for equality between men and women', setting out concrete actions designed to help bridge the gender gap (Commission 2006). It remains to be seen whether the actions proposed will be applied within the Commission itself.

Despite the attention paid to equal opportunities between sexes, there has been no similar attention to equal opportunities between persons of different ethnic origins. Citizenship of the EU is regarded as automatically conferring equal opportunities for all, regardless of ethnic origin, and not until recently has attention been drawn to the likelihood that the Commission staff may not reflect the ethnic diversity of the citizenry (*European Voice* 21 March 2002). But there is no monitoring and no reference to the issue in the EU's annual reports or the reform white papers.

Language

Everything the European Union does, especially its directly applicable legislation, must be accessible to people in the 25 Member States, though Commission officials may agree to use French or English in internal meetings. Under the revised Staff Regulations all officials seeking promotion out of the entry grade must demonstrate ability to work in three of the official languages. Until the mid 1990s French was the de facto language of the Commission but by the turn of the century English had become the dominant, though not exclusive, working language (Stevens 2001, 129). In 1986, 58 per cent of Commission documents originated in French, in 2003 only 30 per cent (*The Guardian* 6 March 2004). It does not follow, however, that all officials, especially older ones, are comfortable using English and 'it seems difficult to imagine how a senior official could do an effective job without a working knowledge of French' (Hooghe 2001, 170 footnote 2). However documents addressed to other European institutions, the Member States, the social partners and the general public are made available in all official languages of the Community. The principles are outlined in Article 217 of the EC Treaty and in Council Regulation No 1 of 15 April 1958. The fact that EU legislation covers most areas of traditional domestic legislation in Member States demands the use of more languages than in traditional international organisations. EFTA, after all, worked only in English, the 26-member NATO works in English and French, and the United Nations uses only six languages (see table 9).

As a result, the Commission has a large language staff. The translation service of the Commission is the largest in the world. It not only translates texts from their original language into 20 languages but also ensures that the end result is as if it were the original text. The number of cases before the European Court concerning different interpretations of Community law in Member States because of linguistic differences in texts shows the importance (and difficulty) of accuracy (Braselmann 1992; Usher 1992). Some 27 per cent of university graduates employed by the Commission (other than on the research budget) in 1999 were directly engaged in language work. In addition, the Commission's language services have a large clerical support staff processing the different language versions of each document and providing technical support for meetings. In 1999 the Commission calculated that the provision of specialised linguistic services occupied nearly 8 per cent

Table 9: *International institutions and language*

International Oganisations	Member States	Languages	Pairs	Number of interpreters**
United Nations	191	6	30	18
NATO	26	2	1	6
Council of Europe	46	2	1	6
EFTA	4	1	0	0
EU12	12	9	72	27
EU 15	15	11	110	. 33
EU 27*	27	21/22***	231	63

*With additional members from 1 May 2004 – Cyprus, Czech Republic, Hungary, Malta, Poland, Slovenia, Slovakia, Latvia, Lithuania and Estonia – and also Bulgaria and Romania
** Assumes one interpretation booth per language, with standard allocation of three interpreters per booth (Source EU Directorate General for Interpretation).
*** 22 includes Maltese

of its total staff resources and over a thousand person years per annum (European Commission 1999b, Annex 4), while with the 2004 enlargement staff numbers in DG Translation have currently risen to 2,081, though finding adequate numbers of competent translators for languages such as Latvian, Lithuanian and Maltese proved to be a problem (*European Voice* 1-9 November 2004). And this bald total seriously underestimates the number of those engaged on language work, because many other officials undertake some translation and processing of different language versions of texts as part of their routine tasks.

The Commission shares its interpreting services with the other institutions (except the Court of Justice and the Parliament) through the Directorate General for Interpretation (formerly the Joint Interpreting and Conference Service). Very substantial use is also made of freelance interpreters. The difficulty of finding suitable interpretation for some of the language pairs – Finnish and Greek, for example – has resulted in growing resort to 'relay interpretation'. The source language is interpreted into a core language, such as English or French, and taken from that version into the target language.

Since language use is an inevitably delicate topic, there has been an understandable reluctance to regulate it officially; unofficially for working purposes in the Commission French and English dominate, if in idiosyncratic versions. One consequence of the domination of French until the 1990s is that concepts which developed within the French-speaking environment of the early years remain difficult to translate into English. These terms include *l'acquis* – the Treaties and the body of law which set out the EU constitution and its policies – and *la construction européenne* – the process of integration. The same applied to procedural matters. McDonald quotes everyday speech: 'Don't forget the *fiche financière*' and 'DG IX is trying to *supprimer la filière papier*' (McDonald 1998, 72). Thus the working English or French of the EU is not quite the language of Paris and London. There are 'oddities of language followed even by the native speakers' which are the result of 'multicultural tolerance' especially at the working level (Bellier 1997, 95). Grammar, vocabulary and syntax intermingle and interfere, and the results are generally acceptable for spoken communication, although written texts cause more difficulties, since idiosyncrasies have to be ironed out when communication with the outside world is required. Nevertheless, linguistic diversity has its costs. There may be a loss of nuance, and particularly of humour and of the small ways in which communication is eased (Abélès and Bellier 1996, 435; Hooghe 2001, 170). More crucially, linguistic features enhance the propensity to cultivate personal networks. It is always easier to telephone or e-mail if one is sure of ready mutual comprehension.

Conclusion

During the 1990s the dilemmas of the staff and personnel policy of the European Commission, too long ignored or circumvented, eventually engendered acute crisis. At the turn of the century a number of clear decisions were made. These seem to indicate a new sense of direction. At the very least the future direction of the administration will depend upon the nature and success of their implementation.

The first dilemma was the tension between regulation and policy, a dilemma also experienced in a number of national administrations, principally those which belong to what Pierre (Pierre 1995, 8) calls a public law Weberian model. The independence and uniformity which are the premise of the *statut* stem from a tradition of administration that has been identified as depending upon a 'public authority' concept of legitimacy (Page and Wright 1999, 273). Hood (2000, 16) characterises this approach as a Hegelian or Confucian 'public service bargain'. Structures of clear and legally based regulation have long seemed in such systems a necessary guarantee against political instability and ideological whim. If they become too constraining then they can be circumvented by local arrangement or personal favour, and accountability involves essentially the demonstration of a willingness to take responsibility for the delivery of benefits, not a detailed justification of the procedures and ethics by which delivery is achieved. As a result, senior management is often politicised and closely linked to the party in power and information retained as a constituent element of a bureaucratic and political power base. In such a system it will not be improper to claim, as a senior official from the Personnel and Administration Directorate General did to Cris Shore (Shore 2000, 198): 'There is no personnel policy. Or rather, the policy is to have *no* policy. What we have instead are the "Staff Regulations"'. On the other hand is the tradition of human resource management common in the Anglo-Saxon tradition, typified by civil service neutrality, the formal absence of nepotism, a high degree of delegation and the principle of sharing information with colleagues.

Whether the two can be resolved in a synthesis containing the positive features of both is a moot point. The discrediting of the 'regulation' system by the 1999 crisis made the attempt inevitable, since in the face of change stemming from enlargement, from the 'banalisation' of European Union policy-making, from rapid expansion of responsibilities, and from the stringency resulting from constrained staffing resources, a human resources policy of 'no policy' proved inadequate. The proposed reforms in structures and career development, described in chapter 17, which attempt to marry the development of a policy with a respect for statutory protection and autonomy, are a response to this dilemma.

The continued existence of the networks is a notable feature which the new personnel policy will need to confront, if the watchwords are to be matching resources to activities, evaluating competences and providing career advancement as far as possible on the basis of performance. The networks are by no means exclusively national. In the 1980s and 1990s, so an interviewee told Cris Shore 'You either have to belong to the Catholic Left, the Socialist Party, come from the Ecole Nationale d'Administration...' (quoted in Shore 2000, 198). Another long serving official said 'To survive you need to see where you work and who you work with; you need a clientèle... Yes there is a French Mafia in the Commission. But there is also an English Mafia... there is a gay Mafia, a freemasons' Mafia, an Opus Dei Mafia, a Socialist and a Communist Mafia.' He went on to allege that the trick was to make sure that they neutralised each other, to know them and to work with them (quoted in Shore 2000, 199). The influx of new officials following the enlargement of 1995, and the much greater influx anticipated following the enlargement in 2004, has disrupted some of these networks and will continue to do so. They have been weakened as recruitment by the back door has lessened and deployment of *piston* has been discredited. But they will not disappear, and the implementation of reform will need to be robust if their effects are to be reduced to a relatively harmless level.

National networks are a consequence of the role of national balance within the Commission. Liesbet Hooghe (2001, 172-5) compares the mechanisms of the EU's policy-formulating and implementing executive to the consociational systems found in certain nation states which possess both a high degree of more or less irreconcilable cultural diversity and considerable political stability. They require a counterbalance to pure majoritarian government through systems of proportionality which ensure 'an association between "one group, one voice" and decision-making'. Within the Commission she finds a tension between mechanisms which seek precisely to ensure that each Member State's vital interests at least have a voice – mechanisms strongly supported by the Member States through the insistence on 'geographical balance' and the seconding of DNEs – and the formal framework of the Staff Regulation and management structures which emphasizes autonomy, refuses to acknowledge 'national flags' and develops a rhetoric of the general European interest. The Kinnock reforms can be seen as a very necessary swing of the pendulum away from the consociational practices of recent decades, even if geographical balance is merely to be kept within tight bounds, and by no means abandoned. Hooghe found that officials operating within strong national networks were most supportive of the continuation of consociational practices if only, she concludes, because 'whether the Commission bureaucracy becomes more or less consociational could boost or shrink a top official's professional fortune. It affects who is hired, promoted or fired. That is why Commissioner Kinnock's reforms have caused great unease in the Commission's ranks' (2001, 192).

The events around the turn of the century have given strong impetus towards the development of a new balance in Commission staff and personnel policy. A positive attempt has been made by reformers since the end of the Delors era to induce some degree of change within the highly complex organisational culture of the Commission. The parallel and informal personnel systems of the 1970s, 80s and 90s have diminished. And the status of geographical (national) balance has been clearly recognised, so that, potentially at least, it can become more accountable. The almost missionary zeal of the first generations of officials has been tempered by an alternative ethos where the Commission is deemed to offer opportunities for valuable, fascinating, but essentially administrative, work, rather than to participate in 'political construction'. The principal advantage over similar policy-making and implementation roles elsewhere is held to lie in the multicultural and multinational environment. The shape of the 'European project' has become more contentious than ever in the context of the stalled ratification process for the proposed Constitutional Treaty. The changes in personnel policy that might have derived from that treaty would have been most marked in the sphere of the external services (see chapter 15) and the process of implementing internal reform in the Commission is likely to continue relatively unchecked even if the treaty is not ratified. Nevertheless, as the the legitimacy of the project comes increasingly into question its continuation may depend, at least in part, upon the satisfactory resolution of the dilemmas outlined above and the successful enhancement – despite the many obstacles – of the reforms already initiated.

7.   The Commission and the Council

Udo Diedrichs and Wolfgang Wessels

Introduction: the Commission and the Council – key actors in the political system of the European Union

The EU system has evolved over the years as the Single European Act and the Treaties of Maastricht, Amsterdam and Nice gradually endowed the institutional framework of the EU with new incentives and constraints. Yet, the interplay between the Commission and the Council remains indisputably the key factor for the smooth and effective working of the European Union as a whole. Both need to act effectively and in tandem to produce successful policy outcomes. Their relationship has undergone substantial changes; a process of 'constitutionalisation' (Joerges 2002a) has progressively changed the 'rules of integration' (Schneider and Aspinwall 2001) and the institutional environment in which the Commission pursues its interests and preferences. The classical notion of a Commission-Council 'tandem' (Wallace 2003, 276) for the adoption of legislation has been replaced by more complex and differentiated forms of interaction discussed in detail in other chapters of this book. Most significant amongst these new forms of interaction is the increasingly important role of the European Parliament (EP). This has led to the emergence of a 'triangular' or even de facto 'tricameral' system of EU decision-making (Tsebelis 2002, 1-2; König and Bräuninger 2001, 279), a fact which has undeniable significance for the analysis of the relations between the Commission and the Council.

These new complexities in European governance mean individual assessments of the evolving roles and powers of the EU institutions are more complex – and more contested. They also depend greatly on the theoretical perspective of the analyst. This chapter therefore outlines different theoretical models in order to set the scene for the main focus of the chapter: analysis of the interaction between the Commission and the Council during the various phases of the policy cycle, from preparation to negotiation and from implementation to control of binding EU decisions. Looking also at the implications of the Constitutional Treaty, whose long term prospects for ultimate ratification are uncertain after rejection in the French and Dutch referenda, the chapter distinguishes the requirements that remain for further effective evolution of Commission/Council relations – both because of enlargement and because of the exigencies of a modernised and effective decision-making process as the EU consolidates its position as a global actor and birthplace for new forms of multilevel governance.

The intergovernmentalist model: the Commission as a subsidiary body

The intergovernmental model regards both the Commission's and EP's roles and powers as being less important than those of the Council and the European Council – the primary sources of decision-making in the European Union (Goetschy 2003; Moravcsik 1998). The Commission provides politically low profile, technical input and information. It is not regarded as a supranational entrepreneur shaping EU politics. Instead, it is viewed as an expert administrative body under the control of the Member States in a principal-agent relationship (Moravcsik 1999a; 1999b). Intergovernmentalists postulate that Member States delegate powers to supranational institutions to overcome the inherent problems of collective action and to improve bargaining efficiency (Moravcsik 1993, 507; Kassim and Menon 2002, 6). For intergovernmental theorists, Member State control of the Commission through various institutional mechanisms significantly reduces the scope of its political action and places it under constant supervision, e.g. through the comitology system, described in detail in chapter 8. From this point of view, Hoffman's (1966) distinction between 'high' and 'low' politics remains a useful categorisation, in particular for areas such as foreign and security policy – the Commission is allowed to do its job as long as Member States believe their own prerogatives are not undermined. Although the intergovernmental model is an ideal-type, it is helpful in classifying current developments such as the increasingly important role of the European Council in shaping the EU agenda and in defining concrete policy or the debate in the European Convention, and in shaping the final outcome of the negotiations on the Constitutional Treaty, which contains important institutional innovations such as the appointment of a full-time President of the European Council permanently located in Brussels.

The neofunctionalist model: the Commission as a supranational technocracy

There is a longstanding debate between intergovernmentalists and 'neofunctionalists', which provides clear but controversial definitions of the relationship between the Commission and the Council. If the intergovernmentalist perspective perceives the Council and the Member States as the main controllers of EU decision-making and the Commission as left with only a narrow margin of manoeuvre, by contrast the neofunctionalist perspective describes the Commission primarily as a supranational institution and identifies a growing degree of Commission independence of the Council in shaping EU policy (Haas 1968; Schmitter 1969, Tranholm-Mikkelsen 1991). The neofunctionalist view posits the Commission as a politically active, autonomous institution possessing considerable resources for transforming EC/EU policies into practice. As a result of 'spill-over' processes and bureaucratic drift – fuelled by an in-built propensity for administrative expansion – supranational EU institutions are becoming increasingly independent of Member States and the Council (Schmitter 2004: Bach 1995, 372ff). It is a 'regulatory bureaucracy' (Pollack 1997, 106), which shapes day-to-day decisions in key policy fields such as agriculture, internal market or competition, and, as a 'magistrature d'experts en charge de définir et de défendre l'intérêt commun' (Lamassoure 2004, 396) it is even the expression of the common European will. On this view, the Council has to rely on the Commission to push for European solutions to a growing number of problems, which cannot be efficiently and effectively tackled at the national level. Commission entrepreneurship is thus the catalyst driving European integration forward (Sandholtz and Zysman 1989, 128) and is the key institution for assuring Member State compliance with EU rules (Tallberg 2003).

In contrast to the federal model described below, neofunctionalists view the link to the European Parliament and the role of the latter as the European source of legitimacy as a secondary concern. The Commission, for neofunctionalists, enjoys a legitimacy derived from its expertise and technocratic problem-solving capacity and from its independence of both Council and Parliament (Burley and Mattli 1993, 71). The Commission is thus an innovative, *sui generis* institution, able to act on behalf of the EU interest and thereby foster integration. For neofunctionalists, when the Council and the Member States follow the Commission line, this manifests the superior and ever-improving capacity of the EU to tackle problems facing the Member States and thus secure their welfare.

The federalist model: the Commission as a future European government

Neo-federalists view the Commission as an embryonic government (Pinder 2003), a 'union of states and peoples' based on shared values (Burgess 2004, 30). From a normative perspective, they argue, the European Union should be endowed with an institutional architecture that strengthens and enhances EU decision-making and leads to the creation of a 'parliamentary Europe' (Duff, 1995) or a 'supranational parliamentary democracy' (Laming 1995, 117). It follows that the Commission is regarded as the nucleus of a European government, acting autonomously of the Member States and the Council, while remaining politically dependent on a majority in the European Parliament, the basis of legitimacy through popular vote. Akin to a parliamentary system, the Council would serve as a comparatively weak second chamber, a 'House of States' (Pinder 2003) in which the national interest is represented. Relations between the Commission and the Council would thus not play the central role. Although such clear-cut federalist concepts are not visible in the Treaties or in the Constitutional Treaty, federalists consider the Constitutional Treaty highly significant because it 'goes far to apply the principles of representative government' (Pinder 2003), in particular by strengthening the parliamentary responsibility of the Commission and by making the Council and the EP equal partners in the legislative process.

The neo-institutionalist/rational choice model: the Commission as a flexible agenda-setter and administrator

In addition to the classical branches of EU studies, the theoretical landscape has been substantially enriched since the late 1980s by the emergence of neo-institutionalism. Defying the intergovernmentalist-neofunctionalist divide, neo-institutionalists seek a more differentiated way of analysing and explaining inter-institutional relations. Neither 'continued Member State dominance' nor a 'runaway Commission' is posited (Pollack 1997, 99). Neo-institutionalist approaches reject an 'abstract' definition of interinstitutional relations, focusing instead on the specific institutional context in which decisions are taken, which may vary over time and across policy fields. In addition, rational choice approaches include principal-agent and delegation theories, which deal with the interaction between supranational institutions and Member States (Pollack 2003; 1997; Thatcher and Stone Sweet 2002). Principal-agent theories focus primarily on the mechanisms through which principals – more or less successfully – try to reduce 'agency losses' by preventing agents from acting against their perceived interests (Schmidt 2000, 41ff.; Pollack 1997, 108ff.). Rational choice approaches also include game theoretical models, based upon a power index (Stokman and Thomson 2004, 6; Widgrén 1994) or spatial analysis (Tsebelis 2002; Garrett and Tsebelis 1999; 1996), which analyse agenda-setting and veto power within or among institutional actors in specific decision-making situations (Mattila 2004, 29ff; König and Bräuninger 2000, 107ff.; Holler and Widgrén 1999, 321ff.). They view the interaction between the Council, the Commission and the EP as embedded in a complex set of decision-making rules which determine each institution's scope of action. 'Since institutions determine the sequence of moves, the choices of actors, and the information they control, different institutional structures affect the strategies of actors and hence the outcomes of their interactions' (Tsebelis and Garrett 2001, 384). In particular, voting rules in the Council and different legal procedures – from consultation to co-decision – are viewed as key variables.

On this view, the Commission commands variable degrees of influence in different policy fields, depending on the institutional setting, the specific policy preferences of Member States, varied access to information and the existence of trans- or sub-national constituencies. The model takes into account the substantial changes that have taken place for the European Commission: from the Single European Act (introducing the cooperation procedure), via the Maastricht Treaty (introducing the co-decision procedure), to the Treaty of Amsterdam (modifying the co-decision procedure by eliminating the third reading in the European Parliament). Tsebelis and Garrett conclude that '[t]he evolution of the EU's legislative regime from consultation to co-decision (under the Amsterdam Treaty) has substantially reduced the legislative powers of the Commission' (2001, 374). This loss of power is epitomised by the more limited agenda-setting function of the Commission in co-decision, as it is the EP and the Council which 'make the final deal' in the conciliation committee (Tsebelis and Garret 2001, 274; Crombez 2001). The Commission is thus relegated to a more traditional bureaucratic role in policy-making, while the EU decision making system develops into a 'bicameral legislature'.

On the other hand, Tsebelis and Garrett also posit that the Commission's role as administrator has been strengthened. The broad scope for policy differences between the Council and the EP confers on the Commission a good deal of discretion for implementation (2001, 382). The power of the Commission as administrator is deemed much greater than intergovernmentalist principal-agent approaches would assume, without, however, the bureaucratic drift towards increasing independence that neofunctionalists would predict. Supranational autonomy is regarded as a function of the mechanisms established by the Member States 'to control their international agents', while 'the costs and credibility of these control mechanisms vary considerably from agent to agent and from one issue-area to another for a given agent' (Pollack 1997, 119). Variation of supranational autonomy across issue areas and over time is therefore as much an assumption of this model as the hypothesis that the

Commission is closely controlled by different mechanisms such as oversight committees, sanctions or revisions to mandates given to it (Pollack 1997, 119f.). The rational choice institutionalist model thus posits a flexible role for the Commission, notes its declining agenda-setting power and the constraints of the rules and preferences of other actors, in particular the Council and the EP.

The multi-level governance model: the Commission as an active player and promotional broker

Multi-level governance approaches apply a broad repertoire of options for analysing inter-institutional relations. Some of these approaches underscore the explanatory power of deliberative and discursive processes within the EU (Joerges and Neyer 1997). In particular, these theorists maintain that the creation and development of non-hierarchical policy networks has contributed to the emergence of a 'culture of dialogue' (Jachtenfuchs and Kohler-Koch 2003, 25) within and between institutions, which rational choice approaches – focusing on strategic interaction alone – do not adequately address. Tension between efforts to preserve Member States' autonomy and those promoting Community solutions is accepted as inherent in the political system of the EU, best illustrated by the institutional co-existence of the Commission and the Council. Since both institutions are expected to endure, no neofunctionalist trend towards supranational policy-making is expected to take place (Jachtenfuchs and Kohler-Koch 2003, 21f.). This accounts for the mix of different modes of governance within the EU, where the Commission is a 'promotional broker' in a dynamic multi-level system of governance characterised by a dispersion of competences among different levels of political authority, a loss of control for national governments and the interconnection of political arenas (Hooghe and Marks 2001, 5-6; Jachtenfuchs 2001; Kohler-Koch 2003; Bulmer 1994). The Commission-Council relationship is not regarded as a zero-sum game but as a reflection of the growing inter-connectedness of national and European interests and decision-making structures, further enriched by the active political role of the EP (Wessels 2003b). The Commission, Council and EP are part of an ever more complex political system which lacks the hierarchical structures familiar in national arenas. As active players in the dynamic evolution of the EU system, these institutions find themselves in a constant process of adaptation and adjustment. The Commission attempts to act at different levels, using specific Treaty provisions even in fields where it does not enjoy a strong institutional position. The dynamics of the integration process assume an inherent trend towards increasing integration as multiple stages of decision-making emerge and shifts in competences occur, starting with loose forms of intergovernmental cooperation and proceeding towards supranational decision-making (Wessels 2001b, 197ff.).

In this complex and differentiated context, the Commission is regarded as a key player alongside the Council and EP. It forms part of an institutional triangle combining supranational and intergovernmental procedures and principles and it anticipates the emergence of a new kind of political system, following patterns that have evolved since the 1950s. The Commission's role in this model is not that of a neutral technocracy, but rather an advocate of European positions, while pursuing its own institutional interests (Rometsch and Wessels 1997). Coalition-building, informal politics, multi-level bargaining and deliberative and communicative action constitute key features of this model. Evidence is found in the formal and informal procedures in which the Commission participates with the Council and Parliament in shaping European decisions, acting as a mediator and trusted partner to both. The Commission is thus regarded as a key actor in the emergence of a new 'legislative culture' within the EU (Shackleton and Raunio 2003, 176). In contrast to rational choice assumptions, inter-institutional strategic bargaining is not considered the only or *the* privileged mode of interaction in the EU. Nor are preferences necessarily regarded as fixed over time; they are open to persuasive adjustment. Considerable importance is attributed to 'deliberative politics' (Dehousse 2002; Joerges and Neyer 1997), in which consensus and cooperative behaviour prevail, leading to non-confrontational patterns of interaction.

The Commission and the Council in the EU policy arena: basic trends and developments

Having briefly mapped out the theoretical frameworks, the chapter now turns to the analysis of Commission-Council relations in practice. As chapter 1 underlines, the appointment procedure for the Commission President and the College illustrates the political process of the EU and the inter-institutional dynamics of Commission-Council relations in particular. The Commission and

Survey 1: *Models of the Inter-Institutional Relationship in the EU and Commission-Council Relations*

Models	Inter-institutional architecture	Role of the Commission	Commission – Council relations
Intergovernmental	consensus-based concordance system	technical secretariat	Commission as agent of Council with limited autonomy
Federal	supranational parliamentary system (with two chambers)	future EU government	Commission subordinated to the EP
Neofunctionalist	*sui generis* Community system	ambitious technocracy	Commission as increasingly independent actor from the Council
Rational choice institutionalist	veto player system	agenda setter with variable influence	interest-based negotiations between Commission, Council and EP
Multi-level governance	triangular partnership Council, Commission, EP	promotional broker	inter-institutional deliberation

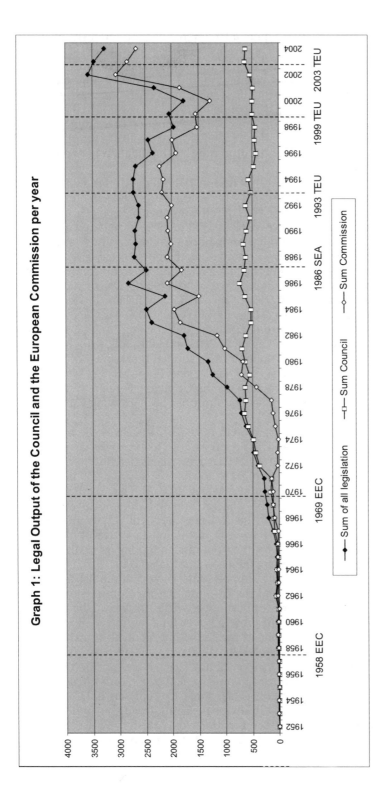

Graph 1: Legal Output of the Council and the European Commission per year

Source: Maurer and Wessels 2001, based on the CELEX data base. From 2002 onwards, figures are based on the EUR-LEX data base. Sums represent every legal event as counted by CELEX/EUR-LEX. Apart from 'real' secondary legislation, CELEX/EUR-LEX also refers to executive acts either by the Commission or the Council. Note that from November 1993 onwards, Council legislation also comprises legislative acts by the European Parliament and the Council (co-decision procedure).

the Council are active players within a Union that has continuously expanded its spheres of legal competence and range of policy instruments. Legislative output has thus increased, though it has arguably reached a degree of saturation in specific areas. As the Commission and the Council adjusted to the increasingly complex nature of the EU system, procedural complexity reached new heights as inter-institutional dependence grew, in part due to the growing involvement of the EP, which dispensed with the notion of a simple Council-Commission tandem. The evolution of the EU since the 1950s, the growth and differentiation of legal output and procedural differentiation between policy areas provide useful insights.

Measured in terms of legal output (graph 1), both the Commission and the Council have made intensive use of the opportunities provided by the Treaties. The activities of the Council, measured in the number of legal acts concluded per year, showed a steady increase from 1958 to 1986/87, entered a phase of moderate decline thereafter and have remained at a comparatively stable level since the 1990s. In the case of the Commission, there was considerable growth in the adoption of legal acts after the mid-1970s, and the trend continued until the early 1990s when a short slump in legal output took place, arguably owing to 'saturation' in the key policy areas of agriculture and fisheries, external economic policy and customs policy (Maurer and Wessels 2003, 44f.). The first years of the new century show a strong upswing culminating in 2002, while the number of legal acts goes down again in 2003 and 2004, following more familiar patterns. So the trends do not point to a sudden breakdown of legal production, since, in other areas, such as justice and home affairs (Müller 2003, 403ff.) and – with slight variations – in the Common Foreign and Security Policy (Regelsberger 2004, 90ff.), legal output has been growing considerably since the 1990s.

Another key indicator for the growth of the EU system is the increase of policy fields dealt with by the EU. The number of Treaty articles covering specific powers and competencies of the EU has grown considerably over the years: from 86 in the EC Treaty of 1958 to 254 in the Nice Treaty and 249 in the Constitutional Treaty (Wessels, Maurer and Mittag 2003, 5). This trend reflects the complex process of expansion of EU policies, though it does not always follow the traditional communitarian path. Instead, new modes of EU governance have been introduced, deviating from the classic institutional patterns of the original Treaties and making it difficult for the Commission to play its traditional role within the decision-making system (Hodson and Maher 2001).

As 'masters of the Treaties', the Member States have continuously expanded the scope of action of the EC and the EU, granting the Commission and the Council new decision-making opportunities. This increases the need for cooperation. The Commission has reacted over time by the creation of additional Directorates General; while at the same time Council formations have become more numerous (Wessels 2003b; Westlake and Galloway 2004, 44).

At the Seville European Council on 22 June 2002, it was decided to reduce the number of Council formations to nine basic types in order to streamline and rationalise working procedures (see table 10; Gillissen 2003, 10). Yet, it is unlikely that this reduction will reverse existing trends, as under each of the nine formations different combinations of ministers will continue to meet. Member States have also stepped up their presence and commitment in Brussels, in particular by adjusting and extending their administrative staff and resources (Wessels, Maurer and Mittag 2003, 4ff.). Indeed, increased involvement of national civil servants dealing with EU matters is a clear trend (Wessels 2003a, 362). At the same time, differentiation of legal procedures has increased. Under the Treaty of Nice, 38 combinations of voting modalities in the Council were created, each with different forms of participation for the EP (see table 11). There were specific implications for the Commission. Under the simple procedure (without EP participation) and consultation, it is mainly the Commission and the Council that adopt legislation. But with the growing influence of the EP this has changed, especially since the Treaty of Maastricht expanded the co-decision and assent procedures. For the Commission, the change implied adjustment to a more complex triangular relationship in EU decision-making. This reduced its formal powers but also offered new opportunities for formal and informal participation (Wessels 2001b). In the last 20 years, one of the most remarkable changes in decision-making in the Council has been the shift from consensus to qualified majority voting (QMV), which, as graph 2 illustrates, has become the single most important decision-making procedure measured by existing Treaty provisions, yet not by actual practice (see table 12).

Despite the growing complexity, Commission strategy towards the Council remains to try to bind national representatives into the decision-making process in a form of 'engrenage' (Bellier 1997, 114; Poullet and Deprez 1976, 120). As a result, the decision-making autonomy of each actor is reduced in favour of a common problem-solving capacity. For the Commission, majority voting offers more influence on decision-making within the Council than unanimity, as majority voting generally enhances the probability that a Commission proposal will be transformed into a legal act (Schmidt 2000, 38). It also enables the Commission to build coalitions

Table 10: *Sessions of the different Council formations 1967-2004*

	1967	1975	1990	1995	2000	2004
General Affairs	7	16	16	14	11	20
Agriculture	8	15	13	10	10	9
Economic and Financial Affairs	1	8	10	9	12	11
Employment and Social Affairs	1	2	3	4	6	4
Transport	1	2	4	4	5	5
Budget	0	3	2	2	2	0
Education	0	1	2	2	2	3
Environment	0	2	5	4	5	4
Development Cooperation	0	3	4	2	2	0
Internal Market	0	0	7	2	4	4
Justice and Home Affairs				4	5	9
Other	2	6	17	20	18	0
Total Sessions	20	57	90	79	82	69
Number of Council formations	7	12	22	21	19	9

Source: Annual Reports of the Council of the European Union

Table 11: *Decision-Making in the Council and the European Parliament under the Treaty of Nice*

Council voting / decision making with the EP

	A	B	C	D	E	F	G	H	I	J	K	L	M	N	O	P
No EP participation		88.2 TEC	104.13 TEC		99.2 TEC		7.3 TEU			24 TEU	207 TEC	289 TEC				
Information		300.2 TEC			60.2 TEC											
Consultation	22 TEC	13.1 TEC	62.2 b) i. TEC		37 TEC	279.1 TEC		62.2 a) TEC			130 TEC	112.2 TEC	117 TEC			
Cooperation					99.5 TEC											
Co-decision		151 TEC			95 TEC											
Co-decision from 1.5.2004 onwards					62.2 b) TEC											
Co-decision if legislative framework decision exists					62.2 a) TEC			63.2 a) TEC								
Assent by absolute majority of votes cast		105.6 TEC			107.5 TEC	161 TEC			214.2 TEC						214.2.2 TEC	

A Unanimity + Ratification
B Unanimity
C 2/3 Majority
D 4/5 Majority
E QMV
F QMV from 1.1.2007 onwards
G QMV minus 1
H QMV if legislation has already been adopted
I QMV by heads of state and gov.
J QMV but referral to European Council
K Simple Majority
L By common accord
M Unanimity by heads of state and gov.
N Assent by Council
O QMV + Assent by COM Pres.
P No role of the Council

Table 11: *continued*

Council voting / decision making with the EP

	A	B	C	D	E	F	G	H	I	J	K	L	M	N	O	P
Assent by majority	190.4	49	2	272.4+5b							223					199
of members	TEC	TEU		7.1 TEU	TEC						TEC		7.2 TEU	190.5.2 TEC		TEC
Assent by 2/3 of votes cast and majority of members																
Assent by 3/5 of votes cast and majority of members														272.6 TEC		
Total cases	2	6	2	1	9	2	1	2	1	1	2	3	2	2	1	1

A	Unanimity + Ratification		G	QMV minus 1
B	Unanimity		H	QMV if legislation has already been adopted
C	2/3 Majority		I	QMV by heads of state and gov.
D	4/5 Majority		J	QMV but referral to European Council
E	QMV		K	Simple Majority
F	QMV from 1.1.2007. onwards		L	By common accord
			M	U by heads of state and gov.
			N	Assent by Council
			O	QMV + Assent by COM Pres.
			P	No role of the Council

Source: Treaty of Nice, 22 December 2000

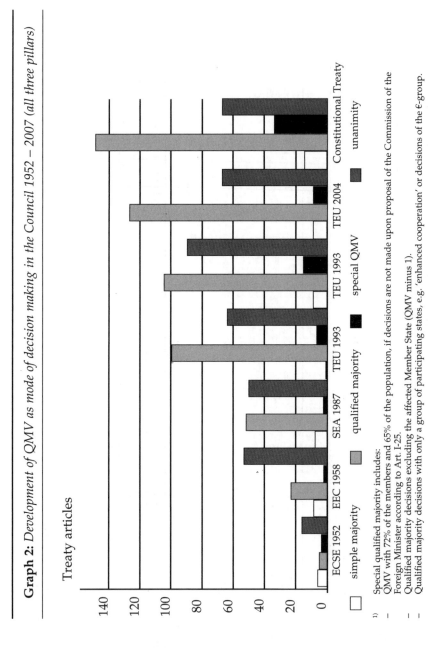

Graph 2: *Development of QMV as mode of decision making in the Council 1952 – 2007 (all three pillars)*

Source: Maurer, Andreas and Wessels, Wolfgang (2003) "The European Union Matters: structuring self-made offers and demands", p. 35, in Wessels et al, *Fifteen into One? The European Union and its Member States*, Manchester. Figures for Nice and TCE added by Funda Tekin, Jean Monnet Chair.

with Member States in order to push proposals through, since changes to a Commission proposal can only be made by unanimity under the EC Treaty, as Usher underlines in chapter 3.

To sum up, the Commission remains an active and productive player in the EU system. Its role is increasingly influenced by the more complex nature of the Union's political process, but there is no evidence suggesting a marginalisation of the Commission or a reduction in its role. Nor is there evidence to suggest the Commission is somehow dormant, as the following analysis of the different phases of the policy-process demonstrates in detail.

The Commission and the Council in the policy cycle: patterns of interaction

The Commission as an 'embedded initiator'

One important role ascribed to the European Commission has been that of an 'engine of integration' (Hayes-Renshaw and Wallace 1997, 185f; Lequesne 1996, 398). As Usher explains in chapter 3, the most important legal provision in this regard is the Commission's monopoly of legal initiative within the Community framework. As the Council – and in cases of co-decision the European Parliament – can only act upon a proposal submitted by the Commission, this rule confers on the Commission a highly strategic role. First, no legal act can be concluded without the Commission submitting a proposal, so all deliberations in the Council are based on Commission texts. In the process of law-making, the Commission thus constitutes the key point of reference, which defines the very nature of the relationship between the Commission and the Council. However, recent Treaty revisions have conferred other actors with the role of initiator of legislation as well. As graph 3 demonstrates, the share of Treaty provisions in which the Commission has an exclusive right of initiative has shrunk in favour of the Council and the Member States. It should be noted though, that it is not the absolute number of cases of exclusive Commission initiative that has decreased (this has in fact increased) but its relative overall share. Clearly, the expansion of EU competence into new policy fields has not been made subject to the (supranational) Community method, but rather to intergovernmental modes of governance (Wessels 2001b, 204). There are varying methods of coordination in different policy areas. Employment (de la Porte and Pochet 2002) or fiscal and economic policy (Wessels and Linsenmann 2002; Hodson and Maher 2001) are cases in point. In addition, different modes of decision-making and control have been used within the second (Regelsberger 2004) and third pillars (Müller 2003; Monar 1997), thus boosting the trend.

Significantly, however, even in the traditional areas of Community competence, the formal right of legal initiative is no longer the exclusive preserve of the Commission. Agenda setting within the EU has become a highly fragmented and pluralist process (Peters 1996, 63; Hix 1998, 39). If the EP has grown in importance, national preferences and priorities still play a role; this influences the Commission in its daily legislative work. The Council and Parliament can request the Commission to submit a proposal for a legal act (Arts. 208 and 192 TEC). The European Council has also begun to pro-

vide input into the European Union's decision-making process (Bulmer and
Wessels 1987), gradually taking over what was hitherto the Commission's
prerogative in agenda-setting and policy-making. The European Council
has not only provided the Union with the necessary impetus for its development, but it also increasingly deals with detailed issues of EU policy, an
evolution accompanied by an increase in the number of European Council
meetings.

The Commission's legislative programme is regularly coordinated with
the Council Presidency in order to streamline and harmonise activities and
ensure smooth cooperation (Hayes-Renshaw and Wallace 1997, 186;

Graph 3: *Evolution of Commission rights 1958-2002 (relative in percent)*

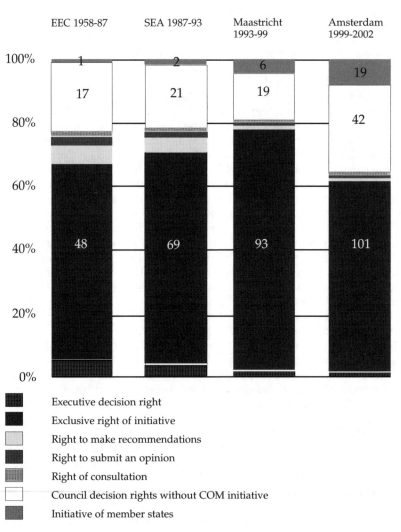

Source: EC Treaty 1958-1997

Schaefer 1996, 11). While the Commission President presents the Commission's annual legislative and work programme to the EP plenary, the Council President customarily has a half-year programme. Yet, effective policy-making outcomes were clearly seen as contingent on enhanced coordination of the two (Hix 1999, 48). Thus, at the Seville European Council of June 2002, it was decided that the European Council would adopt a multi-annual strategic programme for three years, on the basis of a proposal by the Presidencies concerned and after consultation with the Commission. Within this framework, the Council now submits an annual operating programme (European Council 2002, 23f.). Though this might be seen as a further weakening of the Commission's role as initiator, it does open channels of influence for the Commission on the Council's agenda. The procedure may not guarantee smooth interaction, but it very much reduces the risk of political conflict at later stages of the decision-making process. The result of these developments is that important EC/EU initiatives are increasingly developed in close coordination between the Commission, the Council and the European Council (Nugent 1999, 118f.). The White Paper on the Completion of the Internal Market, the Delors-I and Delors-II packages, the process leading to EMU and Agenda 2000, or the recent Agenda 2007 are obvious examples (Weise 2004). In these cases, the Commission gave considerable impetus to the EC/EU process, but it still needed sufficient Member State support to provide its political projects with sufficient credibility (Hayes-Renshaw and Wallace 1997, 187ff.).

As to the Commission's own initiatives, it is significant first that the Commission takes up proposals or requests for legislation from non-institutional actors in the EU, as chapter 10 makes clear. Then there are also legislative requirements resulting from international obligations (e.g. sanctions) or amendments to existing acts. Such legal acts reflect routine administration rather than political initiative, of course. According to Commission data, only 5 to 10% of its proposals could be described as 'pure spontaneous Commission initiatives' (Peterson and Bomberg 1999, 38).[1] Importantly, the Commission is also not the only initiator of consultation processes, since the Council also sets up expert or advisory committees to provide input into the preparation of legal acts (Schaefer 1996, 9). Up to 700 expert, advisory or consultative committees or groups are estimated to work in the EC. Their members may later participate in the working groups of the Council and in the comitology system described in chapter 8.

In sum, therefore, the Commission is obliged to take both the different views and positions of NGOs and Member States into account and investigate the degree of resistance to each potential proposal, but the system of overlapping inter-institutional contacts thereby benefits Commission civil servants by enabling them to network with relevant actors from Member States (Schaefer 1996, 21). To conclude, the role of the Commission as initiator of legislation and engine of integration is not under fundamental threat, but it has become more complex. It is now interwoven with other institutions' activities and preferences. The Commission pools ideas and proposals but is not always the original author of them; its strategy is to serve as an interlocutor and thereby streamline the multitude of European interests and views. It thus remains the prime point of reference for legal initiative in

most fields of Community action, notwithstanding the evolving roles of the
Council, European Council and European Parliament.

The Adoption of legal acts: close involvement, participation and consensus-building

Within the Council arena, an intense dialogue takes place in which
Commission and Member States try to convince each other of their positions
and arguments. This fits the well-known culture of consensus-seeking in the
EU, whereby, '[r]epresentatives from the Member States try at all levels of
Council discussions to influence the behaviour of the Commission within
the Council, just as Commissioners and their officials seek to influence the
behaviour of individual member governments within the Council' (Hayes-
Renshaw and Wallace 1997, 182). But there are various processes involved.

Proposals by the Commission are fed into the hierarchical Council
machinery, with levels of decision-making from working groups of officials
through the (ambassadorial level) Committee of Permanent Representatives
(COREPER) to the ministers themselves, meeting as the Council in its various sectoral forms. Negotiations among the national delegations start in
working groups of which there are around 250 dealing with specific policy
issues, where as a rule, most issues are resolved (Gillissen 2003, 10 and 159).
Where this is not possible they are settled by COREPER or by the ministers
themselves meeting in the Council. COREPER is the main preparatory and
executive body of the Council, bringing together the permanent representatives of the Member States. It deals with all sectoral Council issues, including second and third pillar issues, except agricultural policy, which is dealt
with by the Special Committee for Agriculture (SCA). COREPER meets in
two different formations: COREPER I and COREPER II. COREPER II, composed of the Permanent Representatives themselves, is responsible for the
preparation of General Affairs and External Relations, ECOFIN, Justice and
Home Affairs and Cultural Policy. COREPER I, composed of the Deputy
Permanent Representatives, deals with the remaining policy areas except
agriculture. The Commission is represented in COREPER at senior level; in
COREPER II by the Deputy Secretary-General of the Commission and in
COREPER I by the Director of Directorate D of the Secretariat General,
responsible for relations with the Council. The Permanent Representations
maintain close contacts with the *cabinets* of their home country's
Commissioner – not only to influence the nomination of higher officials in
the Commission, but also to influence the process of policy-making. Despite
rules and rhetoric, no Commission member truly acts in full independence
of external pressure, be it political, ideological or national, as chapter 1
underlines.

The 'Antici group' is a preparatory and supportive body for COREPER II
(Westlake 2004).[2] It brings together the assistants to the Permanent
Representatives to prepare COREPER II, Council and European Council
meetings. The Antici group's role was enhanced by the Council's new code
of conduct in 2003, which was created to cope with the consequences of
enlargement. It serves as a clearing and filtering body, ensuring that only
well-prepared documents arrive at COREPER level and that COREPER's
instructions do not overburden the working groups. The Commission is

represented in the Antici group by the head of unit for relations with the Council in the Commission's Secretariat General, and is thus able to share internal Commission information with national representatives. Over the years, a close and trusting relationship has developed between Commission and Council representatives both in the Antici and Mertens groups and in Council working groups, where the Commission is also represented. The Commission also maintains close contacts with the Council's General Secretariat and staff of Presidencies. As to the 'services', issues arising at COREPER or ministerial level are managed in close consultation with specific Directorates General and, as succeeding Secretaries General testify in this book, the Commission Secretary General attends all European Council meetings and important Council meetings. The legal service of the European Commission also maintains close contacts with its counterpart in the Council Secretariat, a fact which does not preclude differences of opinion and quarrels over legalities between the two.

For the Commission, participation in Council bodies offers important channels of information and influence. The Commission is not only a neutral broker; it can and does take advantage of splits within the Council. This is especially important when majority voting is used, because it allows the Commission and Member States to form coalitions on specific policy issues. The extension of QMV thus suits the Commission's interests, since it increases the probability that a proposal will be adopted (Schmidt 2000, 38; Pollack 1997, 122). But it is also important to take the legal procedure into account. The potential for majorities largely depends on the system of weighted votes in the Council. A number of studies have analysed the voting system under the Nice Treaty (Bilbao et al. 2002; Bräuninger and König 2004) and under the Constitutional Treaty (Baldwin and Widgrén 2004). The 'triple majority system' of Nice was expected to reduce the probability of qualified decision-making considerably and increase the veto power of the big Member States, thus enhancing the danger of complicating decision-making through the building of a blocking minority.

It is crucial for the Commission to be in line with the policy of the 'winning coalition' in the Council. Inter-institutional coalition-building is a key method to achieve this objective. It must however be noted that the use of QMV is still limited (see table 12). Of all legal acts where QMV could have been used according to the Treaties, only a minority of acts has been adopted this way, although the figures are rising. Thus, while QMV is not a 'daily' practice, it is becoming a 'normal' and accepted method of decision-making in the EU.

Varying legislative procedures mean varying levels of Commission influence

The Commission's influence is highly dependent on the legislative procedure used for the adoption of a legal act. The simple procedure, in which the EP is merely consulted, as practised in fields such as agriculture and commercial policy, facilitates Commission influence. Here, the Council remains the central counterpart, and the Commission's ability to modify or even to withdraw a proposal at any stage of the policy-making process is crucial, for there is no extraneous influence of note to the basic 'tandem' model. With unanimity required for the Council to deviate from the initial Commission text, the Commission remains in a strong position.

The picture is different in the case of co-decision. Here, the Commission exerts the same formal influence until it has reviewed amendments of the European Parliament to a common position of the Council. Depending on the Commission's point of view on the proposed amendments, the Council either acts by unanimity to reject it or by QMV if it wishes to approve the EP's amendments. However, when agreement is not reached, a 'conciliation com-

Graph 4: *The Use of Decision-Making procedures EP/Council 1958 – 2004 in absolute numbers (EC Treaty only)*

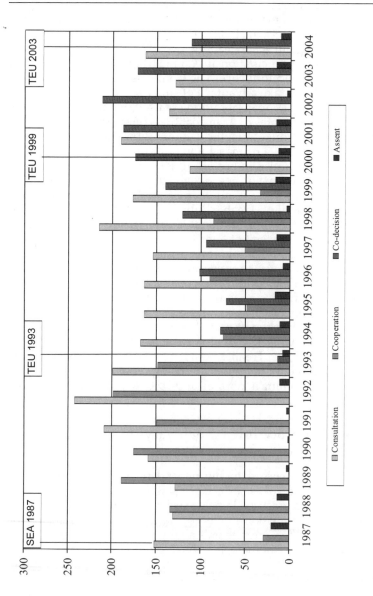

Source: Maurer 1999 and Maurer 2001; further elaborations based on original versions of the Treaties.

mittee' meets. Then, the Commission loses most of its formal influence – though it does gain a mediation role, since the Treaty stipulates that the Commission is 'to take all the necessary initiatives with a view to reconciling the positions of the European Parliament and the Council' (Art. 251 TEC). Thus, during the conciliation committee it can try to mediate between the Council and the Parliament, bringing in its expertise and resources, but without control over the further course of deliberations and decisions. Some observers argue that co-decision has led to a 'genuinely bicameral system' (Crombez 2000, 366), yet with 'semi-tricameral participation' if one still includes the Commission (König and Bräuninger 1997, 8). It is nevertheless clear that the Council and the EP dominate this decision-making procedure (Selck and Steunenberg 2004, 28; Maurer 2003a, 230).

So much for the process of formal interaction; analysis of co-decision would be incomplete, however, without discussion of the informal inter-institutional dimension. The establishment of a 'trialogue' procedure in co-decision has contributed to strengthening inter-institutional links between the Commission, the Council and the EP. Although not formally Treaty-based, trialogue has become an important element in co-decision (Shackleton and Raunio 2003, 178). It brings together one representative of the Council Presidency (usually the deputy Permanent Representative), some members of the EP delegation and one high official from the Commission (Director or Director General), who try to elaborate a compromise before the conciliation committee is called. The

Table 12: *The Real Use of Qualified Majority Voting in the Council 2000-2004*

	2000	2001	2002	2003	2004
Absolute number of cases where QMV was used	16	20	16	29	22
As percentage of all cases where QMV was foreseen in the Treaties	8.4%	15.4%	11.9%	21.5%	17.1%

Source: Council of the European Union, Monthly Summary of Council Acts, 2000-2004.

formal procedure is thereby shortened and there is less inter-institutional confrontation. This has led to a remarkable reduction of the average time span for the conclusion of a legal act (Maurer 2003a, 63). To illustrate the efficiency of decision-making, it should be noted that of the 472 co-decision procedures concluded in 2002, in 69 cases the adoption of a legal act failed, but in only 7 cases was this due to unsuccessful conciliation or because the EP rejected a text adopted by the conciliation committee. Of 348 legal acts finally adopted under co-decision, the conciliation committee was not even called in 236 cases (Maurer 2003a, 232). These figures reflect successful consultation and coordination between the Council, the Commission and the Parliament, leading some observers to speak of a 'new legislative culture' (Shackleton and Raunio 2003, 176). Importantly, a similar practice occurs in the budgetary procedure, where the Interinstitutional Agreement of 6 May 1999 makes the three institutions coordinate their financial priorities and try to ensure a smooth running of the process (Nugent 1999, 402).

To sum up, the Commission can still be regarded as a key actor in decision-making, despite seemingly considerable shifts in its formal and informal powers. In legal terms, its position has been weakened by the introduction of co-decision, while the increased use of its mediation role and trialogue procedures has opened new opportunities for exerting influence. The Commission thus not only behaves as a strategic actor but is also involved in deliberative processes aimed at common problem-solving, in close dialogue with the Council and the EP. The trilateral nature of EU decision-making, reaching well beyond the classical patterns of law-making in the EC, cannot be over-emphasised.

Implementation of EU policy: control and coordination

The Commission defines the detailed arrangements for spending programmes in coordination with Member States. As a comparatively small institution dealing with 25 Member States, it needs their administrative systems to manage policies and programmes effectively. Policy and programme management is thus customarily provided by national bodies; '[h]ence partnership between the national and the European levels of governance has become one of the marked features of EU policy-making' (Wallace 2000, 15). A crucial aspect of implementation – especially with regard to the relationship between the Commission and the Council – is 'comitology', which is discussed in detail by Pedler and Bradley in chapter 8.

The comitology system has doubtlessly contributed to the complexity and differentiation of the EU system. Frequently, members of committees have already been present in Commission or Council working groups. They are thus familiar with the subject matter and contribute to the inter-linkage of actors at the national and European levels (Vos 1999, 46f.). Nevertheless, the Commission influences the agenda and shapes discussions within the comitology committees, where it formally holds the chair. 'Member State officials sometimes complain that within many comitology committees, they feel somewhat powerless in that it is the Commission which is "in the driving seat", which sets the agenda and which is very experienced and effective in chairing meetings' (Schaefer 1996, 21). Although disagreement over the type of committee to be chosen to implement a legal act occurs regularly, Commission-Council interaction within the comitology system is a combination of inter-institutional struggle and strategic bargaining and cooperative and deliberative patterns of interaction (Joerges and Neyer 1997). So the Commission-Council relationship is not characterised by a constant conflict over principle but by a daily, case-by-case approach in which mutual readiness for cooperation prevails (Dogan 1997, 48). Member States also have reasons to accept and even foster implementation by the Commission, despite their efforts to monitor and control it. There is arguably a 'dual-executive' (Hix 1999, 54) of the Council and the Commission, built upon such regular coordination of their activities.

Contrary to intergovernmentalist expectations, the Commission's role in implementation – although closely controlled by Council committees – is not that of an agent exercising limited, delegated powers. It enjoys a considerable degree of autonomy and even at times independence. In contrast to the neo-functionalist model, the Commission is interested in keeping close contacts with Member States and the Council, in order to promote policy options. Comitology is thus not only a forum for conflict and inter-institutional quarrels, but also an arena for dialogue, expert discussion and the formation of epistemic communities, where socialisation of the different institutional actors occurs (Haas 1992).

Monitoring implementation: the Commission as guardian of the Treaties

The Commission plays a key role in monitoring the execution and implementation of EU law. As 'guardian of the Treaties', it is responsible for controlling the correct application of EC law in Member States. In particular, the transposition of directives by Member States must respect deadlines in the original legal act. If the Commission considers the implementation of EC law insufficient in a Member State, it takes action. The procedures are lengthy and multi-staged. As Usher describes in chapter 3, the first step is to inform the Member State and formally ask for a reaction. Where response is unsatisfactory, it issues a reasoned opinion and sets a deadline for compliance. Should the deadline pass without adequate action taken by the Member State, the Commission is within its right to appeal to the Court of Justice, since this constitutes failure to fulfil an obligation arising under the Treaties. In the majority of cases the Commission is successful before the Court. The implicit 'threat' of legal action normally means that Member States comply at an early stage of the infringement procedure. However, as the following table documents, infringement procedures have grown in number in the last years, hinting at increasing problems at the Member State level in correct implementation of Community law (see table 13). Accordingly, the Commission's role as a guardian is of utmost importance.

One specific area of control lies in economic and monetary policy. Here, the Commission fulfils important control functions despite depending ultimately on the Council as the key decision-making actor (Linsenmann et al. 2005; Dyson 2002). The Commission submits recommendations on broad economic policy guidelines under Art. 99 (2) TEC and may voice an early warning in cases where economic developments in a Member State give rise to concern (Linsenmann and Wessels 2002). Additionally, the Commission's authority derives less from its formal Treaty-based competencies than from its publicly acknowledged role as guardian of the Stability and Growth Pact, an expression of informal, soft power which the Commission is able to mobilise for its own purposes. 2004 and 2005 were replete with political and public debate on the limits and benefits of the Commission's role in this area.

In sum, as guardian of the Treaties, the Commission fulfils the classical function of a neutral technocracy acting in the interest of the Community, an assessment close to a neofunctionalist understanding of the Commission. Intergovernmentalist approaches have difficulty explaining the formal power the Commission enjoys to ensure respect for EC law.

The Commission and the Council in external relations: negotiation, representation and a mix of competencies

The Commission's role in external relations and EU foreign policy is fully described in chapters 12 and 14. Suffice to say that there has been an enormous increase in the conclusion of trade, cooperation and association agreements, as Smith underlines in chapter 12. Despite Council monitoring through the 133 Committee, these arrangements have undoubtedly strengthened the Commission's role in external affairs (McGoldrick 1997). The Commission is dependent on the Council in two important stages of the process: when a man-

Table 13: *Infringement Proceedings against Member States (Referrals to the Court 1997-2003)*

	1997	1998	1999	2000	2001	2002	2003
Belgium	18	20	15	5	13	8	19
Denmark	0	1	1	0	2	2	3
Germany	19	5	9	11	12	16	18
Greece	10	16	14	23	16	17	14
Spain	7	6	7	8	14	11	23
France	15	23	35	27	22	31	21
Ireland	6	10	15	17	13	9	18
Italy	20	16	32	24	22	23	18
Luxembourg	8	11	18	16	10	12	16
Netherlands	3	3	1	12	5	7	9
Austria	0	4	9	8	7	15	22
Portugal	14	5	13	10	7	10	10
Finland	0	1	0	4	2	1	6
Sweden	0	1	1	3	3	2	7
UK	1	1	8	4	14	16	11
Total	**121**	**123**	**178**	**172**	**162**	**180**	**215**

Source: XXIth report on monitoring the application of Community Law, COM (2004) 839

date is to be adopted for the negotiation of an agreement and when the final result of these negotiations has to be approved by the Council before conclusion. In both these cases frictions may and do arise. First, some Member States may oppose a Commission recommendation for a mandate because they do not share the objectives and positions defined in it. This necessitates compromise through bargaining between Member States and the Commission. Second, once negotiations are concluded, it is difficult for the Council to reject single elements of a draft agreement without jeopardising the whole text and the Union's international credibility, yet despite these risks there have been several such cases in the past (Monar 1999, 65ff.).

Developments in policy-making have also complicated the Commission-Council relationship in trade policy. In its Opinion 1/94 on the conclusion of the WTO agreement, the European Court stated that EC trade policy mainly covers goods, and only some minor parts of trade in services and intellectual property. The Commission's claim that the Community has exclusive competence overall was hence deemed not to hold (MacLeod, Henry and Hyett 1996, 52ff.). There has thus been an increase in the use of 'mixed agreements', in which the Community figures as a signatory alongside Member States (Bourgeois 1997, 83ff.). Internally, this has arguably weakened Commission influence vis-à-vis the Council and the Member States. It has led to the use of unanimity in the conclusion of certain trade agreements, which would otherwise have fallen under QMV in accordance with the EC Treaty. These trends have certainly increased the need for close Commission-Council coordination in external negotiations, in particular within the WTO (Woolcock and Hodges 1996). The Nice Treaty improved coherence between different sectors of trade policy by bringing agreements on trade in services and commercial aspects of intellectual property into Community competence (Art. 133 (5) TEC), while preserving special provisions for trade in cultural and audiovisual services, educational services, and social and human health services, which fall under the shared competence of the Community and the Member States (Art. 133 (6) TEC). Under the Constitution, these fields were set to come into Union competence, though the conclusion of international agreements in these areas would, nevertheless, remain subject to unanimity in the Council.

EU enlargement is another field of external relations in which the Commission has gained an increasingly important role (Lippert 2004). Formally the Council's turf, enlargement has allowed the Commission to take a leading role in the negotiation and conclusion of accession agreements, making it an increasingly important partner for the Council through its delivery of a considerable proportion of the daily work and preparation of detailed provisions. Unlike the Member States, the Commission is engaged in all stages of the enlargement process: it delivers early estimates and evaluations in the pre-application stage; presents opinions on the applicant's suitability for membership and likely repercussions for the EU; and accompanies the accession negotiations by 'reflection' and 'action', forming the common approaches on which the Council builds its strategy. Thus, the official role of Member States is modified by the Commission's profile as a 'co-negotiator' and as an ever more central player in enlargement negotiations, both in terms of public opinion and the applicant states' perception, which it influences through its delegations in the applicant states. In very real terms, therefore, the Commission is the EU's institutional focus for the enlargement process.

As to CFSP, the Amsterdam Treaty's establishment of the High Representative for CFSP could be said to have considerably reduced the Commission's visibility in external relations as a whole, as chapters 14 and 15 argue. Increasingly, Javier Solana, the High Representative for CFSP, is regarded by the public and by third countries as the spokesman for the EU's foreign policy, while the Commission, as the institution responsible for managing financially powerful programmes and for contractual relations with third countries, remains on the sidelines. As to a theoretical assessment of the Commission's role and influence, the intergovernmentalist model would generally account for its limited role in CFSP, while a multi-level and neofunctionalist approach might focus more on the degree of Commission power through project management and presence abroad.

The Commission and the Council in the Constitution: shifting the balance?

The Constitutional Treaty signed in October 2004 redefined the relationship between the Commission, the Council and the European Council in key aspects of the EU's institutional set-up. With the changes intended by the Constitution in limbo after the rejection of the Constitution in France and the Netherlands, it is difficult to predict those elements of the Constitution which might find alternative means of implementation in due course. It is nonetheless worth reviewing the Constitution's key provisions. One of the central issues of the debates and negotiations in the Convention and the IGC was to find a new institutional balance that would improve the effectiveness, efficiency and legitimacy of the European Union. One highly controversial issue was the creation of a full-time President of the European Council, whose term was set at a once-renewable two and a half years (Art. I-22 Constitutional Treaty). As a politically prominent and influential personality was likely to be chosen, the European Council President could have become a rival to the Commission President in promoting initiatives and providing political impulse to the Union.

Further, as chapter 14 underlines, the simultaneous creation of a Minister for Foreign Affairs under a double hat – as a member of the Commission and representative of the Council – might have raised doubts about the smooth and efficient functioning of the post. The dual nature of the Foreign Minister's tasks and responsibilities would have made it particularly difficult to identify his precise role vis-à-vis each institution. This could have led to political and institutional tensions; in the worst case scenario, the Foreign Minister might have been perceived as a 'Trojan horse' of the Council within the College, using Commission resources and competencies to serve the Council's interests. Conversely, the Foreign Minister could have developed an autonomous position, strengthening his own profile as a political player in EU external relations. A good deal would have depended on the individuals chosen.

In addition, as chapter 1 explains, the provisions on the appointment of the Commission reflected the reduced influence of the Member States within the European Council and the Council. The Commission was to consist of a reduced number of members, which would correspond to two-thirds of the number of Member States (Art. I-26 (6) Constitutional Treaty). The Commissioners were to be selected according to a system of rotation based on equal treatment of all Member States. In fact, the revisions introduced by the Constitution on decision-making and the legal order of the EU in general suited the Commission's views and interests, despite the fact that the establishment of co-decision as the ordinary legal procedure would have provided more formal opportunities to the EP and the Council at the expense of the Commission. The hierarchy of legal acts established by the Constitutional Treaty was set to contribute to clearing the picture (I-33 - Art. 37 Constitutional Treaty) – notwithstanding the fact that it did not overturn the traditional EC system (Maurer 2003b, 444). The legislative 'early-warning procedure' laid down in the 'Protocol on the role of Member States' national parliaments in the European Union' and the 'Protocol on the application of the principles of subsidiarity and proportionality' might have further restricted the Commission's role as agenda-setter and legal initiator. Member States' parliaments were to be

able to scrutinise Commission proposals as to their compatibility with subsidiarity, and might – if a sufficient quorum were reached – call on the
Commission to review its proposal. Member States might even have notified
the Court of Justice on behalf of their parliaments and begun legal proceedings
on grounds of infringement of the subsidiarity principle.

As to the implementation of legal acts, 'European laws and European
framework laws may delegate to the Commission the power to enact delegated regulations to supplement or amend non-essential elements of the
European law or framework law' (Art. I-36 (1) Constitutional Treaty). This provision provided for a special kind of (non-legislative) legal act and a more precise definition of the legal nature compared to the existing EC Treaty. Further,
the objectives, content, scope and duration of the delegation now had to be
defined in the law or framework law, and no essential element of an area was
to be covered by delegation.

Two trends might then have been likely. First, the EP or the Council might
decide to revoke the delegation and voice objections against a delegated regulation within a fixed period of time, thus blocking its implementation (Art. I-36
(2) Constitutional Treaty). This would establish close control over the
Commission by the Council and the EP and might lead to a decrease in the
Commission's room for manoeuvre. Second, the role of the European
Parliament would be substantially upgraded, thus reinforcing its growing role
as legislator together with the Council, consequently sidelining the
Commission.

Conclusion: balance sheet of a complex role

This empirical analysis of the Commission-Council relationship has
revealed a multi-faceted picture. Since the 1950s, the Commission has developed into an important player and shaper of European politics, which continually attempts to enhance its institutional position and its share of influence on
decision-making. Its production of proposals and legal acts still reflects the
basic trend towards a highly active and ambitious role. But this analysis has
generated evidence on the political impact of the Commission on the Council,
whether formal or informal. In external policy, a partnership between the
Commission and the Council is clearly necessary, and both institutions seemingly respond well and in concert, *pace* the comments and analysis in chapter
14. On enlargement, the Commission has increasingly occupied a policy-shap-
ing role. Elsewhere, even where Treaty provisions are weak, as in EMU, the
Commission is able to exert pressure on the Council and the Member States by
using its publicly acknowledged authority.

However, no continuous increase in the Commission's influence has been
identified. What can be observed is a growth in institutional potential.
Undoubtedly, the Commission has had to digest some major changes to the
institutional system of the EU. There are new patterns of decision-making,
principally co-decision. There are new and increasing roles for the European
Parliament. And there are new modes of governance, such as the open method
of coordination, which do not follow the traditional path of supranational
policy-making. On the other hand, the Commission has been endowed with
new – formal and informal – channels of influence, such as the trialogue procedures, which offer opportunities for close involvement and participation in

decision-making. And, within the open method of coordination, the Commission is participating actively and constructively. There is thus no perceptible danger of the Commission being relegated to a technocratic body without major political impact, as predicted in the intergovernmentalist model, despite growing differentiation and complexity in the EU system where an increasing number of options and modes of decision-making have emerged. Neither has the impression prevailed that the Commission's relations with the Council and the European Parliament resemble the classical neofunctionalist model of a technocracy acting under *sui generis* conditions. Rather, a combination of elements from the rational institutionalist and the multi-level governance models seems to hold most explanatory power. The Commission's role is flexible. It adjusts to concrete institutional settings, even where the formal provisions of the Treaty have restricted its room for manoeuvre. The importance of informal politics and deliberative processes can be regarded as a key trend, more than compensating many of the formal constraints. The new provisions of the Constitutional Treaty seem to confirm this trend. There is potential for transforming the Commission-Council relationship, even to the detriment of the former. The crucial question for the future is whether the Commission will maintain its political leverage and perform its role as a promotional broker while at the same time responding to the EP's growing demands and strengthening preferences.

Endnotes

[1]   These data appear in Peterson 1999, p. 59; they were included in a document which the Santer *cabinet* collected for a Commission paper presented to the European Council in Pörtschach in October 1998.

[2]   In a similar fashion, the 'Mertens group' acts in support of COREPER I (Westlake and Galloway 2004, 210) and the Nicolaides group acts in support of the PSC.

8. The Commission, policy management and comitology

Robin Pedler with Kieran Bradley[1]

Introduction: the management of EU policy

It is generally assumed that the Commission is the manager of policy in the EU, yet it is clear both from the Treaties and practice that the Commission is not the only body that exercises management duties, whether within the framework of the European Community (EC) or the European Union (EU). The Council also exercises important executive functions, notably as regards the EU's external relations, and it may also reserve to itself the right, albeit only in 'specific cases', to exercise implementing powers under the Community regime, where the Member States are in any case obliged to adopt the necessary measures in national law to implement legally binding Union acts. Generally speaking, however, the management of EU policies is the responsibility of the European Commission, acting alone or subject to the more or less intrusive supervision of the Member States and/or the Council through various forms of committees acting according to highly structured rules – so-called 'comitology'.

This chapter shows how Community policies are normally managed by the Commission under powers conferred by secondary legislation adopted by the Council, a role specifically provided for under the fourth indent of Article 211 and now under the third indent of Article 202. Legislation conferring management powers in specific areas may be expressly provided for by the Treaty, as in the case of the agricultural and competition regulations under Articles 37 and 83 respectively, or adopted on the basis of more general provisions such as Articles 95 and 308. As a result, the Commission is required to exercise a wide range of executive functions relating to the management, supervision and implementation of Community policies. This executive role has grown considerably as the scope and intensity of Community activities has developed beyond those originally envisaged under the EEC Treaty. The Internal Market programme is one example. Another has been the Commission's responsibilities beyond the scope of Community action, such as the coordination of aid to Central and Eastern Europe under programmes such as PHARE, TACIS and CARDS. Indeed, as manager of the European Development Fund and the new spending programmes for enlargement, neighbourhood policy and stability, the

Commission is seen by the outside world as the prime manager of EU policies and programmes outside the EU.

The Commission's management functions may be divided into four main categories:

- Direct implementation of policy and the management of Community finances, as granted in successive Treaties;

- Rule-making to flesh out policy laid down in primary law, i.e. the Treaties, or derived Council legislation, including supervision of policy implementation by national front-line bodies;

- Coordination of policies agreed by Member States under 'Open Coordination';

- Regulation involving representatives of the economic interests to be affected: 'Co-Regulation'.

This chapter first reviews these four categories and describes the complex comitology mechanisms, whereby the Commission is supported, monitored and controlled by the Council and the Member States in the performance of its management tasks. But, it should be noted that comitology is not the only source of supervised policy management. There has been increasing resort to agencies with their own legal status and separate from any of the three legislative institutions of the EU. The role of these agencies is fully discussed in chapter 5. Suffice to say, their function is usually advisory, so their continuing role in secondary legislation can be viewed as provision of an informed basis for proposals that the Commission will subsequently make to committees. Another alternative is growing resort to Council-managed structures for policy and programme management, which is briefly discussed in this chapter. Importantly, both may undermine the Commission's traditional executive role.

Managing and coordinating – the role of the Commission

Direct implementation of policy

The Commission cannot normally be compared to a national agency carrying out a front-line policy management function, though in some limited areas, notably the management of competition policy, the Commission is able to pursue a 'hands on' role in implementing the relevant Community rules. Within these areas the Commission may even enjoy exclusive executive powers. But such powers are exceptional and subject to significant reservations by Member States, as can be seen, for example, in the history of the powers conferred on the Commission under Council Regulation (EEC) 4064/89 of 21 December 1989 relating to merger control. It took more than 16 years to adopt them and they are limited to much larger-scale (and hence fewer) mergers than the Commission itself had sought. To understand the nature of the Commission's executive role, one should bear in mind that the staff to carry it out – of an overall general total of some 23,000 officials – is comparable in number only to a large European city administration, a fact which led Commissioner Mario Monti (1999-2004) to address the issue by returning some of the Commission's powers in the area of merger control to Member States. The Commission reorganised its Merger Control Task Force on 30 April 2003, both because of the workload on staff in the EU-15 and because it estimated that enlargement to 25 on 1 May 2004 would increase the workload by 30-40%. The reorganisation did not involve an increase in staffing of the competition Directorate General, but sought to improve effectiveness by reallocating officials to sector-specific merger control teams.

Management of Community finances

The Commission is the manager of the EU budget. It is responsible for ensuring that the approved annual budget and the guidelines for expenditure are observed. It takes general management decisions concerning disbursement of the budget, principally within the two main areas of agricultural support and the structural funds, but also across policy areas such as technical assistance and development policy. It also supervises implementation of payments by national authorities acting on behalf of the Community, such as agricultural intervention agencies, exercising specific powers to withhold refunds as a sanction for payments in breach of the rules.

Supervision of policy implementation by national bodies

National bodies such as customs and excise, agriculture and intervention agencies, fisheries inspectorates and even the police all play a role in implementing the bulk of Community policy and combating attempts to defraud the system. But the Commission has a significant supervisory function, both as a line manager and, if necessary, as a 'prosecutor', since it is the 'guardian of the Treaties'. However, despite these powers it relies heavily on the good will and cooperation of national agencies. Its role as the guardian is fully treated in Chapter 3, but it is useful to note that the question of resources plays a determining part in the way the Commission must choose to exercise this function. The Court of Justice and the Court of First Instance have both recognised in very different contexts the limits on the Commission's ability to scrutinise closely all aspects of Community policy. In the *Automec II case* (Case T-24/90 [1992] ECR II-2223), the Court of First Instance recognised that the Commission has discretion on whether or not to take up particular competition complaints, and that it may prioritise its investigations and allocate its resources accordingly. The judgment complemented an earlier judgment of the Court that the Commission's discretion on whether or not to initiate or pursue infringement proceedings against Member States may not be challenged in legal proceedings (Case 247/87, *Star Fruit* [1989] ECR 291 paras 9 – 13). In similar vein, the Court of Justice has recognised the limited extent to which the Commission can supervise national authorities. In a case concerning the issue of special licences to import 'GATT' beef (Joined cases C-106/90, C-317/90 and C-129/91 *Emerald Meats Ltd v Commission* [1993] ECR I-209) under low import levies, the Court found that:

'a Community ... management method does not presuppose that all the decisions should be taken by the Commission but may equally be achieved by decentralised management ... Nor do the requirements of Community management entail that the Commission ought necessarily to be able to correct wrong decisions taken in specific cases by the national authorities.' ([1993] ECR I-209 at paragraphs 39-40)

These pronunciations by the Court are a valuable recognition of the practical constraints placed upon the Commission by its relative lack of resources. The Commission may thus determine its own priorities without being impeded by legal actions alleging maladministration in a situation where, as one commentator points out, 'the Commission is not, in general, well enough resourced for the job'. (Nugent 1999, 128)

Rule-making

The Commission's best-known executive function, and that to which it allocates a significant part of its resources, is the exercise of rule-making powers, laying down, in addition to Community rules, ground rules to be followed by national administrations. The vast majority of conferred rule-making powers concern day-to-day management decisions made by the Commission acting alone as a matter of routine, where little or no exercise of discretion is required. This is the case, for example, where reduction percentages are fixed, if necessary, to equate demands for import licences of agricultural products from outside the Community with the quantities available of those products. Where an exercise of discretion is concerned, however, such as the opening and deciding upon tenders to sell quantities of agricultural products held by intervention agencies or to grant aids to reduce market prices, the Commission will act following one of the committee procedures discussed below. Here, the Commission's function in rule-making may be constrained by involving representatives of the Member States acting in committee, though the practice permits minor modifications of Community legislation to be carried out more informally. Thus Article 12 of Regulation (EEC) No. 1765/92, which implements the 'McSharry reform' of the Common Agricultural Policy, introduced the 'set-aside' scheme (Commission 1992a). It specifically permitted the Commission to amend the list of minor arable crops covered by set-aside via the management committee procedure and set out an extensive list of particular areas where rules have to be adopted by the Commission, such as those enabling the various arable 'quotas', the amount of land to be set aside or the way set-aside is to be applied. The scope of the Commission's rule-making powers of implementation can be extremely controversial and on many occasions Member States have challenged before the Court the exercise by the Commission of its powers. The issue is discussed below. Parliament too has, on one occasion, taken annulment proceedings against a Commission regulation as encroaching on powers which properly belonged to the Council, on the exercise of which Parliament would have been consulted. (Case C-156/93 GMMOs *Parliament v Commission* [1995] ECT 1-2019)

The Open Method of Coordination

In parallel to the development of EMU, the Member States launched the 'Lisbon Process' with the objective of creating by 2010 'the most competitive and dynamic knowledge-based economy in the world, capable of sustainable growth with more and better jobs and greater social cohesion'. (European Council, Lisbon, March 2000) The process is based not on a Treaty amendment but on Council Conclusions and to ensure that it progresses the European Council has adopted the 'Open Method of Coordination'. This determines that the executive task of implementation is to be undertaken by each Member State individually, although they report to each other at the spring European Council every year. This derives from a process instituted by the Luxembourg Presidency in 1997 to encourage all Member States to make good a pledge to reduce unemployment, a Member State responsibility, since control of social security and unemployment policies remained national. It was hoped, however, that the dual forces of 'sharing best practice' and 'peer pressure' would ensure that the situation improved Union-wide. At Lisbon in 2000 it was decided that the issue of reducing unemployment should be addressed on a much broader basis, by seeking to enhance the growth of the Union's Gross Product. Reports to the spring European Council thereby became a review of what each Member State had been able to deliver over the previous twelve months in this regard. They reported initially in Stockholm (2001) and Barcelona (2002) and since the Treaty of Nice came into effect (1 February 2003) they report regularly in Brussels.

It could therefore be argued that the executive role has been pre-empted by the Member States, but it should be noted that they are acting and deciding on the basis of reports by the Commission. The Commission published its own interpretation of the Open Method of Coordination in its White Paper on Governance (2001), which stated, in particular that 'the Commission should be closely involved and play a co-ordinating role' (Commission 2001a). Further, the collective weight of the Member States in favour of liberalising whole sectors of the economy held to be restraining economic growth has strengthened the hand of the Commission, notably in completing the long-running process of liberalising the electricity sector (Greenwood 2002).

Co-regulation

The Commission also defines co-regulation in its White Paper on Governance (2001), stating that it has already been used in agreeing product standards for the internal market under the 'New Approach' and also in the environment sector (reducing car emissions) (Commission 2001a, 21). A novel feature of the Exhaust Emissions Directive adopted in 1994, was a requirement on the Commission to begin work on the norms to be applied from 2000. On this occasion, the car industry – represented by ACEA, the association of European vehicle manufacturers – and the oil industry – represented by Europia, the federation of European oil refiners – were invited to work with the Commission to produce European norms. They set up the 'European Programme on Emissions, Fuels and Engine Technologies' –

EPEFE. The industries jointly provided expertise and laboratory facilities, working with the Commission in a programme worth ECU 10 million. The concrete outcome of the process was new Directives on Exhaust Emissions and on Petrol and Diesel Fuels, adopted by co-decision in September 1998. These required industry to achieve substantial reductions in emissions over the period 2000-5. The co-regulation procedure has since been adapted, so that the norms to be applied from 2005 onwards were analysed and discussed in seven working groups, each chaired by the Commission and including representatives from all Member States, the two industries and an alliance of eight environmentally active NGOs (Pedler 2002). The outcome of their discussions might be described as 'self-regulation'. The car industries involved made three 'voluntary agreements' with the Commission. The Commission set them a target of reducing average CO_2 emissions to 120gm/km by 2010. They undertook that they would achieve 140 gm/km by an earlier date: 2008 for ACEA and 2009 for both Japanese Auto Manufacturers' Association – JAMA – and Korean Auto Manufacturers' Association – KAMA. All three would 'try to close the 20gm gap' (European Automobile Manufacturers' Association – ACEA Commitment on CO_2 Emission Reduction from Passenger Cars (2001), ACEA and Commission Services). While these agreements are voluntary, the process was launched and chaired by the Commission, which also set the target to be achieved.

The Council, the Commission and comitology – the exercise of rule-making powers

A feature common to nearly all the implementing powers conferred upon the Commission by the Council is that they come 'with strings attached'. These relate to the involvement of the Member States or the Council itself in the Commission's decision-making process. In certain cases, this includes the possibility to amend or even block Commission decisions. The key feature of these committees, apart from advisory committees, is that an unfavourable opinion, or in certain circumstances even a failure to adopt an opinion, can result in the decision being referred back to the Council, where it is possible for the measure to be blocked by the Member States. As a result, the Commission is not totally free to act independently, although in practice it is able to exercise its management powers as it wishes in most cases.

The various forms of committee structure imposed upon Commission decision-making within the framework of implementing powers are known collectively as comitology, a set of arrangements which have developed parallel to but outside the original Treaty provisions. The first attempt to codify committee structures occurred as late as 1985 in the Single European Act, when comitology was very much regarded as the 'management' counterpart of the expanded qualified majority voting procedures introduced in the Act itself. Knowledge of the basic elements of comitology is crucial to a proper understanding of the role of the Commission as the manager of Community policy and of the inter-institutional debate on management policy between the Commission, Council and Parliament.

In essence, comitology constitutes an institutional compromise between the need for more effective Community decision-making and Member

States' desire to preserve national influence over Commission decisions. From the Community perspective, the aim of the exercise is to 'speed up decision-making in the Community by more frequent delegation to the Commission of powers to implement Community legislation' (House of Lords 1986, para. 2). From a national perspective, the aim is to retain as much national influence over the Commission as necessary when the Commission exercises powers of implementation. As a result, the Council has consistently sought to adopt stricter forms of committee procedure than those proposed by the Commission, so as to maximise Member States' influence over the Commission's exercise of power of implementation (Engel and Bormann 1991, 55 and 151).

Many aspects of the comitology procedures are no more than the technical or administrative preparation of a decision by the Commission. They are rendered necessary by the EC system of devolved national implementation and administration of EC policies, whereby each Member State is responsible for the implementation of most Community policy within its territory. Indeed, one commentator has concluded that the real impetus behind comitology is Member States' responsibility for the national implementation of policy decided at EC level. Comitology allows for the necessary coordination between the EC and national levels of responsibility:

'The committees... have the purpose both of sensitising and of associating national administrations with the EC legislative and executive rules which they will have to implement' (Blumann 1988, 93-94).

Thus, objections to a Commission draft decision by national representatives on a management or regulatory committee may point to difficulties of implementation at national level, and must if possible be taken into account before adopting that decision. In such circumstances, there will always be a need for procedures to involve national authorities.

The historical perspective

Prior to the Single European Act

Powers of implementation were first subjected to committee procedures in the guise of management committees in agriculture in 1962 and as regulatory committees in customs, health and veterinary legislation in 1968. A basic formula for the organisation of committees has thus emerged. Their members are drawn from the Member States but they are chaired by the Commission, normally the unit dealing with the particular policy area concerned. As early as 1978 the 'Three Wise Men' in their Report on the European Institutions emphasised the need to simplify the range of procedures and to use a much more limited number of procedures for powers of implementation (Committee of Three 1979). In 1986, the European Parliament identified 130 such committees divided into 31 categories of procedure (European Parliament 1986). The House of Lords commented that the range of procedures and variants available to the Council 'defied description' and resulted in a considerable waste of time and energy (House of Lords 1986, para 26). Codification did not take place until the SEA was implemented in 1987.

From the Single European Act to the Treaty of Amsterdam

The Single European Act (SEA) did not settle the differences between the Commission and the Council over comitology, despite strong recommendations to that effect in the preparatory work. However, the SEA did provide for the primary executive role to be exercised by the Commission, subject to the compromises discussed below.

Article 10 of the SEA introduced a new third indent to Article 202 EEC:

'The Council shall ... confer upon the Commission, in the acts which Council adopts, powers for the implementation of the rules which the Council lays down. The Council may impose certain requirements in respect of the exercise of these powers. The Council may also reserve the right, in specific cases, to exercise directly implementing powers itself. The procedures referred to above must be consonant with principles and rules to be laid down in advance by the Council, acting unanimously on a proposal from the Commission and after obtaining the Opinion of the European Parliament.'

In one sense, this was a step forward in that it obliged the Council for the first time to confer implementing powers upon the Commission. However, this progress was qualified by two features. The Council was allowed to impose requirements in respect of the exercise of those powers (subsequently adopted in the 1987 Framework Decision, to be modified by the Council Decision of 28 June 1999 (1999/468/EC)) and even to reserve for itself the exercise of such powers in specific cases. The only caveat to the latter power was the obligation to ensure that procedures are compatible with general rules and principles laid down in advance by the Council.

Article 10 of the SEA was accompanied by a Declaration in the Intergovernmental Conference (IGC) on the powers of implementation of the Commission by the Member States:

'The Conference asks the Community authorities to adopt, before the Act enters into force, the principles and rules on the basis of which the Commission's powers of implementation will be defined in each case. In this connection the Conference requests the Council to give the Advisory Committee procedure in particular a predominant place in the interests of speed and efficiency in the decision-making process, for the exercise of the powers of implementation conferred upon the Commission within the field of Article 100a of the EEC Treaty.'(Article 100a was subsequently re-numbered Article 95 in the Treaty of Amsterdam.)

Thus the Council was mandated to adopt overall rules and to give special prominence to the advisory committee procedure, but the advice was specifically limited to the priority area of the single market. Elsewhere, Member States continued to guard their prerogatives. In response the Council finalised what became known as the Comitology Decision.[2] The procedures laid down were generally held to be complex, so when the EC Treaty was amended in the Treaty of Amsterdam[3], the Intergovernmental Conference on that occasion, in Declaration 31 of its Final Act, called on the Commission 'to submit to the Council a proposal amending Decision 87/387/EC'.

This resulted in the Council Decision of 28 June 1999 (1999/468/EC), which 'repealed and replaced' 87/387/EC.

The 1999 comitology decision

In a clear effort to simplify the decision-making process, the 1999 Decision reduced the number of procedures from seven to four and laid out in detail how they apply to Advisory, Management, Regulatory and Safeguard procedures.

Advisory procedure – I

This is to be adopted 'where it is most appropriate' and where the content of the proposal does not imply that it should follow the Management or Regulatory procedure (see below). In common with the two other forms of committee detailed in the Decision, it is chaired by the Commission and the members are representatives of all Member States. Its distinctive feature is that the opinion of the committee, determined by qualified majority vote, while offering advice to the Commission, is not binding, although the Commission is bound to report back to the committee 'the manner in which its opinion has been taken into account'. There is therefore no detailed procedure to determine what should happen in case of a negative opinion, and in effect the Commission can just ignore it.

In this, as in all committee formats, the Decision takes into account the need for speed in arriving at secondary legislation and states that a Decision must be reached 'within a time limit that the chairman may lay down according to the urgency of the matter'. Experience since 1999 shows that for Advisory Committee as well as other committees the time limit is generally three months.

The reports covering three years of operation (2001-3) show that the Advisory Committee is the least used of the three possible committee structures (excluding Safeguard). It might appear that it is infrequently 'most appropriate'. The Decision's language seems to suggest that it is a fallback when Management and Regulatory formats do not suit. It is also suggested by participants that there is a tension between the Commission, which would prefer to solicit views in a non-binding format, and the Member States, which would prefer to be sure that their voices are heard as part of the legislative process.

Management procedure – II

The management procedure may be adopted for 'management measures, such as those relating to the application of the common agricultural and common fisheries policies, or to the implementation of programmes with substantial budgetary implications'. Again, the committee is chaired by the Commission and assembles representatives of all Member States. Their decisions are taken by qualified majority (QM) vote.[4] In this case, both the Commission and the Member States are bound to act.

Following enlargement and the entry into force of the Treaty of Nice, QM consists of 240/321 votes and must also represent a majority of Member States (13/25). The vote to achieve a qualified majority should also be cast by Member States representing 62% of the population of the EU, though the count is an option, to be exercised at the request of a Member State. The Commission, while it chairs the committee, does not have a vote, but it does retain the initiative, since it is empowered to 'adopt measures to apply immediately'. Disagreement between the Commission and a qualified majority of Member State representatives on the committee will lead to a review by the Council, acting once again by qualified majority, and constrained by a time limit of three months. In reality, it is extremely rare for the Member State representatives on management committees to vote against a Commission proposal. During 2001, for instance, only ten cases out of a total of 5,613 consultations were referred to the Council. These ten cases concerned DG Enterprise (two cases), DG Agriculture (two cases), DG Transport (one case) and DG Health and Consumer Protection (five cases). Pursuant to the comitology decision, measures must be referred to the Council when the Commission fails to obtain the necessary majority in committee. The small percentage of referrals (less than 1%) as compared to the total number of instruments adopted by the Commission (regulatory or management procedures) shows that the proposals submitted by the Commission to the committees normally obtain the necessary majority. Thus, 'the committee's work is characterised by a high degree of consensus.'[5]

Management committees are closely followed by the private sector – farmers and businessmen. This is because, as the Decision says, there are 'substantial budgetary implications' and also because, once the committee has decided, the Commission may 'adopt measures to apply immediately'. To large-scale farmers, and even more so to companies trading in grain futures, the immediate application of a change in the support price for a grain crop is very significant.

Regulatory procedure – III

This procedure may be used for 'measures of a general scope designed to apply essential provisions of basic instruments, including measures concerning the protection of health or safety of humans, animals or plants... where a basic instrument stipulates that certain non-essential provisions of the instrument may be adapted or updated by way of implementing procedures.'

Like the other committees, the Regulatory variant is chaired by the Commission and consists of representatives of all Member States, acting – if they take a vote – by qualified majority. Once again, the initiative remains with the Commission to the extent that the Council, if it wishes to overturn a Commission proposal, is constrained to act within three months and only if it fails to do so, the Commission retains the right to press ahead.

There are specific powers of review vested in the European Parliament. If the EP considers that a proposal submitted by the Commission pursuant to a basic instrument adopted in accordance with the procedure laid down in Article 251 of the Treaty exceeds the implementing powers provided for in that basic instrument, it informs the Council of its position. The power of regulation is a significant part of secondary legislation.

Safeguard – procedure IV

This procedure confers direct powers on the Commission, which does not need to call together a committee to consider its proposals. It 'may be adopted where the basic instrument confers on the Commission the power to decide on safeguard measures.' In this procedure, unlike the Management and Regulatory procedures laid out above, more power of decision passes from the Commission to the Council, in the sense that, if the Council does not act, it is the Commission's proposal that is lost.

'If the Council has not taken a decision within the... time-limit (*usually three months*), the decision of the Commission is deemed to be revoked.'

The working of committees

The 1999 Decision stated that 'the Commission must publish, from 2000 onwards, an annual report on the working of committees'. This was a step towards 'transparency', since the previous report on the working of committees referred to 1995, when it took the form of a review drafted at the request of the European Parliament and sent to Parliament in July 1996.

The Commission duly published reports on the working of committees (Commission 2001b, 2002a, 2003a). It listed the number of committees – 254 in 2000 reducing to 247 in 2001 and increasing again to 257 in 2002 – classified by the Commission Directorate General to which they relate and also by their decision procedure. Following the Decision of 1999, there was initially some confusion about the organisation of committees. It repealed the Decision of 1987, 'pending the amendment of basic legislative instruments putting in place the comitology procedures pursuant to Decision 87/373/EC'. Then, in February 2002 it addressed the situation by publishing Standard Rules of Procedure.

By 2001/2 committees were tabled under the new classifications, as follows:

	2001	2002
Advisory	31	32
Management	76	78
Regulatory	105	97
Safeguard	5	4
'Operating under several procedures'	29	46
Total	247	257

All three reports lay stress on the 'consensual' nature of committee work and demonstrate that in 99% of the numerous proposals listed, the Commission proposal was adopted.

Wessels has underlined the atmosphere of consensus. Though based on interviews with senior German civil servants, his conclusions are likely to be applicable to other Member States. He found 'considerable Europeanisation of national civil services' and concluded that insights into the behavioural patterns within committees indicate 'an interactive style... where daily routine is characterized by business-like workings based on technocratic expertise and camaraderie, and geared to consensus amongst civil servants from several levels.' (Wessels 1998)

Agreement on application of the 1999 Decision

As part of its continuing efforts to complete the Single Market, the Commission set out in 1999 to establish an Internal Market in financial services. This was to be achieved under the Financial Services Action Plan of 1999-2004. It acquired additional force when it came to be seen as part of the 2000 Lisbon process to inject dynamism into EU economies. Part of the action plan involved the establishment of two new committees; the 'classic' Financial Services Committee and the 'new form' of Committee of Financial Services Regulators. The financial services industry was strongly in favour of the details of the plan being handled in committee, citing the benefits of speed and certainty of decision. (Mijs and Caparros 2002) There was however strong opposition from the European Parliament, which saw further committees as eroding its powers in an important area.

The first proposed amendment to procedures under the 1999 Decision occurred when the Commission sent a letter to the Council and the Parliament on 10 January 2003 containing a 'Proposal for a Council Decision (Commission 2002b)[6]. The proposal was made under Article 202 of the Treaty, so Parliament was acting in a consultative role.

'In the Parliament, the President referred the letter to the Committee on Constitutional Affairs as the committee responsible and to all the Committees interested for their opinions. The Committee on Constitutional Affairs appointed Richard Corbett rapporteur.' (European Parliament 2003, 2003a)

MEP Richard Corbett subsequently produced a report.[7] It made 17 amendments to the Commission's text, laying stress on Parliament's 'right to have a say' and therefore 'need of due time', which it defined as three months. The Commission was unable to accept all of the 17 amendments. There thus followed a period of negotiation between the Committee on Constitutional Affairs and the Commission, which resulted in the text of an inter-institutional agreement acceptable to both. As Corbett later concluded in a second report adopted on 11th July by the EP[8], and subsequently agreed by Council, this provided a solution to the long standing controversy on the Commission's implementing powers. It also gave Parliament the opportunity to supervise them.

The agreement goes some way to enhance the Commission's executive powers, but it also gives the Parliament many additional powers:

- a three-month examination period of draft implementing measures (instead of one month);

- a formal role on substance and not just scope;

- incorporation of a 'sunset clause' meaning that if the Parliament and the Council do not renew the delegation of powers after four years it ceases.

More generally, the Commission stated its agreement with the Council's and Parliament's equal role in controlling the way the Commission carries out the executive role in the financial services sector.' (Guéguen and Rosberg 2004)

The Lamfalussy procedure

A group of advisory committees, a recent addition to the system, arises from the creation, in all Member States, of national regulators for a series of industries. In the main, they are concerned with the performance of former state monopolies in transport and energy, but also, and importantly, with the operation of financial and securities markets. Thus in 2001, the Commission set up a new regulatory committee, the European Securities Committee (ESC) 'composed of high level representatives of national competent ministries'. In parallel, the Commission set up the Committee of European Securities Regulators (CESR) from which 'it should receive technical advice in the phase of preparing draft implementation measures'. This committee is not chaired by the Commission, but by Dr van Leeuwen, the Netherlands' regulator (Commission 2002a, and Mijs and Caparros 2002). The establishment of these committees generated opposition from the European Parliament. To seek a solution, the Commission set up a group of 'wise men' chaired by Baron Alexandre Lamfalussy, a distinguished Belgian banker. As the following figure shows, the two committees both play an essential part in the resulting 'Lamfalussy procedure' agreed between the EU institutions and welcomed by the business sector affected.

The number of advisory committees of Member State regulators is growing. A similar situation has been created in the telecoms sector and will shortly be created in the electricity and gas sectors.

Lamfalussy Recommendations

1. *Speeding up the EU legislative process*

2. *New Regulatory Framework based on 4 levels*
   – High Level Principles remain under co-decision
   – Technical Details decided by comitology

3. *Establishment of 2 Committees:*
   – Regulatory Committee – Member States
   – Advisory Committee – Securities Regulators

4. *Transparency and Consultation essential*

Figure 1: *Lamfalussy Procedure – Level 1*

CESR: European Securities Regulator;
ESC: European Securities Committee

Level 2

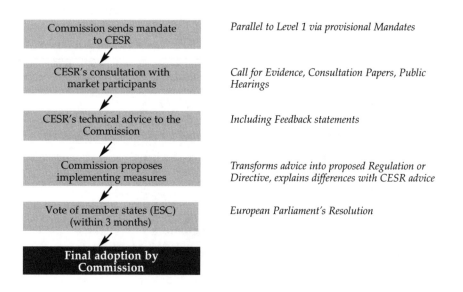

Source: The above figure courtesy of Asunción Caparros, Director ABNAmro

EU comitology: strengths and weaknesses

The comitology procedures have three main strengths: the Commission controls the agenda of the committees; the Commission's draft must be voted upon by the national representatives; and the effect in practice is to guarantee that a decision will be taken within the deadlines laid down.

The weakness of the procedures is that they allow Member States total control over powers of implementation in two situations – either directly, where the Council itself acts, or indirectly in case of doubt or disagreement, where a measure can then be referred to the Council. In these two cases, there is no guarantee that the deadline will be respected, or that there will be any decision at all. In reality, however, as the Commission's annual report on the working of the committees during 2001 underlined, references to the Council are extremely rare, so timely decisions result in 99% of the cases.

Judicial review of the Commission's exercise of delegated powers

The comitology system was nowhere provided for in the original EEC Treaty. It may therefore be considered one of the most significant organic developments of the Community's, now Union's, institutional structures. As a controversial institutional novelty, its establishment, operation and evolution have regularly been subject to the review of the Court of Justice.

The EEC Treaty in its original form did not make an explicit distinction between primary and secondary or 'implementing' legislation, though Article 155 EEC (now Article 211 EC) did enjoin the Commission to exercise any implementing powers the Council conferred on it. In *Köster*, the Court relied on this provision, and on existing institutional practice, to hold that Community law recognised such a distinction, which was also recognised in the legislative practice of the Member States (Case 25/70 *Köster, Berodt & Co* [1970] ECR 1161, para. 6). It followed that the Council, as primary legislator, was only obliged to adopt the basic elements of the matter to be regulated according to the procedure laid down by the Treaty legal basis. Implementing legislation could therefore be adopted either by the Council acting under a different (less cumbersome) procedure, or by the Commission.

The Court has also refined the notion of the 'basic elements' in the German sheepmeat case (Case C-240/90 *Commission v Germany* [1992] ECR I-5383). There it held that the Council was only obliged to adopt 'rules which [are]… essential to the subject-matter envisaged', to wit, 'provisions which are intended to give concrete shape to the fundamental guidelines of Community policy', or more succinctly, policy-defining provisions.

The Court also rejected the charge in *Köster* that the management committee procedure undermined the Commission's independence and distorted the Community's institutional balance. For the Court, the only obligation the procedure imposed on the Commission was to communicate to the Council the measures it had taken, and the committee's function was to 'ensure permanent consultation in order to guide the Commission in the exercise of the powers conferred on it by the Council'. The Court's reasoning may have been influenced by fact that delegation to the Commission was then optional for the Council, which is no longer the case. The 1977 judgment in *Tedeschi v Denkavit* (Case 5/77 [1977] ECR 1555) has been inter-preted by some as demonstrating that the regulatory committee procedure was compatible with the Treaty, though the Court did not in fact address the issue. The relevant Treaty provisions have in any case been significantly modified since.

The issue of policing the boundaries of the Commission's delegated powers has also been considered by the Court. The principal ground on which the exercise of delegated powers may be challenged in the Community system is that the act adopted exceeds the scope of the powers granted to the Commission, i.e. that the challenged act is *ultra vires*, and the Member States are vigilant in ensuring that the Commission does not over-step the bounds of its implementing powers, an area in which the Court has laid down a number of rules. In particular:

- in cases where the Commission must evaluate a complex economic situation, the Court will only annul the measures adopted on the grounds of a manifest error, a misuse of power or lack of compe-tence (Case 29/77 *SA Roquette Frères v France* [1977] ECR 183, para. 20);
- an enabling provision which allows the Commission to adopt implementing measures which impede the achievement of a funda-mental Treaty objective, such as the free movement of goods, must be strictly interpreted (Case 61/86 *United Kingdom v Commission* [1988] ECR 431, para. 16 and 26);
- the Commission may not adopt an implementing measure to govern a matter on which the Council has already legislated exhaustively, or use its implementing powers under the common agricultural policy to pursue objectives in another area of activity falling within the competence of the Council (Case 264/86 *France v Commission* [1988] ECR 973, para. 21; Case 22/88 *Vreugdenhil BV v Minister van Landbouw en Visserij* [1989] ECR 2049, para. 17).

The Court has also laid down a number of other requirements governing the delegation of powers. Thus, for example, unless the basic measure stip-ulates otherwise, the Commission may itself determine the procedure it will follow in adopting implementing measures. Moreover, enabling provisions must in principle be sufficiently specific, 'that is to say, the Council must clearly specify the bounds of the power conferred on the Commission' (Case 291/86 *Central-Import Münster GmbH & Co KG* [1988] ECR 3679, para. 13).

Comitology and the implementation of Article [202], third indent, EC

As noted elsewhere, the growth in the number of committees and variety of supervisory procedures led to the inclusion, by the Single European Act, of a new third indent in what is now Article 202 EC. This was intended to provoke a root and branch rationalisation of the comitology system. Days after the Single Act came into force, the Council adopted a decision laying down the different types of committee procedure which could be used for the adoption of implementing legislation, the 'first comitology decision'.[9] This was immediately challenged before the Court of Justice in the first annulment proceedings ever initiated by the European Parliament; however, the action was rejected on the grounds that Parliament had no legal capacity to take such proceedings (Case 302/87 *Parliament v Council* [1988] ECR 5615). A few months later the Commission challenged one application, rather than the validity, of the comitology decision (Case 16/88 *Commission v Council* [1989] ECR 3457). While the Commission was also unsuccessful, the Court nonetheless provided the most complete interpretation to date of the basic Treaty provisions governing comitology:

- implementation 'comprises both the drawing up of rules and the application of rules to specific cases by means of acts of individual application';
- the legislator is bound by the rules laid down in the comitology decision, and cannot impose any other type of comitology procedure;
- the limitation to 'specific cases' on the Council's right to reserve the exercise of implementing powers to itself requires that it 'state in detail the grounds for such a decision' (paragraphs 10, 11 and 14 of the judgment, respectively).

Certain aspects of the Court's ruling in this case have now been carried over into the second comitology decision of 1999 (Case C-378/00 *'LIFE' Commission v Parliament and Council* [2003] ECR 1-937).

The choice of procedure

For tactical reasons, which subsequently proved to be misconceived, the Commission did not put forward in its proposal for the first comitology decision any principles to guide the choice of committee procedure for implementing provisions in particular areas of activity, notwithstanding the clear injunction in Article [202], third indent, EC that the decision establish such principles. In 'TACIS', the Court recognised that

'the choice of one type of committee or another, in so far as it involves different decision-making procedures and a different division of powers between the Commission and the Council, may have a decisive influence on the operation of the arrangements in question' (Case C-417/93 *Parliament v Council* [1995] ECR I-1185, para. 25).

Somewhat surprisingly, the Court went on to find that there was no significant difference in the instant case between a management and a regulatory procedure, despite the differences in both the level of support required by the Commission to adopt its measures (a blocking minority, as against a qualified majority) and the voting majority in the Council required to amend the text proposed by the Commission (qualified majority as against unanimity).

The second comitology decision went halfway to remedying the matter, by providing criteria for the choice of procedure in Article 2, but then specifying that 'such criteria are of a non-binding nature'. In the so-called 'LIFE' case (Case C-378/00 *Commission v Parliament and Council* [2003] ECR I-937), the Court held that the legislator was not legally obliged to follow the criteria of Article 2, but that if it did so, it was obliged to provide reasons for this course of action.

Operation of comitology procedures

The Court has also ruled on various aspects of the operation of the comitology procedures. The respect by the Commission for the time limits within which it must act has given rise to particular problems, though it is not always possible to draw any general conclusions from these rulings. Thus, for example, where the rules of procedure of a committee provide very precise minimum periods for the submission of the Commission's draft, these must be respected to the letter; submitting a draft 19 days before the committee's meeting will not satisfy a rule stipulating a minimum of 20 days for consideration (Case C-263/95 *Germany v Commission* ('construction products') [1998] ECR I-441; see also Feta II, judgement of 25 October 2005, not yet reported).

On the other hand, the requirement in basic legislation that the Commission 'without delay propose to the Council the measures to be adopted' where a regulatory committee has not adopted the Commission's draft measure, was interpreted as allowing the Commission a certain degree of temporal latitude, here eleven months, in following up on the procedure (Case C-151/98 P *Pharos v Commission* [1999] ECR I-8157). However, the abuse of this latitude, where the Commission has no objective justification for failing to act during a given period, may leave it liable in damages, where it is guilty of a 'clear and serious breach of the principle of sound administration' (Joined Cases T-344/00 and T-345/00 *CEVA Santé and Pharmacia Enterprises v Commission* [2003] ECR II-229, para. 103; in the circumstances of this particular case, the Court of Justice held that the Commission had not disregarded the limits on its discretion; Case C-198/03 P, judgement of 12 July 2005, not yet reported).

Where the Commission's draft measures have not been adopted by a regulatory committee, it is under no obligation to submit the same draft measures without amendment to the Council (Case C-151/98 P *Pharos v Commission* [1999] ECR I-8157). The Court has noted that 'in delicate and controversial cases the Commission had to have a sufficiently broad discretion and enough time', and that it was therefore entitled to withdraw its proposal for measures even after the regulatory committee had met (Case C-352/98 P *Bergaderm v Commission* [2000] ECR I-5291, para. 66).

Transparency

One of the main charges levelled by the European Parliament against the comitology system was the lack of transparency of the work of the committees. While Article 7(2) of the second comitology decision now deals with the matter once and for all by providing that the Commission's régime on access to documents also applies to comitology committees (see above), the Court of First Instance also struck a blow for committee transparency weeks after this decision was adopted. In *Rothmans* (Case T-188/97 *Rothmans v Commission* [1999] ECR II-2463), the Commission had refused a request from the applicant company for access to the minutes of a regulatory committee, on the grounds that it was not the author of the document requested. Finding that such committees were established 'to assist the Commission in performing the tasks conferred on it', the Court held that 'for the purposes of the Community rules on access to documents, 'comitology' committees come under the Commission itself'.

The Court's reasoning is less than convincing; in particular, its reliance on the terminological fact that the committee is said to 'assist' the Commission seems rather strained, not to say naïve. While the Commission certainly may benefit from the expertise of the national administrations, whatever type of procedure is at issue, the fact remains that a regulatory committee can block the adoption by the Commission of legislation merely by failing to provide an opinion. This is probably the kind of 'assistance' the Commission might prefer to do without.

Moreover, even if it were true that a comitology committee assists the Commission, this does not mean that it should necessarily be treated as coming under the latter's rules on access to documents. The Council and the Commission are 'assisted' by an Economic and Social Committee and a Committee of the Regions. Does this mean that a member of the public would be entitled to request the documents of these committees from the Council and/or the Commission? In terms of facilitating public access to 'the information available to the institutions', the judgment might be seen as representing progress. However, the problem the Court sought to resolve in *Rothmans* was in any case dealt with in the second comitology decision. As a result of the judgment, the much more fundamental question of access to documents of other committees and satellite Community bodies, including large numbers of scientific and other advisory committees of the Council and the Commission, remains unanswered.

Committees outside the comitology framework

Committees organised by the Commission

A discussion of committees organised by the Commission would not be complete if it omitted two other areas of committee work which fall outside the comitology structure. The Commission exercises its right of initiative in close collaboration with interest groups on both an informal and formal basis. Mazey and Richardson review the relations between the Commission and the lobby in chapter 10. The following discussion illustrates the more formal committee procedures involved which do not fall under the Comitology Decision.

The many committees and expert groups that assist the Commission in implementing policy fall conceptually into three main categories (Glathaar 1992, 180). The largest category concerns agriculture, where Commission-created committees tend to be set up by formal decision as 'advisory committees'. Thus for example in dealing with the Common Agricultural Policy itself, arable crops, rural development and forestry[10], Commission officials are shadowed by advisory committees. Members of committees are appointed every three years by decision of the Commission on the basis of special interest bodies or associations specified in the Decision setting up the committee. Thus the arable crops advisory committee is composed of representatives of producers, cooperatives, food processors and manufacturers, traders, workers in agriculture, processing and food manufacturing and consumers. Its mandate is to advise the Commission of the views of producers, traders and consumers on the issues arising from the operation of the common market organisation in cereals 'and in particular on measures to be adopted by the Commission'. Such committees should provide valuable expertise to the Commission when contemplating the need for or effect of proposed measures. In practice, however, they are rated by one 'expert' who has served on them as lacking influence (Guéguen and Rosberg 2004). They are precluded from voting, but the views expressed by the various interests represented are reported to the Commission, and on request may be passed on to the Council and to the relevant Management Committees.

The second category mainly concerns the social area, where advisory committees or groups have been created both by formal decision and by informal administrative practice. The Commission has set up a number of joint and tripartite committees where representatives of government and the two sides of industry, or the two sides of industry alone, meet to advise the Commission on the planning and implementation of social policy.

The Advisory Committee on Equal Opportunities for Women and Men was established by Commission Decision 82/43/EEC of 9 December 1981 to provide an institutional framework for consultation of specialised national equal opportunities bodies or their equivalents. Its members range from representatives of autonomous equality bodies such as the Equal Opportunities Commission in the UK and the Employment Equality Agency in Ireland to officials in national ministries handling equality issues in the absence of such specialised agencies.

There is also an advisory committee within this category aimed at the coordination of fraud prevention.[11] This committee serves to complement the work of existing committees by providing a horizontal view of the whole area of fraud against the Community budget and to assist in coordinating the action taken by Member States to protect the interests of the Community and to counter fraud.

The third category consists of groups of experts who provide scientific and technical advice to the Commission in carrying out its policies. Such groups may be set up formally or informally. Examples of the latter are the so-called 'equality networks' composed of diverse specialists such as lawyers, specialists on child care, education and training and small business creation, and representatives of European television organisations (Docksey 1987, 1). These various networks are a source of expert advice to the Commission in their fields of expertise and carry out pilot projects in their sectors.

Scientific groups set up by formal decision are normally expected to back up the rule making function. The two most significant are the Scientific Committee for Food – originally set up by EC Decision of 25 April 1974 – and the Committee for Veterinary Medicine. In both cases, Community legislation has made the consultation of the scientific committee mandatory. 'For example the directive on food additives (EU 1989) states in Article 6 ... "Provisions that may have an effect on public health shall be adopted after consultation with the Scientific Committee for Food ... '" (Gray 1998).[12] The legal basis of these scientific committees was revised in 1995.[13]

The overwhelming majority of commentators, including the authors of a previous version of this chapter, were of the view that '[the] status of scientific groups was revolutionised by the ECJ judgment of 25 January 1994 in Case C-212/91 *Angelopharm v Hamburg*' (Docksey and Williams 1994, 134). According to their interpretation of the judgment, the Court had based its conclusion that consultation of a scientific committee in that case was mandatory essentially on the committee's function of '[ensuring] that measures adopted were scientifically accurate'(ibid). In *Pfizer Animal Health* (Case T-13/99 [2002] ECR II-3305 para 249), however, the Court of First Instance rejected an argument based on exactly this kind of reasoning, to the effect that 'regardless of the working of the relevant legislation, consultation of the competent scientific committee becomes mandatory in all cases'. It noted that the Court's conclusion in *Angelopharm* was based on 'a purposive interpretation of the relevant provisions of the directive' at issue (Case T-13/99 [2002] ECR II-3305 para 262); this is standard interpretative practice at the Court in Luxembourg, rather than a Copernican revolution in judicial reasoning.

The Commission and the Council: major differences in approach

The Commission and the Council remain divided on the question of implementation by the Council itself. The Commission takes the view that the Council can decide to act as the executive only in exceptional circumstances, and subject to the criteria of the Comitology Decisions of 1987 and 1999. Moreover, this view should be interpreted in the light of Article 10 of the Single European Act, confirmed at Maastricht and Amsterdam introducing Article 202 third indent, which transfers administrative competence to the Commission and states that the Council can only award itself such powers in 'specific cases'.[14]

In contrast, Member States consider exercising this right wherever necessary in sensitive areas and do not regard themselves as bound by the criteria of the Decisions. In this respect, the holding in Case 16/88, *Commission v Council*, that the Council may only exercise this right in specific cases and that it must give detailed reasons justifying its exercise, would favour the Commission's approach on this point. This ruling is reflected and strengthened in Article 1 of the 1999 Comitology Decision, which restricts the facility for the Council to exercise implementing power to 'specific and substantiated cases'.

Yet in some key areas the Commission has considerable power. Economic and Monetary Union (EMU), for example, was legally defined in the Treaty on European Union (Maastricht), which came into effect on 1 November 1993. It began to function on 1 January 1999 amongst initially 11 Member States. Greece joined in 2001, bringing the membership to 12. All those Member States have undertaken that they will conduct their economic policies in accordance with the Stability and Growth Pact. This limits the size of their public borrowing and their national budget deficits. The pact was adopted, in accordance with Article 99.2 by 'The Council, acting by qualified majority on a recommendation from the Commission (to) formulate a draft for the broad guidelines of the economic policies of the Member States'.

The definition of the Stability and Growth Pact was undertaken by the Commission and the Council, with the Parliament entitled only to information. Executive powers under the pact are still the prerogative of the first two institutions. Article 99.3 enjoins: 'In order to ensure the coordination of economic policies and sustained convergence of the economic performances of the Member States, the Council shall, on the basis of reports submitted by the Commission, monitor economic developments in each of the Member States and in the Community as well as the consistency of economic policies with the broad guidelines referred to in paragraph 2 and regularly carry out an overall assessment.'

Thus while it is the Member States themselves in Council that have the power to assess each other's economic performance, it is to be done on the basis of the Commission's proposals, and the system is to be operated by the Commission monitoring carefully the economic developments in each Member State and reporting. Exercising its function of ensuring that the Council respects the provisions of the Treaty, the Commission brought a case to demonstrate that the Member States might not exempt some of their number from the Stability and Growth Pact (Case C27/04 13 July 2004).

The Council's follow-up of comitology Decisions

Analysis shows that in the period 1962-1995 management and regulatory committees issued a total of 52,189 opinions, of which only 13 were unfavourable, implying reference to the Council (Falke 1996). In the regulatory committee areas, 98 per cent of proposed decisions had been approved by the committees and almost all of the remaining 2 per cent of measures sent to the Council had been reformulated by the Commission so as to aid the Council to reach agreement. The Commission's reports on the working of committees in 2000 and 2001 show that the high proportion of measures approved in committee without reference to the Council has been continued under the new procedures following the 1999 Decision – see above.[15]

One example cited by the Commission in a 1991 report of where it successfully refused to change its position was the BSE or 'mad cow disease' affair in 1990 (Westlake 1997). In this case, the Commission's draft measures received an unfavourable opinion from the Standing Veterinary Committee, which triggered a referral of the proposed instrument to the Council on 22 January 1990. Under Article 13 of the enabling legislation Directive 64/432/EEC, the Council had a maximum period of 15 days in which it could itself adopt the proposed instrument. However it was unable to act within the time limit and the Commission immediately used the 'net' to adopt its decision on 7 February 1990 (Commission 1990). The Commission concluded that there was 'no objective reason for the Council's hesitancy' and that it was:

> 'deeply concerned by developments in this area which, to its mind, run counter to the spirit of the Single Act and are likely to compromise the efficiency of Community action in the lead-up to the single European market.' (European Commission 1991, 1)

However, the Commission's actions were subsequently strongly criticised by the European Parliament, which established an inquiry committee

that sat in 1996/97 to examine the history of BSE and the way the crisis had been managed by various institutions. The committee's report was adopted by a resolution in plenary on 19 February 1997 by the overwhelming vote of 422 to 49. Although the motion of censure on the Commission for its part in handling the affair voted that session gained only 118 votes in favour with 326 against and 15 abstentions, Parliament did adopt a resolution threatening to adopt such a motion if the Commission did not carry out certain far-reaching reforms within nine months. The most scathing criticism of the report was nonetheless focussed on the UK government and more broadly the Council for supporting the UK position.

The Parliament appointed a second inquiry committee 'to monitor the Commission's response to the first committee's recommendations' (Bradley 1997). The committee was set up in April 1997 and reported in November. 'While globally satisfied with the Commission's response, Parliament complained of the lack of disciplinary measures against the officials concerned... The Commission was invited to use its margin of discretion in selecting the legal basis of legislation in this area in favour of greater parliamentary participation.' (Bradley op. cit)

In summary: 'The affair clearly revealed several shortcomings in the armoury of [Parliament's] supervisory techniques. Parliament clearly took the view that the main culprits were one Member State, a working group of a scientific committee and the Commissioner for Agriculture during the early 1990s; none of those would have been directly affected by the adoption of a motion censuring the Santer Commission.' (Bradley op. cit.)

Comitology and the democratic process: the involvement of the Parliament

While the detailed procedures described above include only the Commission and the Council, Article 7.3 of the 1999 Decision brings in the European Parliament.

> 'The European Parliament shall be informed by the Commission of committee proceedings on a regular basis. To this end, it shall receive agendas for committee meetings, proposals submitted to the committees for the implementation of instruments adopted by the procedure provided for by Article 251 of the Treaty, and the results of voting and summary records of meetings and lists of the authorities and organisations to which the persons designated by the Member States to represent them belong. The European Parliament shall also be kept informed whenever the Commission transmits to the Council measures or proposals for measures to be taken.'

Significantly, however, Article 7 merely lays on the Commission the duty to the European Parliament. But, Article 8 describes how it may act:

> 'If the European Parliament indicates, in a Resolution setting out the grounds on which it is based, that draft implementing measures, the adoption of which is contemplated and which have been submitted to a committee pursuant to a basic instru-

ment adopted under Article 251 of the Treaty, would exceed the implementing powers provided for in the basic instrument, the Commission shall re-examine the draft measures. Taking the Resolution into account and within the time limits of the procedure under way, the Commission may submit new draft measures to the committee, continue with the procedure or submit a proposal to the European Parliament and the Council on the basis of the Treaty. The committee shall inform the European Parliament and the committee of the action which it intends to take on the Resolution of the European Parliament and of its reasons for doing so.'

Article 251 of the Treaty, laying down the co-decision procedure, requires that where the basic act devolves executive powers to the Commission, this must be approved by the European Parliament. This Article reflects the strong feelings of the European Parliament that, under the 1987 procedures, it was effectively excluded from important parts of the decision-making process. Indeed, one of only five cases to date in which Council and Parliament failed to reach agreement in a conciliation committee concerned the application of the comitology procedure: the Securities Committee Directive 1998. Here, the Council took a decision not to reintroduce the common position in anticipation of the Amsterdam provisions (Shackleton 2000, 327).

A major concern of Parliament today remains that of receiving timely information from the Commission on the work of committees. It regards such information as an essential element in reducing the 'democratic deficit', since it cannot react politically and effectively to influence draft decisions if it is not informed in good time. It has therefore developed a policy of seeking broad equivalence with the Council vis-à-vis the Commission. This concern was addressed in the 1999 Decision, which stated that the purpose of the Decision was precisely to involve the Parliament and give it an opportunity to have its views 'taken into consideration'.

The first two years of operation of the new system installed by the 1999 Decision apparently passed off to the satisfaction of both Commission and Parliament. The Commission noted in its Report on the working of committees during 2001 that:

'The previous report was sent to the European Parliament and the Council. Since the Commission received no remarks regarding its structure and content, a similar structure has been used for this report.'

In sum, the 1999 Decision formalised the agreement between Parliament and the Commission described by Westlake in the 1997 edition of the present book. Known as the Plumb-Delors agreement (of 1989), it established a modus vivendi under which the Commission made internal arrangements for informing the Parliament without swamping it with documents. The significance of Parliament being informed of draft measures, on an interim basis under the Plumb-Delors agreement and after 1999 under the new Decision, was to allow an issue to be taken up by Parliament and pressure to be put on the Commission to change a disputed text. Both practical and

procedural avenues are open to Parliament to exert political influence. It can put oral questions to the Commission in Plenary Question Time at any time and on any subject. It can put written questions to the Commission. It can informally question members of the Commission or their officials in committee. It can send a letter to the Commission from its President or the President of the relevant committee. It can also adopt resolutions which are not legally binding, but which do have undoubted political effect.

The 1990s were replete with debates between Parliament and the Commission over the use of executive powers through comitology. They led finally to agreements between the Commission and Parliament in February 2000 and on 14 December 2001, which led, in turn, in 2003/04 to the information flow being developed into electronic transfer, thereby increasing rapidity. The entry into force of the Treaty on European Union (Maastricht) on 1 November 1993 had brought the issue to a head over the co-decision procedure introduced under Article 251. Parliament set out its position in its Resolution of 16 December 1993 adopting the De Giovanni Report (European Parliament 1993) on comitology and the Treaty on European Union. Having become a co-legislator together with the Council, the Parliament claimed that the conferral of powers by instruments adopted under the co-decision procedure was a joint conferral by the Council and the Parliament and that Article 202 and hence the Comitology Decision did not apply to acts adopted under the new co-decision procedure. As a result, Parliament claimed it had corresponding rights to receive information provided to the Council on the work of the committees and to trigger referral back to the Community legislator, the Council and the Parliament. The report accordingly proposed far-reaching negotiations between the three institutions on the consequences for comitology of the new co-decision procedure and the adoption of a new Comitology Decision by the Parliament and Council. The negotiations proved protracted and then, as has been shown above in this chapter, the new Decision was adopted in June 1999, taking into account most of Parliament's claims.

Under the Treaty of European Union (Maastricht) several legislative proposals changed their legal base from the old cooperation base, now Article 252, to the new co-decision base under Article 251. To give teeth to its new position, Parliament began to propose ad hoc comitology procedures for these instruments whereby the conferral of powers by Parliament and Council could be referred back to both co-legislators rather than to the Council alone. An unsatisfactory situation developed where each of the three legislative institutions would have its own proposal for a committee procedure. For example, in the case of the draft directives on sweeteners and colourings, the Commission proposed the advisory committee procedure, the Council opted for the regulatory committee 'net' procedure and the Parliamentary rapporteur proposed a completely new procedure involving Parliament as co-legislator. The positions of the Council and Parliament were poles apart and were in danger of becoming virtually irreconcilable. When discussing the proposed directive on the application of open network provision (ONP) to voice telephony, the issue of comitology and the accompanying question of institutional balance became so sensitive that for the first time under the co-decision procedure the conciliation phase failed. This failure made it possible for Parliament to exercise its veto under that procedure. The co-decision procedure has been in operation since November 1993 and this remains one of only five occasions on which conciliation has not produced a result.

Thus, far from being an abstruse issue for institutional conflict, comitology emerged through the 1990s as a major battleground between the institutions. It was the subject of a series of proposals for working compromise. It then became an issue that was addressed but not resolved in the Treaty of Amsterdam. Finally, the arrangements currently in place were decided not by a treaty amendment in the IGC, but by the Decision of 28 June 1999, explained earlier in this chapter. It is noteworthy that this Decision was reached even as the IGC that led up to the Treaty of Nice was deliberating.

Conclusion: the future of the Commission's management role

This chapter has analysed management functions of the Commission in the light of the debate about the degree of power to be vested in the Commission and the tussle between the institutions and Member States for a right to increase the supervision of the process. In particular, it has highlighted the interplay with representatives of the Member States and the growing supervisory role of the European Parliament. Management is key to the development of Community policy. This chapter has argued that the Commission continues to exercise a central role, even in areas where the Member States are supposedly acting in cooperation and thus in intergovernmental mode. It is the Commission, after all, which manages the CFSP budget!

The chapter has also demonstrated that while comitology is the most frequent, it is not the only method used to supervise or control implementation. But, it does have the advantage for all parties of ensuring that decisions are taken relatively quickly. The alternative, traditional, full legislative process of the EU may be painfully slow. Indeed, the contrast is particularly striking where the EU seeks an executive role in 'new areas' such as financial services and e-commerce. If comitology has created tensions between the institutions and continues to do so, to judge from the experience of the first years of work within the 1999 Decision, it seems to have addressed these tensions successfully. Indeed, the Commission (alone of the three principal institutions) set out in detail its views on how executive powers should be developed in the White Paper on Governance that it submitted to the Convention.[16] It proposed reducing the use of comitology and relying rather on regulation. Regulations, once adopted, are directly applicable in Member States. Unlike Directives, they do not allow for potential adaptation to national law and systems. As one observer put it, the Commission was 'in fact demanding full executive powers to draft and implement the detailed rules and regulations which supplement EU directives.' (Murray 2002, 41). But, the draft Constitution did not adopt the Commission's proposals. Effectively, it continued the system of comitology on the basis of the 1999 Decision.

The Commission's argument had been that this change would speed up the legislative process, but its approach was criticised in the report of the Mandelkern 'high level' group of Member State experts set up 'to explore ways to improve the quality of EU regulation'.[17] The group found that the use of regulations can actually slow down the legislative process. 'Member States may insist that their particular concerns are taken into account during the drafting of the regulation, because they do not have the option of adapting the law to local conditions at a later stage.' Other critics have noted that increased use of regulation would not address the Commission's underlying problem of lack of resources. Ending comitology would deprive them of the assistance of what van Schendelen describes as 'Insourced Experts' (Van Schendelen 2003).

The Constitution, if and when ratified, will simply confirm the Commission's substantial role in the implementation of Union laws, maintaining the Commission's right to adopt delegated legislation. It will also define the powers of each of the three institutions in the control of the process. In this respect, the text of the Constitution is more precise than the Treaties of Amsterdam and Nice.[18] It confers an on-going power of co-decision on the European Parliament. One proposal might, if it were adopted, both enhance the Commission's executive powers and keep all three institutions adequately involved with comitology. This would be for wider, even general use of the procedure proposed by the Lamfalussy group of 'wise men' on the establishment of the Financial Services Committee. Regardless of this eventuality, it seems likely that the significant task of execution of Community policy will remain in the hands of the Commission, though the debate about modifications or limitations is likely to continue.

Significantly, and in closing this chapter, it should be noted that the Framework Agreement of 1999 between the Commission and the European Parliament was revisited in 2004/5 and a new interinstitutional agreement was signed by the Presidents of the Commission and the Parliament on 26 May 2005. The agreement, which is reproduced as annex H of this book, includes an important paragraph (no. 35), which confirms the interinstitutional understandings outlined in this chapter and thereby testifies to a possible lessening of previous parliamentary concern. It may be too early to tell, but the democratic supervision of the Commission's implementing powers, the resolution of previous interinstitutional divergences of view and understanding with regard to the management of financial issues seem, for the time being, at least, to have been achieved.

Endnotes

[1]   Head of Unit in the Legal Service of the European Parliament, responsible for the section 'Judicial Review of the Delegation of Implementing Powers'. The views expressed are personal and may not be attributed to the service or institution with which he is connected.

[2]   Council Decision 87/373 of 13 July 1987 laying down the procedures for the exercise of implementing powers conferred upon the Commission (Council Decision 1987).

[3]   Article 205(2) of the Treaty of Amsterdam.

[4]   Commission report on the working of committees during 2001, Official Journal No. 037, 9 February 2002, p. 37/3.

[5] Reference Commission report on the working of committees during 2001. Official Journal No. 037, 9 February 2002 p. 5 Section ¼ Referrals to the Council.

[6] 2002/298 (CNS).

[7] A5-0128/2003.

[8] A5-0266/2003.

[9] Council Decision 87/373 of 13 July 1987 laying down the procedures for the exercise of implementing powers conferred upon the Commission (Council Decision 1987).

[10] Commission Decision of 11 March 1998 on the advisory committees dealing with matters covered by the Common Agricultural Policy.

[11] Commission Decision 94/140/ec of 23 February 1994, OJ No. L 62/27, 4.3.94.

[12] Gray, 'The Scientific Committee for Food' in Van Schendelen 1998 p. 68.

[13] EC 1974 OJ L 36 20.5.74 p.1, revised on 6 July 1995 (EC 1995 OJ No. L 167, 18.7.95, p. 22).

[14] Council Decision of 28 June 1999 – 1999/468/EC Article 7/3.

[15] 1999/468/EC Council Decision of 28 June 1999 para. 9.

[16] White Paper on Governance adopted 25 July 2001 COM (2001) 428 Final pp. 18-23.

[17] Final Report of the Mandelkern Group November 2001.

[18] Articles 35 and 36.

9. The European Commission and the European Parliament

Martin Westlake

From 'Pangaea' to inter-institutional triangle

According to tectonic plate theory, there once was a single 'super-continent', dubbed 'Pangaea', floating on the earth's crust. Gradually, this super-continent broke up and the pieces began to drift apart, creating the world we know today, composed of several 'tectonic plates' and characterised by slow but constant movement, with friction and seismic activity wherever the plates/continents meet each other.

The European Union's inter-institutional equivalent of 'Pangaea' was the old bilateral relationship between the European Commission and the Council of Ministers. Under this simple model, 'the Commission proposed and the Council disposed.' There was little friction. Unanimity in the Council, combined with 'old-style' Commission proposals, meant that progress was almost entirely consensual and therefore very slow.

The EU's 'Pangaea' first began to break up in the late 1970s, with the advent of direct elections to the European Parliament and several revolutionary Court rulings, including 'Cassis de Dijon' and 'Isoglucose'.[1] The process of fragmentation was accelerated by the 1986 Single European Act (and the associated Single Market White Paper), with its emphasis on qualified majority decision-making in the Council and the counter-balance of the cooperation procedure with the European Parliament (the EP's first true involvement in the legislative process). Fragmentation was further encouraged by the constitutional changes made by the Maastricht, Amsterdam and Nice Treaties, leaving the EU with three large 'tectonic plates'; the Commission, the Council and the Parliament – the so-called 'inter-institutional triangle'.[2]

Over the past quarter-century the European Commission has thus had to face a series of evolutionary processes which have undermined the old institutional certainties of bipolar complicity with the Council and replaced them with a more dynamic situation in which the Parliament has become a far more vociferous and demanding interlocuteur. This new triangular arrangement has required considerable adaptation on the part of the Commission.

This chapter will first examine Parliament's evolving strengths, its current powers and its primary power centres – the political groups and the standing committees. It will then describe a series of essentially administrative and technical agreements and mechanisms into which the Commission has bound itself and which were designed primarily to ensure the free flow of the legislative and policy-making processes. It will consider how Parliament exercises its powers and the daily inter-relationship between the two institutions. It will conclude by considering possible future developments and, in particular, the possibility that the old technocratic arrangements might be replaced by a more politicised executive-legislative relationship.

The Parliament's evolving powers in relation to the Commission

The EP has always regarded the Commission as its primary interlocuteur.[3] The two institutions are kindred, supranational institutions and share a common vision of the EU's development. Prior to direct elections (1979), the Parliament relied heavily on the Commission to be able to play a significant role. Since direct elections, the Commission has drawn heavily on the Parliament's democratic legitimacy. Through that legitimacy, the EP has skilfully and insistently extended its powers, increasingly asserting its role in the EU's budgetary and legislative procedures. A democratically emboldened Parliament has shown increasing willingness to make use of its powers and hold the Commission accountable for its actions, in particular with regard to financial management. A crucial factor in the relationship is Parliament's powers of approval and censure of the Commission.

Replacement of Member State contributions by the Community's own resources led to a first extension of Parliament's budgetary powers under the 1970 Treaty of Luxembourg. A second treaty (1975) further strengthened Parliament's powers, but the EP only gained the political self-confidence to use these to the full after direct elections, first rejecting the budget, for example, in 1980.

The EP used the *Isoglucose* Court ruling and its own rule-making autonomy to create a first sort of weak legislative input (the 'consultation procedure'). The 1986 Single European Act gave Parliament a positive legislative role (through the cooperation procedure) in certain areas and made accession and association treaties subject to its assent. The Maastricht Treaty, by introducing the co-decision procedure in some areas of legislation and extending the cooperation procedure to others, marked the beginning of Parliament's role as a genuine co-legislator. It also gave Parliament the power of final approval over the membership of the Commission.

The Treaty of Amsterdam extended the co-decision procedure to most areas of legislation and reformed the procedure, putting Parliament as co-legislator on an equal footing with the Council. With the appointment of the President of the Commission being made subject to Parliament's approval (after nomination by the Member States), Parliament further increased its control over the executive. The Treaty of Nice, which entered into force on 1 February 2003, marginally enhanced Parliament's role as co-legislator through a minimal extension of the co-decision procedure's scope but also granted Parliament a right to bring actions before the Court of Justice of the European Union, under the same conditions as the other institutions.

The Parliament's main powers in relation to the Commission

Co-decision

The EP participates in the legislative process, in the majority of cases as co-legislator under the co-decision procedure (TEC Article 251). It also participates to varying degrees under the consultation procedure, the cooperation procedure (TEC Article 252) and assent procedure. With the Treaty of Amsterdam, the co-decision procedure became the main legislative procedure outside the areas of agriculture, fisheries and fiscal policy (which remain subject to simple consultation) and EMU (cooperation procedure). With only a few exceptions, co-decision applies to those cases where qualified majority is required in Council.

The co-decision procedure radically altered the relationship between the Commission and the Parliament, in particular by removing the Commission's proprietorial ownership of its legislative proposals at third reading stage, and by introducing a conciliation procedure which puts the Parliament and the Council on a level footing as the twin arms of the legislative authority.

Initiative

The EP has a Treaty-based (TEC Article 192) right to request an initiative from the Commission. The Commission's sole right of initiative, together with its right to withdraw proposals that it considers risk being 'denatured', has been considered to be a key stone of the traditional 'Community method'. As seen above, the co-decision procedure, which foresees a joint Parliament-Council text in the later stages, first undermined the Commission's traditional role. The right to request an initiative might be considered as a further blow. Aware of this, and being a staunch supporter of the Community method, the Parliament has used its rules of procedure to ring-fence its own right to request initiatives with various conditions and an absolute majority requirement. It has thus transformed a breezily granted right into a parsimonious possibility. Of more importance to the Parliament is the ability to influence the Commission's overall policy, and hence legislative, intentions. The mechanisms developed to pursue this end are considered below.

Finance

Parliament participates, as one arm of the budgetary authority, in drawing up the EU's annual budget. Parliament has the last word on non-compulsory expenditure (mainly expenditure not connected with agriculture and structural policies). It definitively approves the budget and can, if there are important reasons, reject it as a whole (TEC Article 272). Parliament's Budgets Committee plays a particularly important role as 'star chamber'.

The directly-elected Parliament soon gave up on the Pyrrhic victories of rejected budgets in favour of discretionary powers within overall budgetary stability, agreed with the Council through so-called 'financial perspectives' on overall EU spending, backed up by inter-institutional agreements on procedures and prerogatives. In its early years, the directly elected EP also used the budgetary procedure as a way of exerting legislative influence. This practice has declined as its real legislative powers have grown.

Over the past quarter-century the Parliament has developed a series of tactics and mechanisms to exert maximum policy influence via the budgetary procedure. By forcing the Commission's hand on budgetary planning, it can also exert influence over the Commission's policy intentions.

Discharge

As the authority granting annual discharge to the Commission for its management of the budget, the Parliament exercises control over the execution of the budget, with Parliament's Budgetary Control Committee playing a particularly important role. In a Union ever more sensitive to charges of corruption and mismanagement, this power has taken on added significance, particularly when combined with Parliament's censure powers. It was Parliament's decision not to grant discharge for management of the 1996 budget that led ultimately to the 1999 resignation of the Santer Commission, which was generally regarded as having fallen on its sword rather than suffer the ignominy of censure (see page 41).

The executive; nomination

Every five years, shortly after direct elections to the Parliament itself, Parliament approves or rejects the European Council's nomination for President of the Commission (by secret ballot – a provision introduced by the EP, through its rules of procedure) after the nominee has made a statement and presented his/her political guidelines to the plenary. Parliament also approves or rejects the Commission as a body, after the nominees for the various posts of Commissioner proposed by the President-elect of the Commission have appeared before the appropriate committees, according to their prospective fields of responsibility (another practice created by the EP's rules of procedure).

Nowhere have Commission-Parliament relations moved more over the past quarter-century than in this field – from no say at all to a definitive say. But it is the nature of that 'say' which, in June/July 2004, also seemed to change in a highly significant way. In a number of public pronouncements Hans-Gert Poettering, the leader of the largest Group in the EP (both before and after the June elections), the centre-right EPP-ED, called for the European Council to take the results of the elections into account when making its nomination for the President of the Commission. Put another way, the leader of the centre-right majority grouping within the EP insisted that the future Commission President had to be drawn from the centre-right – and, in the event, he was.

It is difficult, on the basis of this one experience, to argue that a definite trend has begun. Previously, Commission Presidents tended to alternate between the left and the right, so it could be argued that José Manuel Barroso (from the centre-right) was a natural successor to Romano Prodi (from the centre-left). The proof of the pudding will come in June/July 2009, when Barroso's successor is chosen. By then, as the concluding section will discuss, other factors will have entered into play – including, perhaps most significantly, publicly-funded European political parties. It is, naturally, impossible to predict political developments within the EU with any certainty. At the same time, it should be noted that the directly elected Parliament has proved itself adept at exploiting precedents.

The executive; censure

Parliament can also pass a motion of censure calling for the resignation of the Commission as a body. It is one of the Parliament's most ancient powers, originating in the 1952 Paris Treaty and the old ECSC assembly. It has hung over the Commission like a Damocles' sword for over thirty years and has never been used (though several motions have been tabled), yet it is no exaggeration to argue that this ultimate sanction constantly colours Commission-Parliament relations. The merest hint that a censure motion might be tabled, let alone voted, traditionally sends the Commission into paroxysms of political activity. A graphic illustration of this came in May 2005, when Nigel Farage, a United Kingdom Independence Party MEP, managed to gather more than the 76 MEPs' signatures necessary to trigger a censure motion debate and vote. Although the motion had no chance of being adopted (an absolute majority and two thirds of the votes cast would have been required), the very fact that it had been tabled caused consternation and hectic political manoeuvring designed to ensure that it received as few votes as possible.

Nominating the executive; collegiality

The process leading to the Barroso Commission's 2004 investiture threw up a new form of political conflict, though it was the culmination of an old discussion. Several Commissioners-designate were thought to have performed unsatisfactorily before parliamentary committees during the hearings. The proposed College would probably still have got through, but one candidate, Rocco Buttiglione, a former Italian minister for European affairs, declared before the Civil Liberties, Justice and Home Affairs Committee that 'I may say that homosexuality is a sin, but this has no effect on politics unless I say that homosexuality is a crime.' Buttiglione, who was known to be a devout Catholic and a close friend of the Pope, had sought to indicate that his personal views would have no consequences for the way in which he carried out his political duties. His pronouncement had the opposite effect.

In the ensuing stand off, Barroso at first sided with his proposed team in its entirety, reasoning that he could not afford to cede Parliament the thin end of a thick wedge. Treaty article 214(2) states clearly that it is for 'the Council, acting by qualified majority and by common accord with the nominee for President' to adopt the list of candidate Commissioners. The same article clearly states that the President and the other members of the thus nominated Commission are subject to parliamentary approval *as a body*. Barroso thus sought to defend the Commission's collegial nature.

But on 27 October 2004, just before the EP's investiture vote, Barroso belatedly realised through informal soundings with the political groups that he could not count on a majority – certainly not a sufficient majority to grant his Commission the political authority he wanted. At the eleventh hour Barroso withdrew his proposed College and went back to the European Council. Buttiglione subsequently withdrew his candidature. Another candidate, Ingrida Udre (Latvia), also withdrew. Both were replaced with 'safe hand' candidates. Barroso was able to present his new team to the Parliament in November, and his Commission was duly invested.

The consensus among commentators was that, while Barroso might have over-played his hand at the outset, he had later managed to win back political authority and had been able to transform the initial stand-off between himself and the Parliament into a reinforced position vis-à-vis the Member States meeting together in the European Council.

The executive's collegiality and individual accountability

But there was an underlying issue about the performance of individual Commissioners and possible sanctions against them. It was an issue which had begun at the time of the Delors' Commissions and rumbled on during the Santer Commission's truncated mandate and the parliamentary hearings for the Prodi Commission. Santer's Commission had allegedly been undermined by its inability to force one of its number out. Subsequently, Prodi had famously insisted that each member of his Commission sign a resignation letter in advance – just in case.

The Nice Treaty introduced the following provision (TEU Article 217): 'A Member of the Commission shall resign if the President so requests, after obtaining the approval of the College.' Because of this, in composing his Commission, Barroso had made no Prodi-like demand, but later, in the context of the new, 2005, Framework Agreement (Art. 3 – see below and annex H) his Commission committed itself to the following provision: 'If Parliament decides to express lack of confidence in a Member of the Commission, the President of the Commission, having given serious consideration to the decision, shall either request that Member to resign, or explain his or her decisions to Parliament.'

It was an issue which went to the heart of the Commission's nature and its role. The principle of collegiality was implicit in TEU Art. 201 (the censure motion) but had been explicitly enshrined in the Commission's rules of procedure (Article 1) by one of its 'founding fathers', Jean Monnet. The Commission's collegiality was always considered to be as much a part of the 'Community method' as its right of initiative (on a par, for example, with the doctrine of collective Cabinet responsibility in the UK). The formulation settled on in the Framework Agreement is an uneasy, and so far untested, stand off. President Barroso will have a clear preference for this formulation to remain untested during his watch and so here, as in so many areas, the Parliament has effectively created a precedent.

Foreign and trade policy and the 'third pillar'

The Parliament plays some role in the shaping of the Union's external policy, notably through consultation on 'the main aspects and the basic choices of the common foreign and security policy' (TEU Article 21) and assent to cooperation agreements. Under the Framework Agreement on relations between the European Parliament and the Commission (see point below and annex H), the Commission has undertaken to keep Parliament briefed and informed of the negotiation of international agreements, starting from the preparation stage. Parliament's Rules also address suspension of an agreement (Rule 98 pursuant to TEC Article 300) and hearing a nominee for head of a Commission external delegation (Rule 102).

The European Parliament enjoys consultation rights on the 'principal aspects' of cooperation in the fields of justice and home affairs (police and judicial cooperation in criminal matters) (TEU Article 39). Although consultation powers are theoretically weak, the Parliament can beef them up considerably by encouraging the Commission to be as informative as possible and by insisting that its views be duly taken into account (see Framework Agreement, Art. 9).

In these policy areas, where the Parliament's formal powers are not as strong as it would wish, it relies on the Commission's complicity to enable it to play a more influential role. On occasion, it can also use its budgetary powers to force concessions.

Power centres in the Parliament: the political groups and the parliamentary committees

The political groups

Power within the European Parliament is expressed primarily through its political groups. Parliament's Rules of Procedure (Rule 29(2)) provide that a minimum of sixteen members are required to form a political group, but any group, irrespective of its size, must have members from one-fifth of the Member States (currently five).

Parliament's power-sharing and decision-making mechanisms have been designed in such a way that a persistent oligarchy composed of the larger mainstream political groupings effectively determines the Parliament's stance on most issues. The oligarchy, composed primarily of the largest and second-largest groups (respectively, the EPP-ED, with 267 members, and the PES, with 201 members), was provoked into existence by the absolute majority requirements imposed upon the Parliament by the Single European Act. Since no one group could muster an absolute majority alone, the groups were obliged to cooperate. A third group, the Alliance of Liberals and Democrats for Europe (currently 87 members), has occasionally played a power-broking role. The consensual bloc of the three largest political groups (all are basically pro-integration and pro-single currency) has enabled the European Parliament to assert itself in the budgetary and legislative contexts and to push its institutional agenda of further integration and, in that context, a greater role for itself. Since the Commission shares these general goals, it has fallen into the habit of seeing the bloc as its primary interlocuteur, since it is there that it will find the necessary majority support for its proposals.

However, each successive enlargement has encouraged twin tendencies: on the one hand, the Parliament's composition has become more fragmentary, with, for example, far right, anti-integrationist and single issue MEPs taking their places alongside the traditional European political families; on the other, the largest groupings, which have sought to maintain their relative size and hence patronage powers, have necessarily weakened their ideological cohesiveness in order to absorb greater numbers. The classic example of the latter phenomenon is the uneasy pragmatic alliance between the British Conservatives and the EPP. The overall effect of these twin tendencies is that the votes of the old consensual bloc are no longer as reliable nor as stable as they once were, particularly where votes are secret (as is the case for the investiture of the Commission, for example).

Political groups generally meet during the week preceding Strasbourg plenary part-sessions and just prior to Brussels part-sessions to prepare for votes on the reports on the agenda, for instance. They also meet during part-sessions, in both Strasbourg and Brussels. The political groups in Parliament and the organs of the European party federations and confederations normally welcome the presence of Commission members of their political persuasion, although no official relations exist between them. The Commission has traditionally encouraged its members to attend the political group meetings to act as political antennae and obtain greater support for its proposals. Given the apparent 'politicisation' of Commission-Parliament relations (see conclusions) the Commission's members are becoming increasingly assiduous in maintaining channels of communication to the Parliament's political groups.

Parliamentary committees

– Standing committees

The 2004-2009 legislature has 20 permanent committees and two subcommittees. Their responsibilities do not entirely coincide with the Commission's internal policy divisions. In formal terms, the committees examine questions referred to them by Parliament. This involves debating questions and preparing reports, opinions and resolutions on legislative and non-legislative dossiers. Although superficially similar, the committees vary greatly in their characteristics. As seen above, the Budgets Committee acts as a sort of star chamber. The power and profile of the Budgetary Control Committee waxes and wanes with each discharge procedure, as does the power and profile of the Constitutional Affairs Committee with each IGC. The Foreign Affairs Committee exercises its power primarily through debate, whilst the Environment Committee (to take one example) exercises its power through a particularly heavy legislative load.

Commissioners and Commission officials have a vested interest in keeping on good and close terms with the parliamentary committees responsible for their policy areas. Committees regularly invite Commissioners to address them on topical matters and policy issues. They also expect the Commission officials responsible for dossiers to attend committee meetings to respond to questions on Commission proposals and policy. The Framework Agreement (Art. 11 – see also Art. 40) obliges each Commissioner to ensure a 'regular and direct flow of information.' Particularly where the Commission's and the Parliament's political agendas coincide, Commissioners can develop an almost symbiotic relationship with their 'shadow' parliamentary committee.

– *Temporary committees*

Apart from the above-mentioned standing committees, Parliament may, at the request of a quarter of its members, set up temporary committees with specific powers, composition and term of office (Rule 150). Such committees have been set up on the ECHELON interception system, human genetics, foot and mouth disease, monitoring of the BSE recommendations, and improving safety at sea, by way of example. Unlike temporary committees of inquiry, temporary committees will not necessarily be investigating potential issues of maladministration, though the Parliament may subsequently make operational recommendations to the Commission.

– *Temporary committees of inquiry*

Parliament may also set up temporary committees of inquiry to investigate alleged contraventions of Community law or maladministration in the application of Community law (TEC Article 193 of the Treaty and Rule 151 of the Parliament's Rules of Procedure). In 1997, for instance, Parliament decided to set up two temporary committees of inquiry on the BSE crisis and on the Community transit regime. The former led the Parliament close to tabling a censure motion. With characteristic constitutional ingenuity, Parliament invented the concept of a suspended motion and used this to force the Commission into making administrative and political changes.

Interaction with Parliament's governing bodies

The Conference of Presidents

The Conference of Presidents is composed of the President of the European Parliament and the chairmen of the political groups plus two non-attached members (who do not have the right to vote). The Conference is the Parliament's power centre. Through it, via weighted votes, the oligopoly of the two/three largest political groups expresses itself.

The Conference of Presidents draws up the draft agenda of part-sessions for adoption by the House. It makes proposals to the House on the composition and remit of committees and temporary committees of inquiry and authorises own-initiative reports. It is also involved in decisions on legislative planning based on departmental forecasts for the proceedings in plenary over several months and on recommendations from the Conference of Committee Chairmen.

The Conference of Presidents is also responsible for matters concerning relations with the other institutions and bodies of the European Union, with the national parliaments in Member States, with non-member countries and with international institutions and organisations. The Commission is invited to meetings of the Conference of Presidents when items which concern it are on the agenda (notably this concerns the adoption of the draft-agenda of part-sessions and any inter-institutional legislative planning).

Under the terms of the new Framework Agreement (Art. 10), the President of the Commission and/or the Vice-President responsible for inter-institutional relations meet every three months with the Conference of Presidents 'to ensure regular dialogue between the two Institutions at the highest level.' From time to time, the Conference also holds meetings open to all members, instead of holding an extraordinary plenary part-session, particularly when the Commission may wish to present dossiers of major importance just adopted by the College. The maintenance of good relations with the Conference of Presidents is absolutely essential for the European Commission's political well being. It is primarily in the Conference that, when the political going gets rough, compromise solutions are thrashed out or political deals brokered.

Conference of Committee Chairmen

The Conference of Committee Chairmen consists of the chairpersons of all standing and temporary committees. It can make recommendations to the Conference of Presidents for the agenda of part-sessions and on legislative planning. The Conference of Presidents may instruct it to carry out specific tasks. The Commission's Secretariat General is invited to meetings of the Conference of Committee Chairmen when items that concern it are on the agenda (notably inter-institutional legislative planning and the programming of business for future part-sessions). The Vice-President responsible for relations with Parliament is also invited periodically to address the Conference, particularly in connection with the Commission's Annual Policy Strategy and the Legislative and Work Programme. The maintenance of good relations with the Conference of Committee Chairmen comes only second to the Conference of Presidents in terms of the Commission's political priorities.

Instruments regulating the Commission's relations with the European Parliament

Constitutional glue

Over the years, the Commission and the Parliament have adopted a series of agreements and texts to regulate the conduct of their relations, culminating in the Framework Agreement of 2000, renewed in 2005 (see annex H). Declaration 3 annexed to the Nice Treaty acknowledges the importance of such inter-institutional agreements, particularly in the context of 'loyal cooperation' (TEC Art. 10). Such agreements are perhaps best understood as a sort of 'constitutional glue', filling out and connecting the basic provisions of the Treaties.

Framework Agreement on relations between the European Parliament and the Commission

When the Prodi Commission was confirmed in 1999, a Framework Agreement was negotiated with Parliament and signed in 2000. This built on an existing 1995 Code of Conduct and integrated commitments given by President Prodi in the course of his Commission's investiture procedure. Renewal of the Agreement was negotiated in 2004-5 and signed into being by the Presidents of the two institutions on 26 May 2005. It consists of a main agreement and three annexes that are an integral part of the Agreement. The main agreement covers extending dialogue and political cooperation; political responsibility, the flow of information and organisation of Parliamentary proceedings. Annexes flesh these provisions out in relation to the legislative procedure, involvement of the European Parliament in international relations and transmission of confidential information. After the May signing, Commission President José Manuel Barroso spoke about 'complicity' and 'a strategic partnership'. In effect, the latest version of the Framework Agreement provides a blueprint for the political relationship between the Commission and the Parliament, particularly in the context of the Commission's policy intentions and its legislative programme.

The Commission's Annual Policy Strategy (APS) and its legislative and work programmes

From early on in its directly-elected life, the Parliament has consistently sought to influence the Commission's overall legislative and policy intentions. As matters currently stand, each year the Commission draws up an Annual Policy Strategy and a legislative work programme. Exploiting its internal rule-making autonomy, the Parliament has created a procedure whereby it 'pre-emptively' establishes legislative and political 'guidelines'. The Framework Agreement obliges the Commission to take into account the Parliament's 'priorities' (Art. 29) and even sets out a procedural timetable, or échéancier, as to how this should be done (Annex II), detailing the stages of the process from presentation of the Annual Policy Strategy up to the formulation of its legislative and work programme at the November part-session in question.

In line with Article 28 of the Framework Agreement, an incoming Commission presents its political and legislative programme as soon as it can, listing as far as possible all the actions proposed for its term of office, and establishes 'a dialogue' with the European Parliament. The cumulative effect of these provisions is to tie the Commission in to the Parliament's overall political strategy. Though the Commission continues to enjoy its Treaty-based right of legislative initiative, it does so within this broader political context. The full extent of these provisions will perhaps only become apparent once the current oligopoly of the larger political groups breaks down.

Inter-institutional agreement on better law-making

Signed by the European Parliament, the Council and the Commission on 16 December 2003, the inter-institutional agreement on better law-making was the first inter-institutional agreement signed by all three institutions, as provided for in the Treaty of Nice (Declaration 3). It contains provisions for improving coordination between the three institutions during the legislative process and for ensuring greater transparency and accessibility of the legislative work. This involves information to the Parliament on the draft multiannual strategic programme of the European Council, better synchronisation of the treatment of common dossiers by the preparatory bodies of each branch of the legislative authority, and communication by each institution to the others of its respective annual legislative timetable with a view to reaching agreement on joint annual programming. It prescribes rules on the choice of legislative instruments, on the legal basis and for the consistency with community law of any use of co-regulation and self-regulation as well as measures for improving the quality of legislation and for better transposition and application of Community legislation.

Inter-institutional agreement on budgetary discipline and improvement of the budgetary procedure

The inter-institutional agreement on budgetary discipline and improvement of the budgetary procedure of 6 May 1999, which was adopted together with the agreement on the new financial perspective for 2000-2006, was aimed at implementing budgetary discipline and improving the functioning of the annual budgetary procedure and cooperation between the institutions on budgetary matters. It effectively established stability and coherence, and set parameters for more measured policy debates about particular budgetary priorities. At the time of going to press, the new financial perspective 2007-2013 was still being debated. The Parliament has made its agreement to a renewal of the inter-institutional agreement conditional upon satisfactory political agreement on the financial perspective itself. This is potentially more than a negotiating tactic. The 2000-2006 inter-institutional agreement amounted to a self-denying ordinance, with Parliament foregoing the full extent of its powers in return for overall political stability. If, from Parliament's point of view, the 2007-2013 financial perspective seems insufficient, then it could legitimately decide to forego budgetary stability and aim rather to achieve its political ends through the annual budgetary cycle. In such a scenario, there would be considerable onus on the Commission to assert its role as honest broker.

The parliamentary cycle

Parliament exercises its principal powers through plenary sessions as well as through the work of its committees and by means of parliamentary questions. The rhythm of Parliament's work dictates the rhythm of the working and political relationship between the two institutions (see box below). Commissioners are present in plenary and appear before committees upon request or at their own demand. Commission officials are present in committee meetings. The Secretariat General is present both in plenary and committee meetings. When Parliament is in plenary session in Strasbourg, the Commission holds its weekly meeting there.

As a rule, Parliament works on a monthly cycle of two weeks of committee meetings in Brussels, one week of political group meetings, and one week (Monday afternoon to Thursday afternoon) of plenary session ('part-session') held in Strasbourg. Normally there is no part-session in August. In addition, some shorter part-sessions are held in Brussels. In practice, there are 12 sessions in Strasbourg and 6 sessions in Brussels. Most of the agenda for part-sessions is taken up with the examination of legislative proposals (legislative debates), non-legislative and own-initiative reports. Usually at Parliament's request, Council and/or the Commission are also regularly asked to make statements on topical issues and events of relevance to the European Union.

Annual cycles of Parliament's work on particular subjects

Commission Work Programme (November of the previous year);
Commission's Annual Policy Strategy (APS) and State of the Union address (February/March);
Budget (guidelines April/May; first reading October; second reading December);
Budgetary Discharge (year -2) (April);
Presidency's programme (January and July);
European Council and review of the Presidency (June and December).

Meetings of political groups regularly take place during the session, particularly with a view to finalising group positions on items on the plenary's agenda. During the plenary part-sessions in Strasbourg, extraordinary meetings of parliamentary committees may also take place.

Inter-institutional coordination

Neunreither Group

An inter-institutional coordination group, known as the Neunreither Group (after a former EP official), made up of representatives of the Secretariats of the Parliament, Council, Commission, the European Economic and Social Committee and the Committee of the Regions, meets once a month ahead of Parliament's Strasbourg plenary sessions to prepare for the debates on priority legislative items and the forthcoming part-session(s) as well as to examine questions of inter-institutional procedure connected with implementation of the TEU. This largely technocratic group characterises the administrative approach to inter-institutional cooperation which evolved in the wake of the Single European Act.

High-Level Technical Group for Inter-Institutional Cooperation

The High-Level Technical Group for Inter-Institutional Cooperation was created in 2002 in order to improve dialogue between Parliament, Council and Commission in the light of the new partnership referred to in the conclusions of the Barcelona European Council of March 2002. It is made up of representatives of the three institutions at Secretary General level and discusses political and institutional priority issues on an ad hoc basis. The Seville European Council of June 2002 instructed the High-Level Technical Group for Inter-Institutional Cooperation to draft an inter-institutional agreement on better law-making and this was concluded and signed in 2003 (see above). The High-Level Technical Group, as its title confirms, remains an administration-level device.

Commission procedures

Structures

The Commission has created a number of instruments and procedures for handling parliamentary business. A Vice-President of the Commission has special responsibility for relations with Parliament. The Vice-President, currently Margot Wallström, has specific responsibility for the Directorates of the Secretariat General responsible for relations with the Parliament and the Council and thus provides overall coherence in the Commission's inter-institutional approach.

Each member of the Commission appoints a member of his/her *cabinet* as their parliamentary attaché, who is responsible for relations with Parliament. This *cabinet* member represents the Commissioner in the weekly meeting universally known by its French acronym 'GRI' (Groupe des rélations interinstitutionelles – see below) and maintains the necessary contracts with the political groups in Parliament.

Each Director General appoints a coordinator for parliamentary affairs within their Directorate General. The coordinators meet once a month primarily to review the progress of legislative proposals before the Parliament.

The Inter-Institutional Relations Group (the 'GRI')[5]

The Commission's main instrument in managing its relations with Parliament is the Inter-Institutional Relations Group. It is composed of the institutional relations attachés in the *cabinets* and is chaired by the head of the *cabinet* of the Vice-President responsible for institutional relations. The Legal Service, various departments of the Secretariat General and DG PRESS also participate in the Group's work.

The GRI reports to the heads of *cabinet* meeting and the latter to the Commission. Those matters which cannot be solved at the level of the GRI are passed on to the heads of *cabinet* meeting for consideration and if necessary the Commission meeting itself.

The Group is responsible for coordinating relations with the European Parliament on the political, institutional, legislative and administrative side, and for coordinating the Commission's position before Parliament's bodies and in the conciliation committees.

The Group systematically examines amendments adopted by parliamentary committees under the co-decision procedure, as well as the most important reports under the other legislative procedures and key non-legislative reports, and recommends, where appropriate, a position for the Commission to take on amendments in plenary session. In particular, this involves ensuring that the Framework Agreement is applied.

The GRI assures the political preparation of forthcoming Parliament part-sessions and in particular helps define the Commission's stance on Parliament's amendments, examining certain non-legislative reports and other politically important matters and approving draft answers to parliamentary oral questions to ensure that they reflect the view of the Commission as a whole. The GRI also ensures the administrative preparation of forthcoming Parliament sittings (monitoring Commissioners' attendance in Strasbourg, the handling of items and votes, vetting and handling requests for urgent debate, and making arrangements for Question Time).

The GRI is responsible for all of the Commission's inter-institutional relations, particularly in order to ensure coherence of the Commission's position in the bodies in which legislative procedures are carried out. In particular it is engaged in examining and following up the work of conciliation committees, preparing and monitoring inter-institutional arrangements between the Commission, the Council and the European Parliament, monitoring implementation of the Commission's Work Programme, and any other matters that require the Commission to take a position in any of those bodies (legal basis, rejection of a proposal, withdrawal, committee procedures).

The GRI examines any other questions concerning relations with Parliament, especially the activities of Parliament's committees and political groups and the discharge procedure, and it monitors the work of the Neunreither Group (inter-institutional coordination group).

Future relations

From all of the foregoing it will have been seen that the Commission cannot, and does not, take its relationship with the European Parliament for granted; it has to work hard at it. Indeed, it is in considerable part a tribute to the Commission's determination to maintain and build on a positive relationship with the Parliament that there have been very few troughs in relations between the two, despite the rapid evolution of the Parliament's powers.

Nevertheless, the certainties of the essentially technocratic relationship into which the Commission has bound itself may now be giving way to a more politicised relationship. The essentially administrative mechanisms that have underlain Commission-Parliament relations to date resulted primarily from two factors: mutually-agreed policy goals involving large rafts of legislation (the single market, the single currency, environmental protection) on the one hand; and a stable oligopolistic power centre in the Parliament on the other (itself derived from exogeneously-imposed majority requirements).

The European Union as a whole is perhaps on the cusp of that more politicised world. Whatever fate awaits the Constitutional Treaty, it is already certain that publicly-funded European political parties (a provision of the Nice Treaty) will contest the June 2009 European elections. They will be seeking to make distinctive calls to European voters on the basis of distinctive ideological platforms. Some hints as to the form those platforms may take are already apparent: for example, less legislation versus more; more market-oriented legislation and a concentration on competitiveness versus broader protection of the European social and environmental model. More fundamentally, there is now a sizeable minority within the European Parliament calling for a cap on the European integration process.

Perhaps future relations between the Commission and the Parliament will come more closely to resemble those of an executive and a legislature. A potential obstacle to such a more politicised relationship is to be found in the Constitutional Treaty's provisions on the co-decision procedure, which would still impose absolute majority requirements on the Parliament (Art. III-302), and hence a need for 'technical agreements' between the largest political groupings. But this need not prevent a more politicised approach if, upstream of individual legislative proposals, the Commission has been bound into a legislative and political programme determined by a Parliamentary majority, itself the result of a pan-European contest between European political parties.

Endnotes

[1] See chapter 3

[2] Arguably, the Constitutional Treaty would add a fourth, in the form of the tandem of the European Council and the so called "permanent Presidency" (of two-and-a-half year renewable terms).

[3] The Treaty provisions governing the European Parliament are Articles 189-201 of the Treaty establishing the European Community (TEC). TEC Articles 214 and 215 define its role with regard to the appointment of the Commission and resignation or compulsory retirement of a member of the Commission.

[4] See Westlake 1997, 'Mad Cows and Englishmen, the institutional implications of the BSE crisis', *Journal of Common Market Studies*, Annual Review, Spring 1997.

[5] The GRI came into being in November 2004 and was the result of a merger between two existing groups; the Parliamentary Affairs Group (known universally by its French acronym, le 'GAP' – Groupe des affaires parlementaires), and the Council Affairs Group (Groupe du suivi pour les affaires du Conseil – 'GrAC')

10. The Commission and the lobby

Sonia Mazey and Jeremy Richardson

'By fulfilling its duty to consult, the Commission ensures that its proposals are technically viable, practically workable and based on a bottom-up approach. In other words, good consultation serves a dual purpose by helping to improve the quality of policy outcomes and at the same time enhancing the involvement of interested parties and the public at large'

The European Commission 11.12.2002 (Commission 2002d)

Introduction: the centrality of the Commission

The above quotation, from the Commission's Communication, 'General principles and minimum standards for consultation of interested parties by the Commission' (COM (2002) 704) captures the Commission's strong belief that consultation of interests represents a 'win-win' situation for all parties. In fact, relations between the Commission and the increasingly Europeanised interest group system have developed along quite predictable lines, in part due to the legal obligation of Protocol No 7 on the application of the principles of subsidiarity and proportionality, annexed to the Amsterdam Treaty. This states that the Commission should consult widely before proposing legislation, and, wherever appropriate, publish consultation documents. More recently, the Constitutional Treaty also stressed the importance of open, transparent and regular dialogue between European institutions and representative associations and civil society. But the legal constraint is not the whole story. The Commission also exhibits familiar bureaucratic features, such as sectorisation, problems of coordination, and a penchant for developing close relations with organised interests. Its organisational ideology has thus arguably been more important than legal obligations in fostering the development of an EU level interest group system. For their part, interest groups have been keen to exploit the Commission as a new opportunity structure to gain influence over public policy-making. In practice, most interests are now organised at the European level, yet it seems that there is still scope for new interests to develop a lobbying presence in Brussels, particularly in the field defined as civil society.

The assertion that groups still focus on the Commission may seem odd in the light of the widespread belief that the Commission's powers have declined over the past decade or so. Decline has been attributed to a succession of Treaty reforms which have strengthened the European Parliament (Rittberger 2003; Auel and Rittberger 2005; Rittberger, 2005), greater emphasis on intergovernmental solutions, and a shift in the European policy style towards what has been termed the Open Method of coordination (OMC), which seems much less *dirigiste*. However, the founding Treaties of the EC state that the European Commission is the initiator of Community policies and, formally speaking, it has the sole right to propose Community legislation. The Commission is also the executive arm of Community governance, as chapter 8 amply demonstrates, and is ultimately responsible for ensuring the effective implementation of the policies decided upon by the Council of Ministers. The Commission therefore still plays a pivotal role in translating initiatives (from whatever source) into clear proposals, a fact now widely appreciated by the very large number of lobbyists in Brussels. 'Commission watching' is an essential part of monitoring agenda-setting, the crucial stage of the EU policy process, and the detailed processing of issues through to directives, regulations and soft law.

The European lobby

Effective European lobbying requires a multi-track strategy that utilises the multiple access points and venues that the complex EU policy process provides (Richardson 2000). This chapter's focus on the role that the Commission plays as a broker or bourse for the now high levels of interest group mobilisation within the EU leaves aside the important role played by other institutions in policy initiation and policy decision, which are amply covered in chapters 7, 8 and 9. In performing this function, the Commission has played a crucial role in fostering the structuring and institutionalisation of interest intermediation in the EU. The result is an often symbiotic (though rarely genuinely corporatist) relationship between the Commission and interest groups. Groups are drawn to Brussels by a desire to defend and promote the interests of their members in the context of EU policy-making. Yet the Commission is equally dependent upon groups for two reasons. First, they provide Commission officials with necessary technical information and advice. Secondly – and arguably more importantly – the support of cross-national advocacy coalitions (Sabatier 1988) of groups is essential to the successful introduction of Commission proposals. These functional incentives to consult groups are buttressed by the Commission's political need to demonstrate openness, thus enhancing its own legitimacy. As we discuss below, the Commission makes much of its organisational ideology of openness and consultation. Our central thesis is that incentive structures are in place to encourage the Commission to consult more and more, and interest groups to lobby more and more. The phenomenon of European lobbying is not at all new. Some fairly stable 'policy networks' involving ECSC officials and corporatist interests were apparent as early as the mid 1950s (Mazey 1992). However, the significant expansion of the Community's legislative competence following the adoption of the 1986 Single European Act (SEA) and subsequent Treaty reforms has prompted a sharp increase in the volume and intensity of interest group activity at the European level in the past twenty years.

The general phenomenon which we describe is nevertheless subject to variation. There are considerable differences between sectors in the precise nature of the relationships between Commission officials and groups. As the Commission itself noted in June 2002, there had not been a Commission–wide approach to consultation as 'each of the departments has had its own mechanisms and methods for consulting its respective sectoral interest groups' (Commission 2002c). The adoption of the Commission's Communication on consultation processes in 2002 moved the consultation process towards some common standards and procedures, but stopped short of an overly prescriptive regime for all DGs and Divisions. The Commission argued that the improvements in its consultation practices 'should not be based on a "command and control" approach but rather on providing the appropriate guidance and assistance to Commission officials in charge of consultation processes' (Commission 2002d). One reason for not having total conformity across DGs, of course, is that the size and nature of the constituency of groups varies very considerably across policy sectors.

The Commission is involved in a wide variety of types of policy networks, some of them so loose and unstructured that the term 'network' may have little utility other than to suggest that there are lots of actors involved. Whilst some interests – for example in agriculture and IT – have managed to become part of an identifiable 'policy community', many – for example in social policy and environment – are involved in loose issue networks. The importance of networks in the consultation process was underlined by the Commission in its *White Paper on European Governance*, published in July 2001 and reiterated in the *Report from the Commission on European Governance*, published in 2003 (Commission 2003b). In the latter document, the Commission envisaged 'developing a more systematic and pro-active approach to working with key networks to enable them to contribute to decision-shaping and policy execution…'.

The phenomenon of Euro-lobbying has attracted widespread academic interest; there is now an extensive literature on the EU policy-making role of diverse interest groups (for recent examples, Grossman 2004; Broscheid and Coen 2003; Greenwood 2003; Bouwen 2002; Mazey and Richardson 2001). These studies confirm the diverse nature of relationships that exist between the Commission and interest groups. At a more general level, however, we believe that institutionalisation of relations between the Commission and interest groups is now the norm, not the exception. The exact number of Euro-lobbyists is unknown. However, back in 1992, the Commission estimated that there were some 3,000 interest groups in Brussels, including more than 500 European associations, and that in total some 10,000 people were employed as lobbyists of one sort or another in Brussels (Commission 1992c). By February 2000, the Commission's own directory of non-profit-making European associations had expanded to include some 800 groups. More recently, its 2004 database of 'civil society organisations' listed over 739 such bodies.[1]

Not only has the number of European-focused interest groups increased since 1992, so has the number of professional lobbyists. By 2000 a single firm of political consultants, GPC, had 40 employees based in Brussels (*European Voice*, 3-9 February 2000). Direct EU lobbying by firms has also increased significantly: between 1985 and 1997 more than 350 large firms established their own EU affairs office in Brussels (Coen 1999, 9). In addition, international organisations, national federations, trade unions, regional authorities and voluntary organisations have in recent years recognised the need to have a presence in Brussels. The result is a dense, mature *European* and *transnational* interest group system centred upon the EU. Indeed, there is arguably an *oversupply* of lobbying at the Euro-level (Richardson 2000). Certainly, there has been widespread recognition within the Commission for some time now that the Euro-interest group system has become so extensive and well-organised that some more effective system for 'managing' it has to be introduced. Hence, the emergence of various, loosely defined 'rules' (see below). Yet, the 'problem' of the lobby is not merely a technical one. Concerns regarding the propriety of Commission interest group relations have arisen within the wider context of the debates over the (non)-transparency of EU decision-making procedures and the Union's 'democratic deficit'. These concerns prompted the Commission, in the early 1990s, to review links between itself and special interest groups. It acknowledged the need for these relations to be 'more clearly defined' and to be placed 'on a slightly more formalized footing' (COM 93 285 final). Eleven years later, the Commission has moved far towards a more regularised and transparent system.

The 1993 document cited above is probably still the definitive Commission statement on lobbying as it illustrates so clearly the Commission's fundamental commitment to extensive consultation with organised interests. This commitment is not difficult to explain. Popular mythology notwithstanding, the European Commission is a very small administration. In carrying out their role, officials have somehow to accommodate diverse and often conflicting demands of national governments and sectoral interests within and beyond the European Community. Consequently, there exists a powerful 'logic of negotiation'. Of course, similar pressures exist at the national level, but they are significantly greater in the multinational context of European policy-making. The incremental extension of Community competence together with the recent enlargement to twenty-five Member States, has both increased the need for group consultation and – because of the proliferation of Euro-lobbyists – given rise to a familiar problem in mature democracies, namely the need to balance openness and pluralism with the need for efficiency and stability. Commission officials have sought to resolve this dilemma by means of diverse forms of institutionalisation of group consultation. Below, we examine in more detail recent attempts by the Commission to structure and institutionalise interest group consultation. This analysis highlights the increasing importance of both 'thin' and 'thick' consultative structures.

Open access as organisational ideology

The 'logic of negotiation' encourages groups and Commission officials to seek each other out and groups rarely find it difficult to gain access to officials. Yet, the disparate nature of the Commission's cultural and administrative style is often unappreciated by groups, many of which develop a generalised view of 'the Commission' based upon their experiences with one division or section of a DG. But, the Commission is a particularly extreme example of a fragmented and compartmentalised bureaucracy. Horizontal coordination within the bureaucracy is often problematic, and there is often competition between (and within) DGs over particular policies. Furthermore, different parts of the Commission exhibit different cultural and administrative styles. Thus, whilst Commission structures offer many opportunities for group access, effective lobbying of the Commission requires considerable skill and understanding of the disparate nature of the organisation.

In many respects, the EU administration resembles a typical bureaucracy. In their classic study of the implementation process in the US, Pressman and Wildavsky commented that 'an agency that appears to be a single organisation with a single will turns out to be several sub-organisations with different wills' (Pressman and Wildavsky 1973, 92). The European Commission is exactly such an organisation. Moreover, the pluralistic structure and functioning of the Commission bureaucracy is further reinforced by the fragmentation of political authority within the Community as a whole. The Commission shares power with twenty-five democratically-elected governments and the European Parliament. Within this environment, the Commission performs a pivotal political brokerage role, without which few policies would ever be agreed upon in the Council of Ministers. In order to perform this role effectively, however, the Commission needs to be able both to draw upon the technical expertise and secure the support and compliance of those interests directly affected by EC legislation, who often have close links with 'their' national administration. This need explains, in part at least, the bureaucratisation of the Commission – a development much feared by Jean Monnet, who believed it would undermine its 'supranational' nature.

Bureaucracies have an inexorable tendency to grow, both in size and complexity. In terms of its genesis and subsequent development, the administration of the High Authority offers a good example of bureaucratic dynamics. By 1954, the rudimentary administrative structures established by Monnet had become ineffective. Administrative reorganisation, undertaken in 1954 in the name of efficiency, created a more hierarchical, functionally segmented bureaucracy. This development was entirely predictable. Most bureaux have a notion of 'policy space' and are determined to defend and extend the existing borders of their territory. The benefits of expansion far outweigh the disadvantages to the bureaucrat, added to which the pressures for growth are likely to be particularly strong in new bureaux. This development was accompanied by the blurring of the distinction made by Monnet between the political and administrative functions of the High Authority. As the scope and complexity of the tasks performed by the ECSC expanded, administrative officials became increasingly involved in the daily management, i.e. the execution of Community policies. (Mazey 1992). Inevitably, this brought the Commission into direct contact with interest groups.

Since 1957, this process of bureaucratisation has continued within the European Commission. More importantly for the purposes of this chapter, each Directorate General has become – to varying degrees and in different ways – associated with an expanding base of 'client-groups'. As EU policy has expanded, so has the constellation of groups who are attendant upon each DG and Division in the Commission. Moreover, this dynamic is ongoing: increasing Commission involvement in the second and third pillars of the EU, the recent enlargement of the EU, internal restructuring of the

Commission, and further extension of QMV have undoubtedly prompted further Commission bureaucratisation, increased lobbying and growth in the number of new client groups centred upon the Commission.

The size and density of these constituencies varies. The process of European integration has created winners as well as losers amongst interest groups. Unsurprisingly, those who have gained from this process tend to defend further expansion of the Commission's powers. For example, external threats, increasing competitive pressures and high transaction costs have persuaded many large firms of the benefits of further integration. In November 1999, for instance, the 27-member Association of European Airlines called for the European Commission to be given greater authority to negotiate a common EC-US regulatory framework for all carriers (*European Voice* 25 November–2 December 1999). In 2000, the European Employers' Association, UNICE, also called on the European Commission to push for more powers to vet mergers and acquisitions, because firms 'preferred the "one-stop shop" offered by the Commission's merger task force' to the multiplication of national merger control authorities (*European Voice*, 27 January-2 February 2000). Even when industrialists take a slightly Euro-sceptic turn, such as the Confederation of British Industry's current hostility to many aspects of Euro-regulation, they would not dream of reducing their lobbying of the Commission. Such a response would simply vacate a policy space for others to exploit. However, firms are not the only beneficiaries of European integration: environmentalists and women have also tended to favour further European integration as a means of imposing policy change upon recalcitrant national governments (Mazey 1998).

In those sectors where the Commission has no specific Treaty mandate to initiate EC policies, officials have gradually acquired for themselves a de facto policy role. In most cases, this status owes much to the Commission's cultivation of interest groups and so-called 'epistemic communities' of experts (Haas 1992). Thus, a considerable corpus of environmental law was developed without a strong Treaty base and finally legitimised in the SEA in 1986, long after the event. Only later did Member States realise the huge implementation costs of such environmental policies. An effective advocacy coalition of Commission officials, the international scientific community, and a vociferous and skilful environmental movement acting as a kind of 'megaphone for science', made the running. National governments (including the British government, which now leads the opposition to these laws) agreed to this legislation largely in ignorance of implementation problems ahead. Similarly, in the field of EC social policy, much of the work of (the then) DG V (now DG Employment, Social Affairs and Equal Opportunities) was directed towards mobilising a constituency of support for policies that the Commission wished to pursue, but which had frequently been blocked by some national governments (Cram 1993, 11-13; Mazey 1995; 1998). To this end, the DG promoted and funded research and networks in the fields of poverty, preventive health care provision, violence against women and human rights. Much of the explanation of the resurgence of inter-governmentalism in the EU over the past few years lies in the Commission's success as a policy entrepreneur. This very success has prompted Member States (themselves conscious of growing Euro-scepticism amongst their own electorates) to try to regain 'lost' power in the EU policy process.

As with all bureaucracies, there are often jurisdictional disputes between different parts of the Commission and problems of horizontal coordination across related policy areas. The 'coordination problem' is now well recognised by all observers of the Commission and by the Commission itself. In two areas particularly, environmental policy and gender equality, the Commission has sought to resolve this problem by the introduction of 'mainstreaming' strategies, designed to ensure that all Commission proposals are based upon an environmental and gender audit. These moves have had the (possibly unintended) consequence of forcing groups to lobby across a much wider range of DGs than hitherto, increasing the total amount of lobbying to which the Commission as a whole is subject. They also increase the amount of resources needed by interest groups of all types if they are to be effective.

There is a further complication for groups. As Pollack and Hafner-Burton argue, in order to be effective lobbyists, groups must couch their demands in terms and language that is consistent with the normative and cognitive frame of the DG with which they are dealing (Pollack and Hafner-Burton 2000). Typically, however, more than one DG will have an interest in any policy area. Thus groups must be able to couch their demands in terms which 'speak to' different – and often competing – policy frames (Dudley and Richardson 1999). The most effective lobbyists are those who, by stimulating a process of frame-reflection and negotiation between different bureaucratic interests, are able to assist the Commission in its brokerage role.

The Commission's organisational ideology favouring consultation is now deeply embedded and was aptly summarised by the Commission's then Secretary General, David Williamson, over a decade ago. Introducing the Round Table meeting between the Commission and interest groups, held in Brussels in August 1993, he commented that

> 'from the beginning of the European Community, the Commission has been open to contacts with interest groups and welcomes such contact. A broad spectrum of advice from special interest groups is important in order to arrive at proposals which are practicable. These groups also have a role in relaying information and in helping the understanding of Community action'.

In consequence, the 'early' rather chaotic and ad hoc consultation system has given way to a more institutionalised and structured pattern of interest intermediation. In large part, this development has been driven by the Commission. However, the interest groups have also become better-organised and more European/international in outlook. Mutual institutionalisation produces mutual gains by lowering transaction costs between actors. EU lobbying strategies generally are becoming more sophisticated as groups learn over time and begin to appreciate the complex nature of both the EU policy-making process and the nature of the European Commission itself.

In this context, two developments have significantly enhanced the lobbying capacity of many groups, notably NGOs: the increasing tendency to form effective transnational, and/or 'rainbow coalitions'; and the exploitation by groups of the internet, both as a source of information and transnational mobilisation. Yet, this process of organisational learning by interest groups is uneven. Generally speaking, multinational companies and large firms adapted earliest and best to the EU policy-making environment. Some voluntary associations and advocacy groups, used to cooperating on an international scale outside the EU (e.g. Greenpeace, World Wildlife Fund, Amnesty International) also developed effective cross-national lobbying strategies quite early. However, many smaller firms and national groups still find dealing with the European Commission a rather daunting prospect and may still rely too heavily on contacts with their own national governments. Interestingly, there may be some cross-national variations in the degree of reliance on national administrations as a channel for influencing European policy, with French groups perhaps rather too closely tied to their national government for them to be able to exploit the opportunities of European multi-level games.

Institutionalisation of interest intermediation: managing the flow

A key issue for Commission officials is how to 'manage' the process of consultation to which they are so deeply committed. They are in some respects victims of their own success: their steadfast commitment to consultation and openness has effectively created an oversupply of lobbying. In fact, there is no single or straightforward answer to the question of how they manage this dilemma. The nature of the relationship between officials and interest groups at the EC level varies considerably between policy sectors. The differences are the result of the varying structural characteristics of individual sectors, diverse bureaucratic interests and administrative styles within the Commission, specific policy issue characteristics and differences between groups themselves in terms of their organisational characteristics, resources, ideology and objectives. Notwithstanding this diversity, it is nevertheless possible to identify some important, general trends now emerging at the EU level with regard to relations between Commission officials and interest groups. More specifically, there are definite signs that consultation is becoming more institutionalised within the Commission in two senses. First, there is clear evidence of the evolution of formal and informal behavioural rules regarding how groups should be consulted and how groups should behave. Secondly, there has been a gradual emergence of formal structures, sites or venues where intermediation can take place at various stages of the policy process.

In terms of the EU policy process, effective group consultation is functionally beneficial. However, the considerable influence wielded by organised interests within the European Commission and the close – and often informal – links which exist between some groups and Commission officials, have served to increase public unease about the Community's 'democratic deficit'. The European Parliament began in 1991 to debate the need for a register of lobbyists. Partly in response to these pressures, the Secretariat General of the European Commission in 1992 reviewed Commission procedures regarding group consultation (Commission 1992b; Commission 1993). Possible legal regulation of lobbying has, therefore, been an important agenda item for both institutions.

Throughout this debate, however, the Commission has been greatly con-

cerned to maintain its culture of open consultations with as wide a constituency as necessary. Regulation of lobbying always comes second to the
functional need of Commission officials a) to learn about policy problems
and possible policy solutions and b) to mobilise some form of advocacy
coalition around any solution advanced. As indicated above, the
Commission first needs to ensure that its proposals are technically robust
and politically feasible. Then, it must strengthen its legitimacy as a transparent and accessible institution. To pursue an exclusive rather than an
inclusive policy towards interest groups would be conducive to neither
objective. The Commission's approach to the formal regulation of lobbying
continues to be extremely cautious and has been confined to discouraging
extreme forms of abuse. The formal 'licensing' of groups has been strongly
resisted and self-regulation has been the Commission's preferred strategy.
The Commission has, however, supported the introduction of minimum
standards of behaviour and the use of voluntary codes. In COM (2002) 704
the Commission noted that, just as the Commission had to be transparent in
its operations, then so should interested parties 'operate in an environment
that is transparent, so that the public is aware of the parties involved in the
consultation process and how they conduct themselves' (Commission
2002d). The document added that organisations which are consulted need
to make it apparent which interests they represent and how inclusive that
representation is.

Perhaps more important than formal rules regarding group consultation
are the informal, unwritten rules of the game, which are essential to effective
lobbying and which are widely appreciated by lobbyists and Commission
officials alike. Such norms include the need for groups to lobby early in the
EU policy-making process, the need to present rational arguments based
upon reliable data, the importance of maintaining close professional links
with a wide range of Commission officials, the need to formulate European
rather than parochial policy solutions, the need to be cooperative and trustworthy and the need for modesty and discretion. These 'rules' are unre-
markable and seem fairly well recognised in and around Brussels, again an
indicator of the maturity of the EU lobbying system.

Alongside the evolution of institutional norms and regulatory mechanisms, group participation in EU policy-making has become more clearly
organised within the Commission. In seeking to structure group consultation, the Commission's strategy has been shaped by the need to demonstrate
openness and transparency on the one hand and to establish a permanent,
close relationship with (a smaller number of) key interest groups on the
other hand. Concerns about openness and transparency of EU decision-
making had been highlighted as early as 1992 in the Sutherland report,
which argued that:

> 'Wide and effective consultation on Commission proposals is
> essential. The Commission needs to introduce a better procedure
> for making people aware, at the earliest stage, of its intention to
> propose legislation'. (Sutherland 1992, 30)

In response to this report, the Commission introduced a number of
measures designed to increase openness and transparency. These included
earlier publication of the Commission's legislative programme, a commit-

ment to ensure that target groups are aware of any new policy initiatives, and greater use of Green (consultative) Papers. Prior to 1990, the Commission appears to have published only four Green Papers; in the following eight years approximately fifty were published. The Commission's Report, 'Better Lawmaking in 2003' (Commission 2003c) records that in that year it published five Green Papers and 142 Communications, as well as 73 Reports.

More recently, use of the internet has become an increasingly important characteristic of the Commission's group management strategy. In April 2001, the Commission adopted a Communication on Interactive Policy Making (Commission 2001c). The so-called IPM initiative involves the development of two internet-based mechanisms to assist the consultation processes: a feedback facility, to allow existing networks to report to the Commission on a continuous basis; and an on-line consultation tool, designed to receive and store rapidly reactions to new initiatives. In 2003 the Commission conducted 60 internet consultations through 'Your Voice in Europe', the Commission's single access point for consultations. Current consultations under this initiative include consultations on 'The Future of the Simple Pressure Vessels Directive'; 'Strengthening the EU-US Economic Partnership'; and 'The Green paper on Defence Procurement'. As part of its policy on openness, contributions to open public consultations are published on the internet at the 'Your Voice in Europe' portal. Shortly after the internet consultations on the European Sustainable Development Strategy ended in October 2004, the Commission reported that it had received over 100 answers to its long questionnaire and nearly 700 answers to the online questionnaire and that detailed analysis of the whole consultation would be published in a few weeks.

The Commission has also created a web-based database of formal and structured consultative bodies in the field of civil society, the so-called CONECCS (Consultation, the European Commission and Civil Society). The database provides information on those Commission committees and other Commission frameworks through which civil society organisations are consulted in a formal or structured way and which are relatively permanent and meet at least once a year. The database does not hold information on committees composed solely of representatives of Member States or expert groups or which do not systematically include civil society organisations. Examples of formal committees included on the database include the Advisory Committee on the Common Agricultural Policy and the Advisory Committee on Fisheries and Agriculture. Examples of other structured consultative bodies include Biodegradable Waste – NGOs and Industry and the Satellite Action Plan Regulatory Working Group. For each group, the database lists its objectives, period of mandate, frequency of meetings, secretariat and chair of the body, as well as information on members and links to member organisations. This is a relatively recent development and cynics might wonder how important these bodies really are in terms of influencing policy outcomes, especially as CONECCS does not include what the Commission calls 'open consultation procedures'. These often less visible consultation exercises include bilateral contacts and/or ad hoc consultations between the Commission and interest groups.

For many years the Commission has also funded public interest European lobbies such as the European Women's Lobby and the European

Environmental Bureau. In an attempt to allay public fears about the EU's democratic deficit, the Commission has, since the early 1990s, redoubled its efforts to achieve a more balanced institutionalisation of interest group intermediation, mainly through the construction of a series of inclusive social networks such as the Social Policy Forum. In 1997, the Commission adopted a Communication, *Promoting the Role of Voluntary Organisations and Foundations in Europe*, which stressed the need for NGOs to be consulted more widely and more systematically. As the Commission noted in 2002 (Commission 2002d), this initiative underlined its intention to 'reduce the risk of the policy-makers just listening to one side of the argument or of particular groups getting privileged access'. The increasing institutionalisation of NGO-Commission relations is also reflected in the considerable financial support that NGOs receive from the Commission. Some 2.65m ECU were set aside for funding environmental NGOs during the period 1998-2001 (Commission 1997a). More generally, there is increasing emphasis on involving civil society organisations in the Commission's policy process, as highlighted in the Commission's *White Paper on European Governance* and again, in 2002 in COM (2002) 704, in which it stated 'the Commission particularly encourages a coherent approach to representation of civil society organisations at the European level... belonging to an association is another way for citizens to participate actively, in addition to involvement in political parties or through elections' (Commission 2002d). The role of civil society groups was enshrined in the Constitutional Treaty.

The Commission's need to demonstrate openness and transparency is paralleled by its need to mobilise a consensus in favour of technically sound and politically feasible policies. These potentially conflicting objectives are typically achieved through different institutional structures used at various stages of the policy-making process. Broadly speaking, the Commission employs two different strategies for involving groups in the policy process: large, open gatherings (including consultations via the internet as outlined above), and more restrictive committees and forums. Though it is impossible to generalise about the relative importance of these two types of interest aggregation within the Commission, our own research suggests that there is a pattern emerging. In the early stages of the policy process, consultative structures tend to be open and inclusive, bringing together all potential stakeholders in an open forum, seminar or conference. Generally speaking, the purpose of this form of consultation is to inform potential stakeholders, try out new ideas and obtain early feedback on proposals.

However, the subsequent formulation and implementation of detailed proposals usually takes place within the myriad of formal and informal advisory committees and working parties in the Commission, which comprise group representatives and technical experts. Formal committees include so-called 'expert committees' composed of national officials and experts, who are nominated by government departments. In practice, however, these nominees tend to perceive their role as being that of technical experts rather than national government agents. Generally, the Commission *must* consult the relevant expert committee(s) during the policy formulation process (though it is under no obligation to respond to the advice offered by the experts). The more broadly based 'consultative committees' represent sectoral interests and are composed of representatives of Euro-associations and national groups. Though the Commission has a procedural ambition to deal primarily with the Euro-associations, the latter are not always able to provide the level of expertise (and cross-national knowledge) required. The raison d'être of all these committees is to advise the Commission on the technical details of its proposals. The importance of these committees in the policy process is considerable. Back in 1997 it was estimated that there were some 1,000 advisory committees involving some 50,000 representatives from national administrations and the private sector (Greenwood 1997, 41; see also Van Schendelen 1998a). In addition, the Commission frequently sets up informal, high level groups or working parties to consider a specific problem.

In practice, it is possible to distinguish between rather open and 'thin' institutions such as very large conferences and seminars and the more restricted 'thick' institutions where only the key players are present. Coen, observing this trend with respect to business interests, refers to the emergence at the EU level of 'the creeping institutionalisation of forum style politics' (Coen 1999, 16). This process is described as the Commission acting as both policy entrepreneur and *political* entrepreneur in response to the further explosion of lobbying after the Maastricht Treaty. In short, 'the Commission uses institutional engineering, in the service of political entrepreneurship' (Broschild and Coen, 2003, 180-81). The more open structures facilitate legitimation and identification of key actors and likely 'sticking points'. The more restrictive structures facilitate the detailed technical negotiation and bargaining, resulting in practical proposals. Though some consultative structures are temporary in nature, there is an increasing tendency for them to become permanent structures, which meet irrespective of the legislative timetable. This is particularly true of the thicker structures, which become institutionalised sites for permanent consultation, frame reflection and consensus-building. The fact that it is possible to distinguish between thick and thin institutional structures should not disguise the fact that from the Commission's perspective, consultation is a seamless and long-term process. As one interviewee told us 'we have our style – a process of consultation – not just single consultations, but we consult often… in order to judge people's views and gauge how far people's views have changed during the process.' Thus, institutionalised consultation is as much about mutual learning as instrumental lobbying for short-term, material gain.

Conclusion: orchestrating European interests

The construction of institutions to facilitate learning and consensus-building between competing policy frames and belief systems is especially important in the EU, because the policy-making system is characterised by multiple cultures, languages, policy traditions and national agendas. The potential for conflict is great and there is, therefore, a functional imperative to search for sufficient areas of agreement for workable policies to emerge. For what Sabatier terms 'policy orientated learning across belief systems' (Sabatier 1988, 156) to take place there needs to be a forum which is both prestigious enough to force professions from different coalitions to participate, and dominated by professional norms. As Sabatier suggests, the purpose of these structures:

'is to force debate among professionals from different belief systems to which their points of view must be aired by peers. Under such conditions, a desire for professional credibility and the norms of scientific debate will lead to a serious analysis of methodological assumptions, to the gradual elimination of the more improbable causal assertions and invalid data, and thus probably to a greater convergence of views over time concerning the nature of the problem and the consequences of various policy alternatives' (Sabatier 1988, 156).

In this context, the advantage that the Commission has over other institutional venues is that it is widely perceived as an honest broker. In order to re-enforce the honest broker image and to emphasise the democratic aspects of consultation, the Commission adopted, at the end of 2002, a set of general principles and minimum standards for consultation of interested parties. In many respects, the new statement is not all that new as it restates what we see as an already embedded policy style which has consultation at its core. Thus, the general principles include familiar friends such as 'wide participation', 'openness and accountability' and 'transparency'. However, some of the proposals contained in the statement are rather more specific, such as that consultation should start very early in the policy process where interests 'can still have an impact on the formulation of the main aims, methods of delivery, performance indicators and, where appropriate, the initial outlines of that policy'; that details of any hearings, meetings or conferences should be contained in consultation documents; that the Commission should ensure that it consults all of those affected by a policy and those involved in implementation; that interests should be given at least eight weeks to respond to any consultation document and at least twenty working days notice of meetings (for full details see Commission 2002d).

It is clear, therefore, that consultation with a huge range of interests is the norm within the Commission, that it is increasingly institutionalised, and that it is increasingly governed by a set of codified 'rules'. This long-standing process is presented as part of the democratisation of the EU and seems to have been widely welcomed as shifting the Commission from a closed to an open bureaucracy. No doubt this shift is real, but we end by echoing Broscheid and Coen's caution (cited above) that the Commission should be seen as a *political* entrepreneur and *institutional* engineer. In that sense, the Commission remains the conductor of a large and pluralistic orchestra of European interest groups.

Endnotes

[1] The Commission has adopted the Economic and Social Committee's definition of a civil society organisation. This definition includes:
– the so-called labour market players (i.e. trade unions and employers' federations, also often termed the social partners);
– organisations representing social and economic players, which are not partners in the strict sense of the term;
– NGOs which bring people together in a common cause, such as environmental

organisations, human rights organisations, consumer associations, charitable organisations, educational and training organisations, etc;
– CBOs (community based organisations, i.e. organisations set up within society at grassroots level which pursue member-orientated objectives), e.g. youth organisations, family associations and all organisations through which citizens participate in local and community life;
– Religious communities.

11. The Commission's role in freedom, security and justice and the threat of terrorism

Richard Lewis and David Spence

Introduction: the policy context

This chapter discusses the evolution of the Commission's role in the 'third pillar' policy area, Justice and Home Affairs (JHA), known since the Treaty of Amsterdam as 'an area of freedom, security and justice'.[1] As with the Common Foreign and Security Policy, JHA officially began life as a purely intergovernmental policy area (Title VI TEU). It is not only the subject of political controversy over 'competence' between the Commission and the Council, but it also receives a great deal of media attention since it covers issues high on the public agenda, ranging from policing and criminal justice through to drugs policy, immigration, asylum and counter-terrorism. JHA policy developed during the 1970s on an ad hoc basis in response to increased cross-border terrorism, drug smuggling and international crime. It evolved more rapidly after the signature of the Schengen Convention in 1985 and reached undisputed relevance after the terrorist attacks in New York and Washington on 11 September 2001. The subsequent attacks in Madrid in 2003 and in London in 2005 have ensured that European policymaking in the JHA field remains a firm part of the EU policy landscape.

The Commission began as an observer of this originally intergovernmental process. Gradually, by dint of its expertise and related first pillar competence, it evolved into the policy-making focus of JHA, its responsibilities embedded firmly in Community legal provisions. This chapter examines how JHA evolved to achieve almost full 'communitarisation' in the Constitutional Treaty and how the Commission's role became more central. While the Commission's efforts at policy-making within JHA were long constrained, it must be remembered that the seeds of Community competence in the area were present in the original Treaty of Rome's concern with free movement of goods (Article 3a), services, capital and people (article 3c). Communitarising JHA was thus a logical consequence of integrated policy areas enshrined in the Treaty of Rome and managed by the Commission. But the process was slow and continuously disputed.

The origins of Justice and Home Affairs policies

The philosophy underlying an area of freedom, security and justice had its origins in the minds of the founders of the European Coal and Steel Community, itself part of the wider context of the European desire to prevent war and the totalitarian abuses that led to it in 1939. The challenge of European JHA policies over time has been to translate these concerns and ideals into an acceptable corpus of European law and practice, whilst respecting Member State prerogatives – the principles of subsidiarity and proportionality. The genesis of Justice and Home Affairs policy lay in the Treaty of Rome's commitment to freedom of movement for goods, persons, services and capital. The notion of the free movement of *persons* was a cornerstone of the creation of the original common market. Behind the concept was the assumption that common economic goals required labour mobility and that this mobility would in turn bring about a host of other requirements relating to the transfer of social security rights and the protection of those who took the then relatively courageous step of working abroad in another Member State. Labour mobility became even more important with the advent of a common currency. The idea that this would bring in its wake issues of cross border crime control and, in the ultimate analysis, common frontier control lay far in the future. Indeed, the political implications of freedom of movement did not become apparent until the passage of the Treaty of Maastricht, signed at the end of 1992. Until then, only the economic consequences of free movement of persons were considered. Although the Single European Act of 1986 reiterated the ideals of its treaty predecessor with regard to the four freedoms, the Commission was largely pre-occupied at the time with the freedom of movement for goods and capital. Subsequent Commission Presidents and officials, particularly Jacques Delors, concentrated on these two freedoms, leaving the free movement of services and persons for later. Delors' and Internal Market Commissioner Lord Cockfield's undoubted contribution was the completion of the single market for goods and the laying of the foundations of the single currency. Very little intellectual capital was expended on the future policy area of JHA, despite the budding interest in bringing the content of the Schengen Treaty into the Community sphere. The Schengen system was built on a loose system of border control cooperation agreed in the Luxembourg town of Schengen in May 1985 by France, Germany and the Benelux countries, the latter already having an advanced open frontier system. The objective was free movement of persons within the internal borders of the EU, but this implied an implementing convention designed to ensure that the security of the Schengen Member States would not be compromised as a result of lack of border controls. Implemented in 1990, this principally concerned asylum, visas and immigration.

Cockfield's White Paper on completion of the single market in May 1985 (Commission 1985) did indicate that a Europe without frontiers could not be constructed without affecting a number of areas with which the Commission had never previously dealt. Cockfield articulated the general concern that opening frontiers and allowing goods to pass freely without customs or tax checks at national borders opened the way to potential abuse that would need to be controlled. At the same time, Commission officials concluded that the free movement within the EU had given birth to the notion of external as opposed to internal frontiers and that this had implications for people moving across internal frontiers. By logical extension, if free movement of lorry drivers, holiday makers, and business people were to be allowed within the Union, then admitting an individual and his or her chattels from outside the EU to one Member State meant admitting them to all. The European policy framework came later, despite the fact that the activities of terrorist groups in the 1970s and 1980s, notably the Provisional IRA, the Red Brigade and others, had already begun to set the agenda.

The Schengen agreements were the first solid Commission inroad into immigration and frontier controls, both of which long remained essentially intergovernmental. The Commission was a very present observer of the Schengen process until, in 1989, Adrian Fortescue, later to be the first Director General for JHA, was asked to reflect on the consequences for the EC of removing frontier controls (Fortescue 2002b, 1). The Community then began to move towards the incorporation of the Schengen arrangements into the EU Treaties, though it was only in 1999 with the Treaty of Amsterdam that this formally took place. Until then, they had their own separate institutions deliberately mirroring those of the Council, since the Schengen Agreements were envisaged as EU compatible and eventually absorbable.

There was, and still is, reluctance on the part of Member States to loosen their grip on a policy area which goes to the heart of sovereignty, namely who should be allowed on their territory. Some states, Denmark, the United Kingdom and – largely because of historical ties to the UK – Ireland, were indeed so reticent that they opted out of some or all of the arrangements that ensued – including Schengen. In terms of taking a political lead the Commission was thus demonstrably on sensitive ground. This reluctance of Member States led to the first tentative steps being taken on an intergovernmental basis, on the model of European Political Cooperation (EPC). Indeed, although EPC largely dealt with foreign policy issues, its early committees also touched on matters relating to future JHA questions such as consular cooperation and even terrorism.

As a first step in concrete cooperation in this policy area, in 1975 the so-called Trevi Group was created by the European Council in Rome. It consisted of senior officials meeting in the margins of the EPC framework in three working groups: anti-terrorism, information and security; police cooperation (partly in response to cross-border football hooliganism); and organised crime and drugs. All these fora, including the EPC consular and terrorism working groups, included Commission participation. However, as in the early pre-Maastricht days of all EPC groups, the Commission was an observer and provider of information or occasional practical solutions based on the budgetary weight of the Community institutions. As for terrorism, participants had the impression that the importance or relevance of the information imparted by Member States' representatives was minimal. The detail necessary for meaningful co-ordination of policy or cross-border cooperation was left unspoken. Even in the consular affairs working group, it was difficult to make progress on substantial issues, such as the issuing of visas, and cooperation was confined to relatively trivial matters such as sharing car pools or print-shop facilities. The essential feature of these tentative steps was that the process remained rigorously intergovernmental. The European Parliament was absent from the process, as indeed was any reporting in the media. Yet, the precursors of new forms of terrorism in the new millennium gave momentum to the view that these issues were virtually impossible to contain within the nation state framework and that EU action was needed.

The Single European Act 1986 and the Treaty on European Union 1993

The Single European Act (SEA) was the result of the Trevi Group's first hesitant attempts at cooperation in the field of JHA. De Lobkowicz (2002) describes the process of the idea of free movement coming 'out of hiding' as the completion of the internal market – the so-called 1992 programme – was announced. The SEA reiterated the goal of free circulation of persons in a space without internal frontiers. Whereas the Treaty of Rome did not indicate a date by which free movement should be achieved, the SEA set the time limit of 31 December 1992. The main problem of the SEA text was that legal responsibility for acting on this provision was left unstated. In addition, in a declaration attached to the Treaty, the Member States indicated that their power to act to protect their ultimate control of frontiers to prevent the ills of terrorism and crime, etc., remained. Admittedly, this did not prevent the creation in October 1986 of an Ad Hoc Group on Immigration (significantly by the UK Presidency). The Commission and the Council Secretariat were 'associated' with the process as they were in EPC, though as in EPC, the Commission had no right of initiative.

The real breakthrough in JHA cooperation came with the Treaty on European Union (TEU) signed in Maastricht in 1992. The Treaty set out nine areas of interest: asylum, the crossing of external borders, immigration, combating drug addiction, combating international fraud, judicial cooperation in civil matters, judicial cooperation in criminal matters, customs cooperation and police cooperation. As Monar (1997a) has pointed out, the issues were hardly new. They had been under discussion in various groups for a long time, so the 'new' pillar III was in fact only new in that the issues now had a place in the Treaty. Fortescue argued that momentum had been built up over time for a radical new approach to be incorporated into treaty form: 'for the first time the subjects had been identified as being necessary flanking measures for getting rid of frontier control...' (Fortescue 2002b), thus relating them to core Community competence. This was given form in Title VI of Maastricht: 'Co-operation in the fields of Justice and Home Affairs' – colloquially, but never officially known as 'the third pillar'.

Yet, Fortescue argued that the real achievements under Maastricht were actually few. Weak instruments, lack of clarity in the objectives, virtual exclusion of the European Parliament and the European Court of Justice from the process, lack of budgetary resources and what he called 'the ubiquitous dead hand of unanimity' were all to blame. Dinan (2005, 568) also stresses that:

> 'Given... the cloak of... confidentiality that shrouded the new Council formation and preparatory committee, the imprecision of JHA instruments and the ability of Member States to veto decisions, there was little or no headway on issues covered by the Third Pillar. Yet public support for EU-wide measures to combat illegal immigration and organised crime was remarkably high, despite wide-

spread hostility during and after the Maastricht ratification crisis toward the EU and its institutions.'

This contradiction between public support and governmental reticence is a theme to which this chapter returns below. Importantly, many of the principles enunciated in soft law or in Commission position papers subsequently found their way into binding acts. In fact, 'soft law' measures, consisting of non-binding declarations or recommendations of the Council that might be quietly ignored by the Member States, were in fact precursors of legal change. It was a slow process, but the Commission established itself little by little as a body known for its growing expertise in the field. In 1994, the Member States were somewhat taken by surprise that the Commission could produce a policy document on immigration and asylum[2], a subject they had always believed to be their sole preserve. Yet, the surprise was actually unfounded, for the Commission had invariably been associated with the various pre-Maastricht working groups and its Communication to the Council and Parliament on Immigration and Asylum Policies was a logical extension of the removal of frontiers. It is still cited in discussions on immigration today.

Despite the seeming lack of progress, there were some advances in the field of JHA. In May 1995, a uniform format for visas was agreed and in September, a binding list of countries requiring visas. Another advance of the post-Maastricht period was the passage of the convention establishing Europol.[3] Europol's main objective consisted of collating and disseminating information and facilitating the investigation of crime, whether international or domestic. Yet, as a result of political sensitivities, Europol only entered into force three years after its convention was ratified (in July 1995) and even then its work was initially confined to anti drug activities (Nugent 1999, 334). Hence, although governmental hostility was certainly a reality, the contradictory phenomenon of the popular media calling for action in JHA was clearly a harbinger of further EU efforts, even if Commission initiatives were resisted or downplayed when they were made. In fact, as a concession to the Commission, amongst others, who wished to see greater 'communitarisation' of the field, the Maastricht Treaty designated some subjects, notably asylum, immigration, drugs and civil judicial cooperation, as suitable to pass in due course into the First Pillar. This was the so-called *passerelle* (bridge or gateway) mechanism, which was instrumental in levering certain aspects of JHA into a supranational framework and thus creating some unfinished business to be settled by the next Treaty, signed at Amsterdam in October 1997 and which entered into force on 1 May 1999.

The Treaty of Amsterdam

As Fortescue (2002a) put it, after Amsterdam:

> 'Every chapter was ratcheted up: where Maastricht had given the Commission a right of initiative in the Third Pillar context, Amsterdam 'communitarised'. Where Maastricht had excluded any Commission right to take initiatives, Amsterdam gave it. The European Parliament's role was enhanced; money became avail-

able. The European Court of Justice entered the frame; the subject matter was listed by objective rather than just by catalogue'.

Although the section of the Amsterdam Treaty on police and judicial cooperation in criminal matters still spoke the intergovernmental language of 'closer cooperation' and 'common actions', in sharp contrast, Article 63, relating to immigration and asylum, set a five year timetable within which measures would have to be taken. And there were clear distinctions of procedure and objectives and a strengthening of the role of the Commission in policy formulation, despite its resource constraints, which hampered faster expansion and deepening of JHA. But, Amsterdam underlined three important issues affecting the role and powers of the Commission. First, it failed to gain *sole* right of initiative, despite the Treaty's explicit reference that in the key area of immigration and asylum after 1 May 2004 the Commission would gain that right. Second, unanimity remained the rule until 1 January 2005;[4] and third, certain sensitive issues relating to cooperation in police matters and criminal justice remained in the restrictive intergovernmental Third Pillar. However, this was the principle. In practice, policy-making was somewhat different.

Although the Commission failed to gain sole right of initiative, the Member States used their right of initiative on a limited scale. The Commission's lead in first producing policy papers in the form of Communications or Green Paper consultative documents and then following these up with legislative proposals was preponderant. On the other hand, it may be argued that Member States frequently pre-empted the Commission (e.g. on Eurojust), making the Commission tag along, accommodating national positions as if they had been policy all along. If the Commission were not always successful in convincing some Member States of the added value of collective as opposed to national efforts (Monar 2002 and Guiraudon 2004), its aspiration to play its classic policy motor role was clear. And it was in fact rare that the Member States did not look to the Commission to provide the background information and follow-up even when they themselves made the proposals. All this dovetailed well with Article 67 of the Consolidated Treaties, which laid down the procedure to be followed relating to Title IV (free movement of persons) during the transitional period of five years. It specified that 'the Commission shall (also) examine any request by a Member State that it submit a proposal to the Council'. It thus left a welcome loophole to the Member States and laid the main legal responsibility on the Commission. In sum, the overarching objectives in Article 61 remained what they always were from the time of the Treaty of Rome, namely 'measures aimed at ensuring the free movement of persons', though there was an important rider to the effect that this should be in conjunction with 'flanking measures with respect to external border controls, asylum and immigration'.

The Tampere European Council of October 1999

The key turning point in the process of translating the words of the Treaty of Amsterdam into concrete results was the special European Council held under the Finnish Presidency in Tampere on 15-16 October 1999. It was a strange meeting in that, as is usual with meetings of Heads of State and

Government, the only official invitees, apart from the presidents and prime ministers, were foreign ministers. Ministers of justice or interior ministers were there only as 'guests', akin to the presence of defence ministers in General Affairs Councils. Accounts of the meeting relate that, although consulted, JHA ministers had no access to the meeting itself. In addition, there was an unofficial meeting spearheaded by leading non-governmental organisations (NGOs), especially those concerned with refugee protection and human rights.

A number of delegations, including the Commission, submitted contributions in writing prior to Tampere. The Commission took great care in its own preparations. Commissioner Vitorino visited national capitals to discuss both Commission and national viewpoints. In his speech to the European Council, Romano Prodi referred to the two guiding documents in the process, namely the Amsterdam Treaty itself and the JHA Action Plan adopted in Vienna a year earlier, characterising the EU's cooperation in JHA matters as equivalent in importance and scope to economic and monetary union and CFSP. He argued that 'national administrations should put aside any residual nostalgia for the days of pure intergovernmentalism which Amsterdam finally laid to rest' (Prodi 1999d). He also laid out what he considered the essence of the coming five years, stressing the inclusion of non-EU nationals living in the Member States in the benefits of an area of freedom, security and justice stemming from free movement, and he advocated the use of a so-called 'scoreboard', consisting of a document to be produced every six months by the Commission and listing the obligations required by the Treaty, the proposals that had been made (whether from the Commission or the Member States) and progress or lack of it in the legislative process.

Tampere achieved more than the Vienna Action Plan of December 1998, which had been the forerunner to the provisions in Amsterdam Treaty. It was a political statement of intent that covered all fields of the Treaty. Again, asylum and immigration, as subjects constantly in the headlines, were singled out. In addition, section D of the conclusions of the European Council was devoted to the need to use all the resources of the Union on external issues. Here, the Commission had a distinct advantage. Not only does the Commission's aid budget exceed that of individual Member States, but the Commission Delegations also enhance the Union's international role in promoting JHA ideas and policies. Moreover, it is the Commission which leads the negotiations with applicant states on their ability to implement the *acquis communautaire*, and it is the Commission which manages practical projects for political and administrative adaptation designed to pave the administrative and political way for their entry into the EU. Thus, in asylum and immigration matters, attention was diverted away from purely domestic concerns to dealing with issues that affected third countries from which migrants came. This 'in principle' was covered separately in the 1990 and 2002 Dublin Conventions concerning the Member State where asylum applicants were obliged to first lodge their application. The Commission now began to devote far more intellectual and human resources to coordinating development policies and external relations aspects (brain drain, remittances etc.) than in the past.

9/11 as a catalyst for the Commission's role in JHA

The fight against international crime, terrorism and money laundering was already well underway before the attacks on the Twin Towers in New York on 11 September 2001. Intergovernmental, Europe-wide cooperation had started as early as 1975 on issues of terrorism and internal security in the framework of the Trevi Group alluded to earlier. Twenty years later, the Madrid European Council in 1995 established that terrorism should be regarded as a threat to democracy, to the free exercise of human rights and to economic and social development. Acknowledging that since terrorism increasingly operates on a transnational scale, it could not be dealt with effectively by means of isolated action and national resources alone. The Treaty of Amsterdam itself referred to the fight against terrorism, and terrorism was addressed both in 1998 in the Vienna Action Plan and in the conclusions of the Tampere Council of 1999.

This attention already paid to terrorism explains why the European legal and institutional structures in the area of Justice and Home Affairs were able to adapt rapidly to the increased demands they faced in the wake of 11 September 2001 (Spence 2004). On 20 September 2001, a range of JHA measures to fight terrorism were adopted by a special JHA Council meeting followed by the adoption of a comprehensive EU Action Plan to Fight Terrorism at the extraordinary European Council on 21 September 2001. A detailed 'Road Map' to implement the Action Plan was drawn up in October 2001; it is regularly updated. The Commission subsequently spearheaded counter-terrorism measures within the JHA sphere in the following five areas: (1) judicial cooperation, (2) counter-terrorism services cooperation (police and intelligence services), (3) financing of terrorism, (4) border controls and (5) external JHA measures.

The establishment of a European police college and Eurojust to coordinate national prosecuting authorities were immediate outcomes of a new conducive atmosphere in JHA. The fight against organised crime had already been boosted by the terrorist threat, and the Commission's role in both the external relations aspects (Roma Group) and the internal aspects, including organised crime (Lyon Group), of the G8 grew apace. Adrian Fortescue, the then Director General for DG JHA, was a well respected member of the latter.

Following 9/11, the most significant developments included:

–   Agreement and legislation on a European Arrest Warrant, dispens-
       ing with traditional extradition procedures and expediting the
       arrest and transfer of suspects;
–   Agreement on a common definition of terrorist offences for crimi-
       nal law purposes;
–   Provision for improved joint investigation between national police
       forces, the creation of an anti-terrorism unit within Europol and
       strengthened cooperation between anti-terrorist units;
–   Improved cooperation between the judiciary and prosecutors'
       offices;
–   Measures to give the intelligence services access to parts of the data
       of the Schengen Information System (SIS), and simplification of
       procedures to improve use of the SIS in the fight against terrorism;
–   Enhanced cooperation between Member States on a common list of

terrorist organisations, on strengthening external border checks, on exchange of information on visas and on strengthening internal security;
– Closer cooperation with Canada and the United States, including the appointment of liaison officers to the EU from both countries and mutual visits between Eurojust and Canada and the USA.
– Europol signed a Strategic Cooperation Agreement with the United States on 4 December 2001 and negotiated a second agreement with the USA on 20 December 2002, allowing for the transfer of personal data.

Many of these measures required Commission action. The proposals for a European Arrest Warrant and a definition of terrorist acts, which the Commission tabled immediately and steered through the Council in record time, paved the way for additional penalties for offences involving terrorism and were adopted more rapidly than might otherwise have been the case. Preparatory work had in any event already been done by the Commission prior to 9/11. The Commission had been drafting the texts over the summer and was awaiting a sensible political moment to communicate its legislative intentions. The work was accelerated and repackaged in the weeks following the attacks. Similarly, work by the Commission on the future requirements of the next generation of the Schengen Information System (SIS) included: designing a new, simpler consultation procedure in the context of combating terrorism for alerts issued pursuant to Article 99 of the 1990 Schengen Convention; the possibility of running searches on the basis of incomplete data; access for public authorities responsible for vehicle registration; extended access for the authorities which issue residence permits; and access for Eurojust, Europol and security services to the SIS.

In spite of these efforts, JHA still remained intergovernmental in its inspiration. Despite progress in JHA as an EU policy sector, the Commission was powerless to stop Member States introducing national legislation on issues with high political profile, such as asylum and immigration, where it had hoped that future action would be within the EU framework. The establishment of a coherent EU strategy to address these issues, in the Commission's view, could only be effectively tackled through trans-national cooperation, and national efforts did not help. While the Commission attempted to steer EU measures on asylum and immigration through the Council, the UK and Germany continued to enact national legislation in these fields in 2003, 2004 and 2005. Controversial German legislation on immigration in response to its declining population and need for skilled immigrants obtained political agreement on 17 June 2004. Yet, significantly, many of the concepts in the German legislation, notably the need for better integration of immigrants and the requirements of the labour market, were already present in Commission documents after 2000.

The pressure of events: towards the Hague Programme

JHA issues frequently hit the headlines. The deaths of the smuggled Chinese in Dover in 2000, the ill-fated French Red Cross camp at Sangatte near Calais and cases where illegal immigrants are regularly sent back to Africa by the Italian coastguard, have made the public aware throughout Europe of JHA issues. The Commission often triggered European action after such cross-border crises, though it was sometimes criticised when it did. In June 2004, a Commission Communication[5] assessed achievements and problems in JHA in the run up to the fifth anniversary of the Tampere European Council. The Commission's assessment was that, with the support of the public demon-strated in opinion polls, JHA was now firmly established as one of the Union's priority policy areas. Insecurity, crime and drugs headed the list of public con-cerns, behind only the issue of living standards (Eurobarometer 63).[6] Naturally, there was concern that combating terrorism, racism, illegal immi-gration, people trafficking and other forms of exploitation might imply a measure of curtailment of freedom. A balance between freedom, security and justice and protection of fundamental rights has been a major concern of the EU institutions.[7] While much of the focus of JHA has been on increased coordi-nation on asylum and immigration issues and on criminal matters (den Boer 1996; Monar 2003), the Commission's emerging role in 'human rights' is thus apposite. All Member States and potential Member States of the European Union must belong to the Council of Europe and are *ipso facto* signatories to the European Convention on Human Rights and Fundamental Freedoms which entered into force on 3 September 1953, giving effect to the declaration of the Congress of Europe that took place in The Hague in May 1948. The European Convention is mentioned in the Single European Act of 1986 and in subsequent Treaties. The Council of Europe also passed a Social Charter that came into force in 1960, guaranteeing social rights. Both instruments were reflected in the European Union's own Charter of Fundamental Rights, which would be bind-ing on Member States if the Constitutional Treaty or a version of it were ever to be ratified.

In terms of the number of instruments passed and policy papers published, the Commission clearly made a considerable effort to push through measures in accordance with the Tampere mandate, though it was hampered by the absence of qualified majority voting and by national politics. The 'scoreboard' demonstrates how active the Commission has been in putting proposals to the Council. On the other hand, if rigorous efforts were made on the Commission side, the Council demonstrated somewhat less vigour than the Commission. Where agreements were reached, it was often at the cost of a watered down version of the proposal. The directive on family re-unification is a prime example. It went into three proposals by the Commission before it was accepted by the Council on 22 September 2003 (Directive 2003/86/EC). The directive on long-term residence of third country nationals (Directive 2003/109/EC) was a success for the Commission, however. As the usually diplomatic Fortescue contended (Fortescue 2002a),

> 'JHA is increasingly hostage to outside events and national elec-tion campaigns… In each case immigration and terrorism con-siderations were close to the surface. The subjects have to be kept out of the newspapers; meaning that the Member State concerned can make no concession in the Council because of the risk of atten-tion being drawn to it… Our whole immigration debate was vir-tually on hold for much of 2002 for electoral reasons'.

There was thus perhaps a degree of scepticism present when the

Commission's Communication of June 2004 listed policy areas to which attention ought to be paid. These were:

(a)   A genuine common policy of management of migratory flows, including the facilitation of legal immigrants.
(b)   A common European asylum system and a common status. The Commission laid out its ideas for the second stage of its asylum policy in a Communication in 2004.[8]
(c)   Establishment of a judicial area in civil and commercial matters, especially the continuation of work on mutual recognition.
(d)   Promotion of a coherent criminal justice policy also based on the principle of mutual recognition. This would include 'putting Eurojust at the centre of European criminal justice policy to support and strengthen coordination and cooperation ... relating to serious crime affecting several Member States.' This would involve the creation of a European Public Prosecutor's Office.
(e)   Stronger action to prevent crime and strengthening the fight against terrorism.
(f)   Resolute external action in relation to third countries.

The Dutch Presidency responded with a paper of its own, which was reviewed briefly at the JHA Council of 19 July 2004.[9] It highlighted five similar areas needing attention, echoing the Commission's priority list: adequate access to justice and protection of rights; a coordinated cohesive judicial system for civil and commercial matters that ensures effective jurisdiction and execution of judgements; effective capacity to regulate cross-border movement of persons; the power to protect against external and internal threats; and an integrated capacity to fight organised crime. Subsequently, the European Council of 4-5 November 2004 approved a new blueprint for the future: the Hague Programme.[10] As the Tampere Programme before it, the Hague Programme was an attempt to map out the steps needed to meet particular problems. The policy prescriptions of the Hague Programme were not, however, markedly different from those in the Commission's June 2004 Communication. Based on the Hague Programme provisions, the Commission presented a Five Year Action Plan in May 2005, 'in which the aims and priorities of this programme [would] be translated into concrete actions'. It provided detailed proposals for EU action on terrorism, migration management, visa policies, asylum, privacy and security, the fight against organised crime and criminal justice[11]. The Hague Programme prioritised further development of cross-border police cooperation and amendment of the Convention implementing the Schengen Agreement. The Commission not only had a major role in the drafting of the Hague Programme, but remained the motor in its implementation and monitoring. There seemed little doubt that Member States now saw the Commission in the driving seat in this once purely intergovernmental sector.

The Commission adopted a proposal on the improvement of police cooperation between the Member States on 19 July 2005. The proposal provided a framework to improve information exchange between law enforcement authorities and strengthen structural and operational cooperation between them. It included the creation of a regulatory committee to assist the Commission by reviewing drafts of proposed measures. It would consist of representatives of the Member States and be chaired by the Commission.[12] On the same day, the Commission also adopted a Communication on ensuring greater security of explosives, detonators, bomb-making equipment and firearms[13] as part of its work in developing a coherent preventive strategy in the fight against terrorism. The Communication, which provides the state of play regarding security of explosives and makes a series of concrete recommendations, emphasises improving security arrangements along the production and supply chain, particularly during storage and transport.

External relations and internal implications

An additional Commission obligation in the Hague framework included a joint obligation with High Representative Javier Solana to present by the end of 2005 a strategy 'covering all external aspects of the Union policy on freedom, security and justice'. Following 11 September, the external aspects of JHA expertise were initially used only to a limited extent in the numerous contacts with third countries. There was little formal interaction between JHA and CFSP bodies, and CFSP *démarches* dealing with terrorism in third countries were often not always as infused with the JHA dimension of EU action as they might have been if effective coordination had been the rule (Spence 2004). New, comprehensive anti-terrorism cooperation structures with third countries were initially only developed with the US, though other important partners such as Japan and the Russian Federation followed later, as the G8 became closely involved. There was clearly an initial gap. There was no overall strategy for the fight against terrorism similar to the one which the EU had already had in place since 1997 – through specific action plans – for the fight against organised crime.   The following months and years saw the Commission at first hastily bundling together measures which lacked coordination and which were subject to numerous ad hoc changes (Monar 2003), and then concentrating on a coordinated approach to the interaction between external and internal security. However, despite the amount of practical work involved, the Commission kept a low political profile. When the post of EU Counter-Terrorism Coordinator was created in 2004, the incumbent, Dutch politician Gijs de Vries, was placed in the Council, reporting to the High Representative for CFSP, rather than in the Commission where the staff and financial resources lay.

There is hardly any JHA policy area that does not have an external component requiring negotiation and cooperation, both with individual third countries and in multilateral fora. There is therefore a linguistic irony in the fact that Justice and Home Affairs issues are far from being confined within the borders of the enlarged EU. Enlargement itself has been a major exercise for the Union and the Commission. It is an unfinished process, both in the sense that there are other countries to follow and that, for the new Member States, there are transitional provisions, especially relating to migration. The speed with which the Union embraced working together with the United States and other countries clearly illustrates the salient and rapidly expanding external dimension of JHA. To facilitate trans-national cooperation in Justice and Home Affairs, a Commission official from DG JHA was appointed to the Commission's Delegation in Washington in 2003; similarly, a senior official in the US embassy to the EU in Brussels focussed full time on EU JHA develop-ments (Winard 2004). Transatlantic cooperation has been 'extremely positive', with Commission officials in regular contact with their counterparts at the Homeland Security Department and the State Department. The Commission has also played an important role in negotiating an agreement with the US on air passenger data, despite resistance from the European Parliament on data protection grounds. The agreement required airlines to forward electronically to US Immigration Services an advance passenger list with passport and credit card details for checking prior to the aircraft landing on US soil. Following the London bombings in July 2005, the Council called on the Commission to put forward a proposal on airline passenger name records by October 2005.[14]

The Commission also led discussions with the Chinese government on human rights and illegal immigration from China, as well as the discussions on re-admission agreements which it had either negotiated or had a mandate to negotiate in the future.[15] To prevent money laundering, Commission offi-cials have since its inception been involved in the work of the Financial Action Task Force (FATF), an OECD organisation with primary responsibility for developing a world-wide anti-money-laundering framework. Cooperation on the financing of terrorism has been enormously improved since 9/11, achiev-ing a high degree of sophistication.[16] In cooperation agreements with third countries in general, there is now always a JHA component and there are cor-responding texts inserted in all international agreements on trade and other matters as a matter of principle.[17] Commission officials are also active in the United Nations and other international bodies, including the Global Commission on International Migration, launched by Secretary General Kofi Annan in December 2003, and in regular briefings to the UN's Counter Terrorism Committee. The Commission, together with the Counter-Terrorism Coordinator, is also encouraging the Union to continue its dialogue with rel-evant regional organisations and with its Euromed partners.[18]

Thus, after Amsterdam, JHA became mainstream activity, both within the EU and in the EU's relations with the outside world. As Fortescue put it in 2002, it 'entered the consciousness of other services that the Commission now had a new full-scale Directorate-General dealing with a new area, whose work would certainly impinge on theirs' (Fortescue 2002b). Some powerful DGs such as External Relations and Development have not only been obliged to accommodate this new policy area, but they have also tried to claim some jurisdiction over it, a fact not unnoticed by the Commission's international partners. In some instances, third countries have exploited perceived differ-ences of opinion within the Commission. Clearly, demonstrating a lack of coherence damages the Commission's negotiating position and undermines its credibility. In this regard, the Commission proposal of 11 June 2003 for a regulation establishing a programme for financial and technical assistance to third countries in the area of migration and asylum[19] was a significant advance for the Commission, for it led to enhanced inter-service cooperation, higher visibility for JHA within the Relex family and a concerted effort to make third countries aware of the harmonised nature of JHA issues within the EU.

Technology-based tools and Justice and Home Affairs

The Commission has already financed and developed two out of three major data systems to help manage aspects of border control policy: SIS and Eurodac. The Schengen Information System (SIS I)[20], which enters its second phase in 2006, allows national authorities access to data on persons and property to ensure the smooth running of open borders between Member States taking part in the Schengen Agreement. Thirteen Member States participate in SIS I, but there is only capacity for a further five, hence the need for 'SIS II'. Norway and Iceland, as part of the Nordic Group of states which already had a passport free zone prior to the accession of Sweden and Finland, also take part, as does Switzerland since its referendum on joining Schengen in June 2005. The Commission was responsible for developing SIS II, cooperating closely with Member States, the Council, the European Parliament and a Joint Supervisory Authority. It will also be in charge of its operational management, crucial for the implementation of the European Arrest Warrant and the Dublin Conventions. Finally, the Commission foresees the possibility of transferring SIS II personal data to third countries or international organisations subject to the appropriate legal instruments.[21]

In the field of asylum, the Eurodac[22] system covers the fingerprinting of asylum seekers so that multiple applications can be traced at the touch of a button. All Member States are members of the system, as again are Norway and Iceland. The separate Visa Information System (VIS), on which the principles were adopted by the Council in February 2004, involves the exchange of data on visa applications aimed at helping consular authorities fight fraud, facilitate checks by carriers (especially for airlines), prevent 'visa shopping', facilitate the administration of the 'Dublin 2' regulation on countries of first asylum, and help identify undocumented persons. The Commission's Communication on enhanced interaction between the SIS II, Eurodac and the VIS and a proposal for law enforcement access to the VIS were due by November 2005.[23]

Clearly, Justice and Home Affairs is a complex policy area. Efficient policy-making must rely on unambiguous data and policy monitoring. A report by the Migration Policy Unit at University College London was commissioned in 1996 to report to the Commission on the requirements for information in the field of migration (Salt 1998). The report highlighted the need for accessible data for policy makers. It subsequently led to the creation of a network of the majority of Member States, not only for the exchange of data but also for its analysis. The network is not managed by the Commission, but the Commission did choose the management institute and forms one of its hubs. By providing greater clarity in the field, the Commission thus contributed to output. Similarly, because of its technical nature, the Commission now chairs a committee for the exchange of information between Member States on asylum trends. Known as Eurasil, its task was previously undertaken in the Council framework.

All these sophisticated instruments require a high degree of expertise in computer operations for which the Commission has engaged personnel and set up a specialised unit. The Commission is thereby becoming the focal point of a technological revolution in control of the movement of persons potentially in breach of either Member States' or EU legislation. As discussed below, use of these technologies clearly calls for adequate provisions to uphold civil liberties, for which the Commission is preparing new rules and administrative arrangements on data protection principles in the field of law enforcement at the request of the extraordinary JHA European Council in July 2005.

The Commission's evolving administrative structures for JHA

As with EPC, some administrative and management changes were made to match expanding policy commitments. In 1995, the Commission set up a Task Force on Justice and Home Affairs consisting of some twenty officials within the Secretariat General (SecGen), de facto as a largely autonomous group. The custom of placing a new policy area such as this in the SecGen is more than just symbolic. The SecGen is the nerve centre of the Commission and the funnel through which proposals pass. Although it is placed under the direct authority of the President of the Commission, in the case of JHA between 1995 and 1999, the new Task Force reported to the Swedish Commissioner, Anita Gradin, rather than to the Secretary General or to the Commission President. Gradin was responsible for progressively garnering the confidence of the Member States, though the SecGen provided the administrative strength on which to build the new responsibilities (Nilsson 2004, 124).

In May 1999, the entry into force of the Treaty of Amsterdam transformed the Task Force on Justice and Home Affairs into a fully-fledged Directorate General of the Commission under the Portuguese Commissioner Antonio Vitorino. The establishment of the new DG was amply justified by the scope of the new Treaty. Amsterdam recognised that the model for JHA should not be a carbon copy of the other intergovernmental arm of the Union, the Common Foreign and Security Policy. If the new policy area were to be effective, it would need different instruments – directives (in JHA 'framework decisions') and not simply the joint actions that had been a feature of both policy areas in the Maastricht framework. In addition, it would need more staff. Increased Commission responsibilities justified Vitorino's call to the Council to allocate 250 posts to JHA, a substantial increase over what had become 70 officials in the Task Force. In practice, it took two years to reach even 220, despite Heads of State and Government making it clear that JHA would become a major new area of activity and the workload having tripled by then (Fortescue 2002b). Whether this can be attributed to the reluctance of the Council in general to increase the budgetary allocation for posts or the internal wrangling in the Commission over job allocations is difficult to tell. While Fortescue (2002a) was content that 'money became available', in the Byzantine workings of the Commission, 'money' did not mean human resources, and an almost skeleton staff was obliged to shoulder the considerable new responsibilities; a fact which lead to substantial frustration and left some important tasks undone or placed on the back burner. In mid-2003, DG JHA changed its structure to four Directorates (up from the original three) involving 17 policy units.[24] Yet, DG 'Justice, Freedom and Security', as it is now called, actually remained one of the smallest DGs, numbering only 328 officials even in 2005.

Future perspectives: the Constitutional Treaty and the evolving nature of the Commission's role in JHA policies

Maastricht and Amsterdam clearly constituted tentative steps in the direction of creating genuine Union JHA policies, but the drafting of the Constitutional Treaty provided confirmation that the problems which confront Member States are considered so daunting that recourse to the supranational approach of the Community method was essential, notwithstanding the marked reluctance of the UK and Ireland to participate in instruments relating to external borders, asylum and immigration, using opt-in provisions (mainly for asylum issues) only when they seemed to their advantage. Yet, the cause of further integrated policy in JHA has been well served over the years. The Commission long argued that one of the most important aspects of a European Constitution would be the abolition of the 'pillar' structure and the extension of the Community method to the full range of JHA matters. The pillar structure was hailed as a great triumph, heralding the creation of the European Union to replace the European Community. Despite its commitment to intergovernmentalism, it did allow the measured development of a less intergovernmental approach to JHA over a period of twelve years during which the Commission promoted the JHA agenda, the Community method and its own prerogatives at the same time.[25]

The new Financial Perspectives proposed in 2005 should give a substantial boost to the funding of JHA activities, not least in its external dimension. The budgetary authority had already allocated €250 million over a five year period to external actions relating to migration and third countries, almost a threefold increase over the previous pilot programmes. JHA funding is likely to surpass a billion euros in the multi-annual budgeting 2007-2013, *pace* the fraught discussions on the structure of the EU's budget. This will raise the Commission's international profile since it manages the funds. Comparison with the initial phases of the Task Force in 1994 is striking; officials then had to persuade other departments to allocate small amounts for JHA issues from their own funds.

The Commission's role, of course, is not confined to migration issues. It also runs the Vienna-based European Monitoring Centre on Racism and Xenophobia set up in 1998[26] and the European Drugs and Drug Addiction Monitoring Centre in Lisbon, established in 1994.[27] In each of these fields, it plays a vital part in the analysis of the technical and legal information required for informed policy making at the European level. In addition, the Commission's role in the 'scoreboard' was crucial. The Tampere scoreboard was produced by the Commission for four years of the five-year programme laid down in Amsterdam. It reinforced both the Commission's watchdog role and its right of initiative, and it gave the Commission considerable leverage, by regularly highlighting failures and successes.[28] Member States and interested NGOs knew exactly where responsibility lay for lack of progress – the former through participation in Council working groups and the latter via their extensive lobbying. As a result, Member States and NGOs now increasingly turn to the Commission to find solutions to tricky political issues, and the Commission representative is a key member of the JHA Counsellors' Group, a Council forum for preparing the senior Council working groups that report to the JHA ministers via the hierarchical chain of Council meetings.[29]

Generally speaking, in European affairs, the more complex issues become, the more the Member States turn to the Commission for advice and information.

The Tampere and Hague documents were the precursors of the ill-fated Constitutional Treaty of which Article III-258 indicates that the European Council 'shall define the strategic guidelines and operational planning within the area of freedom, security and justice'. Importantly, if the Constitution were implemented, the three-pillar system would disappear. There would thus be no need to adopt parallel legislative acts under each pillar when cross-cutting policies are made law, such as in areas of money-laundering, freezing terrorists' bank accounts or illicit trafficking in firearms, where UN decisions lead to obligations in terms of EC legislation. The JHA elements of the Constitutional Treaty were prepared by a working group on JHA in the Convention chaired by the current Head of the Commission Delegation in Washington and former Irish Prime Minister, John Bruton. Though the working group swiftly concluded that most of the relevant areas (visas, asylum, judicial cooperation, and immigration) had already been 'communitarised', they also swiftly realised that unanimity remained the stumbling block to further progress, and proposed extension of the Community method and co-decision with the European Parliament. Police and judicial cooperation were two areas where communitarisation could go further by extending to it decision-making by qualified majority vote (QMV). Yet, the end of pure inter-governmentalism in JHA had not yet been reached. The final version of the draft Constitution did opt for QMV, but it retained the 'Luxembourg Compromise' principle of resort to a veto for states believing their vital interests to be at stake. By a process known as the 'brake/accelerator', states in a minority could not be outvoted, but they were to be committed to allowing 'enhanced cooperation' so as not to impede the others (Milton and Keller-Noëllet 2005, 104).

Although largely related to the jurisdiction of the European Court of Justice and not the Commission, two important innovations to the draft Constitution were the incorporation for the first time of the Charter of Fundamental Rights into an EU Treaty, making it binding as opposed to advisory, and the incorporation of the European Convention on Human Rights of the Council of Europe.[30] If the Constitution were ratified, this would place new responsibilities on the Commission as legal watchdog. Likewise, in terms of management of JHA affairs, the Treaty would have set up a standing committee to ensure internal security. While there was no specific mention of the Commission's role in the relevant article (III-261), the Constitutional Treaty does mention 'Union agencies and bodies', and it may be safely assumed that the Commission would, if the Constitutional provisions were implemented, again assume its role of Treaty watchdog.

The Constitutional Treaty also reiterated the basic principle of free movement of persons, including the absence of border controls on both Union and non-Union citizens at internal frontiers. In addition, it envisaged the gradual introduction of integrated border management, a counterpart to the cementing of free movement into the Constitution in that management of external borders needs to be assured, not merely reinforced. The 2004 enlargement, and the associated fears relating to access from the successor states to the Soviet Union and the facilitation of illegal migration, gave rise to new policy elements in the field of immigration policy. Given the enormous difficulty faced by the Commission regarding the failure to pass the draft directive on admission of migrants for employment and self-employment (Commission 2001d), this was no easy task. This draft directive was meticulously prepared by the Commission over a period of eighteen months with a lengthy consultation procedure, including public meetings to gauge opinion in the media, non-governmental organisations, academia and trade unions. The Commission consulted widely on the immigration issue in late 2004 and produced a further Communication by the end of the year.[31] On the substance of the clause on immigration policy, the language of the Constitutional Treaty was more explicit than its immediate predecessor instrument Article 63 (3) of the Amsterdam Treaty. In particular, in order to allay fears on the part of Member States that immigration quotas might be imposed by 'Brussels', Article III-267 paragraph 5 explicitly stated that the Member States would retain the right to determine volumes of admission of third country nationals. The Commission's role was to propose European laws or framework laws for common rules and to guide rather than impose.

In the implementation phase and in contrast with the Treaty of Amsterdam, the Constitutional Treaty outlined an unusual formulation for proposing legislation (Article III-264). Either the Commission or one quarter of the Member States could make proposals to the Council. Based on the experience of Amsterdam, it is likely that the majority of initiatives would have come from the Commission. It would currently have needed seven Member States to fulfil the requirements of Article III-264, and the Commission would undoubtedly have been informed well in advance of any such initiative. It is thus likely that it would have taken over the initiative or at least have been consulted before any concrete proposal were put to the Council, and would thus continue to play its traditional motor role. With the exception of judicial cooperation in criminal matters (Articles III-274, III-275 and III-277) and family law (Article III-269 paragraph 3), qualified majority voting was to apply in the Council.[32] Criminal justice and family law would require a unanimous vote, thus retaining a vestige of the former Third Pillar arrangements.

Conclusion

This chapter has outlined how the Commission demonstrated its commitment to its JHA mission. It consulted widely on the issues arising before Tampere and before The Hague. It published official Communications and discussion papers and held public debates before drafting legislation. And it did all this with minimal staffing, yet fully respecting the Amsterdam schedule and the guidelines of the European Council in Tampere. The agreement to the Hague Programme reached at the European Council of 4-5 November 2004, demonstrated that EU instruments and policies were now viewed positively by Member States, and the Commission was clearly a key component in this success. Armed with the tools mooted in the Constitution, the Commission would have been equipped to deliver more of what the public seems to desire in the field. JHA policies are highly visible and despite the brickbats, this chapter has shown how the Commission is the main architect of EU action. While the Commission will doubtless continue to be constrained to tussle with the awkwardness of intergovernmentalism, and this the more so since the hiatus caused by the breakdown in the process of ratification of the Constitution, the most important constraint is avoiding the risk of further disaffection of a public hitherto purportedly committed to Europeanisation of policy in this politically contested area.

Endnotes

[1] After the appointment of the new Commission in November 2004, the Directorate General for Justice and Home Affairs was renamed 'Justice, Freedom and Security', and given the acronym JLS.

[2] COM(94) 23, 23 Feb. 1994.

[3] For a summary of Europol's history, see Ahnfelt and From (2001).

[4] Since 1 January 2005, QMV and co-decision have been applied except for economic migration. Council Decision 2004/927/EC, 22 December 2004 (OJ L 396/45, 31 December 2004).

[5] Communication on an 'Area of Freedom, Security and Justice: Assessment of the Tampere Programme and Future Orientations', COM (2004) 401 final, 2 June 2004. The Commission Staff Working Document SEC (2004) 680 contains a list of the most important instruments adopted in the Tampere framework.

[6] For the relevant surveys see 'Eurobarometer 63: Public Opinion in the European Union (First Results)', DG PRESS, European Commission, July 2005.

[7] On the relationship between JHA policies, civil liberties and effective human rights protection see Dickson (2005), Amnesty International (2005), Warbrick (2004), Bunyan (2002) and Monar (2003).

[8] Communication on a 'More Efficient European Asylum System: The Single Procedure as the Next Step', COM (2004) 503 final, 15 July 2004.

[9] Note from the Presidency to Coreper/Council, 11122/04 of 9 July 2004.

[10] 'The Hague programme – Strengthening Freedom, Security and Justice', Presidency Conclusions Council Document 14292/04 Annex 1.

[11] COM (2005) 184 final.

[12] Commission Press Release IP/05/970, 'Schengen Area – The Commission Proposes to Facilitate Cross Border Surveillance and "Hot Pursuit" between Member States', Brussels, 19 July 2005.

[13] COM (2005) 329 final, 18 July 2005.

[14] Council of the European Union, 'Press Release of Extraordinary JHA Council Meeting', 13 July 2005.

[15] Readmission agreements are agreements with third countries for their citizens to be returned if their presence on the territory of the EU is unlawful.

[16] Note to the European Council, 16-17 June 2005. Submitted by the Presidency and the EU Counter-Terrorism Co-ordinator.

[17] This was also the case for the negotiations on the transit arrangements through EU territory for citizens of Kaliningrad.

[18] Global Commission on International Migration; Migration in an international world; New directions for action, Geneva 2005; Note to the European Council, 16-17 June 2005. Submitted by the Presidency and the EU Counter-Terrorism Co-ordinator.

[19] Communication on 'Integrating Migration Issues into the EU's External Relations', COM (2003) 355.

[20] Communication on the 'Development of the Schengen Information System II', COM (2001) 720 final.

[21] See the proposal for a Council Decision on the establishment, operation and use of the second generation Schengen information system (SIS II) presented by the Commission on 31 May 2005 (COM(2005) 230 final).

[22] Regulation 2725/ 2000. In 2004, Eurodac processed 232,205 fingerprints of asylum seekers, 16,183 fingerprints of people crossing the borders irregularly and 39,550 fingerprints of people apprehended while illegally on the territory of a Member State. Figures show that in 2004, the number of asylum applications has decreased while the number of registered irregular entrants has increased. The number of checks of illegally present persons has also more than doubled in 2004, see Commission press release 05/214, 21 June 2005.

[23] Council of the European Union, 'Press Release of Extraordinary JHA Council Meeting', 13 July 2005.

[24] The directorates are A: General Affairs, B: Immigration, Asylum and Borders, C: Civil Justice, Rights and Citizenship, and D: Internal Security and Criminal Justice.

[25] For an overview of the Commission's 'shy' approach at the very beginning of cooperation in the field of JHA, see Monar (1994, 69-75) and Nilsson (2004, 136).

[26] Established by Council Regulation 1035/97. It is currently in the process of being transformed into the EU Agency for Fundamental Rights (EP Resolution 26 May 2005).

[27] Established by Council Regulation 302/93.

[28] see http://europa.eu.int/comm/justice_home/doc_centre/scoreboard_en.htm for the link to scoreboard.

[29] For further details on the JHA Counsellors' Group, see Nilsson (2004).

[30] Title II article 1-9

[31] Commission Green Paper COM(2004) 811, 11 January 2005.

[32] The importance of QMV for the effectiveness of the decision-making process in the JHA Council is underlined by Nilsson (2004).

12. The Commission and external relations

Michael Smith

Introduction

The European Community[1] (EC) was from its inception an international phenomenon, and the development of a complex set of external relations has been an integral part of its evolution. Many authors have attributed a major role in the establishment of the Community both to general international conditions such as the Cold War and the Bretton Woods system, and to specific international forces: American foreign policy being the prime example (Milward 1984; Smith 1992, 1999, 2000a). Since its foundation, the Community in its various guises has assumed an ever-growing weight in the world economy, and has become a participant in a wide range of international economic institutions. Indeed, the very existence of the Community has become a central element in the policy concerns of most countries in the international arena. There is a great deal of *prima facie* evidence, therefore, that external relations are an inevitable and growing part of the Community's existence, and that this in turn is a central part of the international life of the European Union (EU). It can be argued that they played a central role in the generation of pressure for the 1992 programme for completion of the single market and the later introduction of the euro, and they are intimately related to the development of 'internal' policy areas such as agriculture, competition policy and transport.

From this initial observation flows a number of more specific issues and problems, many of them directly linked to the role of the Commission as a source of and channel for policy. Although the Treaty of Paris setting up the ECSC contained no explicit Community role in the external field, reserving that domain for the Member States (Kaptein and van Themat 1990), the Treaty of Rome not only made such provision but also gave the Commission a pivotal function (Eeckhout 2004, chapter 2). Successive policy developments and treaties, especially those of the 1990s, beginning with the agreements reached at Maastricht in 1991 and leading to the Nice Treaty of 2000, have confirmed the role of the Commission, but have also raised a number of enduring questions about its relationship both to other Community institutions and to the outside world (Devuyst 1992; Fielding 1991; Meunier 1999; Meunier and Nicolaides 2000; Nugent and Saurugger 2002).

Many of the problems faced by the Commission in the pursuit of external relations are effectively 'boundary problems'. The development of complex linkages in the world economy has made it quite difficult for even the most monolithic of states to say where 'domestic' policy ends and 'external' policy begins. A related problem is that of the boundary between economic issues and political or security issues. In the post-Cold War era and the age of globalisation, it is no longer clear (if indeed it ever were) how this line can be drawn and maintained. As a result, external relations issues increasingly cut across sectors and raise unexpected problems of coordination or action (Smith and Woolcock 1993, 1999; Smith 2001). This is as true for the European Union as it is for the Member States, but in addition to these broad problems of international life in the 1990s and 2000s, the Commission and the Community have a number of other boundary issues with which to contend. The first is the question of competence. Where does the writ of the Commission run, and how are disputes or tensions between the Commission and Member States handled? Closely related to this question is that of institutions. How are the potentially competing interests of the Commission, the Council, Parliament and the Court of Justice to be reconciled in the cause of coherent Community external action? Even within the Commission itself, any clear allocation of policy areas, with DG Trade (formerly DG I) holding the key responsibilities for all external economic relations matters, is challenged by the linkages between sectors and interests.

As chapter 14 describes in more detail, one result of these boundary problems has been the constant re-shaping of the Commission's external relations machinery during the post-Cold War period. The Delors Commission of 1993-95 saw the re-drawing of responsibilities with the creation of DG IA, responsible for external *political* relations, including responsibility for the external delegations. The Santer Commission between 1995 and 1999 undertook further reform, reorganising responsibilities for external economic relations on a geographical basis between DG I, DG IA and DG 18, with all the problems of coordination that such divisions posed. DG IA, however, continued to cover political relations. In the reformed Prodi Commission that emerged after the crisis of 1999, there was a further re-configuration, with what operated in some respects as a 'lead Commissioner' for External Relations (Chris Patten) accompanied by Commissioners for Enlargement (Gunter Verheugen), Development and Humanitarian Aid (Poul Nielsen) and Trade (Pascal Lamy) (Peterson 2002). The changing nature of the international arena has thus been reflected in the re-drawing of internal organisational boundaries, and as a corollary the increasing linkages between the economic and the political have drawn the Commission inexorably into more political areas, where tensions between Union and Member State policies surface more easily and where external relations and foreign policy are very closely in contact – not to mention tensions between Commission DGs and between the Commission and the Council.

This chapter explores the ways in which these developments have modified both the role of the Commission and its relations with other EU institutions and the Member States. It begins by exploring in more detail the foundations for external policy laid in the Treaty of Rome and its successors and the resulting administrative structures in the Commission. Secondly, it identifies the key elements in policy formation and the ways in which the Commission carries out its responsibilities alongside other EU bodies.

Thirdly, it looks at the substance of policy and Commission involvement in a number of issue areas and institutional contexts. Fourthly, it examines the changes in external relations and in the agenda for Union action, which have produced new challenges in the new millennium, including those of enlargement and global governance. Finally, it assesses the ways in which the structure and roles of the Commission might be further adapted to face the changing context and demands of the new agenda, with particular reference to the Constitutional Treaty.

The legal and institutional foundations of Commission responsibility for external relations

The Treaty of Rome gave a central role in external relations to the Commission. Under the Treaty establishing the European Community, Member States of the European Union transferred certain competences to the European Community. In areas of exclusive Community competence, Member States are no longer entitled to negotiate and undertake, individually or collectively, international obligations. However, in areas of shared competence, the European Community and the Member States may both become parties to an international convention, but have a duty to coordinate their positions. For the European Community, the European Commission negotiates on the basis of negotiating directives adopted by the Council of the European Union. It follows from Article 300 (1) of the Treaty, that the European Community cannot be represented by the Presidency of the Council of the European Union during such negotiations. So, it is legally impossible to incorporate the Commission into the delegation of the respective Member State holding the Presidency of the Council, as Presidencies often wish.

Several Community competences, both exclusive and shared, are concerned, for example, in the provisions of the draft UNESCO Convention. For instance, the provisions in Articles 12 and 17 concerning the facilitation of access to global markets for cultural goods and services from developing countries touch upon the Community's exclusive competence to conduct the Common Commercial Policy (Article 133 EC). Other provisions relate to subject matters for which the competences are shared between the Community and the Member States. Examples are Articles 4.4.c, 7.2.b and 19 of the draft Convention which relate to EC competences regarding intellectual property (Article 95 EC), Art 6 of the draft Convention relating to competition policy (Articles 81 et seq. EC) and the free circulation and mobility of artists and creators under Article 12 of the draft Convention.

UNESCO is but one example of the complexity of issues arising in a discussion of who represents the EC or the EU. Problems also arise, for example, in terms of the representation of EC interests and competence in the framework of the Geneva-based Conference on Disarmament, where issues concerning export controls or safety standards for the transport and handling of toxic materials also give rise to questions as to how, institutionally, the Commission can get the EC point across in fora where it has no membership status and is not, by definition, a 'State Party' to a convention. Again, the World Conference on Disaster Relief in Kobe in 2005 saw the Commission struggling for a right to full participation against large non-EU parties to the conference. On the one hand, granting the status of a full participant in the negotiations of a conference is different from membership, particularly where the Community would not enjoy an additional vote. But, on the other hand, and seen from outside the EU, an extra voice might imply extra political weight. Of course, the EC decides in internal coordination whether the Presidency of the Council will speak on an issue, on behalf of the Member States, or whether the Commission will speak on behalf of the Community and the Member States, but it cannot decide how international organisations will rule on the representation issue. This is the crux of the representation issue. Other UN specialised organisations have faced similar situations. In the WHO, also only open to membership by States Parties, the negotiations for the Framework Convention on Tobacco Control were opened to full participation by the European Community (under the wording of a "regional economic integration organisation") by a resolution of the World Health Assembly in 1999. After successful negotiations, the Framework Convention was ratified by the European Community in June 2003, whereas full ratifications by the individual Member States were still underway in 2005. Similarly, the WHO Assembly allowed full participation of the Community for the revision of the International Health Regulations (legally binding standards) in 2003.

The most important area in terms of Community business is trade. The Treaty conferred express powers in the area of Common Commercial Policy (CCP) in Articles 113-114 EEC in conjunction with Article 228 (Devuyst 1992; Fielding 1991; Macleod *et al.* 1996; Young 2000; Eeckhout 2004). Here, the Commission, in principle, had exclusive competence for an area of policy which arose directly from the creation of a customs union and the operation of the Common External Tariff. However, as noted above and as will be seen later, by the 1990s, it was increasingly unclear how the boundaries around the Common Commercial Policy could be drawn or maintained. Although the European Coal and Steel Community (1951) had a number of international implications, particularly in terms of the trade in steel, there was no explicit treatment of policy-making for external relations at Community level in the Treaty of Paris. Over the history of the Community as a whole, this gap in the Treaty of Paris caused a number of uncertainties, not least because of the sensitive nature of industrial policy and competition policy and their growing international ramifications (Meny and Wright 1987)[2]. Thus, it was with the Treaty of Rome that the elaboration of a framework for external policy was undertaken in a conscious and systematic fashion. The core of the Treaty as it affects external relations was to be found in Articles 110-116, which set out the principles of the CCP and some of the mechanisms through which it is to be conducted (Devuyst 1992; Nicoll and Salmon 1992; Eeckhout 2004). Though the Treaty on European Union (TEU) and other treaties of the 1990s made some amendments, and there have been consistent debates about the expanding scope of the Commission's role, the core principles remain the same.

As Devuyst says, 'The Common Commercial Policy is the logical corollary of the customs union set up by the EEC Treaty' (1992, 68; see also Macleod *et al.* 1996; Eeckhout 2004). The establishment of a common external tariff, and thus of a boundary between the internal free trade area and the external world, necessitates common approaches among the members to the issue of international trade, and the development of instruments with which to pursue and defend Community interests. In the case of the EEC, the establishment of the Common Commercial Policy was accompanied by another logical but not self-evident step: the allocation of competence to the European Commission, and the understanding that in matters affecting the CCP this competence was to be exclusive. From the outset, therefore, the Commission was given the power to conduct a common policy, but, while the assumption was that of exclusive competence, there were other aspects of the Treaty which were bound to make this a source of tension and potential conflict (Devuyst 1992; Fielding 1991; Eeckhout 2004).

Articles 110-116 of the EEC Treaty set out both the broad goals of the CCP and a number of specific provisions. It is important to note that the aims set out in Article 110 were cast at least partly in terms not of Community interests, but of those of the international economy as a whole. Thus the Community set out not only to express the external needs of its members, but also: '...to contribute, in the common interest, to the harmonious development of world trade, the progressive abolition of restrictions on international trade and the lowering of customs barriers.' In pursuit of these aims, it was clear that the Community's 'internal' policies could come into conflict with its actual or potential international obligations. As a result, balancing the internal needs of the Community and the demands of the external world has always been a central task facing the Commission in external relations (see below). It has thus been argued that the very foundations of the EEC contained a fault line which was to create considerable difficulty for the Commission (Taylor 1983).

A number of articles in the Treaty of Rome, such as Article 111, dealt with actions to be taken during the transitional period before the establishment of the full customs union, and they withered away as time passed. The Treaty on European Union formally eliminated a number of them. Central to the whole edifice of the CCP, though, was Article 113 (Article 133 in the consolidated Treaties that resulted from the Amsterdam IGC and came into force in the late 1990s). This committed the signatories to the elaboration of common principles for trade policy and included a (non-exhaustive) list of actions and issues covered by the CCP. It was also in this article that the competence of the Commission was firmly established, alongside provisions for qualified majority voting in the Council in the CCP area and the arrangements enabling the Commission to take on a major international negotiating role, for example in the General Agreement on Tariffs and Trade (GATT) (along with Article 229). The strength of the grant of competence, allied to a certain vagueness about the range of commercial policy areas in which it was to be exercised, has proven a major boon to the Commission as an international actor and 'policy entrepreneur'. But it has also led to tensions with the Council of Ministers and with individual Member States, the legacy of which is still visible even in 2005.

While Article 113 (133) was thus the centrepiece of the external relations pursued by the Community, it was supplemented (some would say, qualified) by Article 115, which provided for action to be taken where economic difficulties arose for one or more Member States. Initially, during the transitional period, it also allowed member governments within the Community to take action to protect themselves in cases of emergency. (This was amended under the TEU, whereby governments are to seek authorisation from the Commission to take such action.) Article 116 of the Treaty of Rome further committed the parties to common action in the framework of international economic institutions as they affected the common market and the customs union. (This was repealed by the TEU.) But it was Article 113 (133) which mattered, and on which the Commission erected a complex web of international commercial diplomacy.

A number of other articles in the Treaty of Rome bore on the conduct of external relations under what is known as 'implied powers' – areas where internal competence serves as a basis for external competence. Thus, Article 228 (now with revisions Article 300 EC) gave the Community the general competence to conclude international agreements, including commercial agreements. Other articles, such as those on the common transport policy (original Articles 74-84 EEC), appeared to confer the capacity to negotiate internationally, and to arrive at regulatory agreements on the basis of Community action, although the full implications of this in areas such as air transport were not realised until the turn of the millennium. There was some uncertainty in these cases, though, about the precise extent of Commission competence. It was not clear whether the essentially internal concerns of the common market could give rise to external competences comparable to those explicitly conferred by Article 113 (133). The question of 'implied competence' has not been eliminated with the passage of time. Indeed, the development of ever more intense linkages between internal and external issues relating to the Community has given rise to further uncertainties in areas such as competition law or transport policy (Close 1990; CMLR 1990; Kaptein and van Themat 1990; Cini and McGowan 1999).

The principle according to which external competence arises from internal competence is based on a ruling of the European Court of Justice in case 22/70, *Commission v. Council* (1971) ECR 263 on the European Road Transport Agreement (ERTA). Here, the Court held that treaty-making powers were not confined to the issues covered by Articles 113 (133) and 228 (300). It held that there were implied powers to conclude treaties with third countries, which 'may flow from other provisions of the Treaty and from steps taken, within the framework of these provisions, by the Community institutions'. Thus, where common rules affecting internal policies were laid down, the Member States no longer had the right to conclude treaties with non-Member States.

The judgement has given rise to some tension between the Commission and some Member States who wished to restrict the definition of 'common rules' to areas where binding Community legislation exists, as opposed to the non-binding instruments of Council declarations, resolutions and recommendations often used in such fields as health, culture and education. The Commission traditionally had a more relaxed – or expansive – view of the potential scope of implied powers, and it was a moot point whether the Court would uphold the Commission's or, say, the UK's or France's view on the matter. The problem has been that the Community clearly has competence if there is an indisputable set of internal rules in an area which becomes subject to a Community treaty with a third party. But there are preliminary forms of agreement, for example, in negotiating mandates (discussed below), where the law is unclear as to how binding an agreed policy line becomes in terms of its limitation of an individual state's ability to diverge from an agreed Community position before negotiations with third parties are actually concluded. The apparent breaking of ranks by the French government in the final stage of negotiations in the GATT in 1993 is a case in point (Coleman and

Tangermann 1999). It is, of course, different if there is no agreed Community line. When, for example, the Council has not yet taken a decision on a Commission proposal for a negotiating mandate, there is arguably no binding obligation on the Member States to depart from their own national position. If, however, Member States conduct negotiations or enter into agreements properly within the competence of the Community, which could inhibit or prejudice future Community action in a given field, there may be a case for recourse to the Court for a ruling under Article 228 (300) or, at the very least grounds for a Commission proposal for a Community negotiating mandate in that area. The room for debate about the Commission's rights and obligations in this area is thus considerable.

An important area of 'express powers' in which external relations formed part of the Treaty of Rome was that of associations between the Community and third states or with international organisations. Article 238 (now article 310 EC) has been used as the basis for the development of a wide-ranging network of treaties and cooperative ventures. Among these, the most salient are those concerning the African, Caribbean and Pacific countries in the context of the Lomé Conventions (since 2000 the Cotonou Convention); the EFTA countries (i.e. those that remain outside the European Union after the enlargement of 1995); a number of Mediterranean countries; and the countries of Eastern and Central Europe (most of them now Member States after the 2004 enlargement), particularly in the years immediately following the break-up of the Soviet bloc in the early 1990s. In a broad sense also, the Community provisions for enlargement and the admission of new members can be seen as a form of external relations power. But it must be noted that in neither of these areas (association and enlargement) is the Commission given exclusive competence. While its 'opinion' is the start of the legislative process for enlargement, and the Commission can propose action and provide opinions and information in these areas, the essential powers lie with the Member States acting in the Council of the Union. Action in respect of external associations has also given rise to a wide range of 'mixed agreements', in which the negotiation and the implementation of international accords are subject to both Commission and Member State participation (Kaptein and van Themat 1990; Neuwahl 1990; Macleod et al. 1996; Eeckhout 2004).

'Mixed agreements' occur where the subject matter of an international agreement falls partly within Member State and partly within Community competence. Here, both the Community and the Member States are signatories to agreements. The Commission's view has been that such mixed agreements do not adequately assert the Community's identity, but the European Court has not always supported the Commission. Its Ruling 1/78 (IAEA Physical Protection Convention (1978) ECR 2151) and its Opinion 1/78 (Rubber Agreement (1979) ECR 2871) confirmed the validity of mixed agreements, particularly where individual states provide finance in the framework of such agreements. The Commission and the Member States therefore agreed in this context to suspend judgement on competence on commodity agreements within the UNCTAD Integrated Programme of Commodities and for Community representations with regard to customs arrangements and negotiations within the OECD on accounting standards. Both the Community and the Member States are signatories to these and other similar agreements.

The important point here is not so much the apparent ambiguity in areas of mixed competence as the ways in which this reveals potential sources of tension over boundary disputes between the Commission and the Member States. Community competence is not a static concept. As the European Union gains competence in new areas, as it did in health, environment, culture and education under the TEU, so the scope for Commission responsibility is expanded; its role in external relations as representative of the Community interest and as negotiator in international treaties is extended and enhanced.

To put flesh on the bones of Article 113 (133) and other grants of competence, as it grew the Community acquired a complex set of trade policy instruments. The most notable among these are anti-dumping measures, rules of origin, including such provisions as those on 'local content', and instruments designed to counteract unfair trading practices (Eeckhout 2004: chapter 10). Clearly, the growth and integration of the Community market, and the stakes attached to access to that market, have necessitated defensive measures. At times, these have led to accusations of 'Fortress Europe' policies, particularly from the USA and Japan in the early 1990s and from a range of developing countries, but it is not clear that EC policies have been any more or less restrictive than those of other major industrial trading areas. From the point of view of this chapter, the key factor is that these regulatory and other instruments emanate from the essential grant of trade policy competence to the Commission, and thus are administered by it.

In order to back up its actions and to sustain its capacity to exercise the competence granted to it, the Commission has developed a substantial bureaucratic and diplomatic machinery. In Brussels, the key focus until the reforms of the Santer Commission was DG I (External Economic Relations), which had the lead responsibility for economic relations with non-EU countries. Internally, DG I was structured in accordance with the main concerns of the CCP, although in 1993, there were significant structural changes following the bifurcation of economic and political responsibilities in external relations and an increase from one to two Commissioners. Further changes in 1995 under the Santer Commission increased the number of Commissioners to three (see annex C and also chapter 14), whilst the Prodi reforms after 1999 established a 'team' of external relations Commissioners and DGs nominally headed by Chris Patten as Commissioner for External Relations (and head of DG RELEX). As is the case in many a national foreign ministry, there are both geographical and functional sub-divisions within the broad organisational structure, with particular sections established to handle major international negotiations.

Despite the formal divisions within the structure, the interpenetration of external and internal policy concerns has meant that almost every part of the Commission has an interest in external policy of some kind. In addition, action taken for what appear to be purely internal purposes can have important external policy ramifications. In recent years, the development both of the world economy and of the European internal market has magnified this tendency. The role of DG I and its successors in internal coordination and the achievement of coherent external policy therefore grew apace, and was formalised in the Prodi reforms. As early as 1986, the Single European Act had explicitly provided, as did the TEU and all subsequent treaties, for the maintenance of consistency between different areas of EU activity. External relations is the area par excellence in which this is a central need. In some areas the status of DG I (and now DGs RELEX and particularly Trade) can be likened to that of the US Trade Representative (USTR) in Washington, trying to coordinate and moderate the needs and interests of powerful internal baronies without possessing a great deal of coercive power (Destler 1992). But guaranteeing consistency is not easy. This was recognised by President Santer, who established a more formal coordination procedure among the Commissioners responsible, this being formalised in the coordination arrangements set up after the Prodi reforms. Similar groups have been set up at Director General level to ensure consistency among senior officials' actions and those of their subordinates.

Outside the Community, from the 1970s to the 1990s, DG I developed an extensive mechanism of international representation and reporting, responsibility for which was then transferred to DG IA and later (under the Prodi Commission) to DG RELEX. While some of this relates to specific negotiations and has a temporary air – even when the negotiations extend over a period of some years – there is now an elaborate permanent network reminiscent of many a country's diplomatic service, and there are moves to consolidate matters such as training and human resources development which imply a real sense of institutionalisation. Indeed, as chapter 15 discusses in detail, Commission Delegations in overseas capitals have a formal status akin to embassies, not least in Washington and Tokyo. Other missions are accredited to international organisations such as the OECD, the GATT (since 1995, the World Trade Organisation or WTO) or the UN, where they play an important continuous negotiation role as well as that of representation. Equally important are the many diplomatic missions accredited to the Community (effectively the Commission) itself. By the mid-1990s, there were over 100 of these, and their presence produced a diplomatic network supplementary to, and often replacing, the traditional inter-state network. No clearer indication of the latter trend could be found than the displacement in mid-1993 of the British Ambassador to Belgium from his official elegant residence in central Brussels by the UK Permanent Representative (Ambassador) to the EC. Further evidence of this growth of new diplomatic networks affecting Commission Delegations can be found, for example, in the activities of the Commission Delegation in Geneva. This Delegation maintains contacts with a wide range of international organisations and non-governmental organisations; it participates in frequent EU Heads of Mission meetings, EU Troikas and EU coordination meetings at expert level – to the extent of about 1000 meetings during 2003. In addition, the Delegation often plays a significant role in the preparatory process and negotiations of major UN Conferences or Summits, not only within the framework of trade (the Doha process), but also across the board of the responsibilities of the UN family. Frequently, these activities link economic matters with social and humanitarian concerns in novel ways (see below). Nevertheless, the Delegation to the WTO absorbs more in the way of resources and Commission attention even than these wide-ranging activities imply.

The foundations of Commission action and mechanisms in the realm of external relations are thus not merely those that are found in the Treaties, extensive as they are. These constitutional powers are supplemented by the growth of a bureaucratic and diplomatic network and by the perceived status of the Commission as a focus of attention for outsiders, both at governmental and non-governmental levels. The Community has established a major presence in the international arena, and the Commission is central to this presence.

Policy formation and implementation

As with policy foundations, discussing the Commission's role in external policy formation requires some key distinctions. Perhaps the most important general distinction is that between the formal role of the Commission as set out in the Treaties and administrative procedures, and the informal and often highly political process by which the Commission enters the policy arena. Another important area of distinction is that between policy formation and implementation. In each case, there are several stages and contexts to be considered. As in the earlier discussion, the focus here is on the development of policy and policy-making up to the end of the 1990s, the aim being to establish a framework for later consideration of more recent changes and their implications.

Articles 110-116 of the Treaty of Rome set out not simply the competences of the Commission, but also key aspects of the procedures to be followed. As in other areas of policy, the intermingling of Commission, Council and Member State roles is typical of the external relations domain. Under Article 113 (133), the Commission makes recommendations to the Council concerning the negotiation of trade agreements and the Council then adopts a directive by qualified majority vote. This sets the mandate and the general framework for the negotiations. When the negotiations are concluded, the Commission as negotiator has the power to initial the agreement, but the Council formally 'concludes' the agreement, acting by qualified majority vote. Thus the multilateral negotiations undertaken during the Uruguay Round of the GATT saw the Commission as the sole formal negotiator for the Community, with the Member States as close supervisors both in the context of the GATT itself and in the Council. As will be seen later, this extended to the signature of the agreements themselves and to the involvement of the European Court of Justice in deciding competence.

The 'watchdog' role of Member States is particularly expressed through the 133 Committee, which constitutes a standing check on the negotiators and is, in a sense, the guardian of the negotiating mandate. This situation is not unlike the position in the USA, where Congress produces legislation to empower the Executive to negotiate, but has the right to be kept informed of the negotiations and also the ultimate power to approve or reject any deals made. It could also be argued that the result in policy formation terms is rather like that in the USA, with the constant possibility of rigidity and the difficulty of changing the mandate once it is agreed (Meunier 1998 and 1999). Clearly, this is particularly a factor in the case of long-term and large-scale negotiations, where circumstances (even Member State governments or the number of Member States itself) and the mandate may change, and where there are complex linkages between the various items on the agenda (see below).

In addition to the negotiating roles set out in, and developed under, Article 133, the Commission plays a central role in the monitoring of external policy, and in coping with commercial disputes. The two activities are often closely linked. For example, the Commission's monitoring of trade practices by other countries can lead to anti-dumping findings, to the application of measures under the rules of origin, or to claims of unfair trading practices against a variety of outsiders. Here, the role of the Commission is regulatory and at times coercive rather than persuasive. It is not surprising that its activities have sometimes drawn criticism, not only from outsiders but also from individual Member States. Rather than a general negotiating directive, the instruments of policy can be punitive duties or restrictions, imposed by the Commission though subject to approval by the Council. Perhaps the most obviously punitive or coercive measures in Community external policy are those entailed in commercial sanctions against a range of countries, often for explicitly political purposes. Here, Article 133 can again be used as the basis, although the Treaties also provide a number of other routes with less exclusive Commission competence, for example through Article 301 EC which deals with implementation of measures adopted via the CFSP, and Article 60 which focuses on financial and other measures (Eeckhout 2004: chapter 12).

Moving outside the CCP, there is a range of other policy areas in which the Commission has more or less exclusive competence, and which have external relations effects (although, as already noted, the issue of competence can be hotly debated). Many areas of common policy have inescapable external dimensions. The most dramatic, perhaps, has been the Common Agricultural Policy (CAP), which was built at least in part on the exercise of Community Preference, and thus on variable levies on imports in what has become an increasingly global world food market. From the outset, the CAP meshed uneasily with the CCP, adding a major set of constraints to the external trade policies of the Community. In relations with the USA, in particular, there has been a constant thread of conflict, which has spread to influence the multilateral trading system more generally. The Commission is deeply implicated as the guardian both of the CAP and of the CCP, but the balance has at times been very difficult to strike. Although less dramatic, the development of common policies in areas such as fisheries and air transport, and more recently competition policy, has also led to the need for Commission diplomacy and at times to intense conflict with other countries and organisations.

Outside the common policy arena, the external relations of the Community are less securely within the control of the Commission, and the mixed nature of policy and negotiation becomes apparent. From the early days of the Community, it has been possible for Member States to conclude their own treaties of economic cooperation, reflecting the fact that though the Community may act (for example under Article 228 (300)), it has no exclusive competence. In the autumn of 1993, it was reported that the Commission was anxious to extend its competence, given the persistence of bilateral cooperation agreements which could be used by Member States to circumvent Community measures. The stimulus for this pressure was the attempted evasion by Germany of sanctions imposed by the Community in a dispute with the USA over public procurement regimes (Barber and Gardner 1993). Article 228 (300), used as the basis for a wide range of economic cooperation and assistance agreements, requires the Commission and the Council to receive an opinion from the European Parliament. More specific are the provisions under Article 238 (310) for association agreements. Here, the Commission and the Member States are entangled in mixed agreements, and the Parliament has the right to give its assent by a majority vote of all its members.

It is clear from this review that the role of the Commission is determined not merely by the formal Treaty provisions but also by the nature of the issues at stake and the attitudes of other EU institutions. Even in areas of common policy, it is possible for the Council and for individual Council members to act as a brake on progress. In other domains, it is clear that there is negotiation within the Community as well as between the Community and other entities. The issues are often related to essentially domestic or parochial interests in one or more Member States, producing what can be seen as a multi-level game with complex stakes and rules. The Commission is by no means disadvantaged in this game, but its expanding area of concern has placed a severe strain on its administrative and political resources (Ludlow 1992; Smith and Woolcock 1999).

The process of policy formation and implementation in external relations is thus a political as well as a technical or administrative one. This is not a new insight, but it does contrast sharply with a view based largely or solely on the Treaties, on competence in the legal sense and on the assumption that implementation follows logically from the agreement of measures. Indeed, in this respect, it intersects with one of the central themes about the Commission: the perception that the Commission is not a good implementer, and that it is hamstrung both by its lack of human resources and by constraints exercised by the Council (Peters 2000). Moreover, the political/administrative mix highlights problems of the establishment of boundaries around policy domains. It has often been unclear outside the core of the CCP what the competence of the Commission is or ought to be, and the Commission itself has had to try and redefine the scope of commercial policy as a means of establishing a presence in developing areas such as air transport (see below).

As to coordination between the Commission and the Member States, where Community competence is clear there are few problems. Tensions arise, however, when decisions have to be taken about whether the Commission, the Presidency or individual Member States have policy responsibility. Sometimes, the Community is represented by a bicephalous delegation. Here, the Presidency and the Commission speak on behalf of the Community. Alternatively, a single delegation composed of Commission and Member State officials may exist, though usually the Commission delegate is the spokesman. In a third variant, the Commission heads a delegation supported by representatives from the Member States. The Commission's strategy in this area is to seek to extend its own competence where possible. It does this by building precedents, for example, where preambles to its own texts reflect previous Council declarations in non-related areas, or by using implied competence in one area as a precedent for acquiring competence in another.

The political nature of the Commission's role, and the context within which it operates, is further underlined by the range of influences to which the Commission is subjected or with which it interacts in the area of external relations. It has already been noted that national governments retain a strong watching brief on commercial policy, and that in the context of organisations such as the GATT (now the WTO) and Organisation for Economic Cooperation and Development (OECD), they are present alongside the Commission negotiators – a situation which can lead to confusion about who is really representing the Community (Devuyst 1992; de Burca and Scott 2001). In addition, the Commission is the centre of attraction for a large range of non-member governments and other external lobbies, some of them with a great deal of expertise and clout. In EC/US relations, for example, the Commission deals with the US Mission to the Community in a number of different contexts: with trade associations, with state governments, with multinational firms and with individuals with particular interests or grievances (Hocking and Smith 1997; Pollack and Shaffer 2001). This makes the generation and implementation of policy a matter of complexity, but also a matter quintessentially of politics rather than administration.

Quite apart from the range of influences on Community policy and Commission policy-making in external relations, there is an elaborate set of legal and institutional contexts for the conduct of negotiations and the pursuit of commercial disputes. Some of these are set up by the Community in the context, for example, of the Lomé/Cotonou Conventions or other association arrangements. Others are bilateral, as with the working groups set up under the Transatlantic Declaration and its successors, the Transatlantic Agenda and Action Plan of 1995. Still others are multilateral, ranging from international commodity agreements of many kinds through other regional arrangements and up to the global organisations, chief among them the WTO. The Commission often finds itself negotiating on a wide range of fronts at any given time, thereby increasing the strain on its limited resources and diffusing its attention with potentially damaging results (Smith 2004).

Given the intense dependence of the EU on all kinds of international trade, it is clear that policy-making and implementation in external relations are the highest of high politics, while at the same time being complex and technical in nature. As Nuttall and Spence point out in chapters 13 and 14, there is also an intimate linkage between external relations, foreign policy and security policy in the changing conditions since the 1990s. Here, it is important to register the intermeshing of different policy styles in the Commission's external relations activity. As pointed out by Mazey and Richardson in chapter 10, the Commission finds itself at the intersection of several types of policy network, and has generated its own distinctive brand of 'bureaucratic politics' or 'policy entrepreneurship' as a result (Peters 1992, 2000; Pollack 2000). External relations is subject to this trend as are other areas of policy, but one crucial difference is the intersection of external relations with almost every other area of Commission concern. This is reflected in the substantive agenda of Commission activity in the external policy domain.

The evolving policy agenda

The discussion so far has concentrated on the background to policy-making and the policy process itself. But the substance of policy needs to be explored before we turn to the radical changes in the role of the Commission that have taken place in the past decade. In examining the policy agenda, two issues are of immediate concern: first, the ways in which Community, and particularly Commission, activity is constrained by external forces; and second, the ways in which institutional frameworks operate to focus and channel these forces. The Commission's position at the intersection of a range of economic, political and institutional networks gives rise to a range of specific problems in handling the evolving agenda of policy.

The central thrust of Community external relations towards trade and commercial diplomacy and the key role of the Commission make it natural that much of the activity occurs in the context of the GATT/WTO and, to a lesser extent, the OECD. Here, the Commission functions to a large extent in the same way as the other members (or Contracting Parties as they were called until 1995 in the GATT). In fact, it is not the same as the other members, since the Community Member States maintain individual membership even while the Commission speaks and negotiates for them (de Burca and Scott 2001; Meunier 1999). The issue of voice is thus ambiguous, and there have been a number of episodes in which the Community voice has not made itself heard in a united and effective way. On the whole, though, the pursuit of the CCP has been a matter for the Commission acting in GATT/WTO, while at the same time keeping an eye on its domestic constituency among the Member States (Devuyst 1992; Smith and Woolcock 1999; Smith 2001). Indeed, Sir Leslie Fielding, former Director General in DG I, of his work on the Community's external relations, concluded that the Community (and thus the Commission) had played a vital role in the continuing existence and growth of the GATT, and others have argued that the transition to the WTO was also a key focus for Commission activism (Fielding 1991; Paemen and Bensch 1995; see also Macleod *et al.* 1996). It is thus perhaps fitting that former Trade Commissioner Pascal Lamy became head of the WTO in 2005.

Given the fundamental importance of the WTO to the Community and to the Commission, it is important to distinguish between two types of agenda items arising from it. On the one hand, the WTO is a central mechanism for dealing with specific disputes and crises within the world trading system. Thus, the Commission has found itself over the years engaged in a very wide range of negotiations arising from frictions, either generated by the development of the Community itself or by the policies of its major trading partners. Some of the most notable have arisen in relations with the USA, and particularly in agriculture, from the so-called 'chicken war' of the 1960s to the cheese, citrus, grain and pasta 'wars' of the 1970s and 1980s and other conflicts over food products, food safety, genetically modified crops and other matters since the 1990s.

Alongside these have gone disputes over industrial products in declining sectors, such as steel, or in high-technology developments such as that centring on the European Airbus. This is the type of conflict in which no-one is without sin, particularly the USA and the Community, and it has increasingly extended to include Japan as the competitive interdependence of the world's three greatest industrial powers has intensified. The Commission, as the guardian of Community instruments in anti-dumping, rules of origin and fair trade, has incurred its share of odium, not only for the policies adopted, but also for its inability to demonstrate what to others is the necessary flexibility in their implementation. This reflects to a certain extent the structure of policy-making in the Community as a whole, and it is a problem not unknown in other trade policy machines. Indeed, it may even prove useful for Member State governments to be able to credit (or blame) the Commission for current EU policy (Smith 2000a).

The WTO also functions at a second, more fundamental level. It shapes the framework for the development of world trade and engages in the necessary reforms to respond to changes in the global arena. The negotiating rounds, starting on a large scale under the GATT in the early 1960s and lasting into the new millennium with the so far incomplete Doha Development Round under the WTO, cover virtually the same period as the history of the EEC, then the EC and now the EU. This is no mere coincidence. For many commentators, it was only with the emergence of the Community as a unified interlocutor with the Americans in the 1960s that the development of a truly multilateral world trading system became possible. It also became somewhat difficult, as the development of intense global interdependence tested the capacity both of the Community and of the USA, to find appropriate reforms to meet rapidly changing problems (Preeg 1970; Diebold 1972).

As a result, the competence of the Commission to act for the Community in the GATT and now the WTO negotiating sphere has been exercised in a very challenging context. As with the more specific dispute settlement procedures, the Community Member States retain a voice in the process, and the presence of the 133 Committee provides a constant check on the Commission's activities. As the GATT and now the WTO has extended its attention with successive negotiating rounds from tariffs to non-tariff barriers, and from trade in industrial goods to agriculture, services and issues such as the relationship between trade and the environment, it is also not surprising that the diversity of views among the growing number of EU Member States has become more pronounced. The result has been a more turbulent and taxing political context for the Commission's activities. Perhaps the high (or low) point of this came with the attempt to steer a course between competing national positions on agriculture during the Uruguay Round of negotiations – a problem that re-emerged during the negotiations on the Doha Development Round during the early 2000s. This not only involved frictions between EU members over both internal reform and external negotiation, but was also an issue which cut across several Directorates General in the Commission and which generated intense conflicts between competing groups in the Community. It is thus important to note the different ways in which the WTO can form a context for the conduct of EU external relations and action by the Commission, and can feed into discussions about the role of the Commission itself (see below).

The OECD has a powerful but less well-focused impact on the Community and on the Commission. Here, the aim for a long time was largely the exchange of information and discussion of macro-economic strategies, along with specialist study of such issues as export credit finance. During the 1990s, though, the OECD became the focus for more politicised discussions about investment, the roles of multinational companies and other matters (Young 2002). In many of these areas the Commission has had only conditional competence at best, but it does have the status of active participant in the organisation. Thus, the OECD is an organisation in which the EU can at times speak with 20 voices (those of the 19 current EU Member States that belong to the organisation plus the Commission, which is an observer and participates in discussions on many issues), with only one of them belonging to the Commission and supposedly representing the Union.[3] But the close links between the Commission and the OECD Secretariat make for effective information exchange and the building of the consensus that is vital to the organisation's work (Fielding 1991, 33-34). In a somewhat similar way, the Commission has a role in a number of UN bodies such as UNCTAD, where there is a Community observer delegation consisting of representatives both of the Commission and of the Council Presidency, as well as national delegations from some of the Member States. Since a number of these bodies spend a good deal of their time on trade or trade-related issues, the ambiguous status of the Commission is not always helpful, though it can also be a way of diffusing conflict or embarrassment. As noted earlier in this chapter, in locations such as Geneva or New York, Commission Delegations spend a good deal of their time engaged in what might be termed 'multi-institutional' diplomacy, where specific issues such as human rights or development cross the boundaries between a wide range of international organisations and NGOs.

Intersecting a number of the Community's involvements with international organisations are contacts at the bilateral or limited multilateral level, particularly with other industrialised partners. The Community has a large number of regular consultations with its industrial partners, in which the Commission plays an active role as well as providing a range of facilitating resources. In some cases, such as the Group of Seven industrial countries (G-7) and the annual Western Economic Summits associated with them, the Commission has gradually established itself as a key participant. But there are large areas of policy, particularly those touching on monetary and macroeconomic problems, where the Commission has very little formal standing, even after the establishment of the euro in 2002, and from which it can be effectively excluded. It remains to be seen whether changes either in the EU – for example the extension and consolidation of the euro – or in the world economy will alter this situation. As is to be expected, the Commission is central to the trade-related policy issues discussed in the G-7 context, and during the early 1990s the development of the so-called quadrilateral group became a key feature of the G-7 approach to GATT negotiations in the Uruguay Round and elsewhere. Bringing together as it did the EC, the USA, Canada and Japan, it began to remind some observers of the growth of a 'world of regional blocs'. But it must be stressed that its impact was relatively limited and specifically restricted to trade; indeed, during the negotiation of the Doha Development Round in the early 2000s its profile was markedly lower than before.

Among the industrial partners of the Community, the USA and Japan have long held pride of place, given their dominance in external trade and direct investment, although during the late 1990s and early 2000s China has come to assume a much more prominent position (see below). It is therefore not surprising that there have been moves to institutionalise the links between the Community and these two economic superpowers. During 1990 and 1991, joint declarations were adopted first by Canada and then the USA and the Community, and later by Japan. These established regular processes of consultation, with specific working groups focusing on matters of industrial, scientific and regulatory policy. Although the Commission was heavily involved in both the negotiation and the implementation of these arrangements, the processes were those of a mixed agreement, with the Member States and particularly the Council Presidency holding a central position. Nonetheless, the continuation of the growing infrastructure of specialist policy consultation was both a direct reflection of the changing nature of external relations and a confirmation of the role played by the Commission in facilitating and supporting policies (Fielding 1991; Alting von Geusau 1993). This pattern continued with the conclusion of the Transatlantic Agenda and Action Plan between the EU and the United States in December 1995. This formalised and extended many of the arrangements growing out of the TAD process and the Maastricht Treaty calling for close cooperation on matters falling within both the second and the third pillars (the Common Foreign and Security Policy and Cooperation in Justice and Home Affairs respectively) (Pollack and Shaffer 2001).

Although the main focus of EU external relations has historically been the industrialised countries, there has also grown up a sophisticated infrastructure of institutions and contacts dealing with the Third World. In particular, the Lomé Conventions (of which there were four, with the first taking effect in 1975 and the fourth in 1990) produced a range of preferential trading agreements and technical assistance agreements unique among the links between industrialised and developing countries. These have now been followed up by new types of bilateral and multilateral agreements contained in the Cotonou Convention of 2000, which also added provisions on human rights, good governance and integration into the global economy (Holland 2002). The administration of these agreements and of broader Community policy towards developing countries is entrusted to the Commission, although it is not an area of exclusive Commission competence except insofar as it deals with specifically trade or CCP-related issues. The Lomé Conventions themselves were concluded under Article 238 (310) of the Treaty of Rome, and administered not through DG I but through DG VIII (Development) of the Commission. Significantly, they relied on national allocations of aid and assistance, which had to be negotiated with the Commission on a regular basis (Hewitt 1989; Hine 1985; Lister 1988; Macleod et al. 1996). A distinctive feature of the Cotonou Convention was that this process was re-shaped into a multi-year general programme with more assured budgetary support. A further particular aspect of policy towards the Third World has been the growth of the Commission as a coordinating body for crisis and humanitarian assistance as well as longer term technical assistance. The legitimacy built up in this area has had major implications for Commission activism in the crises of the 1990s and 2000s, both in the Third World and closer to home.

The Commission also has a central role in the initiation and the monitoring of association and cooperation agreements, which fall into a number of categories. In the first place, there are those agreements which are explicitly designed to pave the way for membership by the associated country (as was the case with Greece, for example, before its membership). Secondly, there are agreements which are designed to create free exchange and a close economic relationship but without the presumption of eventual membership, such as those with a number of Mediterranean countries in the framework of the Barcelona Process. The European Economic Area Agreement (EEA), signed in the early 1990s with a number of the EFTA countries, began without the presumption of membership but was later seen as a staging post to full membership for Sweden, Norway, Finland and Austria – an outcome later rejected by the Norwegians in 1992. Finally, there are the partnership and cooperation agreements with, for example, China, Russia and the Ukraine. In these cases, the Commission's role may be at 'arm's length' while in the closer forms of association there is a constant demand on Commission attention and expertise as the detailed arrangements are monitored. By extension, the investigation of applicants for Community membership and the provision of formal opinions on their credentials is a key Commission responsibility, although, as in other areas, the power of decision lies with the Council of Ministers and, by virtue of the assent procedure (see chapter 9), to some extent the Parliament.

A final area of Commission involvement in external relations is in inter-regional arrangements. The Community has developed a series of links with other regional organisations, particularly those of an economic nature, in Latin America and Asia especially (Edwards and Regelsberger 1990; de Cecco 2000). The conclusion of these agreements, and the oversight of the often complex technical activities to which they give rise, is a Commission responsibility, often cutting across a number of Directorates General. In a number of cases, the arrangements have envisaged and developed a political dimension. This was the case, for example, in relation to the Community's links with the Association of Southeast Asian Nations (ASEAN) and with Central American and Latin American organisations. Perhaps the most explicit early example, and one raising the issue of the boundary between economic and political activities, was the Euro-Arab Dialogue of the 1970s. Given the atmosphere surrounding the Arab-Israeli conflict both then and later, the Dialogue was an issue in which the political sensitivities of not only EC Member States but also of powerful outsiders such as the USA were bound to be aroused. The result was a series of 'border incidents' which did little to advance the cause of the Commission in that the Dialogue was organised within EPC, though the bulk of the discussions focused on economic development with which the Commission was closely concerned (Allen 1978). During the late 1980s, the often rather distant relations between the Community and the countries of Eastern and Central Europe, either individually or in the framework of the Council for Mutual Economic Assistance, also underwent considerable development, which raised again the economic/political boundary issue (Pinder 1991). During the 1990s, the development of interregional relations with ASEAN and with a wide range of Asian-Pacific countries through the Asia-Europe Meeting (ASEM) focused the tensions and linkages on human rights policies (for example in Burma (Myanmar)) and these needed careful management by the Commission as well as by Member States.

The question of the boundary between economic and political affairs was also raised during the 1980s and 1990s by a number of episodes in which economic sanctions were either contemplated or used by the Community. At one level, it is clear that the growing economic weight of the EU gives it the potential to mobilise that weight against those of which it disapproves. But given the complexities of both the legal and the political framework of the Union, it is equally clear that the move to economic sanctions poses delicate problems of competence and legitimacy. Not only this, but the increasingly interdependent nature of the world economy gives rise to important operational issues of control and effectiveness attached to any use of the economic weapon. During the 1980s, the Community faced the demand for sanctions several times, either from within its membership or from powerful outsiders such as the USA. Iran, the USSR, Argentina, South Africa and Iraq were all potential targets, and the record of both coordinated action and effectiveness was patchy to say the least (Holland 1993; Macleod et al. 1996). The 1990s brought a new range of episodes, many of them connected to the conflicts in former Yugoslavia but others focused on Asia (such as the tensions with

Burma noted above). The Commission's role in most, if not all, of these cases was a dual one: first, to provide information and estimates of the impact of sanctions, and to coordinate this with national authorities; second, in those cases where Article 113 (133) was the basis of action, to impose, maintain and monitor the effects of the sanctions. As Spence points out in chapter 14, though, the political determination (or lack of it) in all of these cases depended not on the Commission but on the national governments of the Member States, though the Community and the Commission could provide the instruments if the governments had given them the authority.

The picture presented here is one of a growing and elaborate network of contacts between the EU and the outside world, in which the Commission plays a central but sometimes ambiguous role. Its status as repository of expertise and information is widely acknowledged. It often takes a key role in representing the Community, either solely or in conjunction with the Council Presidency; and it is in many respects the guardian of the framework within which the EC's external relations grew until the early 1990s. Despite the fact that until very recently it had exclusive competence only in a limited number of sectors, it was able to establish an effective presence and to operate as an interlocutor at varying levels of authority. It also has the custodianship of a vast infrastructure of working groups and day-to-day relationships which have greatly increased the confidence of partners in both the Community in general and the Commission in particular. But questions are raised precisely by the extent of this commitment. Can the Commission continue to muster the expertise, human resources and attention to play its full effective role in a rapidly changing global political economy?

From development to transformation

It has been argued in many contexts that the affairs of Europe during the 1990s went beyond mere developmental change to a state of radical transformation (Smith and Woolcock 1993; Allen and Smith 1991-92; Alting von Geusau 1993; Laffan, O'Donnell and Smith 1999). The focus of this chapter so far has been on developments in Community external relations at the institutional and policy-making level, but clearly it is of key importance to explore the impact of the political and economic changes of the last decade. These have been such as to throw into sharp relief both the benefits and the limitations of action through the Community, and thus also to throw into question the role of the Commission itself.

In essence, the changes, although not all rooted in the 1990s alone, have reshaped both the context and the agenda of the EC's external relations. The most dramatic has been the disappearance of the division of Europe, carrying with it the need to recreate relationships with a wide range of countries, often in trying economic and political circumstances. Alongside this has gone the already-noted trend towards extensive economic interpenetration between industrial societies and the accompanying need to reform the international economic institutions, including the GATT in its transformation into the WTO. In addition, a major role has been played by the EC's internal efforts to remake itself, particularly through the further development of the Single European Market (SEM), which often intersects with the processes of globalisation.

Three questions emerge relating to the role of the Commission in this context: first, can the Commission maintain its role as provider of information, representation and negotiating expertise in an increasingly demanding world? Second, is the Commission capable of managing and coordinating a transformed policy agenda for external relations? Finally, can the Commission respond effectively to changing political conditions which have clearly affected the conduct and content of external relations in the past ten years and will continue to do so in the future? Before coming to a judgement on these issues, an examination of some key policy problems may prove helpful.

The Single Market, the GATT and multi-level policy-making

The first such problem is the SEM itself, which can form a useful case study of the intersection between internal and external policy processes (Hocking and Smith 1997; Calingaert 1996). Although the SEM might be seen as an internal policy programme, it was clear from the outset in the 1980s that it had international aims and ramifications, and that there would be sharp responses from major trading partners if the programme were not carefully presented. The Commission's initial handling of this problem was not surefooted. Almost the first public recognition of the external implications of the SEM was in a speech made by Willy de Clercq, the External Relations Commissioner, in July 1988, in which he appeared to be arguing that the SEM was too precious to be negotiated away, and that any concessions on market access to (say) the USA and Japan would only be granted if those countries gave equivalent concessions (Montagnon 1988; Hocking and Smith 1997). This aroused predictable fury and predictions of a 'fortress Europe', particularly in Washington, and although the Commission was quick to rectify the situation, the memory lingered. Resentment was also raised in some Member States against the Commission when the latter's defence of the 'European' interest in the SEM conflicted with their national concerns. Such issues as Japanese car and video imports smouldered on well into the 1990s. Other aspects of the SEM were less public but no less potentially the sources of friction. The regulation of financial services, public procurement, technical standards and certification, telecommunications and transportation all held the seeds of conflict with outsiders. The other feature common to all was that they were not the preserve of DG I, a fact which raised problems of policy coordination at the highest level.

Further complications were added to the policy mix by the fact that the SEM programme ran alongside the Uruguay Round of the GATT. Was the SEM to be the basis for a new EC policy on world trade more generally, or the basis for further constructive contributions to the liberalisation of world trade? For the Commission, negotiating in Geneva, a key problem was that the negotiating stance on world trade issues depended heavily on the progress made in the SEM. In fact, this problem was handled with considerable efficiency as the Round progressed, and there were no dramatic confrontations at the multilateral level. The same could not be said for the bilateral relationship with the USA. In the early part of 1993, the Community faced direct threats of retaliation against the effects of newly implemented directives on public procurement, which the Americans saw as damaging their interests. Not only this, but the suspicions of the USA about the effects of EC policies on standards and certification had not been allayed (and were paralleled by European fears of US regulatory competition). These fears focused on sectors such as telecommunications, which were also central to the public procurement dispute (US Congress 1992), but the development of global telecommunications markets during the 1990s defused much of their impact.

The Commission was thus faced with a variety of new challenges in policy coordination which bridged the theoretical gap between external and internal policy. Nor were these confined to the 'new agenda' created by the SEM. The Uruguay Round also threw up coordination issues in 'traditional' areas of trade, particularly in agriculture. Efforts to achieve internal reform of the CAP through the McSharry proposals of 1992 were rendered much more problematic by the fact that they coincided with the most delicate stage of GATT negotiations, and that they engaged the deepest perceptions of national and local interest in Community countries. Thus, the Commission found itself in a double if not a triple bind, between the demands of the GATT (and particularly the Americans), the agreed internal reform programme, and the perceived vital interests of EU members, particularly the French. In November 1992, the so-called Blair House Agreement, reached in Washington between the Community (represented both by the External Relations and the Agriculture Commissioners), appeared to have resolved the issues. But as time passed, the French made increasing efforts to argue for a renegotiation based on the agreement's incompatibility with the CAP reforms. Significantly, their arguments were also based on the fact that the agreement had been initialled by the Commission and the US government, but not 'concluded' by the Council of Ministers – a telling demonstration of the mixed nature of EC decision-making in this area (*Economist*, 1993). Notwithstanding this type of tension, it can be argued that in fact the external relations factor supported those within the EU who were in favour of significant reform, and that this continued into the Doha Development Round of WTO negotiations initiated in 2001.

Not only the process but also the conclusion of the Uruguay Round Agreements created distinctive issues of competence for the Community and Member States. These grew specifically out of the way in which the Uruguay Round had extended to a number of 'new agenda' areas such as trade in services, which came to be covered in the General Agreement on Trade in Services (GATS), and intellectual property, which was dealt with as Trade Related Intellectual Property Measures (TRIPS). When it came to the conclusion of these agreements, the Commission held that the Community was competent. A number of Member States disagreed and asked the ECJ to give a ruling as to whether the GATS and certain other items fell under Article 113 and the CCP. The Court, in Opinion 1/94, held that only certain parts of the GATS and TRIPS agreements were within Article 113, specifically those parts dealing with cross-border supply of services or (in the case of TRIPS) the supply of counterfeit goods across borders. As a result, the Commission and the Member States had to work out a new set of conventions for the handling of what were new or newly recognised areas of mixed competence (see Macleod *et al.* 1996, 268-73; Eeckhout 2004, chapter 2), a process only partly completed by 2004.

The new Europe, enlargement, and a changing world

By 1995, then, the scene in EU external relations was complex to say the least, with a host of unresolved issues even on the well-established agenda of trade and the SEM. But the 1990s also saw a quantum leap in the number of other major external policy areas in which the Commission has a role, and the pressures thus created led to significant issues in the later 1990s. The problem was not merely an increase in numbers or scope, but also an increase in the scale, complexity and political sensitivity of what was being attempted. Four such areas of policy can be identified and briefly reviewed: first, the problems of dealing with new countries in Eastern and Central Europe; second, the related issues of enlargement which became a central preoccupation during the late 1990s and early 2000s; third, new dimensions in the use of economic sanctions and economic and humanitarian assistance; and finally, a new range of global issues arising from the intensification of global interdependence and the need for regulation. In each of these domains, the Commission has been led more or less willingly into new and often uncertain enterprises.

The new Europe

When the Soviet-backed regimes of Eastern and Central Europe progressively collapsed during 1989 and 1990, one of the most pressing needs was for economic and technical assistance. Although there was a massive expansion of bilateral aid efforts, there was a clear need for coordination and the linking of aid to the political reform process. Significantly, the USA was disinclined (some have argued, financially incapable) to undertake the lead role in what some saw as a second Marshall Plan. They actively promoted the Community as the channel for coordination, and the Commission as the lead agency in what became the Group of 24 aid donors (G-24). By 1993, the Community had contributed 60 per cent of the total funds expended through the G-24, and it has continued to be the major source of funding and technical assistance for the CEEC and countries of the former Soviet Union. The Commission became the recognised centre of expertise and the home of coordinated programmes such as PHARE and later SAPARD in East and Central Europe and TACIS, directed at the former Soviet Union itself. There were indeed frictions not only with the Americans, and also between EC policies and extensive national aid efforts, particularly those of the Germans, but the legitimacy of the Commission was firmly established. A linked enterprise, the setting-up of the European Bank for Reconstruction and Development, was less fully subject to Commission control, and has been less successful.

Alongside the innovative Commission role in G-24 went an attempt to establish new trading relationships with countries previously constrained by the bloc politics and economics of the Cold War. One of the first demands of the Central and East European states was for new association agreements with the Community, and for the promise of eventual membership. At one level, this was a technical question, but it was also inescapably political, bearing on the future shape of the Community in an undivided Europe and on the future stability of the new states themselves. The result was a series of so-called Europe Agreements, which granted asymmetrical trade and market access concessions to the East Europeans and foresaw eventual EU membership. But they also reflected the fundamental tensions in the Community position, which extended into the discussion of enlargement as the 1990s wore on. A number of Member States found it difficult to contemplate early membership for new states, particularly in the light of their own domestic economic and social problems. There were also specific areas of tension such as agriculture and steel, where the prospect of free entry for goods from the new states was unattractive to many EC producers and their governments. The Commission was caught in the centre of these tensions, with the capacity to monitor, to provide information and to shape negotiations, but without the competence to determine the shape of any outcome.

Enlargement of the Union

At the same time as it was dealing with the effects of the changes in Eastern and Central Europe, in the 1990s the Commission also became deeply implicated in the negotiations for closer relations, first between the Community and the EFTA countries and then between the Community and what were to become ten new Member States in Central and Eastern Europe and the Mediterranean. The European Economic Area Agreement of December 1992 implied that the EFTA members would accept a very large part of the Community *acquis* without acquiring the benefits of full Community membership. The Agreement reflected a formidable negotiating effort both by the Commission and by the EFTA members. But it also provoked important tensions over such areas as dispute settlement which revealed the underlying problems of EC policy-making in this area. In addition, a number of EFTA members decided to apply directly for entry to the Community, thereby creating a major new commitment for the Commission in the process. In many respects, the Commission could only observe the political process, while continuing to build the necessary infrastructure for management of whatever relationship finally emerged.

After the entry of Sweden, Finland and Austria, the Commission's dealings with the new outsiders, especially Switzerland (which had rejected even the EEA) and Norway continued to be a major area of activity. Bilateral agreements had to be made with the Swiss in a wide range of areas, and these continued into the new millennium as new areas of incompatibility became apparent. In the case of Norway, major negotiations had to be conducted on the extension (for example) of the Schengen agreements to cover what had previously been Nordic agreements on free movement and related matters.

These complexities were of course relatively limited compared to those raised by the moves to admit what eventually became ten new Member States. The scale of the negotiations, and the need to maintain ten sets of bilateral contacts while at the same time balancing the overall costs and benefits between the acceding states and existing Member States, meant that Commission resources were stretched to the limits, as were those of some Council Presidencies. The need to renegotiate a very wide range of existing international agreements for each of the new Member States, and to ensure compatibility with the WTO and other international organisations, meant that this process inevitably had broader implications for relations with the United States and the operation of the multilateral system as a whole.

The politics of humanitarian aid and economic sanctions

Economic and humanitarian aid was always a part of the Commission remit, but the 1990s greatly expanded it and brought it into an ever-closer relationship with political and security issues. The intersection of political turmoil in Eastern and Central Europe with a number of existing conflicts and crises, created new demands on the Commission as the channel for economic and humanitarian measures in the 1990s. At one level, there was a large-scale increase in the application of economic sanctions, most dramatically in the course of the Gulf Crisis of 1990-91 and the break-up of the former Yugoslavia from 1990 onwards. The diplomatic and security aspect of these issues is dealt with further in chapter 14, but it is important to note the ways in which the Balkan conflict in particular increased the load on the Commission as the regulator of the 'economic weapon'. In the case of Bosnia between 1992 and 1994, the addition of large scale humanitarian assistance needs to the already existing economic sanctions meant that the Commission was effectively taking on the non-military aspects of a major war, with all of the administrative (not to mention political) demands that came with it. Moreover, in the Dayton Agreement of 1995 on peace in Bosnia, the Commission was given responsibility not only for the coordination of large amounts of economic reconstruction but also specifically for the administration of the town of Mostar. After the conflict in Kosovo during 1999, similar arrangements for economic and social reconstruction were made, implying yet further expansion of the Commission's role. Each of these expectations and demands added to the burden on the Commission in quite new areas, and it must be remembered that they went alongside the extensive old and new agendas already described. Again, the boundary issues were as prominent as the substance of EU policies and Commission procedures, as Patten was later to lament (see chapter 14).

In the early years of the new millennium, these problems were given additional sharpness and impact through the 'war on terror', the associated war in Afghanistan and later in Iraq. It might have appeared after Kosovo that there was an emerging division of labour between those who fought the wars either individually or as members of 'coalitions of the willing' and those such as the EU (and thus the Commission) who cleared up, reconstructed and stabilised. Yet the new conflicts of the early 21st century made the Commission's role at times exceedingly difficult to maintain in the face of high levels of politicisation and disputes within the Union between Member States with different approaches to the conflicts. Here, the Commission was entering into the political arena in a big way, even if the instruments it was using were often those of traditional external relations. And the questions raised were as much about the legitimacy of any Commission role as about the technical capacity or competence of the Commission as an institution. These questions extended in some instances to the activities of Commission Delegations in centres such as Geneva, where the co-location of a range of economic, social and humanitarian organisations created new opportunities and in many cases requirements for coordination across institutional boundaries. Thus, for example, the need to coordinate policies across areas involving the UN Commissioner for Human Rights, the UN High Commissioner for Refugees, the International Organisation for Migration and the International Committee of the Red Cross has not only created new possibilities for policy innovation but also new tensions between Commission activities, those of the Member States and those of the international organisations, both governmental and non-governmental.

Global interdependence and the need for regulation

A final piece in the rapidly developing jigsaw of EU (and by extension Commission) concerns in external relations is the impact of a series of global and transnational issues, giving rise to moves towards regulation and global governance. Some were given formal recognition as early as 1991 in the TEU agreements. Three examples suffice to highlight issues raised for the role of the Commission by developments in this area. First, there is the problem of international environmental regulation and policy-making. At the global level, this is entangled with other issues such as trade policies in the context of the WTO, or technical assistance activities in the UN framework and elsewhere. On a bilateral level, it enters into relations with the USA and other major industrial partners, for example through the conflicting views of the EU and the US over the implementation of the Kyoto Convention on control of greenhouse gases. At the European level, it engages with the wide range of issues related to changes in Eastern and Central Europe, where enviromental problems have a key role in the development of the CEEC. In all these contexts, the Community is a natural channel for the concerns of West European countries, and the Commission is the natural spokesman for the Community in the broader institutional context – as long as the Member States can achieve a consistent collective position.

A second item on the 'new agenda' is the increasing need to regulate transnational networks in the areas of traditional Community concern. A challenging example is that of air transport, where regulatory issues at the national or the Community level have an inevitable spillover into the global arena. As noted earlier in this chapter, here the Commission has competence, but not of an unchallenged or unchallengeable nature. The question is whether the Commission can or should arrogate competence to itself (for example under the CCP) or whether the solution lies in new forms of cooperative action between the national, the Community and the corporate levels (Macleod et al. 1996).

From the mid-1990s onwards, the Commission made a sustained effort to assert its right to negotiate air routes on behalf of the Member States, and it succeeded in 2002 in establishing the basis for a negotiating mandate. During the mid-1990s also, it became clear that the increasing number of international alliances between airlines could raise important issues of competition policy, thereby leading to further questions of competence between the EC and Member States, but also between the EC and third parties such as the USA. Such questions were given greatly increased point by the escalation of security concerns about air travel in the wake of the attacks on the World Trade Centre and the Pentagon on 11th September 2001; suddenly, the whole issue became inseparable from the 'war on terror', which threw international air transport into turmoil and which led to EU-US confrontations about the release of information about travellers, about security checks on air cargo and related matters. At the same time, the 'rescue packages' given to troubled US airline companies during 2002 and 2003 raised further issues of competition policy.

A third example of global interdependence and the need for regulation is furnished by the increasingly transnational nature of policy-making in competition and anti-trust policy more generally. This had been recognised in negotiations between the EC and the US in the early and mid-1990s (Riley 1992; Pollack and Shaffer 2001). During the late 1990s and early 2000s, the Commission's Competition DG, led by the Italian Commissioner Mario Monti, took an assertive stance on its right to regulate large cross-national mergers and the activities of multinational companies with a major presence in Europe. Two cases became emblematic of this assertiveness and of the problems it could cause. The first concerned a $40 billion merger between GE and Honeywell (two American companies) which was effectively vetoed by the Commission, and the second concerned the attempt to regulate the practices of the US software giant Microsoft, which led in 2004 to findings against the US company and the threat of large fines.

Each of these short examples represents how Commission involvement in new patterns of policy-making is evolving and also where the rules of the game either remain to be worked out or are in some cases non-existent. When they are taken together with the expanding agenda already described in this chapter, major questions arise about the competence of the Commission in formal terms, but also about the ability of the Commission and its members to shape the process of policy making both at the Community and at the broader international level.

Conclusions: the Commission in a new world

There is a lot of evidence that the external relations of the Community are entering a new era of change and challenge. Although the structure and functioning of the Commission machinery and of the Commission itself in external relations were not a central preoccupation of the TEU, they continued to be a significant focus of negotiation throughout the 1990s. By the time of the Nice Treaty, there was a readiness to grant the Commission relatively unqualified competence in the expanding range of trade and commercial policy activities that had caused frictions in the early and mid-1990s. According to some commentators, this was a sharp departure from the relatively minor and incremental treaty changes that had occurred previously, and it framed debate in the Convention on the Future of Europe during 2002-3 (Young 2003, 66-67). Although the European Parliament's right of assent to international agreements was to some extent enlarged during the 1990s, this was not seen as automatically applicable to agreements reached under Article 113 (133) or the CCP in general. The impact of the growing range of association arrangements and inter-regional agreements described above is still to be evaluated in this context. The implementation of economic and monetary union paid little attention to the linkages between external monetary management and the role of the Commission, except to require that the Commission should be 'fully associated' with positions taken in international fora relating to economic and monetary policy, and there remain issues about the international management and status of 'Euroland'.

While the IGCs up to 2000 really contained very little in the way of concrete change to the structure of external economic policy making, less formal factors have been operating to produce change in the Commission's role and status.

But not all the changes are to the Commission's advantage. The increasing role of the Commission on issues affecting Central and Eastern Europe, and the growth of new 'agenda issues' in which national governments have limited competence or interest, clearly made the Commission the target of rising expectations during the late 1990s. The intersection of, say, the CCP with highly charged political issues, or the interaction of the CAP or competition policy with external trade policy, can create severe jurisdictional problems.

Perhaps the most important example of the Commission's response to changing realities is the creation during the 1990s of a new structure for the coordination of external economic relations. For some time, it had been apparent that external relations could not be managed on the assumption that they were all economic in character. The sheer volume and diversity of work in the area made it necessary by the early 1990s to think of institutional innovation. The TEU only added to this tendency by strengthening the relationship between external relations and common foreign and security policy. Thus, successive Commissions during the 1990s moved to foster closer coordination and increased consistency among the core external relations DGs, this culminating under the Prodi Commission with the establishment of the external relations 'team' headed by DG RELEX. This does not mean that there have not been significant 'turf battles' between those responsible for different areas of external economic relations, nor of course that there have not been issues arising from the interaction of the technical aspects of external relations with the more explicitly 'foreign policy' concerns of other areas of the Union. The interaction of the Commission not only with national governments but also with the Council Secretariat is a key determinant here, in a situation where the establishment of the High Representative for CFSP in the Amsterdam Treaty created the potential for new institutional tensions, as Spence discusses fully in chapter 14.

The draft Constitutional Treaty produced by the Convention on the Future of the EU during 2003, and agreed by Member States in June 2004, did not give a central place to developments in the CCP, but nonetheless it proposed a number of significant changes (Eeckhout 2004, 53-55). In Part III of the Constitution, the broad commitment to development of a liberal international trading regime is re-stated, and there is a clear statement of the Union's exclusive competence in the area of external commercial policy[4]. In addition, the Constitution in article III-315, which is an amended version of article 133 EC, makes it clear that all WTO matters are covered, and extends exclusive competence to the area of foreign direct investment where it involves international commercial matters. This is a clarification of the position which had evolved during the 1990s and which had been formalised in the Nice Treaty, and indeed it might be argued that from the point of view of the Commission practice had developed in such a way as to include all of these matters already. No doubt the working out of the implications of these changes (should the Treaty be ratified at some point) would entail further delicate internal negotiations between the Commission and Member States. There would also be intriguing new areas of Commission-Parliament interaction because of the Treaty's provision that trade-related legislation (for example, anti-dumping rules) will be adopted according to the co-decision procedure.

At the beginning of this chapter, it was suggested that one way of looking at the Commission's role in external relations was as a set of 'boundary problems', in which the Commission found itself up against the demands posed by the interlinking and competition of many issues and policy arenas. It is clear from the evidence examined here that this is indeed the case, and in a number of ways. The Commission faces issues of formal competence, of informal status and standing, and of the need to combine several distinct and often competing roles. It also faces the problems created by a rapidly changing external relations agenda, in which the essentially evolutionary processes of its first 30 years have been replaced by processes of radical and even revolutionary change.

Not unnaturally, the responses both of the Commission and of EU Member States have often been hesitant in the face of these new demands. It remains to be seen whether the attempt to bridge 'classical' external relations and the new political and regulatory concerns explored here will be a success. What is clear is that the Commission has over the years developed a powerful set of management procedures for its core external relations business, and that the boundaries of its activity had expanded considerably even before the transformations of the 1990s. A number of long-established problems remain, and should not be obscured by the impact of the new agenda. Indeed, they suffuse the new agenda and give evidence of a solid if sometimes debated core of status and competence for the Commission. One thing is certain: the nature, definition and management of the external relations of the European Union will be central to the development of the Union itself, the wider Europe and the world political economy. The Commission will remain at the heart of this process, but as always, the centrality and boundaries of its role will be contested both from within – and from without.

Endnotes

[1] The term European Community is used throughout this chapter except where the reference is clearly to the EU as a whole, since for all practical purposes in the area of external relations the EC is the key referent.

[2] The Treaty of Paris expired in 2001 and the functions of the ECSC have now been absorbed into those of the EC and the EU more generally.

[3] The accession of the ten new Member States in 2004 added four new OECD Member States to the EU 'team': the Czech Republic, Hungary, Poland and the Slovak Republic.

[4] The Treaty for the first time gave international 'personality' to the Union as a whole rather than just to the Community.

13. The Commission and European Political Cooperation

Simon Nuttall

Introduction

European Political Cooperation (EPC) was the process by which, until the establishment of the Common Foreign and Security Policy (CFSP) in 1993, the Member States of the European Community sought to coordinate their foreign policies. From its beginnings in 1970, it was based on an intergovernmental approach, operating by the rule of consensus. The Community institutions, especially the Commission, were excluded as far as was practicable. Total exclusion proved unsustainable, as Political Cooperation soon operated in areas which impinged closely on matters that were the legal responsibility of the Community. There was thus no choice but to admit the Commission to EPC deliberations, and this occurred on an increasingly less restrictive basis as the years progressed. By the end of the 1980s the Commission was fully accepted as a guest at the intergovernmental table, but even after the Maastricht Treaty's boost to its status, it was still not allowed to perform the role it plays in the Community. This chapter traces the origins of Commission involvement in EPC, describing how the growth in the Commission's role was contingent on its ability to provide, indeed make indispensable, a European Community perspective to the intergovernmental deliberations on foreign policy.

The origins of EPC

Today's European Security and Defence Policy (ESDP) and emerging constitutionally anchored security guarantees underline that the origins of EPC, and the Commission's exclusion from it, must be sought as far back as the political and security origins of European integration after World War II. Frontiers had become permeable and hostility between the United States and the Soviet Union caused doubts in the minds of politicians and publics alike over the ability of nation-state structures to guarantee security. But the first flush of federalist enthusiasm in the 1940s was soon replaced by the hard light of government-to-government negotiation, in which initially popular supranational ideas and mechanisms were rejected for fear of loss of sovereignty. The Council of Europe was set up on intergovernmental lines, and the French attempt to transfer the supranational procedures of the

Coal and Steel Community to a European Defence Community and an incipient European Political Community failed when France's own National Assembly voted down the Treaty in 1954. The history of Europe since then has been coloured by the tensions between those who have desired comfortable maintenance of the nation state and those who have advocated greater integration through supranational institutions and procedures. It was significant that the stumbling block in the 1950s was France, even before General de Gaulle returned to power. René Pleven's bold initiative for a defence community came to nothing, not least because the French government was by then dependent on Gaullist support. One of their most senior representatives, Michel Debré, had made plain the Gaullists' repugnance for federal systems, particularly in foreign policy. In their view, attempts should be made to harmonise national positions, but if these attempts failed, the discussions had to cease. This was the line taken by General de Gaulle when he returned to power in 1958. A text approved by him in August 1958 stated that:

'La coopération européenne doit s'affirmer aussi en dehors de l'Europe, a l'égard des grands problèmes mondiaux . . . des consultations régulières auront lieu entre les gouvernements intéressés. Ce mécanisme de consultations pourra prendre un caractère en quelque sorte organique au fur et à mesure qu'il se développera.' (Nuttall 1992, 37-38)

Thus, the desire for a European foreign policy, previously expressed through attempts to establish a European Defence Community, was counterbalanced by de Gaulle's wish to provide an intergovernmental straitjacket for the Community's supranational institutions. This thinking governed the General's attitude throughout the negotiations for a European Political Community, which he launched in 1960. The so-called Fouchet Plan, named after the French Ambassador in Copenhagen who chaired the negotiations, had to be abandoned in April 1962. Their ultimate failure sprang in part from the requirement of the Benelux countries to have either supranational institutions, or else the United Kingdom in the Community; in both cases as a guarantee that the small Member States would not be subject to a Franco-German directorate. The rift between de Gaulle and the Belgian and Dutch Foreign Ministers, Paul-Henri Spaak and Joseph Luns, over this issue prefigured a long wrangle with the European Commission over its own pretension to power, with de Gaulle insisting at a press conference on 31 January 1964 that 'le pouvoir et le devoir executifs n'appartiennent qu'aux gouvernements' (Grosser 1984, 191).

When the subject was taken up again at the Hague Conference in 1969, President Pompidou continued to adhere to the Gaullist line on foreign policy. As part of a package that also involved enlargement to include the UK and the stabilisation of the EC budget, he obtained agreement that the renewed momentum towards political unification should, in the first instance, concentrate on foreign policy questions and should follow the lines traditionally defended by France. European Political Cooperation as it emerged from the 1970 Luxembourg Report was therefore purely intergovernmental. The machinery which was set up, ministerial meetings and a Political Committee, was largely inspired by the experience of political

cooperation which had briefly flourished at the time of the Fouchet negotiations. France was anxious to ensure that the Community institutions, and
especially the Commission, had no part to play in the new system. Yet, the
French knew that to insist on a replay of the Fouchet debate was to invite a
stalemate. Some concessions were therefore made. The Commission was not
to be regularly associated, but 'should the work of the Ministers affect the
activities of the European Communities, the Commission will be invited to
make known its views' (Luxembourg Report Part II (V) 1970). In paragraph
14 of the 1972 summit, heads of state also recognised the 'implications and
consequences in the international political field of Community policies'
(Bulletin of the EC 1972 no 10).

The implementation of this principle proved tortuous and distressing.
The Commission had to fight for every invitation, sometimes with the support of other Member States, but always against the fierce opposition of
France. The battle began at the first Ministerial Meeting at Munich in
November 1970. The Commission was excluded from the first part of the
meeting dealing with the Middle East and from the discussion which followed on the Conference on Security and Cooperation in Europe (CSCE). It
was ushered in only for the last hour when discussions on the CSCE turned
to the Community aspects of the question. Although Commission President
Malfatti called for the participation of the Community as such in the CSCE,
and was supported by the German and Dutch Foreign Ministers, Walter
Scheel and Joseph Luns, the French Foreign Minister, Maurice Schumann,
was more restrictive, stressing that the Conference would be dealing mainly
with security, not economic questions, and would be between States, not
blocs. Nevertheless, the economic aspects of the CSCE process could not be
denied in the end. The Commission was in fact consulted by France itself,
which then held the Presidency, on a paper on CSCE economic cooperation
prepared by the Political Committee. It was invited to the next Ministerial
Meeting in Paris for the discussion on the CSCE and even to dinner the night
before. However, at that meeting, it was not invited to the discussion on the
Middle East, nor at all to the meeting in Rome the following November.

As discussions on the CSCE proceeded, it became increasingly obvious
that the Commission's presence, and indeed assistance on the economic
side, was indispensable. Initially, the Commission provided input to the
CSCE Subcommittee set up by the Political Committee, though without
being allowed to attend its meetings because of objections raised by France.
It did, however, participate in an ad hoc Group set up to deal with the economic aspects of the Conference. The Group was in EPC but not of it,
designed especially to provide a forum which the Commission might join.
The Commission's status was finally fixed in the formula approved at the
beginning of the second phase of the CSCE in Geneva, whereby 'in order to
give expression to Community views in those areas mentioned in the statement by the [Danish] Foreign Minister, representatives of the Commission
of the European Community appear on the list of the Danish delegation'
(Nuttall 1992, 111).

The Commission thus made slow but steady progress into EPC mechanisms. It made itself acceptable by the modesty of its behaviour and indispensable by its technical expertise, especially on trade policy questions.
From a practical point of view, and setting aside theoretical considerations,

this was something the Member States could not do without. A similar development followed a few years later with regard to the Middle East. This was another particularly sensitive area for the French, who, at the beginning of EPC, strictly denied the Commission access to the discussions. Between 1970 and 1973, the Commission was only associated in discussions on the question of increased financial assistance for Palestinian refugees. The situation changed with the establishment of the Euro-Arab Dialogue, launched by France in 1973 in the wake of the chaotic situation after the October War. The original intention had been for the Dialogue to be primarily political, and hence the exclusive responsibility of the Member States. In the event, because of pressure from the United States, it turned out to be largely economic. The Commission's contribution thus became essential and its presence unavoidable. Commission representatives therefore took part in the work of the Coordinating Group, especially set up to report to both the Political Committee and COREPER, depending on the substance of its discussions. They joined with colleagues from the Presidency in conducting preparatory discussions with the Arab states, and they chaired some of the Working Groups dealing with technical, economic questions. By the time the Dialogue was finally launched in 1976, the Commission had successfully embedded itself in EPC mechanisms and procedures. As in the case of the CSCE, participation was achieved through the provision of indispensable technical expertise. Clear parallel developments can be observed with the Commission's role in conflict prevention, crisis management and the European Security and Defence Policy, as chapter 14 describes in detail.

The successful association of the Commission with work on the CSCE and the Euro-Arab Dialogue began to allay mistrust and thus facilitate participation in other areas, even if the hard-line position still adopted by France continued to act as a brake on many occasions. For example, Commission contributions to studies on developments in Eastern Europe were rejected. Its representatives were excluded from the Mediterranean Working Group dealing with the question of Cyprus. Indeed, as late as 1978, the representative of the Commission at a meeting of that Group had his presence questioned by the representative of France on the grounds that Cyprus was of no concern to the Community. The Commission representative remained in the room but abstracted himself from the proceedings by ostentatiously reading a newspaper; honour was satisfied. But, by the end of the 1970s, the Commission's position in EPC was recognised, though still uncertain. It was represented at Ministerial Meetings and the meetings of the Political Committee, but not at the meetings of European Correspondents, the body which coordinated the work of EPC and advised on practice and procedure. The Commission representative was invited to the Political Directors' luncheon, but not to their dinner. The Commission was not linked to the Coreu network, the confidential telex network linking the Foreign Ministries, but it did receive copies of some telegrams at the courtesy of the Belgian Foreign Ministry. Even then, it was denied a whole category of telegrams. The Commission had to be invited specially to attend any Working Group meeting, and was not always warned when meetings were taking place. The then European Correspondent of the Commission spent much of his time conducting a private intelligence service to find out when items of interest to the Commission were likely to be discussed, and then trying to secure an invitation to attend.

The good offices of Member States, who found the exclusion of the Commission absurd, were helpful, but the same Member States were unable to persuade reticent Member States, especially France, to change their views. Opportunities did arise on a number of occasions to improve the position of the Commission, but they were not seized. The Copenhagen Report of 1973 had limited itself to noting in its Annex the participation of the Commission in discussions on the economic aspects of the CSCE and on the future role of the Council of Europe. Neither the Paris Summit of 1974 nor the Tindemans Report on European Union of 1975 produced any advance on this position. Significantly, the Commission's speed in reacting to the Soviet invasion of Afghanistan between Christmas and New Year in 1979 (and between the Irish and Italian presidencies) stood it in good stead. There was no ministerial meeting in EPC format until 15 January 1980, but the Commission had taken measures on 9 January to prevent Community exports of grain to the Soviet Union to replace the American supplies already blocked by US President Carter on 5 January. The EPC meeting on 15 January merely confirmed the Council's agreement to the Commission's measures. But the significance lay in the demonstration that foreign policy might conceivably need to include Community policies and that there existed in the Commission a mechanism for speedier action than the Member States themselves could muster at the time (Fonseca-Wollheim 1981). Nevertheless, by 1981, although discussions were under way to produce a new Report to follow up the Luxembourg and Copenhagen Reports, there was still no change in the positions of Member States regarding the participation of the Commission.

The London Report

This situation changed suddenly with the arrival of the Socialist government in France in May 1981. The new French Foreign Minister, Claude Cheysson, a former member of the Commission, had suffered from its patchy association with EPC and lost no time in changing the traditional French position. The London Report, adopted in October of that year, finally fully associated the Commission with EPC. The relevant passage read: 'Within the framework of the established procedures the Ten attach importance to the Commission of the European Communities being fully associated with Political Cooperation at all levels' (London Report Part II(12) 1981). This tortuous drafting reflected Denmark's concern to ensure that the Commission did not as a result acquire the sort of powers in EPC that it had in the Community. The Danish Minister was rather embarrassed at the position he was obliged to take. He underwent some gentle teasing at the Ministerial Meeting at the hands of Lord Carrington, who was in the chair. But whatever the formulation, the way was now clear for the full association of the Commission with EPC. What this meant in practical terms still had to be worked out. Although the discussions on implementation were marked by a rearguard action on the part of Gaullist elements in the Quai d'Orsay, it was nevertheless established within a few months that the Commission representatives would take part in all EPC activities without exception, including all meals, and would take part in Groups from which they had previously been excluded, like the Correspondents' Group, the Middle East

Group, the UN-Disarmament Group and the Group of Heads of Communications. The arrangements also included association with Political Cooperation in third countries and a direct link to the Coreu network, so that it could receive all Coreus and in turn be able to send them. In return, the Commission gave written undertakings mainly concerned with security.

The full association of the Commission was timely. Within the next few years came a proliferation of events requiring close interaction between EPC and the Community in which the Commission was called on to play its Community role in EPC policies. Events began in February 1982, with the imposition on the Soviet Union of Community sanctions by Council Regulation following the declaration of martial law in Poland. This was the first time that sanctions had been imposed by the Community as such. The prospect had been mooted in Political Cooperation, but the decision was taken by the Council, which adopted its Regulation on the basis of a proposal from the Commission. This served as a good precedent when, two months later, Argentina invaded the Falkland Islands. The imposition of Community sanctions once again required the Commission to make a proposal to the Council, following deliberations in EPC. The fact that the Commission was represented by the same officials in both fora (while the Member States were not) made the process easier. It certainly enhanced the role of the Commission. The same procedure was followed some years later for the imposition of 'restrictive measures' against South Africa. On that occasion, the legal situation was more complicated because of the diversity of the measures taken, which led to disputes about the legal base of action. The Commission nevertheless played an essential role both in the technical preparation of the texts and in their official tabling as part of the Community institutional procedure.

The budgetary dimension

The Commission's role was not confined to the imposition of sanctions. It also had an important part to play when EPC needed recourse to the Community's financial instruments to further its policies. The preliminary draft Community budget is prepared by the Commission, which must ensure that the necessary appropriations are included for this purpose. The Commission is also solely responsible for the execution of the budget, a fact which often gave rise to tensions with Member States, especially over the selection of projects in politically sensitive areas.

In the early 1980s, the Ten were anxious to conduct an active policy with regard to Central America, an area in which they saw themselves as a neutral point of reference for countries torn between loyalties to the United States and to the Soviet Union. The central point of their analysis was that the tensions and conflicts ravaging Central America frequently stemmed from grave economic problems and social inequalities (Roy 1992, 78). It was therefore logical that part of the Ten's programme in the region should consist of economic assistance. But Political Cooperation had no budget; for this, Ministers had to turn to the Community. It suited the Commission to have political support for its own efforts to secure extra Community funding from the budgetary authority (Council and Parliament). It exploited the situation to secure approval of a special action programme for Central

America in 1982, which the Council would not otherwise have agreed. Moreover, the additional funds made available in the 1985 budget would probably not have been found without the stimulus provided by the conclusion that year, for political reasons, of the EC-Central America Agreement.

A similar situation arose in the case of South Africa. The Member States were anxious to link their restrictive measures to a programme of positive measures to assist the victims of apartheid. This programme was financed by the Community budget and administered by the Commission. The secrecy with which the Commission carried out its duties, which it saw as essential to protect the beneficiaries from reprisals by the South African authorities, was resented by Member States, who therefore demanded a greater share in the decisions on individual projects. An ad hoc arrangement was made to give the Member States an advisory role, but this was centred on the Community framework. Again, similar difficulties arose, and similar arrangements had to be made, in the case of the Community's programme of aid to the Occupied Territories. The Consuls General of the Member States in Jerusalem disagreed with Commission officials in Brussels as to how the Community's money could best be spent. Likewise, in the case of Afghanistan, the provision of aid from the Community budget following the withdrawal of Soviet troops was conditioned by the political framework adopted in EPC. This time, however, the ad hoc Group which oversaw the 'political aspects' of the selection of projects was based on the EPC, rather than the Community framework. The tendency was for Member States in both the EPC and the Community framework to demand closer control over the selection of projects, and for the Commission to attempt to preserve its prerogative as sole executor of the Community budget. Such disagreement was a harbinger of considerable turf battles to come, as chapter 14 makes clear.

The Single European Act

The Single European Act (SEA), implemented in 1987, did not introduce substantial change in the status of the Commission, though by creating an EPC secretariat within the building of (though institutionally separate from) the Council Secretariat it did draw a firm and formal distinction between the intergovernmental and the Community method. The Commission's Secretariat General would clearly have had the necessary expertise and resources to take on the role of the EPC secretariat, but this would have been a supranational hostage to intergovernmental fortune. The importance of the SEA actually lay largely in placing EPC on a legal basis. Its Title III for the most part took up the existing practices and procedures of EPC, confirming the full association of the Commission with the proceedings of political cooperation (Title III Article 30 (3b)). It conferred no new responsibility on the Commission bar the important duty, shared with the Presidency of the Council, of ensuring that consistency between the external policies of the European Community and the policies agreed in EPC was sought and maintained (Article 30 (5)).[1] Even so, it was stipulated that the Presidency and the Commission should act 'each within its sphere of competence', a proviso introduced at the request of Denmark to make it clear that the Commission did not thereby acquire any new powers in EPC. But, as one Belgian official put it:

> 'Toutefois, on peut se demander si le paragraphe 5 de l'article 30 de l'Acte Unique, qui exprime l'obligation de cohérence, ne donne pas à la Commission un droit de s'opposer à des décisions qui ne sont pas cohérentes avec la politique commerciale commune ou avec des conventions auxquelles la Communauté est partie.' (de Ruyt 1987)

In view of subsequent developments, not least a court case which opposed Commission and Council in 2005 (see page 385), the worries inherent in this conjecture were well-founded.

The SEA, in fact, had the unexpected effect of recalling the Commission's rights and duties under the Community Treaties and linking them to the effectiveness of intergovernmental and artificially separate attempts to make European foreign policy. While conferring no new powers, the SEA confirmed the practice which had grown up since the London Report, whereby the Member States and the Commission intensified cooperation between their representatives in third countries and international organisations. This was to be largely through mutual assistance and information. A parallel decision adopted by Foreign Ministers on 28 February 1986, on the occasion of the signing of the SEA, set out a long list of relevant areas for cooperation, ranging from the exchange of political and economic information and pooling of information on administrative and practical problems to communications, consular matters, cultural affairs and development aid. The Heads of Missions and Commission representatives were encouraged to meet regularly to coordinate views and prepare joint reports either at the request of the Political Committee or on their own initiative.

The new European order

The Commission's role in Political Cooperation took on a new dimension in 1989. This was less the result of the entry into force of the Single European Act than of the cataclysmic changes taking place in Central and Eastern Europe. The fall of one Communist regime after another changed the face of politics in Europe and in the Western world as a whole. The situation required an immediate response from the Community to provide economic assistance. Throughout the spring of 1989, negotiations were in preparation or underway for economic agreements of different sorts with Czechoslovakia, Poland, Hungary, Bulgaria and the Soviet Union. The Commission played its normal Community role in the preparation of these negotiations and their conduct. Significantly, however, on two occasions the Member States called for consistency between EPC and Community policies, in the sense of combining the potential of the two frameworks to produce an effective Community policy. The two occasions were illustrative of the fact that EPC was seemingly following events, with political leadership devolving to the Community, and thus the Commission.

The first example was when the Commission leadership was given international recognition when the Western Economic Summit meeting at the Arche in Paris in July 1989 decided – largely because of Commission

President Delors' advocacy and US President Bush's willingness – to entrust the Commission with the task of coordinating international assistance efforts to Poland and Hungary (Ross 1994, 263 footnote 104). By valiant efforts of impromptu organisation during the summer holiday period the Commission succeeded in launching the coordination operation which became known as G24. This brought together 24 donor countries, all members of the OECD. The Community's own aid operation, known as PHARE, was financed by the Community budget and run by the Commission, with the Member States acting in a consultative capacity. The second example was the negotiation of second-generation agreements with the countries of Central and Eastern Europe and the agreements with the Soviet Union and later with its successor States. This was primarily the responsibility of the Commission. The Commission proposed negotiating directives to the Council, played a crucial part in their adoption and subsequently carried them out. Even the discussions with the Community's partners on the tricky political issue of conditionality – the link between the relationship with the Community and the acceptance of democratic principles and the transition to a market economy – were conducted by the Commission.

The policy of the Community towards its Eastern neighbours in Europe at a time of such uncertainty and change may well have been the most important that Political Cooperation had to formulate. Yet it was the Commission which held the levers of power, whether through its control of implementation of the Community budget, its coordination of the international aid effort on behalf of the countries of East and Central Europe, or its mastery of the process of negotiating agreements on behalf of the Community. Small wonder that the Commission seemed to loom large in the counsels of Political Cooperation and to occupy a position which would have raised eyebrows at the time the Single European Act was passed. It would have been deemed rank heresy a decade before that. It was therefore not surprising that the Intergovernmental Conference (IGC) which negotiated the political union part of the Treaty on European Union paid some attention, within the chapter on Foreign and Security Policy, to the role and powers of the Commission. The outcome marked some advances over the Single European Act, but it did not go as far as the Commission had hoped and as its increasing stature might have been thought to justify.

The Treaty on European Union

The Single European Act had given a faithful picture of the state of Political Cooperation at that time. It could therefore have been expected that the Treaty on European Union would at least do the same for its time, including on the status of the Commission. Yet, the ambition was much greater than that.[2] Several Member States and the Commission wished to take the opportunity to bring EPC to a much greater extent within the Community framework. This would have meant merging the EPC and EC machinery within the Council, at least at Ministerial level. It would also have meant introducing a degree of majority voting for foreign policy questions and providing the Commission with a role resembling that which it performed in the Community. Moves in this direction may be seen in various papers circulated in the preparatory stage preceding the Conference.

The Belgian memorandum of 19 March 1990 identified the developments in Eastern Europe as a challenge clearly illustrating the limitations of the existing machinery of EPC. The paper proposed an approach which was pragmatic and prudent, but nevertheless designed to be operational. Ministers should meet regularly in a dual Council-EPC framework, 'so that the General Affairs Council should once again become the Community's political decision-making centre'. COREPER and the Political Directors should together prepare decisions regarding Central and Eastern Europe, 'and the role of the Commission should be better defined, so as to secure the desired consistency'. A specialised task force would be set up, bringing together national diplomats and Commission officials specialising in Eastern European countries, to 'serve as a centre of analysis, study and coordination on Eastern Europe to the benefit of both the Council and the Commission' (Laursen and Vanhoonacker 1992, 269).

This inventive approach had the merit of suggesting practical ways for Member States and the Commission to work together in an area in which there was demonstrable need, where the Commission had already shown that it had much to contribute and conversely had no need to fear a takeover by Member States. Had the Belgian approach been followed, it might have produced procedures and practices with potentially wider application. From the point of view of the integrationists, it was a pity it was not. In fact it was overtaken by the call, launched by President Mitterrand and Chancellor Kohl in their letter of 19 April 1990, for an intergovernmental conference to 'define and implement a common foreign and security policy' (ibid., 276). Subsequently, the European Parliament's Resolution of 11 July 1990 (ibid., 282) called for matters currently dealt with under EPC to be dealt with in the Community framework with appropriate procedures, thereby abolishing the distinction between EPC and the Community's external economic relations. It also urged that the Commission should have a right of initiative in proposing policies and a role in representing the Community externally.

Denmark, however, took a more reserved position. While accepting in its memorandum of 4 October 1990 that a decision-taking structure could be set up in which the General Affairs Council could be a united forum for both EC and EPC questions, with coordinated preparation of dossiers, it was not prepared to say more about the Commission than that its 'current position as an equal partner in European Political Cooperation should be confirmed in the text of the Treaty' (ibid., 293). Portugal's memorandum of 30 November 1990 took the same view on the unitary role of the General Affairs Council and proposed that the Commission 'should be formally accorded a non-exclusive right of initiative in foreign policy matters' (ibid., 304). The United Kingdom was against bringing EPC into the Community framework and opposed a greater role for the Commission in EPC (ibid., 423).

The Commission itself had agreed with the progressive mainstream in its approach to a Common Foreign and Security Policy. In the official opinion it was called upon to produce in preparation for the Intergovernmental Conference, and which was published on 21 October 1990, it suggested a gradual transfer of topics from EPC to the scope of a common policy. It also proposed majority voting on matters other than those directly affecting security. Regarding its own position, it proposed that, together with the Presidency and the other Member States, it should be given the right of initiative in the field of the Common Foreign and Security Policy (Bulletin Supplement 2/91 1991, 75-82). Two months later, the European Council in Rome on 14-15 December 1990 launched the Intergovernmental Conferences (one on economic and monetary union and one on political union). It adopted a measured approach encompassing the different positions expressed. The Council should form a single decision-making centre, and the Commission should have a reinforced role through a non-exclusive right of initiative. On the decision-making process, consensus should remain the rule in defining guidelines, though agreed policies might be implemented through majority voting.

Discussions in the Conference throughout 1991, and the drafting of the Treaty agreed by the European Council at Maastricht in December of that year, did not, on these questions at least, depart greatly from the indications given by the European Council at Rome. At one stage during the Conference proceedings (March 1991), the Commission tabled a draft for the Common Foreign and Security Policy section of the Treaty, with the object of considerably enhancing its own role and making it an equal partner with the Presidency in the conception and management of policy. While not technically going beyond what was finally agreed, the Commission succeeded in presenting itself in such a lurid light that the Member States took fright, and its contribution did not become a basis for discussion. Instead, the Conference concluded on what had previously emerged as the broad consensus. The Council was given a unitary role, the previous Ministerial Meetings of EPC now officially disappearing. The EPC Secretariat was merged with the Council Secretariat, the old bogey of an autonomous political secretariat detached from the Community institutions and operating out of Paris being finally laid to rest; and the Commission was given a non-exclusive right of initiative. It can be argued that this last provision existed already, in that the Commission, at least since the SEA, had not felt inhibited from informally tabling suggestions on matters in which the Community was directly concerned. It was also the case that a non-exclusive right would not allow the Commission to shape the agenda and policy (subject to the final decision of the Member States) or to carry out the medium- and long-term planning function in Political Cooperation that it did within the Community. However, in formalising the right of initiative, the Maastricht Treaty provided the Commission with the opportunity to act in a more structured and consistent way and to make an important contribution to the formation of foreign policy. Provided the Commission made intelligent and sensitive use of its new right, it might lead to a de facto exclusive right of initiative – without raising institutional hackles, as the formalisation of such a right surely would have.

While these three measures marked a coming together of the Political Cooperation and Community frameworks, thereby advancing on the SEA arrangements, in fact they merely reflected existing practice as it had evolved since the SEA. Contrarily, one of the most important innovations was the introduction of majority voting for the implementation of 'joint actions' under Article J3. The decision to decide by majority had to be taken unanimously and progress in defining the areas open to joint action, within

which majority voting would be possible, had been halting. Indeed, the provisions for majority voting were so hedged about with conditions, mainly to
satisfy the United Kingdom, that it seemed unlikely that a vote would ever
be taken. Thus, in sum, the measures introduced under Maastricht were
firmly in the intergovernmental mode within their separate 'pillar' of the
Union. They fell considerably short of what was sought by those who
wanted foreign and security policy questions to be decided by Community
procedures.

The Commission and the operation of EPC and CFSP

Despite the disappointment of the Commission's hopes for greater convergence between Political Cooperation and Community activities, it nevertheless gained responsibilities under the Maastricht Treaty. Bearing in mind
that at the time of signature of the Treaty in February 1992, and until the
Danish referendum in June, the general expectation was that the Treaty
would come into force on 1 January 1993, to coincide with the appointment
of a new Commission, urgent decisions were then needed on how it would
manage these new responsibilities.

The Commission's machinery for dealing with its relationship with
Political Cooperation had grown haphazardly over the years and remained
limited in scope. Responsibility for such participation in EPC as was admitted by Member States, and for the coordination of Commission positions,
rested from the beginning with the Secretariat General of the Commission.
This was because the Secretariat General had overall responsibility for
coordination of the Commission services, and because it was the President
of the Commission, rather than the Commissioner responsible for external
relations, who took part in EPC meetings, especially in the early days. The
only department under direct responsibility of the President, apart from the
Legal Service, is the Secretariat General. It was therefore natural, on both
these counts, that the Secretariat General should be given overall responsibility for the Commission's relations with EPC. Within the Secretariat
General, operational responsibility was given to the Deputy Secretary
General, Klaus Meyer, a senior official originally from the German Foreign
Service. It was Meyer, rather than his counterparts in external relations DGs,
who represented the Commission in the difficult days when the
Commission was trying to secure a toehold in this new intergovernmental
exercise in which it was very definitely unwelcome. Although in the CSCE
exercise the highly technical input came mainly from DG 1 (the Directorate
General for External Relations), the Secretariat General played a strong coor-
dinating role. When it came to the Euro-Arab Dialogue, the Secretariat
General was responsible for the entire exercise within the Commission, with
Meyer devoting personally a great deal of time to the issue.

This administrative arrangement persisted even after the Commission's
position in EPC had eased, and it no longer had to fight so hard for invitations to meetings. When Meyer left the Secretariat General to become
Director General for Development, he took the Euro-Arab Dialogue with
him. But overall responsibility for EPC coordination and the position of the
Commission representative in the Political Committee remained with his
successor as Deputy Secretary General. There was some discussion as to

whether the job would not be better performed by the Director General or Deputy Director General for External Relations; however it remained with the Deputy Secretary General for two reasons. First, increasingly, the Commission's input into Political Cooperation was coming from several departments (the Directorates General for External Relations and for Development, and occasionally others) and only the Secretariat General, under the authority of the President in the Commission's collegiate system, was in a position to exercise overall control. Second, the Deputy Secretary General was also the Commission's representative in COREPER. He was thus able to exploit his dual presence in COREPER and the Political Committee, an advantage enjoyed by no Ambassador or Political Director of a Member State. This maximised the Commission's role as a bridge between the EPC and Community frameworks.

A small unit took shape under the Deputy Secretary General to look after day-to-day contacts with EPC and in-house coordination. In 1981, this consisted of two Category A officials, the 'European Correspondent' of the Commission (who was not allowed to attend the meetings of the European Correspondents) and one colleague. Between them, these two officials attended all EPC meetings to which the Commission was invited, often but not always accompanied by another colleague from the sectoral department concerned. Their duties were to make whatever contribution to the debate was possible and admitted, to make a record of the discussions, to circulate it to those concerned within the Commission and to act as a general channel of communication between EPC and the Commission.

The full association of the Commission with Political Cooperation after the London Report of 1981 had increased the volume, but had not changed the nature of the work. By 1987, when the Single European Act came into force, the unit had grown in size, but still to only four category A officials instead of two. It had also acquired the Commission Cypher Office, as much by chance as by design. One official then working in the Office of the Clerk of the Commission had been responsible for the Cypher Office since it had been set up in 1975, partly to provide cypher communications between the Commission and its Delegations abroad, but also against the day when the Commission would be admitted to the Coreu network. When he was appointed European Correspondent, responsibility for the Cypher Office passed formally into the Commission's EPC machinery. This proved convenient when, six months later, the Commission did indeed join the Coreu network. The episode demonstrates how the Commission, with inadequate financial and staff resources, was able to improvise arrangements for its association with a policy area still seen as outside the mainstream of Community activities.

The steady increase in EPC work, which coincided with the Single European Act and which came to a head with the events in Central and Eastern Europe, meant that these improved arrangements were no longer adequate. Already in 1987, the Commission had appointed a full-time Political Director (of grade A2 standing) in the Secretariat General. He replaced the Deputy Secretary General as Commission representative in the Political Committee. The advantage of the same person being present in both the Political Committee and COREPER was lost, but the change had become inevitable because of the increased pressure of work and the increased travelling created by the surge in EPC contacts with third countries. The change was a forerunner of the separation of the same Political Director post from that of COPS representative after the Treaty of Nice, as chapter 14 outlines. The upsurge in travelling affected the Commission because of its regular association with all 'Troika' activities, a device whereby Political Cooperation conducted contacts with third countries through a team comprising the current, preceding and succeeding Presidencies. It had been used originally for discussions with the Arab League in the Euro-Arab Dialogue, when the Commission had been associated, but its use was generalised from 1978, when the Commission was then excluded. The Troika was put on a regular basis by the London Report of 1981, but the Commission still failed to become a member of it as part of the arrangements then made for its full association with EPC. One of the difficulties which Member States saw, when the possibility was later discussed, was that the Commission would thereby secure a significant advantage over Member States. Each Member State would be in the Troika for only 18 months every six years (in a Community of 12), while the Commission would be permanently present. It was therefore all the more significant that the then President of the Commission, Gaston Thorn, secured in April 1983 agreement on the Commission's presence in the Troika as a general rule.

The appointment of a Director with no responsibilities other than for Political Cooperation (and related duties, such as participation in the political aspects of the Western Economic Summit process) entailed the establishment in the Secretariat General of a Directorate bringing together various activities relevant to the Commission's association with EPC. The Directorate was made up of three divisions. The first, under the European Correspondent, looked after routine and organisational matters. The second division comprised a small planning staff, also responsible for organising seminars on the Community for national diplomats, a function performed with some success and the forerunner of expanded CFSP training offered by the Commission to Member States several times a year. The third covered human rights. By redeployment of staff and a modicum of barrel-scraping, these units were sufficiently manned to give the Commission an embryo of policy-making capacity in the foreign policy field, separate from the desks in the Directorates General, whose main interests were external economic relations. At the same time, the Delegations of the Commission outside the Community were increasingly involved in EPC activities. From a handful in the early 1970s, they had risen to over 100 by the time the Maastricht Treaty was signed and were gradually brought within the normal Community regime. The external Delegations were associated with Political Cooperation in stages in parallel with the Commission in Brussels, as chapter 15 underlines. They were included in the arrangements made for the association of the Commission following the London Report of 1981 – by no means a foregone conclusion at the time, even though the practice had already existed sporadically. They were further covered by the Directives for cooperation in third countries issued by the Political Committee in 1984 and confirmed in the Decision of 28 February 1986 (see above). As a British Ambassador commented, the 'contrast between the close bonds of European Political Cooperation as felt by those engaged at a working level and the doubts about its usefulness in terms of high (Middle Eastern) policy seems to me to mirror a debate which has surrounded EPC since its early beginnings ... day by day, the principal political club to which I felt I belonged in Damascus was that of the European Community. I suspect that, because of EPC, this is true of a growing proportion of British missions worldwide' (Tomkys 1987).

Conclusion[3]

With CFSP's replacement of EPC, the Community was at a turning-point in the development of its foreign policy capability. The Commission was also at a turning-point in terms of the role it might be called upon to play. Both depended not on the text of the Treaty on European Union, but on the spirit in which the text was to be implemented. Importantly, however, the relationship of EPC to Community policies and decision-making processes was set to remain functional rather than institutionally fixed – it might have led to greater flexibility, but in practice it led to greater fragility and often to incoherence (Ifestos 1987, 221). In fact, the dynamism which the absorption of EPC into the Community might have given to the foreign policy process was eschewed. To the extent that public opinion was not yet ready to accept the implications of such a transfer of sovereignty, the decision of Member States was no doubt correct. But the responsibility of the Commission in the intervening years between Maastricht and the Constitutional Treaty was to evolve. By tactful use of its new powers, the Commission was to bring not only greater substance to foreign policy, but also to create a climate of opinion in which the transfer of sovereignty appeared less intimidating. Given the modest institutional role the Commission played in EPC and in the early days of the CFSP, and the unease with which it was regarded by many Member States, it is significant that it was able to consolidate its position. But, despite this it was nevertheless to find itself confronted with the same challenges it faced with EPC, but in different guises as CFSP developed into ESDP. The following chapters analyse these continuing challenges resulting from the conflict between the desire to preserve sovereign rights and the growing need to pool sovereignty in order to enhance Europe's international status, power and security – all criteria in the shifting nature of the national interests of the Member States, and all with major ramifications for the Commission's role and competences.

Endnotes

[1] For an insightful discussion of the consistency issues which were clearly to persist see Bonvicini, 1982.

[2] The issues are discussed in Forster and Wallace, 1996.

[3] By David Spence.

14. The Commission and the Common Foreign and Security Policy

David Spence

Introduction

The Common Foreign and Security Policy (CFSP) had a difficult first decade. Its detractors were many and its failure to meld foreign policy and external relations into a coherent whole hindered the EU from punching its weight in world affairs. A trawl through the literature on CFSP and EU external relations demonstrates that virtually every informed observer, whether official, politician or academic, argues that not only increased political will, but also further institutional adjustments are needed if CFSP is to be successful.[1] Of course, not all observers advocate a greater role for the Commission in CFSP. While enhancement of CFSP is seemingly desired by all, only few argue that the communitarisation of the second pillar is a *sine qua non* of successful foreign policy (Cameron 2004), while foreign ministers, in the UK at least (Hurd 1994 and 2005; Howe 1998), argue that its strength lies precisely in the intergovernmental method which characterises its decision-making. Still others argue that there is not one form of European integration, but several, and that the 'CFSP community' of diplomats is anyway not homogeneous in terms of its views on the institutional end-state of Europe's foreign policy process (Buchet de Neuilly 2005).

In fact, the European Commission's role in CFSP stands at a crossroads.[2] Its future lies in the resolution of a series of bureaucratic and political conflicts, which have marked the history of CFSP. Two issues have brought these conflicts to a head. The first, the Constitutional Treaty, which even though it may have been brought down in its existing form by the French and Dutch referendums, proposed an EU Foreign Minister and concomitantly a European External Action Service, an arrangement which would merge the competing bureaucracies of the Commission and the Council. Both had fundamental implications for the Commission's role, its political and management culture and the commitment of its staff. The second issue lies with the European Court of Justice, which is to pronounce on a Commission challenge to the legality of EU involvement in small arms collections under CFSP. The outcome will have implications in several policy areas in which the Commission has long been active: development, security sector reform, disarmament, demobilisation, reintegration of former combatants and other arms-related issues such as landmines and explosive remnants of war. If the Court does not uphold the Commission's view in its case against the Council, this will be a clear signal that it is time to rethink the bases of the Commission's contribution to foreign policy overall.

This chapter examines the development of the political and institutional setting underlying the resulting dilemmas facing the Commission, arguing that the CFSP's journey so far and the desired arrival for foreign policy making outlined in the Constitution are replete with implications for the Commission's administrative structure, its tasks in international affairs and its overall role in 'Europe's Would-be Polity' (Lindberg and Scheingold 1970). The chapter also questions whether, like it or not, the Commission's involvement in European foreign policy has reached its limit and whether the time may have come either to forestall increasing supranationalism by 're-nationalising' foreign policy (Ginsberg 2001) or to place foreign policy and external relations squarely in the Council. As complex and difficult as that would be, it might prove simpler than ratifying the Constitution.

Problems and prospects for CFSP

Writing forty years ago, Stanley Hoffmann likened the process of European integration to:

> 'swimmers whose skill at moving quickly away from the shore suddenly brings them to the point where the waters are the stormiest and deepest, at a time when fatigue is setting in, and none of the questions about the ultimate goal, direction and length of the swim has been answered' (Hoffmann 1966).

His comment is particularly apposite in relation to CFSP, where the absence of political will and inbuilt tensions between the principles of intergovernmentalism and the supranationalism of the 'Community method' have militated against effective policy formation. Together, institutional tension and lack of concerted political commitment have produced incoherence in policy making and thus reduced the EU's ability to produce an impact commensurate with its economic might. The administrative and political consequences for the EU institutions – not least the Commission – are extensive.

European governments have frequently lamented their collective impotence. Four years after CFSP was established in 1993, they attempted to resolve one of its important weaknesses, demonstrating what many believed was emerging political will by creating the post of High Representative for the CFSP (HR) through the Amsterdam Treaty. Then, a further four years later, they took steps to establish a European Security and Defence Policy (ESDP) embodied in the Treaty of Nice. But weakness and contradictions remained. CFSP still constituted a major challenge to the Community method, bringing into stark relief the basic tenets of the European integration process. The Maastricht, Amsterdam and Nice Treaties all eschewed the Community method, leaving CFSP and its offshoot ESDP in a second, intergovernmental pillar building on the European Political Cooperation (EPC) described in the previous chapter. Importantly, however, CFSP was unlike Justice and Home Affairs, where the Community method gradually replaced intergovernmentalism. Pooling sovereignty in foreign policy was not a foregone conclusion, and this was not only about settling the Commission's role and status or resolving a matter of constitutional theory. It had the practical consequences of debilitating, permanent vying between the Council and the Commission over whether intergovernmental or Community methods should be used in the day to day business of EU foreign policy-making.

Outside the EU, international relations were conducted with foreign states caring little for the vagaries of the EU's internal wrangling over Community or Council competence and with scant regard for the subtleties of European representation abroad, whether through CFSP or the Community's 'external relations', whether by the Council or the Commission, the High Representative for CFSP and the EU Special Representatives, the EU3 (which soon took over the epithet 'troika', though the High Representative made the three into four), the European members of the Quartet or individual Commissioners for External Relations, Trade, Development and Humanitarian Aid. Outsiders concluded that European governments prioritised fidelity to intergovernmental attempts at coordination over the authoritative (and more transparent) arbitration of the Community method. They noted and exploited the results. EU commitment to going it together was the ambition. In reality, EU institutional arrangements were characterised by confusion rather than transparency. And both the aims and means of policy were constrained across the gamut of practical policy making throughout the 1990s. It was easy to divide and rule the Europeans, whether it was the United States or any number of failed states that tried.

Yet, for all the gloom about CFSP, EU cohesion in its policies towards the rest of the world did improve from the start of the Prodi Commission. As External Relations Commissioner Chris Patten put it, there was:

> 'a real change of gear. At long last, European foreign policy is properly linked into the institutions, which manage the instruments needed for its accomplishment; external trade questions, including sanctions, external assistance, external aspects of Justice and Home Affairs including migration policy, terrorism and transnational crime' (Patten 2001).

Patten's optimistic appraisal, though doubted by some, was seemingly shared by governments, for they soon made plans to reinforce further the institutional structures which underpinned this change of gear. In quick succession, a 'Convention' followed by an Intergovernmental Conference decided on a Draft Constitution placing the holder of the post of European Union Foreign Minister in the Commission and creating a European foreign service, clumsily baptised 'European External Action Service'. These fundamental changes were meant to confound analysts like Hoffman by demonstrating new-found political will and engendering groundbreaking improvements both to EU policy-making and to the content of policy itself. The question, of course, was whether institutional change really could somehow consolidate EU political will. Hitherto, the lack of it had gone hand in hand with the commitment to intergovernmentalism, which many saw as a source of weakness. Yet, as the Deputy Secretary General of the Council, de Boissieu, put it 'nobody ever spoke of the weakness of intergovernmentalism when "crisis management" was done by NATO (but) nothing is more intergovernmental than NATO. And seemingly no one says

NATO has failed because it is intergovernmental. This means that the various actors did not want to play the CFSP game' (de Boissieu 2002). De
Boissieu was playing with words. NATO was never intended to be anything
but intergovernmental, and there have arguably been several occasions
when NATO might have acted, had it not been for the refusal of one or other
partner to countenance action, thus preventing potential action from reaching the formal agenda. In fact, many have criticised NATO and for all its
mooted political relevance, it has also suffered from academic neglect
(Schimmelpfenning, 2003). But, if de Boissieu's comparison with the EU was
unusual, his point was clear: given political will intergovernmental methods
could, in principle, work well, and without it neither intergovernmentalism
nor supranationalism was likely to be successful.

The changes proposed in the Constitutional Treaty were intended to tidy
up the existing rather messy EU arrangements for foreign policy making. If
the pillar system disappeared and the proposed post of double-hatted EU
Foreign Minister/Commissioner for External Relations were to materialise,
there would be greater confidence in EU foreign policy making. Its first
prospective incumbent, Javier Solana, maintains these new arrangements
will be introduced – with or without swift ratification of the Constitution
(Solana 2005) – and Patten, too, has surmised that 'Despite the dumping of
the draft treaty, some arrangement like this is likely one day to emerge'
(Patten 2005, 158). There is even support for the idea in the Quai d'Orsay
whose spokesperson, Cathrine Colonna, has formally stated that 'même en
l'absence de traité constitutionnel qui prévoyait des avancées dans le cadre
des traités existants, il est possible de développer ces activités' (Colonna
2005). This is a view which leaves some lawyers perplexed, yet practical
preparation of a new approach is already underway, despite the fact that
ratification of the Constitution is clearly not on the cards for the lifetime of
the Barroso Commission.

The lessons of the 1990s

Welding diverse national perceptions of foreign events into a common
policy constituted the main problem of the 1990s. But, the price was high for
the lesson that uncoordinated national policies rendered CFSP ineffective
and certainly no match for the emerging challenges of a world without the
threat of the Soviet Union, yet with the USA's role changing from avuncu-
lar to proactive and interventionist. As Yugoslavia disintegrated into civil
war, some, such as the much quoted Luxembourg Prime Minister Jacques
Poos, predicted that 'the hour of Europe' had arrived. Chris Patten later
commented ironically that '[i]t should have been the hour of Europe, but we
blew it' (Patten 2002). Far from the EU providing authoritative arbitration
and bringing peace to the warring factions in the former Yugoslavia, it was
regarded as weak and divided, both in the Balkans and in Washington.
Prodi summed up the resulting dilemma well: 'it is not because of our action
that we have lost credibility' he argued, 'but because of our inability to act'
(Prodi 2000). Ending this inability was to be achieved partly by the creation
of the post of High Representative for the CFSP. This was primarily the
result of lessons learned from the Balkans and before that from the Gulf
Crisis in 1990/1991, where the EU response had been a 'cacophonie abom-

inable' (de Boissieu 2002). Events in the Balkans, in Kosovo in particular, and other regional challenges proved salutary experiences for the EU. Indeed, its later success in the Balkans (aided by the growing risk of increased American unilateralism) contributed substantially to the creation of the most significant European institutional development since the creation of Economic and Monetary Union – the European Security and Defence Policy (ESDP).

The concrete lessons from the 1990s both for defence policy (Andréani *et al.* 2001) and for the EU's stance on civilian aspects of conflict prevention and crisis management were indeed many. With 15 separate armed forces, overheads were high and economies of scale low. The Europeans learned that their defence spending, as low as it was, was spent on the wrong things, as if Cold War priorities were still relevant. And they were obliged to recognise that there were inadequate European structures in place to provide cohesive coordination and even basic communication. There was also an embarrassingly clear imbalance in the military contributions provided by the EU and the United States, let alone between the Member States themselves.[3] While the Americans flew 80% of all strike missions in Kosovo, France alone executed half of the remaining (European) 20%. In addition, the EU had problems mobilising sufficient effective ground forces. As these military imbalances became apparent, it was also clear that there had been little or no reflection on how civilian components of interventions abroad were to be coordinated, let alone even conceived. The 'Petersberg Tasks' of peacekeeping and peacemaking were simply unfulfillable. The key conclusion drawn was that enhanced military preparedness was necessary and an integrated civil-military concept was required. EU Member States turned to this with the Helsinki headline goal of 1999 and the subsequent development of ESDP. Community and thus Commission competence was clearly to be affected, but, while the post of external relations Commissioner was held by Chris Patten, there was to be no proactive extension of the Commission's role in CFSP:

> 'Some of my staff... would have preferred me to have made a grab for foreign policy, trying to bring as much of it as possible into the orbit of the Commission. This always seemed to me to be wrong in principle and likely to be counterproductive in practice. Foreign policy should not in my view... be treated on a par with the single market. It is inherently different' (Patten 2005, 155).

During Patten's term as Commissioner, or as he put it 'on his watch', the EU did, however, slowly develop a common policy in the Balkans outside the remit of the specifically security and defence oriented mechanism gradually developed under HR Solana. Foreign, trade and development policies were re-packaged in Stabilisation and Association Agreements, for example, and the EU showed it was realising its potential when EU sanctions on Serbia helped bring down Milosevic, a joint EU-NATO mission, involving Patten, Solana and Lord Robertson, helped defuse an incipient civil war in Macedonia and an EU-brokered deal allowed Montenegro to remain within the Federal Republic of Yugoslavia (now Serbia and Montenegro). Nevertheless, in the minds of the public and policy-makers abroad, the reference points were the ineptitude with which the EU initially handled the major conflicts in the Balkans and the continuing inability of Member States to agree. The EU was clearly not able to build consensus in all areas of foreign policy, and this is what hit the headlines. Indeed, important differences both within the EU and between the EU and its partners split the EU, and disagreement and disarray over the war against Iraq in 2003 proved not only the nadir of EU-US relations, summed up in the US charge that 'Old Europe' had become marginal to the real concerns of post 9/11 realities, but proof to the cynics that CFSP was a chimera. Actually, EU support for counter-terrorism after 9/11 strengthened EU/US relations, as chapter 11 underlines, but persistent disagreement over Iraq dashed the resulting hopes for transatlantic harmony.

CFSP had begun to seem successful when the EU recognised Croatia in 1991. But, 'common' policy in this case followed the whim and national interest of one Member State, Germany. So while this early 'success' for the CFSP was welcomed, it was hardly a model to follow, for it was more imbued with the perhaps laudable will to agree than with insight into the implications, which proved horrendous. As a senior Council official was later to put it, the recognition of Croatia (a catalyst of Yugoslavia's collapse) was a case of most Member States preferring at the time to be wrong together rather than right separately (Crowe 2005). With the appropriate lesson learned, Member States subsequently insisted on attempting to find the most intelligent approach before announcing policy consensus or at least negotiating until (in accordance with the Treaty) the isolated felt able to 'constructively abstain'. The overall lesson learned from the Balkans was that the reality of national interests and the dream of CFSP had been out of kilter. As Patten put it:

> 'Those who criticized the idea of a Common Foreign and Security Policy should study recent history. Europe completely failed to get its act together in the 1990s on a policy for the Balkans. As Yugoslavia broke into bits, Europe was largely impotent because it was not united. Some Member States wanted to keep Yugoslavia together at all costs, some wanted to manage its break-up, and others still felt we should stay out of the whole mess' (Patten 2004).

But there was more. Internal administrative arrangements were clearly revealed as loose and inefficient. The Single European Act and the Genscher-Colombo Declaration had limited cooperation in the EU to the political and economic aspects of security, without producing a mandate for military action outside the EU (SEA III 6 (a)). Danish insistence on limiting the competences of the EU as a whole, coupled with German insistence on subsidiarity, made innovation difficult. Member States obviously knew that the Community pillar contained elements of foreign policy and that the fall of the Soviet Union and EU enlargement would bring implications for security. They knew, too, that the customs union with Turkey and the prospect of Turkish membership would change the security balance at Europe's borders. They knew, furthermore, that the Yaoundé, Lomé and Cotonou agreements contained a clear political dimension going beyond the basic purpose of development policy. But when they developed the intergovernmental CFSP they left these policy areas in the first, Community, pillar, only to find that the implication for cross-pillar management was a lack of coherence that the Treaty itself enjoined them to guarantee (TEU Art. 47).

As for the second, intergovernmental, pillar, the whole of 'foreign' policy was supposed to reside there, but the Treaty's loose wording made it naively permissive; it even allowed for a common defence, which no Member State was really prepared to envisage. Ironically, most of the decisions concerning the Balkans were taken with the first pillar's Article 235 (subsequently 308) as the legal base. This catch-all article enables the Community to act in the absence of a specific legal base, providing the proposed action is compatible with the original aims of the European Economic Community. Aid to the provisional administration in Kosovo and economic assistance to Afghanistan were decided on this basis, but as de Boissieu ironically put it, 'if you can explain how assistance to the provisional administration in Kosovo is necessary for the realisation of the internal market, I wish you luck!' (de Boissieu 2002).

Thus, if after the Nice and Helsinki summits there was a new ambition to act purposefully together and not just, as Patten put it, 'to cluck over the state of the world' (Patten 2001), ambition still did not quite match reality. In September 2000, Solana formally outlined what needed to be done. He argued that the EU was not making the best use of its collective resources, did not exert influence commensurate with the instruments available and did not project itself as a coherent actor (Solana 2000). He made the same case in evidence to the European Convention on the Future of Europe (Solana 2002). His list of complaints was long, and it formed the mainstay of the Convention's later deliberations on the future of CFSP. In sum, for Solana, the lessons of the 1990s were that EU representation needed review, that there needed to be more coordination of ministerial visits abroad, more assistance to the HR, more synergy between Member State embassies and Commission Delegations, more intelligent use of EU weight and influence in international organisations, enhanced CFSP instruments, a review of financial arrangements and more flexible access to CFSP funds. Few would have disagreed, but it was the institutional 'modalities' of such enhanced foreign policy which were to prove the main point of disagreement.

There was another view of foreign policy performance, however. The Commission's contribution to assisting the candidate countries of Central and Eastern Europe prepare for accession to the Union had been crucial not only to their successful entry but to the formation of peaceful and transparent international relations throughout the area for the first time in centuries. Further, the EU, led by the Commission, was successful in negotiating partnership and association agreements with Russia, Ukraine and other former Soviet republics and it also established the Barcelona process, which provided for regular political dialogue and an institutional framework for the Commission to assist the Mediterranean countries in their development. Here, it was the key role of the Commission that was promoted. As the EU became an ever stronger magnet for its neighbours, the Commission gained high profile in negotiating far-reaching conditionality clauses into agreements with them, thus spreading the norms of the Union, whether political, economic or philosophical[4] and advocating 'a world governed by rules created and monitored by multilateral institutions' (Ferrero-Waldner 2005). In sum, while lessons were being learned for CFSP and arguments for change advanced, the 'fully associated' Commission quietly strengthened its position in external relations and gained international visibility. Not only this, the Commission also held the purse strings and sat in the managerial seat of the CFSP in addition to its management of the first pillar policy instruments, even if the precise arrangements involved were rather nebulous.[5] Patten set out to improve transparency and efficiency (see chapter 15). But, as streamlining instruments and introducing modern management techniques became a general clarion call, its counterpart in practice was an immensely increased workload for the Commission both in the field of external affairs and in CFSP.

By 2004, the Commission's External Relations (Relex) family of DGs was managing a budget of some seven and a half billion euros, including pre-accession support, development aid, trade administration and humanitarian aid. DG Relex also managed the administrative and operational costs of CFSP (Art. 28 TEU), a paltry thirty million euros in 2002 as Solana's deputy de Boissieu was cynically to point out to the Convention, arguing 'c'est de la provocation' (de Boissieu 2002), though by late 2005 the CFSP budget was nearing €80 million. Significantly, much of what might have been spent on CFSP came out of the Community budget: for example, spending on human rights, mine clearance, the costs of the Special Representative to Bosnia and Herzegovina and the UN Interim Mission in Kosovo (UNMIK). The financial perspectives for 2006 onwards had not been decided when this book was completed, but proposals for a string of new financial arrangements were being debated (Commission 2004e). The Africa Peace Facility had already been created.[6] In addition, the Commission had proposed four new Community instruments set to streamline a welter of existing separate instruments: Pre-accession Assistance, a European Neighbourhood and Partnership Mechanism, a Development Cooperation and Economic Cooperation Instrument and an Instrument for Stability.

The Council initially welcomed these initiatives. At its meeting on 23 November 2004, in the context of an orientation debate on the effectiveness of EU external action, indeed the first of its kind in the enlarged EU25, it described the Commission's proposal as 'a conducive basis for discussion' (Council 2004). The point of the Stability Instrument was to provide an immediate and effective response to crises in third countries. Seven financial mechanisms have hitherto been available for external crises, each with separate decision-making and budgetary arrangements. By improving crisis response through a streamlining of procedures, the Commission's contribution to EU capacity for response could be enhanced. Though it might sound trite, the coherence between first and second pillar instruments also clearly stands to be improved, as many examples show. In Iraq, a case for CFSP if ever there was one, the Commission was obliged to activate several separate Community instruments: the Rapid Response Mechanism, the Human Rights Regulation, the Mine Action Regulation and Humanitarian Aid. Since then expanded and rationalised financial instruments have reflected growing responsibility and concomitant commitment to efficiency, but there has been serious debate about the Stability Instrument. General agreement exists that it would make sense to reduce the current total of some thirty legal instruments, but placing crisis response under a single Community instrument poses problems for the Parliament and the Council, where there is perhaps justified concern that the Commission would be expanding its competence further than desired.

It is important to retain the point that, as involvement of the EU in the Balkans, Africa, the Middle East, Iran and Iraq grew and underlined how diplomatic carrots and sticks differentiated the EU from the US, it was in the Commission and the first pillar that the operational instruments lay. True, a Council decision was required to introduce sanctions, but the mechanisms involved were Community mechanisms. This was also true of EU policies towards other regions. In Asia, there was a steady deepening of ties with Japan and China, and the EU strongly supported South Korean President Kim's Sunshine Policy, sending a ministerial troika to North Korea in the summer of 2001 to maintain dialogue with Pyongyang and the Korean Peninsula Energy Development Organisation (KEDO) and provide diplomatic counter-balance to the gung-ho attitude of the US. In all these cases the Commission was there managing the detail. In Latin America, where the EU became the principal partner of Mercosur and the Andean Pact, it was the Commission which negotiated the free trade agreements with Mexico and Chile. In Africa, improved development assistance, support for regional economic integration, negotiation of new agreements with individual countries and with the ACP in general and the Africa Peace Facility were managed by the Commission. These initiatives served to strengthen interregional ties not only in the fields of trade and aid, but also through cooperation in conflict prevention, crisis management and peacekeeping. Again, in these areas, the Commission was the de facto operational arm through its driving seat role in management of the crucial first and increasingly third pillar policies and of the budget, including the CFSP budget. It was the Commission that provided the backbone of the negotiating teams, provided the financial and technical resources and played a key role in the long-term prevention of conflict (Manners 2005), even if the star role in the media impact of the EU's international crisis management went to Solana and varying constellations of large Member States. Although the financial and human resources contributed by the Commission and its success in 'conflict prevention' may often pass unnoticed, they amount to 'soft power' (Nye 2004). As Patten frequently stressed, projecting stability may be achieved as much by enlargement, liberal trade policies and effective development assistance as by any number of CFSP 'common strategies' or declarations. That the Commission is the initiator/manager of such policy areas should not be underestimated.

Thus, despite the CFSP's difficult first decade there was a fundamental enhancement of the EU's external relations, which brought about broad changes in the Commission's organisational arrangements both for first and second pillar business. These are discussed below. The Commission's main function in CFSP is rule-making and project management. On the one hand, it proposes legislation in first pillar areas of relevance to CFSP (the introduction of implementing legislation consequent to UN Security Council Resolutions on trade sanctions, for example). On the other hand, there is the Commission's management of the financial aspects of CFSP Joint Actions, such as weapons collection in Cambodia or support for the Palestinian Authority in the area of police training. These are important roles for the Commission, even if in practice the Commission's public image may be weakened by Member States' contentment to do the politics and leave administration to the Commission.

Such reticence to grant the Commission political credit for the role it enjoys in the first and second pillars is costly, not only because it is a decisive factor in the EU's overall inability to provide clear leadership, but because it allows the Council Secretariat and the SG/HR great opportunities to steal the Commission's thunder. It should not be surprising that, as security and defence policy 'completed' the CFSP policy picture after Nice, attempts to marginalise the Commission increased. Whether this was a conscious strategy or simply the consequence of existing procedures is a moot point. From a Commission perspective, the Treaty of Amsterdam's appointment of the HR, originally intended to solve the issue of institutional fragmentation, was already an 'exercise in collusive ambiguity' (Nuttall 1997), enabling Prodi later to argue:

> 'the EU's external policies remain too fragmented. We are still far from having the single telephone number Mr. Kissinger once asked for. In 2004, I would like to see the EU merge all our foreign policy instruments into one single external policy structure. This structure should be located within the Commission, with special rules and procedures tailored to the needs of security and defence. In practical terms this would mean integrating the position of the EU's High Representative for the Common Foreign and Security Policy into the Commission' (Prodi 2001).

The following section outlines institutional developments within the EU and the corresponding changes to the administrative structure of the Commission. But there is an important caveat to the analysis. As the story of the Commission and CFSP unfolds, the reader is asked to view institutional adjustments as a function of political decisions about new procedures for policy-making. But conundrums in institutional developments are often as much part of 'non-decisions' as they are part of the decisions. If institutional developments in CFSP have largely come about through the political decision to add ESDP to the Christmas tree of foreign policy, one important 'non-decision' of enormous relevance for institutional developments and conflict of competences is that there are two conflicting concepts of 'security' upon which decisions are taken (Buzan et al 1998). The 'old' view limits security to military and police concerns. The 'new' view of security questions the primacy of the military and police focus, pointing analysts towards a comprehensive concept of 'human' security to include environmental, developmental and humanitarian issues as worthy of attention for the security analyst. Many of the problems facing the EU institutions arise from a fundamental debate about the concept of security that has not yet taken place. While the Commission espouses (without formally recognising it) the 'new', comprehensive view of security matters and thus brings to bear the wide variety of policy tools at its disposal for the analysis of security issues, the Council has been wedded, until very recently, to a more traditional view. This is not the place for a lengthy discussion of the issue. But it will become clear from the following sections of this chapter, particularly in the discussion of emerging policy in the field of security sector reform, that the absence of a formal attempt to define 'security' and decision-making about procedures, institutions and competence on such an ill-defined basis lie at the heart of the divergence of views and the disagreement over procedures that the rest of the chapter identifies.[7]

CFSP and ESDP – administrative and institutional arrangements

The High Representative for CFSP and the Policy Unit

The most significant political change in CFSP after Maastricht was the enhancement of its operating machinery by the Amsterdam Treaty's creation of the High Representative for the Common Foreign and Security Policy (HR) and his Policy Planning and Early Warning Unit (Policy Unit). These developments and the subsequent creation of ESDP within CFSP, formalised by the Nice Treaty, introduced new committee structures which altered the CFSP landscape (see diagrams in Annex I).[8] The HR, Javier Solana, had previously been Spanish Foreign Minister. His post as Secretary General of NATO was to have expired in December 1999, but he left two months early to take on the newly created position of HR. His appointment was the result of a publicly discussed compromise between intergovernmentalists (UK, Denmark, Sweden), pragmatists (Germany, Italy, Austria) and communitarians (Benelux) (Gourlay and Remacle 1998). But, the post of HR was so circumscribed by Member State prerogative that its final shape depended on how good a fist Solana made of the job and how political will within the Member States evolved. Like many an EU policy or mechanism, the SG/HR and his Policy Unit are considerably different from the model foreseen at the outset. Amsterdam foresaw that '[t]he Presidency shall be assisted by the Secretary-General of the Council who shall exercise the function of High Representative for the common foreign and security policy' (Art 18.3) and that he should also 'assist the Council... contributing to the formulation, preparation and implementation of policy decisions.. acting on behalf of the Council at the request of the Presidency' (Art. 26).

With precise duties – apart from 'assistance' – unassigned, length of appointment and even appointment procedures undetermined in the Treaty, the overall position of the HR was thus precarious. It was clearly to be subject to the whim, size and importance of the Presidency of the day and to the political strength and profile of the Commissioner for External Relations, not to mention his political orientation in terms of the intergovernmental versus supranational divide. Appointment of the HR by the European Council as opposed to European foreign ministers clearly brought status, power and legitimation of the highest order, as it does to the President of the Commission and to individual Commissioners. Yet, the Commission President and the College are arguably more legitimate – they, at least, must gain the assent of the European Parliament and undergo 'hearings' before parliamentary assent to a new Commission is given. An assessment of whether Solana has been used, snubbed or promoted and whether this has varied from small to large Presidencies is not the subject of this chapter, though it would make the now hypothetical debate over whether a single individual should hold both the post of HR and Commissioner for External Relations, as the Constitutional Treaty suggested, more pointed.

In appointing Solana to the HR post, the Member States chose one of Europe's most distinguished statesmen. His stature clearly helped ensure that the EU's voice is heard regularly in Washington and other major capitals. Indeed, as rueful Presidency officials have privately commented, visits to Europe by such foreign leaders as US Secretaries of State Colin Powell and Condoleezza Rice often reversed the expected order of protocol. Meetings between Powell and Solana often took place before meetings with the foreign minister of the Presidency, a fact that particularly vexed some Presidencies. While the choice of a politician as opposed to a senior official for the HR post was by no means a foregone conclusion, such is the political role that Solana carved out that it would now be difficult to envisage his replacement by a bureaucrat.[9] The Council's role has increased significantly and Solana has become a growingly visible and effective figure of European diplomacy, respected by his foreign minister counterparts in Member States and abroad. Indeed, this very success in the post clearly led Solana to let modesty slip over time. He stated early on that his task was to assist the Presidency and the Member States:

> 'to use the post of High Representative to create new momentum within the CFSP. We have to ensure that the EU provides a more coherent approach to the rest of the world. The Council has to guarantee that the Member States deliver on this' (Solana 2000b).

By 2003, he was declaring to the *Financial Times* (2003) that:

> 'As time goes by I do whatever I want. I know what people think. I pursue my own agenda. I don't have to check everything with everyone. I would rather have forgiveness than permission. If you ask permission, you never do anything'.

The fact, however, that most of the practical instruments of political persuasion are usually not his to wield is an obvious straitjacket. Military and economic power lie with the Member States and the Commission, so Solana's undeniable success comes from the respect he has created, and not from his use of the tools of his trade. He has had to outwit and beat the Commission in order to extend his responsibility across the EU foreign policy board. 'Outwitting' and 'beating' are terms redolent with adversarial content and this has clearly affected the HR's and his staff's relations with the Commission. But, Solana's increasing power, both within the EU and abroad, has lent him considerable authority. A single EU Member State would be unlikely to wield the kind of influence Solana offered in mediating a political crisis such as that in Ukraine in November 2004, where he held talks with Ukrainian President Leonid Kuchma and the two contenders disputing the results of the presidential runoff, Prime Minister Viktor Yanukovych and opposition candidate Viktor Yushchenko. The European Parliament had urged Solana to help find a peaceful resolution to the danger of the political crisis escalating into civil conflict between supporters of the two sides. Admittedly, other senior national EU Member State politicians also appeared in Kiev. The Polish and Lithuanian Presidents and the Dutch Prime Minister intervened – the latter as Presidency of the EU, rather than as a spokesman for The Netherlands – but the media focus was on Solana's mediation role. On 21 January 2005, he invited Ukraine's President-elect Viktor Yushchenko to discuss the possibility of future EU membership, just after the Commission had stated the previous week that it had no plans to consider Ukrainian entry into the EU. This may have been a misunderstanding or a simple 'gaffe', but it does demonstrate how powerful Javier Solana had become.

Solana no longer travels with the EU rotating Presidency and the Commissioner of External Relations as the reigning EU 'troika'. Since his mooted appointment as first EU Foreign Minister (EUFM), he now seems to speak and travel as a sole voice rather than as one of three. In 2004 when Israel's Prime Minister Ariel Sharon declined to meet him, arguing that an EU vote against Israel at the UN meant Israel could not cooperate with the EU, despite Solana's participation in the Quartet for Peace in the Middle East, Solana surprised EU leaders and the Israelis alike by replying that like it or not, both he and the EU were there to stay in the Israeli-Palestinian decision making process. The number of national foreign ministers who speak so directly and outspokenly on international issues such as these are few. Solana has clearly been able to focus an enormous amount of media and high political attention on himself, and this has undoubtedly contributed to his unrivalled nomination as first EU Foreign Minister. He may not have power over the Commission in his current role, but a later double-hatted Solana could and would clearly capitalise on the trust Member States have demonstrated in nominating him the first EUFM – if that constitutional change were to come about. However, the role of his personal team in the Council Secretariat, both in his Policy Unit and in Directorate E (External Relations), in contributing to this trust and his reputation overall should not be underestimated.

The Policy Unit, formerly named the Policy Planning and Early Warning Unit, has actually engaged in little planning and hardly any early warning, though it has been strong on analysis. The most salient feature of its brief history has been its transformation from planning and early warning status into a policy-making role under its first Director, Christoph Heusgen. Both the power of the new Policy Unit and the enhanced power and status of the Council Secretariat since the creation of the office of the High Representative have had an important effect in terms of the Commission's changing role. It has been argued that despite the Secretariat's role as 'trusted assistant', it uses 'behind-the-scenes instrumental leadership strategies' and provides itself with 'opportunities to influence the final outcome for private gain, by, for example, shifting final agreement closer to its own preferred outcome' (Beach 2004, 409-11). An amusing incident resulted from the Council Secretariat's forceful advocacy of the creation of legal personality for the European Union, as opposed to the current situation where the European Community has legal personality, with the Commission its flag-bearer. One diplomat (currently Irish representative in COREPER) presented the Secretariat's senior legal advisor with a t-shirt reading 'the legal personality of the Union'; such was the perceived persistence of the Secretariat's advocacy (Beach 2004, 434, footnote 36).

The Council Secretariat's involvement in producing policy papers, often in cooperation with the Commission, though more often using 'informal input' from the Commission's geographical services and Delegations, has been striking. Joint documents included early papers on the Western Balkans in 2000, on the implementation of Common Strategies in 2002, on China in 2001 and 2002 and on the Watch List for Crisis Prevention paper in 2002. But, to the frustration of Commission officials, there were several Policy Unit papers in later years which did not mention considerable – indeed arguably indispensable – Commission input, such as on Colombia, Venezuela, the South Caucasus, Central Asia, Belarus, Moldova, Indonesia and the FRY, to name but a few. In fact, the frequency with which Commission papers have been the basis of Council policy proposals has begun to prompt reflection – in the absence of ratification of the Constitution – on the need for a code of conduct between the Commission and the High Representative's staff. This would not only provide operational guidelines but highlight clear synergies which need to be made explicit in the current absence of the combined foreign service the Constitution was set to introduce.

One relevant area for enhanced synergy is crisis management, for which the Policy Unit was originally created and which is now cooperatively led on the basis of a 'joint watch list'. In the long term it is hardly a sensible use of resources to maintain two 'crisis centres', the Commission's crisis room and the Council's Situation Centre, each replete with state-of-the-art technology and security; and this even more so given the many other Commission crisis mechanisms described in chapter 18. If the EU is to be effective in a real crisis, duplication of resources and input can only hamper its efficiency. Moreover, the EU response in all the relevant issue areas anyway requires a cross-pillar approach involving shared analysis, shared information and joint preparation of EC and EU responses. In turn there is a requirement for a coordinating reflex to overcome the institutionalised differentiation between coordination of Community instruments within the Commission and coordination of other EU instruments in the Council. While many lessons were learned from the failures of the 1990s, coordinating the bureaucracies in the field of security, crisis response and public diplomacy are obvious areas where enhanced cooperation could easily have borne fruit, but it has taken an inordinate amount of time for this lesson to be learned. The proposed creation of the European External Action Service testifies that Member States are cognisant of what is at stake. Meanwhile, the impact of the increased politicisation of the Council Secretariat's role and the arrival on the scene of the Policy Unit has been considerable – both on the functions of the HR and, by extension, on the functions of the Commission. The Policy Unit has wrested political and administrative responsibilities from diffuse power bases in the Council Secretariat and the Commission and made itself the prime focus of foreign policy preparation through its reports and analyses. Meanwhile, the Commission has concentrated on enhancing its role as the EU's project manager.

Rivalries between the bureaucracies of the Commission and the Council were to be expected. After all, in the Community pillar the role of analyst and policy entrepreneur falls to the Commission, while direct management falls to the administrations of Member States, with the Commission ensuring an overall supervisory role. In CFSP the Policy Unit has become a major policy entrepreneur, while the Commission manages CFSP projects and the Council ensures the supervisory role. Unlike the taciturn traditional Council

Secretariat, the Policy Unit has also become the policy advocate in meetings at all levels. The rivalry between the Council Secretariat and both Member States and the Commission in the field of external affairs is meanwhile common knowledge and publicly documented (Beach 2004). Its Directorate E (External Relations) staff are increasingly no longer merely the minute writers and meeting organisers. Like the Policy Unit, they too have become the drafters of authoritative CFSP policy papers.

Outside the institutions this rivalry is often perceived as being between the Commission and the Council Secretariat, i.e. between DG Relex and the Policy Unit, but it also exists within the Council Secretariat, between the Policy Unit and Directorate E. One does not need to have read Max Weber to recognise the trends. The Council Secretariat's external affairs directorate is leaning on the political role created by the Policy Unit to increase its own power. Together, the Council Secretariat and the Policy Unit now rival both the Presidency and the Commission as policy entrepreneur and have become proactive forces in their own right across the gamut of foreign and security issues. Where the Commission lacks sufficient intelligence resources and diplomatic respect, the Policy Unit is gradually gaining them. Whether the Council Secretariat aspires to or could handle a more operational role in CFSP and ESDP remains to be seen. The Deputy Secretary General of the Council has argued defensively that 'everybody has suspected the Council Secretariat of wishing to take over part of the executive functions of the Commission. I reassure you immediately, the General Secretariat and the High Representative are strong because they have no executive tasks. So, I am not claiming any. I ask that we have no executive tasks' (de Boissieu 2002). The Secretariat General is clearly content for the Commission to *manage* policy. But, it is policy-*making* which is at stake.

The Commissioner for External Relations and the issue of coordination

The re-organisation of Commissioners' portfolios and corresponding re-arrangements in the Directorates General (DGs) were many after the Maastricht Treaty led the Commission to convert the special EPC unit of the Secretariat General into a new Directorate General (DG IA), with a Commissioner specifically charged with CFSP. At the same time the increasing volume and range of the Commission's external responsibilities were a key factor in its rapidly changing profile.[10] Over time, the Commission became the principal negotiator for the EU, not only on Common Commercial Policy issues but also when cooperation and association agreements or enlargement negotiations were conducted with non-Member States. But, shifting constellations of internal organisation for the panoply of external relations portfolios resulted in an absence of consensus within the Commission as to what the nature of the Commission's arrangements for coordinated input into external relations and CFSP really should be. There were frequent changes and differences in leadership style within the issue areas involved. Nugent and Saurugger (2002) note that the existence of different visions of how best to attain organisational effectiveness and efficiency, political and bureaucratic jostling, the quality and profile of internal leadership and the occasional existence of 'windows of opportunity' are significant in explaining change in the Commission. At the start of his term Prodi was allocated a mandate to reform the Commission following the debacle of the resignation of the Santer Commission. In addition, the allocation of portfolios between Commissioners had become less subject than hitherto to pressure from national governments. Both Prodi and his successor Barroso were able to profit from the fact that the Amsterdam and Nice Treaties increased the President's powers in this regard. Yet bureaucratic rivalry within the Commission increased because of the uncoordinated division of responsibility for external affairs among several Commissioners and Directors General. The obvious need to coordinate was counter-balanced, even stymied, by the perception that Commissioners' independence and their DGs' autonomy should be preserved. Contributing to effective delivery of policy was as difficult as overall management reform.

The first Commissioner for External Relations, in 1993, was former Dutch Foreign Minister Hans van den Broek. He led the Commission input into the fledgling CFSP. The new Directorate General for External Political Relations was DG IA, its Director General the former Secretariat General EPC Commission expert, Günter Burghardt. DG IA was juxtaposed to DG I, the existing External Economic Affairs DG, reporting to Commissioner Sir Leon Brittan and another German Director General, Horst Krenzler.[11] 'Competition' is the unavoidable description of relations between the two Commissioners and their Directorates General, and it was exacerbated by the largely uncoordinated existence in the 1990s of other portfolios within the Relex family: development, enlargement, North-South relations (itself part of DG I, but reporting to a separate Commissioner, Manuel Marín) and humanitarian aid. Frequent internal disputes were the hallmark of the Commission's foreign relations. Coupled with the reticence of the Commission throughout the 1990s to use its hard-won right of initiative in CFSP, for fear of incurring Member State opposition, this internal rivalry impeded efficient delivery of policy and compounded Commission weakness.[12] Had the EPC section remained in the Secretariat General and reported directly to the Commission President (Delors, after all) or been transferred to the old DG I, where a ready-made system of relations between headquarters and the delegations existed, the history of the Commission's input into CFSP might have been different.

As Director General under Commissioner van den Broek, Burghardt concentrated on the Commission's role in CFSP to the detriment of sound project management. This was subsequently reversed under Director General Legras and Commissioner Patten, as concentration on management became an overall Commission objective in both the Santer and Prodi Commissions and certainly the prime focus in the Relex family.[13] Reform of external assistance was led by Commissioner Patten, but instigated by the Wise Men's Group, which reported on misgivings regarding project management in the Commission. The European Parliament and the Court of Auditors also played an important role through their repeated advocacy of reform. But the counterpart of the concentration on management issues (including the consolidation of the Unified External Service discussed in chapter 15) was less senior enthusiasm for the Commission's role in CFSP. With Patten committed to improving the Commission's ability to deliver effective policy management and further committed to avoiding rivalry with HR Solana in terms of the lead political role in CFSP, there was little likelihood of a high profile for the Commission. Since Director General Legras opted for a managerial as opposed to a political role, the Deputy Director General functioned as the Commission's Political Director. This found the incumbent abroad for most of the year in troikas of political directors and other meetings worldwide. The post of Deputy Director General is not part of the Commission's line management and promotion structure. It is usually staffed by a senior national diplomat on secondment and has at times been left vacant while Member States decide on a candidate. Under van den Broek and Burghardt the senior Portuguese diplomat Vasco Ramos held the post. Then under Patten, Legras and Landaburu (who replaced him as Director General) until the spring of 2005, the Spanish diplomat Fernando Valenzuela held the post until he became Head of the Commission Delegation in New York and the Czech Karel Kovanda succeeded him.

As the workload increased and the Director General was more engaged in management reform than policy-making, the Patten *cabinet* intervened directly in the day-to-day work of the 'services'. Like Pascal Lamy when he was Delors' *chef de cabinet*, Anthony Cary, *chef de cabinet* to Patten until his appointment as UK Ambassador to Sweden in the summer of 2003, developed a network of people from whom he was able to secure new ideas, quick drafts or help with policy briefs. The system was possibly more efficient than working through strict hierarchical procedures. It certainly provided an ego boost to those involved. But it also led to frustration and resentment by those not in the inner circle. The current Director General, Eneko Landaburu, has returned DG Relex to hierarchical order, though the problem of an ever increasing workload remains and the issue of coordination with other DGs in the Relex family remains as important as within the Commission overall and between the Commission and the Council. The joint proposal in 2005 by Solana and Barroso on the future structures of the European External Action Service stressed as much.[14]

Improving external policy coordination by assigning a senior Commissioner an overall coordinating role was tried under Prodi. Patten was made chair of the five Commissioners dealing with external relations. This led to a more coherent Commission approach to CFSP, though the *primus inter pares* principle militated against the creation of really effectively coordinated management of external relations. Resistance to coordinators by the 'coordinated' is not a new phenomenon. Divergences of view between Patten and Development Commissioner Nielson were common knowledge, though overall as Patten was later to note:

> 'Thanks to the friendly, avuncular style of the President of the Commission, Romano Prodi, and to his willingness to delegate to his colleagues, the Commission was a pretty happy team with little acrimonious bickering or bureaucratic turf warfare' (Patten, 2005, 123).

By the time of the Barroso Commission there were four external relations Commissioners managing five Directorates General. In view of the proposed creation of an EU Foreign Minister (EUFM), simultaneously Vice President of the Commission, there was a case in the Barroso Commission for enhancing the coordination role under the Relex Commissioner, yet Barroso himself took the lead. He chairs the Group of Commissioners for External Relations composed of Peter Mandelson (DG Trade), Olli Rehn (DG Enlargement), Louis Michel (DGs Development and Humanitarian Aid) and Benita Ferrero-Waldner (DG External Relations and European Neighbourhood Policy), who functions as vice chair. Should the post of EU Foreign Minister come about, Ferrero-Waldner would presumably drop responsibility for DG Relex, which would report to the EUFM, but continue to preside over European Neighbourhood Policy and simultaneously occupy the Commission seat at meetings of EU foreign ministers, where the EUFM would be in the chair. This may be pure speculation, but the issue itself is highly pertinent.

The Commission in CFSP and ESDP: problems and prospects

The Commission sees its contribution to CFSP/ESDP under the overall theme of conflict prevention, and its internal structures and procedures have been adapted to ensure that hitherto disparate policy areas form part of a coherent and coordinated whole. Many related policy areas, such as development policy and humanitarian aid have hitherto fallen into the Commission's bailiwick, and its long-standing expertise in these areas has led it to focus on key areas where the Policy Unit's growing political strength makes it a rival in terms of policy entrepreneurship. In addition, newer areas for policy, such as in the arms field, from non-proliferation through to security sector reform, disarmament, demobilisation and reintegration into society of former combatants have become areas of rival competence.

When Amsterdam established the post of HR, a separate Commission CFSP Directorate with new units to match the emerging ESDP structures was created in what is now known as DG Relex. Housed on the 12th floor of the Commission's 'Charlemagne' building, it benefits from state of the art security procedures and equipment, in preparation for a Commission role not only in the routine management of policy falling under the term 'conflict prevention' but the operational function of crisis management, in so far as these crises are outside the EU. It also participates in the new Council committee structures with its four units: the Security Unit, the Conflict Prevention and Crisis Management Unit, the CFSP Counsellor's Unit and the European Correspondent Unit. The first Director, Lodewijk Briet, had seen service in many parts of the Commission, not least in Delors' *cabinet*. Briet was both Commission representative to the Political and Security Committee (PSC) and manager of the new CFSP Directorate. His job was a good example of the Commission's work overload. He was obliged to manage the almost one hundred staff and considerable financial resources (the CFSP budget line alone surpassed €60 million in 2005 and in 2006 the total budget was €102 million). To this was added his participation in the PSC almost all day for two, if not three days a week, unlike his Brussels-based PSC ambassadorial colleagues, whose CFSP Directorates were managed back in their capitals. When Briet left Brussels in the spring of 2005 to become Head of the Commission Delegation in South Africa, he was replaced temporarily by Lars-Erik Lundin, Head of the Security Unit, and then finally in the autumn of 2005 by Stefano Sannino, a former member of the Prodi *cabinet*.

At the Nice European Council, several Treaty changes were agreed relating to CFSP and its offshoot the ESDP. The Western European Union (WEU) was incorporated into the EU (Art. 17), and the Political and Security Committee (PSC, commonly referred to by its French acronym, COPS) was anchored in the Treaty and defined (Art. 25) as the locus of decision-making during crisis management operations abroad. The ESDP was later declared operational at the European Council meeting in Laeken at the end of 2001. Since ESDP is an extension of CFSP, the Commission is fully associated and has a right of initiative equal to Member States, albeit not in military matters. While political oversight of CFSP by the European Council and the General Affairs and External Relations Council remains unchanged, the motor running the CFSP is now the Political and Security Committee. The remit of the PSC ambassadorial meetings is to cover all aspects of CFSP, including security and defence issues.

The PSC largely took over the work previously done by the Political Committee, where political directors used to meet on a more leisurely monthly basis – described by Patten as 'the old floating crap game' (Patten 2001). Although it is nominally responsible to COREPER (as overall coordinator of the General Affairs Council), significantly COREPER rarely intervenes in PSC business. The PSC has brought greater urgency to CFSP and a potentially improved capacity to respond swiftly to crisis situations. It meets at least twice a week and forms the diplomatic hub around which the CFSP revolves. Comprising senior diplomats from the Member States, the Council Secretariat, the Policy Unit and the Commission, the PSC monitors international affairs; guides the work of the Military Committee and all CFSP working groups; prepares and oversees the implementation of CFSP decisions; leads political dialogues at official level; and maintains links to NATO. Formally responsible in crisis situations, the PSC has engendered its 'own' ESDP structures adding to those existing in CFSP: the European Union Military Staff (EUMS), the European Union Military Committee (EUMC), the Political-Military Affairs Committee (PolMil) and the Committee on Civilian Aspects of Crisis Management (CivCom). In addition EU Military Staff support the HR and provide military expertise and support to ESDP, with a particular focus on the Petersberg tasks (peacekeeping, peace enforcement and support for humanitarian crisis situations, including evacuation etc.). The EU Military Committee is composed of the national Chiefs of Defence and their military representatives. It is responsible for providing the PSC with military advice and recommendations. As for evaluation of civil-military issues in crisis management, the PolMil and CivCom committees complete the picture. The Commission participates actively in both.

The Commission did not initially seek a role in the military dimension of ESDP. It was agreed within DG Relex that the Commission had neither the resources nor the expertise to contribute meaningfully to the Military Committee. The Commission did, however, argue that it had an important role in non-military dimensions of ESDP such as defence industrial cooperation, funding and training of police, customs officials and border guards, economic sanctions, de-mining operations, security sector reform, demobilisation and rehabilitation, election monitoring, and generally restoring local administrations in societies emerging from conflict. The Commission's seat at meetings of the Military Committee (formally there since the Commission is 'fully associated') was long unoccupied. However, the Barroso announcement at the January 2005 General Affairs and External Relations Council (GAERC) of a 'light platform' for crisis response (Barroso 2005) plus the increased emphasis on crisis response and a new civil-military cell in the Military Staff caused adjustments to Directorate A in the autumn of 2005, including the secondment of two Commission officials to the Military Staff and a re-vamping of responsibilities in the Commission Conflict Prevention and Crisis Management Unit. In mid-2005 the head of the Security Unit in Directorate A, Lars-Erik Lundin, had already become the formal Commission representative in the Military Committee. Lundin had frequently briefed the Military Committee on relevant issues within Community competence and informal contacts between the Military Staff, the Policy Unit and the Commission's staff had also grown apace since the outset. These latest adjustments formalise the process of the growth of cross-pillar discussion on political-military affairs and civilian input to crisis management with a consequent expansion of the Commission's role. The goalposts are clearly set to move further as policy develops and the Commission's input may still increase. This is but one of many areas of responsibility where the creation (or not) of the European External Action Service (EEAS) will have profound implications for the Commission. The future work and status of the CFSP Directorate and its units will depend greatly on their potential fusion into the EEAS.

Meanwhile, since the French and Dutch referenda in 2005 put ratification of the Constitution on hold, DG Relex units contribute as follows. Within the CFSP Directorate, the Security Unit is responsible for input to the Council working groups on political-military affairs (PolMil), terrorism, arms control, small arms and non-proliferation and for input to a new 'crisis room', constructed to provide a secure environment for the Commission's deliberations in times of external threat or crisis. Then, a Crisis Management and Conflict Prevention Unit coordinates the Commission's activities in conflict prevention, crisis management, CFSP in Africa, demobilisation, disarmament and reintegration programmes, and the newly introduced Commission contribution to the EU's rapid reaction capacity, the financial arrangements known as the Rapid Reaction Mechanism (RRM).[15] The unit comprised until late 2005 a team of some twenty officials, of which two managed the RRM.

The CFSP Counsellor, also known as the Relex Counsellor, is responsible for legal oversight of the Commission's input into CFSP, for CFSP project management and management of the EU Special Representatives. Through its budgetary responsibilities under the CFSP chapter (19 03) of the EC budget, the Commission works closely with the Council and the Council Secretariat in the identification and design of civilian crisis management operations, typically through fact-finding missions or as part of 'Crisis Response Coordination Teams', which fine-tune CFSP projects. Once the mandate for an operation has received political agreement, the Commission participates in the drafting of the legal basis to implement the mission (usually 'Joint Actions' under Article 14 TEU) and prepares the correspon-

ding financial statement for agreement in the Foreign Relations Counsellors
Working Group (RELEX Counsellors). Once the Joint Action is adopted and
the financial statement agreed in the working group of CFSP Counsellors,
the Commission is thereafter solely responsible for management throughout
the full project cycle of action financed under the CFSP budget. There are on
average 40 operations under management at any one time.

The European Correspondent's Unit is responsible for coordinating the
Commission's policy input into CFSP and ensuring effective Commission participation in the exchange of views and information between Member States,
both technically and in terms of content, through the transmission and receipt
of Coreus, Cyphers and ESDP-NET messages. It also manages the Cypher
office, the hub of the Commission's secure communications network. It prepares the Commission input to the General Affairs and External Relations
Council, COREPER and the Political and Security Committee, as well as meetings of the European Council. It assists the Commission representative in PSC
meetings and ensures related reporting. It also supports the Political Director
and the Relex Commissioner in political dialogue with a wide range of countries and regional organisations, and within the G8 process.

The evolution of Commission-Council relations: the Commission in retreat?

After the Nice Treaty tried to remedy some of the contradictions born at
Maastricht and only partially remedied at Amsterdam, and with work
having begun on extending CFSP to ESDP, there followed much rhetoric
about the partnership between the Council and the Commission. But the
rhetoric was undermined by widely discussed rivalry in practice. As one
think tank put it:

> 'the "political" foreign policy of the EU, based in the Council
> of Ministers secretariat, has few links to the policies on trade, aid,
> humanitarian assistance, technical co-operation and borders that
> are carried out under the leadership of the Commission. As a
> result, the EU is pursuing a bifurcated foreign policy: politics is
> dealt with in the inter-governmental second pillar as a declara-
> tory and penniless exercise; substantive and funded external
> policies belong to the first pillar and are implemented by the
> Commission' (Andréani et al. 2001, 43).

This substantial contradiction to the principle of consistency strained
relations between the Commission and the Council and between the Policy
Unit working directly to the HR and officials in Directorate E (External
Relations), who perform the Council Secretariat's traditional role of administrative support to the Council and the Presidency. The Council
Secretariat's own internal wrangling further affected the Commission.
While officials of Directorate E continued their cooperative relationship
with officials in the Commission, the newly proactive Policy Unit staff were
frequently at odds with Commission officials, both over who was responsible for policy as well as its content.

Few had predicted the full extent of these institutional difficulties, though
academics and policy-makers had warned that the path of integration in

external relations would not run smooth. After Amsterdam, one leading academic had opined:

> 'Competition between the Commission and the Council for the ultimate control of European foreign policy is here to stay, and the Amsterdam Treaty does not definitely settle the issue, although it favours the Council. Even if the Treaty represents a concerted attempt to clip the Commission's external policy wings, the question remains: is the Commission or the Council most likely to produce something that looks like a European foreign ministry and a European diplomatic service?' (Allen 1998, 58).

This view was shared by the Commission, with President Prodi himself presciently criticising the Amsterdam Treaty arrangements as:

> '... only a provisional response to a lasting need ... the present organisational model is not sustainable in the long term ... (it is) a transitional phase, useful for launching European action in a new area, but destined to be absorbed into the conventional institutional structure ...' (Prodi 2000).

Since the Treaty of Nice failed to tackle many of the unresolved issues of Amsterdam head on, discussions and negotiations in the Convention and subsequent IGC to draft the Constitutional Treaty thus took place against the *leitmotiv* of increased need for coherence in practice, not just Treaty commitment. There were two forces at work. First, for CFSP to be enhanced, the separation between EU policy-making and EC policy instruments had to end. Second, the new paradigm of world affairs after 9/11 and the now indisputable link between internal and external security posed a fundamental challenge to the management of EU external policy-making.[16]

Relations between the Commission and the EU High Representative

Solana and Patten

The idea of a Commission Vice President for External Relations was raised in a declaration to the Treaty of Amsterdam[17], but it disappeared with the appointment of Javier Solana. Both Solana and Chris Patten, his Commission counterpart, had distinguished backgrounds. As mentioned above, Solana had been Spain's foreign minister and Secretary General of NATO. Patten was a former British cabinet minister and last Governor of Hong Kong. Both known for their creative thinking and political nous, their appointments caused considerable speculation about whether the new institutional arrangements would allow them to work together and how their respective staffs would cope with the seemingly inevitable turf disputes. An early assessment of Patten/Solana relations was that 'they are beset by structural problems that no amount of cordiality can eliminate' (*Economist* 2000a). Yet, for public consumption at least, both Patten and Solana usually insisted on their good working relationship. They certainly shared a common approach to the management of their fiefdoms: both introduced radical changes. Solana created the Council's Situation Centre and his Policy Unit to do the thinking, process the information and plan the strategy, leaving the Council Secretariat's Directorate E (external relations) to continue its traditional note-taker/presidency support role in Council meetings.[18] Patten, meanwhile, overhauled the system of delivery of foreign assistance, separating policy-making and project management and streamlining the relationship between Brussels and the Commission Delegations (see chapter 15). Solana took the lead in creating a sound policy-making structure. Patten's reforms ensured the Commission provided more effective policy implementation. While Solana was making political inroads, Patten was honing the existing administrative machine, a fact that disappointed some of his officials who believed that the Commission, under proactive leadership, could aspire to a greater role in CFSP and sought in vain for 'real input' – finding it finally not in Patten's contribution, but in Development Commissioner Nielson's proposal for a 'peace facility'.

In one sense, there was no rivalry. Each knew his place. As Patten put it:

> 'As far as I was concerned, Solana occupied the front office and I was in charge of the back office of European foreign policy' (Patten 2005, 155) and 'in over five years, and thousands of media reports, no one was able to point to a single occasion when one of us had contradicted the other' (ibid., 158).

But Patten, on behalf of his team, did express disenchantment with the distribution of roles. He made no secret of his impatience with arrangements, accusing Member States of making 'ringing political declarations', which they were 'reluctant to underwrite in money and staff', and lamenting the 'unresolved tension' between intergovernmental activities and Community powers, which left the Commission to 'wrestle with the contradictions and blamed for inadequate outcomes', its role 'that of the maid who is asked to prepare increasingly large and grand dinners in a poky kitchen with poor ingredients' (*Economist* 2000c). This was criticism of the system of political and management realities, not the High Representative himself. Patten's point was that 'even with the emergence of the CFSP High Representative, Member States look to the Commission to manage the nuts and bolts of that engagement, and to do much of the donkey work' (Patten 2000c)... 'we are not much helped in that by the new institutional machinery... Javier Solana and I work extremely well together' (Patten 2000b).

> '... [We] have different but complementary roles. We both develop external policies. Javier's role is to help the Council rally the Member States to our common policies and to represent those policies to the world. My role is to ensure that the EU can deliver on those policies, to come up with the necessary ideas and proposals, to implement them and to make sure that Europe's external action is consistent with its internal policies' (Patten 2001).

In fact, they made several joint trips abroad and produced joint papers, such as that on 'Wider Europe' to the September 2002 Gymnich meeting. By stressing tensions, Patten believed, the press may have simply been looking for trouble:

'The media have been slavering for evidence of fights between me and Javier Solana. We have done our best to disappoint them, and it has not been that hard because we get on well. But the institutional relationship between the Commission and the new machinery on the other side of the road is still a work in progress' (Patten 2000b).

As for Solana, he was critical of the Prodi Commission at times, saying, for example, that it had produced no meaningful initiative in its first nine months, apart from an ill-fated invitation to Libyan President Khadaffi, which was subsequently withdrawn. Only once did he criticise Patten himself, saying that he, Solana, had been no 'out-of-work politician' before becoming HR (*Der Spiegel* 2000), implying that Patten's political career might otherwise have ended with his governorship of Hong Kong.

Though Solana came to be regarded abroad as 'the EU's foreign policy chief', he was a 'chief with very few Indians' and very restricted resources. Patten, in contrast, had the resources, both financial and human. He also had a proprietary right to first pillar policies and instruments. The HR is unable to order the use of the new, specifically second pillar foreign policy instruments such as troop deployment or diplomatic demarches, since this relies on a Council decision, while the External Relations Commissioner has considerable autonomous control over first pillar instruments, which make up most of the foreign policy toolbox at the EU's disposal. Patten and his successor Ferrero-Waldner thus have practical power, Solana political profile. Significantly, however, different personalities might have set different political agendas and have had varying success.

Instruments and competence as a source of bureaucratic stress

Issues of disputed competence have been frequently analysed (Gauttier 2004). The Commission has undoubtedly sought to increase its powers and influence in the sphere of external policies by arguing for a holistic approach to foreign relations overall and to security in particular. Solana agreed, but the issue of who was in charge lay just under the surface. The risk, in the Commission's view, was the submission of the Community method to the intergovernmentalism of the second pillar, which insiders refer to as '*pescisation*'.[19] 'Intergovernmentalising' the first pillar was the opposite of the unspoken mandate of the Commission – to 'communitarise' policy where the 'European interest' requires it, though as de Boissieu contends 'quand on parle de communautariser le second pilier, je suis perplexe, car il me paraît difficile de communautariser l'infini!' (de Boissieu 2002). De Boissieu's point is that Member States clearly delineated what, in the foreign policy realm, could be considered Community competence. The rest – 'infinity'- was to be second pillar. This is not merely an issue of equal importance to the debate on the gender of angels. It preoccupies and vexes national and EU officials. They have to deal with the resulting interminable inter-institutional tussles. Even Patten observed that:

'The – welcome – creation of the CFSP High Representative... has not helped... Indeed, it has given rise to some new institutional complications. It may also have increased the tendency for

CFSP to usurp functions, which should be the responsibility of the Commission (e.g. the EC Monitoring Mission to the Balkans, which was dreamt up by CFSP and then left as an expensive baby on the Commission's doorstep) (2000c)... our role cannot be reduced to one of painting by numbers' (2000b).

Since the early years of CFSP, debates on policy have been overshadowed by an ideological argument as to whether action should be funded by the Member States, the CFSP budget or the Community budget. Instruments and competence have clearly been a source of bureaucratic stress, which is why before Amsterdam the Commission had already argued that:

'The hybrid structure of the Treaty, with decisions under one pillar requiring funding under another, has introduced an additional source of conflict. The complexity of the present system gives rise to procedural debates instead of debates of substance... This conflict inevitably hinders constructive cooperation and effective implementation, for each of the institutions is fearful that its own role, and the proper functioning of a part of the Treaty with which it is particularly associated, will be subverted' (Commission 1995, 157 and 158).

If Solana and Patten did not often engage in substantial turf battles, their staffs did. With thinking and policy-making for CFSP in the hands of the Council and CFSP policy management, budgetary power and first pillar management in the Commission, there were increasing tiffs over competence and budgetary issues. Their officials bore the practical brunt of the institutional contradictions Solana and Patten were at pains to play down. From a Commission perspective, Solana and his staff always tended towards *pescisation* of crisis management by promoting the central role of COPS and the HR and the use of CFSP joint actions managed by COPS. '*Pescisation*' questions both the role of COREPER and the Commission itself, arguably extending Solana's role beyond that set out in the Treaty (Articles 18 and 26 TEU), which clearly limits his authority to CFSP. Several issue areas can be cited to illustrate the tensions involved. The debate surrounding the introduction of procedures for crisis management is a prime example. The Commission agreed early on that there was a need for a fully comprehensive approach to crises and had argued forcefully that it had a strong interest in working closely and constructively with the Presidency, the Secretariat General and the Council on the definition of crisis management and the procedures to be put in place to give it shape. The issues at stake were similar to those in later discussions over small arms policy and security sector reform.

On crisis management, a problem arose when a Council Secretariat paper on management arrangements for crisis appeared. The Commission had not been 'fully associated' in the drafting of the paper, despite the offer of its COPS representative and positive noises from the Council Secretariat's security director on the principle of close consultation with the Commission. The paper proposed – and this was at odds with the Treaty – to base all crisis management on the second pillar by subjecting the whole process to the CFSP and giving a central role to COPS rather than COREPER, by giving the

SG/HR a role which went beyond CFSP and by proposing the Joint Action as 'the instrument of choice' – irrespective of whether or not the main action to be undertaken by the EU was based on the first pillar. Despite linguistic precautions on respect of competence and established procedures, the crisis management paper clearly demonstrated *pescisation* of crisis management. It was for COPS to recommend a comprehensive crisis management package, including CFSP and military measures as well as non-CFSP (Community) policy areas. COPS was then to supervise implementation. COREPER and the Commission were lost from the equation. Most importantly, however, COPS would also manage the external representation of EU action, despite what the Treaty foresees in the area of representation and the fact that the HR's role is limited by Articles 18 and 26 TEU to CFSP matters alone. Recourse to joint actions for all civil and military aspects of crises disregarded the fact that most of the civil measures are Community measures. This posed the issue of respect for Article 47 of the Treaty, which requires inter-pillar consistency. In addition, the shared role of the Commission and the Council in guaranteeing coherence (Article 3) was not alluded to. In a letter to Member States' Foreign Ministers, Patten underlined the Commission's concerns:

> 'My problem with Javier's proposal is that as soon as something is designated a "crisis" he proposes it should at once become the object of a comprehensive Joint Action covering both Community and second pillar issues. Yet even in situations where possible military action creates an imperative for immediate decision-making, I would be unhappy about a Joint Action which strayed into the Community sphere'. (Patten 2000a)

Joint Actions are CFSP tools, yet many instruments for crises lie outside the CFSP framework. As Nuttall has suggested, 'consistency', like 'subsidiarity' and 'flexibility', can acquire overtones going beyond dictionary definitions (Nuttall 1997). Consistency might mean simple lack of contradiction between CFSP and first pillar policies. It could also mean 'benignly' harnessing CFSP and the external relations of the Community into one single external policy aim. But, a more Machiavellian view or, as Nuttall puts it, a 'malign' meaning of the term, is that EC policies should be subsumed under national foreign policies, expressed through CFSP. Everybody seeks 'coherence', but the implications are in the eye of the beholder. The impact of such ambiguity on the morale of Commission officials should not be underestimated, and the debates it causes are legion. Indeed, officials are wont to quote Patten himself, who frequently expressed his wish to avoid problems of competence 'on his watch', a common disadvantage in officials' eyes of 'folk who are only there temporarily... we have to pick up the pieces and some of them are difficult to repair'.

In 2003, Solana outlined the main challenges facing the EU in his 'European Security Strategy' (ESS), subtitled 'A Secure Europe in a better world' (Solana 2003). The threats were terrorism, proliferation of weapons of mass destruction, regional conflicts, state failure and organised crime. The ESS stressed that work on conflict and threat prevention 'cannot start too early', seemingly disregarding the fact that the Commission had long been active precisely in that area. 'Effective multilateralism' was announced as the EU's normative ambition, but the Commission had long since maintained close relations with the UN and its agencies, contributing policy papers, desk to desk dialogue and playing a key role in meetings between the UN and other international organisations. For the ESS to describe aspects of Community external relations, such as trade and development,[20] as 'powerful tools for promoting reform' appeared purposely negligent of existing Commission policies. Whereas the Community currently covers the overwhelming bulk of civil crisis management, the Council Secretariat disagrees over whether it should really do so. An example would be emerging police activities and many aspects of security sector reform. They constitute a grey area. Training, technical assistance or capacity-building of police fall, according to the Commission, under the first pillar. CARDS took over the previous WEU police training operation (MAPE) in Albania, for example, though there was some debate about the Council Secretariat's ability to do so, with the Commission arguing (a precursor of its 2005 argument on small arms) that police training missions were 'illegal' under CFSP, since the issue fell squarely into Community competence. Financing executive police missions to substitute for local police in times of crisis is a different issue, however. Thus, the EU Police Mission in Bosnia relies on principles and feasibility studies undertaken by the Commission with regard to police restructuring, but substitution of local police by Member State police forces falls under the CFSP Petersberg Tasks.

Unease over such issues has abounded. The transfer of responsibility for the WEU Institute for Satellite Studies (SatCen) to the Council Secretariat, instead of its becoming a reinforcement of the Commission's Joint Research Centre, with its extensive satellite research programmes of relevance inter alia to landmine detection, international crises or natural catastrophes, is an example. The creation of a European Defence Agency independent of the first pillar regulatory framework which many believed was its natural home, was also a threat to Community logic. These were completely logical decisions in terms of the need to bolster the HR role and to keep security issues within the Council (EU ISS Task Force 2005), but they militated against coherence and the Community method. The SatCen played an important role in terms of security in EU military interventions in the Congo and Bosnia, and it provides information on arms control and environmental monitoring. But, ironically, the foregone advantages of merger with first pillar instruments, if only for financial reasons, are abundantly apparent. The SatCen's Director, Frank Asbek, has argued publicly that lack of funding and staff is affecting efficiency (*European Voice* 2005). There is thus a case for a review of possible duplication and lack of synergy between the two institutions.

The issue of disputed competence came to a head in 2005, when the Commission sought annulment for lack of competence of a CFSP Joint Action (2002/589/CFSP) and a Council Decision (2004/833/CFSP).[20] The issue was a decision by the Council under CFSP to contribute financially to the Economic Community of West African States (ECOWAS) in the framework of the Moratorium on Small Arms and Light Weapons (SALW). The Commission argued that Article 11(3) of the Cotonou Agreement covered action in the area of SALW and that pursuant to that the Commission had concluded a Regional Indicative Programme for West Africa giving support to conflict prevention and good governance and announcing particular support in the field of SALW. The Commission's view was therefore that the CFSP Joint Action and decision infringed Article 47 TEU, which states that policies under CFSP are only permissible in so far as they do not affect Community policies, in this case the Community's development policy (Article 177 TEC). The Commission supported its view by reminding the Court that the budget line (19 03 02) for CFSP specifically indicates that the budget can be used for activities in the field of SALW 'provided that they are not already covered by the provisions of the Cotonou Agreements concerning similar action in the ACP states'.

The Council's Legal Service contended that the fight against SALW was not inherently a Community objective as per Articles 2 and 3 of the TEC, but that it was clearly an EU objective as per Article 11 of the TEU, i.e. 'preserving peace and strengthening international security'.[21] While the Commission's development policy activities might contribute to these objectives, it was not their prime purpose. The Commission's response to these arguments included reference to examples from the work of the United Nations and other organisations where SALW issues fall squarely into a developmental context replete with implications for civilian control in societies often emerging from conflict but certainly on the path to development. The crux of the issue, for the Commission, is whether specific instances of SALW action are operational (in terms of a CFSP crisis action) or part of an ongoing stabilisation programme (potentially as part of a larger strategy for development) of which the purpose is removal of obstacles to sustainable development.

In sum, the Council's view on the issue of whether arms issues can fall within Community competence is that the promotion of international peace and security and conflict prevention are not Community objectives. It argued originally on the same lines against the proposal for a Council Regulation creating the Commission's 'Rapid Reaction Mechanism', which allowed the Community to take action in crisis management and conflict prevention to promote international peace and security, where use of normal procedures would take too long for effectiveness to be guaranteed. Compared with the Commission's proposal, the Regulation adopted by the Council was substantially modified, in particular disallowing areas of potential autonomy of the Commission (yet with comitology guarantees) foreseen in the Commission proposal and incorporation of parliamentary supervision. Again, the Council's concerns regarding the proposed 'stability mechanism' revolve around the Commission's involvement in peace building and political stabilisation through its external assistance programmes. These are foreign policy aims and thus arguably the domain of the CFSP. In particular, the Commission's autonomy, outside the comitology framework, in the first nine months of a crisis is contested. But contesting this autonomy and introducing administrative and consultative procedures *ex ante* are a means of reducing the Commission's ability to contribute rapidly alongside CFSP in times of external crisis.

In similar vein, the Council had opposed the Commission proposal in 2000 for a European Parliament and Council Regulation concerning action against anti-personnel landmines, since it was worded in a way that would have allowed the Community to pursue a general policy of disarmament and non-proliferation in respect of these weapons. If the Commission now claims competence within the landmine sector, this is on the basis of the effect of landmines on development, not on security itself, and does not therefore, in the Council's view, prejudge the issue of the Commission's role in crisis management, itself not mentioned in the TEC, though specifically mentioned in Articles 17 and 25 of the TEU. Council and Commission seemingly view the issue of competence in this area as a zero sum game, while the Parliament is concerned to create democratic accountability (and an enhanced role for itself) by ensuring that first pillar mechanisms are used as a general rule. Further examples are legion. Importantly, whether it is funding conflict prevention programmes (often managed by the World Bank or the UN) in West Africa, Nepal, Aceh, Liberia, Sudan, Bolivia etc. on the basis of its Conflict Prevention Communication endorsed by the Council at Göteborg in 2001, or the small arms support to ECOWAS using the European Development Fund and within the framework of the Cotonou Agreement, Commission/Council competence debates are extensive, debilitating and counter-productive.

Security sector reform is a final example of the issues on which politicians and publics alike must take a view with regard to the institutional arrangements they desire. The European Security Strategy advocated support in third countries for security sector reform (SSR) and there are calls for assistance in this area in conflict situations worldwide. First pillar assistance has existed for years (Hänggi and Tanner 2005). But until late 2005 a coherent EU concept of SSR, despite the existence of guidelines within the OECD of which most EU countries are members (DAC guidelines, OECD 2001) did not exist. Clearly, such an EU concept would require a cross-pillar approach, but the guidelines and authority for such an approach did not exist until their gestation in the second half of 2005. A proposal for a security sector reform strategy emanating from the Council Secretariat in July 2005 focussed primarily on ESDP mechanisms as the overarching structure (Council 2005a). It was argued:

> 'Such a concept should in the immediate future, allow for the improvement of ESDP support to SSR. In the longer term, this work should contribute to the development of a possible overarching EU SSR concept, taking into account that the Commission will develop, in close co-operation with the Council Secretariat, a concept for the developmental aspects of SSR covering first pillar activities. The ESDP and EC work could then be merged at a later stage into an overall SSR concept'.

This raises all the controversial issues of principle mentioned above. An SSR concept would go beyond CFSP and require a cross-pillar approach covering developmental aspects already managed by the Commission within the framework of official development assistance (ODA) and the DAC guidelines, as well as within the European Initiative for Democracy and Human Rights and Justice and Home affairs, not to mention enlargement strategy, country strategies and association agreements such as the Europe Agreements, the MEDA Programme or European Neighbourhood Policy.[22] But, if there is to be a coherent security sector reform policy, then a view has to be taken on whether the Commission or the Council should take the lead. The coming struggle for leadership in EU security sector reform policy-making, falling contemporaneously with litigation over arms policy and debate over the operational coverage of such issues in the new financial instruments, will make or break the Commission's (or the Council Secretariat's) lead role in SSR and related areas.

While many Member States and parts of the Commission accept the notion of overlapping competences in areas such as peace-building and conflict prevention, the ECOWAS small arms case before the Court of Justice in 2005 polarised opinion and encouraged Member States to act defensively, arguing that the Commission does not have competence in these areas. Their fear was that if it did, it would limit the current and future scope of CFSP. The Court's decision is likely to have major implications not only in terms of the continuing clash of views over CFSP and Community competence, but in defining once and for all where the limits of Community and intergovernmental arrangements ultimately lie. Importantly, ideological dispute over the choice of supranationalism or intergovernmentalism means, in practical terms, a dispute about Commission or Council Secretariat leadership. While this bureaucratic debate may be attenuated consequent to the Court's ruling, further conflict is likely as long as the pillar structure remains, despite rhetorical assertions by the Commission and the Council that CFSP and development cooperation are not locked in a zero sum game.[23]

Hence the perceived need finally to settle the issue through the creation of a joint service, the European External Action Service, where former bureaucratic rivals would, in principle, become colleagues in the common cause of coherent foreign policy making. Importantly, all diplomats involved in CFSP, whether the Commission's, the Council's or those of the Member States are gradually forming a kind of 'epistemic community' committed to a vague notion of 'European diplomacy'. But if there is such an epistemic community, it is divided, since each group of institutional actors is tempted to 'façonner la PESC à son image, d'importer dans ce jeu intersectoriel les règles de son propre champ' and thus to 'affaiblir les ressources spécifiques du groupe rival dans l'inter jeu de la PESC et consolider l'autonomie sectorielle' (Buchet de Neuilly 2005, 242). These issues may seem recondite, but they have significant impact on the bureaucracies involved and on those called upon to advise governments on how they can improve arrangements.

The issue of 'voice'

A different form of turf battle surrounds the issue of 'voice' in EU representation. Think tanks often repeat the ironic headline of the *Economist* (1995), 'Who ya gonna call?', and this clearly has remained the pertinent question. Whom you call depends on why you are calling and what the issue is – and similar issues may be treated differently, depending on whether the HR has been mandated or not and whether the issue falls clearly within Commission competence or not. Apart from the specialist lobby, the world still remains at a loss on this issue since Amsterdam. EU 'nerds' revel in their ability to beguile uninitiated observers, whether foreign diplomats or EU citizens. Competence issues and the Treaty are unclear and the fact that Solana often appears together in third countries with the Relex Commissioner, sometimes alone, sometimes with the Presidency, but on other occasions with a different Member State from that holding the Presidency, has maintained the confusion.

In addition, there is further muddle about the very notion of a 'representative'. External representation is complicated by increasing recourse to 'Personal Representatives' of the SG/HR to deal with particular functional issues, such as terrorism, human rights and weapons of mass destruction. DG Relex officials have been perturbed to find that these Personal Representatives have often encroached on their area of responsibility, though this is clearly a harbinger of future strategic direction (*European Voice* 2004). In addition to these Personal Representatives of the High Representative, Article 18.5 TEU allows Member States to nominate a 'Special Representative'. EU Special Representatives (EUSRs) are appointed under the Joint Action procedure and their salaries and expenses are paid by the Commission.[24] Yet, 'despite regular contacts with Member State representatives in the regions concerned, an EUSR's appointment seldom ties together neatly the underlying differences of opinion over how the EU should act' (*European Voice* 2005b), let alone joining up with the content of Member State discussions in Brussels and overall plans in the regions fostered by the Commission. Special Representatives operate in very different circumstances depending on the country concerned. They are resident in the Balkans (Bosnia and the Former Yugoslav Republic of Macedonia), where they head up ESDP missions and dangle the integration carrot before states desirous of later entry into the EU. In the European Neighbourhood Area (South Caucasus, Moldova, Middle East Peace Process) membership of the EU is not a prospect, and EUSRs are not resident. This is also the case for more far-flung missions such as Afghanistan or the Great Lakes.

The number of EUSRs is set to rise, as the EU's presence increases in Asia and Latin America. Yet, they have varied in their ability to ensure added value to the CFSP and have not been formally tasked with ensuring inter-pillar coherence. *De facto* no EUSR or ESDP mission would exist effectively without the daily support and guidance of the Commission. While the Commission tries to locate them in its Delegations, they do not report to the Commission in managerial terms and there has been no serious attempt to structure their relationship with Commission Heads of Delegation. The latter often find themselves in an operational support role without clear line management, though EUSRs' reports to the Council are often co-signed 'in cooperation with the European Commission'. People in the countries where such representatives roam might, despite the often large Commission Delegations, be forgiven for viewing them as the only permanent representatives of the EU. Significantly, the weight of EU representation is clearly higher where there is cooperation and consistency between Special Representatives and Commission Delegations, so it ought not to be beyond the wit of the Commission and the Council, even without the establishment of the European External Action Service, to create more sensible relationships and synergies on the ground. A formal commitment to co-location, combined spokesmen, legal and political advisors would bring clear benefits. Once again, these are not theoretical issues. Whether or not Special Representatives or Heads of Delegation can hold sway across the three-pillar EU structure and whether or not they consult each other are issues of daily practice, where they risk becoming sources of incoherence or inefficiency.

As to meetings with third parties, formally the Treaty of Amsterdam dropped the previous holder of the Presidency from the troika. This left the Presidency, assisted by the Council Secretariat and the Policy Unit – the latter frequently with a speaking brief – and the Commission as the three-some to be known as the troika. While the future Presidency is still custom-arily present, the Treaty states that this is only if 'need be' (Art. 18 Consolidated Text). The only permanent officials on the EU side of the table at troikas in Brussels are the Commission and the Council Secretariat. As to representation abroad, the embassies of EU Member States and the Delegations of the European Commission are also enjoined by the Treaty to cooperate locally and present a united front to their host country or interna-tional organisation, often in troika format. In practice, here the troika format varies considerably from country to country and is often dependent on local personalities. In addition, in many capitals there is no resident Presidency representative anyway, which somewhat complicates matters.[25] To cap it all, the troika is a misnomer abroad in any case, for the Council Secretariat is rarely present abroad, except in the two cities where it keeps a permanent liaison office, New York and Geneva. EU policy coordination requires a per-manent administrative support structure for the EU presidency there because of the location of the United Nations and the World Trade Organisation. The Council Secretariat has argued that it also needs a pres-ence in Vienna for similar reasons. So, the Commission Delegation's Head is actually the only permanent part of the troika abroad, unless Council Secretariat staff fly out from Brussels. They sometimes do, but only when the troika level and subjects covered are politically sensitive.

The G8 framework is an institutional case where the issue of 'voice' is acute. The European Union has long been represented at G8 Summits by the President of the European Commission and the leader of the Member State holding the Presidency of the European Council, though preparatory meet-ings are serviced by the Commission, unaccompanied by Presidency or Council Secretariat staff. Originally, the economic nature of the G8 justified Commission participation on behalf of the EU. But Solana, as High Representative, and, by implication, his staff, are increasingly included, since the agenda now covers the whole gamut of international affairs. There is no formal role for the rotating Presidency of the EU in the G8. Under the Italian G8 Presidency in 2001, the SG/HR, the Relex Commissioner and the Foreign Minister of the EU Member State holding the Presidency of the Council, then Belgium, were invited to the Foreign Ministers' meeting, but the SG/HR was not invited to the summit. The subsequent summit under the Japanese chairmanship of the G8 in Miyazaki set the precedent for the SG/HR's participation, but some non-EU members of the G8 have expressed concern about the proliferation of EU participants, in particular since the presence of high level politicians implies prior presence of senior officials to prepare the meetings. The four current EU members of the G8 and the Commission would be EU overkill if the Council Secretariat were added. Some wonder whether the EU Presidency, when not a G8 member, could systematically call on the SG/HR and his support staff to represent the EU and thereby streamline EU representation. The *chef de cabinet* of the

Commission President (his 'sherpa') traditionally makes an oral report to COREPER on issues arising, so an obvious alternative solution would be for the Commission to have this responsibility. Administratively this would make sense, since the Commission is already present at all preparatory levels. But the issue raises all the political and bureaucratic sensitivities reviewed above.

The fate of the changes proposed in the Constitutional Treaty

Defining the structures

In the Convention on the future of Europe, there was no shortage of ideas on how to strengthen the CFSP and enhance the EU's role on the world stage and no shortage of debate about the Commission's role and weight in the resulting arrangements. The ideas discussed were not new (*Financial Times* 1995 and Buchan 1993). One of the most discussed proposals, advocated by many think tanks (Adréani et al 2001; Rayner 2005; Crowe 2005; Cameron and Grevi 2005) as well as the European Commission (2002a), was an amalgamation of the Solana and Patten functions. Some argued that the merger should take place within the Council; others advocated a merger within the Commission. Independently of where and how policy should be made, the main argument for such a merger was that it would improve coherence and visibility. Some suggested that most foreign ministers would oppose any such merger, as it would inevitably shine the spotlight more on 'Mr CFSP' than on them. They were certainly reticent to envisage a power shift to the Commission.

The decision to create a European Union Foreign Minister (EUFM) with real authority underlines Member States' realisation of the need for more effective leadership to replace the ineffective six-monthly rotating Presidencies, to replace variable capability and credibility with continuity and coherence. The model proposed by the Commission, which would have placed the EUFM squarely in the Commission, was clearly a non-starter. The Constitutional Treaty was signed in October 2004 and it was decided by the European Council in December 2004 that Javier Solana would become the EU Minister for Foreign Affairs, taking over the existing mandates of the Commissioner for External Relations (until November 2004 Chris Patten, and since then Benita Ferrero-Waldner) and the CFSP High Representative. The troika system and the rotating Presidency were set to disappear. Now, the EUFM was to represent the Union. He would thereby consolidate the enormous respect already accrued to Solana as HR and enhance it with the financial and administrative power of the Relex Commissioner.

According to the Constitution, the EUFM would manage the CFSP and chair the External Relations Council, thereby replacing the Presidency. He would make proposals, implement Council decisions and represent the EU in the area of CFSP, ESDP and External Relations overall. He was to have a foreign ministry structure and embassies worldwide answerable to him. He would also be Vice President of the European Commission, which, combined with the chairing of the External Relations Council and the duty to make proposals on CFSP, would give him considerable authority. He would need to manage this carefully, given both his membership of the College of Commissioners and the key but potentially troublesome relationship with the President of the Commission, who would have to reconcile himself to having as a Vice President someone who, as Minister appointed by and answerable directly to the Council, would be in large part removed from his authority.

There were alternatives, which would not have required Treaty change. The HR could have remained in the same position, but been allowed to attend Commission meetings with the right to speak. Commissioners' *cabinet* staff could have visited, had structured relations with and even exchanged posts with the Policy Unit. In fact, such alternatives were lost with the euphoria of the significant change in the new Treaty, which was the 'combining' of the functions of chairmanship of Foreign Ministers' meetings and Relex Commissioner to make a really powerful representative of the EU. The post of EUFM was not actually intended to combine the jobs of the HR and the Commissioner for External Relations. The Constitution retained both posts, but attempted to institutionalise the personal success of Patten and Solana by making one person responsible. This was just one of a new series of 'internal contradictions' with which the Commission would have had to contend. Another, since the EUFM was to replace the rotating Presidency in the external relations field, was that he would chair the Foreign Affairs Council, and his staff would have presumably chaired COPS and even COREPER when the latter were in foreign relations mode, while at the other end of the negotiation room the occupant of the Commission seat remained to be decided. 'Looking around the table at twenty-five other foreign ministers, would the High Representative be their boss – or just their representative?' (Patten 2005, 159).

So, if the old pillar system brought its contradictions and surprises, the new incoherence of Article I-28's call on the EUFM to run the Commission's external relations and guarantee coherence made for a tricky mission, not least resulting from the beguilingly weasel-worded enjoinment that he should do this 'to the extent that this is consistent with paragraphs 2 and 3'. These are precisely the paragraphs bestowing on the EUFM responsibility for the CFSP and chairmanship of the Council. The EUFM was set to be the Council cuckoo in the Commission nest. It is difficult to imagine how the foreign minister role, with its inherent responsibility to the Council, could be reconciled with the obligations on Commissioners to be independent of extraneous influence. At the very least, the principle of *primus inter pares* within the College would have clearly been under threat. A further dilemma lay outside the Commission. The creation of a President of the European Council appointed for 2½ years, who 'shall at his or her level and in that capacity ensure the external representation of the Union' on CFSP matters, albeit 'without prejudice to the powers' of the EUFM, was coupled with the commitment for Community external representation outside the CFSP field to continue to be exercised by the President of the Commission, with the EUFM (the Vice President) enjoined to 'ensure the consistency of the Union's external action'.

Thus, while old conflicts between the Presidency, HR and Commission in the external relations field might have been removed by the Constitution, new ones were in the making. There would have been obvious risks and challenges arising from what Crowe (2005) has called 'triple accountability' – to the Council (which the HR was to chair and lead); to the Commission (of which he was to be Vice-President), both in terms of the College's collective responsibility and in terms of the authority of the Commission President; and finally to the President of the European Council (who was also to represent the EU abroad, albeit 'at his level').

There were also challenges related to the new workload. Even if trade policy remained separate, there was still supervision and coordination of enlargement, development and humanitarian aid to be inserted into the job description. The EUFM would have needed at least one Commissioner (presumably the current External Relations Commissioner) to deputise for him when his presence at College meetings conflicted with a Council meeting, an urgent mission abroad or an appearance at a European Parliament committee. If these political responsibilities were not demanding enough, the weight of time-consuming management of a large budget, trade and cooperation agreements with third countries and the management of resources of the new European External Action Service would also be a challenge. Indeed, a further deputy to manage the administration might have proved necessary. There were precedents in the typical national foreign ministry structure, and the High Representative/Secretary General of the Council, as the title indicates, was also in reality two jobs – unmanageable without a deputy. Hence, Solana's responsibilities at the Council had similarly been divided between him and de Boissieu, a former French Ambassador who had taken over the Council's administration on Solana's original double-hatted appointment as High Representative and Secretary General.

Democratic legitimacy was also an issue. The EUFM was not to be an elected minister with democratic legitimacy and the confidence of the public, parliament and a prime minister. He would not have had the legitimacy conferred by states on their senior politicians or that conferred by the European Parliament on the Commission President and the College. National sovereignty confers weight, yet the new post was set to suffer from the absence of such a power base and the addition of new incoherence. None of these issues was broached in the Constitution. They emerged in the first half of 2005, as officials began to work on the operational implications.

Apart from the high political issues, such as the fate of the military structures, one major issue in these officials' work lay in the effect on the structure and organisation of the Relex services. One internal Commission news briefing was tellingly entitled 'Goodbye Relex, Goodbye'. Many in the Commission feared that the Commission's Relex family and External Service might be relegated to trade and external aid administration, with Member States and the Council providing the (political) heads of unit and heads of EU Delegations and the Commission retaining Counsellor posts with specific technical (first pillar) competence. The worries were understandable. After all, as *European Voice* (2004a) put it, 'disputes... are almost guaranteed, since both jobs and power are at stake'. A Council paper commented ruefully that in the Commission 'there is a widespread feeling... that the EEAS is a takeover by the Council, leading to resentment and defensiveness'. It remains to be seen whether their feelings were justified.

The state of play

Following the signature of the Constitutional Treaty in October 2004, preparatory work on the EEAS began both in the EU institutions and in Member States. Expectations were raised by the European Council at its meeting on 16-17 December 2004, which invited the SG/HR and the Commission to prepare a joint progress report on preparatory work on the European External Action Service for the June 2005 European Council. This, along with five papers by the Council's Legal Service, covering the staff statutes of the EEAS, personnel and budget issues, administrative functions and the management of the EU Delegations abroad, served as the basis for a flurry of political activity, though the ideas in the various papers were already circulating publicly in early 2005 and were the subject of several think-tank papers.[26] Formal discussions began with a first round of discussions in COREPER on 10 March 2005, followed by a series of bilateral meetings between the Presidency, the Council Secretariat, the Commission and all Member States between 27 and 29 April, a meeting of the External Relations Commissioners group on 3 May, consultations with the future new Member States Romania and Bulgaria, a debate in the European Parliament in plenary session on 11 May and a stocktaking of the bilateral meetings in COREPER on 12 May.

The joint issues paper argued that the EEAS should comprise Commission and Council departments already dealing with CFSP and ESDP, together with geographical desks covering all regions of the world and thematic desks dealing with issues such as human rights, counter-terrorism, non-proliferation and relations with the UN. The Council's legal advice was that the EEAS could not be a 'normal service' inside the Commission or the Council, since it would lead to duplication of administrative structures and tasks. But, recruitment of staff would still need to be separated into two categories: Commission or Council Secretariat officials already with EU employment conditions embodied in the staff regulations, and officials from national administrations. The issue was therefore whether there could be two sets of regulations covering the two categories or whether a uniform set should be created. As the Legal Service argued, 'management of staff would not be made easier' (*European Voice* 2005a), as the alternative to a uniform procedure would be employing national diplomats as temporary agents or detached national experts, with disparities in rights and obligations, including salaries. While a European Parliament resolution on 26 May strongly backed the placement of the EEAS in the Commission, the structure advocated in the joint issues paper from the High Representative and the President of the Commission was a 'sui generis' EEAS. The Parliament was attempting (to no avail) to avoid the administrative disadvantages of a dual staffing system and allow itself more supervisory powers by centring the new arrangements within the Commission. The 'sui generis' concept was broadly supported by Member States, so it emerged that the EEAS would be neither a new 'institution' nor simply part of an existing institution. It was to be a service under the authority of the Foreign Minister, with close links to both the Council and the Commission, potentially using support functions of the General Secretariat of the Council and the Commission. Whether this would minimise duplication and save costs was a moot point.

One of the costs of the rejection of the Constitution by the French and Dutch and the perception of crisis reigning in the EU in mid-2005 was failure to deliver on the December 2004 commitment. The European Council of June 2005 did not include a formal declaration on work in hand to create the EEAS. This allowed reflection to continue. At a political level, while all agreed that trade policy should be excluded from the EEAS responsibilities, some Member States considered that the EEAS should be restricted to CFSP/ESDP, while others wished to add enlargement, neighbourhood and development policies. Most followed a line somewhere between the two positions. The EEAS should, in their view, consist simply of the relevant parts of the Council Secretariat (DG E and Policy Unit) and of the Commission (DG External Relations). As to the military staff and the Council's Situation Centre, there remained doubts. An important agreement was that duplication was to be avoided, whether geographical or thematic. Delivering on this ideal was set to be tricky in practice. The Commission hoped to escape unscathed as far as re-organising its DGs in trade, development or ECHO were concerned, but that remains to be seen.

Conclusion

At the outset, this chapter posited that the Commission stands at a crossroads in terms of its role and importance in CFSP and ESDP, and that the outcome of the debate about competence and ratification of the Constitution will determine the fate of the Commission – not only in CFSP but across the gamut of integrated European policy-making for external relations. The chapter has underlined how the personal efficacy of Solana and Patten, which accompanied if not caused the evolution of the EU from ineptitude to effectiveness, threw harsh light on the previous cost of a major constraint in the EU: the absence of political will. Yet, long regarded as the reason for Europe's foreign policy vacuum, political will is toothless without the support of effective procedures and institutional structures. Their absence, in turn, explains continuing lack of coherence and bureaucratic rivalry. It may be true, as Allen and Wallace argued thirty years ago, that decision-makers were too long content with creating procedures as a substitute for policy (Allen and Wallace 1977). Yet, by 2005 there was agreement on the permanent political benefits to be gained by a procedural innovation, the combining of the two important political posts of High Representative for the CFSP and Commissioner for External Relations. The hope, presumably, was that the personal capacities of Solana and Patten might somehow leave their imprint on the new arrangements, engendering the effective policy entrepreneurship, hitherto hampered by complex and contradictory institutional arrangements. But, much still remains to be negotiated before final decisions are reached. In the meantime confusion will continue to reign, bureaucratic rivalry is likely to persist and the Commission's image abroad will suffer.

The view of Europe and the Commission from abroad has not been the subject of this chapter. Foreign views of the EU are not only composed of the attitudes of the more than one hundred and sixty governments accredited to the Commission President in Brussels and their responses to EU policies and international presence. Governments are constrained to deal with the fact that the EU's statements imply that it wishes to be considered as having arrived at the international status to which it aspires. Yet, the image of the European Union is also reflected in a mirror held up by the populations of countries where the EU has a local impact and where its citizens spend their holidays. What the EU is and how it influences the lives of 'foreigners' is as much a function of European tourism, trade policy, immigration, human rights policy and the European 'social model' as it is a function of CFSP. Whether or not a foreigner needs a visa, can gain asylum or can emigrate to the EU are all areas of internal policies which have considerably more impact on individual foreigners than any number of Joint Actions under CFSP or trade and association agreements, which affect their governments' attitudes (*Common Market Law Review* 1999). Importantly, these are all areas within the Community domain, where the Commission is the manager and the voice of Europe, and where the overall effect of European diplomacy can be seen.

Europe's diplomats are now composed of the officials of Member States' foreign ministries and the officials of the Commission and the Council Secretariat. These national and international civil servants share certain assumptions about the role of the EU in international affairs. They believe that individual, competing foreign policies are inimical to enhanced European policy. As 'diplomats', they have shared criteria for weighing and validating knowledge and they consider a coherent and forceful European foreign policy an important objective, with Brussels-based decision-making essential to reaching this objective and ensuring policy effectiveness. EU diplomats are authoritative figures. Their expertise and their readiness to take decisions collectively make them not just any random group of experts. They are authoritative and credible actors both in relation to each other and in their work with diplomats from outside the EU. They have participated in the creation of ever tighter obligations to consult and coordinate as part of the sine qua non of their own new form of foreign-policy. Over the years, this epistemic community has recommended expansive Treaty changes producing clear constraints on national diplomatic practice.

Yet, while EU diplomats advocate a 'European' foreign policy, they remain divided on the institutional implications of their advocacy, so there is a kind of cognitive dissonance at work. While they believe that a shift in the locus of decision-making from the national level to Brussels is a concomitant of efficient common foreign policy making, they are unwilling to cede formal power to supranational mechanisms, in particular the European Commission. European diplomats and their governments have opted in all the intergovernmental conferences for ever increasing Brusselisation, yet simultaneously for a hybrid between federalism and intergovernmentalism; a titular head of foreign policy in Brussels presiding over an administration with built-in rivalry, an intergovernmental decision-making process with distinctly supranational overtones – a measure of qualified majority voting, a shared institutional arrangement with the EC, an operational budget within the EC framework, and a set of policies long in existence in the European Community which they have belatedly found necessary for CFSP to be effective. And they really only realised this when the Commission began redefining development policy, assistance policy, association agreements and enlargement as a form of foreign policy and conflict prevention. They first postponed the evolution of foreign policy to security and defence policy, then added ambiguous wording in the Maastricht, Amsterdam and Nice Treaties with a commitment to revert to the issues for further clarification and evolution into a Constitution. The Treaties thus provided hostages to fortune, for it needed a so far unattainable political breakthrough to boost the process. So, fundamental change remains elusive in the current context of a pending court case and the stalled ratification of the Constitution.

Meanwhile, the Commission is developing a long management agenda. Its advocacy of a comprehensive vision of external relations and CFSP could be the catalyst for a more proactive stance, but the success of such an initiative, were it to come about, would rely on the skill and courage of the Commission President and the Commissioners of the Relex family. In practical terms advocating a comprehensive foreign policy for Europe implies not only better diplomatic training and leadership, but also the promotion of a foreign service culture amongst Commission staff. Meanwhile, many of the issue areas of European foreign policy are up for grabs in terms of the institutional lead. CFSP, and the Commission's role in it, will thus likely limp along, accompanied by the same voices arguing for change, enhancement and effectiveness, and lamenting the fact that, as Carl Bildt has succinctly put it concerning Kosovo, after all the debates 'the hard power of NATO will have to resolve what the failing soft power of the EU has caused' (*Financial Times* 2005). Hopefully, the next edition of this book will be able to record progress for the Commission, but as things stand in 2006 it seems indisputable that the Commission is heeding the bugle call to retreat and that relations between the External Relations Commissioner and the High Representative remain courteous but less than ideal. Notwithstanding this somewhat pessimistic conclusion, the Commission's diplomats stand, rackets ready, waiting for an elusive ball to be in their court.

Endnotes

[1] See Spence and Spence (1998), Hoffman (2000), Cameron (2004), K. E. Smith (2003), M. Smith (2004), Holland (1997 and 2004).
[2] Discussion of the separate 'external relations' of the European Community is covered in chapter 12.
[3] For a precise analysis see Lindstrom (2005) *EU-US Burden-sharing: who does what?*
[4] On the EU as a 'normative power' see Ian Manners (2005).
[5] The European Court of Auditors found in 1997 that the Commission's role 'was not clearly established' (Court of Auditors 1997).
[6] The Africa Peace Facility, created in 2004, financially supports African-led peacekeeping operations in Africa, as well as capacity-building for the emerging security structure of the African Union (AU). Peacekeeping operations financed under this Facility are initiated and implemented by the AU and/or sub-regional African organisations. The Commission allocated 250 million euros to it.
[7] For a useful analysis of these issues, see Sjursen 2004 and Hänggi and Tanner 2005.
[8] For the state of play of institutional developments in CFSP and ESDP see Cornish, P. and Edwards, G. 2005. 'The Strategic Culture of the European Union: a progress report', in *International Affairs* 81, 4 (2005) 801-820.
[9] The UK had originally advocated Lord Hannay, former UK Ambassador to the EU, then to the UN, as HR.

[10] For an insider discussion of the divided loyalties of officials responsible for the CFSP and those responsible for first pillar external relations, see Buchet de Neuilly, 2005.

[11] DG I covered commercial policy and relations with North America, China, Japan, the Commonwealth of Independent States and non-EU Europe, including the crucial Central and Eastern European countries. DG IA duplicated some of the geographical responsibilities, while concentrating on politics.

[12] An overview of the issues from an insider perspective can be found in Gordon (1995) and Buchet de Neuilly (2005).

[13] The title of an article by the Commission's Director General for EuropeAid puts the issue in perspective. See Koos Richelle, 'How Brussels has overhauled its "dire" aid apparatus' in *Europe's World*, No 1, Autumn 2005.

[14] Significantly, this joint proposal was not formally authored by the Relex Commissioner, though her staff had been involved in assessing implications and proposing policy.

[15] The Rapid Reaction Mechanism builds on thematic and geographical regulations. It allows the Community to respond urgently to the needs of third countries threatened with or undergoing severe political instability or suffering from the effects of a technological or natural disaster. It does this by providing financial support (the budget was 30 million euros in 2005) immediately, providing this support is legally eligible under existing instruments, but where 'normal procedures' would take so long that the notion of 'rapid' would need redefining.

[16] For a discussion of the Convention deliberations see Cameron (2004).

[17] Declaration 32 of the Treaty of Amsterdam had noted 'the desirability of bringing external relations under the responsibility of a Vice-President', OJ C 340, 10 November 1997.

[18] On the divergence between the Council Secretariat's traditional roles and the new policy style under Solana see Westlake and Galloway (2004).

[19] PESC are the French equivalent initials for CFSP. So 'pescisation' refers to the trend to 'intergovernmentalise' the first pillar competences.

[20] Action brought by the Commission on 21 Feb. 2005 against the Council. Case C-91/05 O.J. 14.5.2005 (2005/C 115/19).

[21] See its statement of defence in Case C-91/05.

[22] See also *Communication from the Commission on Governance and Development* Com (2003), 615 Brussels, 20 October 2003 and *Communication of the Commission on Conflict Prevention*, COM (2001), 211 11th April.

[23] See Commission reply in case C-91/05.

[24] For a discussion of the machinery see Westlake and Galloway (2004) p 66.

[25] This is because the 25 Member States do not all have embassies in all countries. In fact, many Member States do not have embassies in most countries, though the Commission does (see Annex J).

[26] The most helpful of these was Rayner (2005).

15. The Commission's External Service

David Spence

Introduction: European diplomacy and the Commission's External Service at the crossroads

The creation of a European External Action Service (EASS) and EU Delegations would set a new management framework for national and EU diplomacy; a framework replete with implications for the current work of Commission Delegations and national embassies alike. On one view, it would represent a 'spill-over' from the Commission's administrative, budgetary and project management tasks in the field of aid and technical assistance. On another, it would represent the 'capture' of EC Delegations by the priorities of the CFSP. As chapter 14 outlines, the EU's increasing capacity to speak with one voice in foreign policy and the Commission's potential to play a key part in that endeavour are issues which have long fascinated both academics and practitioners alike. Meanwhile, concrete progress in both areas has been a catalyst for the evolution of the Commission's Delegations (its External Service – ES) from a team of development specialists into a quasi-diplomatic service (Bruter 1999), ready for the challenge of forming an oft-mooted EU diplomatic service. Indeed, rankle as it might with national diplomats, today, as former Commission President Romano Prodi once told heads of Commission Delegations, the Delegations already 'put the EU's common foreign and security policy into practice abroad – [and are] indispensable instruments in the EU's expanding role on the international stage of our globalised world' (Prodi 2003).

This view of the importance of the Delegations may not be shared by national diplomats, but it clearly accords with that of the drafters of the Constitution, which provided for the Delegations not merely to report to the new EU Foreign Minister (EUFM), but also to form the backbone of European diplomacy abroad and be part of his management responsibilities. The appointment of a double-hatted EUFM therefore would not only have implications for inter-institutional arrangements within the EU, as succinctly outlined by Crowe (Crowe 2005). Its impact on the management of the Commission's external relations directorates and its Delegations outside the EU would also be extensive. Though barely analysed by academia and often derided by national diplomats and the press, the ES is now clearly set to form the major component of a new European diplomatic system. Moreover, the changes to European governance outlined in the ill-fated Constitution are significant in a wider sense for the notions of representation and diplomacy in the international relations of the 21st century (Hocking and Spence 2005). They mark a fundamental change in the nature of European diplomacy.[1]

While the implications are many, this book is about the Commission and this chapter therefore focuses on three key areas of relevance to the Commission: the history of the Commission's External Service, the Commission's potential role in the new European External Action Service (EEAS) and some of the implications for national diplomacy, which may later impact on the Delegations. The chapter provides the context of the EU's representation abroad and the Commission's role within it. In tracing the history of the ES, it argues that the frequent reforms of the ES before the arrival of the new (constitutional) agenda were always a response to the outside environment rather than the result of deliberate decisions and strategic policy-making within the Commission itself. They may have resulted in a well-managed system of representation abroad, even one fit to be called an 'EU Foreign Service', but this potential arrival point, though desired by some, was not the objective of its architects, who were less concerned with the arrival than making the journey smooth and efficient. Next, the chapter sets out some practical managerial challenges to both EU and national diplomacy, as the EEAS is created. In conclusion, a practical synthesis between national foreign services and the supranational bent of the Commission is described as the crucial element in the future delivery of coherent European diplomacy.

The EU and international diplomacy: a role for the Commission?

The EU is increasingly expected by foreign governments and European public opinion alike to assume a role on the global political scene commensurate with its economic weight and political potential. With 25 Member States and further enlargements on the horizon[2], the EU is now the largest market, trading bloc and aid donor in the world, and it already speaks with one voice on most issues. It has become an important international player in key areas not immediately associated with the traditional 'high politics' notion of foreign policy, quintessentially first pillar competences such as transport policy, environmental policy, competition policy, and of course agriculture, as well as, latterly, visa policy and other areas of mixed competence such as development, humanitarian aid and conflict prevention. In many of these areas, the Commission is formally the external representative. In CFSP it is usually the Presidency and on occasion the Commission and the Presidency in tandem, or the 'troika'. Soon, under the Constitution, it was to be the EU Foreign Minister and the Commissioner for External Relations, cunningly (or naively?) planned to be the same person with two separate jobs.

In addition, a qualitative change has taken place since 2003, when the EU first ventured abroad with a security and military hat on, undertaking its first assignments under the new European Security and Defence Policy (ESDP). It took over the UN police mission in Bosnia and Herzegovina, ran a stabilisation and police mission (Proxima) in the Former Yugoslav Republic of Macedonia, a rule of law mission (Themis) in Georgia, a police and security sector reform mission in the Democratic Republic of Congo and an integrated rule of law and civilian administration in Iraq after the January 2005 election. In addition it conducted its first military operation in the Democratic Republic of Congo, and, from 2 December 2004, ran EUFOR, its 'Althea' military mission to Bosnia and Herzegovina, comprising seven thousand soldiers and replacing NATO's SFOR forces. When one adds to these developments the creation in 2004 of a European Defence Agency for developing and rationalising EU military capacity, the endorsement in December 2004 by the European Council of a civilian/military cell and operations centre together with NATO by January 2006, an EU cell at SHAPE, direct liaison between the EU Military Staff and NATO, and the creation of a world-wide post-disaster civilian intervention force, the change in the EU's nature becomes even more striking.

The Commission is concerned by and active in all of these operations. It manages through its Delegations civilian projects within generic Commission competence and supervises CFSP policies where financial packages are offered to failing states. The role of the Commission Delegations abroad has thus expanded apace and the trappings of their international 'actorness' are well established, regardless of the outside world's mystification about which country or institution plays the representative role. The creation of a truly European diplomacy to match these developments has been seen by some as the inevitable next step (Allen 1996; European Parliament 2000). But the problem is that while the Commission's role in external relations and CFSP is crucial, it is nonetheless often denigrated. Certainly, its Delegations abroad have been the butt of considerable criticism by the European Parliament, and this is discussed below. The press has also been a constant gad-fly. The *Financial Times*, for example, has castigated staff of the Commission's Delegation in Washington:

> 'With a few notable exceptions, the European Union's diplomatic representation in the US has long been a refuge for backroom bureaucrats with tin ears and continental accents' (*Financial Times* 2005a).

More damningly, though somewhat hysterically and certainly wrongly, one newspaper described EC Delegations as 'missions in paradise', which should be disbanded (*Sunday Express* 1996). As to Member States' appreciation of their role, under questioning from the House of Commons Foreign Affairs Committee in 2004, even the UK Foreign Secretary described the Commission's Delegation staff as 'all sorts of odd-bods from the European Union running all sorts of odd offices around the world... it is not entirely clear what they are doing' (Hansard 2004a, 25 May 2004).

The fact though, as Commissioner Patten appropriately noted in his retort, is that the Delegations

> 'carry out detailed trade and other negotiations, to support and help coordinate the work of the Member States' own embassies, and to provide high quality political and economic reporting, frequently from countries where not all Member States are represented themselves. Perhaps most importantly, they deliver over €5 billion of external and development assistance per year in support of the EU's agreed goals, and in support of the Union's policies' (Patten 2004a).

Formally, the Delegations are the *Commission's* Delegations, though in practice they have increasingly come to represent the EU's collective interests. Delegation staff have, of course, to jockey for power and influence in the countries to which they are accredited, and national diplomats are both partners and rivals in this endeavour. All the more reason to reflect on the salience of the Commission's External Service within the newly emerging diplomatic framework. After all, the Delegations are in place worldwide – passing their management responsibilities to EU embassies or new agencies would be fraught with complexity and pitfalls.

The desire for the Commission to be a world actor actually dates back to Monnet's time, as is described below; and first pillar, Commission-managed (if Council mandated) policies have formed an integral and substantial part of the EU's external relations. But it nevertheless took fifty years of slow evolution for the Commission's policy role to be recognised as so crucial and for the spread of its Delegations to be so wide. Since the 2004 enlargement, there have been 123 Commission Delegations accredited to 155 countries and to the international organisations, thus ranking the Commission's diplomatic representation approximately seventh when compared with the size of geographic spread of Member State representation outside the EU.[3] The Commission's ability to play an important political role commensurate with this geographic spread has suffered greatly from the unwillingness hitherto of Member State governments to create an adequate EU response to the growing desire for a more European and less national policy. As senior Council officials and others have argued, the EU Member States have been markedly unsuccessful in co-ordinating their foreign policy positions on matters of common interest in crisis situations, when the issues have been controversial (Hill 1983; Crowe 2004; Cooper 2004). And even the EU's relations with strategic partners such as Russia and the United States have been hampered by a lack of coherence and forcefulness (Solana 2000).

The Commission is not responsible for this and the reputation of the Commission Delegations cannot be said to have suffered. On the contrary, they are seen by many in the outside world as the natural focus for diplomatic relations with the EU, and they are respected outside the EU for their ability to deliver practical EU policy implementation, even when the formal representational role of the EU falls to the revolving presidency. But, the Commission itself has suffered from the scepticism of governments and publics alike. It does carry a large measure of responsibility for its failure to punch according to its weight. In following the maxim that discretion is the better part of valour, it has failed significantly to engage within the EU in the advocacy and public diplomacy commensurate with its abilities and potential. True, matters might not have improved if the Commission had argued more forcefully during crises, whether with the US or Russia, in the Middle East, Bosnia, South Africa or elsewhere, but the absence of effective public diplomacy, at least before Commissioner Patten arrived, is striking.

The European Parliament has been a consistent critic of the Commission's timidity, inability 'to make full use of its right to submit proposals to the Council' and its general lack of initiative (European Parliament 1998, 5). Yet, again, it is far from certain that the Commission would have had a coherent view given clear differences in interest among DGs, let alone Commissioners. And Member States like France or the UK (or Germany in some instances) might not have welcomed Commission positions if they had countered their own. But, there certainly was failure on the part of the Commission to capitalise on the respect of its international political partners. These are not just the 170 states accredited to the EU in the shape of the European Commission President in Brussels but also, at a different but increasingly significant level, the many international non-governmental organisations which look to the Commission for inspiration – both in terms of ideas and in terms of the considerable financial resources the Commission devotes to them for the exercise of their own contribution to international affairs.

As the international context has changed so with it has the Commission's potential role. Several phases of reform over fifty years have unwittingly prepared the Commission's Delegations for the challenges involved in forming the nucleus of the mooted new Union Delegations. Now, the prime issue of pertinence for the Barroso Commission is whether the political abilities and potential of its External Service will be recognised and rewarded, or whether its project-management functions will determine the Commission's place in the new EEAS. Will the Commission's existing arrangements for external relations form the core of the new system of European diplomatic representation, or will the Commission be relegated to a purely trade, aid and technical assistance role, while the political running is made by others – the Council Secretariat and Member State foreign ministries?

The answer will depend on the roles the EEAS will be called upon to fulfil, and the functions the Commission and the Member State foreign ministries retain. Indeed, if external relations stand at a cross-roads for the EU, one intriguing issue is indeed whether there exists a zero-sum relationship in the division of responsibilities between Member State foreign ministries and the over seven thousand Commission staff involved in external relations. One Head of a Commission Delegation once affirmed that there was merit in the Commission providing a technically oriented diplomatic service, which Member States lack, and that it would be odd for the Commission to start grooming pin-stripe diplomats to 'compete with national diplomats on the cocktail circuit', just when Member States are making their own diplomatic services a bit more technocratic (Buchan 1993, 55). Yet, the shape of future EU diplomacy and thus relations between the EEAS and national diplomatic services will obviously be characterised by the continued sharing of EU representational roles between 'Union' Delegations and Member State embassies. Crucially, most Member States are not present in as many countries as the Commission has Delegations (see Annex J), a fact which begs many questions about the advantages for foreign ministries of sharing embassy facilities or seconding national diplomats to Union Delegations to play both national and European roles, when purse-string, indeed shoestring, constraints make national representation otherwise impossible.

The origins of the Commission's External Service

The history of the Commission presence outside the Member States of the EU is a history of frequent change. It was begun by Jean Monnet, first President of the High Authority of the European Coal and Steel Community (ECSC). Given the risk that the demise of the European Defence Community might signal to the Americans a parallel demise of European integration itself,

Secretary of State Dean Acheson expressed US support by sending Monnet on his first working day in 1952 a dispatch in the name of President Truman confirming full US diplomatic recognition of the ECSC. The creation of an ECSC information office in Washington soon followed – the result of cooperation between Monnet and the ECSC's US lawyer George Ball (later a key figure in the Kennedy and Johnson Administrations of the 1960s).[4] The first Head of this 'Delegation' was Leonard Tennyson, a former Marshall Plan official, and an American national.[5] Two years later, Curt Heidenreich of EURATOM, the first EC diplomat posted outside Europe, joined Tennyson, and a US Ambassador was accredited to the ECSC in 1956. It was the second overseas mission to establish diplomatic relations with the Community institutions. The first had been the UK, which also hosted a full ECSC diplomatic mission, established in London in 1956.

The subsequent Treaty of Rome included measures to associate the then Overseas Countries and Territories of the six founding Member States. This involved the establishment of a five-year development fund, known then by its French acronym FEDOM, the predecessor of today's European Development Fund (EDF). It covered management of some 580 million European Units of Account (ECU) in capital aid programmes to develop physical infrastructure such as roads and irrigation, and it required representation in the field.

The 1960s and 1970s – administrative needs, pragmatism and the expansion of the Delegation network

DG VIII (today's DG Development) focussed on its prime function – development aid, and it is understandable that it did not define the Delegations' role more broadly. But, it did develop a specific management culture and staff loyalties both in Brussels and the Delegations. As the manager of FEDOM, the Commission created contract teams led by a *Contrôleur Technique* usually recruited from European engineering consultancies to be resident in the mainly African beneficiary countries and carry out strictly project management functions. DG VIII was the first DG to run, via its Delegations, expensive programmes (Dimier 2004, 74). These were initially restricted in the 1960s to the former French colonies and the line management was to French Commissioners. The first of these, in 1958, was Robert Lemaignen. His *chef de cabinet* Jacques Ferrandi was a former French colonial administrator and director-general of French West African Development. Ferrandi placed a 'clan' of French former colonial officials in strategic posts in DG VIII. They remained in office after his own appointment by *parachutage* to a directorship in DG VIII, when Lemaignen ceased his functions in 1962. Ferrandi himself was immensely powerful. As he admitted many years later, 'I have never had so much power to dispose of public money. DG VIII was the EDF, and I was the EDF' (Dimier 2004, 78). The power of the Commission was already spread between DG VIII and its Delegations abroad.

But, in 1963, there were only 18 Commission Delegations carrying out these project management functions and their task during the 1960s remained purely to implement Community aid granted through the EDF under the Yaoundé Conventions (1966-75). The subsequent gradual growth in the Delegation network was to result from EC enlargement and the objective need for field work, even if actually the representative role of the Delegations was already growing apace. Development 'cooperation' was seen in the 1960s as a temporary phenomenon that would not require long-term permanent Commission staff with dedicated Commission career structures. Instead, the Commission created in 1964 a semi-autonomous Agency – the Association Européenne pour la Cooperation (AEC) or European Agency for Cooperation (EAC). The AEC managed those Delegations answerable to DG VIII in the ACP states, South East Mediterranean, and Latin American and Asian countries. Staff in these Delegations had contracts under Belgian law, with the exception of some officials seconded by the Commission. EAC was funded under a Commission grant. It recruited and managed the (contractual) Heads of Mission, meanwhile termed 'Contrôleurs Delegués' (the first was appointed to Chad in 1966) and their technical staff in Commission offices in the associated countries. EAC was a hybrid in political and administrative terms. It was composed of former colonial administrators from Member State administrations or development professionals from the private sector, but it reported to a board of senior Commission officials and its Director was seconded from the Commission.

The 1973 enlargement brought a sea-change in the scope of DG VIII, changing its mission, methods and operating assumptions and requiring an expansion of the Delegation network. The UK's accession to the Community and the subsequent signing of the first Lomé Convention between the EC and 46 founding African, Caribbean and Pacific states (ACP) in February 1975 had enormous consequences for the External Service, by then composed of some 320 people serving abroad. They included 120 Europeans, mainly civil engineers and agronomists, and 200 local staff, mainly involved in logistical and administrative support roles. As the former UK colonies were now added to the catchment area, there began a reconciliation between the French and British styles of management of aid – albeit still under the leadership of a French Commissioner, Claude Cheysson, but now with the considerable input of a senior British official, Maurice Foley. Both headquarters and the Delegations underwent considerable reform with aims familiar to Commission reform watchers: efficiency, transparency and rationality. The context – enlargement – was similar to the later reform context under Prodi and Patten, as was the fight against 'nepotism' and the encouragement of 'programming' and 'evaluation'.

The post 1973 reform concentrated on two main features: changing the nature of DG VIII's geographical coverage to encompass the British Commonwealth and departure from a purely project based approach to management into a system whereby projects became tools of wider, coherent programmes. The Ferrandi-based, French inspired bureaucratic empire began to crumble. Ferrandi himself left the Commission in 1975, when the Lomé Convention became the new operating basis for DG VIII and its Delegations. Lomé was hailed as an international partnership, unlike its predecessor the Yaoundé Convention, which had continued the now outdated 'association' policy, considered neo-colonial by many ACP States. The approach under Lomé changed the role of the Commission's representatives in the ACP, both in style and in substance. Lomé still concentrated on development cooperation, but it also covered trade, regional integration and cultural cooperation. Its political profile was much higher, and the leverage afforded the head of the

Commission Delegation reflected the size of the European budget devoted to individual countries. The 'Commission Delegate' became an essential element in the Lomé Agreement. His role was more representational and, significantly, his precise functions were set out in the Convention itself. He represented the Commission in the ACP State for the purpose of implementing the Convention, yet his appointment was subject to the agreement of the receiving ACP state, a procedure akin to classic diplomatic practice.

Gradually, the role of the heads of Delegation began to expand beyond the limited mandate of the 'Contrôleurs Delegués' and their technical teams. Recruitment expanded to include both Commission officials from Brussels and development specialists from Member State administrations, usually on secondment to EAC, which continued to manage the Delegations in the ACP countries. Commission missions in the ACP thus gradually became full 'Delegations' of the Commission and their number increased to 41 between 1975 and 1978, by which time the total staff complement had reached 900, including 250 Europeans. The signing of Community protocols in 1975-77 with eight southern and eastern Mediterranean countries meant that Delegations were opened in all of them by the early 1980s. Delegations also opened in Bangkok, New Delhi, Caracas and Tokyo. Contrary to the EAC system, the new missions were managed by the Commission's External Economic Relations DG (then known as DG I), and contrary to practice in the ACP countries still managed by DG VIII and EAC, there was a more classically diplomatic approach to their establishment. While the emphasis given to their tasks varied according to local circumstances, every external office was equipped – at least in principle – with the staff and support from Brussels to engage in external representation. To reflect the EC's growing economic and political weight in the world Delegations now needed high-level access and diplomatic protection; hence, they gradually evolved. They were not only aid or trade specific, but increasingly tasked with representation of the Commission's growing responsibilities and with the external ramifications of the increasingly integrated policy areas of the European Communities.

The contours of what is now the Commission's External Service were thus becoming apparent. Credentials may not yet have been presented to the President of the host country, as later became the case, but Delegations were taking on new diplomatic roles, with an *accord de siège* or establishment agreement, signed with the host country at political level and based on the 1961 Vienna Convention on Diplomatic Relations, according full diplomatic status to the head of mission and his staff. Though there had been initial hesitation to move in this direction – after the failure in 1960 and 1962, through lack of Member State support, to set up a single diplomatic representation covering the ECSC, EURATOM and the EEC in Washington, London and Latin America – the new-style Delegations soon assumed political and diplomatic functions. The first diplomatic, as opposed to development, Delegation was in Paris (to the OECD) and then Geneva (to the GATT and later the UN organisations there). Meanwhile, the Washington office was transformed in 1971 into a Delegation headed by Ambassador Aldo Mario Mazio, a career diplomat from the Italian foreign service, whose title of 'ambassador' came with the man, rather than reflecting Commission policy.[6] In New York, the Commission Delegation represented the Community at the UN, where it attained observer status in 1974.[7]

Until 1st January 1988, the External Service of the Commission was actually managed by two distinct entities: EAC and the Unité des Bureaux Extérieures (UBE), which was created in 1982 within DG IX. Both were transformed in 1988 into the DAD (Direction pour l'Administration des Délégations). The UBE had managed the Delegations answerable to DG I as well as the Press and Information Offices answerable to DG X, then DG PRESS and now DG Communication. Unlike EAC staff, personnel in these Delegations fell under the Staff Statutes of the European Communities. The creation of the DAD now meant 'titularisation', or 'establishment' as civil servants of EAC's staff. EAC remained as a recruitment agency for technical specialists on contract.

European Political Cooperation: from technicians to diplomats

The evolution from the 1969 Luxembourg Report's creation of EPC, with its regular meetings in European capitals, to the London Report of 1981, which foresaw crisis procedures including meetings of ambassadors within 48 hours, further enhanced the Delegations' role. True, while the Copenhagen Report of 1973 encouraged joint ambassadorial reports from third countries, with the occasional call on a Commission Delegation if Community business was involved, the Commission was often left by the wayside. Meetings were now to be at the request of three Member States and joint reports, either on ambassadors' own initiative or at the request of the Political Committee, composed of the Political Directors of Member State foreign ministries and the Commission, began to draw on Community competence. The Stuttgart declaration of 19 June 1983 called for closer cooperation in the field of external representation and the 1986 Single European Act formalised EPC by treaty and codified the obligation to consult and coordinate on the ground by explicitly requiring Member State embassies and Commission Delegations to 'intensify cooperation' (Single European Act, title III Art. 30 point 9).

As a result, the 1980s saw the evolution of the Delegation network on the model of the new DG I Delegations. As in the early seventies, enlargement played a catalytic role. There was a focus on new Delegations in the Mediterranean and in Asia and Latin America because of the Iberian enlargement of 1986. In political cooperation, Member States were increasingly taking on board the Delegations' expertise in EC policy, its institutional memory and the fact that the Commission was the only stable element in the fluctuating constellation of troikas. In trade relations, Member State officials had only a support role to the Commission's negotiators and Delegation staff, and they looked to the Commission to solve everyday trade disputes. The Commission Delegations also acquired responsibility for assisting high-level Community visitors, increasingly from the European Parliament. As for public diplomacy, the 'mission to explain' begun in Washington in 1954 was now needed everywhere, even if the status of Delegations still varied greatly, from the EAC-run ACP missions with their mainly contracted staff and modest political profile to DG I's increasingly political Delegations.

Two major areas were problematic for the Commission however: collegial respect and human resource issues. From 1986 onwards Heads of Commission Delegations became intimately involved in sensitive and confidential matters with their Member State colleagues on the spot. The problem was that despite their professional competence, Heads of Delegation rarely achieved the full confidence of their EU ambassadorial colleagues. This was not merely a question of diplomats in local post either mistrusting their Commission colleagues or simply not understanding the changing nature of the EU foreign policy game. The Commission's overall role in international diplomacy itself was frequently contested. Indeed, after the Single European Act a specialised unit was set up in the Council to coordinate EPC matters, ensuring that the Commission kept to its proper place and also creating continuity and collective memory, a role the Commission hitherto enjoyed in Community business. In the early days of EPC in Brussels, the then European Correspondent[8] summed up the almost hostile environment surrounding the Commission's participation in the foreign policy process:

> 'the foreign policy establishments of all Member States, confidently reposing on their long-standing traditions of state diplomacy, were at best inclined to treat the Commission with the high courtesy of condescension'(Nuttall 1996, 130).

In time, this 'condescension' gave way, he added, to 'nervous respect', a fact largely due to the Commission's ever-present participation in CFSP and in troikas, and the fact that the Commission is legally the formal external representative of the European Community. Through its Delegations outside the EU, it had become a focus for policy-making towards the EU in capitals world-wide.

There were a number of related internal administrative inconsistencies. A Commission report in 1982 on the external competence of the Community underlined them. Adrian Fortescue, a former UK career diplomat and subsequent Director General for Justice and Home Affairs, drew up the report. It highlighted the fact that:

> 'The Commission has a nucleus of a foreign service. Its external Delegations are doing work directly comparable to Member State embassies. They cover a narrower field but involve the same techniques of negotiation, representation, confidential dealings with governments and international organisations, and political and economic analysis. Like embassies, they need proper back-up from headquarters so that they have the information and instruments to do the job ... They also have the same needs as embassies to cope with the specific requirements of a diplomatic life in distant parts' (Fortescue 1982).

For Fortescue, a key constraint on the future development of the system was the management of personnel. Problems were now arising from the particular situation of the contractual ACP Delegation staff, managed by EAC for the most part, and officials managed by DG VIII, DG 1 and DG IX. Virtually none of the EAC staff had had opportunities to serve in Brussels. And mobility for DG VIII staff, whether between Brussels and the Delegations or between Delegations in different regions, suffered from a lack of career development and inadequate or non-existent training.[9] As for DG IX staff, they had no experience with the Delegations they were called upon to manage. Commission officials in the 1960s and 70s had not been recruited with

'External Service' in mind, so there was often a 'foreign legion' approach to staffing the Delegations. Even in the DG I Delegations, where Commission officials, rather than contractual staff, made up the foreign staff complement, there was little career perspective involved in an overseas posting, and few middle or senior management staff in the 'Relex family' of DGs had any Delegation service behind them.[10] A notable result of discussions on these issues was the creation of Annex X of the staff regulations in 1987, which set out formally the rights and obligations of Commission officials serving in Delegations. Annex X also provided the statutory basis for DG IX's management of External Service staff until the creation of the Unified External Service in 1993 gave personnel management of the ES to the new DG IA. Thereafter there was financial and material support for officials posted overseas comparable to that applicable for Member State diplomats or expatriates in the private sector, and this began to remedy the career development deficiencies exposed in the Fortescue Report.

The 1990s: the demise of the Soviet empire, CFSP and enlargement as catalysts for change

Another qualitative and quantitative leap for the Delegations came after 1989 with the fall of communist regimes in Central and Eastern Europe, the fragmentation of the former Soviet Union and later the perspective of many of the new-born sovereign states attaining membership of the EU – events which led to a diplomatic expansion unprecedented in any foreign service history. The Western Economic Summit, at President Bush's instigation, but with Commission President Delors' willing acquiescence, entrusted the Commission with the coordination of aid to Poland and Hungary and thereby engendered a new phase of expansion of the Delegation network. At the same time there began a conceptual slide from an External Service purely composed of project managers to an evolving diplomatic service, as the Delegations took on much of the work involved in the negotiations for EU membership. The resulting agenda in the Commission's External Service was complex. New Delegations had already been opening at an average of five every year in the 1980s. By 1988, the Commission's 89 missions in six continents meant that the External Service had achieved global presence, and the 1988 'titularisation' of EAC staff brought the number of Brussels-based officials serving in Delegations from 165 to 440, while local staff numbers reached 1440 (Commission 2004b).

By 1990 the establishment of a permanent External Service staff and the upgrade to diplomatic status of Commission Delegations had created a qualitatively different service. With most Delegations accredited as full diplomatic missions by their host countries and most of the Heads of Delegation accredited at Head of State rather than foreign minister level, their credentials signed by the President of the Commission, the Delegations had become a firm feature within the international diplomatic community. Heads of Delegation had the rank and courtesy title of ambassador, though the Commission was at pains to ensure Heads of Delegation made no formal claim to ambassadorial status for fear of rousing animosity within Member State foreign services. In the context of the 'Eftan' enlargement, the (Maastricht) Treaty on European

Union created a diplomatic framework more precise than its predecessor Single European Act:

> 'The diplomatic and consular missions of the Member States and the Commission Delegations in third countries and their representations to international organisations shall cooperate in ensuring that the common positions and common measures adopted by the Council are complied with and implemented. They shall step up cooperation by exchanging information, carrying out joint assessments and contributing to the implementation of the provisions referred to in article 8c of the Treaty Establishing the European Community' (TEU title V J.6).

It also extended and consolidated the Council Secretariat's role in EPC, now rebaptised CFSP, extended EPC to security and defence issues and created a third pillar to add to the SEA's two. Justice and Home Affairs, seemingly the bailiwick of ministries of the interior, had important foreign policy ramifications, as chapter 11 underlines. To mark the change, the Delors Commission shifted responsibility for foreign policy from the EPC unit in the Secretariat General to a new Directorate General, DG IA. Under Director General Günter Burghardt (later Head of the Commission Delegation in Washington), relations with third countries were set to become more effective and coherent. One of the first managerial innovations was the withdrawal of responsibility for Delegation staff from EAC and DG IX, and the creation of a Directorate within DG IA responsible for management of the Delegations and their staff within the framework of a 'Unified External Service' (UES). This was created in 1994 to replace the DAD. The Unified External Service was so called because it brought the disparate elements under one management umbrella, a measure overdue since the Fortescue Report.

Progress began to be made as the Commission identified the main structural problems with the management of the service. David Williamson, then Secretary General of the Commission, produced a key document in 1996 on the professionalisation of this 'unified' External Service (Commission 1996). The 'Williamson Report' recognised the need for the Commission to develop a homogeneous body of people willing to serve overseas as part of a life-long diplomatic career. Its key recommendations included the obligation to serve abroad for all officials working in the external relations field and a commitment to career development and professional training. Staff now had to recognise that their future advancement depended on their willingness to be mobile. 1996 thus heralded significant change in the status of the External Service, and opportunities at Headquarters for staff with Delegation experience rose steadily.

Reflecting the new level of interest in the External Service, the Santer Commission produced policy documents in the form of 'communications' to the Council and Parliament every year. They covered all aspects of External Service management and development, including its role, priorities and resources, and substantial modifications to the Delegation network and its operations. Significantly, however, the adoption of modern management techniques and an enlightened approach to the issue of management change in this part of the Commission were less the result of diligent middle and senior management than might be thought. There had been considerable criticism from within (Alexandrakis 1996) and without (*Sunday Express* 1996). Management was dragged into change in part by these criticisms, but more immediately by the threat of the European Parliament to withhold operational funds from the budget for the management of the Delegations unless criteria for management change were promised – and delivered. The efforts of a former Commission official (former Head of Delegation and Commission Director General) turned MEP (and subsequently Dutch government minister) were not without significance. Laurens Jan Brinkhorst was resented by some, though secretly applauded by the middle management staff tasked with External Service reform, for the quid pro quo of parliamentary pressure was the delivery of reform of the External Service and the professionalisation these officials sought, even if it was not yet a priority at political level.

The European Parliament was thus very influential during the Santer/van den Broek period, playing an increasingly significant part in monitoring and prompting the expansion and professionalisation of the service. A crucial 'incentive' for reform was the 1999 EP Budget Committee's blocking of the External Service budget, sending €13.1 million to the 'reserve'. This was to be released provided the Commission produced by 30 June 1999 a communication[11] on the External Service setting out arrangements for policy concerning the training of applicants to and members of the External Service[12], mandatory rotation (mobility abroad) for officials[13], measures to incorporate Member State diplomats into the staff complement of the external Delegations[14], relations with competent parliamentary committees and inter-parliamentary Delegations[15], a report on the operation of the joint structure for the management of external programmes, management decentralisation (to regional Delegations) measures and monitoring of financial appropriations[16] and a cost-benefit analysis of implementation of decentralisation measures modelled on existing practice in PHARE, MEDA and TACIS.

The resulting Commission Communication (Commission 1999) included measures to ensure contacts between Heads of Delegation and the European Parliament (appearance of newly appointed Heads of Delegation before parliamentary committees) and measures to restructure the external representations and associated staff redeployment. With prescience, given the perspectives in 2005, the Commission also proposed allowing Member States unable to afford their own embassy premises to send serving officers to Commission Delegations. An example of this was the Liberia Commission Aid Coordination Office, where several Member States based their field operations. All these measures were proposed in the framework of an ongoing reform exercise introduced under the patronage of the then Secretary General Carlo Trojan, entitled 'Designing Tomorrow's Commission', discussed in chapter 17.

The Prodi and Barroso Commissions: a technical support structure, or towards a diplomatic service?

During discussions in the IGC of 1996 the Belgians proposed that:

'the diplomatic networks, expertise, personnel and resources available in each of the Member States should be fully utilised in a joint approach with the Commission acting as a catalyst and coordinator' (quoted in Bale 2000).

Yet, the Treaty of Amsterdam did not amend the Maastricht text, though it did strengthen CFSP by creating the post of High Representative (HR). On the Commission side a new CFSP directorate was created, largely as a response to the creation of the Policy Unit, responsible to the HR. Just as the 1993 reforms had been a response to Maastricht, so the Amsterdam Treaty resulted in the gradual reorientation of the Commission Delegations. They now became more involved in CFSP and thus more involved with HR Solana's numerous missions around the world, sending him their political reports and playing an important support role for him and the various EU Special Envoys appointed by the Council. In 2000, the European Parliament, continuing its regular calls for a European diplomacy (e.g. European Parliament 1998), passed a resolution proposing the establishment of a common European diplomacy and calling for a new College of European diplomacy to train professionals from both the EU institutions and Member States in EU policies and diplomatic methods and to enhance basic diplomatic training provisions for Commission Delegation staff. Commission Delegations, argued the report, should evolve into Community Delegations accountable to Council and Parliament, and the External Service should be 'a professional, permanent Community Diplomatic Service'. This frequently made plea by the Parliament was prescient, despite its cautionary rider to the effect that:

> 'The objective is certainly not to create a single diplomatic service to replace the foreign services of the Member States with a European foreign service properly speaking, but simply to improve the quality of the Community's joint External Service and strive for closer cooperation with the External Services of the Member States... (though not ruling out) future... more ambitious steps... setting up Union embassies consisting of a Community Delegation and the missions of Member States wishing to have a presence in the third country concerned' (European Parliament, 2000).

Despite this encouragement to innovate, the Commission concentrated on the reform of its much criticised project and financial management. When the Prodi Commission took office in 1999 its main priority was overall reform of the Commission's management systems. As chapter 17 underlines, it had been a bleak time for the Commission. In answer to the reports of the Committee of Independent Experts (Committee of Independent Experts 1999), there needed to be fast evidence of commitment to modernisation, coupled with the general realisation that Santer's policy of doing more with fewer resources had created more management problems than it had resolved. The consequent ambitious transformation of management culture across the Commission involved the first real overhaul of resource management the Commission had ever seen.

However, the potential change to a culture of diplomacy was never seriously envisaged. This was due both to a lack of creativity and to the prudence with which senior officials positioned the Commission throughout CFSP policy-making. There was an overriding need to prioritise reform through more effective coverage of existing responsibilities and only then, if at all, to consider anew the overall role of the External Service. This was certainly Patten's view. Yet, the contemporary context of reform of the Commission's Delegations was the creation of the ESDP at the Nice European Council, which put crisis management, conflict prevention and international security issues formally on the EU agenda. The Commission had long possessed an interest in all the new areas in the Nice Treaty, but responsibilities were scattered not only throughout the Relex family, but throughout the Commission as well. Just as the post-1993 reforms were largely induced in response to the Maastricht Treaty's creation of an intergovernmental pillar in the EU, the post-Amsterdam reforms obliged the Commission to mirror changes in the Council's creation of the High Representative and his policy unit. A new CFSP directorate and the widening of the Delegations' tasks were the results. There was a need for better coordination in Brussels, and a need for the Delegations to adjust to the implications. The inter-institutional implications, in particular the new ESDP arrangements, are discussed in chapter 14. The importance of the new functional areas for the Delegations was crucial. The work of the Political and Security Committee in Brussels, with its offshoot committees for political-military affairs, civil crisis management and terrorism were all to lead to new involvement for the Delegations in ever closer cooperation with Member State embassies – joint threat analysis by Member State embassies and Commission Delegations was but one such new requirement. Yet advantage was not taken of the potentially permissive environment for the redefinition of the Delegations' role. Paradoxically, the signing of the Constitution in October 2004 seemingly took the Commission by surprise, and it was only in 2005 that serious reflection began on how the Commission's interests could best be defended against the threat of 'pescisation' (see page 379) by the EEAS – and that included the Delegations.

True, in Brussels, and consequent to the Nice Treaty as the Prodi Commission took office, enhanced coordination led immediately to a rationalisation of the Commission's services, all with implications for the Delegations. Directorates General Relex and Trade were housed in one building with their Commissioners and could focus, in principle, on coordinating policy and programming in their respective areas. A new DG, EuropeAid (known internally as AidCo), replaced the 'Common External Service' (*Service Commun Relex* or SCR), a DG created under Santer and van den Broek to manage all external aid and technical assistance except for CFSP actions and humanitarian aid, which remained with DG Relex and ECHO. Despite the intention of letting policy-makers make policy and project managers manage projects, immediate rivalry began between policy-makers and budget managers, which, though much abated, continues to stymie technical assistance to this day.

The External Service was thus not excluded from the Commission's attempt to put its financial house in order (Gray 2004 and chapter 17). But reform was about improved management, not about rethinking the purpose of the ES. Patten's reform of the management of EC external assistance substantially reduced the time it took to implement projects. It made significant improvement in the quality and responsiveness of projects/programme management and ensured robust financial, technical and contractual management procedures in line with the best international standards of propriety and accountability. It clearly improved the impact and visibility of EC development cooperation and aid. As Patten succinctly put it:

> 'external assistance is an area in which EU reality… falls embarrassingly far below its potential. The EU and its Member States account for 55% of all official international development assist-

ance, and some 66% of all grant aid. Yet the money is not well managed. In saying that I do not want to cast aspersions on the many excellent and dedicated staff... But they have been saddled with lousy procedures. And there are too few of them... EC aid volumes have increased two or three times as fast as the staff at our disposal to manage the funds. As a result, our outstanding backlog of committed funds waiting to be disbursed has increased from an appalling 3 years' worth of payments to 4.5 years. For certain programmes the backlog of outstanding commitments is equivalent to more than 8.5 years. We simply cannot muddle on as before' (Patten 2000b).

Under Patten, the Commission carried out a radical reform programme and embarked on a far-reaching adjustment of responsibilities between Headquarters and the Delegations known as 'deconcentration'[17]. Patten's view was that the demarcation line between his and the High Representative's role was clear, Solana's being to rally the Member States to policies and his (Patten's) being to implement them (see page 378). As Patten noted, 'even with the emergence of the CFSP High Representative, Member States look to the Commission to manage the nuts and bolts of that engagement, and to do much of the donkey work' (Patten 2000c).

The result was a radical overhaul of programming of assistance, the rationalisation of the project cycle (previously split between Brussels and Delegations), the creation of the EuropeAid Co-operation Office, the dismantling of Technical Assistance Offices (TAO), usually known by their French acronym BAT, and a package of urgent measures to eliminate 'old' and 'dormant' financial commitments. These new policies had a profound effect on the Delegations. Heads of Delegation with little or no resource management experience found themselves charged overnight with the implications of full deconcentration of responsibility for implementation of assistance programmes to the field. Over time this was to lead to a major redeployment of staff from Headquarters to the 76 Delegations in developing countries, which benefit via the EU countries from more than half the total aid given by the international community. In addition, new Delegations opened in Malaysia, Singapore, Saudi Arabia, Taiwan, Cambodia, Laos, Nepal and Paraguay and, perhaps reversing the historical trend, greater use became made of contracted specialists placed in Delegation offices and of project managers in the field. For example, the number of independent project managers working for ECHO abroad, and CFSP projects, whether assistance to the Palestinian Authority or weapons clearing in Cambodia, expanded apace – the Commission managing them all. During the same period the staffing base of development and technical assistance personnel began to change and several sectoral DGs with important third country agreements or programmes to implement, such as Trade, ECHO, Justice & Home Affairs or Research and Technology, now place staff in Delegations. There is also a small but growing number of officials seconded from Member States in Delegations (46 in 2005). As a result, the average size of many Delegations has increased substantially. What were once relatively small 'family' missions are now in many cases large operations, often housed in more than one building, with 50-100 staff working within them.

A year after the reform of the management of aid and assistance, another report (Commission 2001f) – whose author, Claude Chêne, subsequently became Director General for personnel and administration – recommended a number of further measures to improve the functioning of the External Service, in line with the general process of Commission reform and a Court of Auditors' Report on the management of CFSP (Court of Auditors 2001). For the first time, the Chêne Report clarified the role of the Head of Delegation (HoD) as representative of the Commission as a whole, as opposed to the sectoral interest of a specific DG. The HoD became formally responsible for the organisation and work programme of the Delegation, and a detailed listing of the working rules applicable to relations between Headquarters and Delegations was established. This included standardised organigrammes promoting a consistent structure within Delegations, work programmes, and annual reports to facilitate planning within a new activity-based management framework. In consequence, there was adaptation of resources, a methodology for appraisal of the specific workloads of Delegations, a four year human resource plan responding to the requirements of the UES, and precise individual mandates for Heads of Delegation – all fairly basic management requirements familiar in national foreign ministries and international companies. The Commission simply arrived late on the management scene.

A part of the Chêne Report covered the consolidation of the UES. A major weakness of the staffing system had been the complicated administrative status of officials in Delegations who depended on one or other of the DGs of the Relex family. Of the 733 officials belonging to the External Service, 514 were DG Relex staff, 171 were DG DEV, 24 DG Trade, 1 from ECHO and 23 from other DGs, while none was on secondment from AidCo or DG Enlargement. This militated against coherent personnel and career management. The report proposed that from 1st January 2002 all Delegation personnel should be managed solely by DG Relex. The DG Trade, ECHO and DG DEV staff would thus be formally transferred to DG Relex, implying a shift of 196 posts (182 A grade and 14 B grade staff) and reinforcing the collective management of the External Service, improving transparency within the system, allowing participation by Heads of Delegation in the choice of candidates, and giving priority in selection procedures to officials within DG Relex. All these features were designed to counterbalance the (somewhat resented) obligation for staff to serve abroad, yet opened the door to officials from other DGs whose profiles might correspond to specific needs in Delegations (financial or operational experience for example). Head of Delegation posts were to move gradually, over the course of three years, to systematic publication of all vacancies. Concrete proposals to encourage officials to move to Delegations included the clarification and reinforcement of the obligation to serve abroad, limiting the duration of postings in difficult Delegations, and overcoming difficulties faced by spouses in Delegations. Finally, a general policy on mobility, both within Relex DGs and between Relex DGs and Delegations, was to be put in place within DG Relex, with the aim of finally improving career development.

2005: successful reform of project management?

By 2004 it was time to review the lessons learned from implementation of the Chêne Report and the various commitments made in years of

'Communications' on the development of the External Service. Was there now coherence between overall Commission reform and that of the External Service? Was there now adequate consultation of staff in Headquarters and Delegations, and consultation of staff representatives on each of the measures proposed? As for the Delegations, the extensive deconcentration of project/programme management tasks and responsibilities to Delegations needed review. The Commission had promised an evaluation of the measures taken to make deconcentration effective, to manage external aid reform and to match human resources to increased responsibilities in devolved Delegations. This included the issue of balancing staff deployment in Headquarters and Delegations to manage external aid properly (Commission 2002f and 2003d). Most components of the reform had in fact been implemented by early 2002, but implementation of the deconcentration process only neared completion by the end of 2004. The analysis of the effectiveness of the Chêne Report and deconcentration decisions was undertaken by a Relex family team chaired by DG VIII stalwart David Lipman, Personnel Director in DG Relex. The Lipman Report went to Council and Parliament in May 2004 (Commission 2004g). Its findings were based on research conducted at the end of 2003, relying on nine questions put to the various parties involved and information produced by the services for the evaluation. There was also a review of internal documents and reports. An evaluation questionnaire had been sent to Delegations and Directors from EuropeAid. The final assessment was a joint product of Directors General of DG Relex, DEV and EuropeAid, after an individual hearing with each Head of Delegation. Both the Court of Auditors (2004) and the Lipman Report judged that the deconcentration process had gone according to the initially agreed timetable and was consistent with the parallel process of financial and administrative reform of the Commission in general. In December 2003, 61 of the 78 Delegations due to receive extra responsibilities had already 'devolved', and the process in the remainder was underway in the first half of 2004. Devolved Delegations had become closely associated in the programming process and were now fully responsible for project identification and technical, contractual and financial implementation. Staff numbers in Delegations had increased, resulting in quality improvements and a reduction in the delivery time needed for external assistance. In total 1,559 staff (375 officials and 1,184 external staff) were re-allocated over the 2000-04 period. The external assistance budget managed by the Commission had increased by a factor of 2.8 between 1989 and 1999. However, staffing levels had only increased by a factor of 1.8, so that, even with a limited objective of restoring the staffing ratio of 1989, there was a deficit of 1,300 posts for the management of external assistance (Commission 2000a, 5). And comparison with Member States showed that where they had between 4 and 9 officials to manage €10 million, the Commission only had 2.9 officials (Commission 2000a).

By 2004, the total staff managing external assistance had risen to 3,855, of which two-thirds were in Delegations. The Commission (Delegations plus Headquarters) now has on average 4.8 staff to manage €10 million per year – a considerable increase, yet still putting the Commission within the lower range compared with other important aid donors, though the Commission's is one of the most devolved systems. Lipman proposed 11 follow-up measures covering supply of adequate human resources for the management of external assistance, guaranteeing sustainable financing for the deconcentration process and improving administrative management WTO in Delegations, including a further increase in staff. A separate report by the Court of Auditors (2004) proposed five measures along the same lines. Both fitted the revised general staff regulations in force since 1st May 2004 (Commission 2003b). A major effort has since continued to convert the rudimentary training of External Service staff into a comprehensive programme of training for all aspects of external relations, including modern diplomatic methods (Commission 2003f and Duke 2002). Yet, the management culture clearly remains one of project management, rather than diplomacy.

Commission Delegations and the emerging EU diplomacy

If the culture remains managerial rather than diplomatic, where does external representation of EU interests through Commission Delegations now fit in? Commission Delegations represent the Commission in all areas within its competence, notably economic cooperation and external trade, development cooperation, financial and technical cooperation, and the environment. They are also supposed to ensure consistency in the external actions of the EU. They monitor and report to the Commission and the High Representative on the political, economic and social situation in the host country and serve as a permanent link between Brussels and the local authorities and the socio-economic community of their country of accreditation, informing both sides on EU and Commission-relevant issues. They coordinate and promote dialogue with embassies of Member States, international conferences, and organisations in third world countries. They endeavour to ensure respect, preparation and implementation of common positions and actions decreed by the Council within the framework of CFSP and general EU matters. They promote awareness and knowledge of the European dimension and improve the perception of leaders and Third World public opinion on the role played by the EU. They prepare official visits from the Commission and other EU institutions.[18] They manage food aid, humanitarian aid and technical assistance. They monitor human rights issues, run AIDS programmes and anti-drug programmes, and they maintain a network of relations with NGOs. They support the regional integration favoured by the EU in the African Union, MERCOSUR in South America, ASEAN in South East Asia, the West African Currency Agreement, the creation of a customs union in the UDEAC, and the implementation of reforms to diminish trade and investment constraints as well as intra-regional payments in Eastern and Southern Africa and in the Indian Ocean.

As for EU representation to international organisations, there are Commission Delegations in New York (UN), Geneva (WTO, UN and other international organisations), Vienna (OSCE and other international organisations), Paris (OECD) and Rome (FAO). In New York and Geneva, there are two offices, a Commission Delegation based on diplomatic recognition of the Community as a subject of international law (thus the Commission's formal 'observer' status at the UN) and an 'EU liaison office' of the Council Secretariat without genuine formal status, officially accredited as part of the EC Delegation in New York and sitting with the presidency in Geneva meetings. In Vienna, the Council Secretariat has long argued for the establishment of a separate office in order to strengthen cooperation with the OSCE. In

Geneva, the Commission Delegation and the Council Secretariat liaison office moved into the same building in 2005. Significantly, the walls and dividing arrangements between the two institutions were constructed to allow subsequent easy merger.

Solana has stressed the changing agenda for Delegations that CFSP requires. In a paper to the European Council in Evian in September 2000 (Solana 2000a), he castigated the Member States and set out his plans for enhancement of CFSP. The cumulative diplomatic presence of the EU was, he argued, unparalleled, both in terms of coverage and staff numbers. As a comparison, he quoted the roughly 40,000 EU Member States' diplomats in a network of over 1,500 missions and the US's roughly 15,000 staff and only 300 missions.[19] Yet, output and influence were in inverse proportion he argued. While on-the-spot EU coordination was increasing, and there were more joint reports by heads of mission and more joint debriefings, there was considerable scope for maximising the collective weight and visibility of the EU and more scope for joint action and information exchange. There needed to be analysis of how ESDP issues could be reflected by embassies and Delegations abroad, more synergy of action at the UN and in other international fora and more coordination of EU and Member States' financial action abroad. The subsequent decision to create the European External Action Service may be seen as a vindication of Solana's advocacy.

Commission Delegations certainly do not possess the competence, skills or personnel to deal with ESDP, though some Delegations are sporadically obliged to deal with industrial cooperation or trade related issues in the field of armaments. Nor are the Delegations currently trained or equipped for a culture of confidentiality. Secure communication lines need further improvement, as does the general security situation of Delegations. They have no access to intelligence networks and the system of security clearance is lengthy, cumbersome and insufficient. Know-how as well as staff from Member States would be useful, though improvements in all these areas are underway.

General changes in diplomacy and the implications for Delegations

The diplomat's role was originally personal contact with his opposite numbers in a constant game of information-gathering, persuasion and negotiation. But this role has changed. Foreign policy was long the exclusive province of national foreign ministries. This has also changed. There has been gradual abandonment of the notion that embassies and diplomats are the sole or the most apt defenders of national interests abroad. Foreign ministries were supposedly once the gatekeepers between the domestic and the international arenas. But, in many states the notion that foreign ministries must remain the coordinators of a state's international relations has ceded place to coordination of foreign policy by prime ministerial or presidential offices – the UK Cabinet Office, the French Elysée/Matignon, the Bundeskanzleramt, etc. (Spence 2005a). As EU diplomacy has emerged on the world scene, there has been a detachment of representation from its traditional anchorage in national interests, national foreign ministries and bilateral embassies.

The growth of the Commission's External Service in the last fifty years has accompanied these important developments in the nature of diplomatic representation and practice (Hocking 1999 and Hocking and Spence 2005). There is now a recognisable and distinct European interest, and this European interest needs to be articulated, defended and advocated abroad – a task which Member States and the Commission share. Of course, until, and if, the Constitution enters into force, the Presidency remains responsible for the lead in second pillar affairs. But there were always two important and complicating features of its task. First, most presidencies are simply not present in most capitals around the world, so presidency tasks fall to others most of the time. This can only be exacerbated as the EU expands into a 30-plus membership. Second, as competence in many economic, social and political areas has shifted from the national to the EU arena, so external representation of the resulting interests has evolved. Not only are foreign ministries no longer the gatekeeper between the domestic and the political; there is no firm national line between sectoral concerns and the European level. In both these areas, the Commission's role has increased, since European diplomatic responsibilities overlap the pillars. Indeed, even CFSP and ESDP increasingly require first pillar policy tools and thus a high degree of Commission involvement through its responsibilities for humanitarian aid, nuclear security and disarmament, running project management, the international implications of policies in the area of critical infrastructure protection, terrorism, sanctions and third pillar responsibilities in the areas of asylum, immigration and visa policy.

This evolution in foreign representation has implications for the nature of the new European External Action Service and the EU Delegations. In a globalised world, where the internet and the 'CNN factor' play crucial roles, it is not only financial pressure from ministries of finance that has led governments to take hard looks at external representation and the value for money that it offers. Foreign ministries themselves have all been reflecting on reforms of their foreign services and on the role of embassies abroad. Indeed, a study on the 'cost of Non-Europe in foreign diplomatic representation' might well indicate that the cost of separate diplomatic services of twenty-five, soon over thirty, EU Member States in posts around the world is out of proportion to their added value, a point underlined by Solana (2000a). There is also a 'disjuncture between champagne tastes and a beer budget' (Sharp 1998, 60). As the EEAS emerges, there is thus growing appreciation – not always by national foreign ministries themselves however – of potential resource savings from the creation of single EU embassies, with streamlined and shared consular facilities and pooled administrative and training facilities. One former MEP (and current Dutch MP) has even argued that in the case of her country (the Netherlands), a quarter of the 150 embassies and consulates could be dispensed with altogether (*Telegraaf* 2004). Member States and the Commission are posing hard questions about the efficiency of their systems of representation. An official German report on embassies within the EU has underlined the concerns (Paschke 2003), and an academic survey has confirmed that reform is the order of the day (Hocking and Spence 2005).

Thinking in Member States and elsewhere about the nature of state action in international politics is thus breaking new ground, as decision-makers draw conclusions from changes in the international system with regard to the objectives and modus operandi of diplomatic services. Since it is called upon to represent Member States in all the areas of exclusive competence, has a co-representation role in areas of mixed competence, and is present in many countries where most Member States cannot be present[20], the Commission is able to fulfil functions which many Member States alone may increasingly be unable or unwilling to supply – a fact that fits well with the increasingly widespread acceptance of a cost-benefit approach to public service provision, including in international policy-making. In practice, many governments quietly question whether traditional diplomacy, international project management and the new European diplomacy might be best practised with shared embassies and through public or private agencies. These are now questions asked in embassy inspections and management reviews of foreign services. Financial constraints on foreign services transform the purpose and operational methods of diplomacy. The emphasis is increasingly on commercial rather than political interests, and there is a rise of cost-conscious management – even a cost-benefit approach to the definition of the objectives of diplomacy. The result is often reduction of representation, if not outright closure of embassies. In the case of the UK, a strategic review in 2005 saw around 70 members of the senior management structure (1 in 7 of UK senior staff) and 200 staff in more junior ranks 'axed', and 20 embassies closed or downgraded (*Daily Telegraph* 2005). And as former UK Foreign Secretary Douglas Hurd himself puts it, 'the Foreign Office has to show ingenuity in shifting resources around, for example it decides to run consular posts in Italy or France with locally engaged rather than British-based staff, or to make a splendid – and unsaleable – embassy in the centre of a city earn more of its keep through commercial events' (Hurd 2005).

Yet, there are factors militating against the practical acceptance that traditional diplomacy is on the decline and 'the implicit idea that ambassadors and embassies exist on the margins ...a useful source for anecdotes or historical insight, but otherwise ...of little consequence' (Cooper 1998). The growth in the number of states in recent years has accompanied growth in foreign representation (often on a shoestring). There has been displacement of much traditional diplomatic activity from bilateral fora to multilateral fora such as the UN and EU institutions. Some states have closed embassies in certain countries, although they envisage it reluctantly. They cite fear of offending a host state, the difficulty of reversing a decision to withdraw if conditions change, the fear of disadvantage when rival states do not follow suit, the worry that however much the rise of regional interest has eclipsed specific national interests this phenomenon might prove transitory, the existence of interests difficult to represent without a diplomatic mission, and the inability of sporadic missions or international conferences to fill the gap in continuity of representation of interests. Foreign services tend to justify their existence increasingly in terms of export promotion rather than in terms of the traditional functions of diplomacy, though there is a growing recognition of the need to find alternatives to the simplistic view that representation of interests must either be through embassies or not exist at all. Nevertheless, the search for alternatives has become vital, and it increasingly implies resort to synergy with other Member States and the Commission. In turn, this means the Commission has to adapt to the changing needs and perceptions of Member States' diplomacy. Indeed, most alternatives implicate the Commission Delegations. Non-resident representation may provide an alternative to the traditional form of state representation through embassies. States can turn to

the conduct of relations with some other states from home or from representations in third countries. But, they could also envisage, as the European
Parliament exhorts them, concentrating their efforts on representation
through EU embassies (European Parliament, 1998 and 2000).

The difference between EU Member States and the Commission is that
while the increase in states after the fall of the Soviet Union does not necessarily imply national interests for all EU members in the states concerned, for
the Commission there is a growing role in terms of trade policy (Community
competence) or aid/technical assistance of the PHARE/TACIS variety. There
is thus a need for EU presence everywhere. Of the countries which have
joined the UN over the last few years few are so significant to most EU
Member States that a resident ambassador would be justified, yet there is a
clear European interest in representation. And, significantly, despite the
realisation that purely national interests in a whole series of states may be on
the wane, membership of international fora, such as the EU, the UN Security
Council or the OSCE, brings occasional bargaining interests with concomitant
administrative burdens for non-resident missions.

There is also a series of issues raised for Member States and the Commission
in countries where they have never had missions, have closed missions or have
not yet opened missions. Clearly, the presence of embassies confers status on
the host country, just as the presence of a Commission Delegation, while promoting the European interest and raising the profile of the European Union
itself, also raises the profile and enhances the role of the Commission. Closure
of an embassy or a Delegation can create bilateral tension with multilateral
repercussions. While there is no hard evidence of bilateral relations suffering
because embassies are closed or not yet opened, it might be argued that this is
different for the Commission. The nature of its specific competence in the representation and implementation of Community policies may create special
interests of a different kind from those of Member States.

As to trade promotion, it is hard to establish a causal relationship between
representation or non-representation and trade performance, though there
must be a strong presumption that a diplomatic mission might help secure a
government procurement contract or access to tenders for development aid
funded projects. Indeed, a recent study purports to prove a correlation
between exports and embassy or consular presence, quoting for example the
UK Foreign Office to the effect that 'Nearly 1,500 FCO staff equivalents are
engaged in commercial and investment work (about 350 UK-based and just
over 1,100 locally-engaged)' and arguing that if the resources spent on
embassies and consulates may be questioned, one key justification might be
the linkage between trade promotion and diplomatic presence (Rose 2005).
The essential issue is whether embassies are needed, and how to maximise
effectiveness without them.

Thus, concurrently with their reflections on the EEAS, EU Member States
are re-assessing their global spread and assessing where their focus should be.
They are keen to reduce burdens by multiply-accredited missions and job-
sharing and there is a certain attraction for the cost-cutters in a series of
European solutions. These include the Schengen arrangements and the
increasing currency of the idea of a European visa regime, co-location with
other Member States or with the Commission, or even joint missions[21] –
though in practice the joint embassy compound in Abuja, Nigeria, has not

achieved the success of the commitment of even half the Member States moving their embassies from Lagos to the new Nigerian capital. The Commission maintains Delegations in a large and growing number of countries and its contacts and expertise could provide useful support to visiting non-resident accredited ambassadors or other officials. There may be a risk of loss of continuity and lack of corporate identity, but generalised collaboration through EU missions might outweigh such disadvantages.

As the EEAS emerges, and Member States grapple with these issues, national and EU representation is anyway set to be recast. Could national representation be better managed by others, such as NGOs, specialist cadres, roving ambassadors or by privatising functions? Could diplomacy cost less, by charging for services, and cutting services and functions (trade to new chambers of commerce and consular affairs to a consular agency)? Could some functions be localised on the Commission's 'deconcentration' model or by expanding local staff, expanding IT, reviewing centralisation and decentralisation of functions, sharing on-costs with others, proxy representation and multiple accreditation? As the European Parliament's annual reports on the CFSP consistently stress, there are potential advantages in:

> 'combining the diplomatic missions of states which so desire with the Commission Delegations, resulting in improved coordination of external activities and lower costs deriving from the sharing of infrastructures (while) Member States which so wish (could) be encouraged to use the current Commission Delegations in third countries in which they have no diplomatic representation and assign to them one of their own diplomats who, in addition to contributing to the development of the Community's external policy, would be responsible for maintaining bilateral relations' (European Parliament 2000).

Formally, of course, there is no official attempt to go down such a path. As a UK Foreign Office minister expressed it to a querulous House of Commons, 'there is no suggestion that the external action service would replace national diplomatic representation' (Hansard 2004b, 13 July 2004).

The Union Minister for Foreign Affairs, the European External Action Service and the Delegations

The European Constitution nosedived with the French and Dutch rejection of it in May and June 2005. Solana may have argued that, '[e]ven (so), I think that it is suitable to keep on working on the establishment of the European External Action Service. This service will definitely come into existence sooner or later. …it is not important when this will actually happen – it is crucial that we get mentally and practically used to the fact that the EEAS will become a reality' (Solana 2005a, *Financial Times* 2005a), but senior diplomats and Council officials were of a different persuasion (*European Voice* 2005c). Yet, it is difficult to contest that a link between coherent foreign policy making and foreign ministry structure is crucial. As one observer has put it, '[i]t is hard to imagine a genuine common foreign policy without a common diplomatic service and a means of identifying and operationalising the notion of the European interest' (Allen 1996). Thus, a European diplomacy remains on the cards despite initial rejection of the Constitution, and a key issue is the role the Commission will play. Even if the Santer and Prodi Commissions' focus on managerial reform broke the mould of the Commission's haphazard approach to management change, and the key reforms introduced by External Relations Commissioner Patten clearly made the Commission a more effective donor and manager of aid and technical assistance, it was not the Commission's intention to create a powerful quasi-diplomatic service in parallel to those of Member States. Yet, as the parameters for the EEAS emerge, both the future role of the Commission and the nature of European diplomacy are at stake. Whether or not EU governments intended to see their own diplomatic services and foreign ministers nudged to the sidelines, the Constitution, if ratified, will create an EU Foreign Minister:

> 'The Union Minister for Foreign Affairs shall be one of the Vice-Presidents of the Commission. He or she shall ensure the consistency of the Union's external action. He or she shall be responsible within the Commission for responsibilities incumbent on it in external relations and for coordinating other aspects of the Union's external action' (Art. I-28-4). And, moreover, 'Union Delegations in third countries and at international organisations shall represent the Union... and... shall be placed under the authority of the Union Minister for Foreign Affairs. They shall act in close cooperation with Member States' diplomatic and consular missions' (Art. 328).

The Constitution does not state whether the Union Delegations form part of the EEAS or not, and this seemingly simple omission created doubt and room for negotiation. While it is clear that the Union Delegations were to be placed under the authority of the Union Minister for Foreign Affairs, the practical implications leave much room for negotiation. Reconciling the criteria of Annex X of the staff regulations with new criteria for recruitment of personnel from national foreign ministries is no mean task. Administratively, it would be simple if, in view of the various responsibilities in terms of external representation of the EU, the Delegations could form part of the EEAS. That way, the staff regulations, recruitment of personnel and financial management could remain the same as current arrangements for staff rotation and recruitment. But the independence of the EEAS from the Delegations is just one of many issues occupying planners in foreign ministries, the Commission and the Council Secretariat.[22]

From a common sense perspective, even if the Constitution is not explicit on the issue, it does not make sense to consider the EEAS and the 'Union's Delegations' as two separate or disconnected structures. As with diplomatic services the world over, missions and ministries are inextricably interlinked both in terms of policy management and personnel policy, budget and staff regulations. Embassies cannot function without in-depth knowledge provided by ministries in capitals. And an effective foreign service cannot provide authoritative guidance to embassies without knowledge and skills resulting from the fused diplomatic roles of capitals and missions abroad; lessons the EEAS and Union Delegations would ignore to their cost. The EEAS and the Union Delegations must meet the Constitution's requirements by ensuring coherence and efficiency in external action and by providing the basis for the

Union to play a more active and convincing role in international affairs; in short, providing the instrumental means of the EU's rhetorical ambitions.

As with national embassies, the Union Delegations could easily include personnel seconded from other services to cover trade, JHA, financial matters, agriculture, transport and other areas. But it should be recalled that the EEAS arrangements were positioned in the CFSP chapter of Part 3 of the Constitution (article III-296.3). As they stand, Commission Delegations cannot be considered as a mere instrument of CFSP. Otherwise, the Constitution's commitment to joined-up foreign policy covering all external relations instruments, whether CFSP or Community, would be pointless. In practical terms it also begs the question of the distribution of competence between the EUFM, the EEAS and the Commission's external powers – not to mention the inter-institutional aspects of a potential change to a form of independent management of the EEAS, in practice removing the European Parliament from the policy-making equation by distancing the EEAS from the Community method. This is the political motivation behind the European Parliament's advocacy that:

> 'the Commission delegations in non-member countries and the Council liaison offices should be merged to form 'Union embassies', headed by European External Action Service officials, who would take their instructions from, and be subject to the supervision of, the Foreign Minister, but administratively would belong to the Commission staff, which would not prevent specialist advisers to these delegations being recruited from other Commission or Parliament DGs' (European Parliament 2005).

Somewhat demotivated Commission officials believe they are in a zero sum game. As chapters 13 and 14 underline, gaining competence within EPC and CFSP was a long and arduous battle. If the management of external relations and CFSP is drifting to the Council, as some in the Commission view it, the change, they believe, is in fact from the proven (efficient) Community method to the proven (ineffective) intergovernmental method (Joaris 2005). The major administrative upheaval now beginning has considerable implications. The EUFM will gain extensive powers and responsibility, from aid, through trade, to the EU Association and Partnership and Cooperation Agreements. This could prove the end of the independence of these individual sectors, which Commissioners have long maintained. The Solana argument is that the EUFM will need the geographical expertise in Brussels and in Delegations in order to deliver on the joined up foreign policy commitment under the arrangements for the Commission Vice President. Far-reaching discussion on the future role of the Union Delegations in consular protection and even in the issuing of visas is underway in capitals – a discussion which begs questions about the changing patterns of relations between the EEAS and national diplomatic services, whether it be the simple sharing of information in Brussels and in third countries, unified report writing or the rules on whether and how Heads of EU Delegations might chair all meetings of ambassadors of EU Member States in third countries. The current Commission Delegation network can easily add to its tasks a lead role in implementing the CFSP and its coordination with all other aspects of EU policy. But, if the Delegations replace the rotating EU presidency in the host country and thus become responsible for coordination with Member State embassies, important changes in the political role and management culture of the External Service will be the concomitant, effectively transforming it into a foreign service of the EU as a whole and posing even more fundamental questions for the role of national foreign ministries, embassies and diplomatic staff.

The implications for the Commission's External Service of these emerging changes in European diplomacy are barely understood outside the EU, where confusion as to which institution represents which interest is frequently underlined. The Commission has welcomed the developments in principle (Commission 2003), and it is significant that Member States are already preparing for whatever structure of external representation emerges through the EEAS. In a speech to French ambassadors gathered in Paris in 2004, Foreign Minister (and former Commissioner) Barnier opined that:

> 'en mutualisant leurs actions et leurs initiatives, et d'abord dans nos réseaux consulaires, tous les pays européens se donnent une capacité d'intervention bien supérieure à leurs contributions nationales isolées... la frontière entre l'interne et l'externe n'a plus guère de sens... la mise en place d'un service diplomatique européen ne rend que plus urgente notre préparation... et l'exigence, pour vous,... de renforcer vos relations de travail sur le terrain avec les délégués de la Commission Européenne.' (Barnier 2004).

Clearly, much distance has been travelled since one EU diplomat remarked, '[t]he Commission's fledgling diplomatic service faces one obstacle that will not go away: the strength and solidarity of one of the most formidable trades unions in the world – national foreign ministries' (quoted in Buchan 1993, 55). The Commission's Delegations will certainly cease to exist in their present form, evolving into Union Delegations with staff provided from the EEAS. They might conceivably be divided into a political (CFSP) section headed by an ambassador representing the European Union, with overall responsibility for EU policy and for the coordination of Member State embassies in the host country, and a deputy ambassador responsible for first pillar issues and a separate technical project management service. Now that CFSP and ESDP have become core business for foreign ministry staff, whether at home or serving abroad, the permanent partners of Commission staff are the diplomats from other Member States, to whom the EEAS is set to offer additional potential for postings and career development, as well as work in the field of security and defence.

What then of the newly introduced career development plans in the Commission? The current Head of Delegation to Washington described his appointment quite simply:

> 'It happened back in July 2003 in the Dáil. Bertie Ahern (the Taoiseach) slipped me a note saying he would like a word. Romano Prodi had telephoned that day. My name had been mentioned about a job. I was an opposition front bencher without portfolio, so I accepted immediately' (*Financial Times* 2005a).

If 'placement' of Member State politicians and foreign ministry staff in Delegations becomes the norm, thus rendering the statutory appointment rules obsolete, the Commission clearly stands to lose. In addition, its limited though distinctly expanded political role in CFSP would be compromised, though it could keep its role in the operational field, where its main competence lies and where experienced staff are already in place. Delegations in ACP countries, where most work is development aid related, will need the same number of contract personnel and local agents as before. On the other hand, the more political Delegations in developed countries, such as in Washington, New York, Tokyo, Geneva, Canberra, Ottawa, etc. might need fewer Commission personnel – with the exception of economic advisers from DG Trade. While this might – or might not – produce recognisably enhanced coherence, it might also – or might not – prove the end of turf wars between the Council Secretariat and the Commission. Commission officials have begun thinking that 'their' DGs and Delegations will be the core of a new European diplomacy, though Christoph Heusgen, former head of Solana's policy unit, went on record in December 2004 as believing that the policy unit is 'the embryo of the future European foreign service' (Heusgen 2004). Reconciling these two views in administrative terms is thus the prime task.

Member States debated these issues in the first half of 2005. There was broad consensus that the existing network of Commission Delegations should become the future Union Delegations, and that as a consequence of the provision of the Constitutional Treaty, which places them under the authority of the Foreign Minister, they should be an integral part of the European External Action Service. They also agreed that the new arrangements would respect the treaty provisions covering the institutional responsibilities for external representation of the Union. For most Member States that did not necessarily imply that all staff working in the Delegations would need to be members of the EEAS. Indeed, those covering specific policies such as trade and management of financial assistance would continue to come from the Commission. In March 2005 a joint Solana/Commission issues paper raised the idea that Union Delegations might take on additional tasks such as consular protection and visas. Significantly, a majority of Member States supported the idea, despite the recognition of the complexity of the issue. But no formal Declaration was made at the June European Council.

Conclusion

This chapter has shown that the origins of Commission diplomats were diametrically opposed to those of their nation state counterparts. Whereas the purpose of national ambassadors was to represent authority, convey messages, negotiate, gather information about their country of residence and disseminate information about their own country, these were not the original terms of reference of the Commission's Heads of Delegation, though they are indeed theirs today. As former UK Foreign Secretary Hurd puts it, EU diplomatic 'activities do not replace national diplomacy but provide a forum for old techniques' (Hurd 2005). On this reading, the emerging European diplomacy will likely anchor new tasks along traditional lines. But, Commission diplomats came from humble origins: the need to manage assistance projects and supervise spending on public works. This was a more prosaic calling than the avid search for information and influence which customarily characterised the diplomatic profession.

Reform of the Commission could have formally created old-style diplomats, but it always focussed on internal organisation and management processes, rather than on the raison d'être of EU diplomacy itself. Even under the reform-minded Santer and Prodi Commissions, reform was limited to changes that upgrade and strengthen the existing organisation without challenging or questioning its basic purpose. Opportunity to make concrete the underlying practical shift in nature of the External Service from project management to diplomacy was lost. The Commission perhaps lacked a strategic view of the purpose of its External Service and thus limited itself for that reason to tinkering with management and personnel policy for its staff. Yet, opting for gradual reform through pragmatic adaptation might well have been the only workable strategy, indeed a more suitable focus than a potentially lost cause based on a notion of logical and thus inevitable spill-over from project management to diplomacy. In short, the reformers of the External Service perhaps rightly focussed on the trees rather than espousing a lofty call for grandiose schemes for the wood, as federalists, not least in the European Parliament, might have wished. The result, however, is an efficient machine. Whether it is ready to take on the challenge of a new, more political mission is a moot point. In sum, the Commission has secured greater efficiency in performance of the same tasks, but the crucial challenge before it now is finally adjusting to the accelerating shift to a new diplomatic system.

Endnotes

[1] The prospect has created a rash of academic comments on the likely mechanics of this transformation of diplomacy: Bátora 2005; Keukeleire 2003; Grevi, Manca and Quille 2005; Maurer and Reichel 2005; Cameron 2003, 2004, 2005; Buchet de Neuilly 2002; Dassu and Missiroli 2002; Hocking and Spence 2005; Duke 2003 and 2004; Rayner 2005.

[2] Eight more countries, or eleven including the permanent, yet reticent, invitees Norway, Iceland and Switzerland, are on the enlargement map. Bulgaria and Romania are due in 2007, while Turkey gained candidate status at the Helsinki summit in 1999. Croatia and the Western Balkans states of Serbia-Montenegro, Bosnia-Herzegovina, Macedonia and Albania complete the tally, though there also remain the wishful thinking Ukraine, Belarus, Moldova, Georgia and Armenia.

[3] After enlargement Delegations in the 10 new Member States were transformed into information offices on a par with the 20 existing offices in the 15 Member States. Comparative figures over the years need to concentrate on embassies/Delegations outside the EU to make sense. See table in annex J, which compares the numbers and staffing of EU national embassies and Commission Delegations.

[4] An anecdotal history of the External Service is contained in 'Taking Europe to the World', a publication by the European Commission (Commission 2004b). For details on the specific case of the USA see Winand, 2004.

[5] The political orientation was clear. His first ECSC Bulletin in October 1954 was headlined 'Towards a Federal Government of Europe' (Burghardt 2004).

[6] In those days accreditation was to the US Secretary of State, William Rogers, and not to the President.

[7] Since 1974 the Commission representing the European Community has observer status at the UN but cannot vote, while observer status has not been extended to the EU which has no legal personality. On the other hand, the Community does have full

membership in the Food and Agriculture Organization (FAO), which is a UN body (Winand 2004, 138-9).

[8] The post of the European Correspondent covers the coordination of briefings for foreign affairs meetings at all levels and the exchange and management of the resulting cypher and 'coreu' telegrammes.

[9] It was not until December 2002 that a specific personnel development and training unit was established in DG Relex, responsible for all staff serving abroad and local agents.

[10] By 'Relex family', Commission staff currently mean DG Development, DG Trade, DG Relex (External Relations), DG Enlargement, EuropeAid or AidCo and the European Community Humanitarian Aid Office (ECHO).

[11] There had been similar communications in previous years: Sec (1996) 554 approved 7 March 1996; SEC (1997) 605 approved 8 April 1997; and Sec (1998) 1261 approved 22 July 1998. The Communications had set conditions to implement the Williamson Report (*Report on the Longer Term Needs of the External Service*) (Commission 1996).

[12] Yearly, the Commission organises several training courses on CFSP and EU affairs for Member State diplomats. It has a training programme now rivalling that of Member States' foreign ministries.

[13] Implemented in 2000 as per the communication of 8 April 1997 (Sec (97) 605).

[14] The Commission participates in the CFSP working group on administrative affairs (COADMIN) and its training sub-group. There is a so-called 'Partnership Programme' with Member States' foreign ministries allowing the secondment of national officials to Commission Delegations. The problem has been that Member States prove reluctant to send diplomats and prefer placing technical specialists. This is clearly set to change as the new EEAS is put in place.

[15] Delegations provide considerable support to visiting parliamentary Delegations, but there had not existed a formal responsibility to do so.

[16] The *Service Commun Relex* (SCR) was set up by Sec (1997) 1813/5 of 10 October 1997 and its budgetary responsibilities were later defined in Sec (97) 2305 of 10 December 1997. It required the transfer of approximately 600 posts from Relex family DGs and became operational in summer 1998. The SCR managed the EDF, 70 budget lines, 80 different legal bases, and 30,000 contracts with between eight and ten thousand new contracts per year. Total funds managed in 1999 were €18.8 billion, and there were more than 41.000 payments in a typical year.

[17] See 'The development of the External Service' (COM (2001) 381 of 3 July 2001. It is worth noting that deconcentration had already taken place to Delegations in countries covered by the PHARE programme in 1998.

[18] Though there have been complaints of Delegations' reticence to provide appropriate support for Solana. See Hansard 6 December 2004, evidence from Foreign Secretary Jack Straw to the Foreign Affairs Committee.

[19] The table in annex J relativises these figures somewhat.

[20] Both budgetary reasons and the absence of 'national' interest explain this.

[21] It should be mentioned that a Common Position (TEU Art. J.2.) on potential collocations of embassies was decided, but not published, on 6th October 1995. See European Parliament 1998 p 32. List of Common Positions. See also chapter 11 on this point.

[22] Declaration 24 on Article III-296 of the draft Constitutional Treaty. 'The Conference declares that, as soon as the Treaty establishing a Constitutional Treaty for Europe is signed, the Secretary-General of the Council, High Representative for the common foreign and security policy, the Commission and the Member States should begin preparatory work on the European External Action Service'. The signing took place on 29 October 2004 and a joint report by President Barroso and High Representative Solana was to be presented to the June 2005 European Council. After the French and Dutch 'no' votes, the commitment was quietly dropped.

16. The Commission and Intergovernmental Conferences

Mark Gray and David Spence

Introduction

Shifts in the balance of power between the Commission, the Council and the European Parliament are a vital factor both in the Commission's self-perception and in the changing nature of the Commission's dealings with other EU institutions, with Member States, the public and the lobby. Yet, adapting the rules of engagement is not an easy task. The revision of the European Union's founding Treaties can only be undertaken through an Intergovernmental Conference (IGC). In fifty years' existence, in comparison to sovereign states or 'federal' systems like Canada or the United States, the European Union's founding Treaties have been amended remarkably frequently. While other political systems have undertaken negotiations on one specific article or amendment to their constitution, the European Union frequently amends or introduces whole policy areas, thus questioning the fundamental spread of policy competence between the institutions and the related political and administrative structures. The EU process is thus unlike the gradual changes to constitutions in most European polities. It compares more readily with the process of reshaping the constitutions of the five successive French Republics.

Recent European IGCs have sparked debate on theoretical approaches to the process of European integration and analysis of the roles of individual Member States and supranational actors (Edwards and Philippart 1999; Wessels 2001; Christiansen, Faulkner and Jorgensen 2002; Dimitrakopoulos and Kassim 2005; Mazzucelli and Beach 2006). Many recent articles have focussed on individual institutions – the Commission, the European Parliament and increasingly the Council Secretariat (Corbett 1998; Christiansen and Jorgensen 1998; Moravcsik 1999; Petite 2000; Dinan 1997 and 2000; Gray 2002; Christiansen 2002; Maurer 2002 and 2006; Beach 2004 and 2006; Christiansen and Gray 2003; Hix 2005; Maurer 2006; Dimitrakopoulos and Kassim 2005 and 2006). But, comparative analysis remains sparse on the role of these actors across a series of negotiations. This chapter sets out to fill this analytical gap, going beyond a strict mandate of examining how the Commission has fared in IGCs and how the Commission's powers and responsibilities have been changed by them. The chapter argues that the legal base may only provide for a role before the start of negotiations, but the reality is that the Commission has a central role throughout. It traces the history of Treaty changes, analysing each major set of proposals over the last fifty years, basing its conclusions on research in the historical archives from the Treaty of Paris (1951) to the Treaty establishing a Constitution for Europe (Constitution) (2004) and analysing what lay behind the negotiators' positions and the over-all role IGCs play in EU politics. Since IGCs change both the substance of policy and policy-making methods, the Commission is concerned by all out-comes, not just the successes or failures to agree at the final European summit. This historical overview forms an indispensable background to the rest of the chapter, which examines the coordinating mechanisms within the Commission for dealing with IGC negotiations. It reviews and analyses the influence of the Commission on negotiations and assesses the changing role of the Commission, not only over time, but in light of the creation of the new mode of preparation for IGCs – the European Convention.

Reflections on the role and function of IGCs

EU Treaty reform has become an almost continuous process, where one stage of reform feeds directly into the next. This is particularly striking when one round of Treaty reform throws up a list of 'leftovers' with an instruction to convene a further IGC to address these unresolved issues (Christiansen and Gray 2003). Meanwhile, as preparations for the next IGC take place, Member States are busy ratifying the outcome of the previous IGC and national admin-istrations are adjusting to the new arrangements. The three most recent IGCs concluded at Amsterdam, Nice and Rome demonstrate that Treaty reform has become a policy arena in itself, with the appendages of a policy-making com-munity, technical experts, the need for institutional memory and an element of path-dependency in the deliberations about reform (Christiansen 2002; Falkner 2002). IGCs are thus the key arena for constitutional choice in the EU and a process to which Member States attach the highest importance. While reducing the focus to the question of inter-state bargaining only, as some ana-lysts have done, may help justify the case that supranational entrepreneurship is 'futile', since supranational actors, in contrast to the Member States, lack the all-important resource of the veto in this forum, this section enlarges the focus to include a wider range of issues and explanatory factors drawn from the preparatory processes.

The Commission's formal role

The Commission lacks formal legal powers in an IGC. The general pro-cedure of Article 48 TEU for amending the Treaties fits into the classical tra-dition of international law: amendments must be adopted by common accord of the representatives of Member State governments meeting in a diplomatic conference. They come into force only once they have been ratified by all Member States 'in accordance with their respective constitutional require-ments'. These requirements, in practice, involve approval by national Parliaments and/or the holding of a referendum. Yet, the Community institu-tions are called on to play a part in the opening stage of the procedure. Thus, the Commission may, like each government, submit draft Treaty amend-ments to the Council. In practice, this power of initiative also gives the

Commission the right to sit at the negotiating table, in contrast to the European Parliament. The procedure then stipulates that the Council may decide by simple majority to call an IGC, but only after consulting the European Parliament and, where appropriate, the Commission, on the advisability of amending the Treaties. The Treaty requirements thus essentially provide a role for the Community institutions in the pre-negotiation stage, although formally the Member States remain the primary actors in the process, as far as both its initiation and its results are concerned. Petite (1998) has underlined the ambiguity of the Commission's role by stating that 'anyone taking part in the Maastricht and Amsterdam negotiations can witness that the very function of the Commission in an IGC is less than obvious.' He concludes that the Commission neither plays the role of honest broker (this task is performed by the Presidency), nor does it attempt to be the depositor of an ideal European model. Neither does it attempt to act as an extra Member State. Using the negotiations during the Treaty of Amsterdam as an example, Petite argues that the Commission constantly attempts to propose the 'highest possible realistic line,' pushing, as much as possible, the outcome of the Conference towards greater integration.

Confining analysis to the Commission's legal position in IGCs therefore only provides part of the picture. The Commission brings a unique mix of political and technical roles to an IGC, and its specific responsibility of promoting the general interest and acting as the 'guardian of the Treaties' puts a special political duty on the Commission negotiators, unmatched by those on any other actor at the negotiating table. At the same time, the Commission brings specific technical expertise to IGCs because of its role in monitoring the implementation of Treaty provisions, its over-arching responsibility for the application of Community law and the technical expertise acquired through 'comitology', which chapter 8 discusses in detail. Together with the Council Secretariat, the Commission is perceived as ensuring the 'institutional memory' of an IGC. Although several Member States – the Netherlands, Luxembourg, Italy and Ireland – have held the Presidency during a number of the recent IGCs, it is unlikely that any one Member State will have extensive experience of previously running such a Conference. The Commission and the Council Secretariat thus provide a form of continuity untainted by electoral and political changes or by the fast turnover within diplomatic services. Indeed, a core of the Commission officials in an IGC have extensive experience of previous Treaty negotiations. The Commission is also able to influence negotiations on a day-to-day basis. Individual Commission officials have affected the outcome of specific Treaty articles and the negotiations more generally. The departure of François Lamoureux from the Delors *cabinet*, during the Maastricht negotiations, underlines the importance of individual officials' impact on negotiations. Lamoureux maintained excellent relations with the Luxembourg Presidency, even to an extent replacing David Williamson, the Commission Secretary General, in the representatives' meetings. The French were seemingly so concerned about his influence that the offer of the post of *chef de cabinet* to Prime Minister Edith Cresson in Paris was made – an offer he could not refuse (having already turned it down once before). His departure from the Commission IGC team had a major impact, and not least on the relationship with the Dutch Presidency, which replaced the Luxembourg team shortly afterwards. In general, as consecutive IGCs have taken place, a strong sense has grown of a Brussels based 'IGC community' focussed on the Commission, the European Parliament, and the Council Secretariat in liaison with Member State officials in the representations to the European Union. The latter often turn to the Commission for an assessment of positions or options available on specific issues.   If the Commission can forge a good working relationship with the Presidency and the Secretariat of the IGC during the negotiations, the three actors can play a pivotal role, making a distinctive contribution to the outcome.

Internal organisation within the Commission

As both a political actor and a technical advisor in the IGC process, the Commission contributions vary between political positions adopted by the full College and technical clarifications submitted directly to the Conference by the services of the Commission. The initial contributions of the Commission are usually an attempt to set the political framework for the IGC, providing an overview of the IGC's scope and importance and an explanation of the Commission's objectives (Dinan 1997a, 251) – customarily advocating a more ambitious agenda.[1] These contributions tend to come before the formal opinion that the Commission submits to the Conference. They are, of course, always approved by the Commission and have always led to extensive debate in heads of *cabinet* and full Commission meetings. The College of Commissioners also adopts the official opinion submitted by the Commission before the start of an IGC. This has traditionally been a short political text; good examples being the opinions adopted on 22 July 1985[2] and 28 February 1996[3] before the Single European Act and the Treaty of Amsterdam negotiations. In the run-up to the Treaty of Nice, however, the approach changed. The Commission believed that following the watered down Presidency paper submitted to the Helsinki European Council in December 1999, it should adopt a detailed set of proposals. The formal opinion before the 2004 IGC adopted on 17 September 2003[4] reflected the special circumstances of an existing draft treaty adopted by the European Convention. It thus concentrated on a limited number of proposals on the most sensitive issues still outstanding, such as the size and composition of the Commission, qualified majority voting and revision of the Constitution.

During negotiations, the Commission forwards a range of specific contributions to the Conference, each approved by the College. These can range from proposals on the hierarchy of norms (1991) or the co-decision procedure (1996) to issues such as the European Prosecutor (2000) or a framework for new provisions on freedom, security and justice, or justice and home affairs, as it was then known (1996).

The dynamics of an IGC with its daily negotiations and intense schedule of meetings limit the College to political guidance on the general approach to be taken, with the Commissioner participating at the IGC (or in the case of the Convention on the Future of Europe, two Commissioners, Barnier and Vitorino) taking political responsibility for the positions adopted in the negotiations. This has led to occasional disagreement with other Commissioners who prefer an alternative position on one or other negotiating point. Other parts of the Commission are also involved in the process through special correspondents in each Directorate General, but these are normally limited in their influence on proceedings as they are only consulted on their specific area of competence. For the most recent IGCs, special Steering Groups have been convened to oversee the work of the IGC team and to ensure that Commission negotiators follow an agreed line at each meeting. The Steering Group is normally composed of the key actors on institutional affairs in the Commission. The majority of contributions, non-papers and background notes submitted by the IGC negotiators of the Commission are approved by the Steering Group under the political authority of the respective Commissioner. The proposed briefing for the IGC meetings is prepared by the IGC team and submitted to the Steering Group, which normally meets a couple of days before an IGC meeting. The line to take is rarely altered at these meetings, but it is an important opportunity for weighing options and strategic decision-making. As the negotiations enter the final phase, the Steering Group tends to take on more significance. As for the Commission's IGC negotiating team, as with all delegations, it rarely acts as a single entity. It is not unusual for slightly different emphasis to be placed on an individual point by each of those present at the negotiating table or in the seats behind the main negotiators at the back of the negotiating room.

Over time, the problem of internal coordination has become more difficult for the Commission. With the steady increase in the number of Commissioners, institutional reform, once the preserve of the President, has become the responsibility of a specific Commissioner. In the case of the most recent IGC, President Prodi and Commissioners Barnier and Vitorino were involved, while there were also formal roles for the Secretary General, the Director of the Institutional Affairs team and members of the Legal Service. At the negotiating table, in addition to the President and Commissioners, the Commission normally had room for 4-5 officials. There is thus a complex structure of reporting in the IGC team. The Head of the IGC Task Force or Unit normally falls under the administrative responsibility of the Secretary General. However, the main day-to-day political authority is exercised by the *cabinets* of the President and the Commissioner(s). This is relatively simple in terms of structure, but not always so easy in terms of coordination. A list of these actors can be found in table 14.

The IGC team has always been one of the most sought after posts within the Commission. The team is hand-picked, and the majority of those chosen are senior officials with a wealth of previous experience in institutional affairs. Emphasis is placed on continuity. Since the Single European Act, members of the team have always included officials experienced in previous IGCs. The size (and name) of the team has varied. For the Single European Act, Maastricht and Nice, the teams were extremely small, 3-4 officials, most already members of the permanent institutional team in the General Secretariat. For Amsterdam and the 2004 IGC, the institutional team of the General Secretariat was transformed into a Task Force of 8-10 officials. Of the vast array of issues debated by the Convention, nearly all had been debated previously by the Commission, so the IGC team had already prepared extensive briefing papers and possessed legal briefings by the Commission's Legal Service on each of the negotiating options.

Table 14: *Commission IGC officials from the Single European Act to the 2004 IGC.*

Single European Act

President:	Jacques Delors
Commissioner:	Carlo Ripa di Meana
Secretary General:	Emile Noël
President's *cabinet*:	Pascal Lamy, François Lamoureux
Legal Service:	Claus Dieter Ehlermann, Alain Van Solinge
Director in Secretariat General:	Giuseppe Ciavarini Azzi

Maastricht

President:	Jacques Delors
Commissioner:	Henning Christophersen (EMU IGC)
Secretary General:	David Williamson (Deputy Carlo Trojan)
President's *cabinet*:	François Lamoureux, Michel Petite
Legal Service:	Jean-Louis Dewost, Jörn Pipkorn, Jean Amphoux, Denise Sorasio
Director in Secretariat General	Giuseppe Ciavarini Azzi
IGC Task Force/unit Head:	Alain van Solinge
Members of IGC Task Force/unit	Philippe Godts, Véronique Warlop

Amsterdam

President:	Jacques Santer
Commissioner:	Marcelino Oreja
Secretary General:	David Williamson (Deputy Carlo Trojan)
President's *cabinet*:	Jim Cloos, Diane Schmitt
Commissioner's *cabinet*:	Daniel Calleja, Thierry Bechet
Legal Service:	Jean-Louis Dewost, Ricardo Gonzalez Bono
IGC Task Force/unit Head:	Michel Petite
Members of IGC Task Force/unit:	Nigel Evans, Alain van Solinge, Francisco Fonseca Morillo, Andrea Pierucci, Dominique Maidani, Paraskevi Gilchrist, Angela Bardenhewer, Véronique Warlop, Mark Gray

Nice

President:	Romano Prodi
Commissioner:	Michel Barnier
Secretary General:	David O'Sullivan (Deputy Bernard Zepter)
President's *cabinet*:	Michel Petite, Ben Smulders
Commissioner's *cabinet*:	Christine Roger
Legal Service:	Jean-Louis Dewost, Claire Durand
IGC Task Force/unit Head:	Pieter van Nuffel
Members of IGC Task Force/unit:	Véronique Warlop, Mark Gray, Kerstin Jorna

Convention on the Future of Europe (IGC 2004)

President:	Romano Prodi
Commissioners:	Michel Barnier, Antonio Vitorino
Secretary General:	David O'Sullivan
President's *cabinet*:	Stefano Manservisi, Ben Smulders
Commissioner's *cabinets*:	Christine Roger (Barnier)
	Francisco Fonseca Morillo (Vitorino)
Legal Service:	Michel Petite, Alain van Solinge
Director, IGC team	Paolo Ponzano
IGC Task Force/unit Head:	Pieter van Nuffel
Members of IGC Task Force/unit:	Paolo Stancanelli, Jean-Francois
	Brakeland, Véronique Warlop, William
	Sleath, Nathalie Berger, Kristin
	de Peyron, Floriana Sipala, Alexander
	Winterstein, Dimitris Triantafllou,
	Stephane Verwilghen, Michael Reuss,
	Alexander Stubb, Sylvie Goulard

A chronological perspective: Treaty change from Paris to Rome

The Commission enjoys a privileged position at IGCs, in part due to its historical role in European integration. While it has not been involved in every Treaty revision, it can claim to have been present at every IGC convened in accordance with the revision procedure set out in the founding Treaties (Article 236 EC, Article N TEU, Article 48 TEU). The Commission also has a fundamental role to play in the IGCs to conclude the Accession negotiations for new Member States to join the EU (Article 49 TEU). The IGCs convened for the enlargement negotiations are not covered in this chapter.

The origins of Treaty reform

The origins of Treaty reform in the European Union date back to the drafting sessions on the Treaty establishing the Coal and Steel Community (ECSC), signed on 18 April 1951, in Paris. The High Authority and the Commission had not been created at this point and thus were clearly not involved in the negotiations, although Jean Monnet, who held the pen for the Schuman Declaration, did go on to become the first President of the High Authority. The Treaty provided the first legal basis in Articles 95 and 96 ECSC for the convening of an IGC. During the nine months of negotiations for the Schuman Plan, the revision article was not a fundamental part of discussions. The minutes of the negotiations do not mention the proposed article (French Ministry of Foreign Affairs, 1950). The wording is believed to have been inserted at the last moment, almost as an afterthought. Whatever the reasoning, the drafting sessions produced a main revision procedure (Article 96) and a minor revision procedure (Article 95). As the ECSC Treaty did not allow for further progress towards greater European integration, in 1955 the Benelux countries issued a memorandum calling for further development of cooperation between the six founding members and suggesting that economic and atomic energy should be the subject of further treaties (Benelux Memorandum, 1955). The six founding members accepted the suggestion, and at the Messina conference of July 1955, a committee headed by Belgian Foreign Minister Paul-Henri Spaak was entrusted with the examination of greater integration of the ECSC members (Resolution of Foreign Ministers, Conference at Messina, 1955). The resolution called for a committee to be formed, consisting of 'governmental representatives' of the Six, as well as experts and representatives from the ECSC, OEEC, and the UK.

In 1956, the Spaak Committee's recommendations were presented to the Venice Conference of representatives of the six governments. They called for the formation of a European Economic Community and for a European Community for nuclear energy. After lengthy negotiations, agreement was reached to form these two communities in Rome on 25 March 1957, subsequently ratified by the national parliaments of the Six, and brought into effect on 1 January 1958. Significantly, the discussions did not take place with the presence of the High Authority or on the basis of Article 96 of the ECSC Treaty. The Spaak Committee was not a formal IGC, although it had many elements that were later used in the formal IGC procedure. Even though Article 96 ECSC was not used, additional treaty revision possibilities were adopted in Article 236 TEC, and Article 204 Euratom, which provided for revision procedures virtually identical to those envisaged in Article 96 ECSC.

The First Intergovernmental Conferences

The start of the 1960s saw the first formal IGCs in line with Article 236 TEC. The relatively minor issue dealt with at the first formal Conference was the question of extending the area of territorial implementation of the association system of countries and territories to the Dutch West Indies. After the amendment to the Treaties was agreed, it was signed on 13 November 1962 (OJ L 150, 01.10.64), following a formal Council opinion on 22 October 1962. It did not require an opinion from the High Authority of the ECSC or the Commission of Euratom or of the European Community, at the time headed by Walter Hallstein. The Commission had no role in the negotiations, so this first IGC cannot be compared to the IGCs of the last twenty years. The negotiations to conclude the Fouchet plan (1962) marked another high watershed in the debate on the method of Treaty change. Again, the formal IGC procedure was ignored, and changes to the revision clause were dropped in the final amendments proposed by Emilio Cattani, the Italian ambassador, who had replaced the French diplomat Fouchet as chair of the Committee. These were rejected by Foreign Ministers on 17 April 1962, thus bringing the Committee's work permanently to an end.

The second formal IGC took place from 1964-1965, resulting in the agreement of the Merger Treaty, which fused the organisational structures of the then three European Communities, thus establishing a single Council and a single Commission of the European Communities (8 April 1965, OJ 152, 13.07.67). Here, the High Authorities and the Commission were central to the negotiations. IGCs were then convened on three occasions during the 1970s. Although often forgotten, formal IGCs, based on Article 236 TEC, were used for the Treaty of Luxembourg (22 April 1970) which granted the European

Parliament certain budgetary powers and the Treaty of Brussels (10 July 1975), where the Parliament obtained the right to reject the budget and to grant the Commission a discharge for implementing the budget. The same Treaty established the Court of Auditors. The amendment of the status of the European Investment Bank was also agreed on 22 July 1975. On each occasion, the Commission issued an opinion and was involved in the negotiations. A number of reports throughout the 1970s recommended that the procedure for Treaty revision be changed. The Vedel Report (European Commission 1972) suggested that the co-decision power (today's assent procedure) should be a uniform procedure for Articles 236 EEC, 204 EAEC and 96 ECSC. The committee of 'Three Wise Men' to consider adjustments to the machinery and procedures of the institutions also made suggestions on ongoing Council business and on relations with the Commission and Parliament. But only a limited number of the resulting proposals were taken up.

Moving and shaking: Spinelli, the Single European Act and the Maastricht Treaty

Debate sharpened in the 1980s following the first direct elections to the European Parliament in 1979. Parliament blamed the failure of the Declaration of the 1972 Paris Summit, the Tindemans Report, the Report of the Three Wise Men and the Genscher-Colombo Initiative on the continuous watering down by Member State officials of proposals for change. A group of MEPs drafted a new Treaty, which they sent to Member States, without recourse to Article 236 EC (Crocodile Letter 1983). The 1984 Draft Treaty creating the European Union was written largely by Altiero Spinelli, a former Commissioner (European Parliament 1984). Although the Draft Treaty was a fundamental institutional text, the suggestions for Treaty change were not used during the preparations for the second Intergovernmental Conference of the 1980s leading to the Single European Act. The Report of the Ad Hoc Committee chaired by James Dooge (European Council 1985) and established by the European Council in Fontainebleau in June 1984 to prepare the institutional elements of the Single European Act, underlined that the Member States and the European Commission would be the parties in the IGC. The European Parliament was to be closely associated with the Conference and its outcome was to be submitted to the European Parliament, a disappointment for the Parliament as political reality had again shifted the discussions back to the basis of Article 236 – not to the drafting of a Constitution. Amusingly, at the same time, on 13 March 1984, a further minor IGC was taking place on the withdrawal of Greenland from the territory of the Community (OJ L 29, 01.02.85).

The decision to call an IGC following the Dooge Report led to controversy. At the instigation of Commission President Jacques Delors at the European Council held in Milan on 28-29 June 1985, the Italians called for a vote on whether an IGC was necessary. Against strong opposition from Denmark, Greece and the United Kingdom, the simple majority required was achieved through the support of Belgium, Germany, France, Ireland, Italy, Luxembourg and the Netherlands. Delors attended in his capacity as Commission President, so he was unable to cast a vote. His role in the Milan

European Council 'personified the Commission's role in the IGC process: present but not quite a full participant'; however, this did not prevent the Commission from taking an assertive and active behind-the-scenes role (Dinan 1997a, 250). Margaret Thatcher, the UK Prime Minister, was furious (Thatcher 1993). The IGC leading to the Single European Act was formally convened by the Council of Ministers on 23 July 1985. Foreign Ministers met eight times. They were assisted by a group of senior officials who prepared the amendments to the Community Treaties, while the provisions on cooperation in foreign policy were elaborated by separate groups. The work of the IGC was close to completion at the European Council in Luxembourg on 2 and 3 December 1985, but final agreement was reached on outstanding points by Foreign Ministers on 16 December 1985. The formal text of the Single European Act was then approved on 27 January 1986, and signed by Member States on 17 and 28 February 1986. It was a 'single' act, bringing together the deliberations on foreign policy and reform of Community policy in one legal document.

Negotiations on the TEU at the start of the 1990s were based on two almost completely separate IGCs: one on economic and monetary union and the other on political union. They took place at a time of economic downturn, political crisis (Iraq/Kuwait, the Soviet Union, Yugoslavia) and as a swift follow-up to German reunification, which had accelerated political action in both areas (Spence 1991). Preparations for an IGC on EMU were underway in the so-called Delors Committee from June 1988, an interesting indicator of the way in which the Commission uses expert groups to promote ideas and set unofficial agendas which official procedures subsequently come to adopt (Verdun 1998). The second IGC on political union was less well prepared. Dinan (1997a) argues that 'it is unlikely that the European Council would have agreed in 1989 to convene the EMU IGC without Delors' dogged advocacy... [and lobbying] at the Madrid and Strasbourg Summits for a decision on whether and when to hold an IGC on EMU'. In contrast, Kohl and Mitterrand had pushed for an early IGC on political union, a trade-off for the otherwise reticent Germans in exchange for French support for German reunification. The Commission, 'already over-extended preparing for the EMU IGC and coping with a host of unexpected demands on its time and... slender resources', would have preferred to hold this Conference at a later date (Dinan 1997a, 252).

On 15 December 1990, at the European Council in Rome, the two IGCs were formally opened, and on 10 December 1991, the representatives of the twelve Member States of the European Community reached agreement on the TEU in Maastricht. The Treaty was signed on 7 February 1992, and entered into effect on 1 January 1993. It instituted a European Union destined to mark a new stage in the process of creating a new and even closer union and marked a turning point in the integration process, establishing the European Union and creating the subsequently much maligned three-pillar structure divided into seven titles. It strengthened the Treaty provisions on foreign policy, justice and home affairs, economic and monetary union (including the single currency), European citizenship, culture and education. As to the Commission's success in advancing its own priorities, unlike the EMU IGC, prepared over the past three years, the Commission had mixed results in the political union IGC. It was an effective operator behind the scenes with frequent informal drafting sessions with the various Presidencies and Council Secretariat. However, most outside observers believe that it made the tactical mistake of overestimating the threshold for deeper integration of the large Member States when it tried unsuccessfully to get rid of the Luxembourg Presidency's 'non-paper' – in effect a draft treaty – which had proposed the pillar structure and limited Community competences. The Commission was isolated for the remainder of the IGC (Dinan 1997a, 254-8).

The negotiations on the TEU included a debate on the involvement of the European Parliament in IGCs and on the provision of a parliamentary assent procedure for Treaty change. Before and during the IGC the European Parliament organised a series of 'Inter-institutional Conferences' where the Commission President and Foreign Affairs Ministers were invited. This provided an additional influence point for the European Parliament but they were also keen to obtain a formal status. The Parliament contended that although the Article 236 procedure did not envisage EP participation at IGCs, neither did it envisage participation of the Commission. There was thus no formal reason why another European institution could not be present. An understanding was finally reached that the President of the Parliament would be invited to the opening of IGC Ministerial-level meetings, but adoption of the provision of an assent procedure failed owing to the opposition of Denmark, France, Portugal and Spain. Nevertheless, other changes were made for the first time since 1957. In the final text of the TEU, signed on 7 February 1992 (OJ L 224, 31.08.92), a new article N replaced Articles 96 ECSC, 204 Euratom and 236 TEC. The aim was to make the necessary additions for a future revision in 1996, to allow the additional consultation of the European Central Bank and to provide for a revision procedure common to all the Treaties which would in turn contribute to the coherence of the three pillars of the TEU.

'Unfinished business': from Amsterdam to Nice

The TEU (Maastricht) identified a number of issues that negotiators had failed to resolve during the negotiations. These included the future security and defence arrangements, justice and home affairs, co-decision, hierarchy of legislative acts and possible Treaty provisions on civil protection, energy, tourism, the composition of the Commission, the Ioannina compromise and the weighting of votes in the Council after the accession negotiations of Finland, Austria and Sweden.[5] A 'Reflection Group' to prepare the IGC was suggested in January 1994 by the Greek Presidency, and confirmed at the Corfu European Council in June 1994.[6] The Group, chaired by the Spanish European Affairs Minister Carlos Westendorp, commenced its work in Messina on 2 June 1995, following a series of reports adopted by the institutions in May 1995, and presented its final report at the beginning of December 1995. The Madrid European Council on 15-16 December 1995 then set the starting date for negotiations as 29 March 1996 in Turin. The Commission adopted its formal opinion on 28 February 1996.

As in previous IGCs, a working group was established under the responsibility of Foreign Ministers. This time the group included a number of politicians who had not been members of the Reflection Group. While the Commission had been represented by the Secretary General, David

Williamson, during the Maastricht negotiations, this time the decision was taken to appoint Commissioner Oreja, a former Spanish Foreign Minister and a former chairman of the EP Institutional Affairs Committee. The preparations for the 1996-97 IGC were again complicated by debate on the role of the European Parliament. Following intense lobbying in 1995, the Parliament was given a formal role in the preparation of an IGC for the first time. The Reflection Group had recommended full participation of two EP representatives, but the Parliament again requested participation of the entire EP in the IGC. France and the United Kingdom were opposed to this, so finally two EP representatives were invited to address occasional working groups of representatives. Their impact was limited, with meetings often taking place in two parts, one with and one without the parliamentarians.

The combined effect of the British policy of non-cooperation due to the 'mad cow crisis' and the collapse of the Italian government stymied the first IGC meeting on 2 April 1996. It took until 5 December 1996, for the Irish Presidency to present a general outline for a draft revision of the Treaties, which served as the basis for the Netherlands Presidency's further addendum on 20 March 1997, and updated drafts on 14 and 30 May. The final draft Treaty was presented on 12 June 1997, and the negotiations closed on 17 June 1997. The Treaty of Amsterdam was signed on 2 October 1997, and entered into force on 1 May 1999. It introduced substantial changes, strengthening the rights of citizens, enhancing cooperation in the area of Justice and Home Affairs, appointing a High Representative for the CFSP and adopting a general principle of 'enhanced cooperation' between like-minded Member States when unanimity proved impossible.

With the prospect of enlargement of the European Union, the Treaty of Amsterdam included a protocol on the institutions. It stated that one year before the membership of the European Union exceeded twenty, a new IGC was to be convened. With the shift towards an enlargement strategy based on ten countries quickly joining the EU, Member States needed to amend the institutional 'balance of power' before the new Member States joined. At the informal European Council in Pörtschach on 25 October 1998 during the Austrian Presidency, Europe's leaders accepted that negotiations could not formally begin until the ratification of the Treaty of Amsterdam in 1999, but they held a wide-ranging discussion on the Future of Europe based on a non-paper prepared by the Presidency. The Vienna European Council of 11-12 December 1998 formally requested that the following European Council, to be held in Cologne, take a decision on how and when to tackle the institutional issues not resolved at Amsterdam. After a first round of official meetings in May 1999, the Cologne European Council defined the four issues to be covered by the IGC. These were the size and composition of the Commission, the weighting of votes in the Council, possible extension of qualified majority voting (QMV) in the Council and other necessary amendments. Following disagreement on whether to establish a group of 'Wise Men' or a group of representatives to prepare the IGC, it was agreed that the Finnish Presidency would prepare a report under its own responsibility.

There were also calls for a more fundamental rethink of how the very process of changing the 'constitutional 'basis of European integration should be managed and conceived. The 'Wise Men' appointed by the European Commission (Jean-Luc Dehaene, Richard Von Weizsäcker and Lord Simon) argued in their report of 18 October 1999 not only that the Commission should produce a first draft Treaty, but also that it should be re-organised. The Treaties should be divided into 'constitutional' parts, for which the revision procedure could be 'super-qualified' majority or unanimity, with the assent of the European Parliament. Although the paper's ambitious, integrationist agenda proposals ended up being 'trashed by European leaders' at the subsequent Helsinki European Council, they nevertheless 'gave ammunition to [Member State] governments that wanted to widen the Nice IGC beyond the narrow "Amsterdam left-overs"' (Peterson 2004, 20).[7] Finally, in the run-up to the IGC 2000, attention again largely focused on the type of preparation and the role of the European Parliament, the latter almost causing a procedural conflict. Following the formal Commission Opinion on 26 January 2000[8], serious discussion took place in the European Parliament on whether or not to delay the start of the IGC by refusing to present an opinion. MEPs were not satisfied with the Helsinki mandate and the EP's 'observer' status. The Parliament finally decided that from a presentational point of view it could not be seen to delay enlargement and eventually adopted its formal opinion on 3 February 2000.

The European Council in Helsinki (10-11 December 1999) decided the mandate for the IGC 2000, which began in Nice on 14 February 2000. The Treaty of Nice negotiations focused on some of the most sensitive institutional issues, including the composition of the Commission, weighting of votes in the Council, extension of qualified majority voting and enhanced cooperation. The IGC concluded at dawn on 11 December 2000, and the Treaty was signed in Nice on 26 February 2001. This had been an intense year of negotiations with thirty representatives meetings, ten Ministerial meetings and three European Councils. In preparation for imminent enlargement, the Treaty, which entered into effect on 1 February 2003, introduced a number of important innovations regarding the composition of the Commission, the seats of the European Parliament, the reconsideration of votes by the Council and the extension of majority voting.[9]

Post- Nice: the Convention – a new method for Treaty revision

The Nice European Council is more famous for its disagreeable discussions and political outbursts than for its substantial decisions. While it agreed on revising the Treaties to adapt them to an enlarged European Union, it was obvious that more work was needed on institutional reform and a broader and deeper debate on the future of the EU. Declaration No. 23 to the Treaty of Nice, envisaged three phases: a phase of open debate, a phase to be decided on by the Laeken European Council in December 2001, and a new IGC to be convened in 2004, to decide on the necessary changes to the Treaties. On the basis of four issues set out at Nice, the Laeken European Council during the Belgian Presidency in December 2001, adopted a second and broader declaration on the Future of Europe. The Laeken Declaration set limits to the exclusive intergovernmental method for revising Treaties and, for the fourth revision in slightly more than ten years, it called for a Convention composed of government delegates, representatives of national parliaments, the European Parliament and the European Commission. This ambitious Declaration asked 60 questions about the future of the EU, revolving around four themes: the division of powers, simplification of legislative instruments, the institutional architecture, and the way towards a Constitution for the people of Europe. This was to be presented in a document which would serve as the point of departure for negotiations within the IGC, which would then take the final decisions.

The Convention began its work on 28 February 2002, but not all the participants seemed committed to the process. Concerns were expressed about the rules of procedure and the possibility that discussions would be on the basis of drafting behind closed doors in the Praesidium. Valéry Giscard d'Estaing was a controversial choice as President. The European Parliament remained suspicious of his motives and Member States remained relatively detached from the process. Indeed, until the adoption of the Seville European Council conclusions in June 2002, it can be argued that two parallel processes were running on institutional reform. While the Convention considered the list of questions identified by the Laeken European Council, the European Council was separately debating its own future role and its organisation.

It quickly became clear that the Convention had undertaken a massive task and that it would be virtually impossible to debate the drafting of each proposal and the amendments of the different representatives in the time available. The 'lack of time' was often used as a political device to limit debate or to push through compromises. In the end, large sections of the final text were not adequately reviewed – especially by legal advisors – and extra time was needed to consider the third part of the draft Constitution: the policies of the Union. The result was largely a 'copy and paste' of the existing Treaties, owing to the lack of time for skilful re-drafting. Although seen as the most transparent and democratic IGC preparation at the time, the Convention has subsequently been criticised for failing to connect with EU citizens. The main criticisms have been that few decisions were taken in plenary sessions, the working groups were focused on technical debates and the Praesidium, which was the main decision-making body, took place behind closed doors with no minutes ever produced.

Although the Convention met for its first session on 28 February 2002, a number of key decisions had already been taken by this time. In addition to the choice of the President, Vice-Presidents, Praesidium members and other *Conventionnels*, the work format for 2002 had also been pre-determined by Giscard d'Estaing and Sir John Kerr, the Secretary General to the Convention and the Praesidium. The first phase, 'listening', was an important stepping-stone for the ability of the Convention members to work together. While they did not fully trust Giscard, they learned to respect his authority. The crucial point was that the Convention started to move towards the concept of a single Constitutional Treaty and away from the suggestion that the Convention should prepare a set of options for the IGC. In response to frustration expressed by some of the more experienced members of the Convention at the slow pace of events, the Praesidium proposed the establishment of working groups, of which eleven were eventually formed.[10] The working groups were each chaired by a member of the Praesidium and consisted of up to as many as 30 members. There was also pressure by some to begin work on a draft Treaty, and one specific request that the Commission be invited to undertake this task. However, the President rejected this request on the grounds that it would be tantamount to the Convention shirking its responsibilities. The

working groups – charged with examining topics in greater detail and reporting back to the Convention with specific recommendations – issued their
reports throughout the autumn of 2002, with the final group on Social Europe
presenting its report on 4 February 2003. On 28 October 2002, Giscard
d'Estaing had issued his preliminary draft Constitutional Treaty. This 'skeleton treaty' not only provided the bones on which the results of the working
groups would be added in late 2002, but it also served to '[pull] the rug from
under the feet of the Commission' when the secret draft European
Constitution (code-named 'Penelope') accidentally became public in
December 2002 (Milton and Keller-Noëllet 2005, 41). Penelope was a feasibility study prepared by a working group of experts headed by François
Lamoureux at the request of President Prodi, but without informing the
College of Commissioners. This inevitably led to recriminations within the
College. Penelope sought to provide a general idea of the possible content of
a future Constitution (Commission Feasibility Study 2002). It made a number
of far-reaching proposals, including proposals on the ratification of the future
Treaty and its entry into force. Moreover, it called for a declaration by each
Member State 'confirming the resolve of its people to continue to belong to the
Union' and proposed that defence policy become an 'integral part of the
Union's external relation policy'.

As the working groups completed their work in late 2002, the dynamics of
the Convention were rapidly changing. Member States started to accept that
they could not run a parallel process on institutional questions in the
European Council and started to commit their heavyweights to the
Convention. The Greek Presidency began its work at the start of 2003 with
real uncertainty and some apprehension over the chance of a positive result
by the Thessaloniki European Council in June 2003. A huge amount of work
still needed to be done, and the thorny institutional issues had not even been
debated yet. The task now facing the Convention was to turn the various concepts and positions into formal Treaty language: the Convention had entered
into its decisive third stage. Its work was made all the more difficult by splits
between Member States on institutional issues and divisions emerging
between the Praesidium and the plenary as drafting of Treaty articles began.
Politically, this was all set against the backdrop of serious divisions emerging
on the European response to the war in Iraq.

Although the draft Treaty structure included no less than 13 articles on the
institutional framework of the Union, the first debate in the Convention plenary did not take place until January 2003. Both Giscard d'Estaing and Kerr
had ensured that institutional issues would not be debated any earlier. Now,
in January 2003, the debate on institutions was overshadowed by the debate
on the role of the European Council and the possibility of a long-term and
possibly full-time President of the European Council proposed by Aznar,
Blair and Chirac. The UK was informally circulating detailed proposals for a
full-time President of the European Council, supported by a reduced number
of sectoral Councils with team Presidencies. Although a number of
Conventionnels such as Fischer, Duff, Dini and Lequiller supported a unified
President of the Commission and Council, this proposal never obtained the
support it might conceivably have warranted.

A joint Franco-German proposal of 15 January 2003, shifted the
Convention debate and had a major impact on the final outcome. Essentially,

the proposal was a compromise between the positions of the two governments: a full-time President of the European Council and an elected President of the European Commission. The governments also suggested a double-hatted Foreign Minister for the Union, more qualified majority voting, a restructured Council and greater Commission powers over economic policy. The proposal dominated the Convention plenary on 20 January 2003, and effectively led to a revolt by the small Member States. Over two-thirds of the 91 interventions at the two-day plenary stressed their opposition to the Franco-German proposals. The plenary showed the first signs of close cooperation between Amato, Brok and Duff, who respectively headed the Socialist, Christian Democrat and Liberal groupings in the EP. It also underlined the reality that Member States were not yet the dominant force in the Convention – even on institutional issues. Following the publication of the Franco-German proposal, the small and medium sized Member States began to coordinate and organise their opposition.

While the Iraq crisis did not have a direct impact on the positions in the Convention, it did have an indirect bearing on events. The presence of Foreign Ministers became more infrequent, and the conflict highlighted the impotence of Solana and Patten and the continuing weaknesses of the Common Foreign and Security Policy, described in chapter 14. Following criticism by Chirac of their support for the US/UK coalition, accession country representatives assumed a more active role at the Convention. And as the Iraq conflict escalated, the Convention became the scene of a conflict in its own right. Between January and May 2003, a steady stream of draft Treaty articles was issued by the Praesidium. Nearly all were criticised, re-drafted and subject to a large number of proposed amendments. The drafting of Treaty articles was more difficult, time-consuming and politically charged than even the most optimistic Convention member had imagined.

By the time of the signature of the Accession Treaty on 16 April 2003, where Europe's leaders also agreed to discuss progress in the Convention, major progress had been achieved. The division of competences, legal personality of the Union, the incorporation of the Charter of Fundamental Rights and the area of freedom, security and justice were broadly agreed. Yet, the Convention had failed to reach consensus on part one of the draft Treaty by Easter, as envisaged at the end of 2002. The Convention had also not been presented with any draft articles on institutional issues due to the insistence of Giscard d'Estaing and Kerr that they should be held back. This was in part due to Giscard d'Estaing's belief that these issues should only be debated by his peers – Heads of State and Government. At the meeting on 16 April, Giscard d'Estaing requested responses to five questions on the EU's institutional architecture covering the role of the European Council, the size of the Commission, the appointment and powers of the Commission President, the appointment and powers of a Foreign Minister for the Union and – his pet subject – the role of the Congress of national Parliamentarians. He did not receive the answers he hoped for. Worse, he was rebuffed in his attempts to obtain an extension to his deadline. The Convention now had only two months to complete its work, but Giscard d'Estaing was proposing to re-write the institutional framework with an elected President of the European Council supported by a board, a 'double hatted' Foreign Minister only partly bound by Commission procedures, a revised re-weighting of votes in the

Council, a 'proportional' composition of the Parliament up to a ceiling of 700 members, and a Commission consisting of a President, two Vice-Presidents and up to ten other members. The role of the Commission was to be weakened and the Council was to be streamlined to five distinct Council formations.

Ironically, the proposals themselves were a masterstroke. They were so extreme that integrationist members had to focus their energy over the next month on retaining the status quo of the Community method. In effect, Giscard's real agenda was to seek compromise and consensus on the middle ground. Although his proposals did not survive the Praesidium meeting of 22-23 April, and he was perceived to have conceded considerable ground, this was only in relation to the extreme proposals and not in relation to the positions he had sought to achieve from the start of the Convention. The (conditional) trust had nevertheless disappeared. Member State representatives felt that the responses to the five questions posed on 16 April had been ignored at the plenary on 15 May 2003. Consequently, 650 amendments were submitted to the watered down Praesidium compromise text. Some felt that the Praesidium, by amending Giscard's proposals, had inadvertently accepted them as the basis for negotiation and had merely magnified existing divisions in the Convention. However, as time constraints started to mount, so the first signs of compromise started to emerge. The small and medium sized countries did not seem to be as solid as they first claimed, and key members, such as Amato and Duff, began to envisage compromise packages.

The run up to the draft Constitution

On 26 May 2003, a first, incomplete draft Constitutional Treaty was issued. While many were hoping that the six founding members or the Commission would come to the aid of the Convention by suggesting compromises, these never materialised. While the Convention was genuinely a departure from the preparation phase before previous IGCs, it is questionable whether the final phase from 4 June 2003 was really any different to the 'horse-trading' in the final stages of an IGC. Perhaps the only difference was the actors – this time, it was not only government representatives that were bargaining. The Convention, however, did not end at the Thessaloniki European Council as intended. The final text was not presented to the Italian Presidency until 18 July 2003, after further work on part three on the policies of the Union was undertaken.

The IGC called in 2003 was unlike any that had taken place before. The first question the IGC faced was whether simply to accept the text proposed by the Convention. This was advocated by a number of key Member States. While it quickly became clear that a majority of delegations wished to revisit sensitive institutional provisions, the desire to retain the Convention text produced a negotiating dynamic unique to this IGC. This can largely be explained by four factors. Firstly, 'against the expectations of many, the Convention had produced a single text'. Secondly, the fact that two of the largest Member States 'defended so strongly the Convention text put significant pressure on others to follow suit'. Thirdly, the Convention was legitimate, and fourthly, the Members States wished to avoid a re-run of Nice at all costs (Milton and Keller-Noëllet 2005, 87-8). The principle was therefore established that the text would not be amended unless there was unanimity to do so. The Convention had become the negotiation and not the preparatory session of the IGC!

The Italian Presidency opened the IGC on 4 October 2003, in Rome, on the basis of the draft prepared by the Convention. The IGC met at Foreign Minister level with the Italians resisting the temptation to establish a representatives' group, although a 'focal points' group was later convened. The Presidency also established a group of experts, with the task of undertaking a legal review of the Convention text. Its mandate was then expanded to consolidate the protocols annexed to the successive Treaties. This work was undertaken on the basis of drafts prepared by the Commission and the Council Secretariat. But, it proved impossible to conclude the IGC negotiations at the Brussels European Council on 12-13 December 2003. A critical number of important and politically sensitive issues had not been addressed sufficiently by the Italian Presidency, most notably the extension of qualified majority voting and the lack of consensus on the weighting of votes in the Council. The summit was seen to be badly prepared and handled by the Presidency which was unable to produce a series of promised compromises, and it soon became clear that the absence of an agreement would actually be in the interest of a number of delegations for domestic political reasons.

It fell to the Irish Presidency to pick up the pieces following the chaos of the Brussels summit. Between January and March 2004 the Irish Presidency entered into a series of discrete bilateral meetings with the other Member States. These 'confessionals' forced Member States to make their real intentions clear and allowed the Irish to test out a series of possible compromises. They were also helped by external factors such as the change of government in Spain which shifted the dynamics on the thorny issue of weighting of votes in the Council. Following an upbeat report to the European Council in March 2004, the Irish Presidency saw the opportunity to re-launch full negotiations and conclude the negotiations by June. A series of 'focal points' meetings took place in May and ministerial meetings resumed. The Irish Presidency steadily narrowed down the list of 'open' issues so that by the time of the June 2004 European Council the only outstanding issues were institutional issues. Final agreement was eventually reached at the European Council on 17-18 June 2004, and the Treaty was signed on 29 October 2004.

The Constitution is currently in the 'deep freeze' following its rejection in the French and Dutch referenda. The European Union is therefore stumbling along on the basis of the Treaty of Nice, with no solution in sight on how to move forward. Heads of State and Government have called for a 'period of reflection', essentially to buy some time until they decide how to proceed. They must now decide either to abandon the Constitution, agree to make changes in an attempt to appease the French and Dutch citizens or hope that public opinion will change over time, perhaps after leadership changes in a number of key Member States.

Influencing outcomes: the role of the Commission in IGCs

Given that Treaty change is the most obvious example of intergovernmental cooperation, one might be surprised to find that the Commission influences these proceedings. On the one hand, liberal intergovernmentalists like Moravcsik and Nicolaïdis (1999) state that there is 'little evidence that either

the Commission or Parliament provided either initiatives or compromise proposals that were unique and thereby altered the outcomes of the negotiations',
and that 'there appears to be no correlation between Commission support and
the final outcome.' Yet, each set of negotiations is unique in terms of its own
dynamics, circumstances and personalities, and the amount of influence that
the Commission can exercise on the negotiations varies accordingly. By
analysing the different stages within negotiations and comparing negotiations
across the board, a different view of the role of the Commission emerges.[11]

The agenda-setting phase

The Commission normally has three opportunities to influence the agenda-
setting phase. First, as do all delegations, the Commission tries to define the
agenda of the next stage of Treaty reform during the final phase of negotiations of the Treaty. Second, the Commission has always been present in the
preparatory or reflection groups convened to discuss the IGC agenda,
whether in representatives' groups or in the secretariat of the group in question. Finally, the Commission seeks to influence the debate through its official
opinion to the IGC in accordance with Article 48 TEU.

Towards the end of an IGC negotiation, the question arises whether further
Treaty changes are necessary, and more importantly whether a next 'ren-
dezvous' should be stated in the Treaty. In Maastricht (Article N(2)),
Amsterdam (Protocol 7 on the institutions with the prospect of enlargement
and declaration No. 32 of Belgium, France and Italy), and Nice (Protocol on
the institutions in the perspective of enlargement) a rough agenda was
already envisaged. The Treaties of Maastricht and Nice even fixed a specific
date for the next negotiations. The Commission has always supported these
calls, largely because it viewed Maastricht, Amsterdam and Nice as unfinished business, failing to meet the requirements of an enlarged Union. The
Commission has also sought, and often succeeded, in influencing the drafting
of these clauses.

The Commission has also tended to be effective in setting the agendas of
negotiations, especially in the preparatory groups that define the agenda and
conduct the first review of Member State positions. In preparation of the
Single European Act, the Commission was both a member of the Dooge
Committee and placed an official in the Secretariat. Before Maastricht, Jacques
Delors chaired the 'Groupe des Sages' on Monetary Union, effectively called
the Delors Committee. In contrast, political union discussions were not
covered by a preparatory group. For Amsterdam, the Reflection Group
chaired by Carlos Westendorp set much of the agenda for the IGC, and
Commissioner Oreja had very good links with his Spanish counterpart, even
if his influence within the Group proved to be limited. During the preparation
for the Treaty of Nice, the Commission struggled to influence the debate
during the German and Finnish Presidencies, partly because the preparation
was undertaken by an extension of COREPER II (EC Ambassadors), where a
Deputy Secretary General of the Commission does, however, represent the
Commission. The Commission even resorted to the establishment of a Group
of 'Wise Men' headed by Jean-Luc Dehaene in an attempt to raise a number
of issues it felt unable to propose directly. That Dehaene was later appointed
Vice-Chairman of the Convention on the Future of Europe (along with former

Italian Prime Minister Giuliano Amato) was (formally at least) an unexpected advantage. In the Convention, the Commission provided two Commissioners, both of whom sat on the Praesidium responsible for the bulk of the preparation for the meetings. However, the strong leadership of Valéry Giscard d'Estaing, the personalities involved and the general shift of positions by a number of key Member States meant that the Commission struggled to gain a foothold in the negotiations.

The only formal right the Commission has in an IGC process is to submit an opinion before an IGC is convened (Article 48 TEU). Yet, an interesting legal question is whether an IGC can begin without receiving a Commission – or for that matter a European Parliament – opinion. The Commission has tended to vary in its approach to IGCs in recent years. For the Single European Act, the Commission issued a short political opinion (22 July 1985)[12] setting out the key political lines for the institutional framework for adoption by the forthcoming IGC. For Maastricht, the Commission issued an extremely detailed opinion (21 August 1990)[13] which set out the framework for the Treaty provisions on economic and monetary union and then followed this up with a formal opinion on the establishment of political union (21 October 1990).[14] For Amsterdam, the Commission adopted a detailed report on the operation of the European Union (10 May 1995)[15] and then adopted a short political text as its formal opinion (28 February 1996).[16] At Nice, the Commission did the reverse, adopting a short political statement on 10 November 1999, and then a detailed technical formal opinion on 26 January 2000.[17] Although these reports and opinions have varied in quality and in influence on the process, the Commission has always defended the need for an ambitious approach to Treaty reform. In the Dooge, Delors, Westendorp and IGC 2000 representatives' groups and the Convention on the future of Europe, the representatives of the Commission always called for a widening of the IGC agenda and an increase in the level of ambition. This is its role. But it inevitably has to accept compromises short of its initial demands.

Overall, during the 1985 Single European Act negotiations, the role of the Commission was strongly linked to its success in shaping the IGC agenda, most notably through its influence on the Luxembourg Presidency. The Commission was in a privileged institutional position, not least because the majority of the issues discussed were on the Commission's home-turf such as research and development, social policy, environment and cohesion policy. The Commission was successfully able to link the White Paper on the Internal Market with the IGC discussions. The Commission helped the Italian Presidency to convene the IGC, and widened the scope of the agenda by linking issues with the White Paper. For the Maastricht negotiations, the Commission had a privileged role in the agenda setting phase of the EMU IGC while the Council Secretariat was more dominant in the Political Union IGC. The Commission lobbied to create the Delors Committee and skilfully shifted the agenda with a stronger economic pillar of EMU in the final report which was then followed by a full draft EMU treaty prior to the start of the IGC. This did not mean, however, that the Commission was absent from the Political Union IGC agenda-setting: while it had little control over the discussion on Justice and Home Affairs, the Commission was able to shape the discussions on the new policy areas introduced at Maastricht.

During the agenda-setting phase for the Treaty of Amsterdam, all three

Presidencies relied heavily on the Council Secretariat. This was most prevalent during the political vacuum created by the Italian elections in 1996. While the Commission was successful in helping to frame the agenda, its influence during this phase often came from working together with the Secretariat. The main agenda-setting contributions of the Commission were the substantial assessment of the Treaty of Maastricht issued in May 1995 and the contributions to the questionnaires prepared by the Spanish Presidency during the Reflection Group. The 2000 IGC leading to the Treaty of Nice was effectively a worst-case scenario in terms of agenda-setting for the Commission and the Secretariat. The more defined institutional agenda allowed limited room for manoeuvre and the agenda-setting phase was effectively controlled by COREPER. While the Portuguese Presidency sought assistance, the French Presidency concentrated the preparation of the most sensitive issues in Paris. The Prodi Commission failed in its aim to widen the agenda, even after resorting to the establishment of its own wise persons' group. The agenda was widened during the Portuguese Presidency but the Commission always struggled in its attempts to set the agenda. The one notable exception was the negotiation of reforms to the Court of Justice and Court of First Instance where the Commission effectively drove the process.

The decision-making phase

It is rare for participants to pinpoint exactly when a specific decision was taken or finally agreed, so it is difficult to describe accurately the decision-making process in an IGC. This is in part because 'nothing is agreed until everything is agreed'. The opaque nature of negotiations and the multiple layers of decision-making also add to the difficulty in explaining how decisions were taken. Each delegation produces a different set of minutes with different nuances and interpretations of what was discussed and agreed. Analysis of the influence of any one delegation must be set against this background. Even ignoring the limits of confidentiality imposed on those involved in the negotiations, tracing an individual proposal from formation to inclusion in the final Treaty demonstrates that it is extremely rare for a Member State or Commission proposal to be adopted without debate or amendment. An important exception is the declarations by delegations at the end of the Conference, which are often annexed to the Treaty.

When is the Commission most effective in making its view hold sway? The Commission has achieved varying degrees of success with proposals or attempts to influence the decision-making process. Success has depended on the specific dynamics of the negotiations, the personalities of the actors involved and the policy area under discussion. IGCs normally meet at four levels: Heads of State or Government, Foreign Ministers, Personal Representatives and 'Friends of the Presidency'. Although Commission influence is different at each level, it has been most effective when discussions have concentrated on the Community area of policies as in the Single European Act, Maastricht (IGC on EMU) or Amsterdam (employment, environment, social policy, public health, consumer protection). The Single European Act, in particular, has been widely regarded as the high watershed for the role of the Commission, not least due to the part played by its President, Jacques Delors. During the negotiations for the SEA, the

Commission had a significant impact on the institutional changes and on the development of policies. This was partly due to the crucial role the Commission played in the Dooge Committee preparing the Conference. In addition, the Commission was thoroughly familiar with the institutional and policy issues to be addressed at the 1985 IGC, allowing it 'to enter negotiations with a number of well-crafted demands' (Dinan 1997a, 254). Finally, Delors' mastery of the subject, commitment, and his negotiating and coalition-building skills were crucial in ensuring Commission success. They were particularly well suited to the personalised bargaining of the European Council. However, as the IGCs in 1985 neared completion, the Commission's influence diminished as national governments took almost complete control of the agenda, a clear feature of subsequent IGCs (Dinan 1997a).

In contrast, the Commission generally struggles to influence debates on Common Foreign and Security Policy, not least because it is not able to use previous experience in the area to justify change. It is true that while the Commission failed to succeed with its suggestion of a double-hatted Foreign Minister during the Amsterdam negotiations, the suggestion was taken up in the 2004 IGC. However, there were many voices, not just the Commission's, in favour of it. The influence of the Commission in the area of Justice and Home Affairs has been more mixed. During the Maastricht negotiations, the Commission did not have the experience necessary to be able to respond to the German proposals to include a Treaty pillar on Justice and Home Affairs. Nevertheless, the failure to make substantial progress in this area, due to the intergovernmental approach, provided the opportunity for a major Commission role in drafting the new provisions at Amsterdam. Commissioner Vitorino had a similar influence during the 2004 IGC.

The Commission has been more effective when seeking to argue for new policy areas to be addressed or amended. The Single European Act is the best example, but even the Maastricht negotiations on political union illustrate that a more nuanced assessment of the Commission impact is required. The common wisdom is that the Commission was influential during the EMU IGC but less during the Political Union IGC, especially during the final Dutch Presidency. In reality, the Commission was relatively successful in ensuring that its individual proposals on Community policy areas like social policy and cohesion policy were taken up in the final text, even though they were part of the end-game negotiations. This fact is overshadowed by the perceived failures on the pillar structure and foreign policy. During the Amsterdam negotiations, a similar picture emerged, with proposals from the Commission on employment policy, environment, social policy and fraud having a significant bearing on the final outcome.

As to reforming its own structures and procedures, such as the size of the Commission, or the power of the other institutions – such as the number of votes in the Council and number of members of the European Parliament – the Commission cannot claim to have seriously affected the final outcome of negotiations. Maastricht and Nice and the debates of the Constitutional Convention illustrate this well. However, the Commission did have a notable impact on general institutional questions such as the extension of the co-decision procedure (Amsterdam) and the framework and justification for the extension of qualified majority voting (all recent IGCs). In addition, the Commission has tended to be more effective when negotiations took place at the level of the Personal Representatives or the various Friends of the Presidency groups on specific issues (e.g. Court of Justice during the negotiations at Nice and the re-drafting of Protocols during the 2004 IGC), or indeed in the working groups of the Convention on the Future of Europe. Knowledge of issues and the ability of Commission representatives to provide the technical detail on the development of policies and on how decisions have been taken, clearly weigh heavily in terms of influence.

Foreign Ministers have been unable to exercise effective influence over negotiations in IGC proceedings. Chapter 14 partly provides an explanation. Foreign policy is not only a contested area between Member States, but it is also the focus of a clash of institutional competence. In addition, the Foreign Ministers' undefined role between the Personal Representatives and Heads of State and Government levels is a hindrance to direct influence. In 2004, unlike in previous IGCs, almost no technical level preparatory groups were convened. This was partly because 'the Convention had already carried out all the necessary preparatory work', but also because it was perceived as unjustified to allow civil servants to 'call into question' the results of a legitimate political body like the Convention. Having the IGC conducted at political level also had the interesting result of sidelining COREPER, 'although many of its members were individually active behind the scenes' (Milton and Keller-Noëllet 2005, 89-90).

Finally, in the different assessments of the influence of the Commission on Treaty reform, the role of the Commission President in the European Council receives the most focus. This is in part due to the controversy that surrounded the role of President Delors in the negotiations for the Single European Act and the Maastricht Treaty. Since then, the relative decline in influence of the Commission President in European Councils is most clearly demonstrated by the lack of Commission impact on the Amsterdam and Nice negotiations in the final European Councils. However, this picture is still too simplistic. It is not possible to gauge the influence of the Commission at the final European Council as many of its proposals were also supported by other delegations. Collective pressure is often the catalyst of the final compromise, and all delegations have varying degrees of impact on the final text. It should also be noted that, although it is argued that the Commission is at its weakest in an IGC context in the final European Council, the Commission is the only delegation, apart from the Secretariat of the IGC, entitled to have officials, as opposed to ministers, present in the negotiating room. This leads to a reporting role and dependence on other delegations, which in itself can influence the nuances of the final compromise texts.

Ratification and legitimation

The Commission has no formal role during the ratification of a Treaty stemming from an IGC. However, it has become almost expected that the Commission will support the outcome of the negotiations and make public pronouncements in support of ratification. This can leave the Commission in a difficult position in a number of ways. First, the Commission is expected to support the final compromise even though it does not have a final vote on its content. Within an hour of the end of negotiations in the European Council, the Commission and the Presidency give a press conference. The President of the Commission makes an immediate comment on the final text and the prognosis of the Commission in terms of ratification. This does not cause significant difficulties if the new Treaty is perceived to have further increased integration, but this is not always clear-cut. The situation was particularly difficult for the Commission at the Nice European Council. Only two hours before the announcement, the Commission had seriously considered rejecting the compromise on the negotiating table. The outcome of the Convention put the Commission President in a similarly awkward position.

If, on the other hand, the Commission is too fulsome in its praise for a Treaty and its ratification, it can lead to accusations of attempting to influence the ratification process. Criticism was made of President Delors during the ratification of the Maastricht Treaty and President Prodi during the ratification of the Treaty of Nice. In addition, during the ratification of the Treaty of Amsterdam, the Commission was threatened with legal proceedings by the 'no' campaign in Ireland after the distribution of an explanatory brochure on the Treaty. This was typical of the binds in which the Commission frequently finds itself. On the one hand, the Commission has a responsibility to publish material on the working of the European Union and changes to it when the founding Treaties are amended. On the other, it must avoid the risk of seeming to interfere. Damned if you do, and damned if you don't, would be an apposite aphorism. The Commission somewhat shifted its position in 2005 by making it clear that it did not see itself as a neutral actor in the process. It strongly supported ratification of the Constitutional Treaty but was also careful to ensure that it only assisted Member States where specific requests were made. Practically, the onus must be on the Member States to explain the Treaty to their citizens and justify their actions during negotiations, not least to ensure that the new Treaty is not viewed as imposed by 'Brussels'.

The Commission also has influence – whether inadvertently or not – over the fate of the ratification of a Treaty revision through controversial decisions it may take (or decide not to take) in the policy-process, or even through statements made in other contexts. Thus, even doing its routine job can create clear difficulties for the Commission. The negative assessment by the Commission of Irish economic policy in the context of the EMU stability pact, and the impact that this is considered to have had on the initial 'no' vote in the first referendum on the Treaty of Nice in Ireland is one example. During the ratification process in 2005, the Commission was heavily criticised for the impact of the services directive on the debate in France. To the extent to which the Commission is desirous of ensuring a safe passage of ratification instruments, it may be well advised – and presumably is under much pressure – to avoid 'rocking the boat' before ratification takes place. Thus, positive influence of the Commission on ratification may arise from abstention from routine declarations and lack of visibility to the outside observer.

The Convention method and Treaty reform

Article IV-433 of the Constitutional Treaty specified that future IGCs would also be preceded by a Convention, but the wider significance of the Convention method remains to be seen, especially given the rejection of the Constitution in some countries. However, experience so far provides valuable insights. One concerns the nature of the procedure and the substantive outcomes. In terms of procedure, the Convention method can be seen as a supra-national move. First, it establishes a new EU-level quasi-institution – the Convention – and new EU-level actors – the Convention President and Vice-Presidents. Second, through the Convention method, a range of actors tra-ditionally disenfranchised in the Treaty reform process – the EP and national parliaments – are given a much greater voice in the debate on Treaty reform. Third, the role of these supranational actors is elevated. They are effectively empowered not just to set the detailed agenda of the IGC, but in fact to draft the actual Treaty. National governments, whose ultimate veto over the out-come is never far from the minds of the Convention members, are neverthe-less reduced to responding to the agenda and the proposals emerging from the Convention. They may score 'victories' such as the British government's success in banishing the term 'federal' from the preamble of the draft Treaty, but this also comes at the cost of trade-offs in other areas. In principle, the Convention method gives governments a reactive role – a position that is a far cry from the image of Member States coming to the conference table with fixed preferences and thus setting the goalposts.

However, while the Convention method can be conceptualised as a more supranational form of negotiating, the outcome was not, in fact, more supra-national. Indeed, the Convention on the Future of Europe has had the para-doxical result of producing proposals which seem generally to strengthen the intergovernmental features of the Union at the expense of the supranational institutions. Whether this is due to the indirect influence Member States have had over the Convention Praesidium, a recognition within the Convention of what is politically acceptable to the Member States and the wider European public, or whether the outcome simply reflects in practice the worldview of the Convention leadership, in particular that of Giscard d'Estaing, are all moot points. Only after – and if ever – the European Constitution is ratified will it be clear whether the Convention method constitutes an important shift in the development of the European Union. Indeed, there are conflicting views on the direction of such a shift and the French and Dutch rejections of the Constitution and the resulting 'crisis' in the European Union have further complicated the debate. The issue now is not only the content of this latest round of constitutional tinkering but more generally what the Union is and ought to become.

For some, the purpose of a European Constitution would be to enshrine a constitutional settlement, be this the status quo or a further development of it. This would be in line with the traditional understanding of the term 'Constitution', which is to provide a firm and largely unchanging foundation for politics. On the other hand, there are those who see the European Constitution as a fluid text, 'a living text', evolving in congruence with the political, economic and social changes in Europe, and thus requiring frequent review and reform. On this view, the Constitutional Treaty is not the end, but quite simply one part of a process of drafting the ideal Constitution for the EU. Future enlargements and other changes in EU politics would, on this reading, necessitate further reform.

What is clear is that for at least the coming years, institutional reform and the future of the Constitution will be put to one side. The priority has now turned to protecting what already exists in the European Union and demon-strating the added value that the European project brings. Thus, whether the

Constitutional Treaty is a (final) constitutional move for the European Union – recognition of how close the EU is towards statehood – or whether it is merely another in a succession of treaties completing the business, unfinished at Nice, of giving the larger Member States greater control over EU decision making, strengthening the Council over the Commission and ending the rotating Presidency, lies in the eye of the beholder. For the moment, the Constitution has been relegated to the archive shelf dedicated to institutional tinkering.

As to the institutional process, a more detailed look at the Commission's involvement in the Convention is required. Among the 102[18] members of the Convention two were Commission representatives. Although not a large representation in such a deliberative forum, these two representatives (Commissioners Barnier and Vitorino) were also members of the 12-strong Praesidium, where most key decision-making took place.[19] Furthermore, the Convention Secretariat, influential behind the scenes in assisting the Convention President prepare meeting agendas and draft articles of the proposed draft Constitution, was staffed with Commission and European Parliament officials, as well as those of the Council Secretariat. Since the Convention Secretariat drafted all the papers forming the basis for the Convention's discussions, its role contrasted with the practice of previous IGCs where the Secretariat was solely responsible for assisting the Presidency. Moreover, the Convention Secretariat's composition 'ensured that its products remained balanced and objective', taking into account the views of the various institutions (Milton and Keller-Noëllet 2005, 38).

The Commission had been an early champion of the Convention method, arguing that the IGC method must be altered. Its positive experience with the Convention on the Charter of Fundamental Rights and the influence of Commissioner Vitorino in that process had been a key lesson. As with an IGC, each Convention needs to be analysed in the context of the specific dynamics of the time, the personalities involved and the issues discussed. While the Convention on the Future of Europe made substantial progress on a number of issues that were previously blocked in the IGC context (competences, instruments, legal personality, legal status of the Charter of Fundamental Rights), it meant hard work for the Commission. Like Member State representatives, it did not have a strong role within the plenary of the Convention. It was not able to coordinate and influence the debate in the same way that the European Parliament nominees could. So its technical expertise was of little use in a forum that had opted for far-reaching strategic bargaining over detailed substantive outcomes. In such a politicised context, the Commission had difficulty overcoming the self-imposed limitations resulting from internal divisions within the College and its lack of resources in the political game of Treaty reform. The Commission has constantly struggled with the issue of the number of Commissioners and again in the 2004 IGC struggled to come to a collegiate position. The IGC also rejected the Convention's proposal for Member States to put forward three candidates for the post of Commissioner, from which the President-elect would choose one, a change that would have greatly enhanced the Commission's democratic credentials (Milton and Keller-Noëllet 2005, 107).

Within the Praesidium the Commission should have been a major force – not least since the majority of members of the Praesidium indicated their preference for a strengthening of the Community method. This was not borne out in practice. The President of the Convention and the Convention Secretariat were successful in isolating the Commission because it lacked support from other members of the Praesidium, themselves undermined by the approach of the President. The negotiating style of Giscard d'Estaing prevented Praesidium members from amending texts, instead forcing them to defend the texts as the common position of the Praesidium. This left the two Commissioners in a difficult situation, not least with the rest of the College. Towards the end of the Convention, some in the Commission negotiating team believed it more prudent to deal with sensitive issues in the IGC rather than in the Convention, such were the attempts to marginalise the Commission on institutional and external relations issues.

The Convention method therefore creates a broad dilemma for Commission representatives. Should they provide support for the more abstract idea of the Convention format, or should they concentrate on the parochial representation of specific Commission interests? At the Convention, the Commission decided to support the final text of the Convention, as it was generally acknowledged that only with broad support would the Convention text have a chance of adoption by the IGC. However, this meant abandoning particular Commission interests. As a result, the Commission was unable to influence the Convention, either in the debates in the plenary or in the work of the Praesidium. In addition, there was only limited opportunity to influence the proceedings of the working groups set up to prepare specific aspects of the Treaty. Given that the Commission lacked representation in a number of these working groups, it was unable to participate in negotiations across the board of the agenda. This, in turn, hampered its ability for issue-linkage – a capacity traditionally a major asset in the Commission's conduct of negotiations.

If Commission influence has waned, the role of the European Parliament and national parliaments has increased, for they have partly taken over the accountability role of the Commission. The Commission thus needs to reconsider its role within the Convention method; in particular its current position in the Secretariat, the plenary, the Praesidium and in a number of working groups. It may have to decide whether it will seek to portray itself as the technical advisor or the political impetus behind the Convention approach as such. It may be early days for the Convention method, but on current evidence it does not appear to favour the Commission. The greater degree of politicisation diminishes the Commission's ability to rely on technical expertise to influence the course of negotiations. The greater openness of the forum towards non-state actors and parliamentarians detracts from the Commission's traditional role of representing the European interest in Treaty reform. And the explicit focus on constitutional issues makes it more difficult to link Treaty reform to the EU policy process in which the Commission has a pivotal role. If the Convention continues to form part of the IGC process in the future, further decline of the Commission as an actor in Treaty reform may be the outcome. This would mirror the broader development in the EU where the Commission has lost influence in the wake of the fall of the Santer Commission and the shift of leadership in the Union to key Member States. The days in which the Commission, led by Jacques Delors, could determine the direction of Treaty change are probably distant history.

In conclusion, it must be recognised that the continuance of the Convention

method will fundamentally change the nature of Treaty reform. While it provides more openings for non-state actors to influence the outcome of Treaty
reform and provides potential for the Commission to play a more effective
role, the size and dynamics of the Convention place greater emphasis on
agency. Individual actors such as the Convention President can significantly
influence the outcome and, in the process, side-line the Commission. Whether
the Commission can adapt to these new circumstances and play a more effective role in Treaty reform than it has recently managed remains to be seen.
One thing that remains certain, even if the Constitution is currently in the
'deep freeze', is that planning is already starting for the next Intergovernmental Conference.

Endnotes

[1] See, for example 'Proposal for a Draft Treaty Amending the Treaty Establishing
the European Economic Community with a View to Achieving Economic and
Monetary Union', 21 August 1990, which was followed by a formal opinion on
'Establishing Political Union' on 21 October 1990; 'Commission Report on the
Operation of the Institutions', 10 May 1995; 'Adapting the Institutions to Make a
Success of Enlargement – Contribution by the European Commission to
Preparations for the IGC on Institutional Issues', 10 November 1999; 'Contribution
on the Future of the European Project', 22 May 2002.
[2] Commission Opinion 1985, COM (85) 445.
[3] Commission Opinion 1996, COM (96) 90.
[4] Commission Opinion 2003, COM(2003) 548 final.
[5] The Ioannina Compromise is explained in Westlake (2004) pages 244-5.
[6] A detailed analysis of the work of the Reflection Group can be found in
Chryssochoou, D; Tsinisizelis, M; Stavridis, S; and Ifantis, K. (1999).
[7] The Amsterdam left-overs were rebalancing (national) voting weights under
QMV on the Council, the size of the Commission and the extension of QMV to more
types of decision'.
[8] Commission Opinion 2000, COM (2000) 34.
[9] Details of these changes can be found in chapter 1 of this book and in the com-
panion volumes on the Council and the European Parliament.
[10] Much of the following discussion draws on first hand observation by two participants in the process. See Milton and Keller-Noëllet 2005.
[11] This section draws extensively on an earlier article on the Commission's influence over the three phases of the IGC process. See Christiansen and Gray 2003.
[12] Commission Opinion 1985, COM (85) 445.
[13] Commission 1990, SEC (90) 1659.
[14] Commission Opinion 1990, COM (90) 600.
[15] Commission Report on the Operation of the TEU, SEC (95) 731 final.
[16] Commission Opinion 1996, COM (96) 90.
[17] Commission Opinion 2000, COM (2000) 34.
[18] If one includes each Convention member's alternate and the observers, the total
participants numbered more than 200 (Milton and Keller-Noëllet 2005, 32).
[19] Following lobbying from the candidate countries, Alojz Peterele, former
Slovenian Prime Minister, was nominated to serve as a guest to the Praesidium. He
subsequently became a full member, increasing the number of members to 13
(Milton and Keller-Noëlet 2005, 37).

17. The internal reform of the Commission

Handley Stevens and Anne Stevens

Shortly after midnight on Monday 15 March 1999, President Jacques Santer and his whole team of Commissioners resigned, engulfed by allegations of fraud, mismanagement and nepotism. The high drama of these events gave the new team under President Romano Prodi a uniquely favourable opportunity to devise and carry out the comprehensive reform programme which had long been needed, under the direction of Neil Kinnock as Vice-President and Commissioner for Administrative Reform. This chapter describes the long history of failure, over a period of at least twenty years, to address with sufficient priority or urgency the concerns widely expressed about the Commission's inadequate processes of management and administration. It analyses the crisis which thrust reform to the top of the Commission's agenda in 1999 and the steps taken under the leadership of Prodi and Kinnock to remedy the situation. It concludes with a provisional assessment of the adequacy of these measures and their likely impact.

The failure to reform

Administrative cultures

The key choice when the Commission was established in 1958 was whether to follow the model of national or international administrations. The closely circumscribed role of an international secretariat was rejected (Siotis 1964, 228, 244) in favour of a model more analogous to that of a national administration. The reasoning was that the European Community was destined to be an evolving institution moving towards political and economic integration. Thus, it should have a permanent staff of its own, committed to the Community and its institutions, rather than a continually changing cast of seconded staff with careers to make elsewhere (Stevens 2001, 31-32).

Neither Jean Monnet, the first President of the High Authority of the Coal and Steel Community, nor Walter Hallstein, the first President of the Commission of the European Economic Community, were much interested in the details of administration. As a result, there was a natural, unplanned confluence of mainly French and German practices, owing much to the instinctive tendencies of Hallstein and Emile Noël, the Commission's first Secretary General. The Community model which emerged from this process was a hybrid of what Cassese (1987, 12) identifies as the German model 'dominated by legalism, rigidity and administrative planning' and the French, or Napoleonic, model characterised by 'the rigidity of the structures and the flexibility of the bureaucracy'. After British entry in 1973 and particularly after Noël was succeeded by David Williamson in 1987, the Commission became influenced by the British model, characterised in Cassese's terms by the flexibility of both structures and procedures. But other traditions have also left their mark either in the structures created or in the ways they have been adapted and developed. For example, the Nordic countries have brought with them a greater commitment to openness and to equal opportunities for men and women.

One key feature of continental bureaucracies, which shaped the administration of the Commission in its earliest years, was a reliance on basic statutes, which establish the distinctive status of the official, protect his or her autonomous position as guardians of the law and define the rights and obligations of officials and the institutions they serve. Under a national administration, such laws give the official a special role in relation to the state, distinct from any obligation to serve the government of the day. This sometimes finds expression in the tenacity with which officials trained in the continental tradition will defend their exclusive right to exercise the legal authority of the state, resisting any exercise of such rights by those who are not officials. In the European context, this has translated for many into a sense of commitment to the 'European project', and to the protection of their own special status as its guardians.

Given the preponderance among the reformers of relative newcomers from northern Europe (Christophersen, Hay, Smidt, Liikanen, Kinnock), it was tempting for those who were nostalgic about the pioneering years to associate the rising pressure for modern management with what they saw as a declining commitment to the European project, and to resist it on those grounds. One of McDonald's respondents said of the younger generation of staff: 'we had a European ideal, and now they have to go to management courses to learn motivation' (McDonald 1998). Such remarks may be symptomatic of a conflict between two modes of legitimacy (Stevens 2002). The first, deriving from law-based structures designed to embed the administration within society, results in a relatively autonomous administration. The second mode, deriving from a procedural legitimacy based upon outcomes, responsiveness, effectiveness and accountability, results in an instrumental administration (Knill 2002, 107). The origins of the Commission's administration lie mainly within the first model. But its failure to maintain acceptable standards has undermined its own legitimacy and strengthened the case for reforms deriving from the instrumental model, in which the emphasis on performance in the provision of services to the political authorities and beyond them to the citizens is paramount (Page and Wright 1999, 272; Pollitt and Bouckaert 2000, 58).

The twin pillars of the law-based regime, which shapes the Commission's administration, are the Staff Regulations and the Financial Regulation. The annual budget sets out the requirements of the Commission for both manpower and finance, and the framework of resources within which these

Regulations apply. However, it is the Regulations themselves and their day-to-day administration that establish the parameters for management of the Commission. The Staff Regulations were adopted in 1961, and consolidated in 1968 (Regulation 259/68) following the 1967 merger of the three European Communities (ECSC, Euratom and EEC), but the underlying principles reach back to precedents established for the Coal and Steel Community in 1956. The Financial Regulation, adopted following the 1970 reform of Community finance which first gave the Community its own streams of revenue, known as 'own resources', dates back to 1973, though the basic provisions for the establishment and oversight of the budget have their roots in the founding Treaties themselves (now TEC Articles 268-280). The Financial Regulation, continually revised from 1977 onwards, has been completely rewritten since 1999 (Reg 1605/2002). A comprehensive reform of the Staff Regulations (Reg 723/2004) was equally part of the Prodi Commission's reform programme, but it is important to understand what they contained before 1999, since the culture that the old Staff and Financial Regulations formed and reflected will not be changed as quickly as the Regulations themselves.

Management in the Commission before 1999

Even today, with an official payroll in the region of 24,000 (see chapter 6), the Commission is a relatively small administration, with a strong emphasis on the making of policy rather than its detailed implementation. There are exceptions, notably in the application of competition law, in the implementation of the Community's international aid programme, and in the conduct of its own internal administration, but first and foremost the role of the Commission is as the initiator of policy proposals for the Community. The members of an autonomous bureaucracy tend to maintain that they, and only they, have the intellectual and technical capacity to know what the nation – or in this case, the European Union – needs. At all events, it is the traces of this approach within the EU administration that Shore (1999) discerns and condemns, though Hooghe's survey of 106 top Commission officials between 1995 and 1997 found that most of them 'believe that the era of benevolent technocracy in the tradition of Jean Monnet has come to a close' (Hooghe 1999, 358). The emphasis on policy work is even more pronounced than in most national administrations, not least because so much of the responsibility for implementation rests with the Member States. This may help to explain why the bureaucratic but ineffectual financial regime, which was brought from Paris to Brussels in the early 1950s, survived for so long while national administrations elsewhere in Europe were engaged in sometimes radical programmes of reform and modernisation.

The foundations of the Commission's financial management system rest on the annual budget. No revenue may be raised nor expenditure authorised if it is not provided for in the budget. Additional safeguards were established by the system of financial control, under which the official responsible for authorising expenditure (the authorising officer) had to obtain the prior approval of the financial controller (known as the visa) before committing expenditure, whilst the actual payment was made by a third person under the direction of the accounting officer. Further refine-

ments were bolted on after 1990 through requirements for the prior evaluation and subsequent review of expenditure programmes in the interests of
economy and cost-effectiveness, though the utility of these arrangements
has been questioned (Levy 2000). The laudable intention was that no one
person, nor even three people within the same management team, could
sign all the documents required to carry out a financial transaction.
However, the system was fundamentally flawed. Both the financial controller, who had to approve the expenditure in advance, and the staff of the
accounting officer, who had to make the actual payments, were so far separated from the authorising officer, and so overwhelmed by the growing
volume of transactions, that they could not exercise any effective control.
Yet their responsibility diluted that of the authorising officer, creating a
financial management culture more concerned with procedural routines
than with any underlying financial responsibility.

The personnel management systems were equally flawed by rigid structures originally designed to protect the European civil service from undue
national influence. By the late 1990s the very large numbers of candidates
(55,000 in 1993; 30,000 in 1998) had made normal graduate recruitment competitions almost unworkable (see chapter 6). The 1998 competition, which
had to be re-run following revelations of leaked question papers and cheating, was the last EU-wide graduate recruitment competition to be held
under the old Staff Regulations. Subsequent career progression was linked
so firmly to seniority rather than performance and merit that staff could not
easily be managed or even re-deployed. As a result, alternative methods of
entry and career progression had arisen, leading to the frustration and
demotivation of many permanent staff. The astonishing thing is not so much
that the management was found to have failed so spectacularly in 1999, as
that it had continued for so long to deliver such remarkably good results,
particularly in terms of policy development. The commitment and dedica-
tion of many staff of the highest quality had somehow been sufficient to
overcome the weaknesses of the management structure.

Reform and resistance, 1978-1999

The need for reform had thus been apparent for many years. In fact the
Santer Commission had begun to address it, but there must be some doubt
as to whether it could ever have been carried forward with sufficient commitment, leadership and priority if the crisis which overtook the
Commission in 1999 had not forced administrative reform to the top of the
agenda for the incoming Prodi Commission. The need for reform was first
publicly identified in 1978 when an Independent Review Body was set up
under Ambassador Dirk Spierenburg to examine the work, organisation
and structures of the Commission. The context was a parallel review of the
workings of the Community institutions generally, commissioned by the
Council to prepare the Union for the accession of Greece, to be followed by
Portugal and Spain. Spierenburg identified 'a certain lack of cohesion in the
college of Commissioners, an imbalance between portfolios, insufficient
coordination among senior officials, a maldistribution of staff between
departments, and shortcomings in the career structure of the civil service of
the Commission' (Commission 1979, para 1.3.4). In response to the report,

the number of administrative units within the Commission was eventually reduced from 339 to 291, and the first of many 'screening' exercises was undertaken. The aim was to achieve a better allocation of staff to the busiest parts of the organisation, but the terms of the report show just how rudimentary the structures of management still were at that time. For example, the review recommended a series of measures such as the establishment of a central staff register, job descriptions, a more serious system of staff reporting, a more professional approach to promotions and recruitment, the suppression of 'rigged competitions' designed to give permanent status to staff brought in on a temporary basis without proper competitions, the encouragement of staff mobility with suitable training, and an emphasis on experience of management or at least aptitude for it as a qualification for senior posts (Spierenburg 1979). These measures, to say the least, were fairly basic to any well-run organisation. The list of necessary reforms was long. The Commission responded by setting up a further committee to consider their implementation. Although some progress was undoubtedly made over the years which followed, many of the weaknesses identified in 1979 still needed to be addressed in the reforms proposed in the White Paper of March 2000.

The next wave of reform and modernisation was initiated by Henning Christophersen, Commissioner for Personnel and Administration 1985-1988, and Richard Hay, Director General 1986-1991. Starting with senior management, then whole Directorates General, two-day seminars were organised to 'increase awareness of the possibilities and advantages of modern management techniques', to make staff 'aware of the need to improve work organisation and interpersonal relations, and to suggest ways and methods of doing this' (Hay 1989). The new emphasis on management was reflected in the attempt to ensure the development of a 'middle management' tier within the hierarchy, by appointing officials at grade A4 level to posts as section heads (*chefs d'unité*) with management as well as policy formulation roles. Hitherto no one below the rank of Head of Division (A3) had been expected, or even allowed, to exercise management responsibility. At the same time, further screening initiatives were undertaken, and resources were invested in information technology and training. In addition, an equal opportunities programme was launched, and strenuous efforts were made to introduce a regular and open recruitment programme whilst clamping down on irregular back-door recruitment by way of temporary appointments and 'mini-budgets', a device which used programme resources to finance posts not included in the staff budget.

The success of these initiatives was limited. There were two reasons. First, they depended on the leadership of one or two Commissioners and Directors General without strong support from all their colleagues, so that when others less committed to administrative reform succeeded Christophersen and Hay, enthusiasm flagged. Second, the programme encountered deep-seated cultural resistance. Many in the Commission were suspicious of the Nordic approach to management which they identified with the Christophersen/Hay agenda, and later with that pursued by the Finnish Commissioner Erkki Liikanen and Danish Director General Steffen Smidt (McDonald 1998). When senior official Philippe Petit-Laurent was asked to write a valedictory report on the state of the administration and its effectiveness in 1994, he found that many of the problems first identified by Spierenburg in 1979 had never been satisfactorily resolved. However, in a second report, completed in 1995, he concentrated on what might be done to improve the Commission's image, suggesting that the outgoing Delors Commission, which commissioned it, was still reluctant to believe that there was anything fundamentally amiss (Stevens 2001, 186).

In the event Erkki Liikanen, who was Commissioner for Personnel and Administration in the Santer Commission (1995-99), did more to modernise the Commission's administration than any of his predecessors. There were three main elements in the Liikanen reform agenda. First, in the programme for Sound and Efficient Management (SEM 2000), developed in partnership with the Budget Commissioner Anita Gradin, there was for the first time a strong focus on financial management. The first two SEM programmes, launched in March and November 1995, concentrated on the Commission's management of its own resources. The third, in 1997, focussed on the better management of the major Community expenditure programmes administered by the Member States themselves. The two internal programmes reinforced budgetary discipline in three ways. Guidelines were set centrally in advance of receiving bids from the Commission's services. Financial management was strengthened by giving Directors General appropriately qualified staff to support them in the exercise of their financial responsibilities. And a start was made towards shifting the focus of central resources from routine control functions towards systems audit and the prevention of fraud.

Second, alongside these improvements in financial management, Commissioner Liikanen developed a programme for the modernisation of administration and personnel policy (MAP 2000). From 1997 onwards, the aim was decentralisation and simplification of many of the procedures associated with the management and organisation of staff within the DGs. This included the freedom to transfer resources between administrative budgets; for example if more money were needed to pay for agency staff, the cost could be met by squeezing the budget for travel and subsistence. Initially only six Directors General were prepared to accept responsibility for tasks traditionally regarded as an irritating distraction from the real business of policy-making, but the transfers were accompanied by the corresponding staff resources, and within a couple of years the minority accepting decentralisation had become a substantial majority.

A third element in the 1995-1999 reform programme was the attempt to re-allocate staff to the areas of greatest need, based on yet another screening exercise carried out between November 1997 and May 1999. The continual need for such exercises calls for some explanation. Senior managers in every large organisation find it easier to obtain the additional resources they need to undertake urgent new tasks than to give up resources when the pressure has eased. But the obstacles to mobility within the Commission are abnormally severe. One reason is the way staff are allocated to their work. The link between the person and the particular job he or she does is very strong. A successful candidate in a recruitment competition cannot be appointed (see chapter 6) without first being selected to fill a vacant post on the recommendation of the relevant Director General. Once appointed, an official does not have to move to new work in order to gain promotion. This encourages a tendency to identify so closely with a subject as to 'make it objectively harder to achieve staff mobility because knowledge of a subject is concentrated on an individual' (Hay 1989, 28). Management is reluctant to disturb someone whose store of knowledge will be difficult to replace, and individual officials are reluctant to move to unfamiliar new work, which might set back rather than advance their chances of promotion. In these circumstances, a compulsory transfer may even be seen as a disciplinary measure, and challenged accordingly in the ECJ's Court of First Instance (since 2004, the European Union Civil Service Tribunal), to which officials have recourse if they feel they have been unfairly treated. The Commission has suffered from a culture of immobility, which has made it exceptionally arthritic. Be that as it may, another major screening and restructuring exercise was judged necessary after 1997. It was linked to the ongoing processes of SEM and MAP in a multi-faceted reform programme called DECODE, Designing the Commission of Tomorrow.

The plan was to publish in April 1998, as a basis for consultation, an all-embracing programme of further reforms. However, staff and unions were becoming increasingly suspicious of a programme that was not well understood outside the small circle charged with developing it within the Personnel and Administration DG. The members of this group were conversant with the discussions on administrative reform, which had been going on for some years in the OECD's public management group (PUMA). They assumed a far higher familiarity with, and acceptance of, these ideas within the Commission than was actually the case. When they suggested that the Commission's management needed to take account of the requirements of its stakeholders, including the governments of the Member States and their citizens as well as the Commission itself, they encountered strong opposition from many older staff. The staff were deeply attached to the notion that the Commission had been created to pursue the goal of 'European construction', if necessary in opposition to the Member States. The Germans had proposed to the Intergovernmental Conference preparing the 1997 Treaty of Amsterdam, a treaty amendment allowing the Member States to propose amendments to the Staff Regulations. The proposal was rejected, but in the light of Germany's known hostility to what it considered the inflated levels of EU officials' salaries, it was perceived, notably by the unions, as an attack on pay and conditions of employment (*European Voice*, 15-21 May 1997). In this context the idea that the Member States and their citizens were in any sense the customers for a management reform programme was liable to provoke opposition rather than support.

There were two other strands in this deeply rooted cultural opposition. The first related to the concept of management itself. Some longer-serving officials told McDonald in 1998 that 'you can date many of our present troubles from that time' – that time being the first enlargement, and particularly the arrival of the British and the Danes, who brought talk of 'management' and 'were critical of the functioning of the Commission' (McDonald 1998, 23). The second strand, of particular importance to the unions, was the tendency of management reform to entail devolution from the centre, where union influence was firmly entrenched in the development of personnel policy, to Directorates General where it was much harder for them to intervene in the practical decisions of managers.

Liikanen's intention was to discuss the new reform programme within the full Commission in May 1998, and with the unions in June. However, when the unions were informed of these plans at the beginning of April, they immediately objected both to the plan to make the consultation document available not just to themselves but to all staff, and to any discussion by the College of Commissioners until they had had their say. The situation was further inflamed by the leaking of an internal report (the Caston Report, Commission 1998a) which contained radical proposals for reform of the Staff Regulations, affecting many sensitive areas of personnel management and career development. The impression took hold that the Commission was secretly planning a major assault on the cherished rights and independence of the European civil service, and a strike called for 30 April, the day before a public holiday weekend, attracted very wide support from staff including some in management positions. The Caston Report was disowned by the Commission's senior management. But the furore was enough for a wide range of personnel issues to be referred to a group with equal staff and management representation chaired by David Williamson. Williamson had recently retired as Secretary General. Since the Williamson report (Commission 1998b) could not be expected to reach conclusions for some months – in the event it did not report until November 1998 – the Santer Commission's reform programme was in effect stopped in its tracks.

Crisis and resignation

The highly public sense of crisis and mismanagement that these events had engendered in the early summer of 1998 did nothing to help the Commission's cause. Concerns about its mismanagement of financial resources grew ever more insistent when Parliament reassembled after the summer break. The discharge of the 1996 budget, set for agreement by 30 April 1998, was still pending in November when the Court of Auditors delivered another critical report, estimating that as much as €5 billion, or 5 per cent of the Commission's budget, could not be properly accounted for. Much of this would have been the result of maladministration within the Member States, but it played into the hands of political groups in the Parliament competing for public attention in the run-up to their own elections, due in June 1999. The Christian Democrats saw advantage in leading what they expected to be a popular attack against fraud, waste and mismanagement. The Socialists decided that it would be tactically wise to welcome a vote of no confidence in the Commission, in the expectation that the Christian Democrats and their allies would not be able to raise the two-thirds majority required to dismiss the Commission. It was at this point that the Commission was faced by a case of 'whistle-blowing'. Paul van Buitenen, at that time an internal auditor in the Commission's financial control department, had written first to Secretary General Carlo Trojan and then to President Jacques Santer with a whole litany of allegations. Most of these were old but no less damaging for that. Meanwhile, he lost patience with the Commission's cumbersome internal procedures. Having set a deadline for passing the information to Parliament, he loaded the documents into the back of his car and took them to Luxembourg, where he left them with Green MEP Magda Aelvoet. He was immediately suspended on the grounds that he had acted improperly, and although he was eventually reinstated, albeit in a much less central auditing post, he resigned from the Commission in 2003, claiming that the Commission's subsequent reforms had changed nothing.

Back in December 1998, his dossier threw oil onto a fire which was already raging in the Parliament. The Commission escaped an immediate vote of censure in January 1999 by accepting the establishment of a Committee of Independent Experts (CIE). This was required to report by 15 March on the extent to which the Commission as a body, or Commissioners individually, could be held to bear specific responsibility for the instances of fraud, mismanagement or nepotism, which had come to light. The report focussed on the role and responsibility of the Commissioners themselves, with one sentence from the final paragraph summing up the devastating indictment of the Commission's financial management generally. It said: 'It is becoming difficult to find anyone who has even the slightest sense of responsibility' (CIE First Report, para 9.4.25). In January, when the criticism focussed mainly on Commissioners Manuel Marin and Edith Cresson, both Socialists, the Socialist Group in Parliament had contrived to protect them by proposing a general vote of censure against the whole Commission, and then voting to defeat their own motion. However, when the CIE report appeared, criticising the whole Commission in such stark terms, including the President's own negligence in failing to give adequate attention to the management of the Commission's security services, the game was up. At 9 pm on Monday 15 March 1999, the Socialists announced that this time they would support a vote of censure against the whole Commission. At 10.30 pm the Commission met in emergency session, and soon after midnight, President Santer announced their collective resignation.

In the early months of 1999, when the Santer Commission was casting about for measures sufficient to allow it a reprieve, it had already decided to give its anti-fraud unit (UCLAF) a higher status as an Office (OLAF). The original impetus behind the creation of UCLAF in 1987/88 had been the pressure from the European Parliament's Committee on Budgetary Control for a 'flying squad' able to carry out on-the-spot checks in Member States in cases of suspected fraud involving Community funds. This might have suited the supranational ambitions of Commission and Parliament, but the Member States were not so keen. The small unit co-ordinating the fight against fraud had to start life under the authority of the Secretary General, relying to a large extent on cases forwarded to them by staff in the DGs (Agriculture, Customs and Indirect Taxation, Budget, Financial Control) concerned with the programmes thought to be most at risk. The activity was not drawn together within UCLAF until 1995. Then there were problems with staff elsewhere in the Commission withholding documents or failing to report suspected cases to UCLAF. By October 1998, Parliament was calling for the creation of a more autonomous Office, and the Commission made a proposal to the Council to this effect in December 1998. This commitment to a more serious fight against fraud was not enough to save the Commission from having to resign, but the new OLAF was duly established in April 1999 and given more autonomy than its predecessor (Regulations 1073/99 and 1074/99, adopted by the Council on 25 May).

Despite these advances there remained then, and indeed still remains, ambivalence about the EU's commitment to the fight against fraud. Of course all the institutions of the Union proclaim their commitment to the prosecution and eradication of fraud. But it is widely believed that some of the Member States are none too fussy about how their farmers or regional authorities justify payments under the Agricultural and Structural Funds. Their prime aim is to get their share. And the Commission itself has never been keen on washing its dirty linen in public (as the van Buitenen dossiers amply demonstrated), for fear that such revelations will damage its image and set back the grand project of European construction. In these circumstances, it may be more attractive to create an organisation or upgrade it than to give it the necessary powers and resources to do an effective job. Some commentators take the view that this has been characteristic of the Commission's actions in this field (Pujas 2002). The second report of the CIE called for OLAF to be given much stronger powers of criminal as opposed to merely administrative investigation. But this has not occurred. The Commission claims that OLAF investigations have benefited from total operational independence, but the system was still very slow to pick up the danger signals at Eurostat (see below), and the further bout of institutional tinkering (COM(2004)103), with which the Commission responded to the Eurostat affair failed to impress the European Parliament (*European Voice*, 20 November 2003 and 4 March 2004).

The second and final report of the Committee of Independent Experts was delivered in September 1999. Entitled *Reform of the Commission, Analysis of current practice and proposals for tackling management irregularities and fraud*, the second report responded to that part of the Committee's mandate which required them to examine more fully and over a longer period the Commission's practices in the awarding of financial contracts. The report's ninety recommendations made a helpful contribution to the programme of financial management reform on which President Prodi and Commissioner Kinnock embarked as soon as the new Commission took office in the autumn of 1999. This report shifted the focus from the Commissioners themselves to a wide-ranging review of the culture, practices and procedures of the Commission's services, with particular reference to the procedures for the awarding of contracts and related personnel management issues, including the possible adaptation of the Staff Regulations to facilitate holding officials to account. The CIE also recognised the need for a wide-ranging reform of staff policy (CIE II, chapter 6), rehearsing many of the well known problems besetting the Commission's existing policy. But it dismissed the need for a thorough overhaul of the Staff Regulations themselves. The Prodi Commission was to prove bolder than the CIE in this respect.

Reform since 1999

President Romano Prodi signalled his commitment to reform as soon as the new team of Commissioners was provisionally announced in July 1999. He designated Neil Kinnock as Vice-President and Commissioner for Administrative Reform, and underlined the direct responsibility of Commissioners for the services reporting to them by directing that they should be located with their departments, rather than being housed together in a central building as in the past. Moreover, on the basis of the DECODE report, the Commission's structure was reorganised, resulting in a reduction in the number of separate services and Directorates General from 42 to 35. Kinnock himself lost no time in developing his reform programme, announcing his objectives in December and producing a substantial consultative document in January 2000, less than four months after the appearance of the CIE's second report. This was followed on 1 March by a detailed White Paper (Commission 2000). The pace was maintained with the driving through of amendments to both the Financial Regulation and the Staff Regulations, and the publication of annual reports monitoring progress towards the implementation of the White Paper's 98 recommendations. The White Paper proposals were modified in the course of negotiation with key stakeholders. These included the staff associations and the Member States. They were then refined in the light of experience, not least in the wake of the 2003 Eurostat affair, which identified further weaknesses in financial control procedures.

Table 15: *Reform milestones 1999-2004*

March 1999	First CIE Report – Fraud, Mismanagement and Nepotism in the European Commission
September 1999	Second CIE Report – Reform of the Commission
March 2000	Commission White Paper – Reforming the Commission COM(2000)200
July 2000 July 2002 January 2003	Proposal for new Financial Regulation sent to Council Reg 1605/2002 adopted New Financial Regulation enters into force
Spring 2002	An Administration at the Service of Half a Billion Europeans Staff Reforms at the European Commission
April 2002 May 2003 March 2004 1 May 2004	Proposal for new Staff Regulations sent to Council Political agreement in Council Reg 723/2004 adopted New Staff Regulations enter into force
February 2003	Progress Review of Reform, COM(2003)40
February 2004	Completing the Reform Mandate, COM(2004)93

One of the pleas made by the Santer Commission in mitigation of its failure to exercise adequate control over its expenditure programmes, was that it was chronically understaffed as a result of the tight rein on staff numbers maintained by the budgetary authorities (Council and Parliament). There was some truth in this, but the CIE responded that the Commission had failed to press the case for more staff during the lifetime of the Santer Commission, when it had consciously taken the decision to continue the policy of austerity budgets. The Commission had a duty to set priorities in the light of its new management tasks, but it had 'failed to tailor its human resources to its needs' (CIE First Report, 9.4.2-3). The recourse by hard-pressed managers to 'mini-budgets' and Technical Assistance Offices, both of which were devices for getting around strict manpower controls in ways which were legally doubtful or financially irregular – or both – could not be allowed to continue. One of the key challenges facing the reform pro-gramme was therefore how to match tasks and resources on a routine and ongoing basis, without perpetual recourse to such devices.

A new management framework

The response to this challenge, which is central to the reform programme, was the introduction of Activity Based Budgeting and Management (ABB and ABM). The Commission's proposals were laid out in the White Paper (Commission 2000) and their implementation described in successive pro-gress reviews (Commission 2003g; Commission 2004). The cycle commences with the adoption by the Commission of an Annual Policy Strategy, which identifies priorities and corresponding resources, setting the framework for the preparation of both the budget and the work programme. Each Directorate General must then translate this into an Annual Management Plan, and the cycle is closed by the preparation after the year-end of an Annual Activity Report (AAR). The first Annual Policy Strategy was adopted by the Commission in February 2002 for the year 2003, and the first AAR (for the year 2001) was carried out in 2002. Activity Based Budgeting was introduced in 2003 and applied to the budget for 2004. While these new systems were being developed, there was yet another screening exercise in July 2000, this time called a Peer Group Review. This identified the need for 1,254 additional posts, but a combination of redeployment and an offer of some 600 voluntary early retirements reduced the net figure to be financed by the budgetary authorities to 375.

Another exercise to be built into routine management was the 'simplifi-cation of procedures'. Twelve simplification measures were adopted by the Commission in 2000, and a new strategy on simplifying procedures and working methods was defined in July 2002. The aim was to consolidate the change in administrative culture, which was being encouraged by the reform process. Under this new strategic approach, Quality Circles drawing together staff from different parts of the Commission were assembled, one to consider the new concept of service level agreements defining the serv-ices to be provided by the Commission's central departments to its cus-tomers in the operational Directorates General, another to tackle the old chestnut of 'who signs what' (Commission 2003g, 25). These completed their work during 2003. The Commission's *Manual of Operating Procedures* was also updated and put on line in December 2003 (Commission 2004, 5).

The creation of Commission Executive Offices (see below) is intended to rationalise the day-to-day management of administration and support serv-ices by enabling many of these services to be carried out by contract staff employed under simplified employment conditions (see chapter 6) designed for Commission staff outside the career system for permanent offi-cials. These arrangements provide for the externalisation of routine service delivery functions to executive agencies and the better deployment of official staff. The intention is two-fold. The measures are to enable the Commission to discharge more effectively its public service responsibilities for the proper oversight of Community expenditure programmes. And further, they are to strengthen the focus of the Commission's limited official staff resources on what are seen as its core functions – the exercise of the right of policy initiative and its role as guardian of the Treaties.

The introduction of a management cycle focussing on the setting of political priorities and the appropriate allocation of resources to them is central to the Commission's reform strategy. It provides the framework within which a service-based culture of management can be inculcated (Commission 2000, 1-3). The Commission's reforms of financial management and personnel management are designed to fit into this framework.

Financial management

The reform of financial management advanced faster than personnel management, since more progress had been made under the Santer Commission, and the CIE Report contained specific proposals, which could quickly be translated into a reform of the Financial Regulation. The Commission's proposal was sent to the Council in July 2000, and adopted in June 2002 (Reg 1605/2002). It entered into force on 1 January 2003. The CIE was particularly critical of the Commission's procedures for financial control. It argued that the requirement for prior approval from 'a separate financial control service has been a major factor in relieving Commission managers of a sense of personal responsibility for the operations they authorise'. In addition, 'the combination of this function with a (weak) internal audit function in a single directorate-general gives rise to potential conflicts of interest on the part of the Financial Controller' (CIE II, 12). The solution proposed by the CIE and adopted by the Commission was to give authorising officers direct responsibility for prior approval, whilst strengthening the internal audit function and separating it from financial control. Auditing is now carried out at three levels: internally within each DG or Service, centrally by the Internal Audit Service established in September 2000, and externally by the Court of Auditors. With the demise of the old Financial Regulation on 1 January 2003, the last vestiges of the central *ex-ante visa*, the central provision of prior approval for the commitment of expenditure, could finally be abolished. The function of the new Central Financial Service is to provide advice, support and oversight, mainly through the network of Resource Directors, for the implementation in each DG and Service of the Commission's 24 Internal Control Standards. These cover the full range of delegated financial management responsibilities, including the reporting of improprieties and their correction. The Commission also established a Financial Irregularities Panel, under Article 66 of the Financial Regulation, to determine whether such irregularities have taken place, and what the consequences should be (Commission 2004, 11).

Accountability

A new requirement for every DG to publish an annual activity report (AAR) has powerfully reinforced the direct accountability of Directors

General for expenditure authorised by them and by their staff. The AAR not only states how their service has contributed to the achievement of the Commission's strategic objectives, but includes a signed declaration vouching for the correct use of all the budgetary resources for which the DG has been responsible (Commission 2000, 60). Anything unvouched for needs to be explained and justified. Jules Muis, who was recruited from the World Bank to lead the Internal Audit Service at a much higher level than his predecessors, described this reform as his 'silver bullet'. The first AAR exercise in 2002 prompted DGs to make 135 such reservations (COM(02)426 of 24 July 2002). Almost half of the DGs were experiencing difficulties with the new audit-related and financial management control systems (Levy 2003, 560). This prompted the Commission to clarify and strengthen its arrangements for the central overview of delegated financial control and audit (SEC(2003)59 of 21 January 2003). Meanwhile the Eurostat affair was about to shed a cruelly bright light on the continuing weaknesses in the Commission's financial management arrangements, and particularly on the arrangements for reporting adverse audit findings to Commissioners.

The Eurostat affair

There had been numerous internal audit and OLAF inquiries at Eurostat since the late 1990s. Yet, no action was taken against companies with close links to senior Eurostat personnel, even when Dorte Schmidt-Brown, the official supervising one of the relevant programmes, found that one of these companies had provided incorrect details of its financial and personnel resources in order to win a contract. Her findings were confirmed by an internal audit report, and referred to OLAF, but the company continued to receive contracts from Eurostat, as did several other companies subject to internal or external investigations. Ms Schmidt-Brown tried to get action taken, but found herself subjected to such intense professional and personal abuse from the contractors concerned and their allies within Eurostat that she eventually cracked under the pressure and had to retire from the Commission on health grounds. She had appealed to Commissioner Kinnock for legal support in the battle against her accusers at the European Court, and been turned down. Yves Franchet was Director General of Eurostat for 16 years. While it had not been proven that he benefited financially from his association with the companies concerned, he was rapidly moved aside as soon as a court case in France brought the affair into public prominence. He later resigned. Contracts with the companies under investigation were terminated and Dorte Schmidt-Brown received a belated apology together with support, which led to the settlement of her case out of court (*Financial Times*, 17 June 2003).

The Eurostat affair was uncomfortably reminiscent of the financial scandals which unseated the Santer Commission. Once again the Commission was forced by external events to deal with a scandalous situation which had existed for some years, but been brushed under the carpet. And once again the concerns raised by relatively junior officials (van Buitenen in 1998, Schmidt-Brown in 2003) had been dismissed by senior management. The main difference was that as soon as the Eurostat story broke, Commissioner Kinnock took decisive action to deal with it, rather than attempting to cover it up. He also tightened up the reporting procedures which had failed, and he strength-ened the position of whistle-blowers. The measures taken in the wake of the Eurostat affair, summarised in the Commission's report on the completion of the reform mandate (Commission 2004, 14-20) include the following:

–   Commissioners to be informed twice a year of the results of all audits, whether carried out by the Directorate's own auditors, the central Internal Audit Service, OLAF or the Court of Auditors, and the follow-up action taken on them;

–   Code of conduct governing relations between Commissioners and their services revised to include a specific procedure for informing Commissioners of all questions arising from management, espe-cially financial management, which could call into question their responsibility;

–   A new group set up, comprising the President of the Commission and the Commissioners responsible for personnel and financial administration, assisted by an inter-service group comprising the Secretary General, relevant DGs and the Heads of both Internal Audit and the Legal Service, to be informed of all allegations of fraud, irregularity and other reprehensible acts and action taken on them, and to report where necessary to the whole College;

–   The Head of the Internal Audit Service to chair meetings which will receive all reports completed by the Internal Audit Capabilities in the DGs, and to summarise important findings, recommendations and actions taken twice a year;

–   Whistle-blowers, who already have a duty to inform their own senior management or OLAF or the Secretary General, to have the right, after allowing a reasonable period for them to take appropri-ate action, to address such information to the President of the Court of Auditors, the European Parliament, the Council or the Mediator. Staff who have identified themselves as whistle-blowers to be pro-tected from hostile reactions and adverse consequences for their career, if necessary by being moved to another department.

These are significant improvements in the procedures for dealing with adverse audit findings and in the protection afforded to whistle-blowers. It is encouraging to see evidence of the Commission learning from its failures, despite the sound of stable doors being slammed after the horses have bolted. But it is disappointing that the need for such further reforms should be precipitated by another financial scandal four years into the life of a sup-posedly reforming Commission. The whole sorry tale bears witness to the continuing strength of the cultural and institutional barriers to reform, and raises questions concerning the likely impact of the reform programme.

The accounting system

A second major area of financial reform concerns the Commission's accounting system. As part of its reform programme the Commission appointed a new accounting officer, the official responsible for overseeing the Commission's accounts and payments. It appears that Marta Andreasen was appointed by Budget Commissioner Michaele Schreyer, in January 2002, against the advice of the appointing committee and without full exploration of why she had been suspended from a similar post with the OECD in 2000. The appointment was not a success. The Commission needed someone who would buckle down to the complex and difficult task of improving the Commission's accounting systems. However, Andreasen was a broad brush campaigner. She concluded almost immediately that the Commission's Sincom accounting system was vulnerable to fraud and could not be cured by anything less than the introduction of commercial standards of double-entry book-keeping, which are not the norm for government accounting. She very soon found herself at loggerheads with Jean-Paul Mingasson, Director General of the Budget department for fifteen years. According to a memorandum from Audit Office Head Jules Muis to Neil Kinnock, written in May 2002 but leaked to the newspapers in March 2003, Muis had encountered a 'deep state of denial' about the quality of the Commission's accounting systems. Mingasson had apparently told the Court of Auditors that 'he did not see the need for any accounting system at all' (*Financial Times*, 11 and 13 March 2003). Faced with what Muis described as an 'intrinsically hostile work environment', Andreasen took her concerns to the Commission President, then to the Court of Auditors and members of the European Parliament. But the impatience with which she proceeded laid her open to charges that she had breached the Staff Regulations by making her concerns public without first exhausting the internal procedures open to her. She was suspended after eight stormy months in the job, having attended a press conference organised by a critical MEP in London, but failed to attend a disciplinary hearing.

Andreasen was replaced in January 2003 by Brian Gray, who joined the Commission from the Court of Auditors in 1993. Gray had a strong track record of reducing the error rate in the administration of both Agricultural and Structural Funds, two of the largest areas of Commission expenditure. Mingasson was also moved, becoming Director General for Enterprise, and subsequently given Special Adviser status. The Andreasen affair was an unwelcome year-long distraction from the unglamorous hard work to equip the Commission with a reliable modern accounting system. However, it did increase the pressure on the Commission to establish a modernisation programme leading to the introduction of full accrual accounting by 2005, as required by Articles 125 and 181 of the new Financial Regulation, entailing, among other things, the replacement of Sincom (COM(02)755 of 23 December 2002). Such complex projects are notoriously difficult, but the Commission claims to have introduced its accrual based accounting system both on time, at the beginning of 2005, and within budget (COM (2005) 90).

The management of contracts

The third major reform concerns the management of contracts. This was an area of management much criticised by the CIE (CIE II, chapter 2). Partly as a consequence of the rapid increase in the Commission's responsibilities since 1992 and the reluctance of the Commission to request, or the Council to grant, additional staffing resources to manage the work properly, two strategies had been developed to cope with the workload. The first was the system of mini-budgets. These used the operational part of the budget (Part B) to hire staff for tasks normally performed by the Commission's own staff under the administrative part of the budget (Part A). 'Experts' and 'consultants' are frequently and legitimately hired under contract to carry out technically limited tasks, but many of the 'experts' hired under mini-budgets found themselves managing expenditure programmes for the Commission, committing the Commission in contracts with outside firms, and generally performing tasks of a public service nature which should be performed by the Commission's own staff. In certain areas of the Commission, this practice created quasi-private personal administrations (Spence 1997a, 78). Between 1993 and 1998, some 1,830 posts were created to absorb the additional staff hired in this way.

As the mini-budgets abuse was brought under control, the scale of a similar device relating to the use of Technical Assistance Offices (TAOs) grew to the point where these were estimated to represent the equivalent of approximately 1,000 staff. TAOs could take many different forms. In practice they were simply a name given to the Commission's contractors. There was inadequate control over the contracts. As with mini-budgets, TAOs were sometimes entrusted with tasks, such as assessing tenders, managing contracts, supervision and payment of work done, which should properly have been carried out by the Commission's own staff, if the Commission were to provide the assurance that Community resources had been used with due regularity and propriety. The loopholes in the system were vividly exposed by the accounts of mismanagement in the first CIE report (e.g. the Leonardo Programme) and by the court case investigating Claude Perry's involvement in the Commission's humanitarian aid programme. Perry was a contractor to the Commission, who described himself as a shadow boss, 'working for that "old whore", as we call the Commission' (Stevens 2001, xxi-xxii). If the mini-budgets did much to undermine the integrity of the Commission's formal recruitment policies, the TAOs must bear a similar responsibility for undermining the integrity of the Commission's financial management.

The CIE took the view that the fault lay not so much with the TAOs as such as with the contractual relationships under which they provided services to the Commission. The CIE thus made fifteen recommendations concerned with tighter contract management and the framework of control required by the Financial Regulation. They recognised the increase in the range and scope of the Commission's management tasks, and the need to employ external resources to carry them out. In particular, they insisted that public service responsibilities must never be entrusted to TAOs, and that authorising officers should be appropriately resourced both to draw up sound contracts and to monitor their execution. They therefore suggested the creation of a new category of Commission executive agency to take on such tasks. The Commission seized on this latter suggestion as a means to bury the discredited TAOs. It moved rapidly both to reshape the Financial Regulation in the way recommended by the CIE, and to establish the new form of agency, not least as a vehicle for the management of its external aid programmes, some of which (e.g. ECHO) had been particularly criticised.

The White Paper of March 2000 identified three types of externalisation –

delegation, decentralisation and subcontracting. Decentralisation related to tasks manageable by networks of national bodies. Effective and financially secure delegation required the definition and creation of a new type of executive agency. The scope of subcontracting needed to be strictly defined to avoid any recurrence of the problems identified by the CIE. A Planning and Coordination Group for Externalisation developed the necessary guidelines and draft legislative measures during 2000 and 2001. This was too late for the first draft of the Financial Regulation, sent to Council and Parliament in July 2000, but its final version, adopted two years later as Regulation 1605/2002, was able to include a legal framework for the new executive agencies and appropriate provisions to govern subcontracting. The main Financial Regulation was followed in December 2002 by the necessary implementing regulations and a separate statute for the new breed of implementing agency (Regulation 58/2003).

Meanwhile the Commission's international aid activities were totally restructured after 1st January 2001 under a new organisation called EuropeAid. Its programme management responsibilities were to be progressively delegated to the Commission's Delegations in the countries where the programmes were being carried out as soon as this could be accomplished within the terms of the new Financial Regulation. Management of the Community's aid programme is a critically important aspect of the Commission's financial stewardship. It accounts for more than 60 per cent of all directly managed expenditure (€5.3bn from the Community budget plus €4.3bn through the European Development Fund in 2000), with the involvement in 2000 of some 80 Technical Assistance Offices (Commission Communication of 16 May 2000).

The Commission has undoubtedly embraced a radical and thoroughgoing programme of financial reform. In its Annual Report for the financial year 2003 the Court of Auditors noted the positive impact of the Commission's reform of its internal control system on the legality and regularity of its own directly managed operations (CA 2004a, 12-14). However, two issues remain. First, will financial reform be implemented with the continuing commitment and resources required? The Court of Auditors noted that 'progress is still required in terms of actual implementation'. Second, even when implementation is complete, how successful will the reforms be in changing a culture inclined to regard financial management as a series of irritating hoops to be jumped through, rather than a valued safeguard for the highest standards of probity and accountability? In the case of indirect centralised management (e.g. the research programmes) or decentralised management (of external actions, such as the aid programme), the Court remarked that 'a greater effort must be made to apply the supervisory systems and controls in an effective manner'. There were long delays in tackling the allegations of mismanagement and fraud before they came to light at Eurostat in the summer of 2003, and troubling cases of fraud continue to come to light in the administration of the EU's humanitarian and development aid programmes, as noted for example in OLAF's annual activity report for the year ending June 2004 (OLAF 2004). Since the reform programmes were put in place, Parliament has not had grounds to refuse the discharge of the Commission's budget, as it did to such dramatic effect at the end of 1998, but these examples suggest that there is still some way to go before they would be justified in relaxing the watchfulness which precipitated the crisis that engulfed the Commission in 1999. A sober warning was delivered by Jules Muis, the Commission's widely respected Head of Internal Audit, when he announced his early resignation. He reckoned that he had achieved only '40% of what I wanted to do, and all of it has been uphill' (*Economist*, 9 August 2003).

Personnel management

The Commission's formal proposals for the amendment of the Staff Regulations were not ready to go to the Council until April 2002, and were finally adopted only in March 2004 (Reg. 723/2004), in each case some two years later than the corresponding stages in the reform of the Financial Regulation. They entered into force on 1 May 2004, to coincide with the enlargement of the European Union from 15 to 25 Member States. The longer gestation period was partly because much less progress had been made under the Santer Commission, particularly in its last year, and partly because changes to the Staff Regulations have to go through a lengthy process of consultation, first with staff representatives, and then with the inter-institutional staff regulations committee, before a formal proposal can be sent to Council and Parliament. Even then, although the legislation is not formally subject to the co-decision procedure, there is an extensive process of consultation and negotiation. Given the wide range of conflicting interests to be reconciled, these procedures are at best time-consuming, even if the proposals themselves are relatively innocuous.

In this case, the Commission's proposals were bound to be subjected to the closest scrutiny, bearing in mind that the most recent attempt to launch a radical reform of personnel management policies, the Caston Report of April 1998, had precipitated a widely supported strike and the establishment of a 'Reflection Group' under David Williamson. This produced a thoughtful report ranging widely across recruitment, career development and planning, promotion, discipline, training and mobility, but adopted a firmly traditional stance in relation to grading structures and the protection of more or less guaranteed career paths (Stevens 2001, 192-3). Guided by the principle of 'avoiding ill-conceived reforms aimed at increasing short-term "productivity" if there is a chance that they could jeopardise the long-term prospects for a motivated and efficient European civil service', the specific proposals of the Reflection Group were prefaced with a trenchant defence of the status quo as enshrined in the Staff Regulations and a ringing declaration that 'we do not need an administrative earthquake to achieve' the 'up-to-date procedures' which they did advocate (Commission 1998b, 10-13). In particular the Reflection Group, which recalled that proposals for a single-scale grading structure had been considered in the Commission between 1984 and 1988 and in an inter-institutional group in 1990, came down firmly in favour of keeping the existing system of four distinct staffing categories, whilst reforming the procedures for moving from one category to another (Commission 1998b, 30-32). They also dismissed any system of financial incentives or bonuses in the most categoric terms: 'Experience shows that in time all systems of this type, which are supposed to be flexible and adaptable in relation to individual merit, tend to become automatic and inclusive', though they did favour the use of non-financial incentives to motivate staff performance, including specifically 'increased responsibility and promotion, which should be based more clearly on merit than on age and seniority' (Commission 1998b, 59-60).

The Williamson Group's report put an end to any hope the Santer Commission may have had of launching a radical reform of the Commission's personnel management policies. Nor did the Parliament's Committee of Independent Experts offer much of a lead in its chapter on staff policy, which advocated an in-depth reform, but concluded that 'what is really required is not an overhaul of the Staff Regulations, but simply correct application of the rules and principles set out therein'(CIE II, 92). With their focus on the financial scandals which had led to their appointment, they were more concerned to bring order into the Commission's extensive use of external staff to carry out functions which ought to have been controlled by the Commission's own established civil servants. The CIE therefore followed the Williamson Group in accepting the existing structure of grades and categories. Their report advocated the principle of rewarding merit, and called on the Commission to formulate a dynamic careers policy, but failed to recognise that this was almost impossible to achieve within a structure which brought most officials to the end of their career development prospects at the age of 50-55 (CIE II, 68), yet had a pensions system which was structured to discourage retirement before 60 and offered positive incentives to hang on to the age of 65 (Commission 1998a, 41-48). Whilst Williamson and the CIE had both contributed useful insights into the problems which faced the Commission in seeking to reform its personnel policies, building on similar reports going back many years, both continued to advocate the conservative approach which had been followed without success for many years. The earlier Caston report contained a range of more radical options, but had of course been disowned, and could not be put back on the table.

The events of 1998-99 presented Neil Kinnock with a starting position which was far from promising, but he managed to seize and hold the initiative, by using the political impetus behind the new Commission's reform agenda to force the pace and reopen the debate. Amidst a blaze of publicity and an intensive schedule of meetings with a wide range of stakeholders, Kinnock set out his first set of 21 objectives in December 1999. He followed this with a consultation paper sketching the broad sweep of his reform proposals in January 2000 and a White Paper on 1 March (Commission 2000). One of the reasons why the unions had been able to attract massive support for the 1998 strike was because the discussion of reform took place largely behind closed doors, allowing rumour and misinformation to flourish and be fed by inadequate information from management and a stream of jaundiced tracts from the unions. The strike was essentially about the lack of trust, which this situation had created, and part of the strike settlement was an agreement with the unions that direct communications should cease (Interviews, September 1999). Kinnock had a better understanding of the importance of good internal communications to the management of change. At his first meeting with the unions, he insisted on his right to communicate directly with all staff, and when one of the union representatives suggested that such direct democracy was dangerous, he 'went ballistic.' But his reaction was not merely an emotional outburst, however deliberate. He also took care to establish an effective internal communications strategy, which aimed to support the management of change by providing all staff with accurate, timely and extensive information throughout the reform process, sharply focussed on their legitimate concerns (Bearfield 2004). This left the unions much less room to exploit the climate of uncertainty and suspicion which had undermined reform in the past. Given the support of the leadership and the high profile of reform, the sheer pace and openness of these procedures enabled Kinnock to re-establish the control of the agenda which the Commission had lost to the unions in 1998, and then to the Parliament, and to maintain it throughout his tenure.

Section IV of the Reform White Paper (Commission 2000) outlined a human resources policy designed to emphasise merit in career development by replacing the four separate categories A to D into which staff had hitherto been recruited and managed (see chapter 6) with a unified grading structure. Within each grade, promotion would still be based on seniority, but there would be more grades than before, and promotion would depend essentially on merit rather than seniority. To make this work properly, staff would need clear job descriptions and objectives, and a much more rigorous, professional system of staff reporting on an annual rather than, as hitherto, on a biennial basis. The new staff appraisal system, known as the Career Development Review, was introduced in 2003. Each official is now assessed against three criteria: performance relative to objectives; demonstration of abilities; and conduct. Merit points are awarded on the basis of this assessment, up to a maximum of 20, with a target average of 14 for each Directorate General. These points accumulate over time, and when a given threshold is reached the individual is entitled to be considered for promotion. Management training is now compulsory for promotion to Head of Unit, as well as being required for all current managers at this level. At the other end of the performance scale, where promotion is held back because few merit points have been allocated, the intention is that the jobholder will be motivated to seek help through a process of dialogue with his or her reporting officer, leading to appropriate remedial action which may include training. If performance remains insufficient when these procedures have been exhausted, there are new procedures under Article 51 of the Staff Regulations, which may lead to dismissal or downgrading. These procedures are now distinct from those applying to disciplinary cases arising from allegations of serious wrongdoing, which have also been thoroughly overhauled. In the past the use of disciplinary procedures to deal with poor performance, described as tantamount to using a sledgehammer to crack a nut (Commission 2004h, 49), had proved so burdensome that only one official had ever been sacked on such grounds, and then only after nine years of legal debate, culminating in the European Court of Justice (Coull and Lewis 2003). These career development policies, based on a linear grading structure (see below) flew in the face of the Williamson Report's endorsement, only four months earlier, of the existing structure of four separate categories. This was sure to alarm the unions, but the White Paper was skilfully presented as part of the continuing programme of consultation. It would have been premature for the unions to reject this out of hand.

The unavoidable confrontation came to a head a year later following adoption by the Commission on 28 February 2001 of a package of proposals for personnel management reform. These were still based on the concept of a linear grading structure. Although further consultations were offered, the Commission insisted that these must now be conducted on the basis of the decisions adopted by the College, and could not go right back to basic reform principles. Following the 1998 precedent, a strike was called for 19 March, but there was not the same support as there had been three years earlier – a general assembly called by the unions to discuss the Reform White Paper in July 2000 attracted only 300 staff. So the strike was called off and the unions settled for a review in a group chaired by Niels Ersbøll, a former Secretary General of the Council of Ministers. The Ersbøll group was given only four weeks to complete its work, with a view to reaching agreement on proposals to be put to the inter-institutional staff regulations committee. In the event agreement was reached quickly on recruitment and disciplinary reforms, but it was the end of October before there was sufficient agreement on the grading structure to enable the Commission to finalise its proposals for the amendment of the Staff Regulations, and to take them to the next stage of consultation within the inter-institutional committee.

The new grading structure which emerged from this intensive negotiation, replaces the four old categories not with a single linear grading system as Kinnock had originally proposed, but with two overlapping function groups for administrators and assistants, situated on a linear single spine of 16 grades (see chapter 6). Although the adoption of two function groups might appear to be a concession to the unions' point of view, it is interesting to note that Caston had suggested 'a single career structure with two entry points, one at a junior training grade and the other at the present level of the 'A' category' (Commission 1998a, 22). The importance of management responsibilities is recognised by allowing Heads of Unit with responsibility for managing the work of others to be appointed at any level from grade 9 upwards (equivalent to former A6). In addition, at least two years of satisfactory management experience is now required for promotion to a more senior Head of Unit post at grades 12/13, equivalent to the old grade A4. Although the Commission accepted two groups rather than just one, with distinct but overlapping career paths, it will be considerably easier to move between the new Assistant and Administrator groups than it was between the four old categories. An internal attestation procedure opens the way for C and D grade staff to progress upwards within the new Assistant group, whilst transfers from the Assistant group to the Administrator group will be governed by a new Certification Procedure. Assistants in grade AST5 or above with good reports may be placed on a list which makes them eligible for a training programme, leading to written and oral examinations supervised by the European Personnel Selection Office (EPSO). If they pass these, the higher educational entry requirements which normally apply to candidates for appointment to the Administrator group are waived, and they are entitled to apply for Administrator posts (Staff Regulations Article 45a, and Commission 2004h, 30-31). One consequence of the new scheme is that new entrants will enter at lower grades and lower salaries than would previously have been the case for recruits to the former A and B categories. Promotion will occur when an official has accumulated sufficient merit points (awarded annually based on appraisal against a reasonably precise job description), to take him or her over the threshold level for the next grade. Officials will carry their accumulated points with them, thus removing one significant disincentive to mobility. Since the accumulation of sufficient points will take a number of years, the scheme is also intended to ensure a continued balance between merit and seniority. The points threshold for promotion will be determined annually depending on what the Commission can afford within its budget. Elaborate disincentives have been built into the system to discourage line managers from over indulgent appraisals or the competitive inflation of merit points. However, there are widespread allegations that managers are still tending to side-step the awkwardness of invidious comparisons by narrowing the range of points awarded to 13-15. Rigorous standards will have to be energetically defended if the system is not to slip back into the old habit of progression by seniority rather than merit, but since there are more grades than in the past, and therefore more promotions to be won in a successful career, the structure is potentially less automatic, and thus more competitive than before.

By October 2001 a complete package of amendments to the Staff Regulations, including proposals on pay and pensions, was agreed within the Ersbøll group by unions representing a 59 per cent majority of the votes cast at the elections to the joint union committees (Commission 2002, 62). The Commission evidently judged it necessary to do enough to secure the consent of the moderate centre represented by the Union Syndicale (US, centre left), which commands 48 per cent of the votes, and the Syndicat des Fonctionnaires Européens (SFE, centre right, 11 per cent), but declined to pursue a consensus to which all the unions could sign up (Georgakakis 2002). Such a consensus was probably unattainable in any event, since some of the other unions were formed as a result of divisions within US and SFE, defining themselves in part by their opposition to their former colleagues, and union elections, which would turn on attitudes towards the reform project, were due towards the end of 2002. Although Kinnock can take credit for successfully defending the essential features of his reform project, the unions could also derive considerable satisfaction from what they had achieved in the Ersbøll group. The extension of its deadline was itself an achievement, but of more significance was the fact that they managed to get the Williamson Report back on the agenda. The proposals for less automatic career progression within a unified or linear grading structure were at the heart of these negotiations. The retention of two distinct groups defined by educational qualifications, albeit with provisions for that requirement to be set aside on the basis of the certification procedure, was a significant concession from the original White Paper proposals, as were the detailed assurances on rates of promotion from one grade to the next, written into Annex I of the Staff Regulations, which allow the Commission to give staff the assurance that average career profiles under the new system will be equivalent to what was more or less guaranteed under the old system. Moreover there are generous transitional arrangements, guaranteeing staff at least the same pay rises as they would have received under the old grading system. The formal retention within the Staff Regulations of the procedure for agreeing annual pay increases (known as The Method) was also an important trophy for US to defend, since this was one of their major past negotiating achievements. The Ersbøll group also negotiated the detail of the significant improvements which have been made in the provisions for part-time working, maternity and paternity allowances, and other family-friendly policies.

Following further consultation within the inter-institutional staff regulations committee in January 2002, the proposals passed to the Council and Parliament at the end of April 2002. Political agreement was reached within the General Affairs Council in May 2003. The Council insisted on some reductions in pension benefits mainly affecting new recruits (see chapter 6), but viewed in the round, the package on offer was still sufficiently attractive to head off any serious strike action. The Parliament welcomed the proposals, but took time to comment in detail and to negotiate amendments of particular importance to its own staff. For example, Article 29.4 requires the Parliament to hold internal competitions at least once every five years to give permanent status to staff originally appointed on a temporary basis, whereas the other institutions, more concerned to close such loopholes in the recruitment procedure, are not bound to any such timetable.

There was a separate proposal for the establishment of a joint recruitment organisation, to be known as the European Personnel Selection Office. This was a sensible measure of professionalisation which had been under consideration since at least 1990. It was adopted by Council and Parliament in July 2002 (Decision 2002/620), partly under pressure to gear up the recruitment process for the appointment of 3,900 staff from the new Member States, but its position is also embedded in the new Staff Regulations.

While these measures were making their way through the legislative procedure, the Commission was implementing those reform proposals which did not require the prior alteration of the Staff Regulations. Prominent among these, alongside annual staff reports and the introduction of Activity Based Budgeting and Management, was the implementation of a programme of mobility. This applied not just at ordinary working level, where the volumes of staff in different parts of the Commission needed to be adjusted, but also at the highest levels, where Directors General had frequently remained in the same post for as many as ten years. Mingasson (DG Budget) and Franchet (Eurostat) had occupied their posts for 15 and 16 years respectively. A major shuffle of some twenty DGs took place in January 2003, and by the end of that year no Director General had been in the current post for more than five years. The shuffle also provided the opportunity to demonstrate that no Member State can plant its national flag indefinitely on a specific desk. At less exalted levels the expectation of mobility was reinforced by the establishment of benchmark time-limits for staying in any one job (two to five years) and the setting up of a career guidance function within the personnel and administration DG to assist officials to find satisfactory ways of moving. Mobility will remain voluntary, however, other than at the highest levels or in jobs designated as sensitive, for example because they involve the award of contracts or subsidies (Commission 2002, 9). For such posts, mobility is regarded as essential to avoid the development of unduly cosy relationships.

Finally, it should be noted that the reform of the Commission owes more than is sometimes admitted to those members of its staff, such as Paul van Buitenen and Dorte Schmidt-Brown, who had the courage to become whistle-blowers. Any large organisation, particularly one that feels that it has to fight for every scrap of its authority, prefers to wash its dirty linen in private. However, the experience of the past few years has obliged the Commission to make extensive provision for members of staff to disclose cases of wrongdoing.

Conclusion

The reforms of financial management and personnel management introduced since 1999 build on those which had begun under the previous Commission (see table 16).

Following the crisis of 1999, which made reform a key objective for the Prodi Commission, these reforms had the benefit of a stronger, more united leadership than at any time in the past, as well as the sharp focus and detailed analysis provided by the two CIE reports. The Santer Commission laid some of the foundations, particularly in respect of financial management, the CIE reports helped to point the way forward and the crisis of 1999 created a window of political opportunity. But even when due weight is given to these factors, the rapid pace and comprehensive scope of the Prodi/Kinnock reform programme remains impressive. The main legislative and procedural changes were all substantially complete in advance of enlargement (May 2004), so that the Commission which took office in November 2004 inherited an administration which, for the first time in fifty years, had a well-conceived and coherent, modern structure.

Some might argue that these reforms, which seek to remedy the long-standing weaknesses of the Commission's internal management, are insufficient because they do not address the larger management deficit relating to the Commission's potential role at the centre of policy networks steering the continuing evolution of European governance (Metcalfe 2000; 2004). However, the Commission can hardly aspire to play a leading role on the wider European stage unless and until it can demonstrate an assured capacity to manage its own affairs without waste or scandal. Inward-looking as they may be, the reforms undertaken by the Prodi Commission probably created a situation difficult to reverse to the haphazard informality of the pioneering spirit, which had survived for so long with all its charm and despite the attendant risks. On the other hand, the Eurostat affair reminded a sceptical public and Parliament that it takes a long time to inculcate a new culture. Kinnock argues that the culture of an organisation is formed by its systems and structures (Kinnock 2003; 2004), but those who have been accustomed to different and perhaps more comfortable ways of doing things will not necessarily change their behaviour just because they are faced with a new set of rules. Old habits die harder than that. It is only when the rules are rigorously and regularly enforced at all levels, and with effective sanctions, as seemed to occur rather belatedly in the Eurostat case, that an old culture will give way to a new.

The Commission made a determined effort to put its house in order after 1999. Kassim goes so far as to describe the reform programme as 'an extremely significant, even historic, accomplishment' (Kassim 2004, 58), but there are concerns about implementation, which Kassim recognises, and reform still has far to go before it can confidently be asserted that the new framework has permanently changed the culture. There are grounds for questioning whether the drive towards reform is sufficiently well rooted to

Table 16. *Reform at a glance*

	Pre-1995	1995-99	1999-2004
Policy and Resources	Policy and resource planning managed separately	From Budget 97, Commission lays down priorities and guidelines before DGs bid for resources	Strategic planning and programming cycle integrates activity based management and activity based budgeting
Financial Management	- budgeting managed centrally; - payments authorised by Services; - prior approval and payment of invoices administered centrally; - adversarial relations with Court of Auditors	SEM 2000 programme - Stages 1 & 2 (1995) strengthen internal financial management; - Stage 3 (1997) strengthens oversight of Community expenditure in member states; - enhanced fraud prevention under UCLAF (1995), OLAF (1999); - constructive relations with Court of Auditors	- new Financial Regulation adopted 2002; in force 1/1/03 - Services assume full financial responsibility; - enhanced Internal Audit Service - central financial service lays down rules, provides advice, monitors performance - Accounting system to be reformed by 2005 on accrual basis
Personnel management	- appointments, training, pay, pensions, allowances all centrally administered; - formal appointment procedures widely evaded; - promotion by seniority or national influence; - little mobility; - management regarded as a distraction from policy work.	Under MAP 2000 - from 1997, DGs begin to take responsibility for internal organisation, management of own staff and services; - but radical reforms (Caston Report) blocked by strike action (April 1998) leading to Williamson Report (Nov 1998)	- European Personnel Selection Office (EPSO) established 2002; - Staff Regulations amended March 2004; in force 1/5/04 - back door entry routes closed; - annual staff reporting links performance to promotion; - training required for management posts; - compulsory mobility at senior levels, and in posts with significant financial responsibility

survive the loss of impetus, following the departure of Commissioner Kinnock and his team (Levy 2003). After the enlargement competitions have run their course, how will recruitment on merit be managed satisfactorily across 25 Member States when it was already so difficult before enlargement? Another major challenge is the extent to which staff will be ready to implement the rigorous, and to some rather alien appraisal regime. But it is certain that promotion on merit will be a meaningless concept unless they do. Will Commissioners and their *cabinets* really be willing to allow their nationals to take their chances unaided in the promotion stakes, and will they cease to care on which desks their national flag has been planted? Will busy managers at all levels who have established convenient relationships with contractors, on which they have come to rely perhaps over many years, be willing to put all that at risk for the sake of a new managerial culture, particularly if the contractors concerned drop hints that they might have damaging stories to tell? As the Commission itself has acknowledged, reform is not so much an event as a process (Kinnock 2004, 9). The process is underway, but it will take many years to establish itself as the normal way to do things (Commission 2004, 22). The political imperative which favoured reform under the Prodi Commission, skilfully and energetically exploited as it was by Neil Kinnock, probably enabled the Commission to undertake as thorough a programme of reform as could reasonably be expected in such a complex multi-cultural organisation. Yet, it is too soon to be confident that the new and still fragile culture of management will have strong enough roots to survive and flourish. Under the Barroso Commission the responsibility for administration, audit and anti-fraud activities has passed to Siim Kallas, a former Prime Minister of Estonia. It will be no easy task to defend and carry forward the reforms which have been launched since 1999 in a Commission whose priorities will have more to do with absorbing the influx of ten new Member States than with responding to the reform imperative which loomed so large over the Commission which took office in 1999.

18. The Commission and crisis management

Arjen Boin, Magnus Ekengren, and Mark Rhinard

Introduction[1]

The prospect of unexpected threats from unpredictable sources is a growing source of concern for the modern state. The threat of military attack from clearly defined enemy states, especially salient in the Cold War era, has shifted to threats from non-state actors employing unconventional means to strike anywhere. Threats can also combine in new and dangerous ways: fundamentalists operating in war-torn states to produce biological weapons, computer hackers backed by rogue states wreaking havoc on international monetary systems, and criminal organisations capitalising on accidental catastrophes to extract profit and even territory (Solana 2004). Of course, threats arise not only from intentional and criminal sources. Natural disasters such as floods, forest fires, and earthquakes can also compromise public safety, territorial integrity, and the values a government purports to uphold.

The expanding array of threats over the past decade casts ample doubt over the ability of individual European states to manage such crises – and directs attention to the collective efforts of the European Union. Over the years, the EU has developed formal instruments and administrative capacities to deal with a variety of crises: from operating in conflict-torn countries to providing humanitarian assistance, and from assisting in civil protection emergencies to building alert systems for communicable diseases.[2] The EU is thus becoming increasingly involved in crisis management across the spectrum of policy sectors, threat sources, and emergency situations. If a flurry of policy papers and public pronouncements over the past few years is any indication, expectations of an even greater role for the EU in crisis management are on the rise.[3] Yet there has been little critical discussion regarding the EU's capacities to manage crises now and in the future.

Analysis of the EU's capacities to manage different crises must include the crisis management capacities of the European Commission. The Commission houses most of the EU's policy knowledge and supplies the bulk of the EU's bureaucratic functions. The Commission is a key participant in Pillar II (CFSP) and Pillar III (JHA) activities. It has participated in a range of actual crises, from the BSE crisis to Italian forest fires, and from civilian protection exercises in Macedonia to a military mission in the Democratic Republic of the Congo.

The following discussion examines the Commission's role in crisis management from a specific angle: research by crisis scholars, who argue that the fundamental issue at hand is not the nature of the threat or the type of crisis that can strike a society, but the organisational capacity of government to respond to those challenges. This approach fits well with the widening conception of threats in the EU, drawing attention away from the particulars of the threat source (although this is acknowledged as important) and towards government capabilities across an array of crisis management dimensions: preventing threats from materialising, preparing for potential crises, coping with them when they occur, and redressing the damage after a crisis. Through this analytical lens, the chapter examines the strengths and weaknesses of the organisational capacity of the European Commission to address crises throughout the EU policy portfolio.

The chapter first assesses the concept of 'crisis' and 'crisis management' in the field of crisis studies, applying those concepts to the EU by discussing what exactly entails a crisis for the EU and what values the EU claims to uphold. The chapter then reviews the Commission's experience in dealing with several recent internal crises in the EU and analyses the Commission's role in external crisis management, thereby providing the empirical foundation for the subsequent analytical discussion. The chapter juxtaposes the potential strengths as well as the institutional weaknesses that should inform any assessment of the EU's crisis management capacity and, more specifically, the Commission's role in this. The conclusion sets out some thoughts on future EU threat and crisis management.

Defining European crisis

News headlines regularly inform the public of an impending 'crisis' for or in the EU. In this chapter, we leave aside those 'crises' that signal simply moments of stress within the EU such as the 'crisis' over the Dutch and French referendum results on the Constitutional Treaty. In this chapter, the term 'crisis' pertains to widely perceived threats that require immediate response. The events of 11 September 2001 (New York and Washington), 11 March 2004 (Madrid), and 7 July 2005 (London) centred discussions of crisis management on the threat of terrorism, but terrorism is but one type of adversity. Other types of crisis have visited Europe in the past: public health scares, natural disasters, transport failures and factory explosions. What such crises have in common is not their origin but their effects: each crisis arose unexpectedly, stretched the organisational capacities of governments, and had to be dealt with under conditions of complexity and uncertainty (Rosenthal *et al.* 2001). And each required reflection on the instruments and arrangements to ensure better performance the next time around. At the national level of analysis, researchers speak of a crisis when the core values of a society are at stake and when immediate intervention is required to safeguard those values against threat. If a government cannot preserve and protect those core values, the underpinnings of its legitimacy will erode quickly and the central functions of government may become overloaded or even collapse.

This seemingly uncontroversial use of the term 'crisis' might not apply at the EU level. The unique character of the EU – neither a conventional government nor an international organisation – makes it hard to determine what constitutes a crisis for it and what should be described as its 'legitimate' core values.[4] The core values of the EU are far from self-evident. Judged by the *raison d'être* of European integration and the pattern by which the EU has accumulated policy competences, its values have continually shifted and evolved. In the 1950s and 1960s, a crisis for the European Community was a threat to cooperation, linked directly to the need for peace and stability. In the 1970s and 1980s, economic welfare and stability came to be perceived as a critically important value, one that underlay collective policymaking at the EU level. In the 1990s, the outbreak of war and violence in the Balkans was interpreted by EU leaders as a crisis worth addressing. The value of peace and stability in the 'near abroad' seemed to gain salience in relation to the EU's core goals. The result has been the creation and expansion of the European Security and Defence Policy (ESDP), including new decision-making organs and civilian crisis management instruments alongside military response groups. A threat or event that undermines this 'third value', peace and stability in neighbouring areas, thus also presents a potential crisis for the EU.

Finally, the events of 11 September 2001 sparked a reaction from EU governments that suggests an emerging fourth set of EU values. The 'solidarity clause' in the Constitutional Treaty (agreed in the wake of the Madrid train bombings in 2004) pledges an all-for-one response to 'protect democratic institutions and the civilian population' not only from terrorist attack but also from natural or man-made disasters (Art I-43).[5] Moreover a whole range of security and crisis management instruments, across the EU's three-pillar structure, are being put in place (Boin, Ekengren and Rhinard 2005; Jarlsvik and Castenfors 2004). In this great variety of EU instruments and practices, we can discern a new basic fourth EU value: the safeguarding of governmental and societal institutions. This is not just a matter of 'infrastructure' or traffic flows, but also about the ability to govern society and to articulate political goals effectively (Sundelius 2004). We might then speak of a crisis in and for the Union: when there is an urgent threat to the basic systems that enable European society to function (Ekengren 2004a).

An unresolved question is whether a fifth core value is emerging for the EU. Increasingly, the EU seems to be taking part in military and civilian missions far away from its borders, such as in the Democratic Republic of Congo (DRC). EU efforts to carve out a global security role indicate that underlying values are shifting even further. The potential crisis may threaten not just European citizens, or European neighbours, but be deemed to occur where human rights, 'universal values', and/or international law are being violated anywhere in the world. The EU's 2003 Security Strategy takes just such an approach, and ESDP missions can thereby be justified on the basis of keeping the peace, preventing conflict, and contributing to international security. Thus, events worldwide can be construed as a crisis for the EU, meriting political declarations, carrot and stick threats, sanctions and, since the creation of the ESDP, civilian and military intervention.

In short, the current spectrum of areas in which the EU governs, and in which a crisis might emerge, covers the gamut of a national government's typical responsibilities, ever since the Maastricht Treaty added to the EU competences in practically every policy field. The Charter of Fundamental Rights even explicitly includes values such as the 'protection of the fundamental rights, the right to life, physical integrity, liberty, security, freedom of thought'. The development of the EU has thus been marked by an expansion of its competence and a broadening over time of the set of values underpinning its activities – what is usually termed the *acquis communautaire*, plus what one might sensibly call the *acquis* of the other two Maastricht pillars. A crisis for the EU may be defined as an immediate threat to any of the resulting core values and policy competences, but just as the EU is in constant evolution, so the nature of its 'crises' is also subject to change.

The nature of future threats appears to be changing as well. The global context in which new threats emerge reflects societal, technical, and administrative innovations that bind countries together in ever-closer ways, while simultaneously enabling the rapid proliferation of crises. As a result, seemingly innocent failures in one system may rapidly snowball into others and gather destructive potential along the way. Removing borders increases economic efficiencies, but it also facilitates health epidemics or the free movement of terrorists. Faster computer systems improve service delivery and boost productivity, but also increase vulnerability to security breaches from within or outside the EU. And the same channels that move capital across the world in seconds can plunge entire regions into economic distress. Complex and intertwined systems allow crises to emerge in unpredictable ways. Preventing crises will thus be well-nigh impossible. Moreover, stopping an emerging crisis might involve a worrisome 'Catch 22': shutting down the basic functions of society to arrest an escalating crisis or having that crisis shut down those functions for you. So, European integration may have brought Member States economic dividends and peace, but, at the same time, 'ever closer union' has become vulnerable to these crises of the future.

If European leaders call on supranational authorities to take a more active role in dealing with these threats, what can the EU offer? The management of crises comprises a wide array of activities and substantial organisational, political and even societal capacity (Boin *et al.* 2005). Crisis management begins with attempts to prevent crises from materialising in the first place: the capacity to recognise emerging threats and 'nip them in the bud'. However, as many crises cannot be foreseen (or even imagined for that matter) preparation is crucial. Crisis preparation involves the difficult task of 'planning for the unknown' – a paradoxical mission in most governmental settings. When threats materialise, crisis management is usually understood in terms of making critical decisions, coordinating the actions of all those involved, and communicating to the public an explanation of 'what is going on.' When the threat has faded, crisis management enters the politically charged phase of recuperation, restoration and reform. This phase includes the delicate acts of learning the right lessons and rendering accountability to media and political forums. Crisis management thus comprises a wide variety of activities, policies and mechanisms – a variety that increases when we consider crises that find their origin outside the EU borders.

Managing crises within the EU

The following four cases allow us to see in practice the core values and policies the EU purports to uphold and the instruments used to do so. The Commission played a substantial role in each event.

BSE crisis

The so-called BSE crisis in 1996 comprised two related phases (Grönvall 2000, 2001). The first phase involved the threat to human health posed by tainted meat, including the closing of borders to British cattle and beef. The second was the breakdown of European decision-making processes that began in this phase and culminated in the British 'non-cooperation' policy in protest at EU actions.[6]

The first phase of the crisis followed the announcement by the UK government of a potential link between the animal and human forms of bovine spongiform encephalopathy (BSE) or 'mad cow disease.' The announcement caught other countries and the Commission by surprise. It ran counter to conventional wisdom in many of the EU scientific committees. Several EU Member States responded to the announcement by imposing unilateral bans, immediately closing their borders to British meat after little consultation with the Commission or in relevant EU committees.

The Commission found itself caught between conflicting pressures: the need to preserve the internal market against illegal import bans versus the requirement to protect consumers. The Commission turned to its Scientific Veterinary Committee (ScVC) of experts for advice. The committee's ruling on 22 March 1996 followed its earlier opinions on BSE: that it remained primarily a veterinary issue with insignificant implications for public health (Grönvall 2000, 57). From the ScVC perspective, the UK's measures to control the spread of BSE were sufficient.

The Council's Standing Veterinary Committee (SVC) took a contrary opinion. There, national experts viewed import bans as both legally and scientifically necessary, backing those countries concerned about the public health risks of BSE. Communication between these two expert groups was very poor, with the ScVC's deliberation records not released to the SVC in the early stages of the crisis (Grönvall 2000, 89). Further, Commission efforts to reassure European citizens by releasing expert opinions merely led to more confusion and concern when such opinions conflicted. Facing pressure from powerful Member States such as France and Germany, the Commission ignored the advice of its own expert group and proposed a provisional ban on British beef on 23 March 1996. The two UK Commissioners lodged protests and drew the personal intervention of the British Prime Minister. With the proposal on hold, the debate turned into a technical discussion amongst contending scientists and experts (Grönvall 2000, 87). After six more days, and despite UK pressure, the SVC affirmed the proposed ban and the Council of Agriculture Ministers adopted it on 1 April 1996.

The second phase of the crisis shook the political foundations of the EU. In early May 1996, the Commission proposed to lift the ban on non-consumable beef products from the UK (gelatine, tallow, and bull semen), a ban Commission officials admitted was a mistake made in the heat of the earlier crisis phase (Grönvall 2000, 67). Another round of technical debate followed, with the result that neither the SVC nor the Council of Agricultural Ministers could reach agreement. In the absence of agreement, the decision was referred back to the Commission. Legally required to take a decision, the Commission was forced to lift the ban against the wishes of six Member States. The UK was nevertheless incensed by the continuing lack of support from its EU partners and the consequent collapse of its beef market. The government retaliated by imposing a 'non-cooperation' policy against the EU institutions. British officials strategically blocked an array of Council decisions, while simultaneously launching proceedings against the Commission in the European Court of Justice. Only in late June 1996 was the ban lifted. It took a change of government in the UK in 1997 to fully repair relations.

Dioxin scandal

Dioxin, a toxic substance with serious human health risks, was discovered in Belgian chicken products in April 1999. Yet it was not until 27 May 1999 that the Belgian government officially notified EU authorities of the contamination of poultry, eggs, and derived products. The delay in notification annoyed EU officials and Member States alike, but the more serious problem was the perception by the Commission and the Council's SVC that Belgium had done too little to contain the spread of contaminated products. As news of the dioxin scandal spread within hours, countries outside the EU began closing their borders to Belgian poultry. Several tense days passed as EU Member States prepared to take similar steps (Olsson 2005).

The Commission ordered Belgian authorities to trace and destroy all poultry products with potential dioxin contamination. Unlike the BSE case, the speed with which the Commission responded to the dioxin scandal was largely achieved by bypassing the formal scientific consultation process. The Commission mostly ignored its own ScVC and relied on the tacit support of the Council's SVC to support its swift response (Olsson 2005). As evidence of additional contamination emerged, the Commission issued more measures to the Belgian government in a bid to prevent tainted bovine and pork products from reaching markets. The Belgian authorities complied with the initial requests but balked at the subsequent demands. They viewed the Commission as 'overreacting', especially on measures concerning milk and products derived from milk (such as chocolate, see Olsson 2005). To verify suspicions that the Belgians were not doing enough to limit the crisis, the Commission sent its own inspection teams and devised its own tracking system for Belgian foodstuffs. By June a new government took office in Belgium and agreed to implement fully the Commission's measures.

The 'Prestige' accident and floods in Central Europe

In 2002, the EU experienced two classic disasters. Its response to both was based on a newly created Community mechanism for civil protection. The floods in Central Europe occurred in the summer of 2002, affecting 40 percent of Czech territory, while 6 percent was completely inundated. In Prague, 50,000 residents required evacuation. On 13 November 2002, the *Prestige*, a 26 year-old single hull tanker carrying 77,000 tons of heavy fuel oil, began leaking off the coast of Spain. Six days later the tanker split open and sank, causing major environmental damage and polluting more than 2,000 km of Spanish and French coastline. The spill also had disastrous economic consequences on fishing and shellfish industries in the area.

Spanish authorities informed the Commission's civil protection unit in DG Environment when the *Prestige* first began leaking (Ekengren 2004b). Through the Monitoring and Information Centre (MIC) – the office used to coordinate requests and mobilise Member State experts and equipment at short notice – the Commission acquired information on the extent and pace of the oil spill. Spain requested the Commission to identify and mobilise resources in France, the Netherlands and the UK that could be used for the cleanup operation. The Commission turned to its database on experts and equipment in various EU Member States and issued a general call for assistance. Further, a Community task force was planned for the event of explicit authorisation by the Spanish authorities. The Czech authorities had taken longer to make a formal request to the Commission's civil protection unit, and even had to be encouraged to do so. But, DG Environment's MIC functioned as a focal point, linking Czech requests for help with offers of assistance from EU Member States (Ekengren 2004b).

Since the use of the Community mechanism is voluntary, the Commission could not force Member States to provide assistance, nor could it control the types of resources ultimately provided. But, overall, the Commission experienced few problems in allocating resources in the aftermath of both crises. Special emergency measures made resources available to help Galician fishermen survive the economic fallout of the *Prestige* disaster. And in the flooding case, the Commission reallocated money from the EU structural funds and pre-accession budgets to flood-stricken areas.

Managing crisis outside the EU

Crises that occur outside the EU can also undermine core values the EU professes to uphold in its neighbourhood and as a global actor committed to effective multilateralism and universal principles. To be sure, it is not always immediately clear which external crises constitute a potential threat to EU values. ESDP is an emerging policy area, and though it does harbour spoken and unspoken implications for crisis intervention, there is a 'loud silence' on the geographical extent of the EU's readiness to respond. It is unlikely that the EU will respond everywhere when a situation abroad conflicts with EU 'core values' such as peace and stability, and human security and rights. But, there will, on occasion, be a resort to crisis response mechanisms in response to man-made threats to international security or natural disasters abroad.[7]

Natural catastrophes abroad: the case of the earthquakes in Turkey

On 17 August and 12 November 1999, Turkey was hit by two earthquakes measuring 7.8 and 7.2 on the Richter scale. The first killed 18,000 people and injured another 40,000. The second killed 790 people while 5,000 were injured. The heavy toll on life and property, along with Turkey's geo-political position in the EU's 'backyard', prompted EU action. The Commission's Humanitarian Aid Office (ECHO) took the lead, dispatching a handful of experts to the site and releasing material and financial aid totalling €60 million. ECHO made the decision to act within hours of the first earthquake, in the absence of detailed information about the humanitarian consequences of the disaster (Ramberg 2005). Relying on routine procedures and practices for the dispersal of aid, ECHO issued a call to international organisations (IOs) and non-governmental organisations (NGOs) for funding proposals. By 'lunchtime' on the day of the first earthquake, the Commission's first aid package of €2 million was approved (Ramberg 2005). ECHO used an inter-service process involving a decision mechanism available in times of acute crisis for the dispersal of aid below €10 million.[8] The second earthquake brought additional aid, with €3 million approved in the immediate aftermath of crisis and a further €30 million transferred from other budgets (namely DG External Relations) to ECHO for use in Turkey (Ramberg 2005).

ECHO does not implement humanitarian assistance itself. It relies on bids proposed by other IOs and NGOs. In the case of the Turkish earthquakes, the lack of agencies on the ground in Turkey meant that ECHO had to rely upon the International Federation of the Red Cross (IFRC) as the main recipient of funds. It maintained close contact with the UN Office for the Coordination of Humanitarian Affairs (UN-OCHA) and the Council of Europe's Agreement on Major Hazards (EUR-OPA). But crisis management from a distance has its drawbacks. For instance, ECHO had virtually no contact with NATO's Euro-Atlantic Disaster Response Co-ordination Centre (EADRCC). Despite over-lapping membership and competences, ECHO and the EADRCC were unaware of similar contributions to the relief effort, and the emerging EU-NATO relations within the ESDP were neither designed nor structurally receptive enough to entertain coordination.

In 2005, in the aftermath of the Turkish earthquakes and tsunami disaster, the Commission presented a proposal for a Council Regulation establishing a Rapid Response and Preparedness Instrument for major emergencies, planned to enter into force in 2007. The regulation will apply to preparedness for emergencies regardless of their nature. It develops the Community mech-anism for civil protection intervention assistance by providing Community financial assistance to support and complement the civil protection efforts of Member States.[9] The Commission has also proposed a package of measures to reinforce the EU's own disaster response capacity. The package will fund new specialist planning teams to strengthen the effective delivery of long term aid, strengthen the civil protection mechanism by setting up standby national teams for European responses to major disaster, and improve the delivery of humanitarian aid, by doubling ECHO field experts (in health, water, sanita-tion, provision of food, shelter and housing) by up to 150. The experts, located in 30 ECHO field offices worldwide, will be organised in multi-sector rapid response teams ensuring that the Union can provide immediate civil protec-tion assistance when disaster strikes.[10] The proposals can be seen as a further tool to protect both the fourth and the emerging fifth core value of the EU, i.e. the protection of EU citizens, but also the defence of human security wherever it is threatened.

Man-made crises outside the EU: the European Security and Defence Policy

The EU's first independently launched military operation, Operation Artemis in the Democratic Republic of Congo in 2003, was carried out at the request of the UN (Chapter VII)[11], a practice likely to set a precedent for future ESDP operations. 'EU security' as a core value might increasingly refer to all humans in grave international crisis.[12] The evolving security role of the EU might perhaps best be characterised as a regional body for the implementation of UN decisions. In that case, Union crisis would – in the global context – equal international crisis (Ekengren 2005). This would make it even more urgent to answer the question of the nature and geographic focus of crises where Union crisis management resources should be used.

Whatever the definition in principle, the Commission can play a role in the management of crises that occur outside the EU and are considered a threat to Union values. The EU may consider intervention justified on humanitarian grounds (the so-called Petersberg tasks) and involvement of the EU will usually result from its political role and operational experience in emergency relief, political stabilisation, post-conflict reconstruction and institution build-ing. This notion of 'civilian crisis management' developed in response to the growing understanding that military intervention in the case of failing states, or states involved in or emerging from violent conflict, was unlikely to be suc-cessful unless accompanied by the rapid re-establishment of economic activity and the creation of structures for civil administration, police and the administration of justice. This realisation led the Feira European Council in 2000 to conclude that the EU needed to develop civilian capabilities to balance its build up of military capabilities. Concrete goals were set in the four priority areas of police, rule of law, civilian administration and civil protection. The new capabilities are complementary to the existing EC instruments for the delivery of aid and are separate from the mechanisms foreseen for the man-agement of crises within the territory of the EU, despite the fact that these are increasingly believed capable of playing a key role outside the EU as well. The new crisis management capabilities represent a relatively minor contribution in financial terms, but a highly significant one to the Member States in politi-cal terms.

The Commission originally took the view that all areas of civilian crisis management – except the deployment of Member States' policemen in execu-tive functions – fall within existing Community competences. However, such a position proved politically untenable. Member States and the staff of the High Representative (see chapter 14) regard much of the decision-making in the field of 'civilian crisis management' as falling under the ESDP. A clear definition of civilian crisis management remains lacking and this may exacer-bate the functional tension between the Council and Commission (see below). The latter fears that the former may impose what the Commission believes to be the rigidity of CFSP decision-making on significant areas of Community external relations activity. The Commission also worries that the Council will fail to consider the contribution of the Community pillar and the available human, technical and material resources that the Commission harbours. The coherence of EU action is thought to suffer when the analysis of crisis situa-tions is divorced from the long-term political, trade and economic assistance relationships managed by the Commission. The unanimity requirement of CFSP is thought less effective than the Community method, adding to the Community's reservations with regard to the potential proliferation of over-lapping administrative structures.

In response to these challenges, the Commission has attempted to improve the quality of its crisis response assistance, both by proposing better legisla-tive and budgetary arrangements, and by developing a well-resourced spe-cialist service to deliver crisis management assistance. It has promised to be more responsive to the priorities of the Council in crisis management, and more forthcoming with information on its political analysis of situations of potential crisis and its programme priorities.

A widespread view, and one supported by concerned Commission officials, is that conflict prevention is a particularly important policy dimension. Conflict prevention lies at the intersection of development and security agendas and hence cuts across the Community/CFSP distinction. The Commission has direct responsibility in many areas: development cooperation and external assistance, trade policy instruments, humanitarian aid, social and environmental policies, cooperation with international partners and NGOs, as well as instruments in the field of crisis management and full association in the new instruments of ESDP.[13]

The Commission has seen a shift in attention to areas such as security sector reform and disarmament, demobilisation and reintegration, and to early warning and rapid reaction arrangements. It has established a 'Rapid Reaction Mechanism' in the form of a financial facility that provides for fast payment of civil crisis management missions. It uses conflict indicators to identify risk factors in each partner country and to systematise the information that already exists within the Commission and its delegations. It performs so-called Country Conflict Assessments for more than 120 countries and keeps an EU 'watch-list' of the most critical countries or regions.[14] As to practical mechanisms in the external sphere, there is both cooperation and rivalry with the Council Secretariat's crisis management mechanisms. Clearly, military mechanisms are irrelevant to this discussion of civilian crisis response.[15] As to the purely civilian mechanisms, duplication is obvious – both with the Commission's various crisis response mechanisms and the Council Secretariat's Situation Centre.

The Commission's Crisis Room facilitates initial reactions to a variety of threatening events (such as terrorism incidents, acts of war, and natural emergencies). It produces open source intelligence for the RELEX family of DGs, using a web-based information resource system called Tarîqa, which offers internal capacity for early warning and analysis in the security field.[16] In crisis situations, the Room is the sole entry point for the flows of information between the Commission and the Council's SITCEN.[17] In addition to these coordination and communication tasks, risk analysis is at the core of the Crisis Room activities.[18] The Room gathers and analyses all Country Conflict Assessments, producing risk rankings of priority countries. The Crisis Room has also created a network of country specialists and experts in disciplines such as geopolitics, trafficking, Islamic studies, terrorism and political violence.

Developing EU crisis management capacity: potential and constraints

The above examples of crises and crisis management tools shed light on the EU's capacity to manage adversity. Detailed analysis illuminates the potential role the Commission may play, but it also highlights the constraints operating on the Commission. The Commission holds the bureaucratic capacity and institutional position needed to assist in crisis management. At the same time, internal coordination problems, institutional rivalries, and national-supranational divisions in approaches to crisis management constrain what the Commission can do. This section explores these themes in more detail.

The Commission's potential to manage crises

The Commission may be a small bureaucracy by national standards, but its evolved competences and its supranational vantage point give it considerable potential to observe and report on emerging crises at the European level. Competences vary widely: in some sectors the Commission can only issue reports and advise Member States (e.g. healthcare provision or defence contracting) whereas in others the Commission takes day-to-day decisions in market management (e.g. agriculture). Yet virtually all of the Commission's sectoral responsibilities involve some degree of information collecting, trend mapping and risk monitoring. Its transnational focus, monitoring developments across territorial borders, gives it potential to catch 'creeping crises' that national authorities might miss. While not created or engineered explicitly for crisis management, these responsibilities are nonetheless as critical to preventing crises as they are to crisis management itself.

In some sectors, such as agriculture, transport and monetary policy, a permanent process of information collection and analysis is required. Member States tolerate and even encourage the Commission's role because it both provides a useful service and does not conflict with national decision making. Since the Commission has historically played this key role in tracking trends and notifying national and EU policymakers of potential disturbances, it has little difficulty in justifying its role. The centrality of monitoring and surveillance to effective policy management is clear to most Member States. Another potential strength of the Commission role in European crisis management is its ability to make swift decisions. This may seem counter-intuitive but the cases above demonstrate the potential, under some conditions, for the Commission to shortcut tedious decision-making processes. Quasi-agencies such as ECHO can even rely on standard operating procedures to trigger a fast response during acute crises. Of course, the Commission's ability to make use of these procedures ultimately depends on the consent of Member States, but the potential is worth noting with an eye to future developments.

The sectoral character of the Commission's crisis management capacity has been a weakness in cases of crisis that span several issue areas. The idea of a central crisis centre in the Commission is gaining ground. It would bring together representatives of all Commission services in an emergency (see above). The Commission is establishing Argus – a new coordinating system – as a logistical interface that will ensure rapid information flow between all existing Commission emergency rapid alert systems (listed in table 17) aimed at maximising safety and security (although not those concerned with ESDP). Given the ambiguity at times as to the source of the incident (terrorism related or not?) the scope of the system cannot be restricted purely to the terrorist threat. The Crisis Centre would co-ordinate efforts and practical options for action and decide the appropriate response. There will be a system of uniform risk assessment based on Member States' threat assessments, capabilities, training, joint exercises and operational plans for civilian crisis management.[19]

The Commission's de jure autonomy from intergovernmental forces and national interests offers additional potential benefit. Member States have been willing to grant the Commission institutional latitude in order to prevent policy capture by one set of national interests and empower it as an honest broker and enforcer (Majone 1996). Crisis management can benefit from such independence, given the tendency of individual governments to focus on national interests rather than the European whole. Indeed, its independence might justify granting the Commission additional policymaking powers in crisis management, though questioning Member State control in today's climate is risky at best.

Finally, the Commission offers potential capacity in one area of crisis management, often neglected, which becomes important only after the flashpoint of crisis has faded. The ability to 'learn' from past crises and institute new plans and procedures is a crucial part of comprehensive crisis management, even if it proves highly problematic for most organisations (Boin *et al.* 2005). Yet the Commission does appear to learn from past crises. Its response to the dioxin scandal, for instance, revealed that officials were keen to avoid a repeat of the delay and infighting that characterised the BSE crisis. New procedures implemented in the aftermath of the event were used to accelerate EU response times in the dioxin crisis. In addition, new plans are in place in such DGs as Consumer Protection and Public Health as a response to perceived failings in the past. And the assignment of crisis management responsibilities to several of the new EU agencies attests to some degree of learning in light of past crises (Boin, Ekengren, and Rhinard 2005).

Learning is, of course, not just an altruistic endeavour. The Commission is keen to showcase problems as a strategy for accruing more policy competence. And Member State coalitions sometimes propose new European policies to assure domestic publics that governments are 'doing something' to solve pressing issues. The result over time has been the incremental accumulation of crisis management capacities, occasionally punctuated by major new initiatives, across the Commission's policy sectors.

Constraints on the Commission's crisis management capacity

The Commission's present and future organisational capacity to manage crises is significantly constrained by three institutional features. First, the pattern of bureaucratic politics that characterises intra-Commission communication and cooperation processes impinges upon its capacity to coor-

Table 17: *Commission Emergency Rapid Alert Systems and information systems for crisis management**

EU Value	Policy Sector	DGs Involved in Crisis Management	Rapid Alert Systems
Securing Peace and Stability among the EU Member States			
The European Economy	Economic Affairs	DG Internal Market and Services (MARKT)	

Table 17. *continuation (1)*

EU Value	Policy Sector	DGs Involved in Crisis Management	Rapid Alert Systems
The European Economy	Economic Affairs	DG Trade (TRADE)	
The European Economy	Economic Affairs	DG Taxation and Customs Union (TAXUD)	**Customs Information System (CIS)**, (tool for customs' monitoring of criminal activities crossing the border). **Schengen Information System (SIS)** (system for monitoring of stolen goods and wanted persons used by both DG JAI and DG TAXUD).
The European Economy	Economic Affairs	DG Economic and Financial Affairs (ECFIN)	
The European Economy	Economic Affairs	European Anti-Fraud Office (OLAF)	**Anti-Fraud Information System (AFIS)**, (system for rapid exchange of information on fraud between member states).
The European Economy	Economic Affairs	DG Enterprise and Industry (ENTR)	
The European Economy	Energy and Transport	DG Energy and Transport (TREN)	**European Radiological Data Exchange Platform (EURDEP),** (system for exchanging information and monitoring environmental radioactivity). **European Community Urgent Radiological Information Exchange (ECURIE)**, (system with early warning and rapid information exchange function in case of emergency). Web tool named **ENSEMBLE** (tool for dealing with weather predictions that might appear in case of a radiological emergency). **Community Database on Accidents on the Roads in Europe, (CARE)** (system for monitoring accidents across the EU)
The European Economy	Agriculture and Rural Development	DG Agriculture and Rural Development (AGRI)	**'Crop yield forecasting system'** (used by DG AGRI but managed by DG JRC).
The European Economy	Fisheries and Maritime Affairs	DG Fisheries and Maritime Affairs (FISH)	
The European Economy	Regional Policy	DG Regional Policy (DG REGIO)	
Securing Peace and Stability in the Neighbourhood	External Relations	DG External Relations (RELEX)	**Tarîqa** (internal platform for the production of Open Source Intelligence developed by the Commission Crisis Room)
	Enlargement	DG Enlargement (ELARG)	

Table 17. *continuation (2)*

EU Value	Policy Sector	DGs Involved in Crisis Management	Rapid Alert Systems
Protection of People and Society	Environment and Civil Protection	DG Environment (ENV)	**Water level forecast system (LISFLOOD)**, (used by DG ENV for monitoring floods but operated by DG JRC). **Common Emergency Communication and Information System (CECIS)**, (system for direct communication and information sharing between the Monitoring and Information Centre (MIC) and the designated contact points in the member states).
Protection of People and Society	Health and Consumer Protection	DG Health and Consumer Protection (SANCO)	**Early Warning and Response System (EWRS)**, (system for prevention and control of communicable diseases). **Rapid Alert System for Biological and Chemical Attacks and Threats (RAS-BICHAT)**. **Rapid Alert System for Food and Feed (RASFF)**. **Animal Disease Notification System (ADNS)**, (rapid alert system in the area of animal health). **Rapid alert system for veterinary controls (SHIFT)**, (system for health controls on imports of veterinary concern). **Rapid alert system for plant health (EURO-PHYT)**, (phytosanitary network on the interception of organisms harmful to plants). **Rapid alert system (RAPEX)**, (system for consumer health and safety focusing non-food aspects).
Protection of People and Society	Justice, Freedom and Security	DG JLS (Justice, Freedom and Security)	**Schengen Information System (SIS)**, (for detecting wanted persons and stolen objects). (A newer and more advanced Schengen Information System II (SIS II) is set to be operational in 2007.) Further steps in monitoring criminal matters in the Union will be taken when the **Europol Information System (EIS)**, a database on organised crime, starts running. **Europol Computer System (TECS)** (a database on suspected criminals and stolen goods). **Fingerprint database (EURODAC)**, (database with fingerprint files from all asylum-seekers to the EU over fourteen years of age and persons who are found to have illegally crossed an external border.)
Securing Universal Values	External Aid	ECHO (Humanitarian Aid Office)	**Early warning system (ICONS)** (system containing information on natural and man-made disasters.)
All values			A 'secure general rapid alert system' co-ordinating all the rapid alert systems for emergencies (**Argus**)

* Data from *Communication from the Commission to the Council and the European Parliament, Preparedness and consequence management in the fight against terrorism*, Brussels, 20.10.2004. COM(2004)701 final (p. 10) and Annex to Report, Boin, Ekengren, Rhinard, 2005.

dinate efforts across policy domains. Second, the institutional friction that exists between Commission and Council can be detrimental to any form of crisis management in the EU, since coherent, joint efforts of both institutions, the sine qua non of effectiveness, might remain elusive. Third, the asymmetric distribution of resources (and decision-making authority over these resources) between Member States and the Commission has consequences for Commission participation in crisis management operations. These crucial constraints require further review.

The tensions of bureaucratic politics

The Commission is without doubt a bureaucratic organisation (Christiansen 2001a; Peters 1992). Functional specialisation has led to Directorates General organised around well-defined policy fields and based on specialist knowledge. Consequently, fragmentation has emerged as a prevailing feature of this 'multi-organisation' (Cram 1994). Many of the activities identified as relevant to crisis management – mapping for potential disturbances, developing crisis plans, designing mechanisms for coordination – also take place along sectoral lines. Officials focus on known threats and disturbances to 'their' respective policy field, and work within networks similarly focused on 'their' issues. When it comes to coordinating resources and sharing information, the process can be incremental, slow and plagued by different 'policy styles' (Cram 1994) and perspectives (Christiansen 2001a).

However, the agents of crisis do not respect functional boundaries. To 'prepare for the unknown', the Commission needs to build capacity rapidly to combine specialist knowledge across its policy sectors. Coordination requires the flexible adaptation of multiple actors, and collective action based on shared outlooks and common values (Chisholm 1989; cf. Ekengren and Sundelius 2004). Yet, horizontal coordination mechanisms in the Commission are problematic on the best of days (Patterson 2000; Peters 1992). Policy formulation takes place within specialised units, which guard their role over policymaking as long as possible. Differing perspectives and outlooks persist throughout the policy process, and are reconciled only with the intervention of high-ranking officials and against the backdrop of rancorous debate. The risk that the effectiveness of crisis management in the EU might be shaped by bureaucratic politics in the Commission and its DGs is thus high. It is sometimes thought that a crisis automatically breaks down organisational walls; that it unifies the perceptions and incentives of policymakers. Yet, the contrary may well be the case: because crises revolve around core values, they may actually spark or deepen existing tensions within the organisation (Rosenthal, 't Hart and Kouzmin 1991).

Another feature of the Commission bureaucracy is the enduring tension between 'political' and 'bureaucratic' logics. Political elements of the Commission, especially high-ranking officials and Commissioners themselves, must be sensitive to political realities as well as their own professional survival. On the other hand, bureaucratic elements emphasise the benefits of standard operating procedures and prioritise technical policymaking and concomitant legal formalities. The resulting tensions are finely balanced during day-to-day policymaking (Hooghe 2003), but the onset of a crisis risks exposure of the tension in dramatic fashion. The perplexing uncertainty

caused by crises creates opposing strategies from both logics. The bureaucratic logic prescribes a return to standard operating procedures, whereas the
political perspective typically produces the rhetoric of change, creativity and
renewal. The BSE crisis showed how Commissioners can become caught up
in the politics of crisis management: the two UK Commissioners backed their
government's position against a ban, even when this conflicted with the collegiality principle in the College.

When making policy, large-scale bureaucracies must abide by complex
rules, which reflect historically rooted sensitivities and volatile environ-
ments. Bureaucracies are not designed to suspend their own rules, leave
routines behind and flexibly adapt to the contingency at hand. Unless they
experience multiple crises, their organisational culture is best suited to
incremental politics and policymaking. These commonplace reflections fit
the Commission style and it thus seems likely that an increased capacity to
manage crises would require substantial redesign of its institutional characteristics.

The tension of inter-institutional politics

The Commission's bureaucratic constraints may, however, prove of
slight importance compared with constraints arising from the relationship
between the Commission and the Council. Here, paradox and contradiction
in times of crisis are to be expected, since they exist already in the management of routine matters. Of the two institutions, the Commission commands
most of the expertise and resources for effective crisis management.
However, the Council is where political gravity shifts during an actual
crisis, and the longer and deeper the crisis, the more the role of the
Commission is likely to become constrained. This seemingly inevitable
development stems from the defining characteristic of crisis. Crises threaten
the underlying values of a society. Core values are defined through political
competition and politicians can be expected to uphold and defend them.
Yet, crisis prevention and preparation are often relegated to the techno-
administrative domains of governance, as opposed to the political. When an
actual crisis materialises, crisis management falls squarely within the political domain and thus to political crisis leaders (Boin *et al.* 2005).[20]

The BSE crisis illustrates this crisis-induced shift of gravity. In the initial
phases of the crisis, the Commission had room to employ a rather technical
problem-solving perspective, which flowed naturally from its bureaucratic
culture. As the crisis escalated, the Council became involved. The resulting
tensions between various bodies of expertise – a division that remained
incomprehensible to outside observers – fuelled further escalation of the
crisis. It was finally resolved within the Council (Grönvall 2001). Preparations
for future contingencies – imagine an attack with biological weapons or a
massive disturbance of transport systems – foreshadow a similar dynamic.
The Commission may be called upon to wield its expertise in preventing and
preparing for such contingencies, but when major crises do strike, the Council
is the likely arena for the most crucial decisions to be made.

The resulting institutional tensions and rivalries might be eased by
stronger attention to the complementary roles that both institutions can and
should play, an intuitive conclusion nevertheless belied by recent develop-

ments. Indeed, the perception that the Commission might have too much control over crisis management policies abroad has prompted the Council to place new initiatives within Pillar II, rather than the traditional Pillar I, where the Community method applies. Pillar II policymaking, in which the Commission tends to take a back seat to the Council, is thus the new home for the ESDP's civilian crisis management initiative. The Commission is thereby further distanced from EU crisis management abroad. The Council justifies such moves by the sensitive, political nature of crisis and security policies. Yet, by removing, rather than integrating, the Commission from future crisis management, the Council may be reducing the EU's aggregate capacity to deal with such crises. Significantly, however, as push comes increasingly to shove, the sheer weight of first pillar competences and their related crisis mechanisms may yet prove an insurmountable hurdle to the intergovernmental method and its proponents.

Arguably, there remains a critical space to be filled by an overarching crisis mechanism that would bring together the disparate response mechanisms in an inter-pillar jamboree. For the present, however, it is the case that foreign, security and defence policies merge at the level of the Council and crisis responses are guided by the Political and Security Committee (PSC), in which the Commission does participate, bringing to the toolbox of EU response the civilian instruments of the first pillar. These range from development policies to humanitarian emergency aid. Crisis response mechanisms in CFSP remain extremely few, and meaningful sharing of military intelligence remains rudimentary, despite considerable strides since the creation of ESDP in 2000. In addition, Member States continue to cultivate national crisis responses and effective European crisis management is hampered by the ability of Member States to prioritise between joint and unilateral action. As Tonra puts it:

> 'While path dependency may predispose Member States toward Union-centred policy-making and while they are obliged by treaty provision not to frustrate the creation or implementation of a collective policy, Member States nonetheless retain their sovereign rights. They therefore have the option of dealing with any particular crisis unilaterally, multilaterally (through other institutions such as the UN and NATO or through ad hoc coalitions), or collectively through the EU. This menu of crisis management options provides Member States with a crucial capacity to establish their own agenda in crisis management' (Tonra, 2001).

Thus, the problem for European Union attempts at crisis management abroad is similar to that faced within the EU polity. The knee-jerk reaction by decision-makers in crisis situations remains national. Coordinating twenty-five reactions at EU level is at the very least a challenge for the EU institutions.

Until potential tools, capacity and reactive reflexes come together in a single operational space, crisis management is likely to be less than optimal. It may well prove easier for the intergovernmental High Representative to join the Commission to gain access to first pillar tools rather than hope to minimise Commission influence through an intergovernmental ideology which repeatedly manifests its inability to provide what effective crisis management requires – a judicious mix of speed and coherence.

The national divide

The national-supranational divide presents one of the more fundamental constraints on the Commission's role in crisis management. The vertical relationship, between supranational institutions and national governments, has evolved into a rather sophisticated one, but not without tensions. After the 'major leaps' towards integration embodied by the Single European Act (1988) and the Maastricht Treaty (1993), Member States became more critical of the Commission and its accumulated powers. In a variety of areas, there have even been demands for 'decentralisation' – 'often little disguised attempts at repatriation of Commission powers back to national administrations' (Christiansen 2001a, 103). The national divide manifests itself both in the EU's inputs and in response to its outputs. EU governments are increasingly cautious about what competences they choose to delegate to 'Brussels'. New institutional structures give Member States more control over the EU policy process than hitherto and Member States have proved reluctant (e.g. over BSE) to comply with policies that emerge from the the supranational policy process.

Any efforts to organise for crisis management at the supranational level thus meet with a primary constraint: despite ownership of the mechanisms, the Commission's crisis management capacity depends on Member State resources (Tonra 2001). Whether it is critical information about the situation at hand or the ability to make things happen (securing public order; fixing system breakdowns; providing medical care etc.), the Commission must rely on Member States. The capacities of individual Member States may not always be robust, nor are they always used to manage crises effectively, but they remain the central focus of governments' efforts to protect their citizens. Rapid development of a supranational crisis management role in Europe is thus heavily constrained by this reality.

Commission efforts to map and monitor trends, for instance, are constrained by the need to reconcile many different sources of information. Moreover, planning at the supranational level requires considerable thought as to how to integrate twenty-five different emergency response systems. Crisis management at the supranational level will always involve national crisis management structures. In turn, usually well aligned with the subsidiarity principle, the 'first responders' are typically found at the local level, which is endowed with substantial discretion to manage breakdowns. The tensions between central coordination needs and decentralised coping techniques are continuously evolving – and the more so in the wake of 9/11, 3/11, and 7/7. Yet, national systems remain inward oriented, and this creates all sorts of difficulties in establishing cooperation between neighbouring states. It is hard enough effectively to facilitate communication between emergency organisations of neighbouring states, let alone across the gamut of those potentially concerned by terrorist threats or deadly pandemics.

Thus, despite declarations that supranational crisis management cooperation is crucial, Member States in fact retain a strongly national focus when it comes to crisis management. As a result, national crisis management systems are still not designed for supranational input or collaboration. Even in times of crisis at supranational level, Member States first consider the implications for their own citizens. They may call upon neighbouring countries through a bilateral request (the Dutch and German emergency services collaborated in the wake of the Enschede fireworks factory explosion in 2001 for instance). They may even call on the Community mechanism or some other higher capacity. But they do not seem ready to take their orders from a supranational authority – a stark reality check on any ambitions to enhance the Commission's crisis management capacity.

Conclusion

In spite of all these constraints, hardly a major crisis happens in Europe without some call for the EU to take a more active role in crisis management. Most recently, such calls emerged in the aftermath of the Asian tsunami. Before that, they could be heard after the New York and Madrid terrorist attacks, the Balkans conflicts, and the BSE crisis. As the EU has moved into an ever expanding number of policy fields, and has taken on many of the characteristics of a modern state, expectations are growing that it should also take a greater role in tackling crises with trans-boundary consequences – both at home and abroad.

Crisis researchers suggest that crisis capacity is best developed in a generic rather than a specific way. Crises cannot be predicted or prevented, but as Machiavelli pointed out with chilling prescience to the post tsunami period, long before the arrival of the EU on the world scene:

> 'many men have had, and still have, the opinion that the affairs of the world are in such wise governed by fortune and by God, that men with their wisdom cannot direct them and that no one can even help them; and because of this they would have us believe that it is not necessary to labour much in affairs, but to let chance govern them... Nevertheless, not to extinguish our free will, I hold it to be true that Fortune is the arbiter of one-half of our actions, but that she still leaves us to direct the other half, or perhaps a little less... I compare her to one of those raging rivers, which when in flood overflows the plains, sweeping away trees and buildings, bearing away the soil from place to place; everything flies before it, all yield to its violence, without being able in any way to withstand it; and yet, though its nature be such, it does not follow therefore that men, when the weather becomes fair, shall not make provision, both with defences and barriers, in such a manner that, rising again, the waters may pass away by canal, and their force be neither so unrestrained nor so dangerous' (*The Prince*, chapter XXV 'What Fortune can effect in man's affairs and how to withstand her').

Developing the resilience of the administrative system – the capacity to bounce back in the wake of adversity – may be the key, though this is easier said than done. Bureaucratic configurations within the Commission, the tense relationship between Commission and Council, and the asymmetric distribution of crisis capacity between supranational and national levels, constrain the development of crisis management capacity at the European level. Calls for more supranational crisis management capacity will thus likely remain unheeded unless they consider these strengths and weaknesses. Formal initiatives to bolster the EU's crisis response capacities in the Council, for instance, rarely make a clear connection with the more informal capacities already in existence in the Commission. This type of disconnect reflects not only a lack of awareness about the strenuous requirements of crisis management. It also reveals the enduring tension between Member States' desires to reap the benefits of collective action yet maintain their concerns not to relinquish sovereignty.

Endnotes

[1] This chapter is based on the research project 'Functional Security and Crisis Management Capacity in the EU: Setting the Research Agenda' conducted by the Forum for Security Studies (EUROSEC) at the Swedish National Defence College (SNDC) and the Leiden University Crisis Research Center (CRC) in the Netherlands. More information at www.eucm.leidenuniv.nl. The project is supported by grants from the Swedish Emergency Management Agency (SEMA) (Krisberedskapsmyndigheten).
[2] See European Commission 'Proposal for Council Framework decision on combating terrorism' (2001), Council Decision 2001/792/EC 'Establishing a Community Mechanism to facilitate reinforced cooperation in civil protection assistance interventions' (2001), Council and Parliament Decision 2119/1998/EC 'Setting up a network for the epidemiological surveillance and control of communicable diseases in the Community'.
[3] See inter alia 'A Human Security Doctrine for Europe' (2005), Ekengren (2004b), 'A Secure Europe in a Better World' (2003), and the Constitutional Treaty for Europe, Art I-43 (2004).
[4] For a useful reminder of the linguistic and methodological dilemmas involved see Barker, R. 'Legitimacy, Legitimation, and the European Union: What Crisis?' in *Law and Administration in Europe: Essays in Honour of Carol Harlow*, edited by P. Craig and R. Rawlings, Oxford, Oxford University Press 2003.
[5] European Union (2004) Treaty establishing a Constitution for Europe. *Official Journal of the European Union*, C 310, 16 December 2004, p. 32.
[6] For a discussion of the political as opposed to the managerial implications, see Westlake, M. (1997).
[7] Examples of crisis can be found in, for example, Pastore (2001a)
[8] Unlike with other crisis management resources such as the Civil Protection mechanism, ECHO can immediately intervene without awaiting a formal request from the stricken nation.
[9] Commission of the EU, *Proposal for a Council Regulation establishing a Rapid Response and Preparedness Instrument for major emergencies*, COM (2005) 113 final, 2005/0052 (CNS).
[10] European Commission, Press Release, 'Post tsunami: the Commission reinforces its disaster response capacity', IP/05/460, Brussels, 20 April 2005.
[11] Ulriksen, S., Gourlay, C. and Mace, C., 'Operation Artemis: The Shape of Things to Come?', *International Peacekeeping*, vol.11, no. 3 (Autumn 2004), pp. 508-525.
[12] It is perhaps significant that 'A Human Security Doctrine for Europe' was recently proposed as a doctrine for Europe's security capabilities. *A Human Security Doctrine for Europe, The Barcelona Report of the Study Group on European Security*, presented 10 Nov. 2004, led by Professor Mary Kaldor in 2003 at the request of EU Secretary-General Javier Solana.
[13] The Commission's strategy is based on its 2001 Communication on Conflict Prevention and the subsequent adoption by the European Council of the EU Programme for the Prevention of Violent Conflict. Crucially, this asserted that the EU

must draw on all instruments of its external policy in order to achieve conflict prevention objectives and it specified EU interest in addressing potential causes of violent conflict at the earliest possible stage – the so-called 'root causes' approach. This has meant
a commitment by the Commission to mainstreaming conflict prevention.

14 These assessments are based on analysis by the RELEX Crisis Room and the
Commission's Joint Research Centre. The watch-list is drawn up in collaboration with
the Council Situation Centre & Policy unit and agreed in the Political and Security
Committee.

15 A helpful description of military arrangements can be found in Digneffe, 2005.

16 Tarîqa can exploit 36,000 databases in a variety of fields (including medicine, law
enforcement, industry, education, economics, law and legislation, financial services
etc).

17 The room is mandated to support the Geographic Directorates of the RELEX Family,
the Desks, ECHO, SPS, the units active in the field of civil protection, the Crisis
Coordination group (CCG), the Conflict Prevention and Management Task Force
(CPMT) and the Crisis Steering Board.

18 The Crisis Room draws on extensive experience of the Commission Joint Research
Centre in Ispra (Institute for the Protection and the Security of the Citizen) and its team
of cartographers and GIS (geographical information systems) experts.

19 A secure general rapid alert system (ARGUS) linking 'all specialised systems for
emergencies that require action at European level.' (Communication from the
Commission to the Council and the European Parliament, *Preparedness and consequence
management in the fight against terrorism*, Brussels 20.10.2004. COM(2004)701 final, p. 10).
The Commission also suggested in 2004 the creation of a Critical Infrastructure
Warning Information Network (CIWIN). (Communication from the Commission to the
Council and the European Parliament, *Critical infrastructure protection in the fight against
terrorism*, Brussels 20.10.2004, COM(2004)702 final, p. 4; 7.)" (from Annex to Report,
Boin *et al.*, 2005: 75, footnote 446-448.)

20 When a crisis appears to be over, politicians often seek to 'move' crisis management tasks back to the bureaucratic domain, often to no avail. This may prove a
nasty surprise to crisis leaders, who discover that the post-crisis phase – dominated
by accountability and media dynamics – can last much longer than the crisis itself
(Boin *et al*, 2005).

19. Conclusion: where does the Commission stand today?

John Peterson

The last edition of this volume began by noting the mysterious dearth of serious academic work on the European Commission (Edwards and Spence 1997).[1] Now, the new mystery might be why it attracts so much attention despite its apparently precipitous decline (see Nugent 2000; Hooghe 2001; Stevens and Stevens 2001; Joana and Smith 2002; Dimitrakopoulos 2004; Peterson 2006), which itself seemed almost irreversible after the EU's Constitutional Treaty was rejected in referendums in France and the Netherlands in spring 2005. By this point, the more or less consensus view was that 'the decline of the Commission, evident since the early 1990s, has continued...and there seems little possibility that the situation will be reversed' (Kassim and Menon 2004, 102; see also de Schoutheete and Wallace 2002; Hill and Smith 2005, 399). This view is not confined to academics. Even as he launched a bid to take over the Commission Presidency, Chris Patten (2004) acknowledged 'unremitting gloom in the Commission'.

Supporters of this view point to the Commission's recent marginalisation from major EU projects: two intergovernmental conferences (IGCs), the Lisbon process of economic reform, and the creation of a European Security and Defence Policy (though Gray and Spence provide a more balanced perspective in chapter 16). The Commission has been humiliated on the euro, with EU Member States ignoring the Commission's injunctions (when they have been clear) to respect the terms of the Stability and Growth Pact. Perhaps above all, the Commission has lacked powerful political friends. As Romano Prodi prepared to step down in 2004, he lamented 'swimming against the stream'[2] throughout his Presidency, particularly against the resistance of large EU states that seemed to have lost all enthusiasm for an activist Commission.

When it came time to replace Prodi in 2004, EU member governments split over whether to appoint Patten, or the Belgian Prime Minister, Guy Verhofstadt. Eventually, the job went to José Manuel Barroso, the Prime Minister of Portugal. Barroso's name had not even appeared on a (long) short-list of nine names offered in an earlier opinion piece that urged, somewhat forlornly, that this was 'a top appointment Europe must get right' (Grant 2004). One senior EU official described the choice of Barroso as a 'disaster', the product of yet another Franco-UK split and thus 'a replay of the Iraq war'.[3] Sensing that Barroso was starting from a position of weakness,

France and Germany demanded that he designate their own nominees as 'super-Commissioners' with especially weighty portfolios.

Barroso's earliest moves defied the Commission in decline thesis. First, he impressed the European Parliament (EP) in his own confirmation hearings and secured a resounding investiture vote of 413-251 (Jacques Santer had snuck in with an 8-vote majority in 1994). Second, Barroso appeared to take little heed of lobbying by Berlin and Paris (telling MEPs that he needed '24 super-Commissioners') and insisted that his would be a dynamic, reform-minded Commission subject to strong Presidential leadership. Finally, Barroso responded to calls for a more policy-focused and team-oriented Commission (see European Policy Centre 2004; Patten 2004) by announcing the formation of five clusters of Commissioners in key areas: the Lisbon agenda, external relations, communications, equal opportunities, and competitiveness.

Barroso's bright start was short-lived. After first offering the powerful Justice and Home Affairs (JHA) portfolio to the French nominee, Jacques Barrot (who was firm in wanting an economic job), Barroso took the politically ill-judged decision to designate the Italian nominee, Rocco Buttiglione, as JHA Commissioner. After Buttiglione aired his ultra-conservative views on homosexuality and women at his EP confirmation hearing, the civil liberties and JHA committee took the unprecedented step of voting to reject his candidacy. Barroso tried to appease MEPs by delegating Buttiglione's responsibilities for civil liberties to a committee of other Commissioners. However, opinion within the EP did not measurably shift. Then, Barroso made things worse, stating that he was 'absolutely convinced' that his Commission would be approved since only 'extremist' MEPs could possibly vote against it.[4] Ultimately, he had little choice but to withdraw his team from consideration by the EP at virtually the last minute in order to avoid a humiliating rejection.

Barroso's political instincts seemed to return in subsequent weeks. He was helped by Buttiglione's decision to stand down, as well as Latvia's withdrawal of its original nominee, Ingrida Udre, who was dogged by allegations of corruption.[5] Fresh nominations by both states allowed Barroso to propose a new look College, which was overwhelmingly approved, by 449 votes to 149 (with 82 abstentions) in the EP. Afterwards, Barroso could plausibly claim that 'we have come out of this experience with strengthened institutions',[6] including a stronger Commission and, of course, an emboldened EP.

The early days of the Barroso Presidency gave ammunition to proponents of the Commission in decline thesis as well as those who reject it. More generally, while the Commission's best days often seem to be behind it, it retains considerable capacity to defy expectations. This chapter tries to explain why. For the most part, its perspective is contemporary or forward-looking. Its goal is to determine whether the Commission is in permanent decline, has reached a plateau, or may even face a future that is brighter than its recent past.

The Commission under Prodi

The Commission has always been a strange institution in a strange institutional position. It performs a rich variety of functions, and is under pressure to take on unfamiliar tasks in response to the changing demands of European integration (see below). Traditionally, however, the Commission has performed four main tasks, each very different from the others:

- proposing new policies
- overseeing policy implementation
- acting as guardian of the Treaties
- representing the EU internationally.

By the early 21st century, the argument that nearly everything the Commission did was political, in some way determining who got what, when and how, had become credible (see Lamy 2002; Peterson 2006). As Prodi, a former Prime Minister of Italy, put it 'the days of a bureaucratic Commission are over and done with. That has been the case for a long time'.[7]

Still, overseeing policy implementation is mostly an administrative and legal task, requiring the Commission to be an impartial defender of the sanctity of EU rules (Pedler confronts some of the arcane issues arising in chapter 8). Representing the EU internationally, especially in external trade negotiations, is a balancing act: the work is often highly technical but also politically tricky, with the Commission having to conduct two-sided negotiations with both the EU's Member States and its trading partners (as Smith makes clear in chapter 12). Proposing new EU policies is a fundamentally political job, particularly as the Commission has the exclusive right to initiate most European legislation under the so-called Community method of decision-making (Mazey and Richardson, chapter 10; Bomberg and Stubb 2003, 231-2). This monopoly is the Commission's most powerful weapon, which may explain why it has embraced new policy modes such as the Open Method of Coordination, with great reluctance. This party bag of powers, alongside its fundamental role as legal guardian (Usher chapter 3), makes the Commission a unique administration. It has often found it difficult, if not 'impossible to resolve the tension between politics, expertise, and impartiality' which it confronts (Hooghe 2001, 7). Against this backdrop, three observations about the Prodi years (2000-4) are apt.

A 'normal' Commission?

The position of the Commission under Prodi may have seemed unusually weak, but in fact was not far from the norm in the 50-year history of what is now the EU. By most accounts, the Commission has been powerful as a political agent only twice: first under Walter Hallstein in its earliest days (1958-67) and then under Delors (1985-95). Even these Presidencies ended in tears. Hallstein was politically humiliated by Charles de Gaulle (see Loth et al. 1998), setting the stage for a string of faceless and mostly limp Commission Presidents in the 1970s. Delors played the negotiations on the Maastricht Treaty and the 1992 Danish referendum (which rejected it) badly, leaving a critical mass of EU governments wanting a less visionary successor, who turned out to be Santer (1995-99). In retrospect, the power of the Commission under Delors seemed to peak in the 1980s. The mass resignation of the Santer Commission in 1999 probably marked a nadir. The Prodi era seems unlikely to go down in history either as a period of renaissance or a low point in the life of the Commission.

A buoyant policy agenda

Today's Commission has more work to do, and more of far greater importance, than ever before. It has far wider responsibilities than it had during the Delors years, not least because globalisation has made its existing economic policy competences far more formidable. In competition policy, the Commission is judge and prosecuting attorney – sometimes jury – in mergers falling within its purview. The Commission's enormous international power in this realm was illustrated at the end of the Prodi Commission in 2004, when it controversially considered blocking the takeover by one huge US computer firm, Oracle, of another one, PeopleSoft, before waving it through.

Meanwhile, the creation of the World Trade Organisation (WTO) has enhanced significantly the Commission's power in external trade policy. While Member States still aggressively seek to shape EU trade policy, the Union negotiates as one internationally. Internally, the Commission's own clout was reflected in its 2001 'Everything but Arms' initiative, which – against the strong wishes of France – extended duty-free access to the EU's market for nearly all products to least-developed countries.

The Prodi Commission also found itself with as much work as it could handle on issues ranging from electronic commerce to enlargement and to Justice and Home Affairs. There was general agreement in Brussels that the Prodi Commission's economic team – Pascal Lamy, Erkki Liikannen, Frits Bolkestein, Pedro Solbes and Mario Monti – was collectively the best that the Commission had ever had. In many respects, the Prodi Commission was an unusually professional, industrious, dossier-focused Commission, if also one with a relatively low political profile.

The leadership deficit

It might be argued that Prodi's legacy will become more positive over time, rather like – to draw a somewhat implausible analogy – Bill Clinton's. In particular, future historians might decide that the Prodi Commission was successful where it most mattered: on enlargement and internal reform of the Commission. In both areas, Prodi allowed two visibly competent members of his College – Commission Vice-President Neil Kinnock and Enlargement Commissioner Günter Verheugen – to operate with a mostly free rein. Views on Kinnock's administrative reforms were mixed both within the Commission (Spence 2000; Bearfield 2004) and amongst academics (Kassim 2004; Peterson 2004, 26-7). Still, there was little doubt that the Commission was better-managed and less shambolic by the end of the Prodi Commission than it was at the beginning. The Commission was indispensable in ensuring that the 2004 enlargement, perhaps the EU's most important achievement ever (see Lamy 2004), took place smoothly.

Prodi more generally resisted the temptation to meddle in the portfolios of his Commissioners – as Delors frequently could not – insisting that he wanted each to be a 'big star' in their own policy area (see Peterson 2004, 20-2). Still, as one Commissioner put it, 'Prodi got out of the way, but we needed a sort of control tower. We only avoided a lot of plane crashes at the last minute, and some we did not avoid'.[8] A case in point was a

Commission-sponsored (and technically flawed) 2003 study which indicated that EU citizens thought Israel was a greater threat to world peace than any other state. Outraged Jewish leaders accused Europe and even the Commission itself of anti-Semitism, prompting Prodi to organise a conference dedicated to the problem. However, the conference ended up being cancelled after Prodi became entangled in a rancorous dispute with Jewish leaders, culminating in at least four angry telephone exchanges in one day between Prodi's office and the World Jewish Congress in New York.[9]

The leadership deficit was evident even where the Commission had the most talent and expertise. One senior official complained that: 'this [Prodi] Commission has no economic policy. If you look at the Lisbon agenda, it has 200 or 300 priorities. They're trying to do way too much but the Commission is too weak to get the Member States to prioritize'.[10] Perhaps above all, most of Prodi's attempts to lead were undermined by his lack of skill as a political communicator (see Peterson 2006). Interestingly, when Prodi left Brussels, he returned to the front-line of Italian politics. Regardless of what Prodi's standing in Italy said about the difference between what it takes to succeed in EU versus national European politics, there were few within the Commission who were unhappy to see him go.

Sourcing the Commission's problems

With or without Prodi, the Commission has a general problem of credibility, which itself has three main sources. First, the Commission often presents itself as an elitist institution that is intolerant of any dissent from its message of Europhilia. Second, by the end of Prodi's term, it had been years since the member government of any large European state had shown any inclination to defend the Commission. Third and finally, the Commission continues to suffer from what Patten has called 'plumbing problems': it 'leaks' money and is often inefficient in performing its assigned tasks.

The communication problem

Perhaps the Commission's most obvious problem is one of political communication. Especially under Prodi, it was often notoriously bad at explaining to ordinary people why it existed, and why it did what it did. Prodi himself, a frequently poor and sometimes incomprehensible communicator (especially in French or English) was clearly culpable. Notable amongst a series of communications gaffes was the unveiling of the Commission's (2001) White Paper on Governance. In doing so, Prodi stated that he was sorry that the paper was so dull, but that it could not be helped because governance was essentially a dull topic.[11]

The White Paper also illustrated that the Commission often seems entirely immune to self-criticism. Again and again, the White Paper criticised the Member States and the 'intergovernmental' institutions of the EU for their failings. Nowhere did it give the impression that the Commission was reconciled to the possibility that intelligent, knowledgeable people might disagree with the Commission or its actions, or decide that European integration in federalist mode was not a good thing in all circumstances (Wincott 2001).

The White Paper did embrace the idea that a wider range of policy instruments should be used in EU policy-making, including:

–   tri-partite contracts between the Commission, regional governments, and Member States;
–   'co-regulation', or voluntary regulatory agreements between public authorities and private actors;
–   the Open Method, which had already been employed on monetary union, employment policy, and many areas targeted by the Lisbon agenda.

However, never were the merits of these instruments cast in the context of the need for the Commission to alter its ways.

In the Commission's defence, the first lesson of institutionalist theory is that institutions usually change more slowly than the policy agenda or actor preferences. Rarely does any institution promote its own weakening, which is debatably what any turn away from the Community method entails. But as the Prodi Commission's days dwindled, a chorus joined Patten (2004) in condemning its 'dogmatic insistence on institutional prerogatives over substance'. Lamy (2004), the Commission's Secretary General, David O'Sullivan,[12] and others insisted that the Commission had to become refocused on policy, as opposed to its own institutional position, which itself might do a lot to alleviate its communication problem.

The political problem

If the Commission's most glaring problem is one of communication, its most serious is political: the refusal of any government in any large EU Member State to defend the Commission and its prerogatives. Following the 2001 election of the right-leaning government led by Silvio Berlusconi, the point extended to Italy if it was counted – as it often was not – as a 'large state' in terms of political weight. In this respect, 1998 was a defining moment. In the run-up to a domestic election, the German Chancellor Helmut Kohl abruptly stopped defending the Commission, after years of staunch support for Delors specifically and the EU more generally. Crucial to Kohl's calculations was a 120-page dossier of alleged Commission infringements of subsidiarity presented to him by Edmund Stoiber, the Minister-President of Bavaria and a putative political ally. Kohl's successor, the Social Democrat Gerhard Schröder, showed little hesitation to attack 'one-sided Brussels bureaucrats', repeatedly accusing the Commission of bias against German industrial interests in the 2002 election campaign. The clear intent was to avoid being outflanked by the occasionally Eurosceptic Stoiber, who made a strong (unsuccessful) bid to succeed Schröder. The attitude of any German Chancellor could not fail to be influenced by the fact that amongst European publics, few showed lower levels of trust in the Commission than the Germans.[13]

France was no more supportive of the Commission after Delors left Brussels. During the first half of Prodi's term, the French government was paralysed by *cohabitation,* with a Gaullist President sharing power over EU policy with a hostile Socialist government. Neither Lionel Jospin (Prime Minister from 1999-2002) nor President Jacques Chirac showed much inclination to defend the Commission. Little changed after Jospin was replaced by Jean-Pierre Raffarin following a landslide for the right in the 2002 French elections. In fact, Raffarin had campaigned on a pledge to delay a planned reduction in France's public budget deficit, leading France to contravene the EU's Stability Pact – as Germany did for several years running – and landing the Commission with a huge political headache. More generally, in stark contrast to the Kohl-Mitterrand-Delors days, the traditional Franco-German-Commission triad rarely deserved the label 'alliance' during Prodi's term.

For his part, the UK's Tony Blair, speaking in Warsaw in 2001, urged: 'we need a strong Commission able to act independently, with its power of initiative: first because that protects smaller states; and also because it allows Europe to overcome purely sectional interests'. However, in an illustration of how set-piece speeches can give a less accurate reading of a political leader's mind than what they say off the cuff, Blair told journalists at the 2001 Nice summit that 'there is much for us to gain from a [further intergovernmental] conference that sets out clearly where it is that the Brussels Commission operates and where it doesn't', as if that were all that was needed to make the EU work better.[14]

Meanwhile, Blair's government routinely engaged in Commission-bashing to ward off critics or satisfy supporters. Gordon Brown's Euroscepticism seemed to become more virulent over time, even after he swatted away Commission criticism of his April 2002 budget on the grounds that it reflected a 'prudent interpretation of the growth and stability pact not taken by the European Commission but by the European Council'.[15] Environment Secretary Michael Meacher claimed that the Commission was 'wholly responsible' for the refrigerator mountain fiasco, when the UK found itself unable to cope with the disposal of old, environmentally unfriendly fridges as required by new EU legislation.[16] Logically, no British government would ever shy from such attacks as long as only one in four British citizens tell pollsters they 'tend to trust' the Commission.[17]

In large measure, the Commission's political problem was a by-product of the leadership deficit under Prodi (and Santer). A fair précis was offered by one member of Prodi's College: 'the most basic problem with this Commission is its inability to interact with the Member States. We are at the point now where no one cares anymore what the Commission President says'.[18] Paradoxically, the Prodi Commission was packed with strong individuals but was collectively weak, in contrast to the Delors Commissions, which were far less talent-laden but punched above their weight mostly because of the irrefutable aptitude of their President.

The 'plumbing' problem

There is no denying the Commission's plumbing problems, or its frequent inability to manage its assigned tasks effectively and spend money efficiently, as described in chapter 17. The Commission does not spend much money: about 80 per cent of the EU's (generally small) budget is spent by the Union's Member States. Yet, commenting on the Commission's spending on development aid, Patten moaned that, metaphorically, every time he opened a cupboard, another skeleton fell out. Clare Short (2000), the

UK Development Minister, lambasted the Commission as 'the worst development agency in the world'.[19]

Kinnock made a serious effort to repair the Commission's plumbing problems. Yet, even sensible reforms can create new problems in complex institutions. For example, a new, decentralised administrative code made Commission officials who authorised projects more responsible for expenditure, but also for maladministration or fraud. Many officials thus became less concerned with the effectiveness of programmes than with avoiding any risk of mis-spending. A new Financial Regulation had the effect of making it very difficult for the Commission to run even small project programmes involving very little money, including demonstrably effective ones such as Erasmus, fuelling fears that the Commission was being reduced to the status of a secretariat. Meanwhile, at least in the public eye, Kinnock's efforts risked being undermined by the Marta Andreasen affair, which followed claims by the Commission's chief accountant, largely backed by the Court of Auditors, that its accounting system was susceptible to fraud.

In short, Commission units running spending programmes had relatively weak incentives to make them work under Prodi, and powerful incentives to increase detailed rules governing them. The result was probably less leakage. But whether Europe was served by more effective EU policy management as a result was questionable. Indeed, as one expert cogently argued: 'Unless much more is done to improve the quality of European policy management it would be wise to lower our expectations of the future performance and the legitimacy of the EU' (Metcalfe 2004, 93).

Repairing the Commission

Even before he took over from Prodi, it was clear that Barroso had reflected on the Commission's problems. Lacking the run-in of six months that Prodi had (due to Santer's long period as a lame duck), Barroso worked swiftly and in secrecy to design his College, thus minimising lobbying by member governments. It was possible to argue that the strategy backfired, particularly since one result was the assignment of the JHA portfolio to Buttiglione. Still, the appearance of a President determined to be his own man led to fresh hope for the Commission's renewal.

The prospects for further repairs to the Commission, after considerable progress under Prodi/Kinnock, could not be dismissed. First, there was reason to expect better political communication from the Barroso Commission. Barroso's own skills were displayed in his initial EP confirmation hearings, when he effortlessly switched between Portuguese, English and French. Barroso pledged to close the 'communication deficit', and appointed the first Commission vice-president ever for communication strategy and institutional relations, Margot Wallström, a success under Prodi as Environment Commissioner. Barroso made it clear that Wallström would be his second in command and deputise for him whenever necessary. The seemingly fortuitous nomination some months prior to Barroso's arrival of a Portuguese Director General of DG PRESS was undoubtedly helpful.

Second, Barroso seemed likely to be a stronger political leader than Prodi had been. He announced that his College would be housed together (as

Prodi's was not), and insisted that he would give it clear political direction. In distributing portfolios, Barroso defied Berlin and Paris somewhat less than it appeared. Verheugen was given an expanded enterprise and industry portfolio and made Vice-President with responsibility for chairing the group of Commissioners on competitiveness. France's Barrot was also made a Vice-President, despite ending up with the rather secondary transport portfolio. Barroso later declined invitations to appear in the media in France ahead of the May 2005 French referendum after Chirac launched blistering attacks on his Commission and pressured Barroso's office to stay out of the French campaign. On balance, however, Barroso struck a fine balance, refusing to be cowed by France and Germany but trying to avoid offending them.

On the one hand, it was not clear that Barroso's College would be easy to lead, given its inclusion of three former prime ministers (including Barroso himself), five former foreign ministers, and three former finance ministers. Even more than the Santer or Prodi Commissions (see Peterson 1999; 2006), Barroso's line-up defied the notion that Member States nominated mostly grey, apolitical technocrats to the College. One upshot, in the words an EU official, was that 'Barroso doesn't exactly have ideal material to work with. He has experts in finance and foreign policy but not many generalists'.[20]

On the other hand, Barroso could argue that he needed to make his own choices about who did which jobs in the circumstances. Thus two liberals from small states – the Netherlands' Neelie Kroes and Ireland's Charlie McCreevy – were awarded the coveted competition and internal market portfolios (respectively). Barroso could also justify giving the third key economics portfolio, external trade, to Peter Mandelson, on the grounds that he was one of the few nominees to have previous experience of the job, as UK Trade and Industry Secretary. More generally, Barroso signalled that his Commission would have an economic policy – a liberal, reformist one – and would seek allies wherever they might be found, including with small EU states.

Third, Barroso created a new post of Audit Commissioner to work on the Commission's plumbing problems. His choice for the post, Siim Kallas of Estonia, was not without controversy. Although a former Prime Minister, Finance Minister, Foreign Minister, and President of the Estonian Central Bank, Kallas was dogged by (unproven) allegations that he had personally profited from Estonian monetary reform in the early 1990s. Of all the Commission's problems, its plumbing might well prove the most difficult to fix quickly. Still, Barroso at least showed determination to try to tackle it by splitting the budget portfolio and having one Commissioner each for financial planning and auditing.

It was easy to expect too much of the Barroso Commission. Yet, given the gloom surrounding the Commission for more than a decade, it made a change to have a Commission President who admitted that the Commission had problems and was determined to fix them.

The Commission of the future

To simplify, all possible visions of the Commission's future can be distilled down to two basic views. One would consider the Commission's near-term fortunes under Barroso to be much brighter than its recent past. This view starts with the pendulum theory: the Commission always recovers because activist Commissions are typically followed by managerial ones, as illustrated by Santer following Delors. Prodi's Commission broke the pattern for a variety of reasons, but it is now time for the Commission to reassert itself. In seeking to restore its position, Barroso is likely to find the Commission is actually surprisingly easy to reinvent, according to this view. Despite all its problems, one finds huge diversity in how it has worked in practice in recent years (see Joana and Smith 2002). There may be pathologies that have become embedded in its working practices over time. But the Commission remains basically a young and supple institution.

The alternative view is the permanent decline thesis. Its advocates actually downplay the amount of ground lost under Santer and Prodi and instead insist that the Commission has never been very important or powerful (see Moravcsik 1998). According to this view, there is little Barroso or anyone else can do about restoring the Commission's position given, first, its perennial weakness and, second, new and daunting challenges arising from enlargement and an (almost entirely inherited) policy agenda including Turkey, the Doha Development Agenda, Lisbon, and so on. The Commission has always been weak and is likely to get weaker.

Proponents of both views agree on some basics. One is that the Commission has often seemed overly obsessed with its own institutional self-interest. Admittedly, it has had to live with the risk of major emasculation in recent years. What had always been unthinkable became thinkable in the last two IGCs: the proposed dilution of the Commission's monopoly on the right of initiative. In particular, the Convention on the Future of Europe and agreement on a Constitutional Treaty was a time of 'make or break for the Commission as we know it' (Stacey 2003, 952). Thus, the Commission was defensive, muscular and combative in debates about institutional reform.

In the end, as one member of Prodi's Commission put it, 'we've managed to resist the attack on the Commission that was foreseen in the Convention. The Community method and the basic tools that we work with were preserved'.[21] What's more, two of the most significant proposals contained in the Commission's own White Paper on the Convention ended up in the Constitutional Treaty: that the EU's new Minister of Foreign Affairs be a member of the College of Commissioners (as well as chair of the External Relations Council) and that the EU's thicket of legislative procedures be considerably simplified. Both of these changes remained 'live' ones that retained broad political support even after it became unclear, following the 2005 referendums in France and the Netherlands, whether the Constitutional Treaty was dead or alive. Subscribers to the bright view of the Commission's future could still argue that, having survived a dark chapter, the Commission was poised for a comeback. Declinists might concede that the Commission had dodged a bullet, but also deny that anything much had changed.

Regardless of outlook, most students of the Commission acknowledge that its fate will always be tied up with factors that are impossible for it to predict or control (see Ross 1995). However, on the assumption that the Commission can only try to 'control the controllables', it clearly needs to respond to three broad challenges: enhancing its legitimacy, managing new forms of network governance, and adapting to enlargement.

A political or technocratic Commission?

It might be argued that this review of the Commission's problems has failed to single out its most glaring weakness: its own lack of democratic legitimacy. One of the most powerful unelected political institutions ever created, the Commission must earn its legitimacy via its credibility as a creator and enforcer of effective policies. Yet, as Majone (1996) insists, even if we could design a more politically accountable Commission, eventually it would face the same credibility problem faced by all democratic governments, which increasingly find they lack the knowledge or resources to solve the policy problems that matter most to ordinary citizens. What is different about the Commission is that it is always going to be a comparatively weak defender of its own credibility, since the foundations of its powers are intergovernmental agreements and a passive respect for Community law. Neither are solid rocks to stand on when EU policies violate intense national preferences, as logically stands to occur more frequently in a Union of 25 Member States or more.

The counter-argument is that the Commission's legitimacy problem is less severe than it appears. A 2004 Eurobarometer poll suggested that a plurality of EU citizens – 47 per cent – said they trusted the Commission. This share was lower than the 54 per cent who said they trusted the European Parliament but generally higher than the percentages who found national EU governments and institutions trustworthy. The Commission has discernibly regained public support since the Santer years (see figure 2).

In any case, time and practice are working against those who still argue that the Commission is a largely technocratic body doing technocratic work. The clear trend is towards the increasing politicisation of EU policy-making, as more policy tasks involve a shift of political discretion to the European level. As Scharpf (2001) has argued, an important measure of the success of European integration are demands for market-correcting policies (not market-creating ones) which arise from the effects that integrated European markets have on policy areas that are not themselves EU-based, such as pensions, health and taxation systems. European integration now has direct consequences for these and other thoroughly nationalised policy areas, but problems are often manifest in very different ways in different Member States.

A natural response is the Open Method. Another is the creation of new European regulatory agencies, such as the European Environment Agency, the European Defence Agency and the European Food Authority (see Flinders 2004; Majone 2006; chapter 5 above). These agencies have been created for good, functional reasons as new and highly dissimilar policy tasks – such as the regulation of medicines or monitoring pollution flows – have been shifted to the European level, but often without increasing the EU's own powers. All of this is very problematic for the Commission, which lacks the competence, resources or expertise to handle these tasks.

One logical step is to recast the Commission as a manager of networks of national regulatory agencies. Some of these networks would end up being formally organised as single European agencies, which are both distinct from the Commission and endowed with decisional autonomy. The problem with the current stable of European agencies is that they are in many

Figure 2: *Trust in the European Commission*

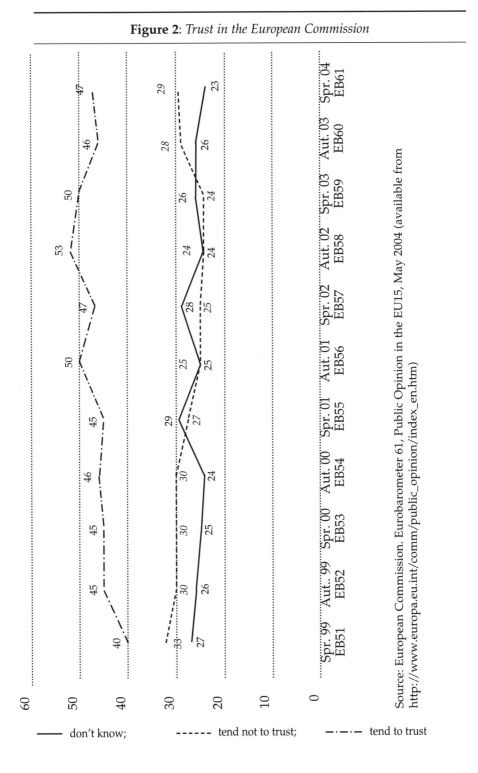

Source: European Commission. Eurobarometer 61, Public Opinion in the EU15, May 2004 (available from http://www.europa.eu.int/comm/public_opinion/index_en.htm)

ways beyond the scope of public scrutiny, without any generalised administrative rules to govern their operations. The Commission could usefully take on the job of scrutinising the activities of these agencies and ensuring that they respect their own behavioural standards and working practices.

In this context, Majone has argued tirelessly for the European equivalent of the American Administrative Procedure Act. The AAPA lays down strict procedural requirements that constrain the discretion of American agencies, requiring them to make their activities transparent, justify their decisions publicly, and submit to judicial review (Majone 2006). Agencies such as the US Food and Drug Administration or Federal Communications Commission operate independently and free from political pressures, but are also accountable for what they do.

A European equivalent of the AAPA could be made obligatory for all EU bodies, including the Commission itself and the various EU regulatory agencies. Independence and accountability need not be mutually exclusive values, and the Commission could play a role in ensuring that European agencies are accountable but also independent. In short, the Commission will always play an overtly political role. But it is plausible to think that the Commission's credibility could be boosted by making it more of an essentially apolitical watchdog of European agencies.

Managing Network Europe

The Commission and the EU remain objects of fascination (if also confusion) for many non-specialists. They are widely seen to be at the leading edge of experimentation with new forms of governance, or the imposition of overall direction or control on the allocation of valued resources. Far less governance is now performed by governments than was the case in the early days of the EEC. Far less policy is imposed hierarchically from the top down, exclusively by public bodies, and without reference to international agreements. An increasingly large share of policy-making is performed by informal clusters of different kinds of stakeholder in discrete policy sectors, who are bound together by mutual dependency, shared values and some kind of common identity. In the EU, but also elsewhere, new modes of governance increasingly favour voluntary performance standards over compulsory regulation.

There is now plenty of evidence to suggest that EU governance is mostly governance by different kinds of network (see Peterson and Bomberg 1999; Metcalfe 2000; Dehousse 2003; Skogstad 2003; Schimmelfennig and Sedelmeier 2004). What Leonard (1999) calls 'Network Europe' is less the result of any conscious plan than an unintended consequence of a truce between advocates of a federal Europe on one hand and a loose free trade area on the other. If network governance is what is available to build on, it makes sense to try to create a Network Europe that actually works better.

One promising avenue is to go beyond the Open Method that, as applied to the Lisbon agenda, has been slow at delivering results, and formally designate the Commission as responsible for the management of independent networks of national regulators. As Metcalfe (2000) has argued, the under-management of networks is a chronic problem because constituent organizations have weak incentives to invest resources in managing them in the absence of any hierarchy. There exists no generic model for managing, or even organising, networks in all of the different areas where Europe now regulates or creates pressures for new regulation. Nevertheless, the new European agencies – provided they are given autonomous powers of decision – offer a basic template. The Commission is both a logical manager and scrutineer of Network Europe.

The idea of turning the Commission into a sort of coxswain for independent regulatory networks will always face resistance on the grounds that it threatens the traditional balance of power between EU institutions. For example, the Governance White Paper expressly stated that: 'agencies *cannot* be given responsibilities for which the Treaty has conferred a direct power of decision on the Commission' (emphasis in original). However, if European integration is to extend to new areas of cooperation, there are a lot of reasons to think that Network Europe, featuring steadily more, and more intensive, cooperation within networks of national agencies, is the future of the EU, and one to which the Commission has much to contribute.

The 'enlarged' Commission

As on so many other issues, two broad views about the effects of enlargement on the Commission are detectable. One holds that enlargement might be the best thing that has happened to the Commission in years. The 2004 accession states appointed leading members of their political classes to the College: four of the 10 original 'shadow' Commissioners (appointed without portfolios of their own in May 2004) were former foreign or finance ministers, and another two were former European affairs ministers. Of the three new Commissioners then nominated to the Barroso Commission, one (Laszlo Kovacs of Hungary) was a former Foreign Minister, another (Vladimir Spidla of the Czech Republic) a former Prime Minister, and a third (Andris Piebalgs) was previously Latvia's ambassador to the EU. Thus, most 'accession Commissioners' had in-depth knowledge of the EU after scrutinising the fine print of its legislation and helping to negotiate their country's accession.

At the level of the Commission's services, enlargement promised to have the desirable effect of lowering the age profile of the Commission. The average age of Commission officials in 2004 was around 50 (down from 52 prior to Kinnock's reforms). Yet, it was not unusual to find officials in their early 40s in senior positions in the (say) Slovenian or Latvian civil services. Case study evidence suggested that the more officials from the accession states interacted with the EU, 'the more they like it' (Drulãk et al. 2003). This rosy view of the Commission was partly rooted in the assumption that enlargement would infuse it with a dose of new vitality and energy.

The pessimistic view saw the Commission becoming a tower of Babel. The College swelled to 25 members after absorbing 10 new Commissioners with limited experience of modern democratic politics. The linguistic consequences of enlargement were daunting: no Commission proposal could become law unless it was translated into a total of 20 official EU languages, including micro-languages such as Estonian and Maltese. Paradoxically, however, the new Commission struck a body blow against multilingualism. Even by a liberal count, only 12 of 25 nominees to the Barroso Commission could claim to be close to fluency in French, while no fewer than 24 could work in English. The formal equality of Commissioners was becoming a fiction, with one member of Prodi's team observing, 'it is just not credible to pretend that the Commissioners from Malta and Germany have the same weight and influence'.[22]

As for the services, a period of considerable adjustment was ahead. The Commission had somehow to digest quotas set for each of the accession states, which meant a total influx of 3,900 officials by 2009. Without question, the relatively long enlargement process – seven years separated the landmark 1997 Luxembourg summit decision and enlargement itself – gave the accession states time to build their administrative capacity, not least through the EU's own PHARE programme. However, capacity-building mostly took place by 'twinning' accession state bureaucracies and those of EU-15 states (Bailey and De Propis 2004). Even accession state officials with experience of working with or in national EU administrations were likely to find the Commission to be a very different sort of place to work.

Ultimately, it is hard to predict with precision how and how much the Commission will change as a consequence of the 2004 enlargement (see Peterson 2005). Past enlargements, always involving fewer new Member States and less dramatic changes generally, are not much help. Still, enlargement is another reason to think that the Commission stands at a major crossroads.

Conclusion

By early 2006 a clear answer to the question of whether the Commission was in decline or undergoing renewal was impossible. The early days of the Barroso Commission were a particularly difficult time to judge the Commission's fate. On the one hand, few claimed that the Commission under Prodi had gained back the ground the Commission lost after the disgrace of the Santer years. Popular rejection of the Constitutional Treaty in France and the Netherlands was as hard a body blow to the Commission as it was to any other institution, or the EU system more generally. On the other hand, the Commission retained control of both old and new levers of power in Brussels. Since its origins, it has always found itself in a strong position whenever major economic, political, or legal changes land the EU with a problem to which nearly any policy solution is better than the status quo. It was not difficult to think of many recent illustrative cases: the regulation of electronic commerce, border controls after 11 September 2001, or the European Court of Justice decision in the 2004 Manninen case (which appeared likely to force reform of national tax systems along lines favoured by the Commission).

The Commission will inevitably find itself with new opportunities to assert itself in the years to come. As argued in chapters 13 and 14, a prime area might be foreign policy, given strong public support for common EU policies (much stronger than for other core policies, such as the Euro or enlargement), yet modest achievements in this area thus far. The Commission might well find its role as an honest broker elevated in the more complex and multi-cornered policy debates of a Union of 25 plus. Alternatively, of course, the EU could become an increasingly less important supplier of policy solutions because so few will suit such a diverse array of Member States working according to rules in the Treaty of Nice that were widely considered unworkable.

It is, of course, impossible to study or gauge the credibility of the Commission in isolation from that of the EU system as a whole. A central feature of the 'new governance' is that the boundaries between institutions inevitably (and often desirably) blur in the modern world of policy design and shaping. In an EU of 25 plus, the Union's institutions will logically need to work harder to identify where compromise can be found among so many diverse national agendas. The new Constitutional Treaty acknowledges the *collective* responsibility of the EU's institutions as never before, giving a political signal to what has long been accepted in practice: that at the end of the EU's legislative process, no one ever remembers which institution was responsible for which specific provision of any policy. At the level of national political and popular opinion in Europe, as the 2005 referendums on the Constitutional Treaty clearly illustrated, 'Brussels' is often held collectively responsible for what the EU does (Peterson and Shackleton 2006).

In this context, the Commission has no monopoly on institutional weaknesses and pathologies. Enlargement had an earlier and arguably more dramatic effect on the European Council than it did on any other EU institution. Participants often bemoaned its inability actually to negotiate when meetings contained no fewer than 26 summiteers. The Council of Ministers per se underwent a programme of much-needed reform and rationalisation after 2002, but with decidedly mixed results. An illustrative example was the newly-created Competitiveness Council, which its Dutch chair in 2004 condemned as a 'Mickey Mouse' institution, featuring a rotating cast of disengaged ministers.[23] As for the EP, the ballooning of its membership to 732 (from 626 in 1999) stood to make it more unwieldy and less capable of collective action. The main talking points of the 2004 EP elections were high rates of voter abstention (even in new Member States) and a rise in support for Eurosceptic parties.

If it seemed improbable in these circumstances that the EU's institutions might provide leadership, individually or collectively, it was not obvious that the old ways of giving political impulse to European integration would work in the new EU. The Franco-German alliance, the main source of political leadership in the past, fell on hard times. Many EU governments seemed positively averse to following the lead of Berlin and Paris when both violated the Stability Pact, were seen to engage in political opportunism over Iraq, and were run by governments that suffered humiliating political setbacks in 2005.

At the same time, it was clear that Barroso would need stronger backing from Berlin and Paris than Prodi had enjoyed. There were good reasons to doubt it would be forthcoming given the perception that Barroso was, in the words of the respected French MEP, Jean-Louis Bourlanges, privileging a 'liberal Atlantic' clique within the Commission.[24] The charge was difficult to deny but also reflective of how the political ground seemed to have shifted in the new EU.

So had the administrative ground. The Council Secretariat invested considerably in developing its own policy resources after the 1990s, especially in external policy. By 2004, it was hard to argue that it remained a purely non-political body. One gauge of its muscle was the fear of many within the

Commission – reportedly including Barroso – that the Council Secretariat would simply swallow up and neuter the Commission's own considerable resources and staff for external policy in the new External Action Service foreseen in the Constitutional Treaty (but whose future fate obviously remains unknown). Spence reports graphically on the likely turf battles in chapter 14.

More to the point, the Council had sprouted more than 170 working groups and COREPER had steadily gained power in the early 21st century. As one senior Commission official put it:

> 'From the 1960s until the early 90s, we were really the only European administration and could call the shots. Now, the Council machinery is much more powerful...and there are lots of other European administrations. We need to reposition ourselves and get away from this idea that only we know what's best for Europe. We have no monopoly on good ideas.'[25]

This plea was indicative of new, modern thinking, especially among younger Commission officials, of a sort rarely found in the past. It also suggested that not everyone in the Commission rejected the idea of more collective EU governance, with the Commission repositioned as a manager and scrutineer of a Network Europe. The Commission's prospects for renewal remain somewhere on a spectrum between very dim and vibrantly bright.

Endnotes

[1] Some of the ideas in this analysis first saw light of day in Peterson 2003a; b. I am grateful to the editor and Martin Westlake for useful comments, ideas and inspiration on earlier drafts.

[2] Quoted in *Financial Times*, 16 March 2004, p. 8.

[3] Interview, EU Council General Secretariat, 30 June 2004.

[4] Quoted in *Financial Times*, 22 October 2004, p.1.

[5] See the profile of Udre in *European Voice*, 21-7 October 2004, p.10.

[6] Quoted in BBC News, 'MEPs approve revamped Commission', www.newsvote.bbc.co.uk (accessed 19 November 2004).

[7] Quoted in *Financial Times*, 16 March 2004, p.8.

[8] Interview, 29 June 2004.

[9] See http://news.bbc.co.uk/2/hi/middle_east/3237277.stm (accessed 31 May 2005).

[10] This view was seconded by the so-called Kok report on the Lisbon agenda, which was published near the end of the Prodi Commission. See Report from the High Level Group chaired by Wim Kok, *Facing the Challenge: the Lisbon Strategy for Growth and Employment*, November 2004 (available from http://europa.eu.int/comm/lisbon_strategy/index_en.html).

[11] See *European Voice*, 25 July-1 August 2002.

[12] See interview with O'Sullivan in *European Voice*, 29 January-4 February 2004, p.2.

[13] For example, only 39% of Germans in the spring 2004 Eurobarometer poll (number 61) said they 'tended to trust' the Commission, a lower share than in any of the EU 15 except Austria (37%) or the UK (26%). No fewer than 62% of Germans reported having a generally favourable impression of the Commission in

1990 (Eurobarometer 34). Annual Eurobarometer polls are available at: http://europa.eu.int/comm/public_opinion/index.htm.

[14] Quoted in Peterson (2002), 92.

[15] Quoted in *Financial Times*, 25 April 2002, p.4.

[16] Interview with Meacher on BBC Today programme, 20 June 2002.

[17] It is worth pointing out that levels of trust in the Council of Ministers are even lower (18%) in the UK as well as in most other Member States, and that Europeans generally exhibit more trust in the EU than they do in their national institutions. See the European Commission's spring 2004 'Eurobarometer' (61) survey (URL reference in note 13).

[18] Interview, Brussels, 29 June 2004.

[19] Short (2000). See also 'EU aid is a disgrace says Short', available from http://news.bbc.co.uk/1/hi/uk_politics/2163865.stm (accessed 27 September 2002).

[20] Quoted in *Financial Times*, 5 August 2004, p.8.

[21] Interview, Brussels, 29 June 2004.

[22] Interview, 29 June 2004.

[23] The Dutch economic affairs minister (and former senior Commission official), Laurens Jan Brinkhorst, quoted in *Financial Times*, 2 September 2004, p.9.

[24] 'Barroso wants to marginalize Franco-German "motor", says Bourlanges', EurActiv.com, 3 September 2003 (available from http://www.euractiv.com).

[25] Interview, Brussels, *chef* of a Commission *cabinet*, 29 June 2004.

Annex A: The Commission in the Nice Treaty

Treaty establishing the European Community (consolidated text) Official Journal C 325 of 24 December 2002

ARTICLES CONCERNING THE COMMISSION

Article 211

In order to ensure the proper functioning and development of the common market, the Commission shall:
– ensure that the provisions of this Treaty and the measures taken by the institutions pursuant thereto are applied,
– formulate recommendations or deliver opinions on matters dealt with in this Treaty, if it expressly so provides or if the Commission considers it necessary,
– have its own power of decision and participate in the shaping of measures taken by the Council and by the European Parliament in the manner provided for in this Treaty,
– exercise the powers conferred on it by the Council for the implementation of the rules laid down by the latter.

Article 212

The Commission shall publish annually, not later than one month before the opening of the session of the European Parliament, a general report on the activities of the Community.

Article 213

1   The Commission shall consist of 20 Members, who shall be chosen on the grounds of their general competence and whose independence is beyond doubt.

The number of Members of the Commission may be altered by the Council, acting unanimously.

Only nationals of Member States may be Members of the Commission.

The Commission must include at least one national of each of the Member States, but may not include more than two Members having the nationality of the same State.

2　The Members of the Commission shall, in the general interest of the Community, be completely independent in the performance of their duties.

In the performance of these duties, they shall neither seek nor take instructions from any government or from any other body. They shall refrain from any action incompatible with their duties. Each Member State undertakes to respect this principle and not to seek to influence the Members of the Commission in the performance of their tasks.

The Members of the Commission may not, during their term of office, engage in any other occupation, whether gainful or not. When entering upon their duties they shall give a solemn undertaking that, both during and after their term of office, they will respect the obligations arising therefrom and in particular their duty to behave with integrity and discretion as regards the acceptance, after they have ceased to hold office, of certain appointments or benefits. In the event of any breach of these obligations, the Court of Justice may, on application by the Council or the Commission, rule that the Member concerned be, according to the circumstances, either compulsorily retired in accordance with Article 216 or deprived of his right to a pension or other benefits in its stead.

Article 214

1　The Members of the Commission shall be appointed, in accordance with the procedure referred to in paragraph 2, for a period of five years, subject, if need be, to Article 201.

Their term of office shall be renewable.

2　The Council, meeting in the composition of Heads of State or Government and acting by a qualified majority, shall nominate the person it intends to appoint as President of the Commission; the nomination shall be approved by the European Parliament.

The Council, acting by a qualified majority and by common accord with the nominee for President, shall adopt the list of the other persons whom it intends to appoint as Members of the Commission, drawn up in accordance with the proposals made by each Member State.

The President and the other Members of the Commission thus nominated shall be subject as a body to a vote of approval by the European Parliament. After approval by the European Parliament, the President and the other Members of the Commission shall be appointed by the Council, acting by a qualified majority.

Article 215

Apart from normal replacement, or death, the duties of a Member of the Commission shall end when he resigns or is compulsorily retired.

A vacancy caused by resignation, compulsory retirement or death shall be filled for the remainder of the Member's term of office by a new Member appointed by the Council, acting by a qualified majority. The Council may, acting unanimously, decide that such a vacancy need not be filled.

In the event of resignation, compulsory retirement or death, the President shall be replaced for the remainder of his term of office. The procedure laid down in Article 214(2) shall be applicable for the replacement of the President.

Save in the case of compulsory retirement under Article 216, Members of the Commission shall remain in office until they have been replaced or until the Council has decided that the vacancy need not be filled, as provided for in the second paragraph of this Article.

Article 216

If any Member of the Commission no longer fulfils the conditions required for the performance of his duties or if he has been guilty of serious misconduct, the Court of Justice may, on application by the Council or the Commission, compulsorily retire him.

Article 217

1   The Commission shall work under the political guidance of its President, who shall decide on its internal organisation in order to ensure that it acts consistently, efficiently and on the basis of collegiality.

2   The responsibilities incumbent upon the Commission shall be structured and allocated among its Members by its President. The President may reshuffle the allocation of those responsibilities during the Commission's term of office. The Members of the Commission shall carry out the duties devolved upon them by the President under his authority.

3   After obtaining the approval of the College, the President shall appoint Vice-Presidents from among its Members.

4   A Member of the Commission shall resign if the President so requests, after obtaining the approval of the College.

Article 218

1   The Council and the Commission shall consult each other and shall settle by common accord their methods of cooperation.

2   The Commission shall adopt its Rules of Procedure so as to ensure

that both it and its departments operate in accordance with the provisions of this Treaty. It shall ensure that these Rules are published.

Article 219

The Commission shall act by a majority of the number of Members provided for in Article 213.

A meeting of the Commission shall be valid only if the number of Members laid down in its Rules of Procedure is present.

Article 201

If a motion of censure on the activities of the Commission is tabled before it, the European Parliament shall not vote thereon until at least three days after the motion has been tabled and only by open vote.

If the motion of censure is carried by a two-thirds majority of the votes cast, representing a majority of the Members of the European Parliament, the Members of the Commission shall resign as a body. They shall continue to deal with current business until they are replaced in accordance with Article 214. In this case, the term of office of the Members of the Commission appointed to replace them shall expire on the date on which the term of office of the Members of the Commission obliged to resign as a body would have expired.

Article 210(26)

The Council shall, acting by a qualified majority, determine the salaries, allowances and pensions of the President and Members of the Commission, and of the President, Judges, Advocates-General and Registrar of the Court of Justice and of the Members and Registrar of the Court of First Instance. It shall also, again by a qualified majority, determine any payment to be made instead of remuneration.

Article 275

The Commission shall submit annually to the Council and to the European Parliament the accounts of the preceding financial year relating to the implementation of the budget. The Commission shall also forward to them a financial statement of the assets and liabilities of the Community.

Article 276

1   The European Parliament, acting on a recommendation from the Council which shall act by a qualified majority, shall give a discharge to the Commission in respect of the implementation of the budget. To this end, the Council and the European Parliament in turn shall examine the accounts and the financial statement referred to in Article 275, the annual report by the Court of Auditors together with the replies of the institutions under audit to the observations of the Court of Auditors, the

statement of assurance referred to in Article 248(1), second subparagraph and any relevant special reports by the Court of Auditors.

2   Before giving a discharge to the Commission, or for any other purpose in connection with the exercise of its powers over the implementation of the budget, the European Parliament may ask to hear the Commission give evidence with regard to the execution of expenditure or the operation of financial control systems. The Commission shall submit any necessary information to the European Parliament at the latter's request.

3   The Commission shall take all appropriate steps to act on the observations in the decisions giving discharge and on other observations by the European Parliament relating to the execution of expenditure, as well as on comments accompanying the recommendations on discharge adopted by the Council.

At the request of the European Parliament or the Council, the Commission shall report on the measures taken in the light of these observations and comments and in particular on the instructions given to the departments which are responsible for the implementation of the budget. These reports shall also be forwarded to the Court of Auditors.

PROTOCOL ON THE ENLARGEMENT OF THE EUROPEAN UNION

Article 4

Provisions concerning the Commission

1   On 1 January 2005 and with effect from when the first Commission following that date takes up its duties, Article 213(1) of the Treaty establishing the European Community and Article 126(1) of the Treaty establishing the European Atomic Energy Community shall be replaced by the following:

"(1) The Members of the Commission shall be chosen on the grounds of their general competence and their independence shall be beyond doubt. The Commission shall include one national of each of the Member States. The number of Members of the Commission may be altered by the Council, acting unanimously."

2   When the Union consists of 27 Member States, Article 213(1) of the Treaty establishing the European Community and Article 126(1) of the Treaty Establishing the European Atomic Energy Community shall be replaced by the following:

"(1) The Members of the Commission shall be chosen on the grounds of their general competence and their independence shall be beyond doubt. The number of Members of the Commission shall be less than the number of Member States. The Members of the Commission shall be chosen according to a rotation system based on the principle of equality, the implementing arrangements for which shall be adopted by the Council, acting unanimously. The number of Members of the Commission shall be set by the Council, acting unanimously."

This amendment shall apply as from the date on which the first Commission following the date of accession of the 27th Member State of the Union takes up its duties.

3   The Council, acting unanimously after signing the treaty of accession of the 27th Member State of the Union, shall adopt:
– the number of Members of the Commission,
– the implementing arrangements for a rotation system based on the principle of equality containing all the criteria and rules necessary for determining the composition of successive colleges automatically on the basis of the following principles:

(a) Member States shall be treated on a strictly equal footing as regards determination of the sequence of, and the time spent by, their nationals as Members of the Commission; consequently, the difference between the total number of terms of office held by nationals of any given pair of Member States may never be more than one;

(b) subject to point (a), each successive college shall be so composed as to reflect satisfactorily the demographic and geographical range of all the Member States of the Union.

4   Any State which accedes to the Union shall be entitled, at the time of its accession, to have one of its nationals as a Member of the Commission until paragraph 2 applies.

Annex B: Presidents of the High Authority and the Commissions (before the merger of the Institutions in 1967)

High Authority of the European Coal and Steel Community

August 1952 – June 1955	Jean Monnet (F)
June 1955 – January 1958	René Mayer (F)
January 1958 – September 1959	Paul Finet (F)
September 1959 – October 1963	Piero Malvestiti (I)
	Resigned May 1963
June 1963 – July 1963	Albert Coppe (B)
October 1963 – July 1967	Rinaldo Del Bo (I)
	Resigned March 1967
March 1967 – June 1967	Albert Coppe (B)

Commission of the European Atomic Energy Community (EURATOM)

January 1958 – January 1959	Louis Armand (F)
	Enrico Medi (I)
	Acting President from September 1958
February 1959 – January 1962	Etienne Hirsch (F)
January 1962 – July 1967	Pierre Chatenet (F)

Commission of the European Economic Community

January 1958 – January 1962	Walter Hallstein (D)
January 1962 – July 1967	Walter Hallstein (D)

B = Belgium   D = Germany (Federal Republic)   F = France   I = Italy

Annex C: Presidents of the Commission of the European Communities

July 1967 – July 1970	Jean Rey (B)*	14 Members
July 1970 – March 1972	Franco Maria Malfatti (I) Resigned	9 Members
March 1972 – January 1973	Sicco Mansholt (NL)	9 Members
January 1973 – January 1977	François-Xavier Ortoli (F)	13 Members
January 1977 – January 1981	Roy Jenkins (UK)	13 Members
January 1981 – January 1985	Gaston Thorn (L)	14 Members
January 1985 – January 1989	Jacques Delors (F)	14 Members**
January 1989 – January 1993	Jacques Delors (F)	17 Members
January 1993 – January 1995	Jacques Delors (F)	17 Members
January 1995 – March 1999***	Jacques Santer (L)	20 Members
September 1999 – Nov. 2004	Romano Prodi (I)	20 Members****
November 2004 – Nov. 2009	José Manuel Barroso (P)	25 Members

* First Commission following merger of the institutions.

** 17 Members from January 1986

*** Having resigned on 15 March 1999, the Santer Commission stayed in office until midnight on 15 September 1999, the day before the Prodi Commission took office. As a 'caretaker' Commission it limited itself to managing 'current affairs'.

**** For a transitional period, from 1 May 2004 to the installation of the Barroso Commission, the ten new Member States also contributed one member each to the Prodi Commission, thus raising the number of Commissioners to 30.

B = Belgium	F = France	I = Italy
L = Luxembourg	NL = Netherlands	P = Portugal
UK = United Kingdom		

Annex D: Members of the Commission, 1958-2005

Commission of the European Economic Community

10 January 1958 to 9 January 1962

President:	Walter Hallstein (DE)
Vice-Presidents:	Giuseppe Caron (IT) (from 9 December 1959)
	Piero Malvestiti (IT) (resigned 15 September 1959)
	Sicco Mansholt (NL)
	Robert Marjolin (FR)
Members:	Hans von der Groeben (D)
	Robert Lemaignen (FR) (until 9 January 1962)
	Lionello Levi Santri (IT) (from 22 February 1961)
	Giuseppe Petrilli (IT) (resigned 8 February 1961)
	Jean Rey (BE)
	Lambert Schaus (LU)

10 January 1962 to 5 July 1967

President:	Walter Hallstein (DE)
Vice-Presidents:	Giuseppe Caron (IT) (until 16 May 1963)
	Lionello Levi Sandri (IT) (VP from 30 July 1964)
	Sicco Mansholt (NL)
	Robert Marjolin (FR)
Members:	Guido Colonna di Paliano (IT) (from 9 September 1964)
	Hans von der Groeben (D)
	Lionello Levi Sandri (IT) (till he became VP on 30 July 1964)
	Jean Rey (BE)
	Henri Rocherau (FR)
	Lambert Schaus (LU)

Commission of the European Communities (following the Merger Treaty of 1967)

6 July 1967 to 30 June 1970

President:	Jean Rey (BE)
Vice-Presidents:	Raymond Barre (FR)
	Fritz Hellwig (DE)
	Lionello Levi Sandri (IT)
	Sicco Mansholt (NL)
Members:	Victor Bodson (LU)
	Guido Colonna di Paliano (IT) (resigned on 8 May 1970)
	Albert Coppé (BE)
	Jean-François Deniau (FR)
	Hans von der Groeben (DE)

Wilhelm Haferkamp (DE)
Edoardo Martino (IT)
Emmanuel Sassen (NL)
Henri Rochereau (FR)

1 July 1970 to 5 January 1973

President(s): Franco Maria Malfatti (IT) (resigned on 21 March 1972)
Sicco Mansholt (NL) (from 21 March 1972)
Vice-Presidents: Raymond Barre (FR)
Wilhelm Haferkamp (DE)
Sicco Mansholt (NL) (became President on 21 March 1972)
Carlo Scarascia-Mugnozza (IT) (from 22 March 1972)
Members: Albert Borschette (LU)
Albert Coppé (BE)
Ralf Dahrendorf (DE)
Jean-François Deniau (FR)
Altiero Spinelli (IT)

6 January 1973 to 5 January 1977

President: François-Xavier Ortoli (FR)
Vice-Presidents: Wilhelm Haferkamp (DE)
Patrick Hillery (IE)
Carlo Scarascia-Mugnozza (IT)
Henri Simonet (BE)
Sir Christopher Soames (UK)
Members: Raymond Vouel (LU) (nominated 20 July 1976)
Albert Borschette (LU) (died on 8 December 1976)
Jean-François Deniau (FR) (resigned on 11 April 1973)
Claude Cheysson (FR) (from 19 April 1973)
Ralf Dahrendorf (DE) (resigned on 31 October 1974)
Guido Brunner (DE) (from 11 November 1974)
Altiero Spinelli (IT) (resigned on 1 July 1976)
Cesidio Guazzaroni (IT) (from 13 July 1976)
Finn Olav Gundelach (DK)
Petrus Josephus Lardinois (NL)
George Thomson (UK)

6 January 1977 to 5 January 1981

President: Roy Jenkins (UK)
Vice-Presidents: Finn Olav Gundelach (DK)
Wilhelm Haferkamp (DE)
Lorenzo Natali (IT)
François-Xavier Ortoli (FR)
Henk Vredeling (NL)
Members: Guido Brunner (DE) (resigned on 4 November 1980)
Richard Burke (IE)
Claude Cheysson (FR)

Etienne Davignon (BE)
Antonio Giolitti (IT)
Christopher Samuel Tugendhat (UK)
Raymond Vouel (LU)

6 January 1981 to 5 January 1985

President: Gaston Thorn (LU)
Vice-Presidents: Etienne Davignon (BE)
Wilhelm Haferkamp (DE)
Lorenzo Natali (IT)
François-Xavier Ortoli (FR) (resigned on 26 October 1984)
Christopher Samuel Tugendhat (UK)
Members: Frans Andriessen (NL)
Michael O'Kennedy (IE) (resigned on 3 March 1982)
Richard Burke (IE) (from 1 April 1982)
Claude Cheysson (FR) (resigned on 23 May 1981)
Edgard Pisani (FR) (from 26 May 1981, resigned
3 December 1984)
Giorgios Contogeorgis (EL)
Finn Olaf Gundelach (DK) (died on 13 January 1981)
Poul C. Dalsager (DK) (from 20 January 1981)
Antonio Giolitti (IT)
Karl-Heinz Narjes (DE)
Ivor (Seward) Richard (UK)

6 January 1985 to 5 January 1989

President: Jacques Delors (FR)
Vice-Presidents: Frans Andriessen (NL)
Henning Christophersen (DK)
Lord Cockfield (UK)
Karl-Heinz Narjes (DE)
Lorenzo Natali (IT)
Members: Claude Cheysson (F)
Stanley Clinton Davis (UK)
Willy de Clercq (BE)
Nicolas Moser (LU)
Alois Pfeiffer (DE) (died on 1 August 1987)
Peter Schmidhuber (DE) (from 22 September 1987)
Carlo Ripa Di Meana (IT)
Peter D. Sutherland (IE)
Grigorios Varfis (EL)

1986 – Following Enlargement to include Spain and Portugal, the following Commissioners were appointed:

Manuel Marín (ES)
Abel Matutes (ES)
Antonio Cardoso e Cunha (PT)

6 January 1989 to 5 January 1993

President: Jacques Delors (FR)
Vice-Presidents: Frans Andriessen (NL)
                        Henning Christophersen (DK)
                        Manuel Marín (ES)
                        Filippo Maria Pandolfi (IT)
                        Martin Bangemann (DE)
                        Leon Brittan (UK)
Members: Carlo Ripa Di Meana (IT) (resigned June 1992)
                        Antonio Cardoso e Cunha (PT)
                        Abel Matutes (ES)
                        Peter Schmidhuber (DE)
                        Christiane Scrivener (FR)
                        Bruce Millan (UK)
                        Jean Dondelinger (LU)
                        Ray MacSharry (IE)
                        Karel van Miert (BE)
                        Vasso Papandreou (EL)

6 January 1993 to 24 January 1995

President: Jacques Delors (FR)
Vice-Presidents: Henning Christophersen (DK)
                        Manuel Marín (ES)
Members: Martin Bangemann (DE)
                        Sir Leon Brittan (UK)
                        Raniero Vanni d'Archirafi (IT)
                        Hans Van den Broek (NL)
                        Abel Matutes (ES) (resigned on 27 April 1994)
                        Peter Schmidhuber (DE)
                        Christiane Scrivener (FR)
                        Bruce Millan (UK)
                        René Steichen (LU)
                        Pádraig Flynn (IE)
                        Yannis Paleokrassas (EL)
                        João de Deus Pinheiro (PT)
                        Antonio Ruberti (IT)
                        Karel van Miert (BE)
                        Marcelino Oreja (ES) (from 27 April 1994)

25 January 1995 to 15 September 1999

President: Jacques Santer (LU)
Vice-Presidents: Sir Leon Brittan (UK)
                        Manuel Marín (ES)
Members: Martin Bangemann (DE)
                        Ritt Bjerregaard (DK)
                        Emma Bonino (IT)
                        Hans Van den Broek (NL)

Edith Cresson (FR)
Franz Fischler (AT)
Pádraig Flynn (IE)
Anita Gradin (SE)
Neil Kinnock (UK)
Erkki Liikanen (FI)
Karel van Miert (BE)
Mario Monti (IT)
Marcelino Oreja (ES)
Christos Papoutsis (EL)
João de Deus Pinheiro (PT)
Yves-Thibault de Silguy (FR)
Monika Wulf-Mathies (DE)

16 September 1999 to 21 November 2004

President: Romano Prodi (IT)
Vice-Presidents: Neil Kinnock (UK)
Loyola de Palacio (ES)
Members: Mario Monti (IT)
Franz Fischler (AT)
Erkki Liikanen (FI)
(Erkki Liikanen resigned in July 2004 and was replaced by Olli Rehn)
Frits Bolkestein (NL)
Philippe Busquin (BE)
(Philippe Busquin resigned in September 2004 and was replaced by Louis Michel)
Poul Nielson (DK)
Günther Verheugen (DE)
Chris Patten (UK)
Pascal Lamy (FR)
David Byrne (IE)
Viviane Reding (LU)
Michaele Schreyer (DE)
Margot Wallström (SE)
António Vitorino (PT)
Anna Diamantopoulou (EL)
(Anna Diamantopoulou resigned in March 2004 and was replaced by Stavros Dimas)
Michel Barnier (FR)
(Michel Barnier resigned in March 2004 and was replaced by Jacques Barrot)
Pedro Solbes (ES)
(Pedro Solbes resigned in April 2004 and was replaced by Joaquin Almunia)

For a transitional period, from 1 May 2004 to the installation of the Barroso Commission, the ten new Member States contributed one member each to the Prodi Commission. Each of them worked alongside one of the members above.

Peter Balázs (HU)
Danuta Hübner (PL)
Siim Kallas (EE)
Joe Borg (MT)
Sandra Kalniete (LV)

Dalia Grybauskaite (LT)
Janez Potocnik (SI)
Jan Figel (SK)
Markos Kyprianou (CY)
Pavel Telicka (CZ)
(Replaced Milos Kuzvart before the latter took office)

22 November 2004 –

The final Barroso Commission was an adaptation of a proposal for a College in which individual Commissioners were either rejected by the European Parliament or were subsequently replaced as a result of changed governmental nominations and consequent reshuffle.

President: José Manuel Barroso (PT)
Vice Presidents: Margot Wallström (SE)
                  Günter Verheugen (DE)
                  Jacques Barrot (FR)
                  Siim Kallas (EE)
                  Franco Frattini (IT)
(Franco Frattini replaced Rocco Buttiglione as Italy's proposal for the Barroso Commission following European Parliament threats to vote down the whole Commission should the latter not be withdrawn)
Members: Viviane Reding (LU)
                  Stavros Dimas (EL)
                  Joaquín Almunia (ES)
                  Danuta Hübner (PL)
                  Joe Borg (MT)
                  Dalia Grybauskaite (LT)
                  Janez Potocnik (SI)
                  Jan Figel (SK)
                  Markos Kyprianou (CY)
                  Olli Rehn (FI)
                  Louis Michel (BE)
                  László Kovács (HU)
(In the original proposal for the Barroso Commission, László Kovács was assigned to the Energy post, but following the reshuffling of the Commission after EP discontent he was transferred)
                  Neelie Kroes (NL)
                  Marianne Fischer Boel (DK)
                  Benita Ferrero-Waldner (AT)
                  Charlie McCreevy (IE)
                  Vladimir Spidla (CZ)
                  Peter Mandelson (UK)
                  Andris Piebalgs (LV)
(Andris Piebalgs replaced the originally proposed Latvian Commissioner Ingrida Udre and changed post with the Hungarian Commissioner following the reshuffling in the second proposal for the Barroso Commission)

Legend

AT =	Austria
BE =	Belgium
CY =	Cyprus
CZ =	Czech Republic
DK =	Denmark
EE =	Estonia
ES =	Spain
FI =	Finland
FR =	France
DE =	Germany
EL =	Greece
HU =	Hungary
IE =	Ireland
IT =	Italy
LT =	Lithuania
LU =	Luxembourg
LV =	Latvia
MT =	Malta
NL =	The Netherlands
PL =	Poland
PT =	Portugal
SE =	Sweden
SI =	Slovenia
SK =	Slovakia
UK =	United Kingdom

Note: Following the EU Interinstitutional style guide, the names of the Member States are abbreviated according to the two-letter International Organisation for Standardisation (ISO) code, except for Greece and the United Kingdom for which the abbreviations EL and UK are used.

Annex E: Commissioners' responsibilities in the Barroso Commission

with corresponding Directorates General, Services and Agencies

Name	Responsibilities	Directorates-General, Services and Agencies
José Manuel Barroso (PT) *President*	– *Political guidance of the Commission* – *Organisation of the Commission in order to ensure that it acts consistently, efficiently and on the basis of collegiality* – *Allocation of responsibilities* – *Chair of Group of Commissioners on Lisbon Strategy* – *Chair of Group of Commissioners for External Relations*	– *Secretariat General* – *Legal Service* – *Spokesperson* – *Group of Policy Advisers (GOPA)*
Margot Wallström (SE) *Vice President* *Commissioner for Institutional relations and Communication Strategy*	– *Relations with the European Parliament* – *Relations with the Council and representation of the Commission, under the authority of the President, in the General Affairs Council* – *Contacts with National Parliaments* – *Relations with the Committee of the Regions, the Economic and Social Committee, and the Ombudsman* – *Standing in for the President when absent* – *Coordination of press and communication strategy* – *Chair of Group of Commissioners for Communications and Programming*	– *Press and Communication DG including Representations in the Member States*
Günter Verheugen (DE) *Vice President* *Commissioner for Enterprise and Industry*	– *Enterprise and industry* – *Coordination of the Commission's role in the Competitiveness Council* – *Chair of Group of Commissioners for the Competitiveness Council*	– *DG Enterprise and Industry (renamed) adding:* – *Space (from DG RTD)* – *Security-related research (from DG INFSO/RTD)* – *Application of treaty rules on free movement of goods (from DG MARKT)* **Agencies:** – *EMEA (European Agency for the Evaluation of Medicinal Products)* – *ECA (European Chemicals Agency)*

Name	Responsibilities	Directorates-General, Services and Agencies
Jacques Barrot (FR) *Vice President* *Commisisoner for Transport*	– *Transport*	– *Transport activities in the Transport and Energy DG* **Agencies:** – *EMSA (European Maritime Safety Agency)* – *EASA (European Aviation Safety Agency)* – *ERA (European Railway Agency)*
Siim Kallas (EE) *Vice President* *Commissioner for Administrative Affairs, Audit and Anti-Fraud*	– *Consolidation of Administrative Reform* – *Personnel and Administration* – *Budgetary discharge* – *Internal Audit* – *Fight against Fraud* – *Security* – *Chair of the Audit Progress Committee*	– *Personnel and Administration DG* – *Internal Audit Service* – *European Anti-Fraud Office (OLAF)* – *Informatics DG* – *Office for Administration and Payment of individual entitlements* – *Office for Infrastructure and Logistics, Brussels* – *Office for Infrastructure and Logistics, Luxembourg* – *Relations with the inter-institutional European Personnel Selection Office*
Franco Frattini (IT) *Vice-President* *Commissioner for Justice, Freedom and Security*	– *Justice and Home Affairs*	– *Justice, Freedom and Security DG (renamed)* **Agencies:** – *EMCDDA (European Monitoring Centre for Drugs and Drug Addiction)* – *EUMC (European Monitoring Centre on Racism and Xenophobia) will be combined with Fundamental Rights* – *Border Control (European Agency for the Management of Operational Cooperation at the External Borders)*
Viviane Reding (LU) *Commisisoner for Information Society and Media*	– *Information Society* – *Audiovisual Policy* – *Coordination of Media Affairs*	– *Information Society DG adding:* – *Audiovisual policy and media programme units from DG EAC* **Agencies:** – *ENISA (European Network and Information Security Agency)*

Name	Responsibilities	Directorates-General, Services and Agencies
Stavros Dimas (EL) *Commissioner for Environment*	– *Environment*	– *Environment DG* **Agencies:** – *EEA (European Environment Agency)*
Joaquin Almunia (ES) *Commissioner for Economic and Monetary Affairs*	– *Economic and Financial Affairs* – *Monetary matters* – *Statistical Office*	– *Economic and Financial Affairs DG* – *Statistical Office*
Danuta Hübner (PL) *Commissioner for Regional Policy*	– *Regional Policy* – *Cohesion Fund* – *Solidarity Fund*	– *Regional Policy DG*
Joe Borg (MT) *Commissioner for Fisheries and Maritime Affairs*	– *Fisheries* – *Coordination of Maritime Affairs* – *Chair of Commission Taskforce to develop a Green Paper on maritime policy*	– *Fisheries and Maritime Affairs DG (renamed) adding:* – *Transfer of responsibility for law of the sea from RELEX* **Agencies:** – *CFCA (Community Fisheries Control Agency)*
Dalia Grybauskaite (LT) *Commissioner for Financial Programming and Budget*	– *Financial Programming* – *Budget*	– *Budget DG*
Janez Potocnik (SI) *Commissioner for Science and Research*	– *Science, Research and Development* – *Joint Research Centre*	–*Research DG* – *Joint Research Centre*
Charlie McCreevy (IE) *Commissioner for Internal Market and Services*	– *Internal Market* – *Financial Services*	– *Internal Market and Services DG (renamed) adding:* – *Free movement of capital from Economic and Financial Affairs DG* – *Responsibility for business related services and management of notifications by Member States of draft rules on services from ENTR DG* **Agencies:** – *OHIM (Office for the Harmonisation of the Internal Market Trade Marks and designs)*

Name	Responsibilities	Directorates-General, Services and Agencies
Vladimir Spidla (CZ) *Commissioner for Employment, Social Affairs and Equal Opportunities*	*– Employment* *– Social Affairs* *– Equal Opportunities* *– Chair of Group of Commissioners for Equal Opportunities*	
Peter Mandelson (UK) *Commissioner for Trade*	*– Trade Policy* *– International dimension of competitivenesss*	*– Trade DG*
László Kovács (HU) *Commissioner for Taxation and Customs Union*	*– Customs* *– Taxation*	*– Taxation and Customs Union DG*

Annex F: Commission Staff Grading System for Administrators

Old Grading System	New Grading System applicable from 1 May 2006	Posts[1]
A 1	AD 16	Director-General
A 2	AD 15	Director-General / Director
A 3	AD 14	Director/Head of unit/Adviser linguistic expert; economic expert; legal expert; medical expert; veterinary expert; scientific expert; research expert; financial expert; audit expert
	AD 13	Head of Unit/Adviser linguistic expert; economic expert; legal expert; medical expert; veterinary expert; scientific expert; research expert; financial expert; audit expert
A4	AD 12	Head of Unit principal translator, principal interpreter, principal economist; principal lawyer; principal medical officer; principal veterinary inspector; principal scientist; principal researcher; principal financial officer; principal audit officer
A 5	AD 11	
A 6	AD 10	Head of Unit senior translator; senior interpreter; senior economist; senior lawyer; senior medical officer; senior veterinary inspector; senior scientist; senior researcher; senior financial officer; senior audit officer
	AD 9	
A 7	AD 8	Translator; interpreter; economist; lawyer; medical officer; veterinary inspector; scientist; researcher; financial officer; auditor
A 8	AD 7	
	AD 6	Junior translator; junior interpreter; junior economist; junior lawyer; junior medical officer; junior veterinary inspector; junior scientist; junior researcher; junior financial officer; junior auditor
	AD 5	

[1]The description of posts corresponds with the new grading system only. There is no correspondence between current post descriptions and the old grading system.

Annex G: Commission Salary Scales

Salary scales in effect from 1 July 2005; base amounts in € per month

	steps				
Grades	1	2	3	4	5
16	15,255.00	15,896.04	16,564.01		
15	13,482.88	14,049.45	14,639.82	15,047.12	15,255.00
14	11,916.61	12,417.36	12,939.16	13,299.15	13,482.88
13	10,532.30	10,974.88	11,436.06	11,754.22	11,916.61
12	9,308.79	9,699.96	10,107.56	10,388.77	10,532.30
11	8,227.42	8,573.15	8,933.40	9,181.94	9,308.79
10	7,271.67	7,577.23	7,895.64	8,115.30	8,227.42
9	6,426.94	6,697.01	6,978.42	7,172.57	7,271.67
8	5,680.34	5,919.04	6,167.76	6,339.36	6,426.94
7	5,020.47	5,231.44	5,451.27	5,602.93	5,680.34
6	4,437.26	4,623.72	4,818.01	4,952.06	5,020.47
5	3,921.80	4,086.60	4,258.32	4,376.79	4,437.26
4	3,466.22	3,611.87	3,763.65	3,868.36	3,921.80
3	3,063.56	3,192.29	3,326.43	3,418.98	3,466.22
2	2,707.67	2,821.45	2,940.01	3,021.81	3,063.56
1	2,393.13	2,493.69	2,598.48	2,670.77	2,707.67

Source: Official Journal, 22 December 2005

Note: The base figures are guidelines. Actual salaries vary according to individual entitlements (size of family, etc.), geographical location of the post held (weighting factors increase or decrease the basic sum according to the cost of living in countries of residence) and special levies agreed between the staff associations and the Commission for various reasons. They are also currently subject to transitional arrangements which have the effect of fractionally lowering actual salaries.

Annex H: Framework Agreement on relations between the European Parliament and the Commission

The European Parliament and the Commission of the European Communities (hereinafter referred to as "the two Institutions"),

having regard to the Treaty on European Union, the Treaty establishing the European Community, and the Treaty establishing the European Atomic Energy Community, (hereinafter referred to as "the Treaties"),

having regard to the Inter-institutional Agreements and texts governing relations between the two Institutions,

having regard to Parliament's Rules of Procedure[1], and in particular Rules 98, 99 and 120 as well as Annex VII,

A.   whereas the Treaties strengthen the democratic legitimacy of the European Union's decision-making process,

B.   whereas the two Institutions attach the utmost importance to the effective transposition and implementation of Community law,

C.   whereas this Framework Agreement does not affect the powers and prerogatives of Parliament, the Commission or any other institution or organ of the European Union but seeks to ensure that those powers and prerogatives are exercised as effectively as possible,

D.   whereas it is appropriate to update the Framework Agreement concluded in July 2000[2] and to replace it by the following text,

agree as follows:

I. SCOPE

1.   The two Institutions agree on the following measures to strengthen the political responsibility and legitimacy of the Commission, extend constructive dialogue, improve the flow of information between the two Institutions and improve the coordination of procedures and planning.

They also agree on specific implementing measures for the forwarding of confidential Commission documents and information, as set out in Annex 1 and on the timetable for the Commission's legislative and work programme, as set out in Annex 2.

II. POLITICAL RESPONSIBILITY

2.   Each Member of the Commission shall take political responsibility for action in the field of which he or she is in charge, without prejudice to the principle of Commission collegiality.

The President of the Commission shall be fully responsible for identifying any conflict of interest which renders a Member of the Commission unable to perform his or her duties.

The President of the Commission shall likewise be responsible for any subsequent action taken in such circumstances; if an individual case has been re-allocated, the President shall inform the President of Parliament thereof immediately and in writing.

3. If Parliament decides to express lack of confidence in a Member of the Commission, the President of the Commission, having given serious consideration to that decision, shall either request that Member to resign, or explain his or her decisions to Parliament.

4. Where it becomes necessary to arrange for the replacement of a Member of the Commission during his or her term of office pursuant to Article 215 of the Treaty establishing the European Community, the President of the Commission shall immediately contact the President of Parliament in order to reach agreement on the manner in which the President of the Commission intends to ensure the presentation of the future Member before Parliament without delay and in full compliance with the prerogatives of the Institutions.

Parliament shall ensure that its procedures are conducted with the utmost dispatch, in order to enable the President of the Commission to be informed of Parliament's position in due time before the Member is called upon to exercise duties as the Commission's representative.

5. The President of the Commission shall immediately notify Parliament of any decision concerning the allocation of responsibilities to a Member of the Commission. Where the responsibilities of a Member of the Commission are changed substantially, that Member shall appear before the relevant parliamentary committee at Parliament's request.

6. Any changes to the provisions of the Code of Conduct for Members of the Commission relating to conflict of interest or ethical behaviour shall be sent immediately to Parliament.

The Commission shall take into account the views expressed by Parliament in that regard.

7. In conformity with Rule 99 of its Rules of Procedure, Parliament shall communicate with the President-designate of the Commission in good time before the opening of the procedures relating to the approval of the new Commission. Parliament shall take into account the remarks expressed by the President-designate.

The procedures shall be designed in such a way as to ensure that the whole Commission-designate is assessed in an open, fair and consistent manner.

The Members of the Commission-designate shall ensure full disclosure of all relevant information, in conformity with the obligation of independence laid down in Article 213 of the Treaty establishing the European Community.

III. CONSTRUCTIVE DIALOGUE AND FLOW OF INFORMATION

(i) General provisions

8. The Commission shall keep Parliament fully and promptly informed about its proposals and initiatives in the legislative and budgetary fields.

In all fields where Parliament acts in a legislative capacity, or as a branch of the budgetary authority, it shall be informed, on a par with the Council, at every stage of the legislative and budgetary process.

9.   In the areas of the Common Foreign and Security Policy, police cooperation and judicial cooperation in criminal matters, the Commission shall take measures to improve the involvement of Parliament in such a way as to take Parliament's views as far as possible into account.

10.   The President of the Commission and/or the Vice-President responsible for inter-institutional relations will meet the Conference of Presidents every three months to ensure regular dialogue between the two Institutions at the highest level. The President of the Commission will attend meetings of the Conference of Presidents at least twice a year.

11.   Each Member of the Commission shall make sure that there is a regular and direct flow of information between the Member of the Commission and the chairperson of the relevant parliamentary committee.

12.   The Commission shall not make public any legislative proposal or any significant initiative or decision before notifying Parliament thereof in writing.

On the basis of the Commission's legislative and work programme and of the multi-annual programme, the two Institutions shall identify in advance, by common agreement, the proposals and initiatives of particular importance, with a view to presenting them at a plenary sitting of Parliament.

Similarly, they shall identify those proposals and initiatives for which information is to be provided before the Conference of Presidents or conveyed, in an appropriate manner, to the relevant parliamentary committee or its chairperson.

These decisions shall be taken in the framework of the regular dialogue between the two Institutions, as provided for in point 10, and shall be updated on a regular basis, taking due account of any political developments.

13.   If an internal Commission document – of which Parliament has not been informed pursuant to points 8, 9 and 12 – is circulated outside the Institutions, the President of Parliament may request that the document concerned be forwarded to Parliament without delay, in order to communicate it to any Member of Parliament who may request it.

14.   The Commission shall provide regular information in writing on action taken in response to specific requests addressed to it in Parliament's resolutions, including in cases where it has not been able to follow Parliament's views.

As regards the discharge procedure, the specific provisions laid down in point 26 shall apply.

The Commission shall take account of any requests made, pursuant to Article 192 of the Treaty establishing the European Community, by Parliament to the Commission to submit legislative proposals, and shall provide a prompt and sufficiently detailed reply thereto.

At the request of Parliament or the Commission, information on the follow-up to Parliament's significant requests shall also be provided before the relevant parliamentary committee and, if necessary, at a plenary sitting of Parliament.

15.   Where a Member State presents a legislative initiative pursuant to Article 34 of the Treaty on European Union, the Commission shall inform

Parliament, if so requested, of its position on the initiative before the relevant parliamentary committee.

16. The Commission shall inform Parliament of the list of its expert groups set up in order to assist the Commission in the exercise of its right of initiative. That list shall be updated on a regular basis and made public.

Within this framework, the Commission shall, in an appropriate manner, inform the competent parliamentary committee, at the specific and reasoned request of its chairperson, on the activities and composition of such groups.

17. The two Institutions shall hold, through the appropriate mechanisms, a constructive dialogue on questions concerning important administrative matters, notably on issues having direct implications for Parliament's own administration.

18. Where confidentiality is invoked as regards any of the information forwarded pursuant to this Framework Agreement, the provisions laid down in Annex 1 shall be applied.

(ii) External relations, enlargement and international agreements

19. In connection with international agreements, including trade agreements, the Commission shall provide early and clear information to Parliament both during the phase of preparation of the agreements and during the conduct and conclusion of international negotiations. This information covers the draft negotiating directives, the adopted negotiating directives, the subsequent conduct of negotiations and the conclusion of the negotiations.

The information referred to in the first subparagraph shall be provided to Parliament in sufficient time for it to be able to express its point of view if appropriate, and for the Commission to be able to take Parliament's views as far as possible into account. This information shall be provided through the relevant parliamentary committees and, where appropriate, at a plenary sitting.

Parliament undertakes, for its part, to establish appropriate procedures and safeguards as regards confidentiality, in accordance with the provisions of Annex 1.

20. The Commission shall take the necessary steps to ensure that Parliament is immediately and fully informed of:

(i) decisions concerning the provisional application or the suspension of agreements; and

(ii) a Community position in a body set up by an agreement.

21. Where the Commission represents the European Community, it shall, at Parliament's request, facilitate the inclusion of Members of Parliament as observers in Community delegations negotiating multilateral agreements. Members of Parliament may not take part directly in the negotiating sessions.

The Commission undertakes to keep Members of Parliament who participate as observers in Community delegations negotiating multilateral agreements systematically informed.

22. Before making, at donors' conferences, financial pledges which imply new financial undertakings and require the agreement of the budget-

ary authority, the Commission shall inform the budgetary authority and examine its remarks.

23.   The two Institutions agree to cooperate in the area of election observation. The Commission shall cooperate with Parliament in providing the necessary assistance to delegations of Parliament participating in Community election observation missions.

24.   The Commission shall keep Parliament fully informed of the progress of accession negotiations and in particular on major aspects and developments, so as to enable it to express its views in good time through the appropriate parliamentary procedures.

25.   When Parliament adopts a recommendation on matters referred to in point 24, pursuant to Rule 82 of its Rules of Procedure, and when, for important reasons, the Commission decides that it cannot support such a recommendation, it shall explain the reasons before Parliament, at a plenary sitting or at the next meeting of the relevant parliamentary committee.

(iii) Budgetary implementation

26.   In connection with the annual discharge governed by Article 276 of the Treaty establishing the European Community, the Commission shall forward all information necessary for supervising the implementation of the budget for the year in question, which the chairperson of the parliamentary committee responsible for the discharge procedure pursuant to Annex VI of the Parliament's Rules of Procedure requests from it for that purpose.

If new aspects come to light concerning previous years for which discharge has already been given, the Commission shall forward all the necessary information on the matter with a view to arriving at a solution which is acceptable to both sides.

IV. COOPERATION AS REGARDS LEGISLATIVE PROCEDURES AND PLANNING

(i) Commission political and legislative programmes and the European Union's multi-annual programming

27.   The Commission shall present proposals for the European Union's multi-annual programming, with a view to achieving consensus on inter-institutional programming between the Institutions concerned.

28.   An incoming Commission shall present, as soon as possible, its political and legislative programme.

29.   When the Commission prepares its legislative and work programme, the two Institutions shall cooperate in accordance with the timetable set out in Annex 2.

The Commission shall take into account the priorities expressed by Parliament.

The Commission shall provide sufficient detail as to what is envisaged under each point in the legislative and work programme.

30.   The Vice-President of the Commission responsible for inter-institutional relations undertakes to report to the Conference of Committee Chairs every three months, outlining the political implementation of the legislative

and work programme for the year in question and any updating rendered necessary by topical and important political events.

(ii) General legislative procedures

31.   The Commission undertakes to carefully examine amendments to its legislative proposals adopted by Parliament, with a view to taking them into account in any amended proposal.

When delivering its opinion on Parliament's amendments under Article 251 of the Treaty establishing the European Community, the Commission undertakes to take the utmost account of amendments adopted at second reading; should it decide, for important reasons and after consideration by the College, not to adopt or support such amendments, it shall explain its decision before Parliament, and in any event in its opinion on Parliament's amendments by virtue of point (c) of the third subparagraph of Article 251(2).

32.   The Commission shall give Parliament and the Council prior notification before withdrawing its proposals.

33.   For legislative procedures not entailing codecision, the Commission:

(i)   shall ensure that Council bodies are reminded in good time not to reach a political agreement on its proposals before Parliament has adopted its opinion. It shall ask for discussion to be concluded at ministerial level after a reasonable period has been given to the members of the Council to examine Parliament's opinion;

(ii)   shall ensure that the Council adheres to the rules developed by the Court of Justice of the European Communities requiring Parliament to be re-consulted if the Council substantially amends a Commission proposal. The Commission shall inform Parliament of any reminder to the Council of the need for re-consultation;

(iii)   undertakes, if appropriate, to withdraw a legislative proposal that Parliament has rejected. If, for important reasons and after consideration by the College, the Commission decides to maintain its proposal, it shall explain the reasons for that decision in a statement before Parliament.

34.   For its part, in order to improve legislative planning, Parliament undertakes:

(i)   to plan the legislative sections of its agendas, bringing them into line with the current legislative programme and with the resolutions it has adopted on that programme;

(ii)   to meet reasonable deadlines, in so far as is useful for the procedure, when adopting its opinion at first reading under the cooperation and codecision procedures and under the consultation procedure;

(iii)   as far as possible to appoint rapporteurs on future proposals as soon as the legislative programme is adopted;

(iv)   to consider requests for reconsultation as a matter of absolute priority provided that all the necessary information has been forwarded to it.

(iii) Specific legislative and implementing powers of the Commission

35.   The Commission shall give full and timely information to Parliament concerning acts which it adopts which fall within the scope of its own legislative powers.

The implementation of Council Decision 1999/468/EC of 28 June 1999 laying down the procedures for the exercise of implementing powers conferred on the Commission[3] shall be governed by the Agreement between the European Parliament and the Commission[4] on the procedures for implementing that decision.

As regards implementing measures relating to the securities, banking and insurance sector, the Commission confirms the undertakings that it gave at the plenary sitting of 5 February 2002 and which were reaffirmed on 31 March 2004. In particular, the Commission commits itself to taking the utmost account of Parliament's position and any resolutions that it might adopt with regard to implementing measures exceeding the implementing powers provided for in the basic instrument; in such cases, it shall endeavour to reach a balanced solution.

(iv) Monitoring the application of Community law

36.   In addition to specific reports and the annual report on the application of Community law, the Commission shall, at the request of the responsible parliamentary committee, keep Parliament informed orally of the stage reached in the procedure as from the stage when the reasoned opinion is sent and, where procedures have been initiated for failure to communicate the measures implementing a directive, or for failure to comply with a judgment of the Court of Justice, as from the stage of formal notice.

V. COMMISSION'S PARTICIPATION IN PARLIAMENTARY PROCEEDINGS

37.   Parliament shall seek to ensure that, as a general rule, items falling under the responsibility of a Member of the Commission are grouped together.

The Commission shall seek to ensure that, as a general rule, Members of the Commission are present at plenary sittings for agenda items falling under their responsibility, whenever Parliament so requests.

38.   With a view to ensuring the presence of Members of the Commission, Parliament undertakes to do its best to maintain its final draft agendas.

Where Parliament amends its final draft agenda, or where it moves items within the agenda within a part-session, Parliament shall immediately inform the Commission. The Commission shall use its best endeavours to ensure the presence of the Member of the Commission responsible.

39.   The Commission may propose the inclusion of items on the agenda not later than the meeting of the Conference of Presidents that decides on the final draft agenda of a part-session. Parliament shall take the fullest account of such proposals.

40.   As a general rule, the Member of the Commission responsible for an item under consideration in a parliamentary committee shall be present at the relevant committee meeting, when invited.

Members of the Commission shall be heard at their request.

Parliamentary committees shall seek to maintain their draft agendas and agendas.

Whenever a parliamentary committee amends its draft agenda or its agenda, the Commission shall be immediately informed thereof.

Where the presence of a Member of the Commission is not explicitly required at a parliamentary committee meeting, the Commission shall ensure that it is represented by a competent official at an appropriate level.

VI. FINAL PROVISIONS

41.   The two Institutions undertake to reinforce their cooperation in the field of information and communication.

42.   The implementation of this Framework Agreement and its Annexes shall be assessed periodically by the two Institutions, and their revision shall be considered, in the light of practical experience, at the request of one of them.

43.   This Framework Agreement shall be reviewed following the entry into force of the Treaty establishing a Constitution for Europe.

Annex 1: Forwarding of confidential information to the European Parliament

1. Scope

1.1.   This Annex shall govern the forwarding to Parliament and the handling of confidential information from the Commission in connection with the exercise of parliamentary prerogatives concerning the legislative and budgetary procedures, the procedure for giving discharge and the exercise in general terms of Parliament's powers of scrutiny. The two Institutions shall act in accordance with their mutual duties of sincere cooperation, in a spirit of complete mutual trust and in the strictest conformity with the relevant Treaty provisions, in particular Articles 6 and 46 of the Treaty on European Union and Article 276 of the Treaty establishing the European Community.

1.2.   'Information' shall mean any written or oral information, whatever the medium and whoever the author may be.

1.3.   The Commission shall ensure that Parliament is given access to information, in accordance with the provisions of this Annex, whenever it receives from one of the parliamentary bodies set out in point 1.4. a request relating to the forwarding of confidential information.

1.4.   In the context of this Annex, the following may request confidential information from the Commission: the President of Parliament, the chairperson of the parliamentary committees concerned, the Bureau and the Conference of Presidents.

1.5.   Information on infringement procedures and procedures relating to competition, in so far as they are not covered by a final Commission decision on the date when the request from one of the parliamentary bodies is received, shall be excluded from this Annex.

1.6.   These provisions shall apply without prejudice to Decision 95/167/EC, Euratom, ECSC of the European Parliament, the Council and Commission of 19 April 1995 on the detailed provisions governing the exercise of the European Parliament's right of inquiry[5] and the relevant provisions of Commission Decision 1999/352/EC, ECSC, Euratom of 28 April 1999 establishing the European Anti-fraud Office (OLAF).[6]

2. General rules

2.1. At the request of one of the bodies referred to in point 1.4., the Commission shall forward to that body with all due despatch any confidential information required for the exercise of Parliament's powers of scrutiny. In accordance with their respective powers and responsibilities, the two Institutions shall respect:

- fundamental human rights, including the right to a fair trial and the right to protection of privacy;
- provisions governing judicial and disciplinary procedures;
- protection of business secrecy and commercial relations;
- protection of the interests of the Union, in particular those relating to public safety, international relations, monetary stability and financial interests.

In the event of a disagreement, the matter shall be referred to the Presidents of the two Institutions so that they may resolve the dispute. Confidential information from a State, an institution or an international organisation shall be forwarded only with its consent.

2.2. In the event of any doubt as to the confidential nature of an item of information, or where it is necessary to lay down the appropriate arrangements for it to be forwarded in accordance with one of the options set out in point 3.2., the chairperson of the parliamentary committee concerned, accompanied, where necessary, by the rapporteur, shall consult the Member of Commission with responsibility for that area without delay. In the event of a disagreement, the matter shall be referred to the Presidents of the two Institutions so that they may resolve the dispute.

2.3. If, at the end of the procedure referred to in point 2.2., no agreement has been reached, the President of Parliament, in response to a reasoned request from the parliamentary committee concerned, shall call on the Commission to forward, within the appropriate deadline duly indicated, the confidential information in question, selecting the arrangements from among the options laid down in section 3 of this Annex. Before the expiry of that deadline, the Commission shall inform Parliament in writing of its final position, in respect of which Parliament reserves the right, if appropriate, to exercise its right to seek redress.

3. Arrangements for access to and the handling of confidential information

3.1. Confidential information forwarded in accordance with the procedures set out in point 2.2. and, where appropriate, point 2.3. shall be forwarded, on the responsibility of the President or of a Member of the Commission, to the parliamentary body which submitted the request.

3.2. Without prejudice to the provisions of point 2.3., access and the arrangements designed to preserve the confidentiality of the information shall be laid down by common accord between the Member of the Commission with responsibility for the area involved and the parliamentary body concerned, duly represented by its chairperson, who shall select one of the following options:

- information intended for the chairperson of and the rapporteur for the relevant parliamentary committee;
- restricted access to information for all members of the relevant parliamentary committee in accordance with the appropriate arrangements, possibly with the documents being collected after they have been studied and a ban on the making of copies;
- discussion in the relevant parliamentary committee, meeting in camera, in accordance with arrangements which may vary by virtue of the degree of confidentiality involved and in accordance with the principles set out in Annex VII to Parliament's Rules of Procedure;
- communication of documents from which all personal details have been expunged;
- in instances justified on absolutely exceptional grounds, information intended for the President of Parliament alone.

The information in question may not be published or forwarded to any other addressee.

3.3. In the event of non-compliance with these arrangements, the provisions relating to sanctions set out in Annex VII to Parliament's Rules of Procedure shall apply.

3.4. With a view to the implementation of the provisions set out above, Parliament shall ensure that the following arrangements are actually put in place:

- a secure archive system for documents classified as confidential;
- a secure reading room (without photocopying machines, telephones, fax facilities, scanners or any other technical equipment for the reproduction and transmission of documents, etc.);
- security provisions governing access to the reading room, including the requirements of signature in an access register and a solemn declaration not to disseminate the confidential information examined.

3.5. The Commission shall take all the measures required for the implementation of the provisions of this Annex.

Annex 2: Timetable for the Commission legislative and work programme

1. In February, the President of the Commission and/or the Vice-President responsible for inter-institutional relations shall present the Annual Policy Strategy decision (APS) for the following year to the Conference of Presidents.

2. At the February-March part-session, the Institutions concerned shall take part in a debate on the main lines of the political priorities, based on the APS decision for the following year.

3. Following that debate, the competent parliamentary committees and the relevant Members of the Commission shall conduct a regular bilateral dialogue throughout the year to assess the state of implementation of the current Commission legislative and work programme and discuss the preparation of the future programme in each of their specific areas. Each

parliamentary committee shall regularly report on the outcome of those meetings to the Conference of Committee Chairs.

4.   The Conference of Committee Chairs shall hold a regular exchange of views with the Commission Vice-President responsible for inter-institutional relations, in order to assess the state of implementation of the current Commission legislative and work programme, discuss the preparation of the future programme, and take stock of the results of the on-going bilateral dialogue between the parliamentary committees concerned and relevant Members of the Commission.

5.   In September, the Conference of Committee Chairs shall submit a summary report to the Conference of Presidents, which shall inform the Commission thereof.

6.   At the November part-session, the President of the Commission shall present before Parliament the Commission's legislative and work programme for the following year, with the College taking part. This presentation shall include an assessment of the implementation of the current programme. The presentation shall be followed by the adoption of a Parliament resolution at the December part-session.

7.   The Commission's legislative and work programme shall be accompanied by a list of legislative and non-legislative proposals for the following year, in a form to be decided.[7] The programme shall be forwarded to Parliament in sufficient time before the part-session at which it is to be debated.

8.   This timetable shall be applied to each regular programming cycle, except for Parliament election years coinciding with the end of the Commission's term of office.

9.   This timetable shall not prejudice any future agreement on inter-institutional programming.

---

[1]   OJ L 44, 15.2.2005, p.1

[2]   OJ C 121, 24.4.2001, p.122

[3]   OJ L 184, 17.7.1999, p.23

[4]   OJ L 256, 10.10.2000, p.19

[5]   OJ L 113, 19.5.1995, p.2

[6]   OJ L 136, 31.5.1999, p.20

[7]   To be included: calendar and, where appropriate, legal basis and budgetary implications.

The European Parliament's Rules of Procedure can be consulted in full at http://www.europarl.eu.int

Annex I (i)

Commission in CFSP Institutions and Committees: the Current Situation

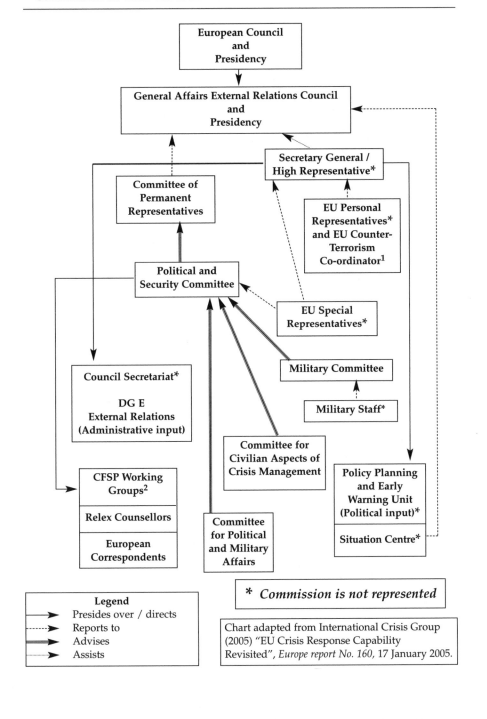

Chart adapted from International Crisis Group (2005) "EU Crisis Response Capability Revisited", *Europe report No. 160*, 17 January 2005.

Annex I (ii)

Commission Role in EU External Action: the Current Situation

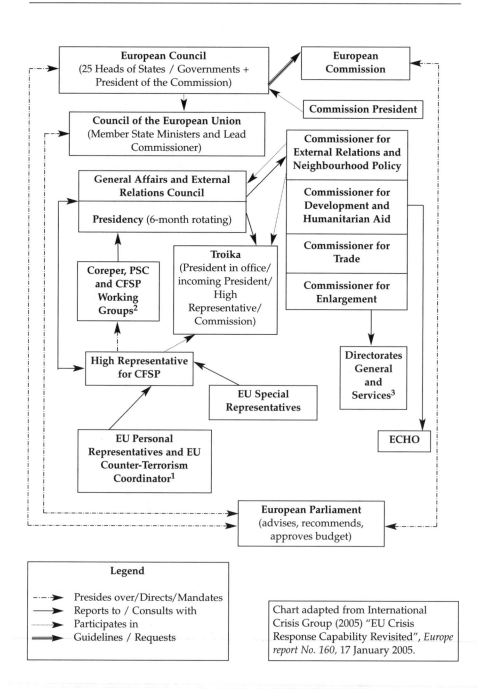

Chart adapted from International Crisis Group (2005) "EU Crisis Response Capability Revisited", *Europe report No. 160*, 17 January 2005.

Annex I (iii)

Commission Role in EU External Action under the European Constitution

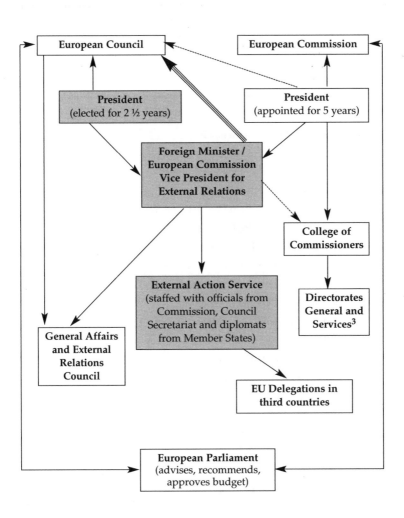

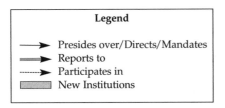

Legend

➤ Presides over/Directs/Mandates
➤ Reports to
┈┈➤ Participates in
▓▓▓ New Institutions

Chart adapted from International Crisis Group (2005) "EU Crisis Response Capability Revisited", *Europe report No. 160,* 17 January 2005.

Footnotes for Annex I:

[1] The SG/HR currently has two EU Personal Representatives: Annalisa Giannella, PR on non-proliferation of weapons of mass destruction (appointed 10 October 2003) and Michael Matthiessen, PR for human rights in the area of CFSP (appointed 16 January 2005). The EU Counter-Terrorism Co-ordinator, Gijs de Vries, was appointed on 25 March 2004. In only one case does the same person act as both the EU Special Representative and the Head of the Commission Delegation – the Former Yugoslav Republic of Macedonia (Erwan Fouéré, Ireland).

[2] The CFSP Working Groups are:

    1. Working Party of Foreign Relations Counsellors

    (a) Sanctions

    2. Working Party on Public International Law

    (a) International Criminal Court

    3. Working Party on the Law of the Sea

    4. United Nations Working Party

    5. Working Party on OSCE and the Council of Europe

    6. Working Party on Human Rights

    7. Working Party on Transatlantic Relations

    8. Working Party on Central and Southeast Europe

    9. Working Party on Eastern Europe and Central Asia

    10. Working Party on EFTA

    11. Working Party on the Western Balkans Region

    12. Ad hoc Working Party on the Middle East Peace Process

    13. Middle East/Gulf Working Party

    14. Mashreq/Maghreb Working Party

    15. Africa Working Party

    16. ACP Working Party

    17. Asia-Oceania Working Party

    18. Working Party on Latin America

    19. Working Party on Terrorism (International Aspects)

    20. Working Party on Non-Proliferation

    21. Working Party on Conventional Arms Exports

    22. Working Party on Global Disarmament and Arms Control

    23. Working Party on Dual-Use Goods

    24. Working Party on European Arms Policy

    25. Politico-Military Working Party

    26. Military Committee Working Group (EUMCWG)

    27. Working Party on Trade Questions

    28. Working Party on the Generalised System of Preferences

29. Export Credits Group

30. Working Party on Development Cooperation

31. Working Party on Preparation for International Development Conferences

32. Working Party on Food Aid

33. Working Party on Commodities

34. Working Party on Consular Affairs

35. Working Party on CFSP Administrative Affairs and Protocol

36. Nicolaidis Group

3 The Directorates-General concerned with external affairs are DG Relex, DG Trade, DG Development, DG Enlargement, EuropeAid and ECHO.

Annex J

Foreign Ministries and Commission Delegations at home and abroad

	MFA Staff Total	MFA Staff in Capital	MFA Staff in Embassies	Local Staff	MFA + Local Staff Total	No. of Embassies	No. of Consulates
Austria	1,314	561	753	620	1,934	86	15
Belgium	1,800	1,400	400	1,800	3,600	86	15
Cyprus	250	160	90	290	540	44	5
Czech Republic	2,200	780	1,420	610	2,810	98	28
Denmark	1,270	1,000	270	900	2,170	75	20
Estonia	600	370	230	90	690	36	4
Finland	2,590	950	1,640	970	3,560	83	7
France	9,400	4,000	5,400	14,300	23,700	182	110
Germany	6,700	2,200	4,500	4,800	11,500	157	58
Greece	2,500	1,000	1,500	320	2,820	87	59
Hungary	2,000	1,000	1,000	*	*	82	28
Ireland	980	490	490	276	1,256	43	7
Italy	5,300	2,500	2,800	2,250	7,550	130	114
Latvia	640	360	280	80	720	60	4
Lithuania	620	340	280	250	870	42	9
Luxembourg	180	90	90	160	340	24	2
Malta	305	220	85	141	446	18	7
Netherlands	3,210	1,970	1,240	1,580	4,790	126	28
Poland	1,800	650	1,150	*	*	106	51
Portugal	950	400	550	1,840	2,790	76	50
Slovakia	750	500	250	*	*	72	11
Slovenia	560	310	250	230	790	67	10
Spain	2,500	1,500	1,000	3,200	5,700	136	67
Sweden	1,450	900	550	1,000	2,450	91	11
United Kingdom	5,900	3,500	2,400	10,000	15,900	163	70
EU 25	**55,769**	**27,151**	**28,618**	**47,766**	**103,535**	**2,170**	**790**
Bulgaria	1,200	600	600	*	*	84	7
Romania	1,950	600	1,350	*	*	103	26
EU 27	**58,919**	**28,351**	**30,568**	**49,766**	**108,685**	**2,357**	**823**
Commission	**3,250**	**2,260**	**990**	**3,765**	**7,015**	**123**	**n/a**
Council Secretariat	**100**	**80**	**20**	**0**	**100**	**2**	**n/a**
For comparison							
United States	44,500	25,600	18,900	18,900	63,400	170	63
Japan	5,290	2,070	3,220	4,894	10,184	139	79

Annex J: Explanatory Notes

Sources:

The data are from varying years between 2000 and 2005, though figures for Poland are from 1998, and figures for the number of 'local staff' for Ireland and Japan are from 1999. Data are derived from several sources including: Ministry of Foreign Affairs (MFA) websites and annual reports, Statistical Yearbooks, written and oral replies from MFAs, OECD Sigma reports, European Council document 1731/6/00 (Solana report to the European Council at Evian). Data for US diplomatic staff are from testimonies by senior State Department officials Joseph E. Kelley at the US General Accounting Office on 6 April 1995 and by Grant S. Green Jr. in Congress on 1 May 2002.

Definitions:

The number of embassies includes states' permanent missions, delegations and representations to international organisations, as well as High Commissions (the name for embassies of the United Kingdom in Commonwealth countries). For the Commission and Council Secretariat, the number of embassies refers to their delegations and representations to international organisations.

Roving Ambassadors are ambassadors that perform their duties abroad, but are based in their Ministry of Foreign Affairs. Roving Ambassadors are classed as Non-resident Ambassadors and are not counted as 'embassies', though they are included in overall 'staff' figures.

The number of consulates does not include honorary consulates, consular agencies and trade representations (e.g. to Taiwan), though it is possible that some overall figures provided by foreign ministries include such representations.

Consular departments within embassies are considered part of the embassy and not counted separately.

Caveats:

The 'local staff' and 'MFA and local staff total' figures are not precise, because national figures for 'local staff' are either missing (denoted with an asterisk) or unreliable. An approximate figure for total 'local staff' for EU 25 could be 47,766 and for EU 27 could be 49,766 and an approximate figure for 'MFA and local staff total' for EU 25 could be 103,535 and for EU 27 could be 108,685, but these figures are guesstimates.

High consular representation of some Member States is partly attributable to specific national inward immigration issues.

Efforts were made to verify that MFAs used the above-mentioned definitions when providing their figures, but this was not always possible. Minor fluctuations in data due to different definitions must therefore be taken into account.

Some Member States include trade and development functions in their MFA, while others have separate ministries.

Some include culture and trade promotion officers as embassy/consular staff, while others do not.

European Commission representations (information offices) in the EU are not included, since they do not provide the same diplomatic functions as Commission Delegations outside the EU. Comparisons between the number of Commission Delegations 'abroad' (i.e. outside the EU) and Member State embassies must take this into account. While total Member State figures include a large number of bilateral embassies within the EU, the Commission figure is thus 25 short, so comparisons of geographic implantation based on overall figures would be misleading. Likewise, for example, whereas Malta has only eighteen embassies world wide, the UK has twenty-four within the EU alone.

Commission staff figures include staff working abroad for DGs RELEX, DEV, TRADE, AIDCO AND ECHO.

BIBLIOGRAPHY

Abélès, M. (1994). "A la recherche d'un espace public communautaire", *Pouvoirs*, 64, pp. 117-128.

Abélès, M. (2004) "Identities and Borders: An Anthropological Approach to EU Institutions", *On Line Working Papers*, Center for 21st Century Studies, University of Wisconsin - Milwaukee.

Abélès, M. and I. Bellier (1996) "La Commission Européenne: Du Compromis Culturelle à la Culture Du Compromis", *Revue Française de Science Politique*, vol. 46, no. 3, pp. 431 - 56.

Abélès, M., I. Bellier and M. McDonald (1993) "Approche Anthropologique de la Commission Européenne", Brussels: unpublished internal report of the European Commission.

Ahnfelt, E. and J. From (2001) "Policy on Justice and Home Affairs: From High to Low Politics" in S. S. Andersen and K. A. Eliasen (eds) *Making Policy in Europe*, London: Sage.

Alexandrikis, N. (1996) *The Lost Union*, London: Minerva.

Allen, D. (1978) "The Euro-Arab Dialogue", *Journal of Common Market Studies*, vol. 16, no. 4, pp. 323 - 342.

Allen, D. (1996) "Conclusions: The European Rescue of National Foreign Policy" in C. Hill (ed) *The Actors in Europe's Foreign Policy*, London: Routledge.

Allen, D. (1998) "Who Speaks for Europe? The Search for an Effective and Coherent External Policy" in J. Peterson and H. Sjursen (eds) *A Common Foreign Policy for Europe? Competing Visions of the CFSP*, London: Routledge.

Allen, D. and M. Smith (1991 - 1992) "The European Community in the New Europe: Bearing the Burden of Change", *International Journal*, vol. 47, no. 1, winter, pp. 1 - 28.

Allen, D. and W. Wallace (1977) "Political Cooperation: Procedure as Substitute for Policy" in H. Wallace, W. Wallace and C. Webb (eds) *Policy Making in the European Communities*, London: John Wiley and Sons.

Allio, L. (2003) "The Case for Comitology Reform: Efficiency, Transparency, Accountability", Brussels: European Policy Centre.

Alting von Geusau, F. A. M. (1993) *Beyond Containment and Division: Western Co-operation from a Post Totalitarian Perspective*, Dordrecht: Nijhoff.

Amnesty International (2005) "Human Rights Dissolving at the Borders? Counter-terrorism and EU Criminal Law", 31 May 2005.

Andréani, G., C. Bertram and C. Grant (2001) "Europe's Military Revolution", Centre for European Reform, April 2001.

Anthropology (1994) "Approche Anthropologique de la Commission Européenne", unpublished report prepared for the European Commission.

Arthur Andersen (2000) "Evaluation of the EEA and the EIONET 1994-2000" as quoted in European Commission, *Meta-Evaluation on the Community Agency System*, Budget Directorate General, Evaluation Unit, Final Report, 15 September 2003, p. 30.

Aubert, F. (1995) *Main basse sur l'Europe*, Paris: Plon.

Auel, K. and B. Ritberger (2005) "Fluctuant nec mergunter: the European Parliament, National Parliaments, and European Integration" in J. Richardson (ed) *European Union: Power and Policy-Making* 3rd edition, London: Routledge.

Bach, M. (1995) "Ist die europäische Einigung irreversibel? Integrationspolitik als Institutionenbildung in der Europäischen Union" in B. Nedelmann (ed) *Politische Institutionen im Wandel*, Opladen: Westdeutscher Verlag.

Bailey, D. and L. De Propis (2004) "EU Pre-accession Aid and Capacity-building in the Candidate Countries", *Journal of Common Market Studies*, vol. 42, no. 1, pp. 77 - 98.

Baldwin, R. and C. McCrudden (1987) *Regulation and Public Law*, London: Weidenfeld and Nicolson.

Baldwin, R. and M. Widgrén (2004) "Winners and Losers under Various Dual-Majority Voting

Rules for the EU's Council of Ministers", *CEPS Policy Brief* no. 50.

Bale, T. (2000) "Field-level CFSP: EU Diplomatic Co-operation in Third Countries", *Current Politics and Economics of Europe*, vol. 10, no. 2, pp. 187 – 212.

Barber, L. and D. Gardner (1993) "Brussels Wants US Treaties Modified", *Financial Times*, 15 July 1993.

Barker, R. (2003) "Legitimacy, Legitimation and the European Union: What Crisis?" in P. Graig and R. Rawlings (eds) *Law and Administration in Europe: Essays in Honour of Carol Harlow*, Oxford: Oxford University Press.

Barnier, M. and A. Vitorino (2002) "Contribution of Mr Barnier and Mr Vitorino to the European Convention on the Community method", CONV 231/02, CONTRIB 80, Brussels, 3 September 2002.

Barroso, José Manuel (2005) "Tsunami and Reinforcing EU Disaster and Crisis Response", speaking points for the General Affairs and External Relations Council, Brussels, 31 January 2005.

Beach, D. (2002) "Bringing Negotiations back into the Study of the European Union – Supranational Actors and the Negotiating Process in the 1996-97 IGC", paper submitted to the International Studies Association annual convention, New Orleans, USA, 24 – 27 March 2002.

Beach, D. (2004) "The Unseen Hand in Treaty Reform Negotiations: The Role and Influence of the Council Secretariat", *Journal of European Public Policy*, vol. 11, no. 3, pp. 408 - 439.

Beach, D. (2006) "The Council Secretariat in the 1996-7 and the 2003-4 IGCs", in C. Mazzucelli and D. Beach (eds.) *Leadership in EU Constitutional Negotiations*, Basingstoke: Palgrave.

Bearfield, D. (2004) "Reforming the European Commission: Driving Reform from the Grassroots", *Public Policy and Administration*, vol. 19, no. 3, pp. 13 - 24.

Beetham, D. and C. Lord (1998) *Legitimacy and the EU*, London: Longman.

Bellier, I. (1997) "The Commission as an Actor: An Anthropologist's View" in H. Wallace and A. R. Young (eds) *Participation and Policy-Making in the European Union*, London: Oxford University Press.

Bellier, I. (1999) "European Institutions and Linguistic Diversity : A Problematic Unity", in H. S. Chopra, R. Frank and J. Schröder (eds.) *National Identities and Regional Cooperation : Experiences of European Integration and South Asia Perceptions*, New Delhi: Manohar, pp. 82-100.

Bellier, I. (2000a) "The European Union, Identity Politics and the Logic of Interests Representation" in I. Bellier and T. A. Wilson (eds) *Anthropology of the European Union*, Oxford: Berg.

Benelux Memorandum (1955) in S. Patijn (ed) *Landmarks in European Unity*, Leiden: A. W. Sithoff, 1970.

Berlin, D. (1987) "Organisation of the Commission" in S. Cassese (ed) *The European Administration*, Brussels: IIAS.

Bilbao, J. M., J. R. Fernández, N. Jiménez and J. J. López (2002) "Voting Power in the European Union Enlargement", *European Journal of Operational Research*, no. 143, pp. 181 - 196.

Blumann, C. (1988) "Le pouvoir exécutif de la Commission à la lumière de l'Acte unique européenne" in C. Engel and W. Wessels (eds.) *From Luxembourg to Maastricht, Institutional Change in the European Community after the Single European Act*: Europa Union Verlag, 1992, pp. 89 - 108 (quoted translation by Docksey and Williams).

Boin, A., M. Ekengren and M. Rhinard (2005) "Functional Security and Crisis Management Capacity in the European Union", report presented at the Swedish National Defence College, Stockholm, February 2005.

Boin, A., P. 't Hart, E. K. Stern and B. Sundelius (2005) *The Politics of Crisis Management: Understanding Public Leadership When it Matters Most*, Cambridge: Cambridge University Press.

Bomberg, E. and A. Stubb (eds.) *The European Union: How Does It Work?* Oxford: Oxford University Press.

Bonvicini, G. (1982) "The Dual Structure of EPC and Community Activities: Problems of Coordination" in D. Allen, R. Rummel and W. Wessels (eds) *European Political Cooperation*, London: Butterworth.

Bourgeois, J. H. J. (1997) "Mixed Agreements: A New Approach?" in J. H. J. Burgeois, J.-L. Dewost and M.-A. Gaffe (eds) *La Communauté européenne et les accords mixtes, Quelles perspectives?*, Brussels: European Interuniversity Press.

Bourlanges, J.-L. (1996) "Achieving a New Balance between Large and Small Member States" in Philip Morris Institute, *In a Larger EU, Can All Member States be Equal?*, Brussels: Philip Morris Institute.

Bouwen, P. (2002) "Corporate Lobbying in the European Union: The Logic of Access", *Journal of European Public Policy*, vol. 9, no. 3, pp. 365 – 390.

Bradley, K. St. C. (1997) "The European Parliament and Comitology – On the Road to

Nowhere?", *European Law Journal*, vol. 3, no. 3, p. 230.

Braselmann, P. (1992) "Ubernationales Recht und Mehrsprachigkeit: Linguistische Uberlegungen Zur Sprachproblemen in EuGH-Urteilen", *Europarecht*, vol. 27, no. 1, pp. 55-74.

Bräuninger, T. and T. König (2004) "Voting Power in the Post-Nice European Union", manuscript.

Brinkhorst, L. J. (1996) "The Future of European Agencies: A Budgetary Perspective from the European Parliament" in A. Kreher (ed) *The New European Agencies, EUI Working Paper* no. 96/49, Florence: European University Institute.

Brittan, L. (1994) *Europe: The Europe We Need*, London: Hamish Hamilton.

Broscheid, A. and D. Coen (2003) "Insider and Outsider Lobbying of the European Commission", *European Union Politics*, vol. 4, no. 2, pp. 265 – 289.

Bruter, M. (1999) "Diplomacy without a State: The External Delegations of the European Commission", *Journal of European Public Policy*, vol. 6, no. 2, pp. 183 – 205.

Bruton, J. (2003) "A Proposal for the Appointment of the President of the Commission as Provided for in Article 18bis of the Draft Constitutional Treaty", Convention on the Future of Europe, CONV 476/03, Brussels, 9 January 2003.

Buchan, D. (1993) *Europe: The Strange Superpower*, Aldershot: Dartmouth.

Buchet de Neuilly, Y. (2005) *L'Europe de la Politique Etrangère*, Paris: Economica.

Bulmer, S. (1994) "The Governance of the European Union. A New Institutionalist Approach", *Journal of Public Policy*, vol. 13, no. 4, pp. 351 - 380.

Bulmer, S. and W. Wessels (1987) *The European Council, Decision-Making in European Politics*, Houndmills: Macmillan Press.

Bulmer, S. and C. Lequesne (eds) (2005) *The Member States of the European Union*, Oxford: Oxford University Press.

Bunyan, T. (2002) "The 'War on Freedom and Democracy': An Analysis of the Effects on Civil Liberties and Democratic Culture in the EU", *Statewatch Analysis* no. 13, 6 September 2002.

Burgess, M. (2004) "Federalism" in A. Wiener and T. Diez (eds) *European Integration Theory*, Oxford: Oxford University Press.

Burgess, N. and D. Spence (2004) "The European Union: New Threats and the Problem of Coherence" in A. Bailes and I. Frommelt (eds) *Business and Security*, Oxford: Oxford University Press.

Burghardt, G. (2004) speech at the 50th anniversary of the opening of the first Commission Delegation in Washington, 6 May 2004.

Burley, A.-M. and W. Mattli (1993) "Europe before the Court: A Political Theory of Legal Integration", *International Organization*, vol. 47, no. 1, pp. 41 - 76.

Burrows, B. et al (1978) *Federal Solutions to European Issues*, London: Macmillan.

Buzan, B., O. Waever, and J. de Wilde (1998) *Security: A New Framework of Analysis*, Boulder: Lynne Rienner.

Calingaert, M. (1996) *European Integration Revisited: Progress, Prospects and Implications for US Business*, Boulder: Lynne Rienner.

Calvert, R., M. McCubbins and B. Weingast (1989) "A Theory of Political Control and Agency Discretion", *American Journal of Political Science*, vol. 33, no. 3, pp. 588 - 611.

Cameron, F. (2004) "The Convention and CFSP/ESDP" in M. Holland (ed) *Common Foreign and Security Policy: The First Ten Years* 2nd edition, London: Continuum.

Cameron, F. and G. Grevi (2005) "*Towards an EU Foreign Service*", *European Policy Centre Issue Paper 29*, April 2005.

Caporaso, J. and J. Keeler (1995) "The European Union and Regional Integration Theory" in C. Rhodes and S. Mazey (eds.) *The State of the Union Vol. 3: Building a European Polity*, Arlow: Longman.

Cassanmagnago-Cerretti, M-L. (1993) "The Role of National Experts and the Commission's Right of Initiative", report of the Committee on Institutional Affairs, European Parliament.

Cassese, S. (1987) "Divided Powers: European Administration and National Administrations" in S. Cassese (ed) *The European Administration*, Brussels: International Institute of Administrative Sciences.

Chisholm, D. (1989) *Co-ordination without Hierarchy: Informal Structures in Multi-organisational Systems*, Berkeley: University of California Press.

Chiti, E. (2000) "The Emergence of a Community Administration: The Case of European Agencies", *Common Market Law Review*, vol. 37, pp. 309 - 343.

Christiansen, T. (2001) "Inter-institutional Relations and Intra-institutional Politics in the EU: Towards Coherent Governance?", *Journal of European Public Policy* , vol. 8, no. 5, pp. 747 - 769.

Christiansen, T. (2001a) "The European Commission: Administration in Turbulent Times" in J. Richardson (ed) *European Union: Power and Policy-Making*, London: Routledge.

Christiansen, T. (2002) "The Role of Supranational Institutions in EU Treaty Reform", *Journal of European Public Policy*, vol. 9, no. 1, pp. 33 - 53.

Christiansen, T., K.-E. Jørgensen and A. Wiener (eds) (2001) *The Social Construction of Europe*, London: Sage.

Christiansen, T., G. Falkner and K. Jørgensen (2002) "Theorising EU Treaty Reform: Beyond Diplomacy and Bargaining", *Journal of European Public Policy*, vol. 9, no. 1, pp. 12 - 32.

Christiansen, T. and K. Jørgensen (1998) "Negotiating Treaty Reform in the European Union: The role of the European Commission", *International Negotiation*, vol. 3, no. 3, pp. 435 - 452.

Christiansen, T. and M. Gray (2003) "The European Commission and Treaty Reform", *EIPAS-COPE* no. 2003/03, pp. 10 - 18.

Chryssochoou, D., M. Tsinisizelis, S. Stavridis and K. Ifantis (ed) (1999) *Theory and Reform in the EU*, Manchester: Manchester University Press.

Cini, M. (1996) *The European Commission: Leadership, Organisation, and Culture in the EU Administration*, Manchester: Manchester University Press.

Cini, M. (2001) "Reforming the European Commission: An Organisational Culture Perspective", *Queen's Papers on Europeanisation*, 11/2001.

Cini, M. (2004) "Norms, Culture and the Kinnock White Paper: The Theory and Practice of Cultural Change in the Reform of the Commission" in D. Dimitrakopoulos (ed) *The Changing European Commission*, Manchester: Manchester University Press.

Cini, M. (2004a) "Reforming the European Commission: An Ethical Perspective", *Public Policy and Administration*, vol. 19, no. 3, pp. 42 – 54.

Cini, M. and L. McGowan (1998) *European Competition Policy*, Basingstoke: Macmillan.

Close, G. (1990) "External Relations in the Air Transport Sector: Air Transport Policy or the Common Commercial Policy?", *Common Market Law Review*, vol. 27, no. 1, spring, pp. 107 - 127.

Cockfield, A. (1994) *The European Union: Creating the Single Market*, London: Wiley Chancery Law.

Coen, D. (1999) "Business Interests and European Integration", paper presented at the conference "Organised Interests in the European Union: Lobbying, Mobilisation and the European Public Area", Nuffield College, Oxford, 1 - 2 October 1999.

Coleman, W. and S. Tangermann (1999) "The 1992 CAP Reform, the Uruguay Round and the Commission", *Journal of Common Market Studies*, vol. 37, no. 3, pp. 385 - 406.

Colonna, C. (2005) Press declaration following visit of Javier Solana to the Quai d'Orsay, Paris, 26 September 2005.

Committee of Independent Experts (1999) "First Report on Allegations regarding Fraud, Mismanagement and Nepotism in the European Commission", 15 March 1999, and "Second Report on Reform of the Commission – Analysis of Current Practice and Proposals for Tackling Mismanagement, Irregularities and Fraud", 10 September 1999.

Committee of Three (1979) "Report on the European Institutions", report presented to the European Council, Brussels, October 1979.

Common Market Law Review (1999) "The Identity of the EU from the Perspective of Third Countries", editorial comments, vol. 36, no. 5, pp. 881 – 886.

Connolly, B. (1995) *The Rotten Heart of Europe*, London: Faber & Faber.

Conrad, Y. (1992) "La Communauté Européenne Du Charbon et de l'Acier et la Situation de Ses Agents. Du Régime Contractuel Au Régime Statutaire (1952-1958)", *Jahrbuch Für Europäische Verwaltungsgeschichte*, 4 (Die Anfänge der Verwaltung der Europäischen Gemeinschaft), pp. 59 - 74.

Coombes, D. (1968) *Towards a European Civil Service*, London: Chatham House/PEP.

Coombes, D. (1970) *Politics and Bureaucracy in the European Community*, London: George Allen and Unwin.

Cooper, A. (1998) "Diplomatic Puzzles: A Review of the Literature" in W. Woolfe (ed) *Diplomatic Missions: the Ambassador in Canadian Foreign Policy*, Montreal: McGill-Queen's University Press.

Cooper, R. (2004) *The Breaking of Nations: Order and Chaos in the 21st Century*, London: Atlantic Books.

Corbett, R. (1998) *The European Parliament's Role in Closer EU Integration*, London: Palgrave.

Corbett, R., F. Jacobs and M. Shackleton (2003) *The European Parliament* 5th edition, London: John Harper.

Cornish, P. and G. Edwards (2005) "The Strategic Culture of the European Union: A Progress Report", *International Affairs*, vol. 81, no. 4, pp. 801 – 820.

Coull, J. and C. Lewis (2003) "The Impact Reform (sic) of the Staff Regulations in Making the

Commission a More Modern and Efficient Organisation: An Insider's Perspective", *EIPASCOPE* no. 2003/3, pp. 2 – 9.

Court of Auditors (1997) "Opinion on the CFSP", unpublished opinion referred to in Court of Auditors Special Report 13/2001 OJ C 338/7 on the management of the CFSP, vol. 44, 30 November 2004.

Court of Auditors (2001) "Special Report no. 13 on the Management of CFSP", OJ C 338, vol. 44, 30 November 2001.

Court of Auditors (2004) "Special Report no. 10 concerning the Audit of Devolution of EC External Aid Management to the Commission Delegations", March 2004.

Court of Auditors (2004a) "Annual Report Concerning the Financial Year 2003", European Court of Auditors, Luxembourg.

Cram, L. (1994) "The European Commission as a Multi-organisation: Social Policy and IT Policy in the EU", *Journal of European Public Policy*, vol. 1, no. 2, pp. 194 - 217.

Crocodile Lettre (1983) aux membres du Parlement européen no. 11, June 1983, pp. 2 – 9.

Crombez, C. (2000) "Institutional Reform and Co-decision in the European Union", *Constitutional Political Economy*, vol. 11, no. 1, pp. 41 - 57.

Crowe, B. (2005) "Foreign Minister of Europe", Foreign Policy Centre, February 2005.

Curtin, D. (2005) "Delegation to EU Non-Majoritarian Agencies and Emerging Practicesof Public Accountability" in D. Geradin and N. Petit (eds) *Regulation Through Agencies: A New Paradigm of European Governance*, Cheltenham: Edward Elgar.

Dahrendorf, R. (writing as Wieland Europa, 9 July 1971) "A New Goal for Europe", *Die Zeit*, vol. 28, translated and reproduced in Michael Hodges (1972) *European Integration*, London: Penguin.

Daily Telegraph (2005) "Diplomats Axed by Whitehall Cost-cutters", 2 February 2005.

Dashwood, A. and C. Hillion (eds) (2000) *The General Law of EC External Relations*, London: Sweet & Maxwell.

Davignon, E. (1995) "The Challenges that the Commission Must Confront" in Philip Morris Institute, *What Future for the European Commission?* Brussels: Philip Morris Institute.

"Davignon Report" (1970) adopted in Luxembourg on 27 October 1970, *Bulletin of the European Communities*, November 1970, no. 11, pp. 9 - 14.

De Boissieu, P. (2002) Oral Contribution to the Convention on Foreign Policy and External Relations: CFSP Financing, 15 October 2002.

De Burca, G. and J. Scott (eds) (2001) *The EU and the WTO: Legal and Constitutional Issues*, Oxford: Hart.

De Cecco, M. (ed) (2000) *European Union and New Regionalism*, Aldershot: Ashgate.

De Gaulle, C. (1971) *Memoirs of Hope: renewal & endeavour*, London: Weidenfeld & Nicolson.

De Gucht, K. (2003) "The European Commission: Countdown to Extinction?", *Journal of European Integration*, vol. 25, no. 1, p. 165.

Dehousse, R. (1997) "Regulation by Networks in the European Community: The Role of European Agencies", *Journal of European Public Policy*, vol. 4, no. 2, pp. 246 - 261.

Dehousse, R. (2001) "European Governance in Search of Legitimacy: The Need for a Process-based Approach" in European Commission, *Governance in the European Union* 'Cahiers' of the Forward Studies Unit Brussels.

Dehousse, R. (2002) "Misfits: EU Law and the Transformation of European Governance", *Harvard Jean Monnet Working Paper* no. 2/02.

Dehousse, R., C. Joerges, G. Majone and F. Snyder (1992) "Europe after 1992: New Regulatory Strategies", *EUI Working Papers in Law* no. 92/31, Florence: European University Institute.

De la Porte, C. and P. Pochet (eds) (2002) *Building Social Europe through the Open Method of Co-ordination*, Brussels: PIE-Peter Lang.

De Lobkowicz, W. (2002) *L'Europe et la Sécurité Intérieure*, Paris: Les Etudes de la Documentation Française.

Delors, J. (1994) *L'Unité d'un Homme: entretiens avec Dominique Wolton*, Paris, Odile Jacob.

Delors, J. (1996) "A Personal Tribute by Former European Commission President Jacques Delors", *European Voice*, 5 - 11 September 1996.

Delors, J. (2004) *Mémoires*, Paris: Plon.

Den Boer, M. (1996) "Justice and Home Affairs" in H. Wallace and W. Wallace (eds) *Policy-making in the European Union*, Oxford: Oxford University Press.

Denman, R. (1990) "There Are not Enough Sir Humphreys in Europe", *The Independent*, 6 March 1990.

De Ruyt, J. (1987) *L'Acte Unique Européen*, Brussels: Université de Bruxelles.

Der Spiegel (2000) 3 July 2000 article quoted in F. Cameron and D. Spence (2004) "The Commission - Council Tandem in the Foreign Policy Arena", p. 137, footnote 6, in D. G. Dimitrakopoulos (ed) *The Changing European Commission*, Manchester: Manchester University Press.

De Schoutheete, P. and H. Wallace (2002) *The European Council*, Paris: Notre Europe.

Destler, I. M. (1992) *American Trade Politics*, Washington, DC: Institute for International Economics / Twentieth Century Fund.

Devuyst, Y. (1992) "The EC's Common Commercial Policy and the Treaty on European Union: An Overview of the Negotiations", *World Competition*, vol. 16, no. 2, pp. 67 - 80.

Dickson, B. (2005) "Law Versus Terrorism: Can Law Win?", *European Human Rights Law Review*, vol. 1, no. 1, pp. 11 - 28.

Diebold, W. Jr (1972) *The United States and the Industrial World: American Foreign Economic Policy in the 1970s*, New York: Praeger for the Council on Foreign Relations.

Dimier, V. (2004) "Administrative Reform as Political Control: Lessons from DG VIII, 1958 – 1975" in D. G. Dimitrakopoulos (ed) *The Changing European Commission*, Manchester: Manchester University Press.

Dimitrakopoulos, D. (2004) *The Changing European Commission*, Manchester: Manchester University Press.

Dimitrakopoulos, D. G. and H. Kassim (2004) "Domestic Preference Formation and EU Treaty Reform", Special Edition of *Comparative European Politics*, vol. 2, no. 3.

Dimitrakopoulos, D. G. and H. Kassim (2005) "Inside the European Commission: Preference Formation and the Convention on the Future of Europe", *Comparative European Politics*, vol. 3, no. 2.

Dimitrakopoulos, D. G. and H. Kassim (2005) "La Commission européenne et la débat sur l'avenir de l'Europe", *Critique Internationale*, no. 29.

Dimitrakopoulos, D. G. and H. Kassim (2006) "Leader or Bystander? The European Commission and EU Treaty Reform", in C. Mazzucelli and D. Beach (eds.) *Leadership in EU Constitutional Negotiations*, Basingstoke: Palgrave.

Dinan, D. (1997) "The Commission and the Reform Process" in G. Edwards and A. Pijpers (eds) *The Politics of the European Treaty Reform – The 1996 Inter-Governmental Conference and Beyond*, London: Pinter Ed.

Dinan, D. (1997a) "The Commission and Intergovernmental Conferences" in N. Nugent (ed) *At the Heart of the Union: Studies of the European Commission*, Houndmills: Macmillan.

Dinan, D. (ed.) (2000), *Encyclopedia of the European Union 2nd Ed.*, The European Union Series, London: Basingstoke.

Dinan, D. (2003) "Governance and Institutions: Anticipating the Impact of Enlargement", *Journal of Common Market Studies*, vol. 41, annual review, pp. 27 – 43.

Dinan, D. (2005) *Ever Closer Union: An Introduction to European Integration*, Houndmills: Palgrave Macmillan.

Dittrich, M. (2005) "Facing the Global Terrorist Threat: A European Response", *European Policy Centre Working Paper* no. 14.

Docksey, C. (1987) "The European Community and the Promotion of Equality" in C. McCudden (ed) *Women, Employment and Equality Law*, London: Eclipse, p. 1.

Docksey, C. and K. Williams (1994) "The Commission and the Execution of Community Policy", in G. Edwards and D. Spence (eds.) *The European Commission*, Harlow 1994, pp.117-144.

Dogan, R. (1997) "Comitology: Little Procedures with Big Implications", *West European Politics*, vol. 20, no. 3, pp. 31 - 60.

Dooge Report (1985) "Report of the Ad Hoc Committee on Institutional Questions to the European Council", *Europe Documents*, nos 1349/1350, 21 March 1985.

Drake, H. (2000) *Jacques Delors: Perspectives on a European Leader*, London: Routledge.

Drulak, P., J. Cesal and S. Hampl (2003) "Interactions and Identities of Czech Civil Servants on their way to the EU", *Journal of European Public Policy*, vol. 10, no. 4, pp. 637 - 654.

Dubouis, L. (1975) "L'influence Française sur la Fonction Publique Communautaire" in J. Rideau et al., *La France et les Communautés Européennes*, Paris.

Dudley, G. and J. Richardson (1999) "Competing Advocacy Coalitions and the Process of 'Frame Reflection': A Longitudinal Analysis of EU Steel Policy", *Journal of European Public Policy*, vol. 6, no. 2, pp. 225 - 248.

Duff, A. (1995) "Building A Parliamentary Europe" in M. Teló (ed) *Démocratie et Construction européenne*, Brussels: Editions de l'Université de Bruxelles.

Duke, S. (2002) "Preparing for European Diplomacy?", *Journal of Common Market Studies*, vol. 40, no. 5, pp. 849 - 870.

Dyson, K. (ed) (2002) *European States and the Euro. Europeanization, Variation, and Convergence*, Oxford: Oxford University Press.

Eberlein, B. and E. Grande (2005) "Beyond Delegation: Transnational Regulatory Regimes and the EU Regulatory State", *Journal of European Public Policy*, vol. 12, no. 1, pp. 89 - 112.
Economist (1990) "Waste a lot, Want a lot", 6 October 1990.
Economist (1993) "France and the GATT: Draw, Partner", 25 September 1993, pp. 50-51.
Economist (1995) "Who Ya Gonna Call?", 5 August 1995.
Economist (1998) "Dishing the Pasta, Not the Dirt", 21 November 1998. Edwards, G. (1984) "Europe and the Falklands Crisis", *Journal of Common Market Studies*, vol. 22, no. 4, pp. 295 - 313.
Economist (2000a) "Chris Patten, Becalmed in Brussels", 22 January 2000, p. 32.
Economist (2000b) "Javier Solana, Europe's Diplomat-in-Chief", 8 April 2000, p. 38.
Economist (2000c) "Who Is Serving Whom?", 31 August 2000, on line edition.
Economist (2005) "Whipping the Commission into Shape", 9 November, 2005.
Edwards, G. and E. Philippart (1999) "The Provisions on Closer Co-operation in the Treaty of Amsterdam", *Journal of Common Market Studies*, vol. 37, no. 1, pp. 87-108.
Edwards, G. and D. Spence (1997) "The Commission in Perspective" in G. Edwards and D. Spence (eds) *The European Commission* 2nd edition, London: Cartermill.
Edwards, G. and E. Regelsberger (eds) (1990) *Europe's Global Links: The European Community and Inter-Regional Co-operation*, London: Pinter.
Eeckhout, P. (2004) *External Relations of the European Union: Legal and Constitutional Foundations*, Oxford: Oxford University Press.
Egeberg, M. (1999) "Transcending Intergovernmentalism? Identity and Role Perceptions of National Officials in EU Decision-making", *Journal of European Public Policy*, vol. 6, no. 3, pp 456 - 474.
Ekengren, M. and B. Sundelius (2004) "National Foreign Policy Co-ordination" in H. Sjursen, W. Carlsnaes and B. White (eds) *Contemporary European Foreign Policy*, London: Sage.
Ekengren, M. (2004a) "Functional Security: A Forward Looking Approach to European and Nordic Security and Defence Policy", proceedings of conference held at the National Defence College, Stockholm, 5 - 6 December 2003.
Ekengren, M. (2004b) "From a European Security Community to a Secure European Community: Analysing EU 'Functional' Security", paper presented at the SGIR Conference, Fifth Pan-European Conference (ECPR), The Hague, 11 September 2004.
Ekengren, M. (2005) "The Interface of External and Internal Security in the European Union and in Nordic Policies" in A. Bailes / SIPRI (eds) *The Nordic Countries and the European Security and Defence Policy*, Oxford: Oxford University Press.
Elgström, O. (ed) (2003) *European Union Council Presidencies: A Comparative Perspective*, London: Routledge.
Elles, J. (1992) "The Staff Policy of the Community Institutions", report of the Committee of Budgets, European Parliament.
"Employer of the Month: European Commission" (2002) *PSM (Public Service Management)* May, 36 - 37.
Endo, K. (1999) *The Presidency of the European Commission under Jacques Delors. The Politics of Shared Leadership*, Basingstoke: Macmillan.
Engel, C. and C. Bormann (1991) *Vom Consensus zur Mehrheitsscheidung. EG-Entscheidingungensverfahren und nationale Interessenpolitik nach der Einheitlichen Europäischen Akte*, Bonn: Europa Union Verlag.
Epstein, D. and S. O'Halloran (1994) "Administrative Procedures, Information and Agency Discretion", *American Journal of Political Science*, vol. 38, no. 3, pp. 697 - 722.
EU ISS Task Force (2005) *Defence Procurement in the European Union: The Current Debate*, report of an European Union Institute for Security Studies Task Force, Paris, May 2005.
Eurobarometer (2004) "Flash Eurobarometer Justice and Home Affairs", March 2004.
European Commission (1958) "Organigramme du Secrétariat de la Commission", COM (1958) 159, 21 July 1958.
European Commission (1972) "Vedel Report", *Bulletin of the European Economic Community*, 25 March 1972.
European Commission (1979) *EC Bulletin 9*.
European Commission (1980) *Bulletin of the EC*, Supplement 2/80.
European Commission (1985) "White Paper on the Completion of the Single European Market", paper presented to the European Council, Milan, June 1985, COM (85) 310 final.
European Commission (1986) "The Week in Europe", 4 December 1986, ISEC/WT42/86.
European Commission (1987) *Bulletin of the EC 6*, no. 2.4.14, pp. 111 – 122.

European Commission Decision (1990) of 7 February 1990 amending Decision 89/469/EEC concerning certain protection measures relating to bovine spongiform encepalothapy in the United Kingdom, OJ No. L 41/23, 15 February 1990.

European Commission (1990a) "Opinion on the Proposal for Amendment of the Treaty Establishing the European Economic Community with a View to Political Union", 21 October 1990, COM (90) 600.

European Commission (1991) "Conferment of Implementing Powers on the Commission", SEC (1990) 2589 final, 10 January 1991.

European Commission (1992) Regulation (EEC) No. 548/92 of 6 March 1992 concerning import licences for milk products from certain Eastern European countries, OJ No. L 62/34, 7 March 1992.

European Commission (1992a) Regulation (EEC) No. 1765/92 concerning the set-aside scheme, OJ No. L 181/12, 1 July 1992.

European Commission (1992b) "Increased Transparency in the Work of the Commission", 2 December 1992, SEC (92) 2274 final.

European Commission (1992c) "An Open and Structured Dialogue between the Commission and Special Interest Groups", 2 December 1992, SEC (92) 2272 final.

European Commission (1993) "Openness in the Community, Communication to the Council, the Parliament and the Economic and Social Committee", 2 June 1993, COM (93) 258 final.

European Commission (1995) "Report on the Operation of the Treaty on European Union", Brussels, 10 May 1995, SEC (1995) 731 Final, pp. 157 - 158.

European Commission (1996) "Report on the Longer-Term Needs of the External Service" (The Williamson Report), approved by the Commission on 27 March 1996.

European Commission (1997a) "Promoting the Role of Voluntary Organisations and Foundations in Europe", 4 June 1997, COM (97) 241.

European Commission (1998a) "Personnel Policy in the European Institutions – Towards the Future" (the Caston Report), DG IX, March 1998.

European Commission (1998b) "Report of the Reflection Group on Personnel Policy", 6 November 1998, Chairman David Williamson.

European Commission (1999b) *Designing Tomorrow's Commission: A Review of the Commission's Organisation and Operation*, Brussels: European Commission.

European Commission (1999c) "Contribution of the Commission to Preparations for the IGC on Enlargement, 'Adapting the Institutions to Make a Success of Enlargement'", COM (1999) 592.

European Commission (2000) "Reforming the Commission. A White Paper – Parts I and II", COM (2000) 200 final/2, 5 April 2000.

European Commission (2000a) "Communication on Reform of the Management of External Assistance", 16 May 2000, SEC (2000) 814/5.

European Commission (2001) "Governance in the European Union", 'Cahiers' of the Forward Studies Unit, Brussels.

European Commission (2001a) "White Paper on Governance", COM (2001) 428 final, Brussels 25 July 2001.

European Commission (2001b) "Report from the Commission on the Working of Committees during 2000", COM (2001) 783/F, 20 December 2002.

European Commission (2001c) "Communication on Interactive Policy Making", 3 April 2001, COM (2001) 1014.

European Commission (2001d) "Proposal for a Council Directive on the Conditions of Entry and Residence of Third Country Nationals for the Purpose of Paid Employment and Self-Employed Economic Activities", COM (2001) 386 final.

European Commission (2001f) "La Réforme administrative du service extérieur unifié" (The Chêne Report), 7 December 2001, Sec (2001) 1954.

European Commission (2001 – 2003) Reports on the working of committees 2000 – 2002.

European Commission (2002) "An Administration at the Service of Half a Billion Europeans: Staff Reforms at the European Commission: State of Play Spring 2002", 17 April 2003.

European Commission (2002a) "Report from the Commission on the Working of Committees during 2001", COM (2002) 733/F, 13 December 2002.

European Commission (2002b) "Proposal for a Council Decision Amending Decision 1999/468/EC Laying down the Procedures for the Exercise of Implementing Powers Conferred on the Commission", COM (2002) 719 final, 11 December 2002.

European Commission (2002c) "Consultation Document: Towards a Reinforced Culture of Consultation and Dialogue - Proposals for General Principles and Minimum Standards for Consultation of Interested Parties by the Commission", 5 June 2002, COM (2002) 277 final.

European Commission (2002d) "General Principles and Minimum Standards for Consultation of Interested Parties by the Commission", 11 Dec 2002, COM (2002) 704.

European Commission (2002e) "Communication from the Commission: A Project for the European Union", Brussels, 22 May 2002, COM (2002) 247 Final.

European Commission (2002f) "Synthesis of the Annual Activity Reports (SAAR) and Declarations of the Directors-General and Heads of Service", 24 July 2002, COM (2002) 426 final.

European Commission (2002g) "For the EU. Peace, freedom and Solidarity", Communication on the Institutional Architecture, COM (2002) 728 final/2, Brussels, 4 December 2002.

European Commission Feasibility Study (2002) undertaken at the request of President Prodi in agreement with Commissioners Barnier and Vitorino, produced by a working party under the responsibility of François Lamoureux, "Contribution to a Preliminary Draft Constitution of the European Union" (Penelope), working document, 4 December 2002.

European Commission (2003) "Communication from the Commission, A Constitution for the Union, Opinion of the Commission, pursuant to Art. 48 of the Treaty on European Union", on the Conference of Representatives of the Member States' governments convened to revise the Treaties, COM (2003) 548 final, Brussels, 17 September 2003.

European Commission (2003a) "Report from the Commission on the Working of Committees in 2002", COM (2003) 530 final, 8 September 2003.

European Commission (2003b) "Report from the Commission on European Governance", Luxembourg: Office for Official Publications of the European Communities.

European Commission (2003c) "Better Lawmaking in 2003", 12 December 2003, COM (2003) 770 final.

European Commission (2003d) "Synthesis of the Annual Activity Reports (SAAR) and Declarations of the Directors-General and Heads of Service", 9 July 2003, COM (2003) 391 final.

European Commission (2003f), 18 November 2003, COM (2003) 4334.

European Commission (2003g) "Progress Review of Reform", 7 February 2003, COM (2003) 40.

European Commission (2004a) "Communication from the Commission: Completing the Reform Mandate: Progress Report and Measures to be Implemented in 2004", COM (2004) 93 final, 10 February 2004.

European Commission (2004b) "Overview on Staff Reform: Annexes". European Commission (2004c) "Report on European Governance (2003-2004)", Commission staff working document, 22 September 2004, SEC (2004) 1153.

European Commission (2004d) "Communication on an Area of Freedom, Security and Justice: Assessment of the Tampere Programme and Future Orientations", 2 June 2004, COM (2004) 401 final.

European Commission (2004e) "Communication on the Instruments for External Assistance under the Future Financial Perspective 2007-2013", 29 September 2004, Com (2004) 626 Final.

European Commission (2004g) "Taking Europe to the World: Fifty Years of the Commission's External Service", promotional brochure.

European Commission (2004h) Reform of Staff Regulations, Explanatory Fiches Committee of Independent Experts (CIE), "CIE I: First Report on Allegations regarding Fraud, Mismanagement and Nepotism in the European Commission", 15 March 1999, and "CIE II: Second Report on Reform of the Commission", 10 September 1999.

European Commission Statistical Bulletin (2005).

European Convention (2003a) "The European Commission: Countdown to Extinction", contribution 313, 2003/705, Brussels, 28 April 2003.

European Council (1985) "Report of the Ad Hoc Committee on Institutional Questions to the European Council" (Dooge Report), 21 March 1985.

European Council (2000) Presidency Conclusions, 23 – 24 March 2000.

European Council (2002) Presidency Conclusions, Seville, 21 and 22 June 2002, Annex II, Measures concerning the Structures and Functioning of the Council.

European Council (2004) "European Council Conclusions", 23 November 2004.

European Council (2005a) "Initial Elements for an EU Security Sector Reform (SSR) Concept", Brussels, 15 July 2005 (11241/05).

EU Observer (2003) "Giscard's Blueprint already under Fire", 24 April 2003, and "Commission Stung by Giscard proposals", 23 April 2003.

European Parliament (1984) "Spinelli Draft Treaty", 19 February 1984, OJ C 77/33.

European Parliament (1986) "Hänsch Report", Doc. A3 0310/90, 19 November 1990.

European Parliament (1993) "De Giovanni Report for the Committee on Institutional Affairs on Questions of Comitology Relating to the Entry into Force of the Maasatricht Treaty", PE 206.619/fin p. 10, cited in the Opinion of the Committee on Budgets.

European Parliament (1998) "The Role of the Union in the World: Implementation of the CFSP for 1997" (Spencer Report), European Parliament Committee on Foreign Affairs, Security and Defense Policy, European Parliament 226.282 final.

European Parliament (2000) "Report on a Common Community Diplomacy 2000/2006 (INI)" (Galeote Report), European Parliament Committee on Foreign Affairs, Human Rights, Common Security and Defence Policy, A5-0210/2000.

European Parliament (2003) "Corbett Report", Doc. A5-0218/2003, 29 April 2003.

European Parliament (2003a) "Corbett Report", Doc. A5-0266/2003, 11 July 2003.

European Parliament (2005) "Resolution on the Institutional Aspects of the European External Action Service", 12 May 2005, B6-0320/2005.

European Policy Centre (2004) "Reworking the Commission", *Ideas Factory Europe* no. 1, June 2004.

European Voice (1999) "Prodi Hatches Plan to Slim Down *Cabinets*", 12 – 19 May.

European Voice (1999a) "MEPs to Scrutinize Integrity of New Commission's Aides", 29 July – 4 August.

European Voice (1999b) "Bonn Bids to Avert Clash with MEPs over Santer's Successor", 4 – 10 February.

European Voice (1999c) "Prodi Struggles to Put together the Right Team" and "Centre-Right Turns up the Heat on Prodi", 8 – 14 July.

European Voice (2004) "Council and Commission Ready for Diplomatic Battle", 2 - 8 December.

European Voice (2004a) "WMD Strategy Hits the Wall in Commission - Council Dispute", 18 - 24 November.

European Voice (2005) "Cash Crisis Weakens Disaster Alert System", 30 June - 6 July.

European Voice (2005a) "Presidency Intensifies Diplomatic Corps Talks", 3 May.

European Voice (2005b) "Managing Crises on a Shoestring", 23 - 29 June.

European Voice (2005c) "Diplomat Corps Joins Treaty in 'Cold Storage'", 9 - 15 June.

European Voice (2005d) "Barroso Told to Reassign His Shipping Portfolios", 4 - 11 May.

Everson, M. (1995) "Independent Agencies: Hierarchy Beaters?", *European Law Journal*, vol. 1, no. 2, pp. 180 - 204.

Everson, M. (2001) "European Agencies: From Institutional Efficiency to 'Good Governance'", *EUSA Review Forum* vol. 14, no. 4.

Everson, M., G. Majone, L. Metcalfe and A. Schout (1999) "The Role of Specialised Agencies in Decentralising EU Governance", report presented to the European Commission.

Falke, J. (1996) "Comitology and Other Committees", in R. H. Pedler and G. F. Schaefer (eds) *Shaping European Law and Policy: The Role of Committees and Comitology in the Political Process*, Maastricht: European Institute for Public Administration, p. 142.

Falkner, G. (2002) "How Intergovernmental Are Intergovernmental Conferences? An Example from the Maastricht Treaty Reform", *Journal of European Public Policy*, vol. 9, no. 1, pp. 1 - 11.

Featherstone, K. and C. Radaelli (2003) (eds) *The Politics of Europeanisation*, Oxford: Oxford University Press.

Ferrero-Waldner, B. (2005) "The EU, China and the Quest for a Multilateral World", speech at conference to mark the 30th anniversary of EU-China relations, Institut Français de Relations Internationales – China Institute of International Studies, 4 July 2005.

Fielding, L. (1991) "Europe as a Global Partner", University Association for Contemporary European Studies, *Occasional Paper*, no.7, London.

Financial Times (1995) "Euro-Structures under One Roof: The EU Needs a Single Foreign Ministry, Not the Half-baked Compromise Set Out at Maastricht", 3 May, p. 20.

Financial Times (1999) "Prodi Names Group to Spur Wide-ranging EU Reforms", 28 – 29 August.

Financial Times (2003) "Follow my Leaders", *Financial Times Weekend Magazine*, 12 July, p. 47.

Financial Times (2003a) "Prodi Prepared to Stay as President if EU Leaders Ask", 3 April.

Financial Times (2005) "Europe Must Keep its Soft Power", 1 June.

Financial Times (2005a) "Diplomatic Mission for a Heavy-Hitter" by Lionel Barber, 31 December 2004 - 1 January 2005.

Financial Times (2005b) "Solana Hopeful EU Diplomatic Service Will 'Forge Ahead'", 31 May.

Fischer, J. (2000) "From Confederacy to Federation – Thoughts on the Finality of European Integration" in M. Leonard (ed) *The Future Shape of Europe*, London: Foreign Policy Centre.

Flinders, M. V. (2004) "Distributed Public Governance in the European Union", *Journal of European Public Policy*, vol. 11, no. 3, pp. 520 - 544.

Flinders, M. V. and M. J. Smith (2003) *Quangos, Accountability and Reform: The Politics of Quasi-Government*, Basingstoke: Palgrave Macmillan.

Føllesdal, A. (2004) "Legitimacy Theories of the European Union", ARENA Working Papers 04/15, Oslo: ARENA.

Fonseca-Wollheim, Da, H. (1981) "Ten Years of European Political Cooperation", March 1981, Brussels: internal document of the Commission of the European Communities, accessed via University of Pittsburg Digit Library, Archive of European Integration.

Forster, A. and W. Wallace (1996) "CFSP: A New Policy or Just a New Name?" in H. Wallace and W. Wallace (eds) Policy Making in the EU, Oxford: Oxford University Press.

Fortescue, A. (1982) "Report to the Council on the External Competencies of the Community", quoted in European Commission (2004a) "Taking Europe to the World: Fifty Years of the Commission's External Service", promotional brochure, p. 29.

Fortescue, A. (2002a) unpublished internal speech to the Legal Service of the European Commission.

Fortescue, A. (2002b) "Justice and Home Affairs DG Moving into the Mainstream of European Commission Work", interview by Fortescue at the launch of the information and communication unit website, December 2002.

French Ministry of Foreign Affairs (May 1950 – October 1950) Archives Diplomatic Serie DE-CE no. 500, CECA A 30-5 (Elaboration des traités).

Galloway, D. (2001) The Treaty of Nice and Beyond: Realities and Illusions of Power in the EU, Sheffield: Sheffield University Press.

Garrett, G. and G. Tsebelis (1999) "Why Resist the Temptation to Apply Power Indices to the European Union", Journal of Theoretical Politics, vol. 11, no. 3, pp. 291 - 308.

Gauttier, P. (2004) "Horizontal Coherence and the External Competences of the European Union", European Law Journal, vol. 10, no. 1, pp. 23 - 41.

Georgakakis, D. (2002) "Syndicats de fonctionnaires et institutionalisation de la fonction publique européenne", unpublished paper presented to the Round Table on L'institutionalisation de l'Europe, seventh congress of the Association française de science politique, Lille, September 2002.

Geradin, D. and N. Petit (2004) "The Development of Agencies at EU and National Levels: Conceptual Analysis and Proposals for Reform", Jean Monnet Working Paper no. 01/04.

Gillissen, A. (2003) "Internal Reform of the Council", paper presented for the conference "Reforming the EU institutions: Challenges for the Council", University of Maastricht, 8 May 2003.

Ginsberg, R. (2001) The European Union in International Politics: Baptism by Fire, Lanham.

Glathaar, C. (1992) "Einflussnahme auf Enscheidingungen der EG durch die Ausschüsse der EG-Kommission", Recht der Internationalen Wirtschaft, Heft 3, pp. 179, 180.

Goetschy, J. (2003) "The European Employment Strategy and the Open Method of Coordination: Lessons and Perspectives", Transfer, vol. 9, no. 2, pp. 281 - 301.

Gordon, T. (1995) "Empire-Building within the Commission: A Case Study of the DGI/DGIA Relationship", College of Europe MA thesis, Bruges (unpublished manuscript).

Gourlay, C. and E. Remacle (1998) "The 1996 IGC: The Actors and their Interaction" in K. A. Eliasen (ed) Foreign and Security Policy in the European Union, London: Sage.

Grant, C. (1994) Delors: Inside the House that Jacques Built, London: Nicholas Brealey.

Grant, C. (2004) "A Top Appointment Europe Must Get Right", Financial Times, 23 February 2004, p. 19.

Gray, B. (1998) "The Scientific Committee for Food", in Van Schendelen p. 68.

Gray, B. (2004) "The Commission's Culture of Financial Management and its Reform", Public Policy and Administration, vol. 19, no. 3, pp. 55 - 60.

Gray, M. (2002) "The European Commission: Seeking the Highest Possible Realistic Line" in F. Laursen (ed) The Amsterdam Treaty: National Preference Formation, Interstate Bargaining and Outcome, Odense: Odense University Press.

Gray, M. and A. Stubb (2001) "The Treaty of Nice – Negotiating a Poisoned Chalice?" in G. Edwards and G. Wiessela (eds) The European Union Annual Review, Journal of Common Market Studies, vol. 39, pp. 5 - 23.

Greenwood, J. (1997) Representing Interests in the European Union, London: Macmillan.

Greenwood, J. (2002) "Electricity Liberalisation" in R. Pedler (ed) EU Lobbying: Changes in the Arena, London: Palgrave.

Greenwood, J. (2003) Interest Representation in the European Union, Basingstoke: Palgrave.

Grevi, G. (2004) "Light and Shade of a Quasi-Constitution, An Assessment", European Policy Centre Issue Paper no. 14, Brussels, June 2004.

Grevi, G., D. Manca and G. Quille (2005) "The EU Foreign Minister: Beyond Double-Hatting", The International Spectator, vol. 40, no. 1, pp. 59 - 75.

Grevi, G. and F. Cameron (2005) "Towards an EU Foreign Service", Issue Paper no. 29,

European Policy Centre, Brussels, April 2005.

Grönvall, J. (2000) "Managing Crisis in the European Union: The Commission and 'Mad Cow' Disease", Stockholm: CRISMART/Swedish National Defence College.

Grönvall, J. (2001) "The Mad Cow Crisis, the Role of Experts and European Crisis Management" in U. Rosenthal, R. A. Boin and L. K. Comfort (eds) *Managing Crises: Threats, Dilemmas, Opportunities*, Springfield: Charles C Thomas.

Grosser, A. (1984) *Affaires Extérieures: La Politique de la France 1944-1984*, Paris: Flammarion.

Grossman, E. (2004) "Bringing Politics Back in: Rethinking the Role of Economic Interests Groups in European Integration", *Journal of European Public Policy*, vol. 11, no. 4, pp. 637 – 654.

Guiraudon, V. (2004) "Immigration and Asylum: A High Politics Agenda", *Developments in the European Union 2*, M. G. Cowles and D. Dinan (eds.), New York: Palgrave Macmillan, 160-180.

Guardian (1999) "Push for an Elected EU President", 16 June 1999.

Guéguen, D. and C. Rosberg (2004) *Comitology and Other Committees and Expert Groups*, Brussels: European Information Service.

Haas, E. (1968) *The Uniting of Europe: Political, Social and Economic Forces, 2nd Ed.*, Stanford: Stanford University Press.

Haas, P. M. (1992) "Introduction: Epistemic Communities and International Policy Co-ordination", *International Organization*, vol. 46, no. 1, pp. 1 – 35.

Habermas, J. (2001) "Why Europe Needs a Constitution", *New Left Review*, vol. 11, September/October pp. 5 – 23.

Hallstein, W. (1972) *Europe in the Making*, London: Allen and Unwin.

Hänggi, H. and F. Tanner (2005) "Promoting Security Sector Governance in the EU's Neighbourhood", *Chaillot Paper no. 80*, Paris: Institute for Security Studies-European Union, July 2005.

Hansard (2004) transcript of 6 December 2004.

Hansard (2004a) uncorrected transcript of oral evidence published as HC 631, 25 May 2004.

Hansard (2004b) "EU External Action Service", 13 July 2004, HC 663, Part no. 116, Column 1132.

Harrison, R. J. (1974) *Europe in Question*, London: George Allen & Unwin.

Hay, R. (1989) *The European Commission and the Administration of the Community*, European Documents Series, Luxembourg: Official Publications Office of the European Community.

Hayes-Renshaw, F. and H. Wallace (1997) *The Council of Ministers*, London: Macmillan.

Hearings (1999) The European Parliament hearings of the Prodi Commission were made available on the Internet via the Commission's server 'Europa'.

Héritier, A. (2001) "The White Paper on European Governance: A Response to Shifting Weights in Interinstitutional Decision-Making", contribution to the Jean Monnet Symposium, paper no. 6/01: Mountain or Molehill? A Critical Appraisal of the Commission White Paper on Governance, New York: New York University.

Herman, F. (1999) "Report on Improvements in the Functioning of the Institutions without Modifications of the Treaties", Committee on Institutional Affairs, PE 229.072/fin, 26 March.

Hervey, T. (2001) "Up in Smoke? Community (anti) Tobacco Law and Policy", *European Law Review*, vol. 26, pp. 101 – 125.

Heseltine, M. (1989) *The Challenge of Europe*, London: Weidenfeld & Nicolson.

Heukels, T., N. Blokker and M. Brus (eds) (1998) *The European Union after Amsterdam: A Legal Analysis*, Leiden: Kluwer.

Hewitt, A. (1989) "ACP and the Developing World" in J. Lodge (ed) *The European Community and the Challenge of the Future*, London: Pinter.

Hill, C. (1983) "National Interests - The Insuperable Obstacles?" in C. Hill (ed) *National Foreign Policies and European Political Cooperation*, London: Allen and Unwin.

Hill, C. (1993) "The Capability - Expectations Gap, or Conceptualising Europe's Role", *Journal of Common Market Studies*, vol. 31, no. 3, pp. 305 - 328.

Hill, C. and M. Smith (2005) "Acting for Europe: Reassessing International Relations and the European Union" in C. Hill and M. Smith (eds) *The International Relations of the European Union*, Oxford: Oxford University Press.

Hill, C. and W. Wallace (1996) "Introduction: Actors and Actions" in C. Hill (ed) *The Actors in Europe's Foreign Policy*, London: Routledge.

Hine, R. (1985) *The Political Economy of European Trade*, Brighton: Wheatsheaf.

Hix, S. (1994) "The Study of the European Community: The Challenge to Comparative Politics", *West European Politics*, vol. 17, no. 1, pp. 1 - 30.

Hix, S. (1998) "The Study of the European Union II: The 'New Governance' Agenda and its

Rival", *Journal of European Public Policy*, vol. 5, no. 1, pp. 38 - 65.

Hix, S. (1999) *The Political System of the European Union*, New York: St. Martin's Press.

Hix, S. (2005) "Neither a Preference-Outlier nor a Unitary Actor: Institutional Reform Preferences of the European Parliament", *Comparative European Politics*, vol. 3, no. 2, pp. 131-154.

Hocking, B. and M. Smith (1997) *Beyond Foreign Economic Policy: The United States, the Single European Market and a Changing World Economy*, London: Cassell/Pinter.

Hocking, B. (1999) *Foreign Ministries: Change and Adaptation*, London: MacMillan.

Hocking, B and D. Spence (2005) *Integrating Diplomats: EU Foreign Ministries*, Houndmills: Palgrave Macmillan.

Hocking, B. and D. Spence (2005a) "Europe Raises its Voice", *The World Today*, March 2005.

Hodson, D. and I. Maher (2001) "The Open Method as a New Mode of Governance: The Case of Soft Economic Policy Coordination", *Journal of Common Market Studies*, vol. 39, no. 4, pp. 719 - 746.

Hoffmann, S. (1966) "Obstinate or Obsolete: The Fate of the Nation-State and the Case of Western Europe", *Daedalus*, vol. 95, no. 3, pp. 862 - 915.

Hoffmann, S. and R. O. Keohane (eds.) (1991) *The New European Community. Decision-making and Institutional Change.* Boulder, CO: Westview Press.

Hoffmann, S. (2000) "Towards a Common European Foreign and Security Policy?", *Journal of Common Market Studies*, vol. 38, no. 2, pp. 189 – 199.

Holland, M. (1993) *European Community Integration*, London: Pinter.

Holland, M. (ed) (1997) *Common Foreign and Security Policy: The Record and Reforms*, London: Pinter.

Holland, M. (2002) *The European Union and the Third World*, Basingstoke: Palgrave/Macmillan.

Holland, M. (ed) (2004) *Common Foreign and Security Policy: The First Ten Years* 2nd edition, London: Continuum.

Holler, M. and M. Widgrén (1999) "Why Power Indices for Assessing European Union Decision-Making?", *Journal of Theoretical Politics*, vol. 11, no. 3, pp. 321 - 330.

Hood, C. (2000) "Public Service Bargains and Public Service Reform", in B. Guy Peters and J. Pierre (eds) *Politicians, Bureaucrats and Administrative Reform*, London: Routledge/ECPR Studies in European Political Science.

Hooghe, L. (1999) "Images of Europe: Orientations to European Integration among Senior Officials of the Commission", *British Journal of Political Science*, vol. 29, no. 2, pp. 345 - 367.

Hooghe, L. (2001) *The European Commission and the Integration of Europe*, Cambridge: Cambridge University Press.

Hooghe, L. (2003) "Europe Divided? Elites vs. Public Opinion on European Integration.", *European Union Politics*, vol. 4, no. 3, pp. 281-305.

Hooghe, L. and G. Marks (2001) *Multi-Level Governance and European Integration*, Lanham: Rowman & Littlefield.

House of Commons (2004) "The EU's Justice and Home Affairs Work Programme for the Next Five Years", 28th Report 2003-2004, 14 July 2004.

House of Lords Select Committee on the European Communities (1986) "Delegation of Powers to the Commission", Session 1985 - 86, 19th Report, para. 2.

Howe, G. (1998) "Towards a Common Foreign Policy" in T. Heukels, N. Blokker and M. Brus (eds) *The European Union after Amsterdam: A legal Analysis*. The Hague: Kluwer Law International.

Hufbauer, G. C. (ed) (1990) *Europe 1992: An American Perspective*, Washington, DC: Brookings Institution.

Hurd, D. (1994) "Developing the Common Foreign and Security Policy", *International Affairs*, vol. 70, no. 3, pp. 421 – 429.

Hurd, D. (2005) "Diplomatic Answers", *The World Today*, March 2005.

Ifestos, P. (1987) *European Political Cooperation: Towards a Framework of Supranational Diplomacy?*, Aldershot: Avebury.

Jachtenfuchs, M., T. Diez and S. Jung (1998) "Which Europe? Conflicting Models of a Legitimate European Political Order", *European Journal of International Relations*, vol. 4, pp. 409-445.

Jachtenfuchs, M. (2001) "The Governance Approach to European Integration", *Journal of Common Market Studies*, vol. 39, no. 2, pp. 245 - 264.

Jachtenfuchs, M. and B. Kohler Koch (eds) (2003) *Europäische Integration*, Opladen: Leske und Budrich.

Jarlsvik, H. and K. Castenfors (2004) *Säkerhet och beredskap i Europeiska unionen*, KBM:S Temaserie, 2004:3. Krisberedskapsmyndigheten (KBM), Stockholm: Edita Ljunglöfs Tryckeri.

Jenkins, R. (1989) *European Diary 1977-81*, London: HarperCollins.

Jenkins, R. (1991) *A Life at the Centre*, London: Macmillan.

Joana, J. and A. Smith (2002) *Les Commissaires Européennes*, Paris: Presses de Sciences Po.

Joaris, A. (2005) "The European External Action Service", *Agora Magazine*, magazine of Commission staff association Union Syndicale, no. 40, March 2005.

Joerges, C. (2002) "Guest Editorial: The Commission's White Paper on Governance in the EU – A Symptom of Crisis", *Common Market Law Review*, vol. 39, no. 3, 441 - 445.

Joerges, C. (2002a) "Das Recht im Prozess der Konstitutionalisierung Europas", *MZES Arbeitspapier* 25/2002, Mannheim.

Joerges, C. and J. Neyer (1997) "From Intergovernmental Bargaining to Deliberative Political Processes", *European Law Journal*, no. 3, pp. 273 - 299.

Joerges, C., Y. Mény and J. H. H. Weiler (eds.) (2001) "Mountain or Molehill? A Critical Appraisal of the Commission White Paper on Governance".

Jørgensen, K. E. (ed) (1997) *Reflective Approaches to European Governance*, Basingstoke: Macmillan.

Kaptein, P. J. G. and P. V. Van Themat (1990) *Introduction to the Law of the European Communities*, Deventer: Kluwer.

Kassim, H. (2000a) "Conclusion: Confronting the Challenge" in H. Kassim, B. Guy Peters, and V. Wright (eds) *The National Coordination of EU Policy*, Oxford: Oxford University Press.

Kassim, H. (2004a) "A Historic Accomplishment? The Prodi Commission and Administrative Reform" in D. G. Dimitrakopoulos (ed) *The Changing European Commission*, Manchester: Manchester University Press.

Kassim, H. (2004b) "The Kinnock Reforms in Perspective: Why Reforming the Commission is an Heroic, but Thankless Task" in R. Levy and A. Stevens (eds) "The Reform of EU Management: Taking Stock and Looking Forward", special issue of *Public Policy and Administration*, vol. 19, no. 3, pp. 25 - 41.

Kassim, H. and A. Menon (2002) "The Principal-Agent Approach and the Study of the European Union: A Provisional Assessment", The European Research Institute, University of Birmingham, *Working Paper Series*, July 2002.

Kassim, H. and A. Menon (2004) "EU Member States and the Prodi Commission" in D. G. Dimitrakopoulos (ed) *The Changing European Commission*, Manchester: Manchester University Press.

Kelemen, R. D. (1997) "The European 'Independent' Agencies and Regulation in the EU", *CEPS Working Document* no. 112.

Kelemen, R. D. (2002) "The Politics of Eurocratic Structure and the New European Agencies", *West European Politics*, vol. 25, no. 4, pp. 93 - 118.

Kinnock, N. (2003) "The Reform of the European Commission", *EIPASCOPE* 2004/1, 6-9.

Kinnock, N. (2004) "Reforming the European Commission: Organisational Challenges and Advances", *Public Policy and Administration*, vol. 19, no. 3, pp. 7 –12.

Knill, C. (2002) *The Europeanisation of National Administrations*, Cambridge: Cambridge University Press.

Kohler-Koch, B. (1999) "The Evolution and Transformation of European Governance" in B. Kohler-Koch and R. Eising (eds) *The Transformation of Governance in the European Union*, London: Routledge.

Kohler-Koch, B. (2003) "Interdependent European Governance" in B. Kohler-Koch (ed) *Linking EU and National Governance*, Oxford: Oxford University Press.

König, T. and T. Bräuninger (2000) "Decisiveness and Inclusiveness: Two Aspects of the Intergovernmental Choice of European Voting Rules", *Homo Economicus*, vol. 17, no. 1 - 2, pp. 107 - 123.

König, T. and T. Bräuninger (1997) "Decisiveness and Inclusiveness: Intergovernmental Choice of European Decision Rules", *European Integration Online Papers*, vol. 1, no. 22.

König, T. and T. Bräuninger (2001) "Decisiveness and Inclusiveness: Intergovernmental Choice of European Decision Rule" in M. Holler and G. Owen (eds) *Power Indices and Coalition Formation*, Dordrecht: Kluwer Academic Publishers.

Kreher, A. (1997) "Agencies in the European Community - A Step Towards Administrative Integration in Europe", *Journal of European Public Policy*, vol. 4, no. 2, 225 - 245.

Laffan, B., R. O'Donnell and M. Smith (1999) *Europe's Experimental Union: Re-thinking Integration*, London: Routledge.

Lamassoure, A. (2004) *Histoire Secrète de la Convention Européenne*, Paris: Edition Albin Michel.

Lamers, K. (1995) "Why the EU Needs to Strengthen its Institutions" in Philip Morris Institute, *What Future for the European Commission?*, Brussels: Philip Morris Institute.

Laming, R. (1995) "Is the European Union Legitimate?", *The Federalist, A Political Review*, no. 2, pp. 114 - 119.

Lamy, P. (2002) *L'Europe en Premiere Ligne*, Paris: Editions Seuil.

Lamy, P. (2004) "EU 25 - Making It Work", address to International Advisory Council, Centre for European Policy Studies, Brussels, 19 February 2004.

Laursen, F. and S. Vanhoonacker (eds) (1992) *The Intergovernmental Conference on Political Union*, Maastricht / Dordrecht: European Institute of Public Administration / Martinus Nijhoff.

Lehning, P. B. and A. Weale (1997) *Citizenship, Democracy and Justice in the New Europe*, London: Routledge.

Lenaerts, K. (1993) "Regulating the Regulatory Process: 'Delegation of Powers' in the European Community", *European Law Review*, vol. 19, no. 1, pp. 23 - 49.

Leonard, M. (1999) "Network Europe", Foreign Policy Centre, London, 10 September 1999.

Leonard, M. (2005) *Why Europe Will Run the 21st Century*, London: Fourth Estate.

Levy, R. (2000) *Implementing European Union Public Policy*, Cheltenham: Elgar.

Levy, R. (2002) "Modernising EU Programme Management", *Public Policy and Administration*, vol. 17, no. 1, pp. 72 - 89.

Levy, R. (2003) "Critical Success Factors in Public Management Reform: The Case of the European Commission", *International Review of Administrative Sciences*, vol. 69, no. 4, pp. 553 - 566.

Lindberg, L. N. (1963) *The Political Dynamics of European Economic Integration*, Stanford: Stanford University Press.

Lindberg, L. N. and S. A. Scheingold (1970) *Europe's Would-Be Polity*, Englewood Cliffs: Prentice Hall.

Lindstrom, G. (2005) "EU-US Burden-Sharing: Who Does What", *Chaillot Paper* no 82, European Union Institute for Security Studies.

Linsenmann, I. and W. Wessels (2002) "EMU's Impact on National Institutions. Fusion towards a 'Gouvernance Économique' or Fragmentation?" in K. Dyson (ed) *European States and the Euro. Europeanization, Variation, and Convergence*, Oxford: Oxford University Press.

Linsenmann, I., C. Meyer and W. Wessels (eds) (2005) *EU Economic Governance: A Balance Sheet of New Modes of Governance*, Houndmills: Palgrave.

Lippert, B. (ed) (2004) *Bilanz und Folgeprobleme der EU-Erweiterung*, Baden-Baden: Nomos.

Lister, M. (1988) *The European Community and the Developing World: The Role of the Lomé Conventions*, Aldershot: Gower.

Loth, W., W. Wallace and W. Wessels (eds) (1998) *Walter Hallstein: The Forgotten European?*, Basingstoke: Macmillan.

Ludlow, P. (1991) "The European Commission" in R. O. Keohane and S. Hoffmann (eds) *The New European Community: Decision-making and Institutional Change*, Boulder: Westview Press.

Ludlow, P. (1993) *Beyond Maastricht*, Brussels: Centre for European Policy Studies.

MacLeod, I., I. D. Henry and S. Hyett (1996) *The External Relations of the European Communities*, Oxford: Oxford University Press.

Magnette, P. and K. Nicolaïdis (2004) "The European Convention: Bargaining in the Shadow of Rhetoric", *West European Politics*, vol. 27, no. 3, pp. 381 - 404.

Majone, G. (1991) "Cross-National Sources of Regulatory Policymaking in Europe and the United States", *Journal of Public Policy*, vol. 11, no. 1, pp. 79-106.

Majone, G. (1993) "The European Community Between Social Policy and Social Regulation", *Journal of Common Market Studies*, vol. 31, no. 2, pp 153-170.

Majone, G. (1996) *Regulating Europe*, London: Routledge.

Majone, G. (1997a) "The New European Agencies: Regulation by Information", *Journal of European Public Policy*, vol. 4, no. 2, pp. 262 - 275.

Majone, G. (1997b) "The Agency Model: The Growth of Regulation and Regulatory Institutions in the European Union", *EIPAscope*, vol. 3, pp. 1-6.

Majone, G. (2000) "The Credibility Crisis of Community Regulation", *Journal of Common Market Studies*, vol. 38, no. 2, pp. 273 - 302.

Majone, G. (2002) "The European Commission: The Limits of Centralization and the Perils of Parliamentarization", *Governance*, vol. 15, no. 3, pp. 375 – 392.

Majone, G. (2002a) "Delegation of Regulatory Powers in a Mixed Polity", *European Law Journal*, vol. 8, no. 3, pp. 319 - 339.

Majone, G. (2002b) "Functional Interests: European Agencies" in J. Peterson and M. Shackleton (eds) *The Institutions of the European Union*, Oxford: Oxford University Press.

Mandelson, P. (2005) "The Idea of Europe: Can We Make It Live Again?", speech to the University Association for Contemporary European Studies (UACES), Crowne Plaza Hotel, Brussels, 20 July 2005.

Mangenot, M. (2001) "La revendication d'une paternité:les hauts fonctionnaires français et le 'style' administratif de la Commission européenne (1958 – 1988)", Pôle Sud, no. 15, pp. 33 – 46.

Manners, I. (2006) "Normative Power Europe Reconsidered", in H. Sjursen (ed) What Kind of Power? European Foreign Policy in Perspective, special issue of Journal of European Public Policy, Vol 13 no.2 2006.

Marjolin, R. (1989) Memoirs 1911-86: Architect of European Unity, London: Weidenfeld & Nicolson.

Marks, G. (1996) "An Actor-Centered Approach to Multi-Level Governance" in C. Jeffery (ed) The Regional Dimension of the European Union: Towards a Third Level in Europe?, London: Frank Cass.

Martin, D. (1995) What Future for the European Commission, London: Philip Morris Institute for Public Policy Research.

Mattila, M. (2004) "Contested Decisions: Empirical Analysis of Voting in the European Union Council of Ministers", European Journal of Political Research, vol. 43, no. 1, pp. 29 - 50.

Maurer, A. (1999) What Next for the European Parliament, London: Federal Trust Series.

Maurer, A. (2002) "The European Parliament: Win-Sets of a Less Invited Guest", in F. Laursen (ed.) The Amsterdam Treaty: National Preference Formation, Interstate Bargaining, Outcome and Ratification, Odense: Odense University Press.

Maurer, A. (2003a) "The Legislative Powers and the Impact of the European Parliament", Journal of Common Market Studies, vol. 41, no. 2, pp. 227 - 247.

Maurer, A. (2003b) "Orientierungen im Verfahrensdickicht? Die neue Normhierarchie der Europäischen Union", Integration, vol. 26, no. 3, pp. 440 - 453.

Maurer, A. and W. Wessels (2001) National Parliaments on their Ways to Europe: Losers or Latecomers?, Baden-Baden: Schriften des Zentrum für Europäische Integrationsforschung.

Maurer, A. and W. Wessels (2003) "The European Union Matters: Structuring Self-made Offers and Demands" in W. Wessels, A. Maurer and J. Mittag (eds) Fifteen into One?, Manchester: Manchester University Press.

Mazey, S. (1992) "Conception and Evolution of the High Authority's Administrative Services (1952-1956): from Supranational Principles to Multinational Practices" in E. Volkmar Heyen (ed) Yearbook of European Administrative History 4: Early European Community Administration, Baden Baden: Nomos.

Mazey, S. (1995) "The Development of EU Equality Policies: Bureaucratic Expansion on Behalf of Women?", Public Administration, vol. 73, no. 4, pp. 591-610.

Mazey, S. (1998) "The European Union and Women's Rights: from the Europeanisation of National Agendas to the Nationalisation of a European Agenda?", Journal of European Public Policy, vol. 5, no. 1, pp. 131 – 152.

Mazey, S. and J. Richardson (2001) "Interest Groups and EU Policy-making: Organisational Logic and Venue Shopping", in J. Richardson (ed.), European Union: Power and Policy-making, 2nd ed., New York: Routledge, pp. 217-237.

Mazzucelli, C. and D. Beach (eds.) (2006) Leadership in EU Constitutional Negotiations, Basingstoke: Palgrave.

McDonald, M. (1995) "'Unity in Diversity'. Some Tensions in the Construction of Europe", Social Anthropology, vol. 4, no. 1, pp. 47 - 60.

McDonald, M. (1997) "Identities in the European Commission", in N. Nugent (ed) At the Heart of the Union: Studies of the European Commission, London: Macmillan.

McDonald, M. (1998) "Anthropological Study of the European Commission", Brussels: unpublished report of the European Commission.

McGoldrick, D. (1997) International Relations Law of the European Union, London: Longman.

Meny, Y. and V. Wright (eds) (1987) The Politics of Steel: Western Europe and the Steel Industry in the Crisis Years (1974 - 1984), Berlin: Walter de Gruyter.

Merritt, G. (2003) "Scandal May Topple Prodi's Team", International Herald Tribune, 7 August 2003.

Metcalfe, L. (2000) "Reforming the Commission: Will Organisational Efficiency Produce Effective Governance?", Journal of Common Market Studies, vol. 38, no. 5, 817- 841.

Metcalfe, L. (2001) "Réformer la gouvernance européenne: anciens problèmes ou nouveaux principes? " Revue internationale des sciences administratives, vol. 67, no. 3, pp. 473 - 505.

Metcalfe, L. (2001a) "More Green than Blue: Positioning the Governance White Paper", EUSA Review, vol. 14, no. 4, Fall, pp. 3 – 5.

Metcalfe, L. (2004) "European Policy Management: Future Challenges and the Role of the

Commission", *Public Policy and Administration*, vol. 19, no. 3, pp. 76 - 91.

Meunier, S. (1998) "Divided but United: European Trade Policy Integration and EC - US Agricultural Negotiations in the Uruguay Round" in C. Rhodes (ed) *The European Union in the World Community*, Boulder: Lynne Rienner.

Meunier, S. (1999) "Who Speaks for Europe? The Delegation of Trade Authority in the EU", *Journal of Common Market Studies*, vol. 37, no. 3, pp. 477 - 502.

Meunier, S. and K. Nicolaïdis (1999) "Who Speaks for Europe? The Delegation of Trade Authority in the EU", *Journal of Common Market Studies*, vol. 37, no. 3, pp. 477 – 501.

Meunier, S. and K. Nicolaïdis (2000) "EU Trade Policy: The 'Exclusive' Versus 'Shared' Competence Debate" in M. Green Cowles and M. Smith (eds) *The State of the European Union Volume 5: Risks, Reform, Resistance, and Revival*, New York: Oxford University Press.

Meyer, K. (1994) "Appendix A. Emile Noël's Contribution to Europe" in S. Martin (ed) *The Construction of Europe. Essays in Honour of Emile Noël*, Dortrecht: Kluwer Academic Publishers.

Meyer, C. (1999) "Political Legitimacy and the Invisibility of Politics: Exploring the European Union's Communication Deficit", *Journal of Common Market Studies*, vol. 37, no. 4, pp. 617 – 640.

Michalski, A. (2002) *Governing Europe: the Future Role of the European Commission*, The Hague: Clingendael Institute.

Michelmann, H. (1978) "Multinational Staffing and Organisational Functioning in the Commission of the EEC", *International Affairs*, vol. 32, no. 2, pp. 477 – 496.

Middlemas, K. (1995) *Orchestrating Europe. The Informal Politics of European Union 1973-1995*, Hammersmith: Fontana Press.

Mijs, W. and A. Caparros (2002) "Making the Single Market in Financial Services a Reality" in R. Pedler (ed) *EU Lobbying – Changes in the Arena*, London: Palgrave.

Milton, G. and J. Keller-Noëllet with A. Bartol-Saurel (2005) *The European Constitution: Its Origins, Negotiation and Meaning*, London: John Harper.

Milward, A. S. (1984) *The Reconstruction of Western Europe, 1945-1951*, London: Methuen.

Milward, A. S. (1992) *The European Rescue of the Nation State*, London: Routledge.

Milward, A. S. et al. (1993) *The Frontier of National Sovereignty: History and Theory, 1945–1992*, London: Routledge.

Missiroli, A. (2001) "Coherence for European Security Policy", WEU Institute for Security Studies, *Occasional Paper* no 27, May 2001.

Missiroli, A. (ed) (2005) "Disasters, Diseases, Disruptions: A New D-Drive for the EU", *Chaillot Paper* no 83, European Union Institute for Security Studies.

Moe, T. (1990) "The Politics of Structural Choice: Towards a Theory of Public Bureaucracy" in O. Williamson (ed) *Organization Theory from Chester Barnard to the Present and Beyond*, New York: Oxford University Press.

Monar, J. (1994) "The Evolving Role of the Union Institutions in the Framework of the Third Pillar" in J. Monar and R. Morgan (eds) *The Third Pillar of the European Union*, Brussels: European Interuniversity Press.

Monar, J. (1997) "Political Dialogue with Third Countries and Regional Political Groupings: The Fifteen as an Attractive Interlocutor" in E. Regelsberger, P. de Schoutheete de Tervarent and W. Wessels (eds) *Foreign Policy of the European Union. From EPC to CFSP and Beyond*, Boulder: Lynne Rienner.

Monar, J. (1997a) "European Union – Justice and Home Affairs: A Balance Sheet and an Agenda for Reform" in G. Edwards and A. Pijpers (eds) *The Politics of the European Treaty Reform – The 1996 Inter-Governmental Conference and Beyond*, London: Pinter Ed.

Monar, J. (1999) "Die interne Dimension der Mittelmeerpolitik der Europäischen Union: institutionelle und verfahrensmäßige Aspekte" in W. Zippel (ed) *Die Mittelmeerpolitik der EU*, Baden-Baden: Nomos.

Monar, J. (2003) "The European Union's Response to 11 September 2001: Bases for Action, Performance and Limits", presentation on 1 May 2003 at Rutgers University, Newark, New Jersey.

Monar, J. and W. Wessels (eds) (2001) *The European Union after the Treaty of Amsterdam*, London: Continuum.

Monnet, J. (1976) *Mémoires*, Paris: Fayard.

Monnet, J. (1978) *Erinnerungen eines Europäers*, München / Wien.

Montagnon, P. (1988) "De Clerq Offers Glimpse of Community Trade Policy", *Financial Times*, 14 July 1988.

Moravcsik, A. (1991) "Negotiating the Single Act: National Interests and Conventional Statecraft in the European Community", *International Organization*, vol. 45, no. 1, pp. 19- 56.

Moravcsik, A. (1993) "Preferences and Power in the European Community: A Liberal Intergovernmentalist Approach", *Journal of Common Market Studies*, vol. 31, no. 1, pp. 473 - 524.

Moravcsik, A. (1998) *The Choice for Europe, Social Purpose and State Power from Messina to Maastricht*, Ithaca: Cornell University Press.

Moravcsik, A. (1999) "The Future of European Integration Studies: Social Science or Social Theory?", *Millennium*, vol. 28, no. 2, pp. 371-391.

Moravcsik, A. (1999a) *The Choice for Europe, Social Purpose and State Power from Messina to Maastricht*, London.

Moravcsik, A. (1999b) "A New Statecraft? Supranational Entrepreneurs and International Cooperation", *International Organization*, vol. 53, no. 2, pp. 267 - 306.

Moravcsik, A. and K. Nicolaïdis (1999) "Explaining the Treaty of Amsterdam: Interests, Influence, Institutions", *Journal of Common Market Studies*, vol. 37, no. 1, pp. 59 - 85.

Müller, T. (2003) *Die Innen- und Justizpolitik der Europäischen Union, Eine Analyse der Integrationsentwicklung*, Opladen: Leske und Budrich.

Murray, A. (2002) "European Economic Reform: Tackling the Delivery Deficit", pamphlet, Centre for European Reform, London, October 2002.

Murray, A. (2003) "The Lisbon Scorecard III: The Status of Economic Reform in an Enlarging EU", CER Working Paper, London: CER.

Murray, A. (2004) "An Unstable House? Reconstructing the European Commission", CER Working Paper, London: Centre for European Reform.

Neuwahl, N. A. (1991) "Joint Participation in International Treaties and the Exercise of Power by the EEC and its Member States", *Common Market Law Review*, vol. 28, no. 4, pp. 717 - 740.

Nicolaïdis, K. and P. Magnette (2005) "Coping with the Lilliput Syndrome : Large Vs. Small Member States in the European Convention", *European Public Law*, Vol. 11, no. 1, pp. 83-102.

Nicolas, J. (1999) *L'Europe des fraudes*, Paris: Editions PNA.

Nicoll, W. (1987) "Qu'est-ce que la comitologie", *Revue du Marche Commun*, 306, April.

Nicoll, W. and T. Salmon (1990) *Understanding the European Communities*, London: Philip Allan.

Nilsson, H. G. (2004) "The Justice and Home Affairs Council" in M. Westlake and D. Galloway (eds) *The Council of the European Union*, London: John Harper.

Noël, E. (1973) "The Commission's Power of Initiative", *Common Market Law Review*, vol. 10, p. 123.

Noël, E. (1988) "Crises et progrès, moteurs de la construction européenne" in *Hommage à Emile Noël*, Luxembourg: Office des Publications Officielles des Communautés Européennes.

Noël, E. (1988a) "The Single European Act", *Government and Opposition*, vol. 24, pp. 3 - 14.

Noël, E. (1992) "Témoignage: l'Administration de la Communauté Européenne dans la Rétrospective d'un Ancien Haut Fonctionnaire" in E. Heyen and V. Wright (eds) *Early European Community Administration, Yearbook of European Administrative History*, 4.

Noël, E. (1992a) "Reflections on the Maastricht Treaty", *Government and Opposition*, vol. 27, no. 2, pp. 148 - 157.

Noël, E. (1998) "Walter Hallstein: A Personal Testimony" in W. Loth, W. Wallace and W. Wessels (eds) *Walter Hallstein. The Forgotten European?* Basingstoke: Macmillan.

Nugent, N. (1995) "The Leadership Capacity of the European Commission", *Journal of European Public Policy*, vol. 2, no. 4, pp. 603 - 623.

Nugent, N. (1999) *The Government and Politics of the European Union* 4th edition, Durham: Duke University Press.

Nugent, N. (ed) (2000) *At the Heart of the Union*, Basingstoke: Palgrave.

Nugent, N. (2000a) *The European Commission*, Basingstoke: Palgrave Macmillan.

Nugent, N. and S. Saurugger (2002) "Organizational Structuring: The Case of the European Commission and its External Policy Responsibilities", *Journal of European Public Policy*, vol. 9, no. 3, pp. 345 – 364.

Nuttall, S. (1992) *European Political Cooperation*, Oxford: Clarendon Press.

Nuttall, S. (1996) "The Commission: The Struggle for Legitimacy" in C. Hill (ed) *The Actors in Europe's Foreign Policy*, London: Routledge.

Nuttall, S. (1997) "The CFSP Provisions of the Amsterdam Treaty: An Exercise in Collusive Ambiguity", *CFSP Forum*, vol. 3.

Nuttall, S. (2000) *European Foreign Policy*, Oxford: Oxford University Press.

Nye, J. S. (2004) *Soft Power: The Means to Success in World Politics*, New York: BBS Publications.

OLAF (2004) "Annual Activity Report, 1 July 2003 – 30 June 2004".

Olsson, E. K. (2005) "The Dioxin Scandal" in S. Larsson, E. K. Olsson and B. Ramberg (eds) *Crisis Decision Making in the European Union*, Stockholm: CRISMART.

Organisation for Economic Co-Operation and Development (2001) "The DAC Guidelines:

Helping Prevent Violent Conflict".

Paemen, H. and A. Bensch (1995) *From the GATT to the WTO: The European Union in the Uruguay Round*, Leuven: Leuven University Press.

Page, E. (1997) *People Who Run Europe*, Oxford: Clarendon Press.

Page, E. (2003) "Europeanization and the Persistence of Administrative Systems" in edited by J. Hayward and A. Menon (eds) *Governing Europe*, Oxford: Oxford University Press.

Page, E. and L. Wouters (1994) "Bureaucratic Politics and Political Leadership in Brussels", *Public Administration*, vol. 72, no. 1.

Page, E. and V. Wright (1999) "Conclusion: Senior Officials in Western Europe" in E. Page and V. Wright (eds) *Bureaucratic Elites in Western European States*, Oxford: Oxford University Press.

Parker, G. (2004) "Unity of Nations Forgotten in Scramble for EU Top Jobs", *Financial Times*, 16 September 2004.

Paschke, K. T. (2003) "Die Zukunft der deutschen Botschaften in der EU" in E. Brandt and C. Buck (eds*) Auswärtiges Amt. Diplomatie als Beruf* 3rd ed., Opladen: Leske and Budrich.

Pastore, F. (2001) *Reconciling the Prince's Two 'Arms': Internal-External Security Policy Coordination in the European Union*, Occasional Paper no. 30, Institute for Security Studies, Western European Union, Paris, October 2001.

Pastore, F. (2001a) "Refugee Crisis Management and the EU – An Emerging Test Case" in A. Missiroli "Coherence for European Security Policy: Debates, Cases, Assessments", WEU Institute for Security Studies, *Occasional Paper* no 27, May 2001.

Patten, C. (2000a) Unpublished letter to Foreign Ministers about the High Representative's powers, 27 November 2000, pp. 23 – 24.

Patten, C. (2000b) "A European Foreign Policy: Ambition and Reality", speech at the Institut Français des Relations Internationales, Paris, 15 June 2000.

Patten, C. (2000c) "External Relations: Demands, Constraints and Priorities", 26 May 2000, Sec (2000) 922.

Patten, C. (2001) "A Voice for Europe? The Future of the CFSP", Brian Lenihan Memorial Lecture, Institute for European Studies, Dublin, 7 March 2001.

Patten, C. (2002) "Speech to UK Conference on Organised Crime in the Balkans", London, 25 November 2002.

Patten, C. (2004) "The Western Balkans: The Road to Europe", speech to German Bundestag, European Affairs Committee, Berlin, 28 April 2004, SPEECH/04/209.

Patten, C. (2004a) unpublished letter to the Chairman of the Foreign Affairs Committee of the House of Commons.

Patten, C. (2004b) "The Next European Commission", speech given at Konrad Adenauer Foundation lecture, 27 April 2004, Brussels.

Patten, C. (2005) *Not Quite the Diplomat: Home Truths about World Affairs*, London: Allen Lane.

Patterson, L. A. (2000) "Biotechnology Policy: Regulating Risks and Risking Regulation" in H. Wallace and W. Wallace (eds) *Policy-making in the European Union*, Oxford: Oxford University Press.

Pedler, R. (2002) "Clean Air and Car Emissions", case study in R. Pedler (ed) *European Union Lobbying: Changes in the Arena*, London: Palgrave.

Penaud, J. (ed) (1993) *La Fonction Publique Des Communautés Européennes. Problèmes Politiques et Sociaux*, vol. 713 - 714, Paris: Documentation Française.

Pentland, C. (1973) *International Theory and the European Community*, London: Faber.

Peters, B. G. (1992) "Bureaucratic Politics and the Institutions of the European Community" in A. Sbragia (ed) *Euro-Politics: Institutions and Policy-making in the 'New' European Community*, Washington, DC: Brookings Institution.

Peters, B. G. (1996) "Agenda-setting in the European Union" in J. Richardson (ed) *European Union, Power and Policy-Making*, London: Routledge.

Peters, G. B. (1999) *Institutional Theory in Political Science: The 'New Institutionalism'*, London: Pinter.

Peters, B. G. (2000) "The Commission and Implementation in the European Union: Is there an Implementation Deficit and Why?" in N. Nugent (ed) *At the Heart of the Union: Studies of the European Commission* 2nd edition, Basingstoke: Macmillan.

Peterson, J. (1995) "Decision-making in the European Union: towards a Framework for Analysis", *Journal of European Public Policy*, vol. 2, no. 1, pp. 69 – 93.

Peterson, J. (1999) "The Santer Era: The European Commission in Normative, Historical and Theoretical Perspective", *Journal of European Public Policy*, vol. 6, no. 1, pp. 46– 65.

Peterson, J. (2002) "The College of Commissioners" in J. Peterson and M. Shackleton (eds) *The*

Institutions of the European Union, Oxford: Oxford University Press.

Peterson, J. (2004) "The Prodi Commission: Fresh Start or Free Fall?" in D. G. Dimitrakopoulos (ed) *The Changing European Commission*, Manchester: Manchester University Press.

Peterson, J. (2005) "The 'enlarged' European Commission", Paris: Notre Europe.

Peterson, J. (2006) "The College of Commissioners" in J. Peterson and M. Shackleton (eds) *The Institutions of the European Union* 2nd edition, Oxford: Oxford UP.

Peterson, J. and E. Bomberg (1999) *Decision-Making in the European Union*, Houndmills: Macmillan Press.

Peterson, J. and M. Shackleton (2006) "Conclusion" in J. Peterson and M. Shackleton (eds) *The Institutions of the European Union* 2nd edition, Oxford: Oxford UP.

Petit-Laurent, P. (1994) "Réflexions sur l'Efficacité de l'Institution et de Son Administration", report submitted to the European Commission, November 1994.

Petite, M. (1996) "L'avis de la Commission européenne: renforcer l'union politique et préparer l'élargissement" in A. Mattera (ed.) *La Conférence intergouvernementale sur l'Union Européenne: répondre aux défis du XXIe siècle*, Brussels: Clément Juglar.

Petite, M. (1998) "The Commission and the Amsterdam Treaty", paper presented to symposium on the Amsterdam Treaty, Harvard University, January 1998.

Philippart, É. and P. Winand (2004) "Deeds not Words? Evaluating and Explaining the US - EU Policy Output" in É. Philippart and P. Winand (eds) *Ever Closer Partnership – Policy-making in US - EU Relations*, European Policy no. 24, Brussels: Peter Lang.

Philippart, É. and P. Winand (2004a) "The Dynamics, Structures, Actors and Outcomes of US - EU Relations: An 'Inside-Out' Approach" in É. Philippart and P. Winand (eds) *Ever Closer Partnership – Policy-making in US – EU Relations*, European Policy no. 24, Brussels: Peter Lang.

Pierre, J. (1995) "Comparative Public Administration: The State of the Art" in J. Pierre (ed) *Bureaucracy in the Modern State: An Introduction to Comparative Public Administration*, Aldershot: Edward Elgar.

Pierson, P. (1996) "The Path to European Integration: A Historical Institutionalist Analysis", *Comparative Political Studies*, vol. 29, no. 2, pp. 123 - 163.

Pinder, J. (1975) "Europe as a Tenth Member of the Community", *Government and Opposition*, vol. 10. no. 4, pp. 387 – 396.

Pinder, J. (1991) *The European Community and Eastern Europe*, London: Pinter for the Royal Institute of International Affairs.

Pinder, J. (2003) "Really Citizens: Contribution to the Website of the UK Federal Union", 23 July 2003.

Piris, J.-C. (1994) "After Maastricht: Are the Community Institutions more Efficacious, more Democratic and more Transparent?", *European Law Review*, vol. 19, pp. 449 – 480.

Pollack, M. (1997) "Delegation, Agency, and Agenda-setting in the European Community", *International Organization*, vol. 51, no. 1, pp. 99 - 134.

Pollack, M. (2000) "The Commission as an Agent" in N. Nugent (ed) *At the Heart of the Union: Studies of the European Commission* 2nd edition, Basingstoke: Macmillan.

Pollack, M. (2003) *The Engines of European Integration: Delegation, Agency and Agenda-Setting in the EU*, Oxford: Oxford University Press.

Pollack, M. and E. Hafner-Burton (2000) "Mainstreaming Gender in the European Union", *Journal of European Public Policy*, vol. 7, pp. 432-456.

Pollack, M. and G. Shaffer (eds) (2001) *Transatlantic Governance in the Global Economy*, Lanham: Rowman and Littlefield.

Pollitt, C. (ed) (2004) *Agencies: How Governments Do Things Through Semi Autonomous Organizations*, Basingstoke: Palgrave Macmillan.

Pollitt, C. and G. Bouckaert (2000) *Public Management Reform: A Comparative Analysis*, Oxford: Oxford University Press.

Pollitt, C. and C. Talbot (eds) (2004) *Unbundled Government: A Critical Analysis of the Global Trends to Agencies, Quangos and Contractualisation*, London: Routledge.

Poullet, E. and Deprez/Gérard (1976) *Struktur und Macht der EG-Kommission. Die Kommission im System der Europäischen Gemeinschaft*, Bonn.

Poullet, E. and D. Gérard (1977) "The Place of the Commission within the Institutional System" in C. Sasse, E. Poullet, D. Coombes and G. Deprez (eds) *Decision Making in the European Community*, London: Praeger.

Preeg, E. H. (1970) *Traders and Diplomats: An Analysis of the Kennedy Round of Negotiations under the General Agreement on Tariffs and Trade*, Washington, DC: Brookings Institution.

Pressman, J. L. and A. B. Wildalvsky (1973) *Implementation*, Berkeley: University of California Press.

Prince, The (c. 1505) by Nicolo Machiavelli.

Prodi, R. (1999) "Address Delivered to Parliament by Romano Prodi, President-Designate of the Commission, on 21 July 1999".

Prodi, R. (1999a) Speech to the European Parliament, 13 April.

Prodi, R. (1999b) Speech to the European Parliament, 4 May.

Prodi, R. (1999c) Speech at the Cologne European Council, 3 June.

Prodi, R. (1999d) speech at the Special European Council, Tampere, October 1999.

Prodi, R. (2000) Speech to the European Parliament before the Biarritz Summit, 3 October .

Prodi, R. (2001) "The New Europe in the Transatlantic Partnership", speech given at the European University Institute, Florence, 9 May 2001.

Prodi, R. (2002) speaking points concerning the Seville European Council, Rapid Database 02/290.

Prodi, R. (2003) address to Heads of Commission Delegations at their conference, 8 September 2003, speech/03/392.

Pujas, V. (2002) "L'Office européen de lutte anti-fraude: Innovation ou mimétisme institution-nel", paper for 7th conference of the Association française de science politique, Lille, September 2002.

Ramberg, B. (2005) "The Two Earthquakes in Turkey in 1999: International Coordination and the European Commission's Preparedness" in S. Larsson, E. K. Olsson and B. Ramberg (eds) *Crisis Decision Making in the European Union*, Stockholm: CRISMART.

Rayner, L. (2005) "The Foreign Ministry and Embassies of the European Union", The Foreign Policy Centre, June 2005.

Regelsberger, E. (1999) "Gemeinsame Außen- und Sicherheitspolitik" in W. Weidenfeld und W. Wessels (eds) *Jahrbuch der Europäischen Integration* 1998/99, Bonn: Europa Union Verlag.

Regelsberger, E. (2004) *Die Gemeinsame Außen- und Sicherheitspolitik*, Baden-Baden: Nomos.

Resolution adopted by the Foreign Ministers of the CSCE Member States, Conference at Messina, 1 - 2 June 1955.

Richardson, J. (2000) "Government, Interest Groups and Policy Change", *Political Studies*, vol. 48, no. 5, pp. 1007 – 1026.

Richelle, Koos (2005) "How Brussels Has Overhauled its 'Dire' Aid Apparatus", *Europe's World*, No. 1, Autumn 2005.

Riley, A. J. (1992) "Nailing the Jellyfish: the Illegality of the EC/US Government Competition Agreement", *European Competition Law Review*, vol. 13, no. 3, May - June, pp. 101 - 119.

Ritchie, E. (1992) "The Model of French Ministerial Cabinets in the Early European Commission", in E. V. Heyen (ed.) *Early European Community Administration*, Baden-Baden: Nomos Verlagsgessellschatt, Yearbook of European Administrative History, 4, pp. 95-106.

Rittberber, B. (2003) "The Creation and Empowerment of the European Parliament", *Journal of Common Market Studies*, vol. 41, no. 2, pp. 203 – 225.

Rittbereger, B. (2005) *Building Europe's Parliament: Democratic Representation beyond the Nation State*, Oxford: Oxford University Press

Rometsch, D. and W. Wessels (1997) "The Commission and the Council of the European Union" in G. Edwards and D. Spence (eds) *The European Commission* 2nd edition, London: Cartermill.

Rosamond, B. (2000) *Theories of European Integration*, Houndmills: Palgrave.

Rose, A. (2005) "The Foreign Service and Foreign Trade: Embassies as Export Promotion", *National Bureau of Economic Research Working Paper* no. 11111.

Rosenthal, U., R. A. Boin and L. K. Comfort (eds) (2001) *Managing Crises: Threats, Dilemmas, Opportunities*, Springfield: Charles C. Thomas.

Rosenthal, U., P. 't Hart and A. Kouzmin (1991) "The Bureau-Politics of Crisis Management", *Public Administration*, vol. 69, pp. 211 - 233.

Ross, G. (1993) "Sidling into Industrial Policy: Inside the European Commission", *French Politics and Society*, vol. 11, no. 1 (winter).

Ross, G. (1994) "Inside the Delors Cabinet", *Journal of Common Market Studies*, vol. 32, no 4, pp. 499 – 523.

Ross, G. (1994a) *Jacques Delors and European Integration*, Cambridge: Polity Press.

Ross, G. (1995) *Jacques Delors and European Integration*, Cambridge: Polity Press.

Roy, J. (ed) (1992) *The Reconstruction of Central America: The Role of the European Community*, Miami: ISI/ECRI.

Sabatier, P. (1988) "An Advocacy Coalition Framework of Policy Change and the Role of Policy

Orientated Learning Therein", *Policy Sciences*, vol. 21, pp. 128 - 168.

Salt, J. et al. (1998) "Feasibility Study for a European Migration Observatory", final report, Migration Research Unit, University College London, Institute of Migration and Ethnic Studies, University of Amsterdam and Centre d'Études et de Recherches Internationales, Paris, published by the European Commission (JV7590 F44 1998).

Sandholtz, W. and J. Zysman (1989) "1992: Recasting the European Bargain", *World Politics*, no. 62, pp. 95 - 128.

Sandholtz, W. and A. Stone Sweet (eds) (1998) *European Integration and Supranational Governance*, Oxford: Oxford University Press.

Sasse, C., E. Poullet, D. Coombes and G. Deprez (1977) *Decision Making in the European Community*, London: Praeger Publishers.

Sbragia, A. (ed) (1992) *Euro-Politics*, Washington: Brookings.

Schaefer, G. F. (1996) "Committees in the EC Policy Process: A First Step Towards Developing a Conceptual Framework", in R. H. Pedler and G. F. Schaefer (eds) *Shaping European Law and Policy: The Role of Committees and Comitology in the Political Process*, Maastricht: European Institute for Public Administration.

Scharpf, F. (1999) *Governing in Europe: Effective and Democratic?* Oxford: Oxford University Press.

Scharpf, F. (2001) "European Governance: Common Concerns vs. The Challenge of Diversity", contribution to *Jean Monnet Working Paper* no. 6/01: Symposium: *Mountain or Molehill? A Critical Appraisal of the Commission White Paper on Governance*.

Schmidt, S. K. (2000) "Only an Agenda-Setter? The European Commission's Power over the Council of Ministers", *European Union Politics*, vol. 1, no. 1, pp. 37 - 61.

Schmidt, S. K. (2001) "A Constrained Commission? Informal Practices of Agenda-setting in the Council" in G. Schneider and M. Aspinwall (eds) *The Rules of Integration*, Manchester: Manchester University Press.

Schmitter, P. C. (1969) "Three Neo-functional Hypotheses about International Integration", *International Organization*, vol. 23, no. 1, pp. 161 - 167.

Schmitter, P. C. (2004) "Neo-Neofunctionalism" in A. Wiener and T. Diez (eds) *European Integration Theory*, Oxford: Oxford University Press.

Schneider, G. and M. Aspinwall (ed) (2001) The Rules of Integration: Institutionalist Approaches to the Study of Europe, Manchester: Manchester University Press.

Selck, T. and B. Steunenberg (2004) "Between Power and Luck, The European Parliament in the EU Legislative Process", *European Union Politics*, vol. 5, no. 1, pp. 25 - 46.

Selznick, P. (1949) *TVA and the Grassroots: A Study of Politics and Organization*, Berkeley: University of California Press.

Shackleton, M. (2000) "The Politics of Co-decision", *Journal of Common Market Studies*, vol. 38, no. 2, pp. 323 – 343.

Shackleton, M. and T. Raunio (2003) "Co-decision since Amsterdam, A laboratory for Institutional Innovation and Change", *Journal of European Public Policy*, vol. 10, no. 2, pp. 171 - 188.

Shapiro, M. (1997) "The Problems of Independent Agencies in the United States and the European Union", *Journal of European Public Policy*, vol. 4, no. 2, pp. 276 - 291.

Sharp, P. (1998) "Who Needs Diplomats?" in J. Kurbalija (ed) *Modern Diplomacy*, Malta: Mediterranean Academy of Diplomatic Studies.

Shonfield, A. (1972) *Europe: Journey to an Unknown Destination*, Harmondsworth: Penguin.

Shore, C. (2000) *Building Europe: The Cultural Politics of European Integration*, London: Routledge.

Short, C. (2000) "Aid that Doesn't Help", *Financial Times*, 23 June 2000, p. 23.

Siotis, J. (1964) "Some Problems of European Secretariats", *Journal of Common Market Studies*, vol. 2, no. 1, pp. 222 - 250.

Sjursen, H. (2004) "Security and Defence" in W. Carlsnaes, H. Sjursen and B. Whitee (eds) *Contemporary European Foreign Policy*, London: Sage.

Smith, K. E. (2003) *European Union Foreign Policy in a Changing World*, Cambridge: Polity.

Smith, M. (1992) "The Devil You Know: The United States and a Changing European Community", *International Affairs*, vol. 68, no. 1, January, pp. 103 - 120.

Smith, M. P. (1997) "The Commission Made Me Do It: The European Commission as a Strategic Asset in Domestic Politics", in N. Nugent (ed.) *At the Heart of the Union. Studies of the European Commission*, Basingstoke: Palgrave.

Smith, M. P. (1999) "European Integration and American Power: Reflex, Resistance and Reconfiguration" in D. Slater and P. Taylor (eds) *The American Century: Consensus and Coercion in the Projection of American Power*, Oxford: Blackwell.

Smith, M. P. (2000a) "The Commission Made Me Do It: The European Commission as a

Strategic Asset in Domestic Politics" in N. Nugent (ed) *At the Heart of the Union: Studies of the European Commission* 2nd edition, Basingstoke: Macmillan.

Smith, M. P. (2001) "European Union Commercial Policy: Between Coherence and Fragmentation", *Journal of European Public Policy*, vol. 8, no. 5, pp. 787 - 802.

Smith, M. P. (2004) "The European Union and the United States: The Politics of Bi-multilateral Negotiation" in O. Elgström and C. Jönsson (eds) *European Union Negotiations: Processes, Institutions, Networks*, London: Routledge.

Smith, M. P. (2004) *Europe's Foreign and Security Policy: The Institutionalisation of Co-operation*, Cambridge: Cambridge University Press.

Smith, M. P. and S. Woolcock (1993) *The United States and the European Community in a Transformed World*, London: Pinter for the Royal Institute of International Affairs.

Smith, M. P. and S. Woolcock (1999) "European Commercial Policy: A Leadership Role in the New Millennium?", *European Foreign Affairs Review*, vol. 4, pp. 439 – 462.

Solana, J. (2000) "Common Strategies Report", Brussels, 21 December 2001, reproduced in Missiroli (2001) "Coherence for European Security Policy", WEU Institute for Security Studies, *Occasional Paper* No. 27, May 2001.

Solana, J. (2000a) "The EU's External Projection: Improving the Efficiency of our Collective Resources", working paper submitted to the informal General Affairs Council at Evian, 2 - 3 September 2000.

Solana, J. (2000b) "Developments in CFSP over the Past Year", *Challenge Europe*, European Policy Centre, 4 October 2000.

Solana, J. (2002) Evidence to the External Action Working Group of the Convention, 15 October 2002, SO 186/02.

Solana, J. (2003) "A Secure Europe in a Better World: European Security Strategy", December 2003.

Solana, J. (2004) "Europe's Growing Role in World Security" in "Fresh Perspectives on Europe's Security", *New Defence Agenda Discussion Paper*, Winter 2004.

Solana, J. (2005) Unpublished reflection paper.

Solana, J. (2005a) summary of remarks to the press by EU High Representative Javier Solana on the results of the referendum in France, Brussels, 30 May 2005, S201/05.

Spence, D. (1991) "Enlargement without Accession: The EC's Response to German Unification", RIIA Discussion Paper no. 36.

Spence, D. (1992) "The European Community and German Unification" in C. Jeffery and R. Sturm (eds) *Federalism, Unification and European Integration*, special issue of *German Politics*, vol. 1, no. 3.

Spence, D. (1997) "Structure, Functions and Procedures in the Commission" in G. Edwards and D. Spence (eds) *The European Commission* 2nd ed., London: Cartermill.

Spence, D. (1997a) "Staff and Personnel Policy in the Commission" in G. Edwards and D. Spence (ed) *The European Commission* 2nd edition, London: Cartermill.

Spence, A. and D. Spence (1998) "The CFSP from Maastricht to Amsterdam" in K. A. Eliasen (ed) *Foreign and Security Policy in the European Union*, Thousand Oaks: Sage.

Spence, D. (2000) "Plus ça change, plus c'est la même chose? Attempting to reform the European Commission", *Journal of European Public Policy*, vol. 7, no. 1, pp. 1 - 25.

Spence, D. (2002) "EU Foreign Ministries between Reform and Adaptation" in D. Spence and B. Hocking (eds) *Integrating Diplomats: Reform and Adaptation of EU Foreign Ministries*, London: Palgrave.

Spence, D. (2004) "The Coordination of European Policy by Member States" in M. Westlake and D. Galloway (ed) *The Council of the European Union*, London: John Harper.

Spence, D. (2004a) "Negotiations, Coalitions and the Resolution of Inter-State Conflicts" in M. Westlake and D. Galloway (eds) *The Council of the European Union*, London: John Harper.

Spence, D (2005a) "The Evolving Role of Foreign Ministries in the Conduct of EU Affairs: Integrating Diplomats" in B. Hocking and D. Spence (eds) *Integrating Diplomats: EU Foreign Ministries*, Houndmills: Palgrave Macmillan.

Spence, D. (2006) "International Terrorism: The Quest for a Coherent EU Response", *European Foreign Affairs Review*, vol. 11.

Spierenburg, D. (1979) "Proposal for Reform of the Commission of the European Communities and its services", report made at the request of the Commission by an independent review body under the chairmanship of Mr Dirk Spierenburg, Brussels, 24 September 1979.

Spinelli, A. (1958) *Manifest der Europäischen Föderalisten*, Frankfurt: Europäische Verlags-Anstalt.

Spinelli, A. (1966) *The Eurocrats: Conflict & Crisis in the European Community*, Baltimore: Johns

Hopkins Press.

Spinelli, A. (1972) *The European Adventure*, London: Charles Knight.

Spinelli, A. (1984) "Draft Treaty Establishing the European Union", reprinted in *Bulletin of the European Communities* 2.

Stacey, J. (2003) "Displacement of the Council via Informal Dynamics? Comparing the Commission and Parliament", *Journal of European Public Policy*, vol. 10, no. 6, pp. 936– 55.

Staff Regulations (2004) "2004 Council Regulation (EC, Euratom) No 723/2004 of 22 March 2004 Amending the Staff Regulations of Officials of the European Communities and the Conditions of Employment of other Servants of the European Communities", OJ L 124 vol. 47, 27 April 2004.

Stevens, A. with H. Stevens (2001) *Brussels Bureaucrats? The Administrative Services of the European Union*, Basingstoke: Palgrave.

Stevens, A. (2002) "Europeanisation and the Administration of the EU: A Comparative Perspective", *Queen's Papers on Europeanisation* no. 4/2002.

Stokman, F. and R. Thomson (2004) "Winners and Losers in the European Union", *European Union Politics*, vol. 5, no. 1, pp. 5 - 23.

Stone Sweet, A., W. Sandholtz and N. Fligstein (eds) (2001) *The Institutionalization of Europe*, Oxford: Oxford University Press.

Strasser, D. (1980) *Les Finances de l'Europe*, Paris: Nathan Labor.

Sunday Express (1996) "Scandal of EU missions in Paradise", 14 January 1996.

Sundelius, B. (2004) "The Seeds of a Functional Security Paradigm for the European Union", paper presented at the Second Pan-European Conference on European Union Politics of the ECPR Standing Group on European Union Politics, Bologna, 24 - 26 June.

Sutherland, P. (1996) "Appreciation: Emile Noël", *Irish Times*, 25 August 1996.

Sutherland, P. et al. (1992) *The Internal Market After 1992*, Operation of the Community's Internal Market after 1992: follow-up to the Sutherland Report. SEC (92) 2277, 2 December 1992.

Tallberg, J. (2003) *Governance and Supranational Institutions: Making States Comply*, London: Routledge.

Taylor, P. (1983) *The Limits of Integration*, London: Croom Helm.

Taylor, P. (1989) "The New Dynamics of EC Integration in the 1980s" in J. Lodge (ed) *The European Community and the Challenge of the Future*, London: Pinter.

Telegraaf (2004) "Kwart van Nederlandse Ambassades Kan Weg", 1 November 2004, interview with former MEP Lousewies van der Laan.

Thatcher, M[argaret]. (1985) "Europe – the future", reproduced in Select Committee on the European Communities, HL226, London: HMSO.

Thatcher, M[argaret]. (1993) *The Downing Street Years*, New York: Harper Collins.

Thatcher, M. (2002a) "Delegation to Independent Regulatory Agencies: Pressures, Functions and Contextual Mediation", *West European Politics*, vol. 25, no. 1, 125 – 147.

Thatcher, M. (2002b) "Regulation after Delegation: Independent Regulatory Agencies in Europe", *Journal of European Public Policy*, vol. 9, no. 6, pp. 954 - 972.

Thatcher, M. and A. Stone Sweet (2002) "Delegation to Non-Majoritarian Institutions", *West European Politics*, vol. 25, no. 1, pp. 1 - 22.

Three Wise Men (1979) "Report on European Institutions" presented by the Committee of Three to the European Council, October 1979, Council of the European Communities, 1980, p. 86.

Three Wise Men (1999) "The Institutional Implications of Enlargement: Report to the European Commission", by Richard von Weizsäcker, Jean-Luc Dehaene and David Simon, Brussels, 18 October.

Tindemans, L. (1976) "European Union: Report by Mr Leo Tindemans, Prime Minister of Belgium, to the European Council", *Bulletin of the European Communities*, Supplement 1.

Tindemans, L. (1998) "Dreams Come True, Gradually" in M. Westlake (ed) *The European Union Beyond Amsterdam*, London: Routledge.

Tomkys, R. (1987) "European Political Cooperation and the Middle East: A Personal Perspective", *International Affairs*, vol. 63, no. 3, pp. 425 – 438.

Tonra, B. (2001) "Setting the Agenda of European Crisis Management – The Challenge to Coherence" in A. Missiroli "Coherence for European Security Policy: Debates, Cases, Assessments", WEU Institute for Security Studies, *Occasional Paper* no 27, May 2001.

Tranholm-Mikkelsen, J. (1991) "Neo-functionalism: Obstinate or Obsolete? A Reappraisal in the Logic of the New Dynamism of the EC", *Millennium*, vol. 20, no. 1, pp. 1 - 22.

Tsebelis, G. (2002) *Veto Players, How Political Institutions Work*, Princeton: Princeton University Press.

Tsebelis, G. and G. Garrett (1996) "Agenda Setting Power, Power Indices and Decision Making in the European Union", *International Review of Law and Economics*, vol. 16, no. 3, pp. 345 - 361.

Tsebelis, G. and G. Garret (2001) "The Institutional Foundations of Intergovernmentalism and Supranationalism in the European Union", *International Organization*, vol. 55, no. 2, pp. 357 - 390.

UK Government Paper on Institutional Reform (1999).

US Congress (1992) "Europe and the United States: Competition and Co-operation in the 1990s", study papers submitted to the Subcommittee on International Economic Policy and Trade and the Subcommittee on Europe and the Middle East of the Committee on Foreign Affairs, US House of Representatives, Washington, DC: US Government Printing Office.

Usher, J. (1992) "General Course on the European Community: The Continuing Development of Law and Institutions", *Collected Courses of the Academy of European Law*, vol. 2, no. 1, p. 371.

Van Miert, K. (2000) *Markets, Influence and Competition*.

Van Schendelen, M. P. C. M. (1998a) "Prolegomena to EU Committees as Influential Policymakers" in M. P. C. M. Van Schendelen (ed) *EU Committees as Influential Policymakers*, Aldershot: Ashgate.

Van Schendelen, M. C. P. M. (2003) "The Insourced Experts", paper.

Van Thiel, S. (2001) *Quangos: Trends, Causes and Consequences*, Aldershot: Ashgate.

Verdun, A. (1998) "The Role of the Delors Committee in the Creation of EMU: An Epistemic Community?", Florence: EUI Robert Schuman Centre of Advanced Studies, *EUI-RSCAS Working Paper No. 44*.

Verheugen, G. (2005) presentation at informal Competitive Ministers Council in Cardiff, 12 July 2005, Press Release IP 05/905.

Vos, E. (1999) "EU Committees: the Evolution of Unforeseen Institutional Actors in European Product Regulation" in C. Joerges and E. Vos (eds) *EU Committees: Social Regulation, Law and Politics*, Oxford: Hart Publishing.

Vos, E. (2000) "Reforming the European Commission: What Role to Play for EU Agencies?", *Common Market Law Review*, vol. 37, no. 5, pp. 1113 - 1134.

Vos, E. (2003) "Agencies and the European Union" in L. Verhey and T. Zwart (eds) *Agencies in European and Comparative Law*, Maastricht: Intersentia.

Wallace, H. (2000) "The Institutional Setting" in H. Wallace and W. Wallace (eds) *Policy-Making in the European Union* 4th edition, Oxford: Oxford University Press.

Wallace, H. (2003) "Die Dynamik des EU-Institutionengefüges" in M. Jachtenfuchs and B. Kohler-Koch (eds) *Europäische Integration*, Opladen: Leske und Budrich.

Wallace, H. and G. Edwards (1976) "European Community: The Evolving Role of the Presidency of the Council", *International Affairs*, vol. 53, no. 4, pp. 535 – 550.

Wallström, M. (2005) "The First Year of the Barroso Commission and Beyond", Meeting at the European Policy Centre, Brussels, 17 November 2005.

Warbrick, C. (2004) "The European Response to Terrorism in an Age of Human Rights", *European Journal of International Law*, vol. 15, no. 5, pp. 989 – 1018.

Weidenfeld, W. (1994) *Europa '96: Reformprogramm für die Europäische Union*, Gütersloh: Bertelsmann.

Wessels, W. (1998) "Comitology: Fusion in Action. Politico-administrative Trends in the EU System", *Journal of European Public Policy*, vol. 5, no. 2, pp. 209 – 234.

Wessels, W. (2001) "The Amsterdam Treaty in Theoretical Perspectives: Which Dynamics Work?" in J. Monar and W. Wessels (eds) *The European Union after the Treaty of Amsterdam*, London: Continuum.

Wessels, W. (2001b) "Nice Results: The Millenium IGC in the EU's Evolution", *Journal of Common Market Studies*, vol. 39, no. 2, pp. 197 - 219.

Wessels, W. (2003a) "Beamtengremien im EU-Mehrebenensystem. Fusion von Administrationen" in B. Kohler-Koch and M. Jachtenfuchs (eds) *Europäische Integration*, Opladen: Leske und Budrich.

Wessels, W. (2003b) "Das Politische System der Europäischen Union" in W. Ismayr (ed) *Die Politischen Systeme Westeuropas* 3rd edition, Opladen: Westdeutscher Verlag.

Wessels, W. and I. Linsenmann (2002) "EMU's Impact on National Institutions. Fusion towards a 'Gouvernance Économique' or Fragmentation?" in K. Dyson (ed) *European States and the Euro. Europeanization, Variation, and Convergence*, Oxford: Oxford University Press.

Wessels, W., A. Maurer and J. Mittag (2003) "The European Union and Member States. Analysing Two Arenas over Time" in W. Wessels, A. Maurer and J. Mittag (eds) *Fifteen into One?*

The European Union and its Member States, Manchester: Manchester University Press.

Westlake, M. (1994) *The Commission and the Parliament. Partners and Rivals in the European Policy-making Process*, London: Butterworths.

Westlake, M. (1997) "'Mad Cows and Englishmen' - The Institutional Consequences of the BSE Crisis", *Journal of Common Market Studies*, vol. 35, annual review, pp. 11 - 36.

Westlake, M. (1998a) "The EP's Emerging Powers of Appointment", *Journal of Common Market Studies*, vol. 36, no. 3, pp. 431 – 444.

Westlake, M. (2001) *Kinnock: The Biography*, Little, Brown.

Westlake, M. and D. Galloway (2004) *The Council of the European Union*, London: John Harper.

Widgrén, M. (1994) "Voting power in the EC Decision Making and the Consequences of Two Different Enlargements", *European Economic Review*, vol. 38, no. 5, pp. 1153 - 1170.

Williamson, D. (1991) Redcliffe-Maud Memorial Lecture, 10 October 1991.

Williamson Report (1998) *Reflection Group on Personnel Policy*, chair D. Williamson, European Commission, 28 July 1998, Brussels.

Willis, V. (1983) *Britons in Brussels*, London: PSI.

Wilson, J. Q. (1989) *Bureaucracy: What Government Agencies Do and Why They Do It*, New York: Basic Books.

Winand, P. (2004) "The US Mission to the EU in 'Brussels D. C.', the European Commission Delegation in Washington D. C. and the New Transatlantic Agenda" in É. Philippart and P. Winand (eds) *Ever Closer Partnership – Policy-making in US - EU Relations*, European Policy no. 24, Brussels: Peter Lang.

Wincott, D. (2001) "Looking Forward or Harking Back? The Commission and the Reform of Governance in the European Union", *Journal of Common Market Studies*, vol. 39, no. 5, pp. 897 - 911.

Wincott, D. (2001a) "The Commission and the Reform of Governance in the EU", *Journal of Common Market Studies*, vol. 39, no. 5, pp. 897 - 911.

Wise Men (1999a) "First Report on Allegations regarding Fraud, Mismanagement and Nepotism in the European Commission", Committee of Independent Experts, 15 March.

Wise Men (1999b) "Second Report on Reform of the Commission. Analysis of Current Practice and Proposals for Tackling Mismanagement, Irregularities and Fraud", Committee of Independent Experts, 10 September.

Wise Men's Report (1979) "Report on European Institutions", presented by the Committee of Three to the European Council, October 1979. Luxembourg: Office for Official Publications of the European Communities.

Woolcock, S. and M. Hodges (1996) "EU Policy in the Uruguay Round" in H. Wallace and W. Wallace (eds) *Policy-Making in the European Union* 3rd edition, Oxford: Oxford University Press.

Yataganas, X. A. (2001) "Delegation of Regulatory Authority in the European Union: The Relevance of the American Model of Independent Agencies", *Jean Monnet Working Papers* no. 03/01.

Young, A. (2000) "The Adaptation of European Foreign Economic Policy: from Rome to Seattle", *Journal of Common Market Studies*, vol. 38, no. 1, pp. 93 - 116.

Young, A. (2002) *Extending European Co-operation: The European Union and the 'New' International Trade Agenda*, Manchester: Manchester University Press.

Young, A. (2003) "What Game? By Which Rules? Adaptation and Flexibility in the EC's Foreign Economic Policy" in M. Knodt and S. Princen (eds) *Understanding the European Union's External Relations*, London: Routledge.

Zabuski, S. E. (2000) "Boundaries at Work: Discourses and Practices of Belonging in the European Space Agency" in I. Bellier and T. M. Wilson (eds) *Anthropology of the European Union*, Oxford: Berg.

Ziller, J. (1988) *Egalité et Mérite - L'accès à la Fonction Publique dans les États de la Communauté Européenne*, Brussels: Institut International d'Administration Publique.

INDEX

Note: The Index should be used in conjunction with the detailed Table of Contents, to which it is intended as a supplement.

Names and terms in the annexes are not indexed.